TRUST MANAGEMENT

IFIP – The International Federation for Information Processing

IFIP was founded in 1960 under the auspices of UNESCO, following the First World Computer Congress held in Paris the previous year. An umbrella organization for societies working in information processing, IFIP's aim is two-fold: to support information processing within its member countries and to encourage technology transfer to developing nations. As its mission statement clearly states,

> IFIP's mission is to be the leading, truly international, apolitical organization which encourages and assists in the development, exploitation and application of information technology for the benefit of all people.

IFIP is a non-profitmaking organization, run almost solely by 2500 volunteers. It operates through a number of technical committees, which organize events and publications. IFIP's events range from an international congress to local seminars, but the most important are:

• The IFIP World Computer Congress, held every second year;
• Open conferences;
• Working conferences.

The flagship event is the IFIP World Computer Congress, at which both invited and contributed papers are presented. Contributed papers are rigorously refereed and the rejection rate is high.

As with the Congress, participation in the open conferences is open to all and papers may be invited or submitted. Again, submitted papers are stringently refereed.

The working conferences are structured differently. They are usually run by a working group and attendance is small and by invitation only. Their purpose is to create an atmosphere conducive to innovation and development. Refereeing is less rigorous and papers are subjected to extensive group discussion.

Publications arising from IFIP events vary. The papers presented at the IFIP World Computer Congress and at open conferences are published as conference proceedings, while the results of the working conferences are often published as collections of selected and edited papers.

Any national society whose primary activity is in information may apply to become a full member of IFIP, although full membership is restricted to one society per country. Full members are entitled to vote at the annual General Assembly, National societies preferring a less committed involvement may apply for associate or corresponding membership. Associate members enjoy the same benefits as full members, but without voting rights. Corresponding members are not represented in IFIP bodies. Affiliated membership is open to non-national societies, and individual and honorary membership schemes are also offered.

TRUST MANAGEMENT

Proceedings of IFIPTM 2007: Joint iTrust and PST Conferences on Privacy, Trust Management and Security, July 30- August 2, 2007, New Brunswick, Canada

Edited by

Sandro Etalle
Distributed and Embedded System Group
University of Twente
The Netherlands

Stephen Marsh
Information Security Group
Institute for Information Technology
National Research Council
Canada

 Springer

Trust Management

Edited by S. Etalle and S. Marsh

p. cm. (IFIP International Federation for Information Processing, a Springer Series in Computer Science)

ISSN: 1571-5736 / 1861-2288 (Internet)

ISBN 978-1-4419-4465-8   eISBN: 13: 978-0-387-73655- 6
Printed on acid-free paper

9 8 7 6 5 4 3 2 1
springer.com

Preface

This volume contains the proceedings of the IFIPTM 2007, the Joint iTrust and PST Conferences on Privacy, Trust Management and Security, held in Moncton, New Brunswick, Canada from July 29th to August 2nd, 2007.

The annual iTrust international conference looks at trust from multidisciplinary perspectives: economic, legal, psychology, philosophy, sociology as well as information technology, is built on the work of the iTrust working group (http://www.itrust.uoc.gr), and has had four highly successful conferences in Europe to date.

The annual PST conference has quickly established itself as a leader in multidisciplinary research on a wide range of topics related to Privacy, Security and Trust, looked at from research and practice, through academe, business, and government. 2007 marks the 4th year of PST's existence.

The two conferences come together in 2007 as the first annual meeting and conference of the newly formed IFIP Working Group on Trust Management (IFIP WG11.11), a major step forward in Trust Management work globally.

IFIPTM 2007 received 76 submission from 25 different countries: Canada (15), USA (10), United Kingdom (8), China (6), Finland, Italy (4), Korea, Switzerland, France, Ireland, Spain, Germany, Denmark, Jordan, Poland, Kuwait, Singapore, Iran, Netherlands, Japan, Luxembourg, Australia, Norway, Austria, Tunisia. The program committee selected 25 papers for presentation and inclusion in the proceedings. In addition, the program and the proceedings include 4 short papers.

The highlights of IFIPTM 2007 included invited talks by industrial and academic experts in the fields of trust management, privacy and security, including Larry Korba from NRC-IIT, Brian O'Higgins of 3rd Brigade, Jim Robbins from EWA, Jonathan Cave from RAND, Roger London, and Bruce Cowper from Microsoft Canada.

Sponsors of the IFIPTM 2007 include the University of New Brunswick, the National Research Council of Canada, Institute for Information Technology, Microsoft Q1 Labs, Third Brigade, Microsoft , EWA-Canada, and VE Networks, to whom our thanks.

There are many people who contributed to the success of the conference, without whom it would not exist, and to whom we owe our gratitude and thanks. PC members and several other external referees provided timely and indepth reviews of the submitted papers, and worked hard to select the best papers for the conference program.

Special thanks are due to Greg Sprague who has worked tirelessly to make the conference a success. William Winsborough and John McHugh have, with Greg, steered the conference from inception to reality. Stephane Lo Presti has worked hard to bring the workshops and tutorials to fruition, with excellent results, and on the ground Georges Corriveau has ensured a conference that's not only academically interesting but culturally enriching also.

Scott Buffett and Ilia Goldfarb have done tremendous work getting the proceedings you have in your hands ready, formatted, and looking as good as they do now.

To all who have helped, our sincerest thanks. We hope you enjoy the proceedings and the conference.

Ottawa, Canada and Twente, the Netherlands.
Sandro Etalle and Stephen Marsh
Program Committee co-Chairs
IFIPTM-07

Organization

IFIPTM 2007 Executive Commitee

Conference co-Chairs:
    John McHugh, Dalhousie University, Nova Scotia, Canada
    William Winsborough, University of Texas at San Antonio, USA

Program co-Chairs:
    Sandro Etalle, University of Twente, the Netherlands
    Stephen Marsh, National Research Council, Canada

Workshop Chair:
    Stephane Lo Presti, Royal Holloway, University of London, UK

Publicity Chair:
    Emmanuele Zambon, University of Twente, the Netherlands

Local Arrangements:
    Georges Corriveau, National Research Council, Canada

Program Committee

Scott Buffett, NRC, Canada
Elizabeth Chang, Curtin University of Technology, Australia
Theo Dimitrakos, British Telecom, UK
Sandro Etalle (chair), University of Twente, the Netherlands
Rino Falcone, CNR, Italy
Javier Garcia-Villalba, Universidad Complutense de Madrid, Spain
Ali Ghorbani, University of New Brunswick, Canada
Jim Greer, University of Saskatchewan, Canada
Milena Head, McMaster University, Canada
Peter Herrmann, NTNU, Trondheim, Norway
Valerie Issarny, INRIA, France
Sushil Jajodia, George Mason University
Christian Jensen, Technical University of Denmark, Denmark
Audun Josang, QUT, Australia
Dawn Jutla, Saint Mary's University, Canada
Yuecel Karabulut, SAP, Canada
Larry Korba, NRC, Canada
Javier Lopez, University of Malaga, Spain
Fabio Martinelli, IIT-CNR, Italy
Steve Marsh (Chair), National Research Council, Canada

Fabio Massacci, University of Trento, Italy
Ali Miri, University of Ottawa, Canada
Yuko Murayama, Iwate Prefectural University, Japan
Mogens Nielsen, University of Aarhus, Denmark
Christos Nikolaou, University of Crete, Greece
Sylvia Osborn, University of Western Ontario, Canada
Stefan Poslad, University of London Queen Mary, UK
Babak Sadighi, SICS, Sweden
Pierangela Samarati, University of Milan, Italy
Ravi Sandhu, George Mason University
Jean-Marc Seigneur, University of Geneva, Switzerland
Simon Shiu, Hewlett Packard, UK
Sean Smith, Dartmouth College, USA
Ketil Stoelen, SINTEF & University of Oslo, Norway
Sotirios Terzis, University of Strathclyde, UK
David Townsend, University of New Brunswick, Canada

Additional Referees

Mohd Anwar	Kwang-Hyun Baek	Adrian Baldwin	Yolanta Beres
Enrico Blanzieri	Damiano Bolzoni	Roberto Speicys Cardoso	Marco Casassa-Mont
Roberto Cascella	Marcin Czenko	Heidi Dahl	Jeroen Doumen
Christopher Dutchyn	Maria C. Fernandez	Farookh Hussain	Apu Kapadia
Yee Wei Law	Mass Soldal Lund	Chris Masone	Ilaria Matteucci
Katsiarina Naliuka	Tomas Olsson	Andrew Patrick	Marinella Petrocchi
Vidyasagar Potdar	Atle Refsdal	Philip Robinson	Rodrigo Roman
Fredrik Seehusen	Ludwig Seitz	Robin Sharp	Bjoernar Solhaug
Terkel K. Tolstrup	Artsiom Yautsiukhin	Emmanuele Zambon	

Table of Contents

Private Distributed Scalar Product Protocol with Application To Privacy-Preserving Computation of Trust 1
Danfeng Yao, Roberto Tamassia and Seth Proctor

Trust Transfer in Distributed Systems 17
Changyu Dong, Giovanni Russello and Naranker Dulay

Trust without Truth 31
Michel Deriaz

Mining and Detecting Connection-Chains in Network Traffic 47
Ahmad Almulhem and Issa Traore

A Privacy-Aware Service Discovery Middleware for Pervasive
Environments 59
Roberto Speicys Cardoso, Pierre-Guillaume Raverdy and Valérie Issarny

Analysis of the Implicit Trust within the OLSR Protocol 75
Asmaa Adnane, Rafael Timóteo de Sousa Jr, Christophe Bidan and Ludovic Mé

Validating a Trust-based Access Control System 91
William Adams and Nathaniel J. Davis IV

Negotiation for Authorisation in Virtual Organisation 107
Shamimabi Paurobally

A Geo Time Authentication System 123
Leonardo Mostarda, Arianna Tocchio, Stefania Costantini and Paola Inverardi

Content Trust Model for Detecting Web Spam 139
Wang Wei and Zeng Guosun

Applied Computational Trust in Utilities Management: a Case Study on
the Town Council of Cava de' Tirreni 153
Pierpaolo Dondio, Edmondo Manzo and Stephen Barrett

A Trust Protocol for Community Collaboration 169
Samuel Galice, Marine Minier and Stéphane Ubéda

Towards an Understanding of Security, Privacy and Safety in Maritime
Self-Reporting Systems 185
    Mark McIntyre, Lynne Genik, Peter Mason and Tim Hammond

Dismantling the Twelve Privacy Purposes 207
    Sabah Al-Fedaghi

A Framework for Privacy-Preserving E-learning 223
    Esma Aïmeur, Hicham Hage and Flavien Serge Mani Onana

Exploiting Trust and Suspicion for Real-time Attack Recognition
in Recommender Applications 239
    Ebrahim Bagheri and Ali Ghorbani

Self-Selection Bias in Reputation Systems 255
    Mark Kramer

Resisting Sybils in Peer-to-peer Markets 269
    Jonathan Traupman

A Trust Model for an Open, Decentralized Reputation System 285
    Andreas Gutscher

Control Flow Based Pointcuts for Security Hardening Concerns 301
    *Marc-André Laverdière , Azzam Mourad, Andrei Soeanu and
Mourad Debbabi*

Design of Trusted Systems with Reusable Collaboration Models 317
    Peter Herrmann and Frank Alexander Kraemer

MUQAMI: A Locally Distributed Key Management Scheme for Clustered
Sensor Networks 333
    *Syed Muhammad Khaliq-ur-Rahman Raazi, Adil Mehmood Khan,
Faraz Idris Khan, Sungyoung Lee, Young-Jae Song and Young Koo Lee*

Trust based Approach for Improving Data Reliability in Industrial
Sensor Networks 349
    Tatyana Ryutov and Clifford Neuman

The AI Hardness of CAPTCHAs does not imply Robust Network Security 367
    Allan Caine and Urs Hengartner

Resilia: a Safe and Secure Distributed Backup System for Small and
Medium Enterprises 383
    Christian Damsgaard Jensen, Fernando Meira and
    Jacob Nittegaard-Nielsen

Integrity in Open Collaborative Authoring Systems 399
    Christian Damsgaard Jensen

Service-Oriented Approach to Visualize IT Security Performance Metrics . 403
    Clemens Martin and Mustapha Refai

From Early Requirements Analysis towards Secure Workflows 407
    Ganna Frankova, Fabio Massacci and Magali Seguran

Monitors for Usage Control 411
    Manuel Hilty, Alexander Pretschner, Christian Schaefer, Thomas Walter
    and David Basin

Author Index **415**

Private Distributed Scalar Product Protocol With Application To Privacy-Preserving Computation of Trust*

Danfeng Yao[1], Roberto Tamassia[1], and Seth Proctor[2]

[1] Department of Computer Science, Brown University
   Providence, RI 02912 USA
   {dyao, rt}@cs.brown.edu
[2] Sun Microsystems Laboratories
   Burlington, MA 01803
   Seth.Proctor@sun.com

Summary. In this paper, we first present a private distributed scalar product protocol that can be used for obtaining trust values from private recommendations. Our protocol allows Alice to infer the trustworthiness of Bob based on what Alice's friends think about Bob and Alice's confidence in her friends. In addition, the private information of Alice and her friends are not revealed during the computation. We also propose a credential-based trust model where the trustworthiness of a user is computed based on his or her affiliations and role assignments. The trust model is simple to compute, yet it is scalable as it classifies large groups of users.

Key words: Private multi-party computation, trust management, location privacy

1 Introduction

Conventional access decisions in stand-alone systems are usually made based on the identity of the entity requesting a resource. By comparison, in open systems such as the Internet, this approach becomes less effective. The main reason is that there is no central authority that can make access decisions. Thus, the resource owner and the requester typically belong to different security domains administrated by different authorities and are unknown to each other. For example, Alice is holding a student credential from an organization A, but Bob, the resource owner, may know nothing about A in terms of its trustworthiness, etc. Therefore, there is a strong need for designing a flexible trust establishment model.

Reputation or trust models [7, 19] provide an open, flexible, and dynamic mechanism for trust establishment, where the requester does not belong to the resource owner. Trust models have applications in distributed systems such as peer-to-peer

---

* Work supported in part by the National Science Foundation under ITR grant IIS–0324846.

Please use the following format when citing this chapter:

Yao, D., Tamassia, R. and Proctor, S., 2007, in IFIP International Federation for Information Processing, Volume 238, Trust Management, eds. Etalle, S., Marsh, S., (Boston: Springer), pp. 1–16.

networks, e-commerce applications such as online auctions, or in resource-sharing systems such as Grid computing. Trust models are typically built on information such as recommendations and previous experiences of individuals. Various algorithms have been proposed to evaluate trust values [6, 30], in particular how transferred trust are computed.

In this paper, we attempt to address two aspects of computational trust models: (1) how to protect the privacy of personal opinions during computation, and (2) how to design a scalable computational trust model.

In computational trust models, the recommendations on the trustworthiness of users are usually assumed to be public. However, recommendations represent one's personal opinions of other entities, and are usually considered *sensitive*. For example, Bob has bad experiences doing business with Paul on an auction site, but, he does not want to publish his negative recommendation on Paul. Alice, who has not dealt with Paul previously, would like to use Bob and others' recommendations to evaluate Paul's trustworthiness. In the meantime, Alice has her own *private* evaluations on Bob and others, which give weights to individual recommendation (e.g., Alice knows and trusts Bob, so Bob's recommendation has a higher weight.) The problem is how to enable Alice to compute the weighted recommendation on Paul without disclosing everyone's sensitive parameters. We formalize this problem as a secure multi-party computation of scalar product, and present an efficient protocol for solving it.

This paper also describes an approach to improve the scalability of trust and reputation models. Ideally, a trust model should be able to accurately and efficiently classify a group of users. In trust management applications with a large number of users, such as Shibboleth [25], the trustworthiness of individual users becomes less important if the resource owner knows the home organization of the individual. For example, if the user is a professor from a reputable college, then he or she is likely to be trustworthy. We aim to improve the scalability of the typical grass-root approach of building trust. Our approach takes advantage of the pre-existing organizational infrastructure, in particular the credential-based administration model. The trustworthiness of an individual is deduced from her digital credentials and the issuers' trustworthiness.

1.1 Our Contributions

The contributions of this paper are summarized as follows.

1. We present a private multi-party computation protocol for computing weighted trust values. The problem is for A to infer the trust value of an unknown entity X based on what other entities think about X together with A's confidence in these entities. In a world where there is no privacy concern or there is a trusted third-party, the problem can be solved by computing the scalar product of two vectors – one vector representing A's confidence values for a set of entities, and the other vector representing recommendations of these entities on X. In real life, this information is usually considered sensitive, e.g., B may not want to disclose that he does not trust X at all, and A hopes to conceal the fact that her confidence

in B is low. Private two-party scalar product protocols are available [1, 13, 31]. However, they are not suitable for our problem, where one of the vectors in the computation is distributed among multiple entities. We design an efficient private multi-party computation protocol for scalar products where individual values of a vector can have different owners. The sensitive information of all parties is not revealed (except the final scalar product).

2. We propose a credential-based trust model for inferring trustworthiness in decentralized environments. Our credential-based trust model not only simplifies and scales the decision-making process, but also improves the reliability of computed trust scores by using role certificates. We describe how to compute trust values from multiple credentials, delegation credentials, and from peers' recommendations. Our model can also be used for computing point values in the existing point-based authorization model.

3. We also describe a location-query system for giving fuzzy location information based on the trustworthiness of the query issuer. This system is a practical application of the point-based authorization model, and demonstrates the ability to give flexible yet confident trust verdicts in open systems. Location-aware applications are made popular by the increasing deployment of sensor networks, RFID, and GPS-enabled cellphone networks.

1.2 Outline of the paper

A private multi-party computation protocol for distributed scalar products is presented in Section 2. This protocol supports efficient and privacy-preserving computation of trust values. Our credential-based trust model is introduced in Section 3. In Section 4, we describe how our trust model can be integrated with the existing point-based trust management model. In Section 5, we present an application of point-based trust management to the location query problem for sensor networks. Related work is described in Section 6. Finally, future work is given in Section 7.

2 Private Distributed Scalar Product Protocol

In this section, we define, construct, and analyze the private distributed scalar product protocol. The private distributed scalar product protocol has applications in privacy-preserving data mining problems. In Section 3.2, we show how it is used to privately compute trust values from peers' recommendations.

2.1 Definitions

In what follows, we define that all arithmetic is done in $\mathbb{Z}_m$ for some m. A private distributed scalar product protocol is to compute $X \cdot Y$, where $X = (x_1, x_2, \ldots, x_n) \in \mathbb{Z}_m^n$ and $Y = (y_1, y_2, \ldots, y_n) \in \mathbb{Z}_m^n$ are vectors of length n.

The protocol is run by l numbers of players where $1 \leq l \leq 2n$, and x_i and y_i are disjointly partitioned among the players. That is, each player knows one or more of the elements in the vectors, and a vector is known by one and only one player. In a centralized case where $l = 1$, the problem is reduced to trivial scalar product computation. If $l = 2$, i.e. a two-party private computation problem, one can use existing private scalar product protocols [1, 13, 31]. If there are $2n$ players, each party knows only one element in X or Y. The goal of the protocol is for the players to jointly compute $X \cdot Y$ without disclosing each own's private information, i.e., x_i or y_i values. The security of the protocol can be intuitively thought of as players do not gain non-negligible knowledge of others' private information (besides the final scalar product). In particular, the property should hold even if players collude. The security of the protocol is further analyzed in Section 2.4.

For our trust model in Section 3, we are interested in a specific scenario with $n + 1$ players: Alice wants to compute the point value for an unknown entity E. She knows n entities $B_1, B_2, \ldots, B_n$, and Alice's point value for entity B_i is x_i. Each entity B_i knows entity E, and has assigned point y_i to E, respectively. Alice and $B_1, B_2, \ldots, B_n$ jointly compute $X \cdot Y$, which is given to Alice at the end of the protocol, but not to any of the B_is. We present our private distributed scalar product protocol for this special case. The protocol can be easily generalized to cases where l is anywhere between 3 and $2n$, where n is the length of the vector.

2.2 Building Blocks

Our private distributed scalar product protocol uses the homomorphic encryption scheme and a private multi-party summation protocol.

Homomorphic Encryption

A homomorphic encryption scheme has three functions (Gen, Enc, Dec), where Gen generates a private key sk and a public key pk, Enc and Dec are encryption and decryption functions, respectively. The encryption function Enc is said to be homomorphic, if the following holds: $\mathsf{Enc}_{\mathsf{pk}}(x; r) \cdot \mathsf{Enc}_{\mathsf{pk}}(y; r') = \mathsf{Enc}_{\mathsf{pk}}(x + y; r \cdot r')$, where x and y denote plaintext messages and r and r' denote random strings. Another property of such a scheme is that $\mathsf{Enc}_{\mathsf{pk}}(x; r)^y = \mathsf{Enc}_{\mathsf{pk}}(x \cdot y; r^y)$. This means that a party can add encrypted plaintexts by doing simple computations with ciphertexts, without having the private key. The arithmetic performed under the encryption is modular, and the modulus is part of the public parameters for this system. Homomorphic schemes are described in [9, 21]. We utilize homomorphic encryption schemes that are semantically secure. A homomorphic scheme is called *semantically secure* when a probabilistic polynomial-time adversary cannot distinguish between random encryptions of two elements chosen by herself.

Private Multi-Party Summation Protocol

Our protocol also uses an efficient private multi-party summation protocol, which was presented by Atallah *et al.* [2]. Their protocol is to make n parties, each with a number V_i, cooperate to *simultaneously* find out $\sum_{i=1}^{n} V_i$ without revealing to each other anything other than the answer. To achieve this, each party chooses a random value, which is used to hide the input. The intermediate sum is additively split among the participants.

The summation protocol by Atallah *et al.* [2] is briefly described as follows. Every party i has a private value V_i. Party i chooses a random number R_i. Every party $2i$ gives to $2i + 1$ his $V_{2i} + R_{2i}$, then every $2i + 1$ gives to $2i$ his R_{2i+1}. Let us denote A_i as the sum $V_i + R_i$ for each party i. The odd (resp., even)-numbered parties together compute the sum $A + R$ (resp., R), where $A = \sum_{i=1}^{n} A_i$ and $R = \sum_{i=1}^{n} R_i$. Note that to compute the sum, the protocol should not let each party send his share in the clear to all other parties, which is obviously insecure. The protocol in [2] gives a non-trivial way to do this by requiring the participants to compute a randomized private sum. We refer readers to the literature for details of summation procedure. Finally, the odd (resp., even) simultaneously exchange their quantities to obtain A. We use their protocol as a black box, and refer readers to the literature for more details [2].

2.3 Protocol Description

Our private distributed scalar product protocol is shown in Figure 1. Alice's input of the protocol is a private vector X. Each party B_i (for $1 \leq i \leq n$) has a private value y_i. At the end of the protocol, the scalar product $X \cdot Y$ is learned by Alice or by every participant, where $Y = (y_1, \ldots, y_n)$.

Alice encrypts each element x_i of her vector X with her public key in homomorphic encryption. The ciphertext c_i is sent to B_i, respectively. Because B_i does not know Alice's private key, Alice's value is safe. Because of the properties of homomorphic encryption, entity B_i is able to compute the ciphertext corresponding to $x_i y_i$, even though he does not know x_i. The resulting ciphertext is w_i in Figure 1. To hide y_i, B_i computes the ciphertext w_i' corresponding to $x_i y_i - s_i$, where s_i is a random number. Alice receives ciphertext w_i' from each B_i, and computes the product of all w_i's, which is decrypted to $X \cdot Y - \sum_{i=1}^{n} s_i$. Next, all of B_is carry out a private multi-party summation protocol that computes $\sum_{i=1}^{n} s_i$. At the end of the summation protocol, every B_i learns the sum. Alice obtains the sum from B_is, and computes $X \cdot Y$ without learning the individual y_i values.

Our private distributed scalar product protocol is based on the private two-party scalar product protocol by Goethalsh *et al.* [13], where each party has a vector and the protocol outputs the scalar product result of the two vectors in a split form. That is, the scalar product result is split between the two parties, and equals to the sum of two shares. The concept of shared private computation can also be found in [1, 12]. A variant of our protocol allows all participating parties to learn the scalar product result $X \cdot Y$. Alice with S_A and all B_is, each with s_i, carry out a private multi-party summation protocol with their inputs. Our analysis is based on the protocol in Figure 1.

PRIVATE INPUTS: Private vector $X = (x_1, \ldots, x_n) \in \mathbb{Z}_m^n$ by Alice; private values y_1 by entity $B_1, \ldots, y_n$ by entity B_n, where $y_i \in \mathbb{Z}_m$ for all $i \in [1, n]$.

PRIVATE OUTPUTS: Alice learns $X \cdot Y \mod m$, where m is a public parameter.

1. Setup phase. Alice does: Generate a private and public key pair (sk, pk). Send pk to all B_i.
2. Alice does for $i \in \{1, \ldots, n\}$: Generate a random new string r_i. Send $c_i = \mathsf{Enc}_{\mathsf{pk}}(x_i; r_i)$ to B_i.
3. B_i does: Set $w_i = c_i^{y_i} \mod m$. Generate a random plaintext s_i and a random nonce r_i'. Send to Alice $w_i' = w_i \cdot \mathsf{Enc}_{\mathsf{pk}}(-s_i; r_i')$.
4. Alice does: Compute the product of ciphertext w_i's as $\Pi_{i=1}^n w_i' \mod m$. Use her private key sk to decrypt the product, and obtain the partial result $S_A = X \cdot Y - \sum_{i=1}^n s_i$.
5. All B_is, each with s_i, carry out a private multi-party summation protocol with their inputs (described in 2.2). At the end of that protocol, each B_i obtains $S_B = \sum_{i=1}^n s_i$.
6. Alice does: Obtain S_B from (any of the) B_is. Compute $X \cdot Y = S_A + S_B$.

Fig. 1. Private Distributed Scalar Product Protocol. m is a public parameter of the homomorphic encryption scheme.

Operation	Scalar Product Phase	Summation Phase	Total
Comp. (Alice)	$O(n)$ homomorphic op.	$O(1)$	$O(n)$ homomorphic op.
Comm. (Alice)	$O(n)$	$O(1)$	$O(n)$
Comp. (B_i)	$O(\log y_i)$ homomorphic op.	$O(1)$	$O(\log y_i)$ homomorphic op.
Comm. (B_i)	$O(1)$	$O(1)$	$O(1)$

Table 1. Computation (Comp.) and communication (comm.) complexities of the private distributed scalar product protocol. We denote by n the length of Alice's vector X. The logarithmic factor is due to using multiplications to compute exponentiation in step 3.

2.4 Analysis of the Protocol

The correctness of the protocol is obvious. Alice obtains from B_i (for all $i \in [1, n]$) an encryption of $x_i y_i - s_i$. Alice multiplies the n ciphertexts, and decrypts to obtain the sum $\sum_{i=1}^n x_i y_i - s_i$. Once Alice obtains $\sum_{i=1}^n s_i$, she computes $X \cdot Y = \sum_{i=1}^n x_i y_i$. The security and efficiency of our private multi-party protocol for distributed scalar product are analyzed.

The security of our private multi-party scalar product protocol is based on the security of the private two-party scalar product protocol [13] and the private multi-party summation protocol [2]. In general, the multi-party protocol among players is secure when the privacy and correctness are guaranteed for all players. It is said that a protocol protects privacy when the information that is leaked by the distributed computation is limited to the information that can be learned from the designated output of the computation [22]. In our problem, Alice's private vector X and each entity B_i's private value y_i are not leaked to each other, besides the scalar product. Note that in almost all existing private scalar product solutions, one player can construct a system of linear equations based on the specification of the protocol, and solve it for the secret values.

Our security is in the semi-honest model, where it is assumed that all players follow the protocol, but they are also curious: that is, they may store all exchanged data and try to deduce information from it. One challenge in designing the multi-party scalar product protocol is to prevent collusions among players. In particular, during the step of summation, Alice may attempt to collude with a subset of players B_is to discover the private values of other players.

As in almost all private multi-party protocols, we assume that each party inputs his or her true private values. Providing skewed values during computation can result in inaccurate results, and wasting the computation power and bandwidth of all participants including the dishonest party. In addition, the effect of providing skewed intermediate value by a participant can be achieved by raising or lowering his or her own input. This issue is standard in multi-party protocols (both semi-honest and malicious models). Suppose A wants to compute the trustworthiness of C with help of $B_1, \ldots, B_n$, and suppose B_i is a friend of C, B_i may modify the output of the protocol by raising s_i in Figure 1. As a result, A gets a higher value for C. However, B_i can achieve the same effect by choosing a different input to begin with. Therefore, this type of attacks is not considered in multi-party protocols including ours. It is worth mentioning that once detected, this type of behaviors could be folded back into the reputation of participants, which can provide incentives for being honest during the computation.

Because of the intrinsic nature of the problems considered, even if the protocol is secure in the malicious model (discussed later), multi-party computation such as ours is still vulnerable to probing attacks. For example, if A wants to learn B_i's private value y_i, A can engage the protocol with input $X = (0, \ldots, 0, 1, 0, \ldots, 0)$ by setting only the i-th entry to be one. After the protocol A learns $X * Y = y_i$, which is the private value of B_i.

The security of our protocol is summarized in the following theorem.

Theorem 1. *Assume that* (Gen, Enc, Dec) *is a semantically secure homomorphic public-key cryptosystem. The private distributed scalar product protocol presented in this section is secure in the semi-honest model. Alice's privacy is guaranteed when for all $i \in [1, n]$, entity B_i is a probabilistic polynomial-time machine. Also, for all $i \in [1, n]$, B_i's privacy is information-theoretical.*

Proof (sketch): Each entity B_i only sees a random ciphertext from Alice, for which B_i cannot guess the ciphertext. This is because of the semantic security of the homomorphic encryption scheme. Hence, B_i cannot guess Alice's value x_i.

During the summation protocol, each B_i only sees random values exchanged. Hence, B_i cannot guess the random secret s_j of B_j for all $j \neq i$.

On the other hand, Alice only sees (1) random value $x_i y_i - s_i$, (2) the sum of all s_i, and (3) the final computation scalar product $X \cdot Y$. She does not gain additional information about Y besides the final scalar product. In addition, the protocol prevents collusions among Alice and a subset D of B_is to discover private y_j value of B_j for $B_j \notin D$, because the summation protocol guarantees that all B_is learn the sum simultaneously. Thus, Alice obtains no information about any B_i except the scalar product $X \cdot Y$, and each B_i obtains no information about Alice and entity B_j for all $j \neq i$. □

The private multi-party summation protocol is efficient, as it does not require any type of encryption schemes. The summation step does not introduce significant overhead. Details of complexities are summarized in Table 1.

Security in a malicious model Malicious adversaries, unlike semi-honest ones, can behave arbitrarily without following the protocol. They may refuse to participate the protocol, abort the protocol without finishing it, and tamper with intermediate values. Any protocol secure against honest-but-curious adversaries can be modified to a protocol that is secure against malicious adversaries using standard zero-knowledge proofs showing that all parties follow the protocol. At each step of the protocol, each party uses their transcripts and zero-knowledge proofs to convince the other parties that they have followed the protocol without cheating. We do not describe the details of how this transformation is done in this paper.

3 Credential-Based Trust Model

In this section, we present a simple credential-based trust model that is useful for the trust management in distributed environments. The main idea is to convert role-based credentials and related information into quantitative trustworthiness values of a requester, which is used for making authorization decisions. Quantitative authorization policies can allow fine-tuned access decisions instead of binary (allow or deny) verdicts, and provide more diversified access options for requesters. In addition, quantitative authorization enables providers to correlate the quality of service with the qualifications of requests (e.g., more rewards or higher resolution with higher trustworthiness). This approach utilizes and leverages existing credential and role-based management infrastructure for autonomous domains (e.g., [28, 36]) and improves the accuracy of trustworthiness prediction.

Our private multi-party scalar product protocol in the previous section can be used to compute trust values from recommendations in Section 3.2.

Terminology: In our model, we define the *administrator* of a role as the organization that creates and manages the role. If a role credential of an entity D is signed and issued by the administrator of the role, that role is said to be an *affiliated role* of D (this type of role is usually obtained through the affiliation with an organization, and thus the name). If a role credential of D is instead issued through delegation and signed by entities other than the administrator of the role, that role is called a *delegated role* of D. We define an *entity* to be an organization or an individual. An entity may issue credentials. Also, an entity may have one or more affiliated roles or delegated roles, which are authenticated by role credentials. An *affiliated role credential* is the credential for an affiliated role, and is signed by the administrator of the role. Similarly, a *delegated role credential* is the credential for proving a delegated role. A *privilege* can be a role assignment or an action on a resource. A role r administered by entity A is denoted as $A.r$. A role defines a group of entities who are members of this role.

3.1 Definitions in Credential-Based Trust Model

A trust value in the credential-based trust model represents what an entity thinks about the trustworthiness of another entity or a role in another entity. More specifically, trust value $t(A, B)$ in the credential-based trust model represents what entity A thinks about the trustworthiness of entity B; trust value $t(A, B.r)$ in the credential-based trust model represents what entity A thinks about the trustworthiness of role $B.r$ administered by entity B. For example, a Grid Computing facility GCLab assigns trust values to types of users, such as role *professor* and role *student* in a university U, and role *researcher* from a research center C. When a user holding a certain role credential requests for access to the grid computing facility, his or her privileges are specified based on the trust value of the role. Note that the credential-based trust model is different from existing trust models that generate rating certificates, which are signed certificates of one's trustworthiness generated by one's peers [23].

Ideally, an entity A maintains a trust value for each role in organization B. For example, GCLab gives different trust value to role *student* and role *professor* in a university. Hence, a requester with a *professor* role credential may be granted a different level of access privileges from a requester with a *student* role credential.

Definition 1. *If an entity A gives a role $B.r$ in B a trust value $t(A, B.r)$, then any individual who has a valid role credential of role $B.r$ issued by B has the trust value $t(A, B.r)$.*

Trust values can be derived from previous interaction experiences and/or others' recommendations, and we focus on the latter. Deriving trust values from previous transactions usually depends on specific applications, and is not discussed in this paper. In what follows, we use *trust value of a credential* to mean the trust value of the credential issuer.

3.2 Derive Trust Value From Recommendations

We describe a *weighted average* method for an entity A to compute a trust value on entity B or role $B.r$. This computation is useful when A does not have any previous interaction experience with B or $B.r$, and A wants to combine others' opinions of B or $B.r$ in forming her trust value.

In the credential-based trust model, the *recommendation* by an entity E on B is the trust value $t(E, B)$ that E gives to B. A *confidence value* represents how much A trusts the judgement of a recommender, and is defined as the trust value of A on the recommender.

Above definitions mean that recommendations are weighted by A's confidence on the recommenders. Formally, we define the weighted average computation of trust value as follows. We denote n as the number of recommenders, and E_i represents the

i-th recommender. Let MAX_TRUST be the public upper bound of all trust values. Without loss of generality, we assume a trust value is non-negative. We assume that A has already obtained her trust values $t(A, E_1)$, $t(A, E_2)$, ..., $t(A, E_n)$ on the recommenders. We also assume that each of the recommenders E_i has formed her trust value $t(E_i, B)$ on the target entity B. (In case no one in the system knows about entity B, a default trust value can be assigned to B to indicate this situation.) The formula for computing $t(A, B)$ is shown as follows, where weight $w(A, E_i) = t(A, E_i)/\text{MAX\_TRUST}$.

$$t(A, B) = \frac{1}{n} \sum_{i=1}^{n} w(A, E_i) t(E_i, B) \tag{1}$$

Value $w(A, E_i)$ represents the weight of E_i's recommendation (trust value) on B for A. Variants of weighted average computation have been used in other reputation systems, such as ordered weighted average [32]. The above description also applies when the target to be evaluated is a role, for example $B.r$, instead of an entity.

Application of private distributed scalar product protocol. Equation (1) is useful for A only when all the trust values $t(E_i, B)$ are available. However, trust value $t(E_i, B)$ is private information of E_i, who has the incentive to hide it, especially when E_i thinks negatively about B. Similarly, A may consider her trust values $t(A, E_i)$ sensitive too. The problem is how to compute the weighted average in (1) without leaking the private information of each entity. Our protocol for private multi-party scalar product in Section 2 solves this problem and satisfies the privacy requirement.

Combining trust values for access. If a requester presents multiple role credentials, then the trust values of the credentials are to be combined. For example, one simple method is to sum the trust values. This means that the requester with multiple credentials of low trust values can gain the same access privileges as a requester with one credential of a high trust value. This combination method is intuitive and is used in point-based trust management model [35].

Delegation [4, 28, 36] is important for transferring trust in decentralized environments. Associating trust values with delegation credentials is different from role credentials because the values should not only depend on the initial credential issuer, but also the intermediate delegators's trustworthiness. Our trust model can be generalized to support delegation credentials. Due to space limit, we omit this description and refer readers to the full version of our paper.

4 Integration With Point-Based Trust Management

Our proposed private multi-party protocol and trust model are useful for general access control in a decentralized environment. In this paper, we describe how it can be used for deriving point values in the existing point-based trust management model [35], which was proposed for the privacy protection of sensitive information in open environments. We briefly introduce the point-based model next.

4.1 Point-Based Trust Management

In the point-based trust management model [35], the authorization policies of a resource owner define an *access threshold* for each of its resources. The threshold is the minimum number of points required for a requester to access that resource. For example, accessing a medical database might require fifty points. The resource owner also defines a *point value* for each type of credential, which denotes the number of points or credits a requester obtains if a type of credential is disclosed. For example, a valid ACM membership might have ten points. This means that a user can disclose his or her ACM membership credential in exchange for ten points. (This is called a trust management model as opposed to an access control model, because the resource owner does not know the identities or role assignments of requesters *a priori* as in conventional access control settings.)

Each user defines a *sensitivity score* for each of their credentials. The sensitivity score represents the unwillingness to disclose a credential. For example, Alice may give a sensitivity score of ten to her college ID, and give fifty to her credit card. The user is granted access to a certain resource if the access threshold is met and all of the disclosed credentials are valid. Otherwise, the access is denied. From the requester's point of view, one central question is how to fulfill the access threshold while disclosing the least amount of sensitive information.

The credential selection problem here is to determine an optimal combination of requester's credentials to disclose to the resource owner, such that the minimal amount of sensitive information is disclosed and the access threshold of the requested resource is satisfied by the disclosed credentials. A private two-party dynamic programming protocol has been proposed to solve the credential selection problem [35].

4.2 Derivation of Point Values

Existing work on point-based trust management [35] does not describe how point values can be obtained or how to systematically derive points corresponding to credentials. The credential-based trust model presented in Section 3 answers this question. Using the described methods, a resource owner computes the trust values of credential issuers and their roles. The resulting trust values are to be used as point values of a resource owner in point-based trust management.

For delegation credentials presented by a requester, a resource owner can use the trust model to compute the discounted trust value of the credential. The trust value can only be computed exactly when the delegation credential is revealed. However, this information is private to the requester in the credential selection computation in point-based trust management. To mitigate this problem, a resource owner can use an approximate trust value during the credential selection computation, and then make adjustments when credentials are exchanged later.

The credential-based trust model completes the description of an important aspect in point-based authorization. Next, we give a concrete application for point-based authorization in location-query systems.

5 Applications to Location Query Systems

Privacy is an important concern in systems that use presence and other real-time user data. Presence provides great utility, but also has the potential for abuse. Managing security and privacy preferences in these systems can be complex. One approach to protect the privacy is to apply distributed anonymity algorithms to sensor networks [16, 17]. Another type of solutions is to augment existing routing protocols to enhance source-location privacy in sensor and conventional networks [18, 27].

However, these existing solutions are not suitable for several types of applications. In many scenarios such as 911 or medical emergency, road-side emergency of a GPS-enabled vehicle, and police enforcement agents, the location information of a subject is critical, and should not be hidden or anonymous. Also for example, in distributed collaboration applications such as Meeting Central [33], being able to share presence information to trusted collaborators is desirable.

Generally, sharing presence information implies sharing sensitive personal data such as computer activity, physical location, IM status, phone use, and other real-time attributes associated with a given user. Managing the privacy of this data requires capturing the user's preferences and concerns, which are typically quite individualistic. Some users feel comfortable sharing any personal details, but most want at least some control over what is shared and with whom.

A presence system can provide a service that runs on behalf of each user, acting as that user's always-online proxy. Through this proxy, the user has ultimate control over all their associated data. The proxy is resolvable based on the user's identity, and can expose services that can be queried by other entities in the system. One such service provides presence querying.

Alice's proxy chooses access decisions through a set of domain-specific entities called advisors. Each advisor provides input on possible decision responses based on its domain of expertise (e.g., reputation, purpose of the query, context of the exchange, value of the requested data). These inputs are then aggregated to determine the overall advice about a possible response. The idea is to provide a flexible mechanism that more accurately represents a user's decision process. Our credential-based trust model and point-based authorization can be used to implement a flexible advisor system.

Alice's proxy contains her policies and preferences, including the trust values of credentials that may be used for authentication. Alice also defines the precision associated with certain trust values. For example, if the trust value of the query issuer is twenty, then she might release her location information exactly. If the trust value is five, then she might release a *fuzzy interpretation* of her location, for example, the building or city where she is currently. Phrased more concretely, if Alice's closest friend, Bob, queries about her location, a precise answer is returned. If a stranger queries her location, nothing about Alice should be disclosed.

The reputation advisor computes the trust value of each query issuer, based on their credential information. The trust value is then compared to Alice's policies, and the corresponding location result is returned. The advisors reside in Alice's proxy that is a tamper-resistant system in order to prevent the leaking of private trust values.

Note that this model makes it easy to use the trust value not just in deciding what to share, but in determining the system's confidence that the right decision is made. A high trust value represents high confidence and can be executed without bothering Alice. A low trust value represents low confidence in a decision, and if low enough, may warrant interrupting Alice to check that the right decision is being made for her. This confidence metric is then fed back into the system for use the next time a similar query from the same entity arrives, and used to provide an aggregate sense of past confidence.

For location-query systems, the main advantages of using point-based trust management as opposed to conventional access control mechanisms are the flexibility of making access control decisions with an arbitrary degree of precision and the ability to derive some simple notion of confidence. In order to achieve the same expressiveness, a boolean-based access control policy would be very inefficient, as one needs to enumerate all of the possible combinations of authorizations.

6 Related Work

Secure Multi-party Computation (SMC) was introduced in a seminal paper by Yao [34], which contained a scheme for secure comparison. Suppose Alice (with input a) and Bob (with input b) desire to determine whether or not $a < b$ without revealing any information other than this result (this is known as *Yao's Millionaire Problem*). More generally, SMC allows Alice and Bob with respective private inputs a and b to compute a function $f(a, b)$ by engaging in a secure protocol for public function f. Furthermore, the protocol is private in that it reveals no additional information. This means that Alice (resp. Bob) learns nothing other than what can be deduced from a (resp. b) and $f(a, b)$. Elegant general schemes are given in [5, 8, 14, 15] for computing any function f privately.

Besides the generic work in the area of SMC, there has been extensive work on the privacy-preserving computation of various functions. For example, computational geometry [1, 10], privacy-preserving computational biology [3], and private two-party dynamic programming for the knapsack problem [35]. Compared to existing private scalar product protocols [1, 13, 31], our protocol is designed for general privacy-preserving distributed scalar product computation, where vector values are distributed among multiple players. The protocol has promising applications in the information discovery of reputation systems. Our security is efficient, and is comparable to the private two-party scalar product of Goethalsh *et al.* [13].

There has been much work on the privacy-awareness for ubiquitous computing environments [16, 18, 20, 26]. An existing approach to protect the location-privacy in sensor networks is through distributed anonymity algorithms that are applied in a sensor network, before service providers gain access to the data [16]. Another category of solutions is to augment existing routing protocols to enhance source-location privacy in sensor and conventional networks [18, 27]. A more fine-grained approach for managing the access to location data is based on privacy-policies [20, 26], which is closer to our solution. Using point-based authorization, we are able to support more flexible trust establishment mechanism without rigid boolean-based policy specifications.

Our trust model work is related to the existing work on recommendation or reputation systems [6, 19] in decentralized models. Trust evidences that are generated by recommendations and past experiences have been used for trust establishment in both ad-hoc and ubiquitous computing environments [11, 24, 29]. This type of trust evidence is flexible and straightforward to collect. The notion of uncheatable reputation was proposed in recent work by Carbunar and Sion [7], who developed a reputation mechanism that prevents untruthful reputation information using witnesses. In comparison, the main property of our trust model is the use of role-based organizational infrastructure to derive trust values, which aims to improve the scalability of trust computation.

7 Conclusions and Future Work

In this paper, we have developed a general protocol for privacy-preserving multi-party scalar product computation. This protocol can be used for peers to jointly compute a weighted trust score from *private* recommendations and *private* weights. We have also presented a simple credential-based trust model for evaluating trustworthiness based on role and delegation credentials, and recommendations. Finally, we have described the architecture of a location-query system for giving fuzzy location information based on the trust score of a requester.

There are several interesting areas to explore for future work. One is to evaluate other types of trust computation besides weighted average. For example, the ordered-weighted-average operator allows the user to weight the input values in relation to their relative ordering [32]. Another promising direction is to design private multi-party protocols for other desirable functionalities in a trust model. For example, an entity wants to find out who else in the system has a similar profile of trust values as his or her own — other entities who have similar likes and dislikes. The problem becomes how to privately compute the distance between two set of trust values according to certain metrics. As part of future works, we also plan to evaluate the effectiveness of credential-based trust model in answering fuzzy location queries. This experimentation involves an implementation of the point-based authorization model, the weighted scalar protocol computation, and the comparison tests with conventional trust models.

References

1. M. J. Atallah and W. Du. Secure multi-party computational geometry. In *Proceedings of 7th International Workshop on Algorithms and Data Structures (WADS 2001)*, volume 2125 of *Lecture Notes in Computer Science*, pages 165–179. Springer Verlag, August 2001.

2. M. J. Atallah, H. G. Elmongui, V. Deshpande, and L. B. Schwarz. Secure supply-chain protocols. In *2003 IEEE International Conference on Electronic Commerce (CEC 2003)*, pages 293–302. IEEE Computer Society, 2003.

3. M. J. Atallah and J. Li. Secure outsourcing of sequence comparisons. In *4th Workshop on Privacy Enhancing Technologies (PET)*, volume 3424 of *Lecture Notes in Computer Science*, pages 63–78, 2004.

4. T. Aura. Distributed access-rights management with delegation certificates. In *Secure Internet Programming – Security Issues for Distributed and Mobile Objects*, volume 1603 of *LNCS*, pages 211–235. Springer, 1999.

5. M. Ben-Or and A. Wigderson. Completeness theorems for non-cryptographic fault-tolerant distributed computation. In *The Twentieth Annual ACM Symposium on Theory of Computing (STOC)*, pages 1–10. ACM Press, 1988.

6. T. Beth, M. Borcherding, and B. Klein. Valuation of trust in open networks. In *Proceedings of the Third European Symposium on Research in Computer Security (ESORICS '94)*, pages 3–18, November 1994.

7. B. Carbunar and R. Sion. Uncheatable reputation for distributed computation markets. In *Financial Cryptography and Data Security Conference (FC '06)*, 2006.

8. D. Chaum, C. Crépeau, and I. Damgard. Multiparty unconditionally secure protocols. In *The twentieth annual ACM Symposium on Theory of Computing (STOC)*, pages 11–19. ACM Press, 1988.

9. I. Damgård and M. Jurik. A generalisation, a simplification and some applications of Paillier's probabilistic public-key system. In *4th International Workshop on Practice and Theory in Public Key Cryptosystems (PKC '01)*, LNCS 1992, pages 119–136, 2001.

10. W. Du. A study of several specific secure two-party computation problems, 2001. PhD thesis, Purdue University, West Lafayette, Indiana.

11. L. Eschenauer, V. D. Gligor, and J. Baras. On trust establishment in mobile ad-hoc networks. In *Proceedings of the Security Protocols Workshop*, April 2002.

12. K. B. Frikken and M. J. Atallah. Privacy preserving route planning. In *Proceedings of the 2004 ACM workshop on Privacy in the Electronic Society (WPES)*, pages 8–15. ACM Press, 2004.

13. B. Goethals, S. Laur, H. Lipmaa, and T. Mielikäinen. On private scalar product computation for privacy-preserving data mining. In C. Park and S. Chee, editors, *ICISC*, volume 3506 of *Lecture Notes in Computer Science*, pages 104–120. Springer, 2004.

14. O. Goldreich. Secure multi-party computation, Oct. 2002. Unpublished Manuscript.

15. O. Goldreich, S. Micali, and A. Wigderson. How to play any mental game. In *The nineteenth annual ACM conference on theory of computing*, pages 218–229. ACM Press, 1987.

16. M. Gruteser and D. Grunwald. Anonymous usage of location-based services through spatial and temporal cloaking. In *ACM/USENIX International Conference on Mobile Systems, Applications, and Services (MobiSys)*, 2003.

17. M. Gruteser, G. Schelle, A. Jain, R. Han, and D. Grunwald. Privacy-aware location sensor networks. In *9th USENIX Workshop on Hot Topics in Operating Systems (HotOS IX)*, 2003.

18. P. Kamat, Y. Zhang, W. Trappe, and C. Ozturk. Enhancing source-location privacy in sensor network routing. In *Proceedings of 25th International Conference on Distributed Computing Systems (ICDCS)*, 2005.

19. R. Kohlas and U. M. Maurer. Confidence valuation in a public-key infrastructure based on uncertain evidence. In *Proceedings of the Third International Workshop on Practice and Theory in Public Key Cryptography (PKC '00)*, volume 1751 of *Lecture Notes in Computer Science*, pages 93–112. Springer, 2000.

20. M. Langheinrich. A privacy awareness system for ubiquitous computing environments. In *In 4th International Conference on Ubiquitous Computing*, 2002.
21. P. Paillier. Public-key cryptosystems based on composite degree residuosity classes. *Advances in Cryptology – EUROCRYPT 1999*, LNCS 1592:223–238, 1999.
22. B. Pinkas. Cryptographic techniques for privacy-preserving data mining. *KDD Explorations*, 4(2):12–19, 2002.
23. P. Ruth, D. Xu, B. K. Bhargava, and F. Regnier. E-notebook middleware for accountability and reputation based trust in distributed data sharing communities. In C. D. Jensen, S. Poslad, and T. Dimitrakos, editors, *iTrust*, volume 2995 of *Lecture Notes in Computer Science*, pages 161–175. Springer, 2004.
24. B. Shand, N. Dimmock, and J. Bacon. Trust for ubiquitous, transparent collaboration. *Wirel. Netw.*, 10(6):711–721, 2004.
25. Shibboleth. http://middleware.internet2.edu/shibboleth/.
26. E. Snekkenes. Concepts for personal location privacy policies. In *In Proceedings of the 3rd ACM Conference on Electronic Commerce (CEC)*, pages 48–57. ACM Press, 2001.
27. P. F. Syverson, D. M. Goldschlag, and M. G. Reed. Anonymous connections and onion routing. In *Proceedings of the IEEE Symposium on Security and Privacy*, pages 44–54, May 1997.
28. R. Tamassia, D. Yao, and W. H. Winsborough. Role-based cascaded delegation. In *Proceedings of the ACM Symposium on Access Control Models and Technologies (SACMAT '04)*, pages 146 – 155. ACM Press, June 2004.
29. G. Theodorakopoulos and J. S. Baras. Trust evaluation in ad-hoc networks. In *WiSe '04: Proceedings of the 2004 ACM workshop on Wireless security*, pages 1–10. ACM Press, 2004.
30. H. Tran, M. Hitchens, V. Varadharajan, and P. Watters. A trust based access control framework for P2P file-sharing systems. In *Proceedings of the Proceedings of the 38th Annual Hawaii International Conference on System Sciences (HICSS'05) - Track 9*, page 302c. IEEE Computer Society, 2005.
31. J. Vaidya and C. Clifton. Privacy preserving association rule mining in vertically partitioned data. In *Proceedings of The 8th ACM SIGKDD International Conference on Knowledge Discovery and Data Mining*, pages 639–644. ACM Press, July 2002.
32. R. Yager. On ordered weighted averaging aggregation operators in multi-criteria decision making. *IEEE Transactions on Systems, Man and Cybernetics*, 18(1):183–190, 1988.
33. N. Yankelovich, W. Walker, P. Roberts, M. Wessler, J. Kaplan, and J. Provino. Meeting central: making distributed meetings more effective. In *Proceedings of the 2004 ACM Conference on Computer Supported Cooperative Work (CSCW '04)*, pages 419–428, New York, NY, USA, 2004. ACM Press.
34. A. C. Yao. How to generate and exchange secrets. In *Proceedings of the 27th IEEE Symposium on Foundations of Computer Science*, pages 162–167. IEEE Computer Society Press, 1986.
35. D. Yao, K. B. Frikken, M. J. Atallah, and R. Tamassia. Point-based trust: Define how much privacy is worth. In *Proceedings of the Eighth International Conference on Information and Communications Security (ICICS '06)*, December 2006.
36. D. Yao, R. Tamassia, and S. Proctor. On improving the performance of role-based cascaded delegation in ubiquitous computing. In *Proceedings of IEEE/CreateNet Conference on Security and Privacy for Emerging Areas in Communication Networks (SecureComm '05)*, pages 157–168. IEEE Press, September 2005.

Trust Transfer in Distributed Systems

Changyu Dong, Giovanni Russello and Naranker Dulay

Department of Computing
Imperial College London
180 Queen's Gate, London, SW7 2AZ, UK
{changyu.dong,g.russello,n.dulay}@imperial.ac.uk

Abstract. Trust transfer is a common technique employed in trust management systems to establish relationships between parties that are strangers. It is also well known that trust is not always transferable. That is, given an existing trust relationship, it may or may not be possible to derive new trust from it. In particular, it is not known under which constraints trust is transferable. In this paper we investigate trust transfer and identify when trust is transferable. Our analysis starts with a simple trust model. By using the model, we find that trust transfer is related to trust policy entailment. We then present a modal logic system which captures how trust and beliefs evolve in distributed systems. With the modal logic system we identify the key constraints on trust transfer regarding the communication between the trustor and the recommender and the trustor's belief state.

1 Introduction

The open and dynamic nature of modern distributed systems presents a significant challenge to security management. Traditional security management systems are centralised and operate under a closed world assumption. All participants must have an identity established by the system and share some secret information with the system for authentication purposes. The centralised model is usually infeasible in open distributed systems. Trust management [1, 2, 3, 4, 5, 6] is an alternative approach that utilises some notion of *trust* in order to specify and interpret security policies and make authorisation decisions on security-related actions.

One of the main objectives of trust management is to build up trust between two strangers effectively. Trust can be established by direct experience [7, 8]. Generally, two parties start from interactions requiring little or no trust, the outcome of each interaction with the trustee affects the trustor's trust towards it. A positive outcome increases the trust while a negative outcome decreases the trust. As trust increases, the parties can engage in interactions which require more trust. However, building trust in this way needs time and is inappropriate when both parties require a quick decision, for example, for a one-off interaction. *Trust transfer* (or trust transitivity) is more useful in such cases. Trust transfer is the process of deriving new trust from existing trust. One example of

Please use the following format when citing this chapter:

Dong, C., Russello, G. and Dulay, N., 2007, in IFIP International Federation for Information Processing, Volume 238, Trust Management, eds. Etalle, S., Marsh, S., (Boston: Springer), pp. 17–29.

utilising trust transfer is *recommendations*. A recommendation is a statement regarding the trustworthiness of the potential trustee from another party, the recommender. The trustor makes its decision based on the recommendation. For example, Alice may trust Bob to be a good car mechanic if her friend Carol says so. This kind of scenario is common in the real-world and seems to work well. But when we try to capture it in computational trust models, we encounter difficulties.

A key problem is that trust is not always transferable [9, 10, 11, 12]. That is, given an existing trust relationship, it may or may not be possible to derive new trust from it. In particular, it is not known under which constraints trust is transferable. Without solving this problem, systems based on trust transfer can be unreliable. Trust may be misplaced when it is not transferable, which may consequently lead to bad decisions.

In the remainder of this paper, we first present a basic trust model and use it to analyse the trust transfer problem. We then develop a modal logic system which captures how trust and beliefs evolve in distributed systems and derive the constraints for trust transfer. We believe that the constraints and the modal logic provide a foundation for constructing more reliable trust management systems.

2 A Basic Trust Model

Our basic trust model is similar to the one presented by Castelfranchi *et al* [13]. It is simple but captures the most important properties of trust. The model is described as follows:

- Trust is a binary relation between two subjects: the trustor and the trustee.
- Trust is a binary decision: trust or distrust.
- Trust is bound to a goal. A goal is what the trustor wants to achieve by relying on the trustee or how the trustee is expected to behave. For example, "be a good car mechanic" or "to read my document".
- Trust is subjective. For the same trustee and goal, different trustors may make a different decision.

In this model, trust is defined as a logic predicate: $Trust(trustor, trustee, goal)$. The predicate is true when the trustor trusts the trustee for the goal, and false otherwise. Each subject has a set of trust policies. A trust policy reflects the trustor's evaluation criteria and sets requirements for certain attributes of the trustee and the environment. A trust policy is modelled as $Trust(trustor, trustee, goal) \leftrightarrow pol$, where the policy body *pol* is a conjunction of predicates. The trustor trusts the trustee for a goal if and only if the trust policy body is true. Trust policies capture the subjectivity of trust.

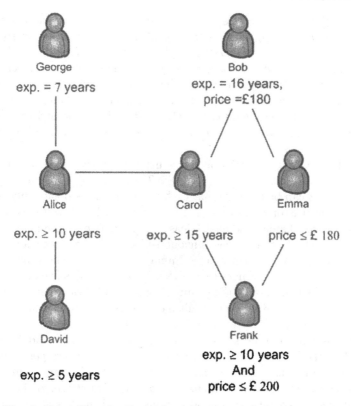

Fig. 1. Trust Transfer Example: subjects and their trust policies

3 Analysis of Trust Transfer

Before we begin our analysis, we need to express the problem more formally. Given $Trust(r, e, g)$ is true if $Trust(t, e, g)$ is also true, i.e. $Trust(r, e, g) \rightarrow Trust(t, e, g)$, then we say trust is transferable from r to t. Our goal is to find the constraints for trust transfer.

It is clear that if the trust policies for subject r and t are $Trust(r, e, g) \leftrightarrow pol$ and $Trust(t, e, g) \leftrightarrow pol'$, then $Trust(r, e, g) \rightarrow Trust(t, e, g)$ if and only if $pol \rightarrow pol'$. Loosely speaking, if pol is more strict than pol', then the trust established by satisfying pol can transfer from r to t. We can explain this using an example (see Fig. 1): Alice will trust anyone to be a good car mechanic if he has at least ten years experience, and Carol will trust anyone to be a good car mechanic if he has at least fifteen years experience. For example, if Carol thinks that Bob is a good car mechanic, Alice can also trust Bob because he satisfies her requirement. In this case, trust is said to transfer from Carol to Alice.

We can derive more rules from the above rule. For example, trust can transfer in a chain. A subject t_1 can derive a trust relationship $Trust(t_1, e, g)$ from $Trust(r, e, g)$, then another subject t_2 derives a new trust relationship

$Trust(t_2, e, g)$ from $Trust(t_1, e, g)$, and so on. According to the above rule, a trust chain $(Trust(r, e, g) \rightarrow Trust(t_1, e, g)) \wedge (Trust(t_1, e, g) \rightarrow Trust(t_2, e, g)) \wedge \ldots \wedge (Trust(t_{n-1}, e, g) \rightarrow Trust(t_n, e, g))$ is possible if and only if $(pol \rightarrow pol_1) \wedge (pol_1 \rightarrow pol_2) \wedge \ldots \wedge (pol_{n-1} \rightarrow pol_n)$ where $pol, pol_1, \ldots, pol_n$ are the corresponding trust policy bodies. In other words, a trust chain can be formed if the trust policies are monotonically relaxed along the chain. Suppose David will trust anyone to be a good car mechanic if he has at least five years experience, then the trust towards Bob can be transferred from Carol to David via Alice.

It is also possible to derive a new trust relationship from a set of existing trust relationships, i.e. $Trust(r_1, e, g) \wedge Trust(r_2, e, g) \ldots \wedge Trust(r_n, e, g) \rightarrow Trust(t, e, g)$. It can be the case that each recommender's policy only subsumes a subset of the trustor's requirements. For example, Frank will trust anyone to be a good car mechanic if he has at least ten years experience and asks for no more than £200, Carol will trust anyone to be a good car mechanic if he has at least fifteen years experience, and Emma will trust anyone to be a good car mechanic if he asks for no more than £180. Each of Frank's friends cannot convince him, but when both of them think Bob is good, Frank can trust Bob. So if $pol_1 \wedge pol_2 \ldots \wedge pol_n \rightarrow pol$, then multiple trust relationships can be combined to derive new trust.

If trust is transferable, so is distrust. If two subjects r and t have trust policies $Trust(r, e, g) \leftrightarrow pol$ and $Trust(t, e, g) \leftrightarrow pol'$, where $pol \rightarrow pol'$, then as we have said, trust can transfer from r to t. At the same time, distrust can transfer from t to r, i.e. $\neg Trust(t, e, g) \rightarrow \neg Trust(r, e, g)$. For example, Alice will trust anyone to be a good car mechanic if he has at least ten years experience, and Carol will trust anyone to be a good car mechanic if he has at least fifteen years experience. If Alice thinks that George is not a good car mechanic, Carol should not trust George because if he cannot satisfy Alice's requirement, he will never be able to satisfy her requirement.

4 A Modal Logic for Trust

With the basic model, we revealed the relationship between policy entailment and trust transfer. But this model is not suitable for analyzing trust transfer in distributed systems. One limitation of this model is that the knowledge is global, i.e. every subject knows everything in the system. But in distributed systems, subjects must make decisions based on their local knowledge. For example, if Alice doesn't know Carol's trust attitude towards Bob, she has no legitimate basis to conclude whether to trust Bob or not. In addition, first order logic is too strong for defining trust policies. When evaluating policies in first order logic, a subject must know the logical truth of the predicates, which may not be possible because the subject has only limited knowledge. In many situations, the subjects make decisions not because a predicate is true or false, but rather because they *believe* that it is true or false based on their local knowledge.

In order to overcome the limitations above, we extend the basic trust model to a modal logic system. The logic is built above an idealised model of a distributed system where each subject has its own local state and communicates with others via messages. Communication changes the subjects' local states and in turn results in the evolving of the subjects' beliefs and trust.

4.1 Syntax

First we define the language for the logic. We assume there exists a set $\mathbb{T}$ of primitive terms. $\mathbb{T}$ contains several disjoint sets of constant symbols: a set of primitive propositions, denoted by Φ_0; a set of subjects, denoted by $\mathbb{S}$; a set of goals, denoted by $\mathbb{G}$. Each individual subject is denoted by a natural number, i.e., $1, 2, ..., n$.

The well formed formulae(wff) of the logic is the smallest set that contains:

- The primitive proposition set Φ_0;
- $T_i(j, G)$, read as "subject i trusts subject j for goal G" where $1 \leq i \neq j \leq n$ are subjects and $G \in \mathbb{G}$;

and is closed under the following rules:

- if ϕ is a wff, then so is $\neg\phi$ where $\neg$ is the Boolean connective "not";
- if ϕ is a wff, then so is $B_i\phi$, read as "subject i believes ϕ" where $1 \leq i \leq n$ is a subject;
- if ϕ is a wff, then so is $S_i(j, \phi)$, read as "subject i sees a message from j containing ϕ" where $1 \leq i \neq j \leq n$ is a subject;
- if ϕ and ψ are wffs then so is $\phi \wedge \psi$ where $\wedge$ is the Boolean connective "and".

Other classical Boolean connectives $\vee$ (or), $\rightarrow$ (if), $\leftrightarrow$ (iff), $\top$ (true), and $\perp$ (false) can be defined as abbreviations.

4.2 System Model

Before giving the semantics for the logic, we first sketch our model of the distributed system in which the logic will be used. The system model is similar to those defined in [14, 15].

The basic elements of a system are subjects. For convenience, we use the same notation $\{1, 2, ..., n\}$ as in the syntax to denote the subjects in describing the system model. A subject can be a person, an organisation, a computer process or any other entity. We assume that subjects can be identified uniquely in the system.

The system is modelled using a state-based approach. At any time point, each subject i in the system is associated with a local state ω_i. The local state is determined by the subject's knowledge, e.g. its trust policies, its beliefs and what it has learned from other subjects etc. The system is also associated with a global state ω at the same time, which consists of all the local states of the subjects in the system.

Subjects can communicate with each other via messages. A message contains a conjunction of wffs and must have a sender. The receiver is optional for the message, that means the message can be sent by a point-to-point channel or by broadcast.We require that messages cannot be forged or modified during communication. If a subject forwards a message it received from another subject, e.g. "Alice says that Bob said that X", the original sender can be identified. Each subject maintains a message history, which is a sequence of messages it received. The messages in the history are ordered by the time they were received. When searching the message history, the subject always starts from the latest one and returns when it finds a match. This means that if there is a conflict in two messages, the subject always gets the newer one. We define a function $MESSAGE(\omega_i)$ which returns a set of messages which are the message history in state ω_i. We also define another function $MESSAGE\_CONTAINS(M, \phi, j)$ which returns true if the message M is from subject j and contains a wff ϕ, false otherwise.

Each subject has its own beliefs. The beliefs may come from the subject's preconceptions which are the initial beliefs when it entered the system, or by interacting with other subjects in the system, or come from outside the system, e.g. by perceiving the real world. The beliefs are uniquely determined by the subject's local state.

To make trust decisions, a subject must have a set of trust policies. A trust policy is based on the trustor's beliefs. For a subject i, the trust policy is always in the form of $T_i(j, G) \leftrightarrow B_i\phi$. This means that i, who is the trustor, will trust j, the trustee, for the goal G if and only if he believes ϕ where ϕ is a conjunction of wff.

4.3 Semantics

The most widely accepted modal logic system for beliefs is KD45 [16, 17, 18]. We follow this convention in our logic. Beliefs are interpreted in the *possible worlds semantics* [16] which is a formal semantics for modal logic and has been used intensively in formulating knowledge and beliefs. The intuition behind the possible worlds model is that there are many global states, or "worlds". In a given world, a subject considers a number of worlds to be possible according to its local state. The truth value of a wff depends on these possible worlds. For example, a subject is said to believe ϕ if and only if ϕ is true in all the worlds that the subject considered possible. The set of possible worlds is determined by the accessible relation (or possibility relation).

A Kripke structure [19] is used as a formal model for possible worlds semantics. A model for our logic is a tuple $(W, \pi, (\beta_i)_{1 \leq i \leq n})$, where:

- W is a set of all worlds,
- $\pi : \Phi_0 \rightarrow 2^W$ is a truth assignment mapping each primitive proposition to the set of worlds in which it is true;
- $(\beta_i)_{1 \leq i \leq n} \subseteq W \times W$ is an accessibility relation for the subject i. By convention, β_i is serial ($\forall w \exists u, \ u \in \beta_i(w)$), transitive ($\forall w, u, v, \ u \in \beta_i(w) \wedge v \in$

$\beta_i(u) \rightarrow v \in \beta_i(w))$ and Euclidean $(\forall w, u, v, \ u \in \beta_i(w) \wedge v \in \beta_i(w) \rightarrow v \in \beta_i(u))$.

We are now ready to present a formal definition of the truth of a wff. Given a model $\mathcal{M}$, we define the truth of a wff at a world ω, denoted by $\mathcal{M}, \omega \models \phi$ by induction on the structure of ϕ:

- $\mathcal{M}, \omega \models p$ iff $\omega \in \pi(p)$ for primitive proposition $p \in \Phi_0$;
- $\mathcal{M}, \omega \models \neg\phi$ iff $\mathcal{M}, \omega \not\models \phi$;
- $\mathcal{M}, \omega \models \phi \wedge \psi$ iff $\mathcal{M}, \omega \models \phi$ and $\mathcal{M}, \omega \models \psi$;
- $\mathcal{M}, \omega \models B_i\phi$ iff for all $u \in \beta_i(\omega), \mathcal{M}, u \models \phi$;
- $\mathcal{M}, \omega \models S_i(j, \phi)$ iff in ω, we can find a message $M \in MESSAGE(\omega_i)$ such that $MESSAGE\_CONTAINS(M, \phi, j)$ is true;
- $\mathcal{M}, \omega \models T_i(j, G)$ iff in ω there exists a policy $T_i(j, G) \leftrightarrow B_i\phi$ and $\mathcal{M}, \omega \models B_i\phi$.

Trust and beliefs are interrelated by the trust policies. This means that trust always depends on the subject's belief state. $S_{ij}\phi$ is totally determined by the subject i's local state. In any state, if i can find a message from j containing ϕ in its message history, then $S_{ij}\phi$ is true.

4.4 Axioms and Inference Rules

The axiom schema consists of the following axioms:

P   All substitution instances of propositional tautologies
B1 $B_i(\phi \wedge \psi) \leftrightarrow B_i\phi \wedge B_i\psi$
B2 $B_i\phi \wedge B_i(\phi \rightarrow \psi) \rightarrow B_i\psi$
B3 $\neg B_i\bot$
B4 $B_i\phi \leftrightarrow B_i B_i\phi$
B5 $\neg B_i\phi \rightarrow B_i\neg B_i\phi$
S1 $S_i(j, \phi \wedge \psi) \leftrightarrow S_i(j, \phi) \wedge S_i(j, \psi)$
S2 $S_i(j, \phi) \wedge S_i(j, \phi \rightarrow \psi) \rightarrow S_i(j, \psi)$
S3 $S_i(j, S_j(k, \phi)) \rightarrow S_i(k, \phi)$

and the following inference rules

R1   (Modus ponens): from $\vdash \phi$ and $\vdash \phi \rightarrow \psi$ infer $\vdash \psi$
R2   (Generalisation): from $\vdash \phi$ infer $\vdash B_i\phi$

Axioms B1-B5 are standard KD45 axioms which capture the characteristics of beliefs. B1 says that a subject believes the conjunction of two wffs ϕ and ψ, if and only if it believes ϕ and also believes ψ. B2 says that a subject believes all the logical consequences of its beliefs. B3 says that a subject does not believe an obviously false statement. B4 and B5 state that a subject knows what it believes and what it doesn't believe.

S1-S3 are axioms for communication. S1 and S2 are similar to B1 and B2. S3 says that a subject can identify the origin of a message forwarded by another subject. This comes from the requirement of our system model that every message must have a sender and cannot be forged or modified.

5 Constraints for Trust Transfer

We now conduct an in-depth examination of trust transfer. As in section 3, let's first formalize the problem. The difference between the modal logic system and the basic model is that trust is determined by the local state of each subject, and one subject's local state is totally independent of the states of other subjects. The only way that a subject can affect the local state of another subject is through communication. Here we redefine the problem as: given $S_k(i, T_i(j, G))$ is true if $T_k(j, G)$ is also true, i.e. $S_k(i, T_i(j, G)) \rightarrow T_k(j, G)$, then we say that trust is transferred from i to k. This means that a subject must know another subject's trust attitude before deriving a new trust relationship.

From $S_k(i, T_i(j, G))$, we cannot derive $T_k(j, G)$ in our logic system. There are many points to consider. First of all, does this message reflect the real local state of i? If subject i says it trusts j for G, is this the real attitude of i? Also, is the subject k willing to believe what i says? i might be telling the truth, but if k doesn't accept it, it still means nothing.

To make trust transferable, the trustor k must have some beliefs in the recommender i. These can be formalised as:

A1 $B_k(S_k(i, \phi) \rightarrow B_i\phi)$.
A2 $B_k(B_i\phi \rightarrow B_k\phi)$.

The first one says k must believe i is honest, i.e. i only says what it believes. The second one says k must be willing to accept beliefs from i.

With these beliefs, k can begin to derive new trust. Given $S_k(i, T_i(j, G))$, by R2, k has:

$$B_k(S_k(i, T_i(j, G)))$$

Recall A1 says that k believes what i said is what i believes. With the above belief and if we apply B2, k has:

$$B_k B_i(T_i(j, G))$$

Taking the above belief with A2 and applying B2, k has:

$$B_k B_k(T_i(j, G))$$

This can be simplified by applying B4:

$$B_k(T_i(j, G))$$

Now k believes that i trusts j for G. It is quite close, but k still cannot conclude that $T_k(j, G)$ is true. k trusts j for the goal G if and only if the trust policy $T_k(j, G) \leftrightarrow B_k\psi$ is satisfied, i.e. $B_k\psi$ is true. If $B_k(T_i(j, G)) \rightarrow B_k\psi$ is true, then the new trust relationship between k and j can be established.

Recall in section 3, that our analysis showed that policy entailment is an important factor for trust transfer. But in distributed systems, trust policies are in each subject's local state, so k will not believe i has a more strict policy until it sees it and believes this is indeed i's policy. i must show its policy to k, i.e. $S_k(i, T_i(j, G) \leftrightarrow B_i\phi)$. If k thinks i is honest, it can get:

$$B_k(T_i(j, G) \leftrightarrow B_i\phi))$$

The above belief with $B_k(T_i(j, G))$ and A2 can then derive:

$$B_k(\phi)$$

If i's policy is really more strict than k's, i.e. $\phi \to \psi$, k can generalise it into $B_k(\phi \to \psi)$ by R2. Then it can finally derive $B_k\psi$, which in consequence, makes $T_k(j, G)$ true.

In summary, our constraints for trust transfer in distributed systems can be stated as follows:

C1 The trustor must know the recommender's trust attitude, i.e. $S_k(i, T_i(j, G))$ is true.

C2 The trustor must believe the recommender is honest, i.e. $B_k(S_k(i, \phi) \to B_i\phi)$ is true.

C3 The trustor must be willing to acquire beliefs from the recommender, i.e. $B_k(B_i\phi \to B_k\phi)$ is true.

C4 The trustor must know the recommender's trust policy, i.e. $S_k(i, T_i(j, G) \leftrightarrow B_i\phi)$ is true.

C5 The recommender's trust policy must be more strict than the trustor's, i.e. $\phi \to \psi$ is true.

Rules for trust transfer chains, trust fusion and distrust transfer as discussed in section 3 can also be derived from the constraints above.

There may be some objections to constraint C4, which says that a trustor must know the recommender's trust policy. Here we make some justification for this. Intuitively, when we seek a recommendation from a friend, we expect the judgement of the recommender is better than ours. But how can we know it is better? We might ask the recommender why does he thinks that it is good or why he thinks that it is not good. In other words, we are trying to figure out his policy and compare it with ours. That is why most online recommendation systems need not only feedback but also comments: comments can provide clues of the reviewer's evaluation standards. It is sometimes possible that we can derive trust without asking for the policy. This usually happens when we already know the recommender very well, so we can infer what his policy is, i.e. we already have $B_k(T_i(j, G) \leftrightarrow B_i\phi))$ and $\phi \to \psi$.

6 Related Work

Trust transfer has been studied for many years as trust transitivity. Researchers have noticed that trust is not always transitive. Grandison [11] concluded that transitivity cannot be used as an axiom for trust relationships because of the diversity of distributed systems. He also concluded that trust is not transitive in general, but can be in some cases. Christianson et al [9] pointed out that modelling trust transitivity requires careful analysis of the beliefs held by principals about each other and the basis upon which these beliefs are held, otherwise using trust transitivity can be harmful.

Abdul-Rahman *et al* [5] studied conditions under which trust transitivity may hold. They came to the conclusion that for transitivity to be held in the simple example "if A trusts B and B trusts C then A trusts C", four conditions must be satisfied:

- B explicitly communicates his trust in C to A, as a 'recommendation'.
- A trusts B as a recommender, i.e. recommender trust exists in the systems.
- A is allowed to make judgements about the 'quality' of B's recommendation (based on A's policies).
- Trust is not absolute, i.e. A may trust C less than B does, based on B's recommendation.

This seems to be a more detailed formulation of trust transitivity, but it can be obscure because the notion of recommender trust does not have clear semantics. They defined it as "closeness of recommender's judgement to the trustor's judgement about trustworthiness", where "closeness" is quite vague. As a result, the computation model for deriving trust value is not concrete.

Jøsang *et al* [20, 21, 12, 4] have done a lot of research on trust transitivity. They argue that for trust to be transitive, trust purpose (scope) must also be considered. Trust purpose expresses the semantic content of an instantiation of trust, i.e. what the trustor wants to achieve through the trust. Trust transitivity can break down because the trust purposes are different and do not fit together for the subject in the chain. So if Alice wants to find a car mechanic and Carol recommends Bob because she trusts him as a good car salesman, this cannot form transitive trust. This result can be explained in our model. Usually with different purposes (goals in our terminology), a subject examines different sets of the trustee's attribute, e.g. for a car mechanic, the subject cares about his experience, and for a car salesman, the subject cares about whether he can offer a good discount. It is hard to form an entailment between policies regarding different attributes, therefore when purposes are different, trust usually is not transferable. In Jøsang's model, trust is expressed as reliability which is the subjective probability by which the trustor expects the trustee to perform a given action. When a transitive trust path is found, the trust value can be propagated from the recommender to the potential trustor, the potential trustor can decide whether to trust the trustee for the trust purpose by calculating a value for the indirect trust. Abstracting trust as a probability makes it easier for computation, but also loses useful information. As a trust value is a subjective probability, it is only meaningful to a particular trustor. When communicated to the other party without justification, this can be misinterpreted.

Modal logic [22] can be used to express modalities such as possibility, necessity, belief, and knowledge etc. It has been used to formalise and analyze trust because trust is closely related to beliefs. Rangan [14] proposed a modal logic for beliefs and presented an axiomatic theory of trust in distributed systems. In his system, trust is modelled as axioms which can provide desirable security properties when added into the logic. The paper discussed how to map certain security requirements into trust axioms and uses the logic to verify the security of distributed systems. Liau [23] presents the BIT logic for belief, information acquisition and trust. In BIT logic, trust is denoted by a modal operator with neighborhood semantics [22] and is used to infer beliefs from acquired information. Liau also discusses trust transfer and gives an axiom to derive new trust when trust is transferable. But he does not address under which conditions trust is transferable. Both works focus on how to use trust as a tool to reason about beliefs, but cover little about how to derive trust from beliefs which is important in the context of building trust management systems.

7 Conclusion and Future Work

In this paper, we considered the trust transfer problem using a simple trust model and then a modal logic system. Our contribution is the identification of the constraints needed for trust transfer in distributed systems, namely that:

- the trustor must know the recommender's trust attitude.
- the trustor must believe the recommender is honest.
- the trustor must be willing to acquire beliefs from the recommender.
- the trustor must know the recommender's trust policy.
- the recommender's trust policy must be more strict than the trustor's.

Besides trust transfer, there are two other mechanisms commonly used to establish indirect trust: credentials and reputation. One area of our future work will be to analyse credential-based and reputation-based trust. For example, a credential is an assertion on the trustee's attributes. It can be viewed in our logic as $S_i(j, B_j\phi)$, where j is the credential issuer. Reputation, on the other hand, can be viewed as the aggregation of trust opinions from a community. We hope to analyse, model and compare these alternatives with each other and with trust transfer.

We plan to apply our results and modal logic system in the implementation of the trust management system for the CareGrid project [24]. CareGrid aims to provide middleware for organising and coordinating trust, privacy and security decisions across collaborating entities using autonomous trust domains and context. The CareGrid trust management system will also be integrated with Imperial's Ponder2 policy management framework [25] and used for developing trust-based distributed, mobile and ubiquitous systems.

Acknowledgments

This research was supported by the UK's EPSRC research grant EP/C537181/1 and forms part of CareGrid, a collaborative project with the University of Cambridge. The authors would like to thank the members of the Policy Research Group at Imperial College for their support and to Marek Sergot for his advice.

References

1. M. Blaze, J. Feigenbaum, and J. Lacy (1996) Decentralized trust management. In: Proceedings of the 1996 IEEE Symposium on Security and Privacy, (Washington, DC, USA), p. 164, IEEE Computer Society.
2. A. Herzberg, Y. Mass, J. Mihaeli, D. Naor, and Y. Ravid (2000) Access control meets public key infrastructure, or: assigning roles to strangers. In: Proceedings of the 2000 IEEE Symposium on Security and Privacy, (Berkeley, CA), pp. 2–14.
3. N. Li, J. C. Mitchell, and W. H. Winsborough (2002) Design of a role-based trust-management framework. In: Proceedings of the 2002 IEEE Symposium on Security and Privacy, (Washington, DC, USA), p. 114, IEEE Computer Society.
4. A. Jøsang, E. Gray, and M. Kinateder (2006) Simplification and analysis of transitive trust networks. Web Intelligence and Agent Systems, 4(2):139–161.
5. A. Abdul-Rahman and S. Hailes (1997) A distributed trust model. In: Proceedings of the 1997 workshop on New security paradigms, (New York, NY, USA), pp. 48–60, ACM Press.
6. B. Yu, M. P. Singh, and K. Sycara (2004) Developing trust in large-scale peer-to-peer systems. in : Proceedings of IEEE First Symposium on Multi-Agent Security and Survivability, pp. 1–10.
7. C. M. Jonker and J. Treur (1999) Formal analysis of models for the dynamics of trust based on experiences. In F. J. Garijo and M. Boman (eds), vol. 1647 of Lecture Notes in Computer Science, pp. 221–231, Springer.
8. A. Birk (2000) Learning to trust. In: R. Falcone, M. P. Singh, and Y.-H. Tan (eds), vol. 2246 of Lecture Notes in Computer Science, pp. 133–144, Springer.
9. B. Christianson and W. S. Harbison (1997) Why isn't trust transitive? In: Proceedings of the International Workshop on Security Protocols, (London, UK), pp. 171–176, Springer-Verlag.
10. E. Gerck (1998) Toward real-world models of trust. http://www.safevote.com/papers/trustdef.htm.
11. T. Grandison (2003) Trust Management for Internet Applications. PhD thesis, Imperial College London.
12. A. Jøsang and S. Pope (2005) Semantic constraints for trust transitivity. In: S. Hartmann and M. Stumptner (eds), vol. 43 of CRPIT, pp. 59–68, Australian Computer Society.
13. C. Castelfranchi and R. Falcone(1998) Principles of trust for mas: Cognitive anatomy, social importance, and quantification. In: ICMAS, pp. 72–79, IEEE Computer Society.
14. P. V. Rangan (1988) An axiomatic basis of trust in distributed systems. In: Proceedings of the 1988 IEEE Symposium on Security and Privacy, pp. 204 – 211, IEEE Computer Society.
15. M. Abadi and M. R. Tuttle (1991) A semantics for a logic of authentication (extended abstract). In: PODC, pp. 201–216.
16. J. Hintikka (1962) Knowledge and Belief. Cornell University Press.
17. W. van der Hoek (1990) Systems for knowledge and beliefs. In:J. van Eijck (ed), vol. 478 of Lecture Notes in Computer Science, pp. 267–281, Springer.
18. N. Friedman and J. Y. Halpern (1994) A knowledge-based framework for belief change, part I: Foundations. In: R. Fagin (ed), TARK, pp. 44–64, Morgan Kaufmann.
19. S. Kripke (1963) Semantical considerations on modal logic. Acta Philosophica Fennica, 16:83–94.

20. A. Jøsang (1999) An algebra for assessing trust in certification chains. In: NDSS 99, The Internet Society.
21. A. Jøsang, E. Gray, and M. Kinateder (2003) Analysing Topologies of Transitive Trust. In: T. Dimitrakos and F. Martinelli (eds) Proceedings of the First International Workshop on Formal Aspects in Security and Trust, (Pisa, Italy), pp. 9–22.
22. B. F. Chellas (1988) Modal logic: an introduction. Cambridge University Press.
23. C.-J. Liau (2003) Belief, information acquisition, and trust in multi-agent systems—a modal logic formulation. In: Artif. Intell., 149(1):31–60.
24. The CareGrid project. www.caregrid.org.
25. The Ponder2 project. www.ponder2.net.

Trust without Truth

Michel Deriaz

University of Geneva, Switzerland

Michel.Deriaz@cui.unige.ch

Abstract. Can we trust without any reliable truth information? Most trust architectures work in a similar way: a trustor makes some observations, rates the trustee, and makes recommendations to his friends. When he faces a new case, he checks his trust table and uses recommendations given by trustworthy friends to decide whether he will undertake a given action. But what if the observations that are used to update the trust tables are wrong? How to deal with what we call the "uncertainty of the truth"? This paper presents how people that publish and remove virtual tags are able to create trust relations between them. A simulator as well as a concrete and widely deployed application have been used to validate our model. We observed good and encouraging results in general, but also some weaknesses, brought out through specific scenarios.

1 Introduction

Spatial messaging, also called digital graffiti, air graffiti, or splash messaging, allows a user to publish a geo-referenced note so that any other user that attends the same place can get the message. For example, let us consider the community of the Mt-Blanc mountain guides. The members would like to inform their colleagues about dangers in specific places or about vacancies in refuges. One guide can publish a geo-referenced message that informs about a high risk of avalanches, and any other guide that attends the same place will get the warning, and comment it if necessary. It is a kind of blog, in which editors and readers share the same physical place.

There are many reasons to believe that spatial messaging will become a wide spread concept in a nearby future. Today, people use the connection capabilities of their mobile phone mostly in one way, to download information. But in the same way that people passed from television to Internet, the next generation of user will probably become "active" and publish information. If we remember how fast the computer power and the communication capabilities of these devices improve, and the fact that there are today more modern mobile phones (with Internet connection) than desktop computers in the world, we can easily paint a glorious future for mobile technology. This assertion can be confirmed by the growing interest for location

Please use the following format when citing this chapter:

Deriaz, M., 2007, in IFIP International Federation for Information Processing, Volume 238, Trust Management, eds. Etalle, S., Marsh, S., (Boston: Springer), pp. 31–45.

awareness. The success of Google Map Mobile [1], a service that allows you to download maps on your mobile phone as well as POIs (Points Of Interest) wherever you are, is an indicator of this growing interest. And Google Map Mobile is not alone. There are more and more applications or Internet services for mobile users that provide maps and other information related to your current position.

There are already some implementations of the spatial messaging concept, but experiences realized with volunteers showed that there is only little interest in posting notes. To our view, the main reason is that there is currently no trust mechanism which informs about the reliability of the messages, thus preventing any serious application. In our Mt-Blanc mountain guides example, even if the security aspects will ensure that the posted messages are really posted by the mentioned author, that no modifications of the original text can be made afterwards, and that the service is available for everyone that is authorized, you still need a trust mechanism to know how reputable the author is.

This paper proposes a generic model to handle the trust component in spatial messaging. We validated it through a simulator and through a widely deployed application called FoxyTag, which allows a driver to publish virtual tags near traffic radars in order to warn the other drivers.

2   A new model is required

Lots of work has already been done in the trust context, and the obvious question that arises is why not just using well-known trust models? The answer is simply that it will not work. Indeed, traditional trust models are mainly designed with file sharing or auctions applications in mind. In this case, people are rating each other and when user A wants to download a file (or buy an item) from user B, he questions the system in order to determine how trustworthy user B is. Currently, commercial systems (like e-Bay) are using very basic centralized systems, and the academics are suggesting solutions to transform such systems into peer-to-peer architectures. But spatial messaging is noticeably different from file sharing or auctioning. First of all, we want to take care about the context. For example time is important. Imagine that you see during summer time a tag that warns about a high risk of avalanches. Even if there is no snow anymore, it does not mean necessarily that the author was lying; it can also mean that the tag has been written six month ago. Second, we believe that trust cannot only be applied to users. The tags themselves have to maintain information so that a user can compute how reliable it is to him.

In traditional computational trust, we usually agree over a set of axioms and hypothesis. For instance, the "truth" is a notion that is common to all. A corrupted file is seen as corrupted by everybody. In spatial messaging however, the truth is context dependant. The truth becomes a subjective and temporal notion. Something that is true for one user is not necessarily true for the others. Something that is true at a certain time is not necessarily true later. We call this new notion the "uncertainty of the truth". If user A posts a tag saying "Dangerous path", user B only knows that user A finds this path dangerous. But A is perhaps just a tourist and the path is in no way dangerous for user B, how can be a confirmed mountain guide. Or this path was maybe dangerous because of the snow, which has melted away by the time.

To our view, trust is not only a tool that can be used to exclude malevolent users from a given system. Trust is also a way of creating relationships between users that behave in a similar way. Like in real life, each user has his own definition of what the truth is. The aim is therefore to create trust relationships between people that share the same definition.

3 Related work

We already tackled the time component in a paper that has been published in the PST'06 proceedings [2]. In the survey, we wrote that several authors are aware about the difficulty to take the time into account, but no one proposed a trust model that gracefully solved the problem, or at least it was not directly applicable to spatial messaging. Dimmock [3], who realized the risk module in the EU-funded SECURE project [4], concluded in its PhD thesis that "one area that the framework does not currently address in great detail is the notion of time." Guha [5] built a generic trust engine allowing people to rate the content and the former ratings. He recognized however that in case of highly dynamic systems (like in spatial messaging where tags can appear and disappear very quickly), "Understanding the time-dependent properties of such systems and exploiting these properties is another potentially useful line of inquiry." Most existing trust metrics update their trust values only after a specific action, like a direct interaction or the reception of a recommendation. The few trust engines that take the time component into consideration simply suggest that the trust value decreases with the time. Mezzetti's trust metric [6] consists in multiplying the trust value at time t by a constant between 0 and 1. We proposed in [7] a similar model that also takes into consideration the dispersion of the outcomes. In Bayesian-based trust metrics [8, 9], the trust value converges to its initial value over time. All these models work in situations where the changes occur slowly, but are challenged in short-lived cases.

Our former time-patterned trust metric, called TIPP GC (TIme-Patterned Probabilistic Global Centralized), was used in a collaborative application allowing to signal speed cameras on mobile phones. A full description of the trust engine and the application can be found at [2]. Even if we brought some novelties about the way we updated the trust values, we still used a "traditional" way to store them, i.e. the number of positive outcomes P and the number of negative outcomes N. The trust value equaled $P / (N + P)$. And under a certain trust value, the malevolent users were simply excluded from the system. The problem with this kind of metrics is that it is difficult to decrease the trust value of a user that behaved correctly for a long time. We suggest therefore, to be closer to the human way of handling trust, that any trust value must decrease quickly in case of bad behavior. An honest user that becomes malevolent must not be able to use its long term good reputation to subvert the system.

4 Our model

4.1 Overview

Spatial messaging is not a new concept [10, 11], but existing systems do not have a trust mechanism, thus preventing any serious application. We can of course build a trust engine for each application, but it is like reinventing the wheel each time. Worse, the trust engine is the more complicated part.

Our solution to this problem consisted in building a framework that provides, among other things, a generic trust engine. So that it becomes very easy to build new applications using trusted virtual tags. Our framework, called GeoVTag, provides an API that eases the development of new applications using virtual tags.

To facilitate further comparisons, we introduce here a second scenario that is quite different from the mountain guides one. It is FoxyTag, a collaborative system to signal speed cameras on mobile phones. The idea consists in posting virtual tags close to radars in order to warn other drivers. These users will then get an alarm when they are closer than 15 seconds to a critical point, and a red point locating the radar appears on their screen. A driver signals a radar by pressing the key "1" of his mobile phone and signals that a radar disappeared (he gets an alarm but he does not see any speed camera) by pressing "0".

Creating a single trust engine that fits all the different applications is a difficult task. One reason is because the way we compute a trust value differs from one situation to another. There are different classes of trust engines. For instance we have situations where changes are unpredictable, like in the FoxyTag scenario where a radar can appear or disappear at any time. What if you get an alarm but you do not see any speed camera? You do not know if the former driver was a spammer (and then you need to decrease its trust value) or if the radar simply disappeared. But there are also situations where changes are more predictable. In the mountain guides scenario, if someone warns about a danger of avalanches, he can easily put a deadline to his tag, thus avoiding disturbing with an outdated tag a user attending the same place six months later.

It is clear that we compute the trust differently when the tags are meant to change often than in situations where the tags are meant to be stable. In the FoxyTag scenario, we could handle differently fixed radars and mobile ones. A mobile speed camera that disappears after a few hours is a "normal" situation. But a fixed speed camera that disappears is an unusual situation, especially if other neighboring radars disappear as well.

The GeoVTag framework provides a generic trust engine that can be easily extended. Updates in the trust table are made according to the behaviors of the users, and each of this update can be redefined and configured via rules and parameters. Roughly speaking, the designer of a new application will have to code "how much a specific behavior in a specific context costs in terms of trust value". He will therefore only have to code behaviors directly related to its application, leaving the framework doing all the job of maintaining and managing the trust information.

The main idea of our trust engine is to remember only important or recent information, like it is done in human communities. Tags and users keep a history of their last or important transactions. To know whether a tag must be shown to the user, the trust engine checks the n last reviews done by trustworthy users. A user is trustworthy if its global trust value, computed has a mix of the trustor's opinion (based on former direct interactions) and the opinions of the trustor's friends (who ask their own friends, and so on until a certain level), is above a certain threshold. A trustor calls friend every user with who he has a good trust relationship, or better said, each user with a good local trust value. That was how to get a tag. When a user rates a tag, he updates the trust values of the author and the former reviewers according to rules and parameters that depend on the application. In certain cases, a review can be done on both directions. For instance an author can update the trust value of every reviewer that gives a positive rating, since they seem to share the same opinion about the tag. However, these "reverse reviewings" must be configured with greatest care, to avoid that a malevolent user rates automatically and positively all the tags he crosses, in order to use its growing trust value to subvert the system.

4.2   A vTag in GeoVTag

A vTag is a virtual tag. It contains the following fields:

- **ID**. A unique identifier for this tag.
- **Author**. The ID of the author. This field, which is an integer, equals -1 when an author decides to revoke its own tag.
- **Position.** The geographical position of the tag. Each tag is attached to a given position, expressed in latitude and longitude.
- **Creation time**. The time when the tag has been created.
- **Deadline**. After the deadline, the tag is removed.
- **RD (Request to delete time)**. To avoid malevolent acts, it is not possible for a user to directly remove a tag. Instead, when certain conditions are met (for instance several users that rated the tag negatively), a "request to delete" is made to the tag. Its value is the time the request is made, and external rules define when the tag should be definitively removed.
- **Content**. The content of the tag. It is the application that decides how to structure the content. For instance an application could decide that the content is always an URL, and that all the tags are coded in HTML.
- **Reviewers**. A user can agree or disagree with the content of a tag. A tag contains a reviewers list that is sorted in an inverse chronological order. Each review contains the current time, the ID of the reviewer, the rating, and possibly some content (same format as the content written by the author).

These are the minimum fields required by the trust engine. An application designer can however add his own ones, like for instance the area where the tag is visible, under what condition it is visible...

4.3   A user in GeoVTag

A user is composed of an ID and a trust table. After an interaction with user B, user A updates the local trust value of B and places B on top of its list, so that there are sorted in an inverse chronological order. Each trust value is simply an integer in the range $[t_{min}, t_{max}]$ so that $t_{min} < 0 < t_{max}$. GeoVTag allows specifying rules to describe how a trust value must be changed according to a given situation. A typical case is to have a linear way to increase a value (for instance adding n when you agree with a tag) and an exponential way to decrease a value (for instance multiplying by m a negative trust value). When $-t_{min}$ is much bigger than t_{max} (for instance $t_{min} = -70$ and $t_{max} = 5$), we imitate the human way of handling trust: Trust takes time to be built, we forgive some small misbehaviors (exponential functions moves slowly at the beginning), but when we loose trust in someone (one big disappointment or lots of small disappointments) then it becomes very difficult to rebuild a good trust relationship. We avoid that malevolent users switch between good behaviors (in order to increase their trust value) and bad behaviors (in order to subvert the system).

It is important that our system forgives small mistakes in cases where the truth is unknown. We recall here the driver that gets an alarm about a speed camera that does not exist anymore. He will disagree with the author of the tag as well as with all the people that agreed. He will therefore decrease their trust values since they are perhaps spammers. But, most likely, the radar simply disappeared in the meantime and they are not spammers. Our model is built to forget easily such mistakes, as long as they do not happen too often, but to decrease quickly the trust values of malevolent users.

The global trust value of a user is relative and is computed by the following function:

$$global\_trust = q * myOpinion + (1-q) * friendsOpinions , \quad q=[0..1]$$

It is a recursive function where *myOpinion* is the local trust value and *friendsOpinions* is the average opinion of the n first friends (where *local_trust* $>= 0$). These friends apply the same function, so they return a mix between their own opinion and the average opinion of their own friends. And so on until we reached the specified depth. This way of processing is fast (all the values are centralized) and gives a good idea of the global reputation of a user. Typically, if we choose $n=10$ (number of friends) and a depth level of 3, then we have already the opinion of $10^0 + 10^1 + 10^2 + 10^3 = 1111$ reliable people, with more importance given to close friends. The more q is big, the more the user gives importance to it own value. In situations where people are susceptible of doing mistakes, this value is usually quite small.

4.4   The GeoVTag framework

The GeoVTag framework facilitates the development of applications using virtual tags. A simplified view of the framework can be seen in figure 1.

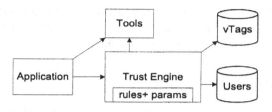

Fig. 1 GeoVTag framework

The Tools box is used by the trust engine and can also be accessed by the application. It contains mostly geographical related tools, like methods allowing conversions or methods handling tags of different formats.

All accesses to the two databases (vTags and Users) are done via the trust engine. The way the trust values are updated is defined via the rules and the parameters. In short, an application designer will have to configure these rules (in practice he will extend the trust engine class and rewrite the methods that code each specific behavior), set the parameters, and then write its application.

The trust engine can be accessed via three main primitives:

- **setTag**. This primitive simply creates a new tag. No trust mechanism is used.
- **getTags**. Returns a list of tags. The requester specifies which filter he wants to apply to the result. For instance, a user can ask to get all the tags in a certain radius, with updated trust values for the author and the reviewers, and let the application decide what to do. But he can also ask to get only the tags that are above a certain trust level and ignore the others. Or he can apply a personal filter and not use the trust mechanism at all, like asking all the tags that are authored or reviewed by Alice.
- **reviewTag**. Reviewing a tag means to rate it, optionally to add a comment, and then update the trust tables of the reviewer, the author and the former reviewers. The way the trust tables are updated is defined through the rules and the parameters. The framework splits all the behaviors so that the application developer can simply write the rules according to the needs of its application.

5   Validation process

We chose a speed camera tagging application to validate our trust engine. The first reason is because the question is quite complex. As we saw previously, radars can appear and disappear at any time, and it is not always possible to know if a wrong alarm is due to spammers or if it is actually the radar that just disappeared. To our view, the speed camera application is a "top" problem, or a problem that deals with all the possible cases. If our trust engine works for speed camera tagging, it should also work for other applications. The second reason is that it was very easy to find volunteers to test our system, since they could save their money while increasing the road safety. We set up a simulator that allowed us to test different scenarios (spammers, users that try to delete all the tags...) as well as a widely deployed application used to confirm the results of the simulator.

5.1   The simulator

Our simulator randomly positions speed cameras on a road and runs the user's cars according to given scenario parameters. An additional user, whose behavior can also be completely specified, logs its observations and returns the number of true positives (alarm: yes, camera: yes), false positives (alarm: yes, camera: no), true negatives (alarm: no, camera: no) and false negatives (alarm: no, camera: yes).
We model our road as a single way on a highway. Exits are numbered between 1 and n. Between two exits there is only one speed camera, numbered between 1 and n-1. So the camera c1 is between exits e1 and e2, the camera c2 is between exits e2 and e3, and so on. Figure 2 shows a road model.

Fig. 2 The road model

This model seems to be very simplistic. It is however sufficient to validate our trust metrics. Of course, we do not take into account some contextual information, like shadow areas (tunnels, urban canyons...) or what happens when the user posts a message concerning the opposite direction. These are more technical issues that need to be validated in the field and it is what we actually did with a real device in a real car. Since we can define the behavior of every user (where they enter and exit, how reliable they are by signaling speed cameras...) as well as the behavior of each speed camera (frequency of turning on, for how long...), we can precisely define which user drives in which area and how many speed cameras he is meant to cross on average. Our simulator accepts an input file that looks like this:

```
cam;1-4;8;15,10  // about three times a day, for 15 minutes, 10 minutes pause
cam;5-5;24;2,0   // about once a day, for 2 minutes, no pause
cam;5-5;240;3,30 // about once every 10 days, for 3 minutes, 30 minutes pause
usr;1-10;1-5;24;95;90  // once a day, 95% true positive, 95% true negative
usr;1-1;3-5;240;80;75  // once every 10 days, 80% true positive, 75% true negative
usr;11-15;1-10;1;10;10 // every hour, 10% true positive, 10% true negative (hacker!)
usr;11-11;1-10;0;20;25 // every minute, 20% true positive, 25% true negative (hacker!)
col;5-7;1-11;6;10;100  // 4 times a day, 10% true positive, 100% true negative
spm;20-23;1-10;1    // every hour
scn;100;2;run(24);pas(1,10);act(1,10,50,60)
scn;10;4;run(2400);pas(3,5);run(1);act(1,10,100,100);run(2);act(1,10,100,100)
```

- In the first line, "cam;1-4;8;15,10" means that cameras 1 to 4 have one chance out of 8 to become active within an hour, and when one becomes active then it stays active for 15 minutes. After it stays inactive (paused) for at least 10 minutes. Note that these cameras will on average become active less than 3 times a day, since they cannot switch to active while there are already active or paused. Precisely, these cameras will become active every 8+(15+10)/60 = 8.42 hours.
- The next two lines define two different behaviors for camera 5.
- In the fourth line, "usr;1-10;1-5;24;95;90" means that users 1 to 10 entry the highway at 1 and exits it at 5, that they run once a day and that they vote 95% of the time correctly when they signal the presence of a speed camera, and 90% of the time correctly when they cancel a camera.
- In the collusion line, "col;5-7;1-11;6;10;100", we deduce that users 5 to 7 are colluding by entering all at the same time on entry 1, exiting on exit 11, and voting (all similarly) about all 6 hours with 10% of true positives and 100% of true negatives.
- In the spam line, "spm;20-23;1-10;1", we deduce that users 20 to 23 spam by entering all at the same time on entry 1, exiting on exit 10, and voting 1 about every hour at every speed camera place.
- The first scenario, "scn;100;2;run(24);pas(1,10);act(1,10,50,60)" contains 100 big loops and 2 small loops. The scenario itself will be executed twice, then the trust engine is initialized, and then we re-execute the scenario twice. And so on (100 times).
- run(t) means that the system will run for t hours (simulation time). Each minute, the go method of each camera and each user is called, allowing them to act according to their specified behaviors.
- pas(e1, e2) means that our test user will passively drive once from exit e1 to exit e2. Passively means that he does not vote. His observations are logged and printed.
- act(e1, e2, tp, tn) means that our test user will actively drive once from exit e1 to exit e2 and has tp (True Positive) chances (in %) to vote correctly if he sees a speed camera, and tn (True Negative) chances (in %) to vote correctly when he tries to cancel a speed camera that does not exist (anymore). His observations are logged and printed.
- Everything after a // is a comment and is ignored by the simulator.

5.2   Real life evaluation: FoxyTag

The simulator allows us to test the trust models, but how to be sure that our simulator acts in a way that is close to reality? To answer this question, we tested our model with FoxyTag [12], a collaborative system to signal radars on mobile phones. FoxyTag motivates neither speeding nor any other risky behavior, but allows the driver to concentrate on the road instead of having is eyes fixed on the speedometer, by fear of being flashed. We observe that drivers tend to brake suddenly when they see a radar (even if they are not speeding), which can provoke traffic jams or even accidents. FoxyTag signals in advance the presence of speed cameras, so that the driver has enough time to check its speed and adapt it if necessarily. A more technical description of this application can be found at [13].

5.3   Rules and parameters for the speed camera application

Each new user has an initial trust value equal to 0. A user is meant to send "1" if he sees a radar, or "0" if he gets an alarm but does not see any radar. If the application gets a "1" and there is no neighboring camera (less than 150 meters), it is considered as a creation of a new tag. If there is a neighboring camera, this "1" is considered as a positive rating for the existing one. A "0" is therefore considered as a negative rating. The main parameters are the following:

- **Minimum trust value.** t_{min} = -70. A malevolent user can have a trust value as low as -70. This is to make sure that a malevolent user cannot easily regain a good reputation in order to subvert the system a second time.
- **Maximum trust value.** t_{max} = 5. It is not possible to have a trust value higher than 5. The reason is that a user can suddenly change its behavior and become malevolent. This means that even if a user behaved correctly for many years, he will not be able to use his past good behavior to subvert the system.
- **Size of the history.** It is the number of ratings that a tag keeps in memory. A new rating will automatically erase the oldest one. If a user already rated a tag, the old rating is deleted and the new one is put on top of the list. We chose 10 for this value, so we keep only recent information. This value could seem small, but is perfectly adapted to an environment where changes can happen very suddenly.
- **Number of contacts.** This is the number of contacts that each user keeps, or the size of its trust table. Each time the user modifies the trust value of another user, the later takes the first place in the trust table. If a new user appears and there is no place in the trust table, the last one (the one that did not get any rating for the longest time) is removed. We chose 1000 for this number.
- **Weight of user's opinion.** We saw previously that the reputation of a user is computed as a mix of the user's own value (local trust value) and the one given by its friends. This parameter defines the weight to give to the user's opinion. We chose 0.2, meaning that we take 20% of the user's own opinion and 80% of his friends' opinions.
- **Number of levels.** When we need the global trust value for a given user, we ask our friends, who ask their own friends, and so on up to a certain level. We chose 2, meaning that we get the opinion of our friends and the friends of our friends.
- **Request to delete threshold.** The number of successive users that must deny the tag (voting 0) in order to make a request to delete. We chose 2 for this value.

The rules are described below:

- **Vote 1 for 1.** Confirming a tag. The 8 first people that confirm a tag increase by 5 the author's trust value and the author does the same with these reviewers.

- **Vote 1 for 0.** The previous reviewer denied the tag, but it seems the radar still exists. Its trust value is decreased by 3. It is not reasonable to decrease by more than 3 since it can simply be a misuse (mixing up buttons...) of the application. And since there must be at least 2 successive reviewers that deny the tag before a request to delete is made, this error will not harm the quality of the system.
- **Vote 1 for 00.** The two previous reviewers denied the tag, but it seems the radar still exists. This time the chance of being a misuse is reduced and this pattern could be considered as two malevolent users trying to remove the tag. Their trust values are updated like $t' = t * 1.5 - 5$, so that a misuse can be easily forgiven but if this behavior is repeated then the trust value falls quickly.
- **Vote 0 for 1.** The previous reviewer confirmed the existence of the speed camera but it seems that there is no radar anymore. It can reflect a normal situation (the radar simply disappeared), so the trust value should not be decreased too much. But it can also be the result of a spammer attack. Since a spammers attack is less dangerous than a deniers' one, we observed that decreasing the trust value by 1 in this case is not too penalizing for honest users, and still sufficient to exclude spammers in a reasonable delay.
- **Vote 0 for 0.** This case happens when a second user denies a tag. The two users increase mutually their trust value by 5.
- **Request to delete.** This rule defines when a tag that got a request to delete order (in our case after two successive disapprovals) should be removed. We decided to keep it for the same amount of time than elapsed between the creation time and the request to delete order, but for at least 6 hours and at maximum 50 days. A long term tag (for instance a fixed speed camera) will therefore need more time to be deleted. The minimum of 6 hours avoids that two malevolent users scan the network and delete all the tags as soon as they appear without being penalized by the trust engine.

These rules motivate the users' participation. Posting or confirming a tag increases trust relationships. We could think that it is not a good idea to deny a tag when the radar disappeared. It is true that in such a case we decrease (-1) the trust value of the previous reviewer who was probably an honest user. But on the other hand, we will build a bidirectional trust relationship with the second user that will deny the tag, and the increase of the trust values (2 times +5) compensates generously the former loss.

6   Results

In addition to our new trust model, we ran also the simulator on two very easy trust engines that have been used for comparison. The first is called "Test" and simply adds a tag when a user sends a "1" and removes it when a "0" is sent. The second one is called "Basic" and works as follow:

- If a user sees and mentions a new camera, a new tag is created. The default value of its counter equals 0.

- If a user sees and mentions an existing camera (one that was signalized by a tag), the corresponding tag counter is set to 1.
- If a user gets an alarm about a camera that does not exist anymore and mentions it, the counter of the corresponding tag is decreased by 1.
- A tag whose counter reaches -1 is deleted.

The main idea behind these rules is that if a user signals by mistake a new speed camera, then the next user can alone cancel the message, but if a second driver confirms the existence of a speed camera, then we need two people to remove the tag.

Now let's see the scenarios and the results. Scenario 1 tests our trust engine when malevolent users try to remove all the tags.

Scenario 1

cam;1-10;0;9999999;0

usr;1-100;1-11;24;100;100

usr;101-105;1-11;1;0;100

scn;100;100;run(24);act(1,11,100,100)

	tp - yy	fp - yn	tn - nn	fn - ny
Test	43470	0	0	56530
Basic	59450	0	0	40550
SC	99781	0	0	219

We have 10 radars that are always turned on, a hundred users that behave always correctly and five users that systematically try to cancel all speed cameras they cross. Each hacker runs on average 24 times more often than an honest user. In the results table we compare the Test, the Basic and the SC (we call our new trust engine SpeCam) trust engines. We used also the following abbreviations: "tp - yy" means true positives (alarm: yes, camera: yes), "fp - yn" means false positives (alarm: yes, camera: no), "tn - nn" means true negatives (alarm: no, camera: no) and "fn - ny" means false negatives (alarm: no, camera: yes).

With the Test trust engine, we see that there are more false negatives (alarm: no, camera: yes) than true positives (alarm: yes, camera: yes). This is normal since the malevolent users are driving more than the honest ones. But our SpeCam trust engine eliminates quite well these malevolent users, since less than 0.22% (219 / 99781) speed cameras where not tagged.

Scenario 2

cam;1-10;9999999;0;0

usr;1-100;1-11;24;100;100

spm;101-105;1-11;1

scn;100;100;run(24);act(1,11,100,100)

	tp - yy	fp - yn	tn - nn	fn - ny
Test	0	20550	79450	0
Basic	0	36110	63890	0
SC	0	240	99760	0

Scenario 2 tests how the trust engine reacts against a spammers attack. This time the cameras are always turned off and the malevolent users vote "1" for each radar position. Again we observe a significant improvement with our new trust engine.

Scenario 3

cam;1-10;48;360;720

usr;1-100;1-11;24;100;100

scn;100;100;run(24);act(1,11,100,100)

	tp - yy	fp - yn	tn - nn	fn - ny
Test	8736	346	90572	346
Basic	8734	688	90245	333
SC	8692	674	90304	330

In scenario 3 we have 10 radars that are turned on every 66 hours (48 + (360 + 720) / 60) for 6 hours, and 100 users that vote always correctly. We expected therefore similar results than for the Basic trust engine, which seems to be the case.

Scenario 4

cam;1-10;48;360;720

usr;1-100;1-11;24;95;95

scn;100;100;run(24);act(1,11,95,95)

	tp - yy	fp - yn	tn - nn	fn - ny
Test	8356	350	90510	784
Basic	8751	750	90090	409
SC	8710	836	90056	398

In scenario 4 the users are voting incorrectly 5% of the time. This figure is clearly overrated (according to the tests realized with FoxyTag where this number is less than 1% in practice), but it let us to prove that our trust engine is tolerant with unintentional incorrect votes made by honest users.

Scenario 5

cam;1-10;48;360;720

usr;1-100;1-11;24;100;100

usr;101-105;1-11;1;0;100

scn;100;100;run(24);act(1,11,100,100)

	tp - yy	fp - yn	tn - nn	fn - ny
Test	3885	58	90901	5156
Basic	5123	115	90873	3889
SC	8726	820	90047	407

In scenario 5 we added 5 deniers that try to remove all the tags they cross. The honest users are behaving correctly 100% of the time. We have clearly more false positives than for the Basic trust engine. This is normal since the deniers removed all the tags, whether there is a camera or not. If we compare the results with the ones from scenario 4, we see that our trust engine eliminates efficiently deniers, since the number of false positives and false negatives are similar.

Scenario 6

cam;1-10;48;360;720

usr;1-100;1-11;24;95;95

usr;101-105;1-11;1;0;100

scn;100;100;run(24);act(1,11,95,95)

	tp - yy	fp - yn	tn - nn	fn - ny
Test	3653	67	90927	5353
Basic	5051	129	90717	4103
SC	8623	920	90020	437

In scenario 6 the users vote incorrectly 5% of the time. Unfortunately, we observe that the number of false negatives and false positives increase a little bit (compared to scenario 5). It seems that 5% of incorrect votes is a critical limit for this scenario.

Scenario 7

cam;1-10;48;360;720

usr;1-100;1-11;24;100;100

spm;101-105;1-11;1

scn;100;100;run(24);act(1,11,100,100)

	tp - yy	fp - yn	tn - nn	fn - ny
Test	8656	18348	72768	228
Basic	8910	32978	57937	175
SC	8777	1591	89223	409

In scenario 7 we replaced the deniers by a spammer team, who votes "1" at every radar position. The other users are voting correctly 100% of the time. Even if the number of false negatives is correct (compared to scenario 3), we observe a high number of false positives. We first thought of a weakness in our trust engine, but further investigations concluded that it is actually the simulator that presents a weakness. The problem is that the positions of the radars are always the same (which is not the case in reality), and that sometimes, by chance, a spammer really signal a new speed camera, which generously increases its trust value. In reality this would not be a problem, since signaling randomly a real speed camera at the right place is almost impossible.

Scenario 8

cam;1-10;48;360;720

usr;1-100;1-11;24;95;95

spm;101-105;1-11;1

scn;100;100;run(24);act(1,11,95,95)

	tp - yy	fp - yn	tn - nn	fn - ny
Test	8440	19048	71941	571
Basic	8867	35156	55769	208
SC	8652	1761	89176	411

In scenario 8 the honest users are voting incorrectly 5% of the time. We face the same weakness as in scenario 7. However, to scope with this problem, we tried to remove from the system all the users where the mean trust value (average of the local trust values of all the users) falls under -2. We got then similar figures than in scenario 3, meaning that these "bad" values are mainly due to the simulator and not to the trust engine.

7 Conclusion

We set up a trust engine that deals with what we call the "uncertainty of the truth" or a situation where a trustor rates a trustee according to an observation that not necessarily reflects the truth. Our trust engine is generic and can be adapted through rules and parameters to any application using virtual tags. We chose the topic of speed camera tagging since it is a complex problem in terms of uncertainty (speed cameras can appear and disappear in a very unpredictable way) and since it was easy to find volunteers to test our application.

The results presented in this paper where computed by our simulator, and some of them where compared with data collected by FoxyTag (a widespread application using our trust engine) in order to make sure that our simulator behaves in a way close to reality. We observed that our trust engine excludes malevolent users but "forgives" small mistakes (due to the "uncertainty of the truth") and infrequent misuses (incorrect votes due a mix of the buttons) done by honest ones.

The main weakness we discovered in our work was directly related to the simulator. Since the positions of the speed cameras where always the same, spammers could by chance signal real radars and then have their trust value generously increased. The second weakness was due to our trust engine and precisely with scenario 6. We saw that in case of a heavy attack, the honest users had to do less than 5% of incorrect ratings in order to keep the system reliable. In practice this is not really a problem since we observed that real people using the application do less than 1% of incorrect votes.

The next step in our study will be to use the deadline parameter of our tags. In the speed camera case, we will be able to differentiate mobile radars from fixed ones. We expect then an improvement in the presented figures, since we will be able to set more precise rules.

References

[1]   Website: http://www.google.com/gmm/
[2]   M. Deriaz and J.-M. Seigneur, "Trust and Security in Spatial Messaging: FoxyTag, the Speed Camera Case Study", in Proceedings of the 3rd International Conference on Privacy, Security and Trust, ACM, 2006.
[3]   N. Dimmock, "Using trust and risk for access control in Global Computing", PhD thesis, University of Cambridge, 2005.
[4]   Website: http://secure.dsg.cs.tcd.ie/
[5]   R. Guha, "Open Rating Systems", 1st Workshop on Friend of a Friend, Social Networking and the Semantic Web, 2004.
[6]   N. Mezzetti, "A Socially Inspired Reputation Model", in Proceedings of EuroPKI, 2004.
[7]   M. Deriaz, "What is Trust? My Own Point of View", ASG technical report, 2006.
[8]   S. Buchegger and J.-Y. Le Boudec, "A Robust Reputation System for P2P and Mobile Ad-hoc Networks", in Proceedings of the Second Workshop on the Economics of Peer-to-Peer Systems, 2004.
[9]   D. Quercia, S. Hailes, and L. Capra, "B-trust: Bayesian Trust Framework for Pervasive Computing", in Proceedings of the 4th International Conference on Trust Management (iTrust), LNCS, Springer, 2006.
[10]   J. Burrell and G.K. Gay, "E-graffiti: evaluating real-world use of a context-aware system", in Interacting with Computers, 14 (4) p. 301-312.
[11]   P. Persson, F. Espinoza, P. Fagerberg, A. Sandin, and R. Cöster, "GeoNotes: A Location-based Information System for Public Spaces", in Höök, Benyon, and Munro (eds.), Readings in Social Navigation of Information Space, Springer (2000).
[12]   Website: http://www.foxytag.com
[13]   M. Deriaz and J.-M. Seigneur, "FoxyTag", ASG technical report, 2006.

Mining and Detecting Connection-Chains in Network Traffic

Ahmad Almulhem and Issa Traore

ISOT Research Lab,
ECE Department,
University of Victoria,
Victoria, CANADA

Summary. A *connection-chain* refers to the set of connections created by sequentially logging into a series of hosts. Attackers typically use connection chains to indirectly carry their attacks and stay anonymous. In this paper, we proposed a host-based algorithm to detect connection chains by passively monitoring inbound and outbound packets. In particular, we employ concepts from association rule mining in the data mining literature. The proposed approach is first explained in details. We then present our evaluations of the approach in terms of real-time and detection performance. Our experimentations suggest that the algorithm is suitable for real-time operation, because the average processing time per packet is both constant and low. We also show that by appropriately setting underlying parameters we can achieve perfect detection.

Key words: Connection chain, Stepping stone, Tracing, Traceback, Network forensics, Network security

1 Introduction

In order to provide a stronger level of security, most organizations use a mixture of various technologies such as firewalls and intrusion detection systems. Conceptually, those technologies address security from three perspectives; namely prevention, detection, and reaction. We, however, believe that a very important piece is missing from this model. Specifically, current technologies lack any investigative features. In the event of attacks, it is extremely hard to tie the ends and come up with a thorough analysis of how the attack happened and what the steps were. We believe the solution is in the realm of Network Forensics; a dedicated investigation technology that allows for the capture, recording and analysis of network events for investigative purposes [1]. The current practice in investigating network security incidents is a manual and brute-force approach. Experienced system administrators generally conduct

Please use the following format when citing this chapter:

Almulhem, A. and Traore, I., 2007, in IFIP International Federation for Information Processing, Volume 238, Trust Management, eds. Etalle, S., Marsh, S., (Boston: Springer), pp. 47–57.

it. Typically, investigation proceeds by processing various types of logs, which are located in a number of places. Brute force investigation however is a time consuming and error-prone process. It also can be challenging because the mentioned logs are not meant for thorough investigation. The logs may lack enough details or contrarily have lots of unrelated details. In this regard developing investigative tools that can assist and automate network forensics process is essential. In this paper, we present the foundation of a data mining tool that can assist network forensics analyst in automatically detecting connection-chains in network traffic data, which represent an important but challenging aspect of network forensics.

The term *connection-chain* refers to the set of connections created by sequentially logging into a series of hosts, known as *stepping-stones* [2, 3]. Attackers typically use connection chains to indirectly carry their attacks and stay anonymous. As such, several approaches have been proposed in the literature to detect them. We refer the interested reader to our review paper for a taxonomy and a detailed discussion of these approaches [4].

In this paper, we propose a host-based technique to detect connection-chains. In general, the main disadvantage of the host-based approaches proposed so far in the literature is that they are operating system specific [5, 6, 7]. Specifically, they are expected to be re-designed and re-implemented differently for different operating system. Also, it is not obvious if they can be applied to proprietary operating systems such as MS Windows.

To avoid being operating system specific, we adopt a black-box approach. In essence, inbound and outbound packets at a host are *passively* monitored to detect if there is a connection-chain. In particular, we employ concepts from association-rule mining from the data mining literature. Agrawal et al. were first to introduce association rules mining concepts, and demonstrate their usefulness in analyzing a database of sales transactions (*market basket transactions*) [8].

The rest of the paper is organized as follows. In section 2, we summarize and discuss related work on host-based approaches for connection-chains detection. In section 3, we give some background knowledge on association rule mining. In section 4, we present our detection framework by presenting our connection-chain mining approach and algorithm. In section 5, we describe the experimental evaluation of the proposed approach, and present and discuss the obtained performance results. Finally, in section 6, we make some concluding remarks.

2 Related Work

Several host-based detection techniques have been proposed in the literature. They can be broadly classified into two main classes. In the first class, processes at the concerned host are searched to find out if two connections are part of a connection chain [6, 7]. The idea is that if an outbound connection is created by an inbound one, then their corresponding processes should be "related". The main concern in this approach is that the search process may fail if the link is involved. For instance, this can be the case when the related processes are created through deeply nested pipes.

In the second class, an operating system itself is modified to support linking an outbound connection to an inbound one. Buchholz and Shields proposed special data structures and system calls to achieve the desired linking [5]. In particular, for each process, a new data structure `origin` is stored in its process table. For processes created by a remote connection, `origin` holds the typical 5-tuple information associated with that connection. For locally created processes, `origin` is undefined. When a process `forks` another one, `origin` is as usual inherited. The main concern in this approach is that modifying an operating system can be costly and might break already running software.

3 Background

3.1 Association Rules Mining

In the data mining field, *association rules mining* refers to a methodology that is used to discover interesting relationships in large data sets [9]. Specifically, the term *association rules* is used to denote the discovered relationships, while the process itself is called *mining for association rules*.

Formally, let $I = \{i_1, i_2, \ldots, i_n\}$ be a set of *items*. Let $T = \{t_1, t_2, \ldots, t_N\}$ be a set of transactions, where each *transaction* t_i contains a subset of items from I, i.e. $t_i \subseteq I$. An *itemset* is also defined as a set of items. An *association rule* is an implication of the form $X \to Y$, where X and Y are disjoint itemsets, i.e. $X \bigcap Y = \phi$. The strength of an association rule is typically measured by its *support (s)* and *confidence (c)*. The support implies that X and Y occur together in $s\%$ of the total transactions. On the other hand, the confidence implies that, of all the transactions containing X, $c\%$ also contain Y.

3.2 Connection Chains

A *connection chain* denotes a set of *tcp connections* [10], which are formed when one logs into one host, from there logs into another and so on. From a host perspective, a connection chain appears as a pair of connections through which packets flow back and forth. An important observation is that the time taken by packets inside the host has to be bounded for a connection chain to work [11]. Throughout this paper, we refer to this time bound as Δ.

Furthermore, a connection between two hosts is a bidirectional channel that enables both ends to send and receive data. For convenience, we refer to each channel as a *flow*. Further, an *inbound flow* refers to the flow of traffic from a remote host to the local host, while an *outbound flow* refers to the reverse direction. Similarly, *inbound* and *outbound packets* refer to packets in the corresponding flow.

4 Connection-Chains Detection

4.1 Connection-Chains Mining Approach

We adapt the traditional association rule mining framework, which originally was geared toward business transactions rules mining, for connection chains mining. In our approach, the items of interest correspond to a set of connections, and the desired association rules correspond to connection chains.

Formally, let $C = \{c_1, c_2, \ldots, c_n\}$ be the set of active *connections* at a given host. As packets flow in these connections, *transactions* are dynamically generated. For a given packet, *transactions* are restricted to be one of the following two types:

- *input transaction* $[c_i]$, where $c_i \in C$, or
- *chain transaction* $[c_i, c_j]$, where $[c_i, c_j] = [c_j, c_i]$, $c_i \neq c_j$ and $c_i, c_j \in C$.

An *input transaction* $[c_i]$ is generated when an *inbound* packet is received on the corresponding connection. On the other hand, a *chain transaction* $[c_i, c_j]$ is generated when an *outbound* packet in one connection follows an *inbound* packet in the other connection within a Δ amount of time. For a transaction of type $[.]$, the *support count* $\sigma([.])$ ~~refers to~~ how many times it has occurred.

A *connection-chain* is an association rule of the form $\{c_i, c_j\}$, with its *confidence* defined as follows:

$$confidence(\{c_i, c_j\}) = \frac{\sigma([c_i, c_j])}{\sigma([c_i]) + \sigma([c_j])} \qquad (1)$$

where $c_i \neq c_j$ and $c_i, c_j \in C$.

Note that a set notation is used to represent a connection chain instead of an implication ($\rightarrow$), in order to emphasize the fact that a connection chain does not imply a particular direction. Intuitively, the numerator of the confidence is a count of how many times a chain transaction has occurred; i.e. packets flow within Δ time unit in either directions: $c_i \rightarrow c_j$ or $c_j \rightarrow c_i$. The denominator represents a count of how may times an input packet is seen on the corresponding connection. Typically, a true connection chain is expected to have a high confidence close to 1, while a false one is expected to have a low confidence close 0.

4.2 Detection Algorithm

In figure 1, we summarize the detection algorithm as a pseudo-code. The input to the algorithm is a stream of packets P, which is either captured in real-time

```
 1: INPUT: P a stream of packets
 2: inboundPackets = {}
 3: for all p ∈ P do
 4:     if d(p) = in then
 5:         generate an [c(p)] transaction
 6:         add p to inboundPackets
 7:     else if d(p) = out then
 8:         for all q ∈ inboundPackets do
 9:             if t(p) − t(q) ≤ Δ then
10:                 if c(p) ≠ c(q) then
11:                     generate an [c(p), c(q)] transaction
12:                 end if
13:             else
14:                 remove q from inboundPackets
15:             end if
16:         end for
17:     end if
18: end for
```

Fig. 1. The detection algorithm.

or read from a saved capture file. Those packets are processed in the order of their timestamps.

For each packet $p \in P$, we define the following operators :

- $t(p)$: the time-stamp of p.
- $c(p)$: the connection to which p belongs.
- $d(p)$: the direction of p; either inbound (in) or outbound (out).

When the processed packet p is an *inbound* one, an input transaction of type $[c(p)]$ is generated. Also, the packet itself is added to the *inboundPackets* set for later comparisons with *outbound* packets.

On the other hand, the processing of an *outbound* packet p is more involved. The packet is compared with all *inbound* packets that were stored in *inboundPackets* set. Then, a chain transaction is generated of type $[c(p), c(q)]$, if $q \in inboundPackets$, $t(p) - t(q) \leq \Delta$ and $c(p) \neq c(q)$.

Although not shown in figure 1, support counts of the generated transactions are maintained in a special data structure. Then, the confidences are computed according to equation 1. Particularly, connection chains corresponds to any pair of connections with a *confidence* exceeding some user-defined threshold (*minconf*).

5 Experiments

5.1 Experimental Settings

We implemented the proposed approach in Java, and run various experimentations on a PC with the following specifications: a 1.3Ghz Intel Pentium m-processor, 2 GB RAM, and 80 GB 7200 RPM Hard drive. The experimentations were performed using a public network trace (*LBNL-FTP-PKT*) [12]. It was selected because it is reasonably large to assess the algorithm. Also, it only contains the interactive part (control stream) of FTP sessions. This means that the characteristics of the traffic in this trace is similar to those generated by applications such as `telnet` [13] and `ssh` [14] that are used in creating connection chains.

The trace contains a ten-day worth of traffic for the period of Jan 10-19, 2003. It contains 3.2 million packets flowing in 22 thousand connections. The connections are between 320 distinct FTP servers and 5832 distinct clients. Initially, we sliced the trace into 320 *subtraces* using the servers' ip addresses; i.e. each subtrace contains the packets exchanged with the corresponding server. In a way, running the algorithm on a subtrace is equivalent to running the algorithm in real-time on the corresponding server.

In the experimentations, we studied the effect of changing Δ. As such, we first analyzed the timing of inbound and outbound packets of those servers, and estimated the response time of the servers to be between 10-90 msec. We used this value as a guidance to set Δ in our test suite. Accordingly, we decided to use the following values of Δ: 1, 10, 50, 100, 200, and 500 msec. They were selected to investigate the effect of setting Δ, *below*, *around*, and *above* the true Δ value.

5.2 Real-Time Performance

To assess the algorithm's real-time performance, we evaluated the processing time per packet. For every subtrace (320 subtraces), we run the algorithm with a Δ of 1, 10, 50, 100, 200, and 500 msec; i.e. a total of $6 \times 320 = 1920$ cases. For a particular subtrace S_i, the processing time T_i is recorded in each case. The results are then plotted in figure 2.

As shown in figure 2, we notice that the processing time exhibits a linear trend as subtraces increase in size. Accordingly, the processing time per packet is almost constant, as it basically corresponds to the slope of these lines. Mathematically, it is given by $\frac{T_i}{|S_i|}$ *seconds/packet*, where $|S_i|$ is the number of packets. For this trace, the average processing time per packet is approximately 35 μsec/packet. Additionally, we noticed that varying Δ does not seem to have a significant effect on the processing time. Accordingly, we concluded that the algorithm is suitable for real-time operation, because the average processing time per packet is both constant and low.

5.3 Detection Performance

To assess the detection performance of the algorithm, we first picked the largest subtrace among the 320 subtraces, although other subtraces give similar results. The subtrace contains 1.7 millions packets that correspond to the traffic exchanged between the server (131.243.2.12) and 236 unique remote

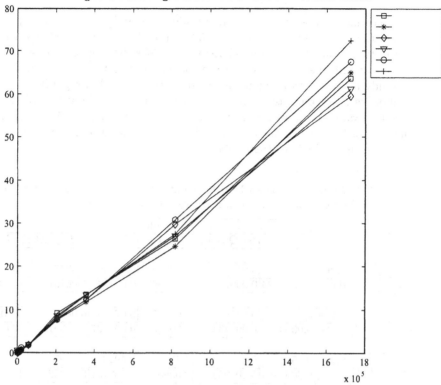

Fig. 2. The processing time of the 320 subtraces for different values of Δ. The subtraces are sorted in increasing order according to the number of packets. As shown, the processing time is approximately linear as subtraces increase in size.

hosts. Among these 236 unique remote addresses, we randomly picked 88 of them to create simulated connection chains as follows. Let L, R and R' respectively stand for the server (local), a remote host and a *fictitious* remote host. Then, the steps to create a simulated connection chain {R,R'} are as follows:

- For an inbound packet (R,L), create an outbound packet (L,R'). The time-stamp of the new packet is set to original time-stamp **plus** some random time t.
- For an outbound packet (L,R), create an inbound packet (R',L). The time-stamp of the new packet is set to original time-stamp **minus** some random time t.
- Merge those generated packets into the original trace.

For the random time t, we use a uniform random variable between 10-90 msec (an estimate of the server response time). Accordingly, the modified subtrace has $236 + 88 = 324$ remote addresses and $\binom{324}{2} = 52326$ possible connection chains. Only 88 out of the 52326 possible connection chains are *true* connection chains ($\approx 0.2\%$). Those are the ones that we actually simulated.

The modified subtrace is then used as an input to the algorithm. In order to study all connection chains detected by the algorithm regardless of their confidences, we compute confidence statistics for different values of Δ. The following values of Δ were considered: 1, 10, 50, 100, 200, and 500 msec. Note that a Δ of 100 msec is the ideal value in this case, because the server response time is estimated to be 10-90 msec.

Table 1. A summary of The Algorithm's output showing confidence statistics for different values of Δ under any non negative value for *minconf*.

		Confidence					
		Min	1st Quartile	Median	Mean	3rd Quartile	Max
$\Delta = 1$ ms	True	0.01429	0.01857	0.02389	0.02639	0.0317	0.04348
	False	0.0002823	0.0007423	0.0009671	0.001242	0.00151	0.0122
$\Delta = 10$ ms	True	0.02439	0.03584	0.06797	0.07214	0.08378	0.1923
	False	0.0003401	0.001433	0.002322	0.002967	0.003913	0.02817
$\Delta = 50$ ms	True	0.2581	0.4756	0.4093	0.4929	0.5595	0.8077
	False	0.0003804	0.002959	0.006042	0.009131	0.01292	0.07726
$\Delta = 100$ ms	True	1.0	1.0	1.0	1.0	1.0	1.0
	False	0.0003623	0.004518	0.01006	0.01599	0.02237	0.1467
$\Delta = 200$ ms	True	1.0	1.0	1.0	1.0	1.0	1.0
	False	0.0003623	0.008181	0.01796	0.03009	0.04302	0.2653
$\Delta = 500$ ms	True	1.0	1.0	1.0	1.0	1.0	1.0
	False	0.0004968	0.01471	0.03562	0.05958	0.08803	0.4173

A summary of the the algorithm's output is shown in table 1. For each value of Δ, we list several descriptive statistical quantities to show the confidences distributions of the true and false connection chains involved in the evaluation dataset.

We visualize the confidences of true and false connection chains in figure 3. In this figure, notice how the confidences of true and false connection chains overlap when Δ is set to very low values (1 and 10 msec). However, once Δ is set around or above the ideal value, true connection chains are clearly separated. In this case, by appropriately setting the confidence threshold (*minconf*) in the separation area, we achieve perfect detection rates. For instance, for $\Delta = 100$ msec, by setting *minconf* $= 0.5$ we obtain a true detec-

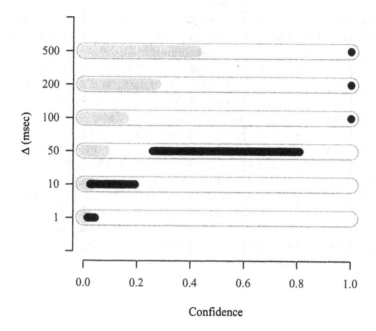

Fig. 3. The range (min-max) of confidences of true and false connection chains for different values of Δ. For each value of Δ, a grey region indicates the range for false connection chains, while a black region indicates the range for true ones.

tion rate = 100% and false detection rate = 0%. Also, notice that increasing Δ beyond the ideal value decreases the *separation* between the confidences of the true and false connection chains. In this case, the maximum separation occurs at the ideal value of Δ (100 msec). However, notice that this separation is reasonably large even when Δ = 500 msec; i.e. 5 times the ideal value. In essence, large separation is desirable because it gives greater flexibility in setting the *minconf* threshold. Such threshold is used to reduce (or eliminate) false connection chains.

6 Concluding Remarks

A *connection-chain* refers to the set of connections created by sequentially logging into a series of hosts. Attackers typically use connection chains to indirectly carry their attacks and stay anonymous. In this paper, we proposed a host-based algorithm to detect connection chains by passively monitoring inbound and outbound packets. We took advantage of the fact that the time taken by a packet inside the host has to be bounded for a connection chain to work. We refer to this time bound as Δ.

In the proposed approach, we employed concepts from association rule mining in the data mining literature. In particular, we proposed efficient algorithm to discover connection chains among a set of connections. Also, a confidence measure is proposed to measure the strength of a connection chain.

We implemented the proposed approach in Java, and run various experimentations to assess the real-time and detection performance. The experimentations were performed using a public network trace.

For processing time, our experimentations suggest that the algorithm is suitable for real-time operation, because the average processing time per packet is both constant and low. For the detection performance, our experimentations suggest that the algorithm is effective in detecting true connection chains. The setting of Δ seems to play an important role. In particular, we found that the confidences of true and false connection chains are clearly separated when Δ is set around or above (even 5 times) the true value. This gives greater flexibility in setting a confidence threshold ($minconf$) to reduce (or eliminate) false connection chains.

References

1. M. Ranum, "Network forensics: Network traffic monitoring," Network Flight Recorder, Inc., Tech. Rep., 1997.
2. S. Staniford-Chen and L. T. Heberlein, "Holding intruders accountable on the internet," in *Proceedings of IEEE Symposium on Security and Privacy*, May 1995, pp. 39–49.
3. Y. Zhang and V. Paxson, "Detecting stepping stones," in *9th USENIX Security Symposium*, Aug 2000, pp. 171–184.
4. A. Almulhem and I. Traore, "Connection-chains: A review and taxonomy," ECE Department, University of Victoria, Tech. Rep. ECE-05.4, 12 2005.
5. F. Buchholz and C. Shields, "Providing process origin information to aid in network traceback," in *Proceedings of the 2002 USENIX Annual Technical Conference*, 2002.
6. B. Carrier and C. Shields, "The session token protocol for forensics and traceback," *ACM Trans. Inf. Syst. Secur.*, vol. 7, no. 3, pp. 333–362, 2004.
7. H. W. Kang, S. J. Hong, and D. H. Lee, "Matching connection pairs," in *Lecture Notes in Computer Science*, vol. 3320, Jan 2004, pp. 642–649.
8. R. Agrawal, T. Imielinski, and A. Swami, "Mining association rules between sets of items in large databases," *SIGMOD Rec.*, vol. 22, no. 2, pp. 207–216, 1993.
9. P.-N. Tan, M. Steinbach, and V. Kumar, *Introduction to Data Mining*. Addison-Wesley, 2006.
10. J. Postel, *Transmission Control Protocol*, RFC 793, sep 1981.

11. D. L. Donoho, A. G. Flesia, U. Shankar, V. Paxson, J. Coit, and S. Staniford, "Multiscale stepping-stone detection: Detecting pairs of jittered interactive streams by exploiting maximum tolerable delay," in *RAID 2002: Proceedings of the 5th International Symposium on Recent Advances in Intrusion Detection,*, october 2002, pp. 17–35.
12. "Lbnl-ftp-pkt," http://www-nrg.ee.lbl.gov/anonymized-traces.html.
13. J. Postel and J. Reynolds, *Telnet Protocol Specification*, RFC 854, May 1983.
14. C. Lonvick, *SSH Protocol Architecture*, Cisco Systems, Inc., December 2004.

A Privacy-Aware Service Discovery Middleware for Pervasive Environments

Roberto Speicys Cardoso, Pierre-Guillaume Raverdy, and Valérie Issarny

INRIA Rocquencourt 78153 Le Chesnay, France
{first-name.last_name}@inria.fr

Abstract. Pervasive environments are composed of devices with particular hardware characteristics, running various software and connected to diverse networks. In such environments, heterogeneous devices must cooperate to offer meaningful services to users, regardless of technological choices such as service discovery and access protocols. Interoperability thus is a critical issue for the success of pervasive computing. In this context, we have previously introduced the MUSDAC middleware for interoperable service discovery and access across heterogeneous networks. Still, data exchanged in pervasive environments may be sensitive, and as service information is forwarded to unknown or untrusted networks, privacy issues arise. In this paper we present a privacy-aware solution for service discovery in heterogeneous networks, based on the MUSDAC platform. Specifically, we discuss privacy issues that arise during service discovery and mechanisms to control disclosure of private information contained in service-related data.

1 Introduction

Today, individuals carry various wireless-enabled multi-purpose digital devices, and applications that exploit their cooperative possibilities begin to emerge. Middleware systems are in particular being introduced to handle the richness of the services available in the environment, and the high heterogeneity of the various hardware, software and wireless network technologies. Heterogeneity has been primarily addressed by providing *multi-protocols* interoperability layers, and by managing network overlays atop dynamic *multi-networks* compositions. These solutions however further aggravate the issue of handling the multitude of networked services available to users.

A major trend to handle such service richness and provide localized scalability, is to rely on context information to infer mobile users' needs and autonomously locate the most appropriate services. However, as more applications and system services on mobile devices start to disseminate context data containing users' personal information (e.g., interests, location), it becomes critical to protect the users' privacy and therefore control this diffusion. One crucial middleware service in particular that must be considered is service discovery (SD), which provides information about the user's on-going interests and activities. Indeed, service discovery requests may disclose information such as user profiles,

Please use the following format when citing this chapter:

Cardoso, R. S., Raverdy, P.-G. and Issarny, V., 2007, in IFIP International Federation for Information Processing, Volume 238, Trust Management, eds. Etalle, S., Marsh, S., (Boston: Springer), pp. 59–74.

preferences, relations with other users, mobility pattern, and so on. Correlating multiple discovery requests from a single user would then quickly provide extensive knowledge about a user and reveal critical private information.

In this paper, we analyze how personal information is disclosed during service discovery in a heterogeneous environment, and propose various mechanisms to increase the level of privacy, and in particular prevent the correlation of multiple discovery requests. We base our work on the MUlti-protocol Service Discovery and ACcess (MUSDAC) middleware [13], a platform introduced to provide context-aware service discovery and access in pervasive environments by combining well-established patterns to address protocol interoperability (i.e., common representation) and multi-network discovery (i.e., ad hoc network composition). We therefore believe that the issues discussed and the mechanisms proposed are general enough and can be integrated also into other discovery platforms. In Sect. 2 we discuss challenges in service discovery for pervasive environments and analyze the MUSDAC platform impact on the privacy of clients and service providers. After that, we introduce in Sect. 3 the mechanisms that allow for privacy-aware multi-protocol service discovery. We assess our solution in Sect. 4 and present our concluding remarks in Sect. 5.

2 Service Discovery in Pervasive Environments

In this section, we first review the challenges and standard solutions for SD in multi-protocols, multi-networks environments, and present the MUSDAC platform. MUSDAC combines solutions for interoperability and multi-networking that specifically address the context requirement of pervasive computing. We then identify the inherent privacy issues caused by the use of such SD platforms.

2.1 The MUSDAC Platform

We assume an environment with various highly heterogeneous networks running the IP protocol, but without global IP routing. Each network is managed independently, and applications within each network may use various service discovery and service access protocols. We also assume that some devices with multiple network interfaces may connect to different networks simultaneously. In this context, the MUSDAC platform was designed to support the discovery of services (i) advertised using legacy SD protocols (interoperability) and (ii) hosted on any device in the environment (multi-networks).

A typical mechanism for supporting SD protocol interoperability is to rely on a common representation for service advertisements and discovery requests (either in the form of enriched advertisements and requests [1] or as sets of elementary events [2]). The interoperability layer may either be transparent for clients and services, with messages being translated on the fly between the different protocols [2], or may be explicitly accessed by clients through an API [7]. While the former approach generally leads to better performances and does not require any adaptation of the client applications, the latter allows the enhancement of service descriptions and requests with additional information (e.g., QoS, semantic). The dynamic composition of heterogeneous networks may be either achieved at the network level, providing a global IP network, or at the application layer with the deployment of a network overlay. Again, the network-level approach offers better performance and a straightforward support of legacy applications, but prevents each network from defining its own access policies and prevents the choice of a service instance based on communication cost and quality, or other contextual information related to the network path.

As previously established [3, 9], the use of context information is crucial in pervasive computing. We therefore designed MUSDAC to provide an explicit SD interface to clients, and to provide a SD overlay by managing the dynamic composition of nearby networks. MUSDAC is composed of (i) a set of Managers, each processing discovery and access requests of local and remote clients within a single network, (ii) sets of SD Plugins and Transformers, associated with each Manager, that interact with legacy SD protocols on behalf of their Manager, and (iii) Bridges that forward service discovery and access requests to remote Managers, enabling clients located in any network of the pervasive environment to use services available on another network. Figure 1 shows how these components interact. A more detailed presentation of the MUSDAC platform can be found in [13].

MUSDAC enables clients to add context information to their SD requests, and enables Bridges and Managers to exchange context information about the network characteristics and policies. This context information is used by Managers to select the most relevant services, and by Bridges to control the propagation of clients' requests. A complete description and evaluation of the context-awareness mechanism of MUSDAC is detailed in [14].

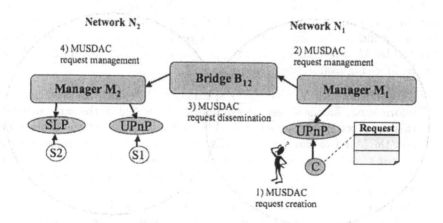

Fig. 1. Interaction Between MUSDAC Components

It is not required for each device in the environment to execute the MUSDAC platform. Indeed, a device may just host Manager/Plugins or the Bridge component. Within a network, one of the devices hosting a Manager component is elected to control the network, and registers the MUSDAC SD service to be used by clients using various SD protocols. This Manager in turn selects among the potential Bridges which one to activate based on various criteria (connectivity, performance, cost). While services just register with their preferred SD protocol, MUSDAC-aware clients first discover the MUSDAC SD service using any legacy SD protocol, and then use the MUSDAC API and formats to discover services in the pervasive environment.

2.2 A Trust Model for Multi-Network Service Discovery

Service discovery information is sensitive. Service request messages and service descriptions contain private information that can be later used to infer personal data such as users' desires and intentions or to link consecutive requests. Storage and analysis of service descriptions and requests over a period of time can increase the precision of inferred personal information. Service-related data hence must be carefully disclosed, particularly when it is going to be handled by untrusted entities. In the current MUSDAC middleware, users are assumed to trust all Bridges and Managers to fairly use their personal information. This trust model, however, is not appropriate for a real world multi-network scenario. Pervasive environments connect networks in different domains using distinct administration policies. Devices in remote networks may not have any reason to fairly use clients personal information or may even join the environment only to abuse personal data available through the platform.

We must define a trust model for MUSDAC consistent with the multi-network pervasive scenario. Consider a pervasive environment comprising n networks $N_1, ..., N_n$. Each network has a single Manager M_i responsible for handling requests from all clients belonging to network N_i. Two distinct networks N_i and N_j can be connected by a Bridge B_{ij}, in which case requests handled by M_i can be forwarded to M_j through B_{ij}. Our trust model is based on the following assumptions:

1. Clients in network N_i trust the local Manager M_i to fairly use their personal information. As clients and the Manager are located in the same network, their trust relationship can be created based either on a contract that defines how the Manager can use client information (and possible countermeasures in case of abuse), on the client's personal experience when using Manager M_i, or any other trust establishment protocol. In Fig. 1, client C trusts Manager M_1 to fairly use its personal information.

2. Clients in network N_i do not trust any Bridge $B_{kl}, \forall k, l \in \{1, ..., n\}, k \neq l$ to fairly use their personal information because they are not directly responsible for Bridge election and their requests are forwarded to Bridges regardless of their trust judgment. Besides that, clients do not know critical

information about the networks connected by the Bridges such as topology or network technology in place, which are important to support the clients' trust decisions. For instance, a client may not trust WiFi networks with low encryption levels. In Fig. 1, client C does not trust Bridge B_{12} to fairly use its personal information.

3. Clients in network N_i do not trust any other Manager M_j, $j \neq i$ to fairly use their personal information. As clients do not interact directly with remote Managers and their association is transient, it creates additional obstacles for trust establishment protocols (for instance protocols based on past experiences). In Fig. 1, client C does not trust Manager M_2 to fairly use its personal information.

4. All the entities in the environment trust that Bridges and Managers will correctly execute the MUSDAC protocols. We assume that every Manager can determine if Bridges are running the right software version and vice-versa. We also suppose that one MUSDAC component can detect another MUSDAC component misbehavior, and exclude ill-behaved components from the platform in later interactions. We are not investigating issues that arise when components maliciously run MUSDAC protocols.

2.3 MUSDAC Privacy Pitfalls

As the term privacy may assume different meanings depending on the research context, it is important to define its scope in the service discovery scenario. In this paper, privacy is defined as the *control over information disclosure*. As such, a privacy invasion is considered to occur when information regarding an entity is disclosed without the entity's explicit consent. When the trust model defined above is taken into account, it is possible to identify many channels for privacy invasions in the original MUSDAC design.

First of all, service requests are gradually flooded to MUSDAC components through successive multicasts: the local Manager forwards each client request to the group of Bridges connected to it, Bridges to neighbor Managers, and so forth until all the networks compatible with context rules and within a certain distance to the client are reached. As a result, personal information contained in requests is disseminated to multiple MUSDAC components even if relevant services have been found early in the discovery process.

Service descriptions may also contain private information about the service provider, and its access must be controlled. In pervasive computing, the roles of clients and service providers are not fixed, and users may even perform both at the same time. This creates yet another possibility for privacy invasions: service request data can be used along with service descriptions to identify a user and to infer more personal information, by combining both sources of private data. MUSDAC does not provide any specific mechanism to control access to service descriptions, so any service published by a user can be discovered by the whole environment and the service description can be potentially disclosed to a great number of entities, amplifying the privacy risks for the user.

Request routing can also be a vector for privacy invasion attacks. The current algorithm was designed to minimize MUSDAC components processing, by reducing the quantity of routing state information required to be cached in intermediary nodes. Addresses of Bridges and Managers along the path between a source and a destination Manager are appended to the request, so that they carry all information required for routing back the response. Routing data included in the request, however, can reveal details about the requester identity, such as the address of the source Manager and the path used to reach the destination Manager, and could be later used to relate consecutive service requests and infer clients' personal data.

Routing data is not the only source of identity information contained in service requests. Request contents may also contain personal data, especially if context information is included. For instance, requests from a client looking for content adapted to his mobile device can be linked to each other if the device model is not popular. As MUSDAC originally forwards requests in clear-text, all entities of a path have access to its contents and can use it to correlate distinct requests. Not every MUSDAC component needs to be able to read request details, though: Bridges, for instance, are only responsible for transport and should only access data relevant for routing.

3 Privacy-Awareness Mechanisms in MUSDAC

Privacy enhancements in MUSDAC aim at dissociating the source of a request from the request message and reducing the access of untrusted entities to service request contents. In this section, we present the modifications introduced into MUSDAC to achieve these goals. They can be divided into: (i) mechanisms to give clients control over their service discovery data propagation, presented in Sect. 3.1 and (ii) techniques to increase client privacy during request routing, introduced in Sect. 3.2.

3.1 Control over Discovery Data Propagation

MUSDAC's original design floods the networks with service requests and asynchronously waits for discovery results. Although this propagation strategy can produce results faster, it also exposes client's requests to a higher number of untrusted entities. According to the trust model defined in Sect. 2.2, clients trust only the local Manager to fairly use their personal information. The other entities, such as Bridges and remote Managers are not trusted by the client and can misuse request data to invade his privacy. The decision to trade-off performance for privacy should not be imposed by the platform, but rather left at the client's discretion. To enable clients and service providers to have more control over service discovery data disclosure, we enhance MUSDAC with mechanisms to define *how* requests must be propagated and *where* they should go.

Incremental Service Discovery: The original MUSDAC design provides only a **parallel** discovery strategy, which gradually floods platform components with client requests, reaching all significant networks. If sufficient results are found in networks closer to the client, the parallel strategy unnecessarily exposes personal information contained in service requests to all reachable MUSDAC components. To avoid needless service data disclosure, we propose two alternative propagation strategies: **progressive** and **one-by-one**. In the former, the local Manager initially sends the request to all the networks that are one hop away and waits for the results. If more results are necessary, the local Manager sends the request again to networks two hops away, and so forth. In the latter, the local Manager sends the request to a specific Manager one hop away and waits for results. If more results are needed, the request is sent to another Manager one hop away and so on, until all the Managers in neighbor networks are queried. Only then the request is sent to a Manager two hops away. Figure 2 shows the three strategies. The parallel strategy is asynchronous, so requests are forwarded independently of replies and quickly reach various MUSDAC components. The progressive strategy waits for results from networks one hop away before deciding if the discovery process should go on. Finally, the one-by-one strategy may disclose the request contents to a single Manager, if it provides sufficient results.

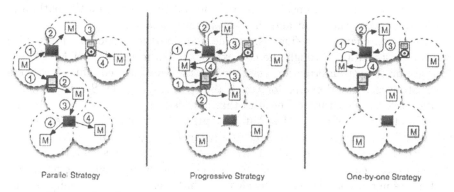

Parallel Strategy   Progressive Strategy   One-by-one Strategy

Fig. 2. Parallel, Progressive and One-by-One Propagation Strategies

Clients can define which strategy to use on a per-request basis. When using the progressive strategy, users can inform the number of results that must be obtained before stopping discovery and the maximum distance of Managers that should receive the request in terms of hops. With the one-by-one, strategy users can also define the maximum number of Managers that can receive the request. Implementation of new propagation strategies demands two modifications in MUSDAC. First, Bridges must be able to directly forward requests to other Bridges in order to bypass Managers that already processed the request. Second, a unicast mechanism is necessary to enable a Manager to send a discovery request to another specific Manager. Local Managers must have network topology information to be able to determine the route to a destination Manager. This is obtained by running a routing protocol based on OLSR (Optimized Link-State Routing) [8] on each MUSDAC component. Periodically, each component uses the beacon message to also advertise its neighbors. Other components use that data to compute a local view of the network and to determine how to route packets to specific destinations.

Privacy-Compliant Dissemination: The second mechanism introduced allows clients to control where their requests go. The original MUSDAC platform forwards requests to all connected networks, disregarding the clients' trust level on destinations. Nevertheless, users may establish trust relationships with companies or services, and expect those relations to be respected when using pervasive computing systems. This work extends the original MUSDAC platform by enabling service discovery to comply with two types of trust relationships concerning private data usage: between citizens and governments based on **privacy protection laws** and between consumers and corporations based on **privacy agreements**. Privacy protection law coverage is related to geographical boundaries, such as state, country, or group of countries. Privacy agreements on the other hand cover relations between a consumer and services provided by a company, possibly hosted in different domains. It is important to notice that, as service requests traverse several components before reaching the destination Manager, the trust relationship must hold for all the entities on the path, and not only between the client and the destination Manager.

To enable clients to define geographic and domain restrictions for service request propagation through the context-awareness mechanism of MUSDAC, Bridges must keep information about where they are located while Managers must store also the domains for which they are responsible. Service requests contain a list of geographical entities that adopted privacy laws trusted by the client and the list of companies that have privacy agreements accepted by the client. Privacy-related context is disseminated to neighbor MUSDAC components so that they can verify client-defined context rules to decide if the request can be forwarded or not. We developed two elementary ontologies for geographical and domain context data specification that increase the flexibility of this mechanism removing the need for exact matches between context rules and context data (recognizing that a request from a client who trusts the European Union privacy legislation can be forwarded to a Manager in France, for instance). Recent work in our group proposes directions on how to efficiently use ontologies for service discovery [10].

Privacy-related context data can also be used by service providers to control access to service descriptions. Service providers may want that only clients on a given geographical region under a certain legislation, or coming from a given domain administered by a trusted company are able to discover a service. In this case, the service provider includes in the service description its privacy preferences concerning domain and geographic location of the request source. Instead of requiring clients to include that information in the request – which would ultimately disclose their location and domain – service provider's privacy preferences are included in the discovery results. As they are forwarded back to the client, privacy preferences are checked and the response may be filtered out at one of the MUSDAC components along the path.

3.2 Privacy-Enhanced Routing

In Sect. 3 we stated that one of the goals of privacy-enhancements in MUSDAC is to dissociate the source of a service request from the request message. If a service needs to identify a client before allowing access, this identification should be explicitly performed at the application level, so that the client can evaluate what are the effects of revealing his identity, and act accordingly. Service discovery requests have two sources of identifiable information. First, request source address and routing information can reveal the request starting point. Second, service request contents along with source addresses can be used to correlate consecutive requests and reduce the set of possible origins of a message. We enhance MUSDAC with mechanisms to protect request source address and contents during multi-network message routing.

Hop-by-Hop Routing: Ideally, every communication should be anonymous, with identification provided by the application level. Anonymity, however, is a relative concept. An individual is never completely anonymous; his anonymity degree when performing some action depends on the anonymity set, the set of all possible subjects who could have caused the same action [11]. We are interested in reducing the probability of identifying the entity responsible for sending a service request by increasing the set of entities that could have sent the same request. However, it does not suffice to consider anonymity for each message independently. If different messages can be related, the anonymity set for the group of messages is smaller than the anonymity set of each message individually. Unlinkability [11] between messages is hence another important requirement to increase the anonymity set of multiple messages.

As described in Sect. 2.1, MUSDAC components add their identification to each message for routing purposes, including the local Manager that originated the request. Even though the client address is not included on service request messages, routing data narrows the set of possible sources and can be also used to correlate consecutive requests. We modify MUSDAC's original routing algorithm to increase the sender anonymity set for service discovery messages by performing hop-by-hop routing. After receiving a local request for a service, the local Manager creates a unique ID for the request and sends the requests to a neighbor Bridge. Before forwarding the request to the next MUSDAC component, the Bridge generates a new ID for the message and stores the original ID, the new ID and the local Manager address. This information is used afterwards to identify the reply message and send it back to the request source. Every other entity that forwards a message caches its original ID, new ID and source. This entry can be later deleted if no reply is received after a pre-defined timeout. As a result, intermediary components know only the previous and the next hops of a message. The sender anonymity set for the message increases on each hop, since all the messages coming from a MUSDAC component have the same source address information. The destination Manager, in particular, can only identify the last Bridge that forwarded the request.

End-to-End Anonymous Encryption: Even though some MUSDAC components are only responsible for routing packets during a service discovery, all of them have access to the request contents. Clients, however, may consider that service discovery information in a particular request is so sensitive that only the destination Manager should have access to the message contents. Still, clients must be able to receive discovery results without disclosing their identities. The straightforward solution of using public key encryption to protect service requests and discovery results, in that case, is unsuitable since it would require disclosure of client or local Manager identities. We add to MUSDAC two protocols for end-to-end service discovery encryption that provide clients with different anonymity levels.

A common solution to provide network communication anonymity is the use of mixes. They were first introduced by Chaum [5] as a mechanism to protect the relation between sender and receiver of a given message, providing *relationship anonymity* [11]. In its simplest form, it consists of a single trusted server that receives encrypted messages from different sources and forwards them to different destinations adding delays as needed, as illustrated by the left side of Fig. 3. To increase resistance against malicious mixes, Chaum proposed the use of cascade of mixes: users define a path of mixes and encrypt messages with different encryption layers, one with the public key of each mix on the path. As messages traverse mixes, encryption layers are removed and the message is delivered to the final destination, as showed by the right side of Fig. 3. This way, a single honest mix along the path suffices to guarantee the cascade secrecy.

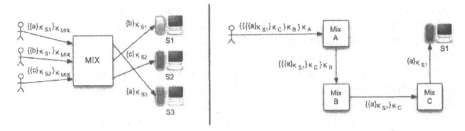

Fig. 3. A Simple Mix and a Cascade of Mixes

The privacy-aware version of MUSDAC uses the protocol proposed by Tor [6], a real world implementation of the Mix approach, to provide strong anonymity for service discovery. The protocol provides unilateral authentication (request sources remain anonymous), forward secrecy and key freshness.

A local Manager increasingly establishes symmetric keys with every MUSDAC component on the path to a destination Manager, one at a time, using their public keys. Symmetric keys are used afterwards to encrypt messages with multiple layers, that are decrypted by a cascade of mixes. For instance, if Manager M_1 wants to establish a key with Bridge B_{12} that possesses public and private keys $\{K_{B_{12}}, K_{B_{12}}^{-1}\}$, it first sends a request containing the first half of a Diffie-Hellman key agreement protocol and a circuit ID, encrypted with the Bridge's public key $(M_1 \rightarrow B_{12} : \{g^{x_1}, ID_1\}_{K_{B_{12}}})$. The Bridge answers with the second part of the Diffie-Hellman key agreement in plain text, along with a hash of their common key k_1 $(B_{12} \rightarrow M_1 : g^{y_1}, H(k_1))$.

This protocol provides strong anonymity since only the destination manager is capable of accessing the request contents, and intermediary MUSDAC components cannot relate the source and destination Managers of the service request. If we take into account the environment dynamics, however, this protocol may be too costly for a single service discovery transaction. We also introduce a lighter version of the protocol that offers weaker anonymity but better performance for anonymous end-to-end encrypted service discovery. Instead of negotiating a key with every MUSDAC component on the path, a local Manager runs the above protocol only with the destination Manager and uses the agreed key to encrypt the service request. In this protocol, however, the relation between source and destination Managers of a request is no longer protected. The first MUSDAC component of the path, particularly, knows exactly the source and destination of a service request. Groups of compromised components can also reveal that information. Nevertheless, intermediary MUSDAC components are still unable to read the request neither the reply contents.

4 Solution Assessment

Privacy-protection usually has an effect over resource consumption. Some mechanisms proposed by this work, however, allow for a more rational use of network resources and may actually have positive impacts on the MUSDAC performance. In this section, we perform a qualitative and a quantitative evaluation of the privacy-enhancement mechanisms proposed. Whenever it is relevant, we discuss the impacts on users as well as on MUSDAC components.

4.1 Qualitative Assessment

Most part of the privacy protection mechanisms proposed in this work is not mandatory, and clients can use it independently or in combination to increase their control of how and when they want to release personal data. Implementation of these mechanisms requires the introduction of a pro-active routing protocol in MUSDAC. Nevertheless, routing data dissemination improves MUSDAC support for mobility. In the original design, routing information is appended to messages as they traverse the platform. If a modification happens to the route, such as a Bridge that moves to another location, the path stored in the message is not updated and the request or the response is lost. With routing dissemination in place, every MUSDAC component has a partial local view of the network and thus can determine the new location of another component that moved. When a message's next hop is no longer available, a MUSDAC component is able to find an alternative route to that hop.

Also, the progressive and one-by-one discovery strategies contribute to a better resource usage by reducing message processing during service discovery. Experimental data shows that inter-network connectivity degrades substantially after three Manager hops [12]. The two new dissemination strategies take that into account and provide a more rational use of resources by performing service discovery first in closer networks, and only forwarding service requests to other remote networks if more results are needed. As a consequence fewer service discovery messages are generated, offloading the platform components. Reduction of component resource usage is an important incentive for entities volunteering to run MUSDAC services. Even though those strategies take longer to produce discovery results when compared to the parallel strategy, this delay may be acceptable in service discovery since it is a non-interactive process. Furthermore, users needing faster responses can always choose to use the parallel strategy.

Malicious components can disrupt the protocol or abuse it to invade the privacy of clients. Misbehaving Bridges can ignore the propagation strategy chosen by the client and forward requests to every MUSDAC component on the network, or announce fake geographical or domain information to receive undue requests. To prevent these attacks, honest MUSDAC components can examine the behavior of neighbor components during protocol execution to identify if they are working as expected or not. For example, a Bridge that announces that is located on a given country but never returns results from that country may be advertising a false location, or two identical requests with different propagation strategies may suggest that one of them was modified by a malicious Bridge. An intrusion detection protocol could use this kind of information, provided by multiple MUSDAC components, to identify rogue protocol participants. After identification, the MUSDAC overlay network could be reconfigured to avoid malicious components or MUSDAC components could be adapted to tolerate misbehaving participants, for instance by using end-to-end encryption which is resistant even to groups of malicious nodes along a communication path.

4.2 Quantitative Assessment

Even though the greatest part of the privacy protection mechanisms in MUSDAC is optional, the new routing capabilities impose a permanent overhead on the architecture and can be considered as the only fixed cost of the new platform design in terms of resource utilization. We first analyze the quantitative impact of hop-by-hop routing on resource consumption and after we discuss the effects of introducing a pro-active routing protocol into MUSDAC. Finally, we detail the performance impact of the other remaining privacy-enhancing mechanisms.

Hop-by-hop routing requires MUSDAC components to cache routing data for each message they handle and to search cached data for next hop determination. This data consists of an original message ID, the message last hop identification, and the new message ID. Message IDs are 128-bit random values, while hop identifications are 128-bit MD5 hashes of Managers and Bridges network information such as domain name and IP address. Each MUSDAC component thus has to store 48 bytes of routing data per message and this data can be discarded after a pre-specified timeout. According to our experiments, a service discovery takes at most 2 seconds to finish [13]. Based on that data, we estimate that 30 seconds is an adequate timeout for routing data and we do not expect that MUSDAC components will have to process more than 50 messages during that time interval [12]. Bridges and Managers, hence, will have to store a route state table of at most 2.4 KB, which we do not consider as too constraining. Also, search and update operations on a table with 50 entries should not impose a great overhead on MUSDAC components, especially when taking into account that context-aware service request processing already takes at least 40 ms to complete on each MUSDAC component [14]. Regarding proactive routing, we use a protocol based on OLSR optimized to only discover routes at most four Manager hops long. Already existing beacon messages are used to disseminate route information causing only a small overhead on the beacon message size. We expect that Bridges and Managers on a pervasive environment will form a weakly connected graph. In that case, as MUSDAC components only store routes four hops long, the required storage space and processing to compute routing tables is not significant.

Besides this small but permanent overhead, other optional privacy features can affect service discovery performance. User-defined restrictions on service request propagation based on geographic and domain data is implemented as MUSDAC context rules. Previous results show that service discovery time increases by 1.0 ms to 1.6 ms for each context rule [14]. Based on that data, and as request propagation restrictions can be implemented by two context-rules, we expect that processing of service requests that define restrictions on propagation will be at most 3.2 ms slower, representing a processing time increase of 6.8% on each MUSDAC component per message, which we believe to be acceptable. As service providers may also specify privacy-related context rules, the total delay for processing a service request and its corresponding result is 6.4 ms for each hop and can be at most 51.2 ms for messages passing through 8 hops considering Bridges and Managers.

Service discovery strategies and end-to-end encryption introduce a higher delay for discovery results. The progressive strategy for service discovery can be much slower than the parallel strategy, especially for networks many hops away. However, for networks one hop away, their performance is identical, since all networks one hop away are discovered in parallel. The one-by-one strategy always performs poorer than the other two strategies, and the delay increases as the number of networks visited by the request also increases. Regarding MUSDAC components, the progressive and one-by-one strategies may require

Bridges and Managers to process the same message more than once, when discovering services in networks more than one hop away, but the protocol can be optimized to avoid this situation. Nevertheless, the user can choose among the three options, which one provides the best balance between privacy protection and performance according to the request privacy requirements.

Finally, end-to-end encrypted requests using the weaker anonymity protocol require local Managers to perform one public-key encryption and remote Managers to perform a public-key decryption operation per request. Public-key encryption using the RSA algorithm and 1024-bit keys can be achieved in less than 50 ms even in computers with processing power equivalent to today's mobile devices [15]. The processing cost of encrypting and decrypting service discovery requests with the agreed symmetric key is negligible. If the stronger anonymity protocol is used, two public-key operations are required for each message hop. As we expect service requests to traverse at most 8 hops (including Bridges and Managers), the total encryption overhead for a service request can be as high as 800 ms at the worst case. However, clients can limit end-to-end encrypted service discovery to neighbor networks or networks two-Managers away, and in that case the encryption cost would be of 400 ms at most per request. Table 1 summarizes the costs involved in adding privacy-protection mechanisms to MUSDAC. The table enumerates expected delays for the client and compares the overhead between the native and privacy-aware (P-A) versions of MUSDAC.

Table 1. Privacy Performance Overhead

	Client	MUSDAC	P-A MUSDAC
Hop-by-hop Routing (storage)	-	0 KB	3.2 KB
Privacy Related Context	6.4 ms - 51.2 ms (per request)	2.1% - 3.4% (per rule)	6.8% (plus rules)
Progressive Service Discovery	0 - 4 times slower	-	-
One-by-one Service Discovery	0 - n times slower (for n networks)	-	-
End-to-end encryption (weaker)	100 ms (per request)	0 ms (no encryption)	50 ms (Mgrs.) 0 ms (Bridges)
End-to-end encryption (stronger)	200 ms - 800 ms (per request)	0 ms (no encryption)	50 ms

5 Conclusion

Interoperability between heterogeneous devices, networks and protocols is a fundamental factor for the success of pervasive environments. As we move towards this objective and the flow of information among different systems and applications is simplified, privacy issues arise. In service-oriented architectures, particularly, data associated to services such as service descriptions and requests become accessible to a greater number of entities. This data can contain sensitive information and malicious entities may abuse it to infer personal details such as activities and preferences.

In this work, we discussed privacy issues raised by service discovery in pervasive environments, particularly when context information is used to increase the relevance of the results. To address these issues, we proposed a trust model consistent with multi-protocol and multi-network service discovery, identified four complementary mechanisms to increase the privacy protection of mobile users interacting with the environment and performed an initial assessment to evaluate the impact of implementing those features. Figure 4 summarizes the mechanisms we propose (solid lines) and the modifications necessary to implement them on MUSDAC (dashed lines).

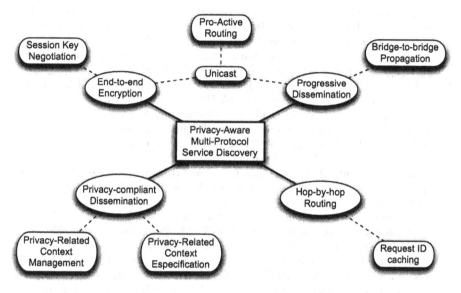

Fig. 4. Privacy-Awareness Features and Required MUSDAC Modifications

Even though our implementation is based on a specific platform, we believe that the problems discussed in this paper are common not only to other middleware for multi-protocol service discovery but also to other systems that distribute data to heterogeneous networks, such as content-based networking [4]. We also believe that the solutions proposed can be easily adapted to increase privacy protection on such systems. As part of the IST PLASTIC project[1] we are developing a privacy-aware service discovery service based on the MUSDAC platform, and also studying how to enhance other systems that present similar characteristics with privacy-awareness features.

Acknowledgment This work is part of the IST PLASTIC project and has been funded by the European Commission, FP6 contract number 026955.

---

[1] http://www.ist-plastic.org/

References

1. J. Allard, V. Chinta, S. Gundala, and G. G. Richard III. Jini Meets UPnP: An Architecture for Jini/UPnP Interoperability. In *SAINT '03: Proceedings of the 2003 Symposium on Applications and the Internet*, January 2003.
2. Y.-D. Bromberg and V. Issarny. INDISS: Interoperable Discovery System for Networked Services. In *Proceedings of the 6th International Middleware Conference*, November 2005.
3. L. Capra, S. Zachariadis, and C. Mascolo. Q-CAD: QoS and Context Aware Discovery Framework for Mobile Systems. In *Proceedings of the International Conference on Pervasive Services (ICPS'05)*, July 2005.
4. A. Carzaniga and A. L. Wolf. Content-Based Networking: A New Communication Infrastructure. In *IMWS '01: Revised Papers from the NSF Workshop on Developing an Infrastructure for Mobile and Wireless Systems*, October 2001.
5. D. Chaum. Untraceable Electronic Mail, Return Addresses, and Digital Pseudonyms. *Communications of the ACM*, 24(2), February 1981.
6. R. Dingledine, N. Mathewson, and P. Syverson. Tor: The Second-Generation Onion Router. In *Proceedings of the 13th USENIX*, August 2004.
7. A. Friday, N. Davies, N. Wallbank, E. Catterall, and S. Pink. Supporting Service Discovery, Querying and Interaction in Ubiquitous Computing Environments. *ACM Baltzer Wireless Networks (WINET) Special Issue on Pervasive Computing and Communications*, 10(6), November 2004.
8. P. Jacquet, P. Mühlethaler, T. Clausen, A. Laouiti, A. Qayyum, and L. Viennot. Optimized Link State Routing Protocol for Ad Hoc Networks. In *Proceedings of IEEE INMIC 2001*, December 2001.
9. C. Lee and S. Helal. Context Attributes: An Approach to Enable Context-awareness for Service Discovery. In *SAINT '03: Proceedings of the 2003 Symposium on Applications and the Internet*, January 2003.
10. S. Ben Mokhtar, A. Kaul, N. Georgantas, and V. Issarny. Efficient Semantic Service Discovery in Pervasive Computing Environments. In *Proceedings of the 7th International Middleware Conference (Middleware'06)*, December 2006.
11. A. Pfitzmann and M. Köhntopp. Anonymity, Unobservability, and Pseudonymity - A Proposal for Terminology. In *International Workshop on Designing Privacy Enhancing Technologies*, July 2000.
12. P.-G. Raverdy, S. Armand, and V. Issarny. Scalability Study of the MUSDAC Platform for Service Discovery in B3G Networks. In *Proceedings of Wireless World Research Forum Meeting (WWRF-17)*, November 2006.
13. P.-G. Raverdy, V. Issarny, R. Chibout, and A. de La Chapelle. A Multi-Protocol Approach to Service Discovery and Access in Pervasive Environments. In *Proceedings of MOBIQUITOUS - The 3rd Annual International Conference on Mobile and Ubiquitous Systems: Networks and Services*, July 2006.
14. P.-G. Raverdy, O. Riva, A. de La Chapelle, R. Chibout, and V. Issarny. Efficient Context-Aware Service Discovery in Multi-Protocol Pervasive Environments. In *Proceedings of the 7th International Conference on Mobile Data Management (MDM'06)*, May 2006.
15. M. J. Wiener. Performance Comparison of Public-Key Cryptosystems. *RSA Laboratories' CryptoBytes*, 4(1), July 1998.

Analysis of the implicit trust within the OLSR protocol

Asmaa Adnane[1], Rafael Timóteo de Sousa Jr[2], Christophe Bidan[1], and Ludovic Mé[1]

[1] Supélec - Equipe SSIR (EA 4039) {aadnane, cbidan, lme}@rennes.supelec.fr
[2] University of Brasília - LabRedes desousa@unb.br

Abstract. Trust is an interesting criterion for analyzing and comparing network protocols. The goal of this paper is to explicit the different types of trust relations between entities which exchange routing information and establish a routing infra-structure based on the OLSR protocol. One such entity assumes the other entities will behave in a particular way and the relations coming from this trust behavior are expressed in this paper using a formal language. This approach highlights the process of trust construction in OLSR and allows the analysis of trust requirements for this protocol, as well as the expression of attacks related to the betrayal of trust relations. Besides, this analysis allows the description of indicators for OLSR entities to have a protective mistrust behavior when effectively acting based on trust relations.

1 Introduction

Several research studies were conducted the last few years aiming at developing protocols for networks whose nodes communicate directly with each other to relay messages without the support of a central entity. This operating mode characterizes the ad hoc networks, for which the Internet Engineering Task Force (IETF) standardized some routing protocols such as the Optimized Link State Routing Protocol (OLSR) [3].

The objective of this paper is to identify and formalize trust assumptions that are implicitly used by the OLSR protocol. One of the goals of this analysis is to propose extensions to OLSR in order to make it more flexible to the variations of the environment and more resistant against security treats, while avoiding excessive restrictions on the auto-organization capacities and the dynamics of the network.

For this purpose, we begin from the idea of trust classification, which consists of a delimitation of the circumstances where a trust relationship is established, and we analyze the classes of trust present in OLSR. Initially, we present the language used to formally express trust clauses and the definition of trust subjacent to this language. Then, we expose the general characteristics of the OLSR protocol and its security problems. Finally, we present the OLSR implicit trust clauses and analyze the attacks against this protocol according to these implicit clauses.

Please use the following format when citing this chapter:

Adnane, A., de Sousa, R. T., Jr., Bidan, C. and Mé, L., 2007, in IFIP International Federation for Information Processing, Volume 238, Trust Management, eds. Etalle, S., Marsh, S., (Boston: Springer), pp. 75–90.

The paper is organized as follows. Section 2 surveys related research works. Section 3 presents the formal language for the expression of direct and derived trust clauses. The OLSR protocol is briefly described in section 4. The analysis of implicit trust within OLSR is presenteted in section 5. Section 6 is a study of some attacks against OLSR, from the point of view of trust. Finally, the conclusion sumarizes the results and indicates possible directions for future research.

2 Related works

The concepts of trust, trust models and trust management have been the object of several recent research projects. Trust is recognized as an important aspect for decision-making in distributed and auto-organized applications [5] [4]. In spite of that, there is no consensus in the literature on the definition of trust and what trust management encompasses. Many authors propose their own definitions of trust, each one concerning a specific research domain [13]. As a result, a multitude of formal models for trust calculation and management emerged, but this also lead to similar concepts appearing under different names and reciprocally [13] [14]. To mitigate this situation, in this paper we use the trust definition and a language to express trust proposed by [4], which permit to formalize and clarify trust aspects present in communication protocols.

A framework for specification and security analysis of mobile wireless networks communication protocols was proposed by [16], specifically for studying the SAODV routing protocol. However this study was not interested in the concept of trust. Other studies treat trust management and its relation to the routing operation in ad hoc networks [10],[7],[3].

Other authors [10] explored this subject to solve the problem of cooperation (one of the concepts related to trust) in ad hoc networks and to constrain the selfish nodes to cooperate.

The CONFIDANT project [7] proposes an extension of the DSR protocol providing nodes with a special component to observe and adapt to the behavior of the neighbors according to their reputation. Paper [9] proposes an extension to DSR, which selects the route based on a local evaluation of the trustworthiness of all known intermediary nodes on the route to the destination. The TRANS protocol [11] proposes a location-centric architecture for isolating misbehavior and establishing trust routing in sensor networks.

Reference [17] proposes a mechanism of anonymous signature bound to the record of a node's interactions history and associated to a proof of proximity, in order to allow the establishment of trust relations based on the history of interactions among the concerned nodes.

The OLSR specification [3] does not establish any special security measures, but recognizes that, as a proactive protocol, OLSR is a target for attacks against the periodic broadcast of topological information. Several efforts were made with the objective of finding security solutions for OLSR [6] [7] [8]. A survey on these solutions is presented by [6] which proposes a security architecture based on adding a digital signature to OLSR control messages, together with methods to validate the actual link state of nodes and to control intra-network misbehavior. One of these methods is based on the use of a protocol to detect misbehaving nodes using a reputation evaluation system. Other more traditional solutions, based on cryptography and authentication, are developed in [2].

However, these proposals do not provide an analysis of implicit trust in ad hoc routing protocols (especially OLSR), which is the basic contribution of this paper.

3 Expressing trust relationships

We use the language proposed by [4] for expressing the clauses concerning trust in a networking protocol. The concept of trust subjacent to this language is expressed by the fact that if an entity A trusts an entity B in some respect, informally means that A believes that B will behave in a certain way and will perform some action in certain specific circumstances.

The trust relation is taken into account if the possibility of realization of a protocol operation (the action) is evaluated by entity A on the basis of what it knows about entity B and the circumstances of this operation. According to the considered action and its circumstances of execution, it is necessary to distinguish various trust classes as defined by [4] and [13], so, for the sake of precision on the formalization of trust relations required by OLSR, in section 5 we propose appropriate classes to the actions performed by this protocol, such as the trust in another entity to route messages (routing trust). Still in accordance with [4], we distinguish the direct trust relations and the derived trust relations, the last ones being established from recommendations of other entities. Given the presence of several types of entities in the execution environment of a protocol and the existence of indirect relationship between the entities, it is necessary to distinguish these two types of trust relations. Thus, the clauses relating to trust are expressed with the following notations:

- each entity is identified by a single name; the terms A, B, C indicate specific entities, while the terms R, S indicate sets of entities;
- a specific class of trust is noted cc;
- the expression $A\ trusts_{cc}(B)$ means that A trusts B with respect to the action cc;
- $A\ trusts_{cc}(S)$ means that A trusts the set of entities S with respect to action cc, S being defined as the set of all entities for which a certain predicate holds;
- $A\ trusts_{cc-C}(B)$ means that A trusts B to perform action cc with respect to the entity C (but not necessarily to other entities);
- $A\ trusts.rec_{cc}(B)when.path[S]when.target[R]$ means that A trusts the recommendations of entity B about the capacity of other entities to perform

action *cc*. The *when* clauses allow the specification of constraints on the recommendations. The trust recommendation *path* is a sequence of entities such
that each one is recommended by its predecessor, so the *when.path* specifies
the only set of entities to be considered, at each point in some trust recommendation path, as candidates for the next step in the path. The *target*
clauses specifies the only set of entities to be considered as candidates for
becoming target entities in some recommendation path.

In the following sections, the use of this language, together with the mathematical set theory, allows us to reason about the trust required by the OLSR
protocol and to explicitly express trust relations between the entities executing
this protocol. This formal approach also has the interest to allow the analysis
of certain attacks against OLSR by revealing the implicit trust relations these
attacks exploit.

4 Characteristics of the OLSR protocol

OLSR is a proactive link-state routing protocol, which uses an optimized flooding mechanism to diffuse partial link state information to all network nodes.
The protocol uses multi-point relays (MPRs) which are selected nodes that
forward broadcast messages during the flooding process. The link state information is generated only by nodes elected as MPRs and each MPR must only
report on the state of links between itself and its selectors. Two types of control messages, HELLO and TC, allow each node to obtain and declare network
topological information.

HELLO messages are sent periodically by a node to advertise its links
(declared as asymmetric, symmetric or MPR) with neighbor nodes. Received
HELLO messages allow a node to memorize information about links and nodes
within its 2-hop neighborhood, so as to constitute the internal mental state
of each node, which is represented in the form of sets, including the link set
(LS), the neighbor set (NS), the 2-hop neighbor set (2HNS), the set of nodes
selected as MPR (MPR Set - MPRS) and the set of neighbor nodes who chose
the node as MPR (MPR Selector Set - MPRSS). These sets are updated and
used continuously for MPR selection, in such way that a message sent by the
node and relayed by its MPR set (i.e., elements of its MPRS) will be received
by all its 2-hop neighbors. Each node also records the addresses of its neighbors
who selected it as MPR (what constitutes the MPRSS). Thus, HELLO messages allow a node to establish its view of the "small world" (within the 2-hop
neighborhood).

The TC message conveys the topological information necessary for computing routes to the whole network, the "big world". The reception of TC messages
allow a node to obtain information about destination nodes and to keep this
information in its Topology Set. A node which was selected as MPR periodically
broadcasts TC messages advertising symmetric neighbors and these messages

are flooded in the whole network allowing the nodes to compute the topology to be used for routing (routing table).

With regard to the security aspects, the RFC 3626 does not specify any security measures for OLSR, even though this RFC describes the vulnerabilities of the protocol. The principal security problems are related to the facts that the topology of the network is revealed to anyone who listens to OLSR control messages, that nodes may generate invalid control traffic, that interferences may come from outside the OLSR environment and that the protocol operations assume the unicity of the IP address to identify a node. Traditional solutions based on cryptography and digital signature of messages, authentification of the origin and time-stamping of the messages, as well as address restriction and filtering, are indicated in the standard to mitigate these security problems. An implementation of these solutions is presented by [2]. Still, it should be noted that trust is not treated by this reference.

Given the general description of the protocol and the definition of the sets maintained by the OLSR node, it is possible to use the language described in section 3 to express the trust relationships in this protocol. Generally, the nodes (N) are considered to be cooperative and to trust the fact of obtaining the cooperation of the neighbor nodes. This behavior corresponds to the concept of general trust as defined by [5]. For example, the RFC 3626 [3] states that "a node should always use the same address as its main address" (p. 5), which is the basic belief of a node in the identity of others. This statement is translated using the formal language presented in section 3 to the expression:

$$N_i \; trusts_{id}(N_j), i \neq j$$

In the same way, other similar expressions are employed in the following sections for the analysis of the implicit trust required by OLSR and the description of attacks against OLSR.

5 Analysis of OLSR implicit trust aspects

In this section, while expressing the implicit trust rules in OLSR, we present reasonings on trust which could be used for selecting the MPRs of a node and for computing its routing table. We show that trust, if "explicitly" expressed, can be a reasoning factor of a node about its small world and about the routing towards the big world.

The node collects information about link configuration (small world) and routing topologies (big world) from the exchanges of HELLO and TC messages, respectively. The analysis below allows us to extract OLSR implicit trust rules and to suggest that the protocol should also integrate the concept of mistrust towards its choices of MPR and routes. For this purpose, we use the following definitions:

- *MANET*: the set of the whole MANET nodes,

- LS_x (Link Set): the link set of the node x,
- NS_x (Neighbor Set): the set of symmetric neighbors of the node x,
- $2HNS_x$ (2-Hop Neighbor Set): the set of 2-hop neighbors of the node x,
- $MPRS_x$: the set of nodes selected as MPR by the node x ($MPR_x \subseteq NS_x$),
- $MPRSS_x$ (MPR Selection Set): the set of symmetric neighbors which have selected the node x as MPR,
- TS_x (Topology Set): the set containing the network topology as seen by the node x,
- RT_x (Routing Table): the routing table of the node x.
- $dist : MANET^2 \rightarrow \aleph$: the function which provides the distance, expressed as the number of hops, between two nodes of the network.

The following sections present the evolution of a node's trust during the operations of link sensing, MPR selection (computation of MPRS), MPR signaling (computation of MPRSS), and routing table calculation.

As indicated before, initially the nodes are generally trustful [5], since they do not know anything on their environment and believe in all information that they receive from others without checking its validity.

5.1 Discovering the neighborhood - Link sensing

Initially a node X does not know any neighbor, therefore it does not have any view of the network. The node starts to build its view with the reception of HELLO messages coming from the neighbors. We note $X \overset{HELLO}{\leftarrow} Y$ as the reception of a HELLO message coming from Y. Firstly, these messages allow the node to detect asymmetrical links, leading to a modification of the mental state of X about its trust in node Y, i.e., X knows Y but does not trust it yet, because X is not sure that Y functions in accordance with the OLSR specification, with regard to the reception and sending of HELLO messages:

$$X \overset{HELLO}{\leftarrow} Y, \; X \notin LS_Y \implies X \neg trusts\,(Y) \tag{1}$$

This expression means that X does not trust Y neither to be a symmetrical neighbor, nor to be a MPR, although X receives HELLO messages from Y. However, being an agent generally trustful [5], X diffuses HELLO messages that can be received by Y, which in turn will be able to take them into account and to add X to its set of symmetrical neighbors NS_Y.

If Y acts according to the protocol, i.e., if it sends HELLO messages informing that it has a link with X, then a new situation of trust is reached:

$$X \overset{HELLO}{\leftarrow} Y, \; X \in LS_Y \Rightarrow X \; trusts_{ID \cup NI}(Y), LS_X = LS_X \cup Y$$
$$2HNS_X = 2HNS_X \cup (NS_Y - X) \tag{2}$$

A trust relation has just been built which is concretized by the fact that now X regards Y as its symmetrical neighbor, and the symmetrical neighbors of Y as 2-hop neighbors. In addition, this trust relation is seen as symmetrical, since Y is expected to behave in the same way as X:

$$Y \stackrel{HELLO}{\longleftarrow} X \Rightarrow Y\ trusts_{ID \cup NI}(X)$$

This symmetrical relation is the base for future decisions which will be taken by X about its small world (MPR selection), but also, indirectly, for the routing towards the big world (calculation of the routing table) through the exchange of TC messages.

5.2 MPR selection - Computing the $MPRS$

In OLSR, the only criterion for MPR selection by a node X is the number of symmetrical neighbors of a candidate node Y, which defines the degree of Y, noted $D(Y)$ and calculated by the formula:

$$\forall Y \in NS_X : V_Y = NS_Y - NS_X - \{X, Y\}, D(Y) = card\{V_Y\} \qquad (3)$$

Firstly, the choice concerns the MPRs for relaying to nodes in the 2-hop neighborhood that can be reached only through paths including the chosen MPRs:

$$MPRS_X = MPRS_X \cup \{Y \in NS_X : \exists Z \in 2HNS_X : Z \in NS_Y,$$
$$\forall V \in NS_X : Z \notin NS_V\} \qquad (4)$$

Then, while there are nodes in $2HNS$ which are not covered by at least one node in the MPR set, this set is extended with other MPRs whose selection is based on their reachability to the maximum number of nodes in $2HNS$ (in case of multiple nodes providing the same reachability, the node whose D(Y) is greater is selected as MPR) until all nodes in $2HNS$ are covered:

$$\exists V \in 2HNS_X : \forall Y \in MPRS_X : V \notin NS_Y \Longrightarrow MPRS_X =$$
$$MPRS_X \cup \{Y \in NS_X : D(Y) = MAX\{D(Z) \forall Z \in NS_X\}\} \qquad (5)$$

In terms of trust, this means that X trusts the nodes in its MPR set for routing:

$$\forall Y \in MPRS_X : X\ trusts_{fw}(Y) \qquad (6)$$

Consequently, the nodes in $MPRS_X$ are required to recommend to X the routes to the distant nodes:

$$\forall Z \in MANET : X\ trusts.rec_{fw}\ (Y)\ when.path[MPRS_Y]\ when.target[Z]$$

Considering that the nodes $MPRS_Y$ themselves trust other MPRs, the route from X to Z is formed by a sequence in the form of the predicate: $route_{Y_1 \rightarrow Y_n} = Y_1, ..., Y_n$ with $Y_{i+1} \in MPRS_{Y_i}$, which allows to extend the expression above to obtain:

$$\forall Z \in MANET : X\ trusts.rec_{fw}(Y)\ when.path[route_{Y \rightarrow Z}]when.target[Z]$$
$$(7)$$

This expression presents the general rule of trust recursivity for the routing in the networks operating under OLSR.

5.3 MPR Signaling - Computing the $MPRSS$

This calculation allows a node X to discover information about the trust that other nodes place on X itself. The calculation of the $MPRSS_X$ is expressed by the following formula:

$$X \xleftarrow{HELLO} Y, X \in MPRS_Y \Rightarrow MPRSS_X = MPRSS_X \cup \{Y\} \qquad (8)$$

As X allows the nodes of its $MPRSS$ to use its resources for routing, which constitutes a form of access trust as discussed in Section 3, the calculation of $MPRSS_X$ implies that X trusts Y to use X resources for routing without causing any harm and also that X trusts Y for advertising that X is a MPR. These trust relations correspond respectivelly to the following expressions:

$$X \; trusts_{at} \; (Y), X \; trusts_{dt} \; (Y)$$

5.4 Computing the routing table

The routing table is computed from the information contained in the local link information base and the topology set. Therefore, the routing table (RT) is recalculated if the node detects a change in either of the sets LS, NS, $2HNS$, TS, $MPRS$ or $MPRSS$.

Each entry in RT consists of: ($R\_dest\_addr, R\_next\_addr, R\_dist,$ R_iFace_addr), and specifies that the node identified by R_dest_addr is located R_dist hops away from the local node, that the symmetric neighbor node with interface address R_next_addr is the next hop node in the route to R_dest_addr, and that this symmetric neighbor node is reachable through the local interface with the address R_iface_addr.

Each node X has its view of the network topology and selects the shortest path to reach any other node Z passing through a selected MPR Y. The routing table is thus computed using a shortest path algorithm [18]. From the point of view of trust,this calculation will allow X to trust Y for the routing towards Z. If we note $T = (Z, Y, N, I)$ for a tuple of RT_X, the following relation is obtained:

$$\forall T \in RT_X \Rightarrow X \; trusts_{fw-z}(Y) \; or \; X \; trusts_{fw-R\_dest\_addr} \; (R\_next\_addr) \; (9)$$

Moreover, the routing table is calculated so that there is only one route towards each destination:

$$\forall X, Z \in MANET, \; Z \notin NS_X \Rightarrow \exists ! \; T \in TR_X : \; T.R\_Addr\_Dest = Z \; (10)$$

and each selected route is the shortest among the routes starting from MPR nodes, which defines a predicate that we call $MinDist(X, Z)$:

$$Y \in MPRS_X : \; MinDist(Y, Z) = MIN\{dist(A, Z)/A \in MPRS_X\}$$
$$\Rightarrow T.R\_Next\_Addr = Y \quad (11)$$

The inherent risk in the choice of only one route towards any destination is to choose, as router, a corrupted or misbehaving node. In the following section, we explain how this vulnerability can be exploited by the attackers, who give false information about the network topology in order to direct all the traffic of the network towards them and/or to disturb the operation of the protocol.

According to the expression (11), even if there are several paths towards Z, X will only choose the shortest route starting from one of its MPR. The routing table calculation is a reasoning based on the distance and results in the set of routes which the node considers as the most adequate for the routing. Actually, the goal of this calculation is to suitably choose the MPRs among those which offer routes towards the destinations. After computing the distances to destinations, the node will place more trust in those nodes which offer the shortest paths towards the destinations (9).

The selection of Y as MPR by X for routing towards a node Z implies that X, not only trusts Y for routing (6), but also trusts the choices of the routes made by Y (7). Actually, there is a chain of this indirect trust relation between X and any relay forwarding the packets to Z and this chain has the particularity that only the last relay before Z, being a MPR of this target node, exchanges control messages directly with Z (HELLO messages). This sequence expresses the transivity of MPR recommendations in OLSR, a property which allows us to use the deduction algorithm presented by [4] to obtain the following trust relation:

$$X \; trusts.rec^*_{fw-Z} \; (Z) \; when.target[Z] \; when.path[Z] \qquad (12)$$

This expression means that the routing target node is itself the starting point of the trust chain, and its $MPRS$ should be properly chosen so that every other node can correctly communicate with this node.

That suggests the existence of a spreading of the trust placed in the MPR. Certain attacks against OLSR exploit the vulnerability resulting from the absence of validation of this derived trust chain. The node should have a degree of mistrust concerning the information used for the calculation of the routing table. This mistrust could be associated to the use of a procedure for validating the routing information which is spread in network (TC messages).

Two results are put forward by this analysis. In the first place, the operations of OLSR generate information related to trust and present implicit trust rules that, as such, are not taken into account by the nodes, but which can be actually exploited to contribute to the security of the protocol. Secondly, the analysis shows that the nodes create trust relationships without validated evidence, not measuring the consequences of these relationships and thus without any mistrust in their choices.

6 Trust-based synthesis of OLSR vulnerabilities

With respect to routing choices, the OLSR reasoning is aimed at calculating the routing table, a behavior that implies thereafter the implicit use of trust relationships between nodes. In other words, OLSR effectively generates information about trust between nodes, but the nodes firstly cooperate and then, without any validation, implicitly deduce information about the other nodes in which they have to trust. The only criterion for this reasoning is the distance between the nodes, an aspect of which they should be careful. Otherwise, mistrust would be a more appropriate behavior in the beginning of a relationship which can lead to cooperation with mischievous nodes. Moreover, the information related to trust is obtained, but is neither used for the future cooperations, nor exploited to improve the operation of the protocol.

To accept information that comes within the received messages, without using a security mechanism (i.e., authentication) or a validation procedure (i.e., checking the protocol logic), is the principal vulnerability exploited by certain attacks against OLSR. These attacks are analyzed hereafter, considering the trust clauses that were explicitly expressed for OLSR in section 5.

In a previous work [15], we proposed a classification (table 1) of these attacks against OLSR. Any node can either modify the protocol messages before forwarding them, or create false messages or spoof an identity, and each one of these actions can be at the base of an attack. As the HELLO message is sent to the 1-hop neighbors and is not relayed, this message is not prone to modification attacks, but rather to fabrication attacks. On the other hand, the TC message is sent to all the network and can thus be used either for modification and fabrication attacks (before the relaying).

Table 1. Vulnerabilities of the OLSR Protocol

Attack	OLSR message	Falsified Routing Information	Origin information in the Corrupted Message
Fabrication	HELLO	Neighbor List	Any
Fabrication and impersonation	HELLO	Link-status	IP Address of the impersonated node
Fabrication	TC	MS list	Any
Modification and impersonation	TC	Sequence Number	Originator IP Address

6.1 Attack 1: Fabrication of HELLO Messages

In this attack (figure 1), the adversary wants to be selected as MPR and fabricates a HELLO message advertising all the nodes previously announced in any HELLO message it has already received, together with an additional unused address, this one with symmetric link status. On receiving this message, all of the attacker's neighbors choose it as sole MPR (according to the rule 4). Thus all traffic originated in these nodes towards destinations outside the 1-hop neighborhood is then forwarded to the attacker. Before the attack, A chooses B as

Fig. 1. Hello message fabrication

MPR to transmit data to C. The attack takes place according to the following steps:

1. $att \xleftarrow{HELLO} B$: the attacker identifies A and C as neighbors of B;
2. $att \xleftarrow{HELLO} A$: the attacker identifies B as a neighbor of A;
3. After receiving a new HELLO message from B, the attacker fabricates a HELLO message announcing $LS_{att} = LS_A \cup LS_B \cup X = \{A, B, C, X\}$ (X is an additional fictitious address announced with symmetric link status).

In consequence of this attack, according to the rule (4), A and B will select att as MPR:

$$A\ trusts_{fw}(att),\ B\ trusts_{fw}(att)$$

The attacker acquires the trust of A and B which will choose it for routing towards any node Z in the network, without having a proof of the existence of a path between the attacker and Z. In this example, A will select the attacker to route towards C because it seems to A that this is the shortest path (11), leading to the situation expressed by the rule (7):

$$A\ trusts.rec_{fw}\ (attacker)\ when.path[route_{attacker \to C}]\ when.target[C]$$

The fact that there is no path $route_{attacker \to C}$ proves that the nodes A and B should mistrust the information provided in the HELLO message. A trust-based reasoning allows the nodes to check the validity of the topological information so that the nodes A and B can detect the attack without calling upon heavy cryptographic mechanisms.

One of the possible verifications consists in reasoning based on subsequent TC messages. Before the attack, A held B as MPR for routing messages to C and C held B as MPR for routing messages to A, thus $MPRS_A \cap MPRS_C = \{B\}$. After the attack, since B remains as a MPR of C, it will broadcast a TC message advertising C as a symmetric neighbor. In the other hand, the attacker will also broadcast a TC message advertising A and B as neighbors. The reasoning from the point of view of A will lead to contradictory conclusions. By receiving a TC message from B, A will deduce:

$$A \xleftarrow{TC} B,\ NS_B = \{A, att, C\} \Rightarrow \exists\ Z \in NS_B :\ B \in MPRS_Z$$

To the contrary, node A, after receiving a TC message from the attacker, will also deduce:

$$A \xleftarrow{TC} att, \ NS_{att} = \{A, B, C, X\} \Rightarrow \exists \, Z \in NS_{att} : \ att \in MPRS_Z$$

To discover the node which selected B as MPR, A reasons by elimination on the set NS_B. Given that $B \notin MPRS_A$ then it is not A which selected B as MPR. To check if it was the attacker that chose B as MPR, A compares the respective neighbourhoods of B and att, by checking whether the smallest neighbourhood is included in the largest :

$$[NB_B - \{att\}] \subset [NB_{att} - \{B\}]$$

Then, A deduces that it was not the attacker which selected B as MPR. Thus, it is the node C which did it, establishing the following trust relation:

$$B \in MPRS_C \Rightarrow C \ trusts_{fw-A}(B) \tag{13}$$

Moreover, the degree of reachability of B is lower than the degree of the attacker. Thus, based on clause (5), A deduces that C should also choose the attacker as MPR:

$$D(B) < D(att) \Rightarrow att \in MPRS_C$$

In terms of trust, C should use att for routing towards A:

$$att \in MPRS_C \Rightarrow C \ trusts_{fw-A}(att) \tag{14}$$

Considering that it should exist only one route for each destination (10), there is a contradiction between (13) and (14), which leads node A to mistrust the received information, since its view of the network topology indicates that C should have chosen att as MPR and not B. The problem arises from the link between att and C. Thus, A must be mistrustful regarding these two nodes. But, C should not represent a danger given that it selects B as MPR and thus behaves correctly; on the other hand, the attacker, which was selected as MPR, presents a real risk. The trust-based analysis of this attack shows the importance of message correlation to establish a mistrust-based control in OLSR, according to the following assertions:

- The node has to mistrust another node who declares to be neighbor of all other nodes until these other nodes confirm it effectively as a symmetric neighbor;
- The node has to look for contradictory topological information by correlating the received message contents (HELLO and TC messages).

6.2 Attack 2: Fabrication and Impersonation in HELLO Messages

In this type of attack, the attacker aims at destroying a symmetrical link that exists between two neighbors. After reception of a legitimate message, the attacker generates a spoof HELLO message advertising the link which it wants to destroy with "lost" status. When the target neighbor receives the false HELLO, it will update its link set. Thus no traffic will be forwarded to the target node through the lost link. This attack, which is illustrated in the figure 2, proceeds according to the following steps:

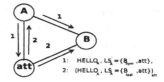

Fig. 2. Fabrication and impersonation in HELLO Messages

1. A and B establish a symmetric link by exchanging HELLO messages. Thus, they trust each other (rule 2):

$$B \xrightarrow{HELLO} A \Rightarrow A\ trusts_{ID \cup NI}(B),\ A \xrightarrow{HELLO} B \Rightarrow B\ trusts_{ID \cup NI}(A) \quad (15)$$

2. by capturing a HELLO from A, the attacker identifies B as a symmetric neighbor of A.
3. after receiving the HELLO message from A, the attacker fabricates a HELLO message impersonating A, advertising B with lost link status. This message makes B alter to asymmetric its link status towards A, thereby blocking any traffic to be forwarded via this link. This implies (according to (1)):

$$B \xleftarrow{HELLO_A} att,\ B \notin LS_A \Rightarrow B\neg trusts(A) \quad (16)$$

As OLSR specifies an interval value for the periodic emission of HELLO messages, but does not specify measures to check if messages are received in a very small interval, if this attack occurs, B will continue to receive HELLO messages from A advertising the link to B as symmetrical and spoofed HELLO messages from the attacker declaring the opposite. Thus, B receives two contradictory pieces of information (15 and 16) in a small time interval (lower than the standard interval defined by OLSR), and so must mistrust this information before destroying its trust relationship with A.

The analysis of this attack confirms the potential of the correlation between received messages to establish a control based on mistrust. In the present attack, the node must take into account the factor of time before destroying a trust relationship, according to the following assertions:

- following the reception of a HELLO message advertising a lost link status, the node should not destroy the trust relation and declare the link as lost immediately. It must exchange other HELLO messages to check with the neighbor whether they continue to hear each other;
- as before, the node must mistrust the neighbor who will benefit from the destruction of the link, for example which will be selected as MPR.

6.3 Attacks 3 and 4: Fabrication and modification of TC messages

The objective of these attacks is to provide false network topological information. The attacker fabricates a TC message advertising remote nodes (2 hops or more) as being within its neighbor set (NS). This means that the attacker will be chosen by its neighbors to route traffic to the falsely advertised nodes. A similar outcome can be obtained if the attacker modifies a received TC message. The attacker proceeds according to following steps (Figure (3)):

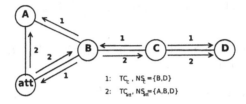

1: TC_c, $NS_c = \{B,D\}$
2: TC_{att}, $NS_{att} = \{A,B,D\}$

Fig. 3. Fabrication of TC message

1. by receiving a TC Message from C, the attacker identifies D at a distance of 3 hops;
2. the attacker fabricates another TC message, advertising D as part of its NS (symmetric neighbors). This causes A to update its routing table so as to stop routing traffic to D via B and start routing it via the attacker.

In this situation, the attacker takes advantage of the rule (9), leading to the following trust relationships:

$$A\ trusts_{fw-D}(att) \Rightarrow A\ trusts.rec_{fw}(att)\ when.path[route_{att \to D}]\ when.target[D]$$

This is a situation similar to attack 1: the trust relationship above is established without evidence because there is no $route_{att \to D}$. Node A should check this information before changing its routing table. To proceed this verification, A has to wait messages coming from D, which will allow the correlation of network topology information. Initially:

$$A \overset{TC_C}{\longleftarrow} B,\ NS_C = \{B,D\} \Rightarrow \exists Z \in NS_C : C \in MPRS_Z$$

Then, A will receive a TC message from the attacker:

$$A \overset{TC_{att}}{\longleftarrow} att,\ NS_{att} = \{A,B,D\} \Rightarrow \exists Z \in NS_{att} : att \in MPRS_Z$$

The node A can deduce that: $Z \neq A$, because $att \notin MPRS_A$ and $Z \neq B$, otherwise A would have received the TC_C messages from B and from att. Therefore, $Z = D$, which implies:

$$att \in MPRS_D \Rightarrow D\ trusts_{fw-A}(att) \qquad (17)$$

On the other hand, D continues to have C as MPR for routing towards A. Therefore, A will receive data from D via B and will be able to deduce:

$$A \overset{data_D}{\leftarrow} B, \ D \notin NS_B, \ D \in NS_C, \ C \in NS_B \Rightarrow C \in MPRS_D \qquad (18)$$

According to the rule (9), A can deduce that:

$$C \in MPRS_D \Rightarrow D \ trusts_{fw-A}(C) \qquad (19)$$

Given that a node should have only one route towards each destination (10), this expression represents a contradiction with expression (17).

7 Conclusions and future works

The trust aspects of OLSR ad hoc routing could be formalized with the chosen language, which allowed us to interpret attacks against OLSR in terms of trust classes and relations. As a result, we put forward the conditions to use trust-based reasoning as a solution to mitigate certain vulnerabilities of the protocol.

Indeed, the analysis highlights possible measures to render OLSR more reliable and this by means of operations and information already existing in the protocol, without resorting to cryptographic mechanisms. We arrive at the conclusion that a mistrust-based control can be set up to detect suspect behavior using the correlation between information provided in the subsequent received messages. For example, the discovery of neighborhood (link sensing), which is limited to the information provided by HELLO messages, can be strengthened by exploiting the topological information (TC messages) to validate the acquired knowledge and deduce other criteria which a node can use to select its MPR set. Some relationships between nodes can be derived exclusively from a trust-based reasoning. These derived relationships could be used for MPR selection. It is also possible to consider the use of trust as an additional criterion to calculate the routing table, besides the degree of the nodes (number of declared neighbors).

Finally, it is possible for a node to discover the information about the trust the other nodes place on it. By principle, any node could consider the possibility of having a behavior of reciprocity towards these nodes.

We plan the simulation of an extension to OLSR using trust rules for MPR selection and routing table calculation. Another possibility is to set up a trust management module to be tied to the structure of the nodes without modifying the protocol. Our goal is to measure the impact of these solutions on the protocol, while preserving the auto-organization and the dynamic of the adhoc environment. With regard to the usage of an explicit specification of direct and derived trust relations, it is worth, in the view of trust, to compare OLSR with other protocols, for example AODV, and report the contribution of trust to the security of both protocols.

Acknowledgements. Rafael Timóteo de Sousa Jr. is supported by CNPq - Brazil and would like to thank Supélec - France for its support during his postdoctoral program.

References

1. Mui L (2003) Computational Models of Trust and Reputation: Agents, Evolutionary Games, and Social Networks, PhD Thesis, Massachusetts Institute of Technology.
2. Clausen T, Laouiti A, Muhlethaler P, Raffo D, Adjih C (2005) Securing the OLSR routing protocol with or without compromised nodes in the network, HAL - CCSd - CNRS, INRIA - Rocquencourt.
3. Clausen T, Jacquet P (2003) IETF RFC-3626: Optimized Link State Routing Protocol OLSR.
4. Yahalom R, Klein B, Beth T (1993) Trust Relationships in Secure Systems - A Distributed Authentication Perspective. In: SP'93: Proceedings of the 1993 IEEE Symposium on Security and Privacy. IEEE Computer Society, Washington, USA.
5. Marsh S (1994) Formalising Trust as a Computational Concept, PhD Thesis. Department of Mathematics and Computer Science, University of Stirling.
6. Raffo D (2005) Security Schemes for the OLSR Protocol for Ad Hoc Networks, PhD Thesis, University of Paris 6 Pierre et Marie Curie.
7. Buchegger S (2004) Coping with Misbehavior in Mobile Ad-hoc Networks, PhD Thesis. IC School of Computer and Communication Sciences, Lausanne university.
8. Fourati A, Al Agha K (2006) A Shared Secret-based Algorithm for Securing the OLSR Routing Protocol. Springer Netherlands, Telecommunication Systems, Volume 31, Numbers 2-3, pp. 213-226.
9. Jensen C D, Connell P O (2006) Trust-Based Route Selection in Dynamic Source Routing. In: Trust Management, 4th International Conference, iTrust 2006. Springer, Volume 3986/2006, pp.150-163, Pisa, Italy.
10. Michiardi P (2004) Cooperation Enforcement and Network Security Mechanisms for Mobile Ad Hoc Networks, PhD Thesis, Ecole nationale supérieure des télécommunications, Paris.
11. Tanachaiwiwat S, Dave P, Bhindwale R, Helmy A (2004) Location-centric Isolation of Misbehavior and Trust Routing in Energy-constrained Sensor Networks. IEEE International Performance, Computing, and Communications Conference (IPCCC), pp. 463-469.
12. Liu J, Issarny V (2004) Enhanced Reputation Mechanism for Mobile Ad Hoc Networks. In: Trust Management. 2nd International Conference, iTrust 2004. Springer, Volume 2995/2004, pp. 48-62, Oxford, UK.
13. Grandison T, Sloman M (2000) A Survey of Trust in Internet Applications. IEEE Communications Surveys and Tutorials, 4th Quarter, Vol. 3, No. 4.
14. Viljanen L (2005) Towards an Ontology of Trust. In: Trust, Privacy and Security in Digital Business. Springer, Volume 3592/2005, pp. 175-184.
15. Puttini R S, Mé L, Sousa Jr R T (2004) On the Vulnerabilities and Protection of Mobile Ad Hoc Network Routing Protocols. In: Proceedings of the 3rd International Conference on Networking ICN'2004. IEEE, pp. 676-684, New Jersey, USA.
16. Nanz S, Hankin C (2006) A Framework for Security Analysis of Mobile Wireless Networks. Theoretical Computer Science, Volume 367, pp. 203-227.
17. Bussard L (2004) Trust Establishment Protocols for Communicating Devices, PhD Thesis, Eurecom - ENST.
18. Johnson D B (1973) A Note on Dijkstra's Shortest Path Algorithm, Journal of the ACM, Volume 20, pp. 385-388, New York, USA.

Validating a Trust-based Access Control System

William J. Adams[1] and Nathaniel J. Davis, IV[2]

[1]Department of Electrical Engineering and Computer Science,
United States Military Academy, West Point, NY 10996
Joe.adams@usma.edu
[2]Department of Electrical and Computer Engineering, Air Force Institute of Technology,
Wright Patterson AFB, Dayton OH 45433 USA
Nathaniel.Davis@afit.edu

Abstract. Over the last few years researchers have recognized the need for adaptive access control mechanisms for dynamic collaborative environments. As a result, several mechanisms have been proposed and demonstrated in academic literature. Although these mechanisms have been verified to perform as advertised, few of them have been validated to work within an operational environment. Using a decentralized trust-based access control system of their own design, the authors validated their system using a narrative technique to develop a realistic operational scenario. They tested the system within the scenario and then applied a cost and a success metric to the results to determine the efficiency of their mechanism. The results show how the authors' narrative approach and success metric combine to provide more efficient and effective analysis of how an access control mechanisms will perform when used in an operational environment.

Keywords: validation testing, access control, trust management

The views expressed are those of the authors and do not reflect the official policy or position of the US Army, the US Air Force, the Department of Defense or the US Government.

1. Introduction

During development, programmers typically verify a system's output to ensure that the system is performing as expected and producing credible results. To complete testing, however, a system must be validated to ensure that it performs reliably in situations that are present in its intended operational environment. In the case of a trust-based access control (TBAC) system, these situations include misbehaving users and temporary collaborations. This paper looks at the validation of a TBAC system

Please use the following format when citing this chapter:

Adams, W. and Davis, N. J., IV, 2007, in IFIP International Federation for Information Processing, Volume 238, Trust Management, eds. Etalle, S., Marsh, S., (Boston: Springer), pp. 91–106.

called the Trust Management System (TMS) and examines its performance in terms of effectiveness and cost to make correct decisions.

TBAC validation required more than getting the TMS to produce reputation or risk assessments. Our approach started by describing our system's expected operational environment and then deriving specific tasks that needed to be tested in that environment. After executing the tests, we applied specific metrics to measure the TMS' performance in that environment.

Dynamic collaborative environments (DCEs) formed to enable participants to share information while, at the same time, allow them to retain control over the resources that they brought with them to the coalition [1]. The trust management system (TMS) [2] developed through this research effectively implemented a decentralized access and permission management scheme. User permissions were determined using a combination of behavior grading and risk assessment without the need for preconfigured centrally managed roles or permission sets. Because the TMS tracked a user's behavior, using past behavior as an indication of future performance, no pre-configuration of users or resources was required.

The TMS also offered a unique ability to enforce multiple access levels without the burden of implementing and managing multiple cryptographic keys or hierarchies of roles. A user provided its peers customized views of its contents and services based on its trust profile and its individual assessment of the peer's trustworthiness. As the user's evaluation of a peer's reputation changed, the peer's access changed to safeguard the user's resources, restricting access to those peers that have contributed to the user's and the coalition's goals.

The contribution of this paper lies in its application of contextually derived objectives and requirements to validate a TBAC system. We use a narrative technique that is based on a realistic operational scenario. The scenario not only defines the operating environment but it also constrains testing so that results are pertinent and justified by real requirements. Having defined out test environment, we developed a success metric that assesses the TBAC system. Our results show that our TBAC implementation is far more effective and efficient than other current systems.

The rest of this paper is organized as follows. The next section describes our TMS, an implementation of a TBAC system, and then presents some related work in the field of trust-based access control and access control validation. Section 4 describes our validation test and the metrics used to gauge performance effectiveness. Finally, we conclude the paper and describe the future work that is ongoing with the TMS.

2. System Description

The TMS was developed to provide a trust-based privilege management mechanism in a fluid, collaborative environment. Users were initiated information sharing with a new peer in the DCE through an introduction process. This process in an exchange of lists of DCE members that can refer the user to strangers. Once introduced, the user collected behavior observations collected behavior observations from its trusted peers on members of the DCE called Feedback Items (*FI*). *FI* were weighted with the reputation of the observer and placed in a temporally-ordered queue called a Reputation Indexing Window (*RIW*).

When a peer requested a resource, a user applied a quantitative method (called the 3Win method) to the *RIW* to compute a Reputation Index (*RI*) for that peer before allowing access to any of his or her resources. Once the *RI* was computed, the TMS stored the *RIW* in its trust store (*TS*). The *RI* was compared against the user's trust thresholds and the decision to extend or deny trust was made.

3. Related Work

Access control systems have been implemented to grant or deny the ability to use a resource or perform an operation in almost all computer systems. Before fielding, they have been verified to perform as expected given a wide range of statistically valid input. Few access control systems have been validated, however, because of the number and complexity of operating environments. One exception was dRBAC [3] that proposed an operational environment and then used this setting to derive the operational requirements for system testing.

TBAC systems used behavior grading to assess the trustworthiness of a prospective associate. They allowed or denied access based on a comparison of a quantitative reputation rating and a trust threshold. Previous work by the authors [2] discussed how the TMS was designed and verified to operate correctly. Other TBAC projects, such as SECURE [4] and Vigil [5] also verified the operation of their systems but stopped short of validating them in any realistic operational environment.

Validation testing was considered crucial to the success of a fielded system, as it provided the engineers and users some certainty that the system could withstand the demands of the specific operational environment and still perform as expected. Lo Presti [1] presented one method of using an operational scenario to derive user requirements for testing. The application of this method formed the first part of the validation process presented in this paper.

Once the requirements were derived, the system's success at accomplishing the tasks was measured quantitatively. Assessing the efficiency of an access control system [6] involved examining a ratio of three parameters: the number of correct decisions, the number of false positive decisions, and the number of false negative decisions. Linked to the efficiency rating, the cost of making decisions was also considered. This evaluation included the amount of memory and communications required by the system to make trust decisions. These criteria are explained in more detail in the next section.

4. Validation

Validation ensured that the system met the user requirements. In our case, validation guaranteed that the modules of the TMS worked together to make access control decisions correctly under a variety of network conditions. Validation differed from verification testing in that the system was tested against operational requirements instead of purely quantitative comparisons.

The requirements used in validation testing came from two sources. The first source was verification testing. These requirements, derived in part from the analysis presented in previous work [2], placed the system in a test environment that simulated the target operational conditions. The points of failure identified in each module during verification testing were added to the validation test profile to determine the impact of a module's limitations on the system as a whole. The goal was that the system continued to operate or at least failed in a safe state when these points of failure were reached. For an access control system, such as the TMS, failing in the "closed to all" state was desirable, since it was better to deny access to everyone at the expense of false positive responses than to fail in the "open" position and suffer false negative responses, which were more costly.

The second source of validation requirements was an operational scenario. In our case, the scenario needed to involve mobile, collaborating users asking each other to share resources. Once the general conditions of the scenario were determined, we applied a narrative technique to construct the test environment for the system [1].

Task 1: A user should be able to enter the community.
Condition: A user enters a location with an established identity.
Standard: The user joins the community and can interact with altruistic users or the control plane until he or she establishes a reputation with other users.

Task 2: A user should be able to meet another user through the introduction process.
Condition: A community member meets another community member and wants to establish an association. Other members, known to one or both of the prospective associates as trusted peers, are available to provide references.
Standard: The prospective associates request and receive information on each other from their trusted peers. This information is processed to determine the reputation index of each other.

Task 3: A user should be able to move between sites (i.e., geographically separate sub-networks) and continue to operate.
Condition: A user enters a location with an established identity.
Standard: The user joins the community and can interact with established trusted peers, members of their own organization, altruistic users, or the control plane until he or she establishes a reputation with other users.

Fig. 1. Enumeration of Validation Testing Objectives

4.1 Describing the Validation Test Objectives

First, the objectives that needed to be tested within the system were enumerated. These objectives addressed operational issues within the broad topic areas, such as mobility, network density, and general peer behavior. Objectives were expressed in the form of task-condition-standard in order to be evaluated. Figure 1 presents three tasks that were included in the validation testing. The benefit of using the task-condition-standard format was that the task's context and the conditions for its success were explicitly described. This format was also extensible, so that tasks that could be performed in different contexts were identified, described, and evaluated separately. By describing the context of each task, we also helped build the operational scenario we used as the background to the test.

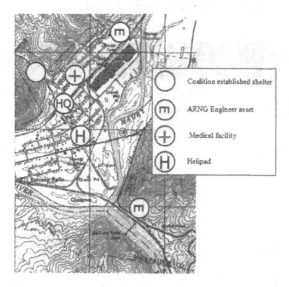

Fig. 2. Operational Scenario Map

4.2 Operational Scenario

The scenario provided a framework for user requirements within realistic vignettes for the purpose of testing interaction. In this scenario, we detailed the composition and deployment of a notional disaster response task force. Since the system was specifically concerned with the access control of resources within a collaborative environment, users were assigned as resource providers in specific locations.

Figure 2 illustrates how a coalition might deploy in response to the notional emergency response situation. The operational scenario was developed using Training Scenario 2: Slow Building River Flood – Natural Disaster [7]. This scenario called for cooperation between a variety of government organizations and local volunteers to evacuate the inhabitants of a small riverside town and secure the town's infrastructure against damage. The local Emergency Management Services (EMS) office coordinated the efforts of law enforcement agencies, local fire department, volunteer rescue squad, and county health facility to form the coalition. EMS directed the evacuation of the town's inhabitants to the higher ground behind the town, where the Red Cross established a shelter. Medical units treated injured people and evacuated a senior citizen home, assisted by the helicopters and rescue squads. An Army National Guard (ARNG) engineer unit provided technical or specialist assistance to contain contamination from the town's two sewage disposal sites and to reinforce the Balcony Falls Dam. The coalition formed using the Incident Command System (ICS) [8] and established a public information cell (PIC) to provide media services with information, in accordance with the ICS guidelines.

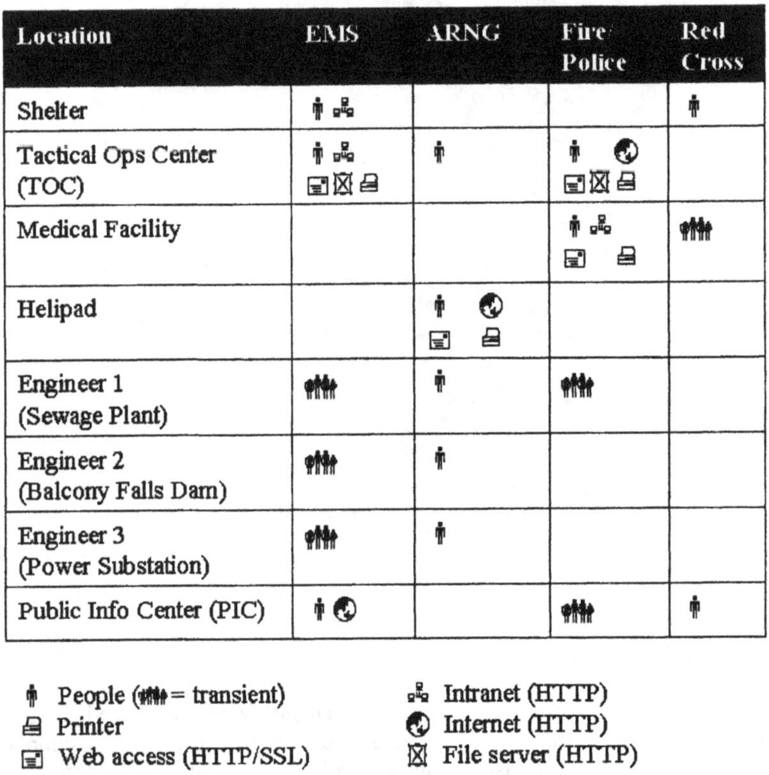

Location	EMS	ARNG	Fire Police	Red Cross
Shelter	👤 🖧			👤
Tactical Ops Center (TOC)	👤 🖧 💻 🗄 🖨	👤	👤 🌐 💻 🗄 🖨	
Medical Facility			👤 🖧 💻 🖨	👥👥
Helipad		👤 🌐 💻 🖨		
Engineer 1 (Sewage Plant)	👥👥	👤	👥👥	
Engineer 2 (Balcony Falls Dam)	👥👥	👤		
Engineer 3 (Power Substation)	👥👥	👤		
Public Info Center (PIC)	👤 🌐		👥👥	👤

👤 People (👥👥 = transient)	🖧 Intranet (HTTP)
🖨 Printer	🌐 Internet (HTTP)
💻 Web access (HTTP/SSL)	🗄 File server (HTTP)

Fig. 3. Coalition Locations and Resources

Although this scenario included severe inclement weather, members of the coalition and the outside populace were able to move about the scenario location. Communications, although unreliable, were present between the coalition locations and the unaffected "safe" areas.

Figure 3 provides an example of the resources that require access control. In terms of information resources, the coalition represented a hastily formed DCE. Users possessed a variety of computing and communications platforms that utilized both wired and wireless communications. This research focused on the ability for users to access coalition resources and, similarly, for the resource owners to maintain control and protect their resources for the use of contributing coalition members. Validation testing analyzed the TMS from the role of the Tactical Operation Center's (TOC) file server to assess system performance.

Given the composition and deployment of the notional coalition, we distributed resources for coalition use. For example, the coalition might leverage the connectivity present at the police building to co-locate the TOC and coalition Headquarters (HQ). The community fire department and clinic would provide a location for the medical unit.

Finally, vignettes were written to frame the points within the scenario that tested the objectives. The scenario not only provided a realistic approach to developing the vignettes but also helped order the tests if need be. Lo Presti's narrative technique [1] mapped objectives to vignettes and this exercise is demonstrated in the next section.

Task Vignette	1	2	3
Dave meets Alex, the task force engineer.	X		
Dave and Alex move to the Balcony Dam site to perform an assessment and rejoin network			X
Dave is introduced to Alex's colleague Bob at Balcony Dam. Bob shares his most recent assessment with Dave.		X	

Fig. 4. Mapping Tasks to Vignettes within the Scenario

4.3 Vignettes

A vignette described a scene within the scenario. Each vignette was developed to be as realistic as possible. Individual experiences contributed background details such as terrain, weather, and timing. Technical details were derived from more quantitative sources, however, and are described in Section 4.4.

A vignette established context within the test scenario in terms of time, location and actor participation. Most importantly, the vignette's description specified which task it was exercising for the purposes of the test. Figure 4 illustrates how three tasks (described in Figure 1) were tested within the scenario. Because the mapping of objectives to vignettes was done before the test started, the test ran through several vignettes in sequence, collecting data that was analyzed using the metrics described in the next section.

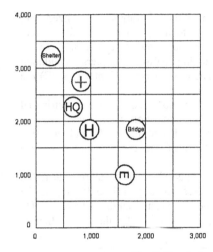

Location	X	Y	Attrac-tion	Std. Dev.
Shelter	300	3200	1.5	20
Hospital	800	2800	2.0	20
TOC	600	2200	4.0	20
Helipad	1000	1900	2.0	10
Bridge	1800	1800	5.0	10
Dam	1600	1000	2.0	10

Fig. 5. Simulation Location Parameters

4.4 Simulation Testing

Testing the TMS involved simulating user interaction in a mobile, dynamic environment. A four-step process was developed to create scripts that simulated behavior reporting and resource requests from the user's peers. These scripts were used by both the TMS and the base system (described below) during the simulation.

The first step constructed a simulation area using parameters applicable to the operational scenario. The resulting Cartesian representation of the simulation area is shown in Figure 5. BonnMotion 1.3a [9] simulated node movement inside a 3,000 x 4,000 meter bounded area. Attraction points mimicked the effect of roads and facilities on nodal movement. Each Attraction Point was given an (x,y) coordinate, roughly corresponding to the map in Figure 2. The intensity value of the point weighted the attraction points so that a point with an x intensity level attracted nodes with a probability x times higher than an un-weighted point. Locations with higher intensity values were predicted to have heavier traffic. Nodes would approach an

Table 1. Individual Mobility Simulation Parameters

Duration	5000 secs.
Warmup	3600 secs.
Sim area	3000 x 4000 meters
Nodes	100
Speed	Min = 0.5 m/s Max = 10 m/s
Pause Time	60 sec. (Max.)

Table 2. Group Mobility Simulation Parameters

Average Nodes per Group	3 (Std. Dev. 2)
Group Change Probability	0.01
Distance to Group Center	2.5 meters

attraction point to a location within the point's standard deviation from a Gaussian distribution with a mean of 0 in meters.

The second step of the process involved three mobility models. The first model was static, meaning that the nodes (i.e., users) were homogeneously distributed over the simulation area and did not move. The second mobility model was the Random Walk (RW) model [10]. Simulations run using the RW model used the node speed and pause time parameters indicated in Table 1.

The reference point group mobility model (RPG) was used to simulate group mobility. In addition to the speed and pause parameters that it shared with the RW simulations, RPG required settings to describe the group dynamics in the simulation. These settings, shown in Table 2, show that the simulation had groups of one to five people. These groups were stable, in that the chance of people changing groups was low. Raising this probability skewed the RPG results toward those seen in individual mobility models, such as RW. The groups moved in open order, as the group members could be as far as 2.5 meters from each other. Each mobility model was executed on the same area mentioned above with and without attraction points. By executing the chosen parameters on the selected grid and mobility model, BonnMotion created a movement trace file for all the nodes in the network.

The third step in creating the scenario script fed the movement trace into BonnMotion's companion program, LinkDump. This program read the movement trace and applied a transmission range of 100 meters (selected to simulate 802.11b traffic) to determine when pairs of nodes could interact. The interaction file that was produced listed each node and its unidirectional communications link. Having each interaction listed twice reflected the "one-way" nature of the link. For example, if Alice could interact with Bob, two links were listed: "Alice to Bob" link was listed in Alice's part of the file and the "Bob to Alice" link was listed in Bob's portion. Having the links listed in this manner facilitated the next step, which was determining who could provide performance observations on whom.

The fourth and final step of the script generation process was to generate behavior and trust related network traffic. A reporting period was set and had each node generate a behavior grade once every ten seconds. A bin in a linked list represented each reporting period. Each bin was itself a linked list of behavior grades for that time period. A C++ program called Builder read the interaction list and populated the bins with observations and reports. These transactions placed associates in the TMS's Trust Store. Once an associate was known, the generated traffic represented the flow of behavior observations and reports.

As Builder read each link from the interactivity list, it called on the behavior model to determine a grade for the observed node for that reporting period. That grade was then adjusted based on the observer's behavior model. Once Builder had read the entire interactivity list and filled all of the appropriate bins, the behavior grades were written to a script file of network traffic formatted for the TMS.

Initializing the scenario required that the user (e.g., Joe) be introduced to someone by the KMS. Once Joe had an initial trusted peer (TP), he could participate in the scenario and make other TPs. This startup requirement was viewed as feasible; since Joe would be introduced to the people he would be working with when he arrived at the TOC, thus allowing Joe to start associating in the DCE.

Testing the TMS required a means of simulating service requests received by a resource providing DCE member from associates. Our simulation assumed the viewpoint of the server in the TOC and processed requests for files via a HyperText Transfer Protocol (HTTP) user interface. Modeling requests typically made to the resources illustrated in Figure 3, we examined the process of modeling a typical wireless system [11]. Given a generic inter-arrival rate we determined the number and period of resource requests in our notional scenario.

Requests were classified by the nature of information being sent or received. There were two general types of information: simple files and composite files. Simple files were single data type (text or graphics) files. Examples of these included email, web page (without graphics), or text files that were exchanged through an HTTP process. Composite files were multiple simple files linked together. Web pages with graphics were the most common examples. Each file type could come in one of three sizes. After determining the type and size of a request, the request duration was determined by approximating the times depicted in a "slow Internet" connection [12], again following Ost's example.

Table 3. Probability and Duration of Resource Requests in a Simulated Collaborative Environment

Request Type	Probability	Duration (secs)
Small Simple File	0.6	1
Medium Simple File	0.1	2
Large Simple File	0.05	8
Small Composite file	0.15	1
Medium Composite File	0.075	6
Large Composite File	0.025	27

The test system simulated resource requests in a three step process. First, the system determined if there was a request being serviced. If the system was free, it checked to see if there was a request. Requests were serviced on a first come, first served basis, with no attempt being made to restore or save requests that might be lost if a system was busy. When there was a request, the system determined the type. The system was then flagged as busy for the duration specified for that type of request. The probability and duration for each type of request is shown in Table 3.

In order to provide a frame of reference for the results gathered during testing, a base system was constructed using the basic reputation aggregation equations and principles developed by Buchegger [13] and through the SECURE project [4]. The base system utilized an exponential weighted moving average equation for reputation scaling. It had fixed trust thresholds and exchanged reputation index values during a modified introduction process.

In addition to the work of the previously mentioned authors, the base system was equipped with a trust store-like reputation storage to enable the system to weight behavior grades upon receipt. During all tests, the same underlying interactivity traces and behavior models were applied during the creation of the test scripts. Although the simplicity of the base system appeared beneficial at first glance, testing revealed serious deficiencies in its performance. The most notable deficiencies were found in the investigation of the success metric.

4.5 Success Metric

The TMS was an access control system, so its efficiency was determined by examining how often the system correctly allowed access. The cost of making the decisions, in terms of communications and storage overhead, was also included in the determination. While acknowledging that the success metric of an access control system was comparative (i.e., one system performs better than another given a set of circumstances), we also experimented with critical settings to determine a feasible parameter range within which the system was effective.

In the most basic sense, the system was efficient when it correctly allowed access more often than it made incorrect decisions. Incorrect decisions came in two forms. False positive decisions occurred when a trustworthy user was incorrectly denied access. False negative decisions occurred when untrustworthy users were incorrectly allowed access [6].

We examined the ratio R of correct answers to false negative and false positive answers, shown in Equation 1. D was the total number of trustworthiness decisions the TMS was asked to make. P was the number of false positive answers and N was the number of false negative answers.

$$R = (D - (P + \omega N))/ D \qquad (1)$$

We differentiated between false positives and false negatives and applied a weighting factor in recognition of the fact that the cost of a false positive was much less than the cost of a false negative. The cost weight (ω) was a value selected to represent this difference in cost and, in these experiments, was set to ($\omega = 1$) to show the basic effectiveness of the TMS.

Having examined the efficiency of the TMS, we evaluated the overhead required by the system to render its decisions. The general intent of the overhead metric (C) was to determine the cost of the level of efficiency. Two forms of overhead were included in the calculation of C.

Communications Overhead (C_C) was defined as the number of Feedback Items (FI) that needed to be sent between trusted peers to gain enough information to determine a trustworthiness decision on a specific peer. Equation 2 illustrates how the system divided the number of Introduction transactions (I) by the size of the weighted queue of I, which is called the RIW. This computation assumed that the user would, in the worst case, attempt to fill their RIW before calculating a new associate's Reputation Index (RI). This assumption is not as far-fetched as it may seem, especially if the number of reports was few.

$$C_C = I * |RIW| \qquad (2)$$

Storage Overhead (C_S) was defined as the number of FI each node stored to create a decision. Equation 3 determined C_S by multiplying the amount of memory designated for the TMS (TS) by the amount of memory used to store reputations that are being actively calculated (e.g., the size of the RIW).

$$C_S = |TS| * |RIW| \tag{3}$$

Adding the two costs together yielded the number of FIs maintained by the TMS over a period of time. Equation 4 used this result, divided by the number of correct access control decisions $(D - (P+N))$, to provide the total cost for each correct decision.

$$C = (C_C + C_S)/(D - (P+N)) \tag{4}$$

When we executed the test scenarios, each scenario yielded independent values for R and C, as shown in the following charts. We called these values $R(S)$ and $C(S)$, where S was the scenario number that was used. In analyzing $R(S)$, we wanted a value as high as possible. The opposite was true of $C(S)$, where we wanted the smallest number possible.

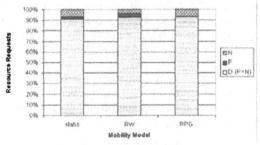

Fig. 6. Components of the Success Metric

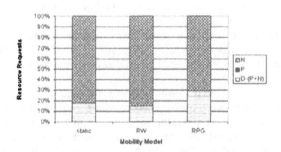

Fig. 7. Success Metric Components of the Base System Test

The a success metric, explained in Equation 1 expressed the number of correct decisions the system made as a ratio against the number of false positive (P) and false negative (N) decisions. Ideally, the column should be 100% correct (i.e., $P+N=0$) to represent that the system answered all of the requests correctly. Barring this situation, the goal was to minimize the number of false negative responses and then to eliminate the number of false positive responses.

Figure 6 shows the three components of the success metric. These tests, performed in a 100 node network with 30% misbehaving or non-contributing users, illustrated how well the TMS responded to resource requests in three mobility cases. The graph shows the proportional contribution of each response category to the over success rate.

The TMS performed well in the static case, having 91% overall success in responses, but had moderate numbers of false positive and false negative responses. The overall success rate improved slightly in the RW case to 93% but the incidence of false positives almost doubled as a proportion of the incorrect responses. These false positive responses are of concern because they represent missed opportunities for information exchange and the possibility for a trustworthy peer to submit negative behavior reports on an otherwise "good" user. The RPG case was the most worrisome. Although the overall success rate increased to 94% and there were no false positive reports, the proportion of false negative reports doubled once again to represent 6% of the total number of requests. This testing illustrated the importance of examining the contributing components of the metric in addition to examining the overall percentage of correct responses.

The ratios presented in the previous tests are put into a better frame of reference when the TMS results are compared against those of the base trust system. Figure 7 shows how the base system performed. In addition to having a lower overall success percentage, the base system exhibited an extraordinarily high percentage of false negative responses. This high proportion was due to the lack of historical knowledge maintained by the TMS for dynamic weighting of behavior grades [2].

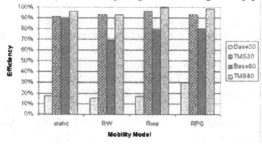

Fig. 8. Comparison of Base and Trust Management System Success Rates

The comparison between the TMS and the base system clearly showed the benefits of the 3Win method and the impact of dynamic grade weighting [2]. Figure 8 shows the comparison of success of the TMS and the base system in different mobility models. Tests using a general peer behavior condition of 30% misbehaving users, for example, are entitled TMS30 and Base30, respectively. While it had been expected that the base model performed would show less efficiency than the TMS, the poor success percentage in the static and RW models was surprising considering the general ratio of good users to bad was rather high. While the base system efficiency increased slightly in the RW models with attraction points (RWa) and group mobility (RPG), it never demonstrated better than 30% efficiency.

As the proportion of bad users increased, the TMS efficiency remained at or over 90%. The base system reached its highest performance level when there were 80% bad users (see Figure 8, TMS80 and Base80, respectively). This case simulated a situation where the TBAC system was effectively presented with fewer trustworthy associates to select from.

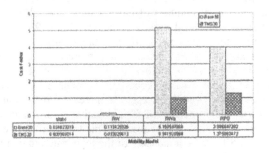

Fig. 9. Comparison of Cost Factors between TMS and Base System

4.6 Cost Metric

Using Equation 4, the communications and storage costs of each system were combined to convey a sense of the behind the scenes requirements for making trust-based access control decisions. The TMS incurred a fixed cost of having to store and exchange all of the *FI* in its *RIW* while the base system only maintained an *RI*, so the general expectation was that the TMS would be at a disadvantage in this comparison.

What tests determined, however, was that the TMS cost was far lower than the cost incurred by the base system under the same test conditions, as shown in Figure 9. This phenomenon occurred because, while the amount of data exchanged by the base case during introductions was much smaller than used by the TMS, the number of introductions was an order of magnitude higher. In most cases, the difference between the base system and the TMS was 3:1 but, under RW mobility tests, the difference grew to four or five to one bias against the base system.

When success and cost were combined and displayed, the overwhelming efficiency of the TMS was reinforced. The TMS costs were several times less than those of the base system, while providing much higher efficiency. As discussed above, the combination of maintaining historical behavior grades, dynamic weighting of feedback items at every reputation calculation, and adjusting trust thresholds based on current levels of uncertainty have resulted in a much more robust trust system.

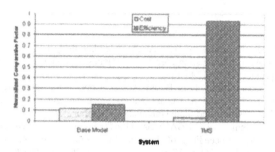

Fig. 10. Comparison of TMS Success Rate to Base Case System

Figure 10 illustrates this point using the RW mobility model and a network of 30% misbehaving users. The TMS displays low cost and high efficiency while the base system provided less success and more cost. Although changes to the base system might compensate for some of the deficiencies, the use of a memory-less computation method like the exponential weighted moving average puts and keeps the base system at a disadvantage. Furthermore, the implementation of adjustable thresholds and dynamic weighting in the TMS make it more flexible and able to adapt to a wider range of network conditions.

5. Conclusion and Future Work

Validation ensured that the system was ready for the intended operational environment. Using narrative techniques, we derived realistic requirements and assessed the TMS's efficiency and cost in meeting the demands of a TBAC system. The key to appreciating the impact of these results was that the findings would have less meaning were they not framed within a realistic operational scenario. While both TMS and the base system were verified to produce expected results, validation testing demonstrated that the TMS outperformed the base system in the expected operational setting. This conclusion could not have been determined without establishing the tasks to be accomplished, the conditions under which the task would be called for, and the standard to which the task would be accomplished successfully.

Throughout its development, the TMS was applied to inter-personal access control situations in mobile, often ad-hoc, networks. Currently, the TMS is being investigated for use as an inter-organizational access control mechanism. In this new incarnation, security policies and best business practices are applied to generate verifiable behavior observations. Studies are ongoing to create a framework for evaluating observed practices.

References

[1] Lo Presti, S., M. Butler, et al.: A Trust Analysis Methodology for Pervasive Computing Systems. Trusting Agents for trusting Electronic Societies. R. Falcone, S. Barber, J. Sabater and M. Singh, Springer (2005) 129 - 143

[2] W. J. Adams. Decentralized Trust-Based Access Control for Dynamic Collaborative Environments, Ph.D. Dissertation, Department of Electrical and Computer Engineering, Virginia Polytechnic Institute and State University, Blacksburg, VA (2006)

[3] Freudenthal, E., T. Pesin, et al.: dRBAC: distributed role-based access control for dynamic coalition environments. Proceedings of the 22nd International Conference on Distributed Computing Systems (ICDCS 2002). Vienna, AU, 2 - 5 July 2002, (2002) 411-420.

[4] Cahill, V., Shand, B., Gray, E., Bryce, C., Dimmock, N.: Using trust for secure collaboration in uncertain environments. IEEE Pervasive Computing 2 (2003) 52—61

[5] Kagal, L., T. Finin, et al.: A framework for distributed trust management. Proceedings of International Joint Conference on Artificial Intelligence (IJCAI-01), Workshop on Autonomy, Delegation and Control, 2001, Seattle, WA (2001) 73-80.

[6] Bryce, C., N. Dimmock, et al.: Towards an Evaluation Methodology for Computational Trust Systems. Proceedings of the Third International Conference in Trust Management (iTrust 2005), Paris, FR (2005) 289-304.

[7] FEMA: Scenario and Incident Action Plan Catalog. Retrieved from http://www.nwcg.gov/pms/forms/compan/iap.pdf (1994)

[8] FEMA: Incident Command System. Retrieved from http://training.fema.gov/EMIWeb/IS/is195.asp (2004)

[9] de Waal, C. and M. Gerharz: BonnMotion. Retrieved from http://web.informatik.uni-bonn.de/IV/Mitarbeiter/dewaal/BonnMotion/ (2005)

[10] Camp, T., J. Boleng, et al.: A Survey of Mobility Models for Ad Hoc Network Research. Wireless Communication & Mobile Computing (WCMC): Special issue on Mobile Ad Hoc Networking: Research, Trends and Applications 2(5) (2002) 483 - 502.

[11] Ost, A.: Performance of communication systems: a model based evaluation with matrix geometric methods. New York, Springer (2001)

[12] Heidemann, J., K. Obraczka, et al.: Modeling the performance of HTTP over several transport protocols. Networking, IEEE/ACM Transactions on 5(5) (1997) 616-630.

[13] Buchegger, S. and J.-Y. Le Boudec: A Robust Reputation System for Mobile Ad-Hoc Networks. Lausanne, Switzerland, Ecole Polytechnic Federal de Lausanne (2003)

Negotiation for Authorisation in Virtual Organisations

Shamimabi Paurobally

Department of Information Systems and Computing, University of Westminster
115 New Cavendish Street, London W1W 6UW, U.K.
S.Paurobally@westminster.ac.uk

Abstract. In virtual organisations, the authorisation and expression of policies in terms of direct trust relationships between providers and consumers have the problems of scalability, flexibility, expressibility, and lack of policy hierarchy because of interdependent institutions and policies [7]. This paper proposes a bilateral negotiation protocol and an English auction to negotiate a list of credentials to be exchanged after a service level agreement has been drafted, and that would provide sufficient trustworthiness for the parties in the negotiation. We implement and evaluate our algorithms as grid services in a virtual organisation (VO) to show the effect of negotiation on the trustworthiness achieved within a VO.

1 Introduction

The long-term Grid vision involves the development of "large-scale open distributed systems, capable of effectively, *securely* and dynamically deploying Grid resources as required, to solve computationally complex problems" [1]. Thus, traditional centralised methods needing complete information for system wide optimisation of performance, reliability and security are not enough. In current Grid applications, heterogeneity and dynamic provisioning are limited, and dynamic virtual organisations (VOs) are restricted to those parties with a priori agreements to common policies and practice. To remedy this, there is a drive towards service-oriented architectures and virtual organisations which can support a broad range of commercial applications and authorisation mechanisms [9], [5]. Grid computing research is investigating applications of virtual organisations for enabling flexible, secure and coordinated resource sharing among dynamic collections of individuals, institutions and resources. The virtual organisations and usage models include a variety of owners and consumers with different security requirements, credentials, usage, access policies, cost models, varying loads, resource requirements, and availability. The sharing and coordinated use of resources may involve not only file exchange but also direct access to computers, software, data, and other resources, as is required by a range of collaborative problem-solving and resource-brokering strategies emerging in industry, science, and engineering, each with their own access policies and credentials.

Please use the following format when citing this chapter:

Paurobally, S., 2007, in IFIP International Federation for Information Processing, Volume 238, Trust Management, eds. Etalle, S., Marsh, S., (Boston: Springer), pp. 107–122.

In this paper, we focus on facilitating secured and trustworthy interactions between grid services, since a key challenge for the Grid in the coming decade is adaptability to varying security requirements and capabilities. There is a need for complex and dynamic policies governing access to resources. In virtual organisations, the authorisation of policies to form direct trust relationships between producers and consumers has the problems of scalability, flexibility, expressibility, and lack of policy hierarchy because of interdependent institutions and policies [7]. As members of institutions or VOs change, policies change accordingly. We use negotiation mechanisms to address the problem of scalability for authorisation within distributed virtual communities. Another advantage to using negotiation for bringing about trust lies in the inability of current systems to establish trust between complete strangers, as explained in Winsborough et. al. [10]. The requirement for a-priori knowledge to establish trust between interaction partners cannot be met in truly open distributed systems.

There are significant differences between our approach for deploying negotiation in VO authorisation and the current work on trust negotiation by Winslett et. al. [6] and Winsborough et. al. [10]. In contrast to these latter works, we do not send a user's credentials and certificates during the negotiation to respond to a request, rather the user and service provider (or authorisation server) negotiate and agree on a suitable set of credentials for resource access. The actual credentials are exchanged on both sides only after the negotiation has terminated with a service level agreement. Our approach has the advantage of preventing malicious parties from obtaining sensitive information from others through negotiation without having any intention of reaching an agreement. Thus, the certificates are sent at the end, and thereby also preventing repeated authentification and decreasing the probability for the encryption keys to be compromised. This paper also advances the state of the art by considering *1-many* negotiations in the form of English Auctions. Here the auctioneer is a service provider whose goal is to maximise secure access to its resources by choosing out of a number of consumers the most trustworthy one. The bids are offers with a list of credentials that the auctioneer evaluates. Finally, our implemented negotiations are at a higher level than at the Operating Systems or Hardware level. Here, the negotiations are concerned with agreeing on a set of credentials for authorisation to securely access a resource.

This paper is structured as follows. Section 2 provides critical analysis of current forms of negotiation in VOs. Section 3 describes our approach and two negotiation protocols that we deploy in a grid framework. Section 4 describes the strategies used for evaluating and generating credentials offers. Section 5 presents an evaluation of the two negotiation protocols. Section 6 concludes.

2 Related Work

In this section, we analyse the current state of the work on trust negotiation and the need for more flexible negotiation in this area. Our work is mostly relevant to the current research by Winslett et al. [6] and Winsborough et. al. [10]. The former proposes an authorisation broker service that uses negotiation to issue tokens for resources on consumers' requests. The latter defines an architecture to establish mutual trust through negotiation and specifies various strategies, assuming cooperation between participants. In our framework, we do not assume cooperation but rather allow for self-interested agents that most probably have different goals.

Figure 1 depicts the type of trust negotiation developed in [6] in a stock exchange scenario. Alice has a broker ID credential, protected by a policy that requires a certificate from the SEC (Securities and Exchange Commission) showing that the holder is authorized as a stock exchange. Bob is a stock exchange that offers an internet-based exchange service to stock brokers. Bobs authorization policy for the service requires that the customer present a current broker ID from a recognized brokerage firm. Alice tries to access the service and Bob responds by sending Alice the authorization policy that protects this service. Alice is not willing to disclose her credential to Bob, because its authorization policy is not yet satisfied. Alice sends her broker ID policy to him and he sends Alice his certification issued by the SEC and a proof that he owns the certificate. Alice sends her broker ID credential to Bob who grants Alice access.

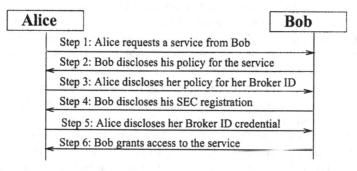

Fig. 1. Example of current forms of Trust Negotiation [6]

Winsborough et. al. [10] also follows such a model of trust negotiation where credentials are requested and exchanged during the whole interaction, whenever required by the participants policies. Although such approaches provide flexibility in acquiring trust between strangers, there are situations that could prove to be insecure, as argued below:

Malicious agents. There can be malicious agents whose goals are to gather as much information as possible about other users without intending to reach the end of the interaction and sending their final credentials. For example in figure 1, Alice could be a duplicitous agent intending to obtain Bob's SEC registration for illegal access or impersonation. After Bob has disclosed his SEC registration, Alice does not disclose her Broker ID credential, and stops communicating with Bob, blaming this on a fake faulty communication or that she is no longer interested in the resource. Bob would not suspect any foul intentions. Here Alice has only disclosed non-vital information about her broker ID policy whilst she has gathered secure information about Bob's policy and his SEC registration. Thus, the problem in this type of interaction is that users are disclosing their credentials during the interaction without any guarantee of a successful negotiation and of a binding agreement.

Non flexible interaction. Negotiation is defined as a form of decision making where two or more parties jointly search a space of possible solutions with the goal of reaching a consensus [3]. Moreover, there is not only one agreement that is possible but a space of possible agreements that represents a convergence between the preferences of two or more parties during the negotiation. The concessions depend on constraints such as time, resource availability and utility valuations. Thus in an auction or a bargaining situation, at the beginning of a negotiation, the final agreement is unknown to all parties. The scenario in figure 1 is a discrete form of negotiation of the request-response type, where neither Alice nor Bob can choose what to request or offer from a set of possible agreements. The contents and sequence of messages are fixed in the above scenario for the exchange of the policies and credentials. What would turn this in a full-fledged negotiation would be if Alice and Bob bargain about what type of credentials each is willing to disclose and to be disclosed in exchange, without any pre-determination of what credentials are to be sent.

Unnecessary credential disclosure. Consider the situation where Alice has disclosed credentials {Ca,Cb}, but does not have the required {Cc}. So Bob back-tracks and instead asks for credential {Cd,Ce}. However, credential Cd subsumes Ca, and Cb is no longer relevant if {Cd,Ce} are sent. Thus, it can again be seen that sending credentials during the negotiation can disclose some credentials that could later prove to be unnecessary. Here also, a malicious agent can exploit this situation by negotiating as long as possible and asking the disclosure of different sets of credentials to gather as much information about other agents. Thus parties should be unwilling to readily disclose credentials. Each exchange of credentials and decryption of the private key of a sender provides another opportunity for the information and the key to be compromised.

No public auctions. Disclosure of credentials prevents the use of open-cry auctions, such as the English auctions, because the bidders will see each other's certificates which will have to be advertised publicly in the bids. Thus the above scenario cannot use auctions for negotiations and misses the advantages that are associated with auctions such as a competitive market.

3 Our Approach: Negotiation of Credentials

To remedy to the above problems, we do not pass actual credentials during a negotiation, but negotiation is on what credentials may be sent at the end and after reaching a binding agreement between the parties. The credentials are exchanged at the end of a successful negotiation, reducing the risks of exploitation from malicious agents and of unnecessary information disclosure in case of back-tracking in a negotiation. Our approach can help advanced Grid applications in which a single interaction may involve the coordinated use of resources at many locations and allows users to access resources without repeated authentication.

We also do not assume cooperation, but instead consider the case of each party being self-interested and having their own goals, as would normally be the case in grid and e-commerce scenarios. On the one hand, consumers have digital certificates that attest to their attributes, membership in VOs, and requirements for resources. A consumer might want to get access the resource as soon as possible. On the other hand, resource owners have access policies for resources, sharing constraints for their resources and wants to collect as much information as possible about the clients attributes before granting access to resources. In some cases, a consumer trusts the server apriori but the server does not trust the client. In our case, we do not assume any prior trust on either side. An acceptable level of trust is established between the parties based on their properties proved through credential disclosure at the end. Negotiation allows to determine in an iterative manner which credentials and policies are to be disclosed between parties at the end. No sensitive credentials are disclosed if anyone party terminates the negotiation prematurely.

In this section, we describe two negotiation protocols which we implement as grid services – the time-constrained bilateral negotiation and English auction.

3.1 Bilateral Negotiation

A bilateral negotiation occurs between two agents, a consumer and a service provider or an authorisation server. Figure 2 shows such a protocol where at the beginning the service provider advertises the set of credentials it recognises. Agreement will be on a subset of these credentials. The service consumer A obtains the interface of the service provider B through service discovery and makes an initial offer with the credentials, for example $\{ C^B_{ibm}, C^A_{GSI} \}$, where the super-script to a credential denotes the owner and sender of that credential. The service provider B evaluates these credentials and either accepts if the proposed credentials from the consumer is sufficiently secure, or it counter-offers with other credentials, for example $\{ C^A_{SSL}, C^B_{TSL}, C^A_{prima} \}$. The negotiation continues until either party accepts or rejects a counter-offer. Acceptance could occur because the counter-offer has reached a required trust threshold for a party, where as rejection occurs if the deadline of the negotiation arrives for a party without reaching its trust threshold.

3.2 English Auction

The other negotiation protocol we implement is the English auction which is a 1-many protocol. This protocol is used when there is a scarcity or excess of resources. For example, if resources are scarce, a service provider acts as the

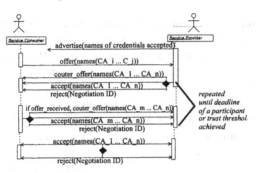

Fig. 2. Bilateral Negotiation Protocol

auctioneer and auctions access to its resources to many consumers and the consumer offering the highest security options wins the auction and thus the service provider maximises the security access to its resources. On the other hand if supply exceeds demand for resources, then there is a reverse auction between 1 consumer and many providers. Here the consumer acts as the auctioneer and has two options – either it chooses the provider that requires the least number of credentials from the consumer, or the consumer chooses the provider offering the most secure information about itself. As future work, we intend to develop many-many double auctions.

In an English auction with time constraints, the auctioneer grid service, for example the service provider, informs bidder consumer grid services the start of the auction and the issues on which to bid, that is the advertised credentials list. Bidder consumer services reply with bids offering their sets of credentials. The auctioneer evaluates the bids, chooses the best bid, called **highest_bid**, and invokes the **Submit_Bid** method on the bidder consumer services with **highest_bid** as parameter. By doing so, the auctioneer is invoking the bidder services to submit counter-bids again respective to **highest_bid**, so as to offer a better *ordered* list of credentials than those listed in the **highest_bid**. The bidder services evaluates whether they can improve on the highest bid and if so send their revised bids. The auctioneer again evaluates received bids and requests higher bids from the remaining bidders with respect to the new highest bid. This process of requesting new bids and submitting higher bids continues until the auction deadline or there is only one bidder left. At these terminating conditions, the auctioneer invokes the **Auction_Result** method on the bidder services indicating the end of the auction and informing the winning bidder of the agreed credential list. Figure 3 shows the English Auction port-type.

3.3 Negotiation Subject

We define the contents of offers and bids for both negotiation protocols. Figure 4 gives the WSDL specification of the credentials that are exchanged between the consumers and service providers. We extend Jonczy and Haenni's definition of

```
<wsdl:portType name="Bidder">
  <wsdl:operation name="Submit_Bid" parameterOrder="bid">
    <wsdl:input message="SubmitBidIn" name="SubmitBidIn"/>
    <wsdl:output message="SubmitBidOut" name="SubmitBidOut"/>
  </wsdl:operation>
  <wsdl:operation name="Auction_Result" parameterOrder="bid">
   <wsdl:input message="ResultIn" name="ResultIn"/>
   <wsdl:output message="ResultOut" name="ResultOut"/>
  </wsdl:operation>
  <wsdl:operation name="getBidderID">
   <wsdl:input message="getBidderIDIn" name="getBidderIDIn"/>
   <wsdl:output message="getBidderIDOut" name="getBidderIDOut"/>
  </wsdl:operation>
  <wsdl:operation name="getMember">
   <wsdl:input message="getMemberIn" name="getMemberIn"/>
   <wsdl:output message="getMemberOut" name="getMemberOut"/>
  </wsdl:operation>
</wsdl:portType>
```

Fig. 3. English Auction Service PortType

credentials [4]. In their work, a credential can have a class, and either a positive, negative or a mixed sign as rating. The class of a credential could be either be a statement about the trustworthiness or the authenticity of the recipient. In contrast to their definition, in our case a credential owner do not disclose to other parties the weight it assigns to the credential, i.e. the importance it attaches to the credential. This is a private matter for the credential owner and would be different for another user.

In figure 4, in the CredentialType which specifies a credential, we include fields to specify membership to any VO, the period of validity of that credential and any registration or cryptographic keys. We also include the negotiable field which if false means that this credential is compulsory the requester of that credential. For example, if A's offer include C_{IBM}^{B} and IsNegotiable is false, then A regards C_{IBM}^{B} as a compulsory credential to be provided by B. It is very important to note that during negotiation, information-sensitive fields in the CredentialType are not disclosed. Sensitive fields, such as sign and private keys are only instantiated when an agreement is reached. Thus there is enough information for a user or a server to evaluate a credential during the negotiation, but not enough to disclose any private information in case of malicious agents. CredentialListType is a list of credentials and *Negotiation_Subject* is what is exchanged in offers and bids. In addition to the list of credentials, the *Negotiation_Subject* include the sender of the bid or offer, which may not be the same as the recipient in CredentialType, for example in the case of a broker negotiating on behalf of another party. The NegotiationID is an identifier for a negotiation instance where a user may be involved in concurrent negotiations.

```
<wsdl:types>
<xsd:complexType name="CredentialListType">
 <xsd:sequence>
    <xsd:complexType name="CredentialType">
     <element name="class" type="xsd:string"/>
     <element name="sign" type="xsd:string"/>
     <element name="issuer" type="wsa:EndpointReferenceType"/>
     <element name="recipient" type="wsa:EndpointReferenceType"/>
     <element name="negotiable" type="xsd:boolean"/>
     <element name="VO_membership" type="wsa:EndpointReferenceType"/>
     <element name="validity_period" type="date"/>
     <element_name="private_key" type="String"/>
     <element_name="policy_details" type="URI"/>
     <element_name="any_other_details" type="any"/>
    </xsd:complexType>
 </xsd:sequence>
</xsd:complexType>

<xsd:element name="Negotiation_Subject">
    <sequence>
     <element name="sender" type="wsa:EndpointReferenceType"/>
     <element name="NegotiationID" type="xsd:string"/>
     <xsd:element ref="tns:CredentialListType"/>
    </sequence>
  </xsd:element>
</wsdl:types>
```

Fig. 4. WSDL Types for the Negotiation Subject

In both the negotiation subject and in the service level agreement, the list of credentials is an *ordered* list. For example, the credential list in the agreement $\{C_{SSL}^A, C_{TSL}^B, C_{prima}^A, C_{IBM}^A\}$ would mean that service A sends its SSL certificate, followed by B sending its TSL certificate and finally by A sending both its PRIMA and IBM-signed certificates. The service provider advertises the negotiation subject allowing the service consumer to share the same structure for the credential list.

4 Negotiation Strategies - Evaluation and Generation of Credentials

We implement strategies for evaluating and generating bids and offers of the credentials names list. In the evaluation strategy, we use a classical summation of the weighted utility of each issue in the negotiation subject, here a credential being an issue. For generation of bids and offers, we implement four strategies: 1) the truth-telling strategy, 2) the constant decrement strategy, 3) the time dependent strategy, and 4) experience-dependent strategy.

4.1 Preferences Modeling for Credentials

In order for an agent to evaluate and generate bids and offers, it needs to know what is a good enough bid and what is a good deal. To this end, a grid service has preferences which captures the profile of the owner of the grid service. From these preferences, a grid service can decide if a bid/offer is good enough by calculating whether its trust threshold has been reached. If a bid/offer is not good enough, then a service can calculate what to send as a counter-offer/bid. These preferences are private and are not disclosed to the other parties. The preferences of a grid service for a credential as an issue are:

- *Preferred value* for an issue is the ideal value for an issue, for example ideally a user might prefer a SSL certificate and a certificate from IBM.
- *Reserve value* defines the limit to which a participant is willing to concede. For example, a service provider will not accept any credentials less secure than those issued by IBM.
- *weight* is used to assign the relative importance of a credential with respect to other credentials.
- *Utility* of a credential specifies how much that credential is worth to a service provider or consumer. A higher utility means a higher worth and utility may change over time or with other environment factors.
- *IsNegotiable* is a Boolean that if false means that this credential must be provided by the other party, and if true means that it can be replaced by another credential. In our evaluation and generation strategies, the first step is to always check that the non-negotiable credentials in the received negotiation subject can be met by the receiver's preferences.
- *PrefersHigh* specifies if a user prefers a high evaluation for that credential or not. For example, a service provider may prefer to receive a high value credential from a consumer, but may also prefer to send a low value credential about itself to disclose the least amount of secure information.

Note that a service provider has to assign quantitative preferences to the list of credentials it advertise at the beginning of a negotiation, and similarly a consumer has to assign values to its known list of credentials, specially to those advertised and known credentials. For example, a service provider knows how much it values certificates from IBM, SSL, PRIMA if these are the certificates it advertises. We denote such a personal valuation for certificate C_i as $v(C_i)$.

4.2 Evaluation of Credentials

We now provide a mechanism for a service provider or consumer to evaluate a list of credentials. Evaluating a list of credentials in a received bid or offer is dependent on a user evaluating each credential in that list. In turn the evaluation of a credential in an offer/bid depends on the specifics of that credential in that negotiation subject and the user's personal preferences. More specifically, we differentiate between the evaluation, $V(C_i)$, of a credential, C_i, in the context of a credential list and a negotiation, and the personal evaluation $v(C_i)$ which is independent of the context and the reserve preferences. This personal evaluation allows a user to know which credential it prefers itself out of 2 or more credentials, but it does not know its opponent's private valuation. It may be that two parties agree on which credentials they prefer which means that their preferences are not always opposing. Moreover, $v(C_i)$ is independent of time or other factors where as the utility can be a function changing over time or with environmental factors.

Evaluation of the credential list yields a quantitative value to the trust level achievable from an offer. The evaluation of a credential, C_i, is given as a function of the absolute value of the difference between the personal value of the credential, $v(C_i)$, and the reserve value, *reserve*, divided by the reserve value and multiplied by the utility of that credential, U_{C_i}.

For example, evaluation of credential C_{IBM} as an issue in an offer is as follows:

$$V(C_{IBM}) = (|v(C_{IBM}) - reserve|/reserve) * U_{C_{IBM}} \tag{1}$$

The valuation of a list of credentials for agent a, $V^a(cred\_list)$, called the trust valuation of such a list, is calculated by the summation of the weighted utility of credentials in that list. Let $V_j^a(cred\_list[j])$ denote the valuation of credential j in list $cred\_list$ for service a.

$$\text{Trust valuation of cred\_list} \quad V^a(cred\_list) = \sum_{1 \leq j \leq n} \omega_j^a \, V_j^a(cred\_list[j])$$

$$\tag{2}$$

We define the *trust threshold* to be the trust valuation of a list consisting only of preferred and ideal credentials for that user. If the trust threshold for a user is reached in a negotiation, then the opponent evaluating the trustworthiness of that user may accept the user's offer or bid. On the other hand, when when the credential list consist only of reserve values for its constituent credentials, then the *minimum acceptable trustworthiness* is obtained. Any offers or bid that are below that *minimum trustworthiness* are rejected.

4.3 Generation Strategies

We specify four strategies for generating a bid/offer in an increasing order of complexity and negotiation cost – truth-telling, constant decrement, time-dependent and experience-dependent strategies.

Truth Telling Strategy. In the truth telling strategy, the participants send their preferred list of credentials, then if an agreement has not yet been reached, then they send the reserve credentials in the second round. The first offer/bid from a service consumer is instantiated with its preferred credentials. On receiving the offer, the service provider evaluates the list according to equation

2 to obtain $V^a(cred\_list)$. If $V^a(cred\_list)$ is less than the service provider's minimum trustworthiness, then the service provider counter-offers with its own list of preferred credentials. The service consumer evaluates the provider's credential list and if this valuation is not equal/greater than its minimum trustworthiness, then the consumer counter-offers with a list of credentials where the issues are now given the consumer's reserve values. If this new counter-offer is not equal/greater than the provider's minimum trustworthiness, then the provider counter-offers with a credential list with its reserve values. This time, the consumer on evaluating the received credential list accepts the provider's counter-offer if it is within its minimum trustworthiness leading to an agreement, otherwise it rejects the received offer.

The English auction truth telling strategy resembles the bilateral protocol truth telling strategy. The first bid contains the preferred values of each bidder. The auctioneer evaluates each bid and chooses the highest bid. If the auction deadline is reached, the auctioneer declares the overall winning bid to be the highest received bid. Otherwise, if there is still time, then the auctioneer calls to submit another round of bids and passes to the other bidders the credential list in the highest bid. In the next round, the bidders submit bids with their reserve values. The auctioneer evaluates the highest bid using equation 2 and if the highest bid is equal/greater than the auctioneer's minimum trustworthiness then it declares the overall winning bid as the second round's winning bid.

Decrement Strategy. In this strategy, the participants evaluate and generate a bid/offer using the reserve values and the minimum trustworthiness, and also using a pre-defined margin above or below the reserve values. This gives the parties a chance to converge to an agreement during the negotiation even though the initial offers/bids are below the minimum trustworthiness, instead of rejecting such bids/offers in the first rounds as would occur in truth-telling. The pseudocode for the evaluation of a credential list here is summarised below:

```
for each issue in the credential list
    if non-negotiable issues in the credential list do not
                match non-negotiable issues in preferences
      return cannot accept
    else {
      if prefers high for that issue {
      marked_reserve = reserve value * (1-margin_outside_preferences)
      if value of issue in subject < marked_reserve
      return cannot accept
      } else { // prefers low
       marked_reserve = reserve value * (1+margin_outside_preferences)
      if value of issue in subject > marked_reserve
      return cannot accept
      }
   return can accept
```

The generation of an offer/bid follows the same trend as for the evaluation. First non-negotiable issues are instantiated with the preferred credential

for that user. As for negotiable credentials, the credential that is offered is one
with valuation closest to
$(margin\_for\_generation * average(V(preferred\ credential),\ V(credential\ in\ received\ offer)))$

Time Dependent Strategy. Both the bilateral protocol and the English
auction are dependent on the time left for the end of the negotiation. In the
English auction, there is a deadline for receiving bids for each round and an
overall deadline for the auction to end. A bidder only has its personal deadline
for the overall auction. The generation of a bid/offer depends on the time left for
the end of the negotiation. A bidder service determines which credential to send
in a bid/offer by calculating how much to concede over the valuation of the whole
credential list and over each credential in that list. Let $V^a(new\_cred\_list)$ denote
the evaluation of agent a for the new credential list such that $V^a(new\_cred\_list)$
incorporates the concession from the previously received credential list. Also,
the credential that has the closest match to the valuation in equation 3 is chosen
to form part of the new credential list, such that the evaluation of the generated
credential list as calculated in equation 2 is nearest to $V^a(new\_cred\_list)$. The
bid $bid_a^t(new\_cred\_list)[cred_j]$ of bidder service b at time t with deadline t_{max}
is calculated from equation 3 for each credential $cred_j$, where max_j and min_j
are preferred and reserve values for that credential.

$$bid_a^t(new\_cred\_list)[cred_j] = min_j + \frac{min(t, t_{max})}{t_{max}}(max_j - min_j) \qquad (3)$$

The pseudocode for this strategy in a bilateral protocol is given below:

```
receive offer with credential list credList_i from opponent
if deadline has been reached
    evaluate credList_i using equation (2) to obtain V(credList_i)
    accept if V(credList_i) ≥ minimum trustworthiness
    otherwise reject
 else  // more time available
    if non-negotiable credentials in credList_i do not match
          non-negotiable credentials in preferences then reject; break;
    accept if V(credList_i) ≥ threshold trustworthiness; break;
    else
       generate counter-offer according to equation (3)
       send counter-offer to opponent
```

From the pseudocode, the time dependent strategy for a bidder implies that
the bidder evaluates the current highest bid through equation 2 and decides
whether to send a counter-bid or not. A bidder does not send a higher bid if
the evaluation of the current highest bid is below its minimum trustworthiness
value. If a bidder decides to send a counter-bid, then it uses equation 3 to
generate a bid.

Experience Strategy. In the experience strategy, a user determines its concessions for the credential list to send based on the previous attitudes and credential lists received from its opponents two or more steps ago. In the auction, the opponent's offers are taken as the previous highest bids two or more rounds ago. If there has only been two offers/bid rounds before, then the time dependent strategy is used. Otherwise, if three or more offers/bid rounds have occured, then the experience strategy is used to generate the bid/counter-offer. As for the time dependent strategy, the credential that is to form part of the generated credential list is a concession on the credential list in the previous offer/bid. So we generate $bid^t_{a \rightarrow b}(new\_cred\_list)[cred_j]$ (or offer) from service a to service b at time t through equation 4.3. max^a_j and min^a_j are preferred and reserve values for that credential for a. The set of credentials service a generates at time t_{n+1} is within a's acceptable values for credentials.

$$bid^t_{a \rightarrow b}(new\_cred\_list)[cred_j] = min(y, max^a_j)$$

$$\text{where } y = max(\frac{new\_cred\_list^{t_{n-2\delta}}_{b \rightarrow a}[j]}{new\_cred\_list^{t_{n-2\delta+2}}_{b \rightarrow a}[j]} \times new\_cred\_list^{t_{n-1}}_{a \rightarrow b}[j], min^a_j) \quad (4)$$

5 Evaluation of Protocols through Trustworthiness

We evaluate the English auction by deploying one auctioneer and 10 bidders negotiating on a list of credentials. Similarly we evaluate the bilateral protocol in 10 different cases by changing the parties. The advertised credential list of the service provider contains 7 possible credentials and an agreement can be reached on a subset of the advertised list.

Parameters and Metrics for Evaluation. In our evaluation, in addition to varying the negotiation protocols and the strategies, we vary the personal deadlines of the participants and their reserve and preferred values for a credential. The preferred and reserve preferences for credentials will in turn yield different values for the threshold and minimum trustworthiness and influence whether an agreement is reached or not. We also consider how far apart are the preferences of the service provider with the consumers and how this factor affects performance. More specifically, to measure the performance of our protocols, we consider the following metrics:

- The number of agreements reached.
- The time to do a negotiation and especially to reach an agreement.
- The quality of an agreement and of exchanged offers and winning bids per round, calculated from equation 2. We call this metric the trustworthiness value. The trustworthiness value shown in our results are from the provider's preferences, and the same trends are obtained when trustworthiness is calculated from the consumer's preferences.

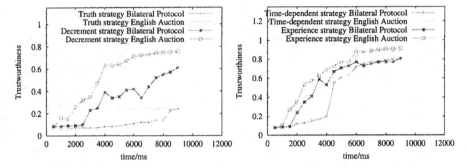

Fig. 5. Trustworthiness of offers/winning bids v/s Time for time-independent strategies

Fig. 6. Trustworthiness of offers/winning bids v/s Time for time/experience strategies

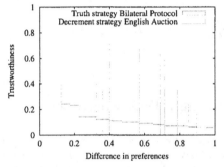

Fig. 7. Trustworthiness v/s preferences differences for time-independent strategies

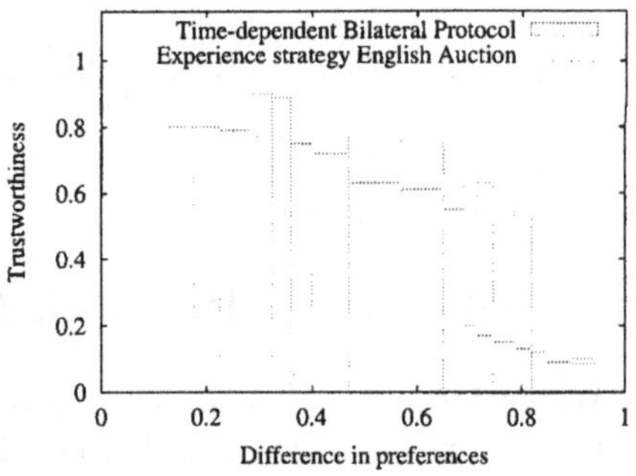

Fig. 8. Trustworthiness v/s preferences differences for time/experience strategies

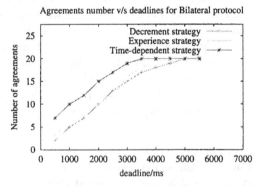

Fig. 9. Number of agreements v/s deadlines for the Bilateral protocol

Figures 5 and 6 show the trustworthiness level reached for a service provider as time elapses, by evaluating received offers and winning bids in each round for time-independent strategies (truth and decrement strategies) and for time or experience dependent strategies. The truth-telling strategy achieves a lower level of trustworthiness than the Decrement strategy, and the time-dependent strategy yields a lower trustworthiness level than the experience strategy. Also the English auction achieves a higher level of trustworthiness in a shorter time than the bilateral protocol. This is because in an English auction, there are competition between the bidders which can see each other's bids and so the trustworthiness level rises more sharply than when the consumers do not compete with each other.

Figures 7 and 8 show that the trustworthiness achieved in the offers and winning bids each round for the service provider decreases with increase in the difference between the provider's and the consumers' preferences. In fact, figure 7 shows that the English auction performs better than the Bilateral protocol, especially when with the added benefit of a more complex strategy for the English auction. With more complex strategies, such as time and experience strategies, there is lesser difference in the level of trustworthiness achieved, although the experience strategy for the English auction performs better of all strategies. This performance occurs because, in an English auction, the experience strategy takes full advantage of watching other bids in addition to choosing the winning bid in each round.

Figure 9 shows the number of agreements achieved with varying deadlines in the bilateral protocol, given that the two participants' preferences intersect and allow for an agreement. As a party's deadline increases, more agreements are arrived upon. However in this case, the time-dependent strategy yields more agreements than the experience strategy if a deadline less than 4000ms. The maximum number of agreements possible, which is 10 here for all the executed 10 bilateral protocols, is achieved within a smaller deadline for the time-dependent strategy than for the other two strategies as shown in figure 9. This is explained by the fact that a time-dependent strategy performs better with a time constraint parameter such as deadline.

6 Conclusions

Virtual Organisations require increasingly complex grid systems and scalable authorisation mechanisms for resource access. Negotiation is a technique that leads to contracts and SLAs between service providers and consumers in a VO, not only for sharing resources but also, as shown in this paper, for agreeing on a list of credentials that would bring about sufficient trustworthiness for the participants. To this end, we have described our development of the time-constrained bilateral negotiation protocol and the English auction. The participants in our approach do not exchange credentials during the negotiation, but they only exchange the names of the credentials that they are willing to disclose at the end of the negotiation once a binding agreement or contract has been achieved. We implemented decision making strategies of varying complexity for these protocols. Evaluation of our negotiation protocols shows that both competition in English auctions and the experience strategy yield a higher level of trustworthiness in a shorter time.

As future work, we intend to perform a more thorough evaluation of our protocols, and to analyse the inter-dependencies between the credentials in an offer or a bid, and to adapt the evaluation and generation decision functions to consider such inter-dependencies.

References

1. I. Foster and C. Kesselman. *The Grid: Blueprint for a New Computing Infrastructure*. Morgan Kaufmann, 2003.
2. Keith B. Frikken, Jiangtao Li, and Mikhail J. Atallah. Trust negotiation with hidden credentials, hidden policies, and policy cycles. In *NDSS*, 2006.
3. N. R. Jennings, P. Faratin, A. R. Lomuscio, S. Parsons, C. Sierra, and M. Wooldridge. Automated negotiation: prospects, methods and challenges. *International Journal of Group Decision and Negotiation*, 10(2):199–215, 2001.
4. J. Jonczy and R. Haenni. Implementing credential networks. In K. Stølen, W. H. Winsborough, F. Martinelli, and F. Massacci, editors, *iTrust'06, 4rd International Conference on Trust Management*, LNCS 3986, pages 164–178, Pisa, Italy, 2006. Springer.
5. N. Kelly, P. Jithesh, P. Donachy, T. Harmer, M. Perrott, R.and McCurley, M. Townsley, J. Johnston, and S. McKee. Genegrid: A commercial grid service oriented virtual bioinformatics laboratory. In *Proceedings of the 2005 IEEE Conference on Services Computing, Orlando*, pages 43–50, 2005.
6. Lars Olson, Marianne Winslett, Gianluca Tonti, Nathan Seeley, Andrzej Uszok, and Jeffrey M. Bradshaw. Trust negotiation as an authorization service forweb services. In *ICDE Workshops*, page 21, 2006.
7. Laura Pearlman, Von Welch, Ian T. Foster, Carl Kesselman, and Steven Tuecke. A community authorization service for group collaboration. *CoRR*, cs.DC/0306053, 2003.
8. Daniele Quercia, Manish Lad, Stephen Hailes, Licia Capra, and Saleem Bhatti. Strudel: supporting trust in the dynamic establishment of peering coalitions. In *SAC*, pages 1870–1874, 2006.
9. Simon Firth. *The Future is Grid*. Hewlett-Packard (HP) Labs, http://www.hpl.hp.com/news/2003/oct_dec/grid.html/, 2003.
10. W. Winsborough, K. Seamons, and V. Jones. Automated trust negotiation. In *DARPA Information Survivability Conference and Exposition (DISCEX 2000)*, 2000.

A Geo Time Authentication System*

L. Mostarda, A. Tocchio, P. Inverardi, and S. Costantini

Dip. di Informatica, Università di L'Aquila, Coppito 67100, L'Aquila, Italy
{mostarda,tocchio,inverard,costantini}@di.univaq.it

In this paper we present Geo Time Authentication (GTA), a prototype system that provides authenticity and integrity of cultural assets information. It has been conceived in the context of the CUSPIS project and afterwards it has been generalized to the context of assets and goods where problems of counterfeiting and thefts are prevalent. To prevent these crimes GTA adds to the usual asset information an additional tag that contains Galileo geo time information and it extends digital certificates with the notion of geographical areas for protecting the origin and the authenticity of the assets. Moreover, GTA makes available several services to protect the assets transport.

1 Introduction

The painting of Jean-Marc Nattier, The Alliance of Love and Wine, 1744, synthesizes the core of this paper strangely. What do a certification of origin and an ancient picture where a man and a woman drink wine share in common? At first sight nothing but cultural assets and wine share a common risk: the possibility of being forged. High quality wines such as Barolo or Chateaux Bordeaux owe their fame to the geographic areas where vineyards are cultivated and wine is left to mature in casks. It is inconceivable to define Bordeaux as a bottle of wine coming from the Nero d'Avola vine in Sicily.

The assurance about the origin and the integrity of a wine is very important and for this purpose in France and in Italy the AOC (Appellation d'Origine Contrôlée) and DOC (Denominazione di Origine Controllata) certifications have been introduced. Their purpose is to protect the reputation of the regional foods and to eliminate unfair competition and misleading of consumers by non-genuine products, which may be of inferior quality or of different flavor. AOP, DOC and other certifications represent a relevant obstacle to the forgeries even if the problem of falsifying data as the geographical origin still remains. Generally speaking, the counterfeiting in the context of alimentary products presents two main branches: the faking of origin and the forgery of the producer. In Italy, in December 2006 the police operation "Nozze di Cana" sequestered a large quantity of low quality wine ready to be sold as Pinot grigio IGP, Prosecco e

---

* We thank the Next S.p.A. research group and the CUSPIS project partners. Their suggestions during the project meetings have improved the quality of this work. Moreover we thank Naranker Dulay who revised this paper

---

Please use the following format when citing this chapter:

Mostarda, L., Tocchio, A., Inverardi, P. and Costantini, S., 2007, in IFIP International Federation for Information Processing, Volume 238, Trust Management, eds. Etalle, S., Marsh, S., (Boston: Springer), pp. 123–138.

Pinot nero DOC. Moreover, it is estimated that in the U.S. the imitation of Made in Italy wine market is in fact almost equal to that which Italy exports. In other words, one out of two bottles of wine are "fakes" and it is easy to come across curious "Italian" bottles of Chianti, Sangiovese, Refosco, and Barbera, even Rosè, Barolo and Super Piemontese that are produced in California. Works of art share with wines the unhappy destiny to be stolen and faked. In Italy, the police operation "Canale" sequestered 20,000 pieces, paintings and graphics works, 17,000 of them were imitations. Works of art stolen belonged, mainly to religious places, houses and museums.

The main reason for the excessive development of this criminal activity is the absent or incomplete cataloguing of works of art and the inadequacy of passive defense systems. Moreover, even with good planning of the journey and an escort presence, sometimes the criminals are able to steal works of art in transit.

Is it possible to cut down the criminal activity on wine, works of art and other goods that ensure huge profits for few people to everybody's detriment? It is very difficult to find a definitive solution for this problem but a relevant role in the prevention of the criminal activities could be assigned to the Galileo satellite[2], a big brother capable not only of certificating the origin of products such as wine but also of following the works of art in museums and during their journeys. Our idea is to combine the Galileo services with public key certificates [12] in order to guarantee the producer, the origin and the destination of products such as wines, to authenticate works of art and to ensure the security in their transport. Both Galileo services and public key certificates have been combined in the Geo Time Authentication (GTA) system in order to enhance security services (i.e., identification, authentication, assets information integrity, secure transport) in the ubiquitous systems constituted by assets.

In the identification phase the Galileo services permit the tagging of an asset with a unique asset identification code (GAID) in which the Galileo coordinates have a relevant role. In particular, the Galileo Open Service (OS) [11, 10] provides to the GAID accurate positioning and timing information to uniquely catalogue an asset while the Galileo authentication service enhances the GAID with integrity and authentication information. GAID combined with 'extended' digital certificates (i.e., certificates that bind a producer to a geographical area) guarantees the precise origin of products and links the origin with the entity that produced them. In some cases it can also be useful to consider in the certification process the product destination. This concept can be applied more rarely to wines but in the context of the works of art transport, the destination authentication guarantees that people are looking at a genuine work in a museum or in a gallery of art.

Identification, authentication and secure transport of assets supported by the satellite could be a good response to the criminal phenomena emphasized earlier. GTA allows us to defend against the imitations of origin wines, dresses,

---

[2] Galileo is Europes own global navigation satellite system.

paintings and other products, allows people to check if an asset is in the place where it is destined to remain and, finally, allows museums to lend more easily works of art by considering the security guaranteed not only by Galileo but also by particular procedures of packing and control. Our approach has been developed and validated in the context of the CUSPIS project [5] by using the Galieo satellite but it can operate also with the support of other positioning infrastructures.

2 Defining the asset life cycle

In this section we introduce step by step the process that, starting by the producer, delivers assets to consumers. We call this process the asset life cycle. The life cycle is divided into four phases: (i) Certification; (ii) Identification; (iii) Transport; (iv) Selling and authentication.

Certification phase: In order to guarantee the traceability of an asset, a unique identifier (AID) must be assigned to it. This identifier is composed of two parts: the first one identifies the company (CI) while the second one is a serial number identifying a product of the company itself (PI). In order to generate the CI identifier, a company (i.e., the producer) can interact with some international organizations. The basic role of the international organizations is to guarantee the uniqueness of the CI. In the context of bar codes [3] in USA and Canada, this role is assigned to the GS1 (Global Standard 1) organization. When a company requests its CI from the GS1 and obtains it, the process of assets identification starts. The CI is joined to the asset serial number according to the Universal Product Code (UPC) standard and to the kind of asset. In fact a bar code does not distinguish among the same kind of assets. For instance, the same brand of wine with the same characteristics has the same bar code. A more promising technology is based on Radio Frequency Identifiers (RFID) [8] that holds both an asset unique identifier (AID) and the related description in a digital form. With respect to the bar code the RFID is able to identify uniquely an item.

Identification phase: In this phase the producer, after creating an asset, attaches to it Asset Data (AD). The AD contains both a description and the Asset Identifer (AID). The description is usually composed of some sentences that describe the product, the producer generalities and the origin (e.g., made in the USA). The AID uniquely identifies an asset and may allow a producer to perform easily an inventory, to verify the status of an asset by means of the tracking process and to oversee the correct assets management.

Transport phase: Transport is the step where products are packed and delivered by the transporter to the markets where they are sold.

Selling and authentication phase: In the selling phase the seller gets in touch with the consumer. The seller has assets equipped with ADs that are used for

---

[3] The printed code used for recognition by a bar code scanner (reader).

inventory purposes. The consumer can access the information in the AD for validating the product authenticity and capturing all data useful to determine the asset qualities and characteristics. The asset authentication process is usually performed by means of empirical rules, e.g., by looking at the description inside the AD and comparing it with the shape and the features of the product.

In the following we describe all attacks that can be performed on the asset description and on the AID (see [8] for a survey). Without loss of generality we will consider attacks that could be performed when the AD is stored on the RFID device. In fact, as we are going to see in the rest of the work, a basic RFID is more vulnerable than the traditional bare code [6].

3 Attacks on AD information

In the following we summarize the attacks that can be performed against an AD:

AD modification: An unauthorized entity can take the AD (i.e., description and/or AID) and tamper with it. This is an attack on the integrity of the AD information. In the context of the wine production and transport, either the carrier or the seller could modify both the AID and the description of a wine in order to change its data and/or its origin.

AD fabrication: An unauthorized entity can introduce counterfeit assets in the market. This is an attack to the authenticity of the product. For example in the field of the wines, an entity could produce a bottle of wine in Italy pretending that its origin was a vineyard located in France. A painter could create a copy of a famous painting and exhibit it as the original.

AD duplication: A malicious entity can duplicate a valid AD generated by an authorized producer. For instance, this is the case in which a malicious producer of wine duplicates AD data of a wine bottle and uses it on its bottles.

AD reuse: A malicious entity can reuse the AD information for other assets. For instance, a malicious producer can copy the AD information, destroy it and reuse the AD data in its product. A seller could misplace the AD from a bottle to another one or a museum employee could remove an ID from a work of art and put it on an imitation. A particular case of this general attack is the swapping one, in which an adversary exchanges two valid ADs.

AD destruction: A malicious entity can destroy the AD. For instance a malicious transporter can destroy the AD related to an asset.

AD access control An authorized entity can attempt unauthorized actions. In this case the device containing the AD must authenticate the AD reader in order to implement access control mechanisms.

Besides the security issues the RFID devices emphasize privacy issues since they do not require a direct line of sight and can be read without bearer authorization. For instance, EPC RFID contains a description field where the asset description can be stored. An attacker could capture information on products bought by a person, his clothing size and accessory preferences violating his privacy. The producer can be affected by similar privacy violation acts. In fact, a competitor could be interested in acquiring information of his production methodologies and processes. This problem has been faced by the work of Juels et al. in [9]. Generally speaking clandestine tracking is a well-known problem that affects other devices such as Bluetooth or Wi-Fi (see [18] for an extended survey).

In order to design a secure system for the products having an AD we first have to define the notions of privacy and security; to this end, we have to know *against what* we want to be secure and private. Therefore, in the next section we will present a rigorous model of the attacks that an adversary can perform against the AD. Under this assumption we will identify interesting attacks that our Geo Time Authentication System is able to prevent.

4 The attack model

In our attack model we assume that an attacker: (i) can read (any number of times) an AD previously written; (ii) can rewrite an AD previously written; (iii) has its own instruments to fabricate an AD; (iv) can read the information flowing between an AD storage device and the related reader; (v) cannot interfere in the AD creation process, when a valid AD is created and stored in the related device by its producer.

In the following we consider the functionalities of AD storage devices (as we have emphasized in Section 2 we adopt RFID storage devices). Devices functionalities and asset life cycle characteristics will be used to validate the reasonableness and the correctness of our attack model. Finally, we provide some related work where other attack models are proposed.

RFIDs range from basic to advanced ones. Basic RFID devices cannot perform cryptographic operations, do not offer cloning resistance and can be easily read/written with a low-cost device. Advanced RFID devices offer some basic cryptographic operations, some form of cloning resistance, one-time writing and they implement basic access control mechanisms. In order to make our system as adaptable as possible we adopted basic RFID devices.

Concerning the asset life cycle, we observe that an asset identified by a producer can be handled by other entities during the asset life cycle. For instance a bottle of wine produced in France can be handled by the carrier that transports it in England or by the restaurant that serves it to the users.

The above considerations lead us to assume that an attacker can read, write, fabricate an AD information as emphasized in (i), (ii), (iii) and he can eavesdrop clear-text information sent between an RFID device and its reader (i.e., (iv)).

Concerning the assumption described in (v), it is consequence of two main considerations. First the supply chains of producers always provide some forms of physical security measures in the asset identification phase (see Section 2). Secondly there must be a physical proximity during AD generation. Therefore, we can assume that a man-in-the-middle attack is not possible during the AD creation.

As described in [8], an important research challenge is the formulation of weakened attack models that accurately reflect real-worlds attacks in the field of AD and RFID devices. For instance in [7] a 'minimalist' security model for low-cost RFID devices is proposed. In this model an adversary can only read an AD on a periodic basis (and also tag release data at a limited rate). In particular, this model assumes an upper-bound on the number of times that an attacker can read the AD or spoof a valid AD reader. It is suitable for proximity cards where an adversary can only read the card. In the context of the asset life cycle, products are handled by different entities, for this reason the 'minimalist' model is not suitable. A more general model is proposed in [2] where all kinds of threats are described and related solutions shown. It has several characteristics in common with our model and this correspondence constitutes for us a validation of the model proposed in this paper.

5 The GTA system

The Geo Time Authentication (GTA) system provides security services in an ubiquitous context where assets equipped with digital devices are put everywhere. The GTA security services address: (i) authentication; (ii) access control; (iii) integrity; (iv) privacy and confidentiality; (v) secure transport of assets; (vi) non-repudiation. These services are countermeasure to the attacks described in Section 4.

The GTA authentication service guarantees the authenticity of an AD. This authenticity ensures that the producer is the one indicated on the AD and that the AD was indeed generated in the origin indicated on it. Moreover, AD authentication prevents an attacker from masquerading as a legitimate producer (more generally that counterfeit objects are introduced in the market). The GTA access control service is able to limit and control the access to the AD. To this aim each entity must be first authenticated so that access rights can be tailored to the individual. The GTA integrity service ensures that an AD is received as sent, i.e, duplication, reuse, destruction cannot be performed. The GTA privacy and confidentially services guarantee that AD information is provided only to authorized people. The GTA secure transport of assets ensures that assets are not stolen or substituted during the transport phase. The GTA non repudiation service prevents a producer to deny a generated AD. We will show that these services are implemented by using well known cryptographic mechanisms combined with Galileo service infrastructures and with the flexibility of the GTA configuration.

The GTA system can run in a completely decentralized configuration or with the addition of logically centralized components. In the decentralized configuration a user can easily use its mobile devices (e.g., a phone or a PDA) to locally check the authenticity and the integrity of an AD. For instance, in a shop a user can verify the authenticity of a shirt without the need of any connection. The advantage of the decentralized solution is in terms of performance and scalability, i.e., an increasing number of users and assets does not affect the AD verification time. However, this solution does not provide access control mechanisms, privacy and secure transport of assets. In order to provide these services the GTA system relies on centralized components.

5.1 The decentralized GTA solution

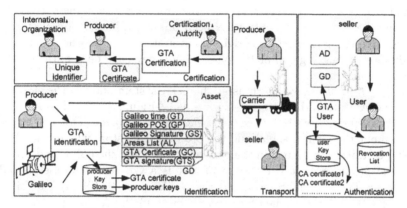

Fig. 1. The addition of the GTA components

In Figure 1 we show how the GTA decentralized solution is added in the asset life cycle. This addition does not affect the normal standard life cycle phases described in Section 2 since it only introduces certification authorities and an additional tag (the GTA tag (GD) shown in Figure 1) to each asset.

Certification phase. In the GTA system, different Certification Authorities (CAs) are equipped with the GTA certification component (see left-upper side of Figure 1). Each authority can release a GTA certificate to a producer. For instance in our application the Certifications Authorities are the Italian and Greek Ministries of Cultural Heritage and the Italian Commercial Entity (CCIAA). GTA certificates associated to museums are released by the Ministries while the Commercial Entity is involved in the generation of certificates for the producers of wine. A GTA certificate is an X509 v3 certificate[12] with the addition of GTA special extensions. A standard x509 v3 extension is a triple (*ID extension* ,*critical*, *extension Value*) used to store additional information in an X509 certificate. *ID extension* is an extension unique identifier. *Critical* is set to true (false) whether or not an implementation trying to process a X.509 certificate should be (should not be) able to understand the extension to correctly process the certificate. Finally, the *extension Value* field contains the data of the extension. For instance, the extension can be used to write in a certificate the Internet address where the List of Revoked

Certificates (CRL) can be downloaded. The GTA system uses the extension mechanism to store in a certificate a tuple (Description, Area) where *Description* is composed of some words that informally describe the field *Area* that is an ordered list of points (i.e., a polygon) identifying the place where products are built. For instance a GTA certificate can have the geographical extension $\{(FranceMargot, \{(46.290763, -0.839555), (46.286302, -0.816752),$ $(46.277241, -0.820633), (46.282811, -0.847808)\})\}$ vouching that the producer bottles its wine in the square geographical area defined by the above points (i.e., France Margot). We point out that when a producer has different vineyards located in different areas, he must have different certificates, one for each area. This uniquely identifies uniquely not only the producer of the wine but also the geographical area where the bottle has been produced. In the case of cultural assets an area can guarantee the origin of cultural assets, i.e., where they have been discovered (e.g. Egypt) or the place where they have been authenticated (e.g. Louvre museum).

Identification phase. For each asset the GTA system adds to the standard AD the GTA Data (GD) (see left-lower side of Figure 1). To this aim each producer is equipped with a *GTA identification component.* This component takes in input the Galileo signal and the producer Key store where holds both the GTA certificate (obtained in the previous phase) and the public and private key of the producer. The component output is a GD for each asset. A GD contains the following information: (i) the Galileo time (GT); (ii) the Galileo position (GP); (iii) the Galileo Signature (GS); (iv) the Areas List (AL); (v) the GTA certificate (GC); (vi) the GTA signature (GTS).

The GP field corresponds to the geographical position (i.e., latitude, longitude and altitude) measured by a Galileo receiver[4]. The GT field is the Galileo time locally measured by means of a Galileo receiver. The use of GT and GP fields is twofold: from one side they are the GD part providing information on the time and on the geographical point where the asset has been created. On the other side they permit to uniquely identify each asset. In fact, we suppose that a producer can create in each instant only an asset and for each geographical point can exist only a producer. In the rest of this work the concatenation of the GT and the GP fields will be referred to as the Galileo Identifier (GAID). The GS is the Galileo digital signature of the GAID data. By using this digital signature, a Galileo receiver is able to authenticate the source of GP and GT data (i.e., the Galileo satellite) and verify their integrity[5]. Moreover, the GS ensures that a producer cannot counterfeit the origin of its product. The AL field defines a list of areas. These areas are useful for 'tracking' the product during its life cycle. For instance a wine producer can generate a list containing all 'destination' areas where the product will be sold, i.e., the areas identify-

---

[4] In closed environments the signal is forwarded from outside to inside by means of special devices.

[5] The Signal Authentication through Authentication Navigation Messages (ANM) is a Galileo service that will be active on 2008 [11]. In our GTA implementation integrity checking is based on cross-checking the Galileo signal.

ing a chain of restaurants. In the case of cultural assets the list can contain one destination area that identifies the museum where the cultural asset will be exhibited. The field GC contains the GTA certificate of the producer. The GTA signature (GTS) is a standard signature (SHA1 With RSA Encryption) of both GD fields (i.e. GAID , GS, AL, GC) and AD (if any) that is performed by the producer with its private key. This signature guarantees the integrity and authenticity of both GD and AD.

In the decentralized GTA implementation the size of a GD is about 1 Kilobyte and can been stored in both RFID devices [6] and bar code form. For instance in the case of cultural assets the RFID has been positioned next to each cultural asset in order to provide its authenticity. Concerning the bar code, it can be added in the label to the usual wine bar code to enhance security issues.

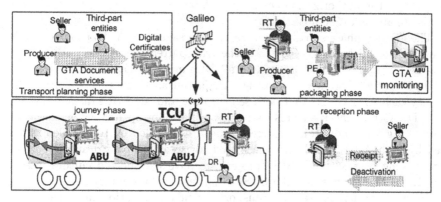

Fig. 2. The addition of the GTA components

Transport phase. In Figure 2 we provide a detailed description of the transport subphases: (i) transport planning; (ii) packaging; (iii) journey; (iv) reception.

In the transport planning phase different entities use the GTA document services component in order to produce different certificates. Entities are the producer (i.e., the owner of the asset), the seller (the entity who wishes to take the assets) and third-part entities (i.e., who vouches the content and the routing of transport). In particular, digital certificates must include an authorization certificate for each package and a unique transport certificate. Each authorization certificate can contain the list of all GDs inserted in the package. The transport certificate contains the correct routing. The routing of the transport certificate is defined in terms of a list of tuples $\{(A_s, T_{A_s}), (A_1, T_{A_1}) \ldots (A_i, T_{A_i}) \ldots (A_n, T_{A_n}) (A_d, T_{A_d}) \}$ where A_s is the starting transport area and T_{A_s} the related date (i.e., day and hour), A_i an area at which the transport must pass and T_{A_i} the related date, (A_d, T_{A_d}) the destination area and its date.

---

[6] There are RFID tags with this size that maintain full EPC compatibility.

We point out that for specific assets transport other certificates (e.g., insurance certificates) can be added, moreover all certificates are signed by all entities. For instance in the context of CUSPIS project we have transported cultural assets. In this case the producer is the owner of the cultural assets, the seller is the renter of cultural assets and third-party entities are the Ministry of Cultural Heritage, the Insurance Company and the Transporter. Those entities cooperate to produce the above digital certificates (i.e., the authorization certificates, the transport certificate and the insurance certificate).

In the packaging phase the above entities in cooperation with a transporter (RT) and the packaging expert (PE) supervise the packaging of assets. Each package is filled with: (i) a set of assets each identified by an AD and the related GD; (ii) an Asset Board Unit (ABU); (iii) a sensor of humidity; (iv) a sensor of light; (v) a sensor of temperature. The ABU is equipped with a GTA monitoring component, the authorization certificate related to the package, the transport certificate and additional certificates.

The journey phase starts with a startup message that the transporter sends to all ABUs. Each ABU verifies: (i) the transporter identity; (ii) the correct starting position; (iii) the presence of all GDs in its package . Moreover, each ABU gathers all distances from other ABUs and all sensors data. During the journey each ABU checks that both sensors data and the ABUs distance do not vary. The former check ensures that packages are not opened while the latter that packages are not stolen. Correct routing is enabled by the Galileo signal used by each ABU in order to check that all areas are passed at the correct time. In the context of CUSPIS project we have transported cultural assets from Rome to Florence (see the CUSPIS [5] project for details).

In the reception phase the transporter sends a reception message to the renter. This renter receives this message and sends a deactivation message to all ABUs. In particular each ABU deactivates its GTA monitoring system component only when it is in the right area (i.e., the destination area), the renter provides a valid certificate and the receipt is correctly formatted.

Authentication phase After the identification phase the assets are delivered to the market where their authenticity will be verified by a user. To this end the user mobile device is equipped with a GTA user component (see right-side of Figure 1) that is able to check the authenticity and the integrity of both the GD and the AD. A GTA user component interacts with a local user key store and a local revocation list. The user key store contains the digital certificates of all valid certification authorities. The revocation list should be updated as often as possible and it contains all GTA certificates that have been revoked. In order to check a GD and AD the GTA component performs the following steps:

- *GTA certificate (GC) verification.* This step involves the usual verification performed on x509 certificates [12]. In the following we describe the most relevant verifications that are performed. The certificate expiration date and its period must be validated. The issuer (i.e., a certification authority) who released the certificate must be a valid one (i.e., present on the local user key store). The GTA certificate signature, which includes signature of subject name (i.e., the producer) and subject key, has to be checked w.r.t. the certification authority key. The GTA certificate must not be present in the certificate revocation list.

- *Galileo signature (GS) verification.* The Galileo signature (GS) must be verified w.r.t. both the Galileo position (GP) and the Galileo time (GT).
- *Origin verification.* This step verifies that the origin of the product (the Galileo position (GP)) is contained inside the area defined in the GTA certificate.
- *Actual position verification.* This step checks if the actual asset position belongs to the area defined inside the areas list (AL) present in the GD.
- *GTS signature verification.* This step verifies that the signature of both AD and GD data is correct (w.r.t. the producer public key contained in the GTA certificate).

In the following we will see that the GD and the AD can be used in order to address the attacks presented in Section 4 (i.e., to provide the GTA services described in the first part of this section).

The GTA authentication services rely on the GTA certificate (GC) verification step and on the Galileo signature (GS) verification. The former guarantees the 'authenticity' of the producer and the latter the origin of the product. The GTS signature guarantees the GTA non-repudiation service since it is based on asymmetric key technology. Moreover, the GTS signature even ensures detection of the AD and GD modifications (i.e., an aspect of the integrity service).

AD and GD reuse and duplication (i.e., the remaining attacks avoided by the integrity service), are addressed by the actual position verification step and/or by the use of a distributed GTA integrity component. The actual position verification ensures that the asset stays in one of the areas included in the GD areas list (AL) so that reuse (i.e., misplace and swapping) and duplication of AD and GD is bounded. In fact, a faked product should be distributed in the same restricted area where the original one resides. For instance suppose that a malicious producer reads the GD and AD of a famous wine in a market of New York in order to put them on a bottle of low quality wine. He cannot duplicate and reuse the GA and AD information in its falsified bottle. In fact, the purchasing of it in a place different from the original destination (e.g., a market of S.Francisco) will be detected by the GTA system through the actual position verification. But, the problems of reuse and duplication in the same area still remain. To address this we introduce the following solutions.

In the same area, swapping and misplacing are under the judgment of a user. We assume that the AD and GD information, received in the GTA user terminal, are coupled with a user's careful asset 'observation'. Observation can include the checking of the AD (e.g., the label information and the bar code), the shape and the form of the asset. For instance a GTA user can receive information on its terminal about a bottle of wine (i.e., the label, the form and the features of the bottle) and identify a possible misplacing or swapping of both AD and GD. Another solution to the reuse threat is to secure physically both the AD and the GD. For instance in a museum both AD and GD should be secured next to the cultural asset in such a way that no unauthorized person can access it. Concerning the duplication prevention it can rely either on GD and AD storage devices (for instance actual RFIDs are equipped with anti-cloning devices [8]) or on a decentralized GTA system integrity component. Each area can have associated a centralized GTA integrity component which is based on a local GTA database. The asset GAID is a unique handler to the local GTA database where are stored information related to the asset purchasing data (i.e., whether or not the asset has been bought). Every time a user authenticates an asset, an enhanced GTA user component forwards the asset location data and the GAID to the GTA integrity component. The GTA integrity component checks if the AD is related to an asset never bought and raises an alarm when both AD and GD have been already checked out. It is worth noticing that the AD duplication is guaranteed by the singleness of each GAID code.

However, in real industrial context it is not always possible to generate GDs that contain the areas list (AL) information. Moreover, unless storage device are equipped with cryptography and access control mechanisms, both AD and GD information are visible and accessible to any user. In order to enhance these security and privacy issues the GTA system provides the following centralized configuration.

5.2 The GTA centralized solution

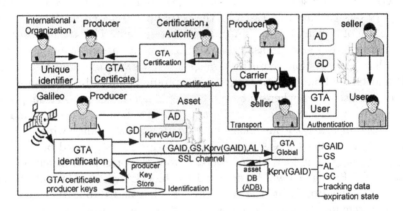

Fig. 3. The addition of the centralized GTA component

In Figure 3 we show how the GTA centralized solution is added in the asset life cycle. As for the decentralized solution the centralized one does not affect the asset life cycle phases but incorporates only a new centralized component, the GTA global component. This component is implemented in terms of different sub-components (see the online official CUSPIS documentation [5] for details) that interact with each other in order to provide the GTA security services. In this paper, for space reasons, we do not describe the sub-components view but we merely consider the GTA global component as a black-box one. It is worth noticing that, as we are going to see in the phases description, both the GTA identification and the GTA user components are named as the ones described in the previous section but they are based on a different implementation.

Certification phase The certification phase is not modified with respect to the previous Section since a producer must still obtain its certificates in the same way.

Identification phase For each asset the GTA system adds to the standard AD (if any) the GTA Data (GD) (see left-lower side of Figure 3). To this aim each producer is equipped with a *GTA identification component*. This component takes in input the Galileo signal and the producer Key store and outputs a GD for each asset. A GD contains the GAID (i.e., Galileo time and the Galileo position) encrypted with the producer private key (this is denoted with $k_{priv}(GAID)$ in Figure 3). After the GD information has been produced the GTA identification component creates an SSL connection (mutual authentication is obtained through digital certificates) with the Global GTA component. This connection is used to transfer both GD data and additional asset data (see Figure 3). Additional data are those described in Section 5.1, the GAID, the areas list AL (if any) and the Galileo signature (GS) (see Figure 3). The global component stores the received data and some additional ones in the assets database (ADB). Additional data are the GTA certificate of the producer (GC) and the tracking and expiration ones. The tracking data contain a list of points where the asset has been observed. The expiration state can be set to 'killed' when the asset information has expired[7].

Authentication phase. After the identification phase the assets are delivered to the market where their authenticity will be verified by a user. The user mobile device is equipped with a GTA user component (see right-side of Figure 3) that is able to check the authenticity and the integrity of both an AD and the related GD. The GTA component sends the GD (e.g., $k_{priv}(GAID)$), the user position (e.g., Ux,Uy) and the related Galileo signature (GS(Ux,Uy)) to the GTA global component that performs the following basic steps:

- *User data verification.* The integrity of the user position is checked by using the Galileo signature GS(Ux,Uy). Moreover, there must exist an ADB entry labeled with key $k_{priv}(GAID)$.
- *Access control verification.* An access control component verifies the user rights in order to provide the asset data.
- *Expiration checking.* The entry $k_{priv}(GAID)$ must not be related to an asset expired.
- *Actual position verification.* The user position and its asset tracking data are matched to verify whether or not the user is looking at the original asset or

---

[7] For instance, an asset information can expire as a consequence of checkout

a duplicated/reused one[8]. Moreover, if the areas list of the asset is available (i.e., the possible asset locations) then it can be used to validate the correct asset location.

The GTA authentication service is based on the user data verification step where the GTA global component uses the $k_{priv}(GAID)$ handler to guarantee the existence of a valid asset entry. The $k_{priv}(GAID)$ signed handler even guarantees the GTA non-repudiation service since it is based on the producer private key.

Both AD and GD modification (i.e., an aspect of the integrity service) is guaranteed by the user data verification which checks the existence of the entry $k_{priv}(GAID)$. The AD and GS reuse/duplication (i.e., the remaining attacks avoided by the integrity services), are addressed by Expiration checking and Actual position verification steps. In the case that the asset expiration data is set to killed the GTA system detects that the asset could be reused. The actual position verification discovers when the asset is in an anomalous position or appears in too many different geographic positions. This check would allow duplications to be detected.

The GTA global component provides access control mechanism, for instance in the case of cultural assets information a user can get them only when they are paid for. For wine a user can get information only when the product has not been destroyed. Furthermore, the GTA system addresses the problem of AD and GD destruction by means of the time-out that expires when a product is unused for too long. The privacy in ensured by the encrypted GD which does not provide asset information.

6 Related work

In this section we cite some systems that face the problem of the origin certification or the secure transport of assets. Some can be compared because they are used to discourage imitation, some because they are based on RFID technology, others because are supported by the Galileo services. In the context of the origin certification, we cite the ETG [14] a system presented recently in Vicenzaoro Winter, capable of defending products against the problem of imitations. ETG (Traceability and Guarantee Label) supports the automatic printing and the reading of informative messages, based on a encrypted bar code. RFIDs have been applied successfully in the context of wines and is reported in WinesandVines, a trade publication for the grape and wine industry [3]. Some wineries adopted RFID tags for tracking data on individual barrels and tanks. For example, Barrel Trak [16] is an advanced process data management system that brings real time, read/write data tracking and process history to the winemaking process. RFIDs containing non-encrypted information are useful for maintaining track of the wines bottles in restricted environments as

---

[8] A similar technique is used for to detect possible credit card cloning.

wineries or restaurants but, what happens if the products of a winery are numerous and exported all over the world? The possibility of duplicating or faking an RFID increases considerably. The support of Galileo in GTA permits the introduction in the bottle identification code of information on the geographical area where it has been bottled. The concept that we intend to emphasize is that the RFID in GTA contains the coordinates where the products has been realized, so increasing the difficulties for faking it. In fact, in the case of the Barrel Trak, a bottle of a forged wine could be equipped with an RFID created in Europe vouching that the product has been bottled in California. Contrary, with GTA for faking the information in a RFID the falsifier should create it in the same geographical area of the Barrel Trak. This decreases the imitation probabilities. A good survey on the techniques for augmenting RFID security and security is [8]. Juels explores several methodologies for avoiding RFID duplications and tampering but none of them use the Galileo signal in order to enhance security issues. Galileo can take on a basic role to ensure the singleness, the authenticity and the origin of the RFID information considering also its relevant role in the information encryption process. RFIDs and cultural assets share the scene in the work of Augello et al. [1]. MAGA is a user friendly virtual guide system adaptable to the user needs of mobility and therefore usable on different mobile devices (e.g. PDAs, Smartphones). In MAGA RFIDs are applied to furnish information to the user but it is not clear if the authors faced the problem of the identification and authentication of cultural assets. In the context of Galileo applications (Agriculture and Fisheries, Civil Engineering, Energy, Environment and so on) [10], GTA confirms its originality in facing the problem of identification, authentication and secure transport of products. Two companies, Texas Instruments and VeriSign Inc., have proposed a 'chain-of-custody' approach that is strictly related to the GTA system [13]. Their model involves digital signing of tag data to provide integrity assurance. Digital signatures do not confer cloning resistance to tags, however. They prevent forging of data, but not copying of data. The EPC global standard for RFID technologies proposes global object naming services [4]. A centralized database stores assets information and can be used for security purposes. The GTA system enhances this with the notion of areas and the Galileo infrastructure. In particular, in the decentralized solution the security services are provided through local databases that do not need any data exchange. Therefore, performance and scalability are enhanced.

7 Conclusions

The GTA system provides novel security services in an ubiquitous system made of assets and the related devices. The combination of both Galileo services and enhanced digital certificates prevents counterfeiting of origins and the introduction of false assets in the market. The GTA limits duplication and reuse of assets information in the same geographical area where a local database can provide a solution. The flexibility of its configuration permits the tuning of the system as needed. For instance when privacy is a relevant concern the centralized solution can be used. In contrast when scalability and performance are relevant concerns the decentralized solution can be applied.

References

1. Augello A, Santangelo A, Sorce S, Pilato G, Gentile A, Genco A, Gaglio S. Maga: A mobile archaeological guide at agrigento. University of Palermo, ICAR-CNR.
2. Bailey D. and Juels A (2006) Shoehorning security into the EPC standard. In: De Prisco R, Yung M (eds) International Conference on Security in Communication Networks, volume 4116 of LNCS, pages 303–320, Springer-Verlag.
3. Caputo T. (2005) Rfid technology beyond wal-mart. WinesandVines.
4. EPC global standard powered by GS1 (2005) Object Naming Service (ONS) 5 Version 1.0. Whitepaper, www.epcglobalinc.org/ standards/ Object_Naming_Service_ONS_Standard_Version_1.0.pdf EPCglobal Ratified Specification Version of October 4, 2005.
5. European Commision 6th Framework Program - 2nd Call Galileo Joint Undertaking. Cultural Heritage Space Identification System (CUSPIS). www.cuspis-project.info.
6. Garfinkel S and Rosemberg B (2005) Hacking the prox card. In: RFID:Applications,Security and privacy, pages 291–300. MA: Addison-Wesley.
7. Juels A (2004) Minimalist cryptography for low-cost rfid tags. In: Proc. 4th International Conference on Security Communication Network, C. Blundo and C. Blundo, Eds. New York: Springer LNCS.
8. Juels A (2006) Rfid security and privacy: A research survey. IEEE Journal on Selected Areas in Communication.
9. Juels A, Molnar D, and Wagner D (2005) Security and privacy issues in e-passports. In: Gollman D, Li G, Tsudik G, (eds) IEEE/CreateNet SecureComm.
10. official web page of Galileo. www.galileoju.com.
11. Pozzobon O, Wullems C, Kubic K. (2004) Secure tracking using trusted gnss receivers and galileo authentication services. Journal of Global Positioning Systems.
12. Stallings W (2006) Cryptography and network security: Principles and Practice. Fourth edition, Prentice Hall (eds).
13. Texas Instruments and VeriSign, Inc. Securing the pharmaceutical supply chain with RFID and public-key infrastructure technologies. Whitepaper, www.ti.com/ rfid/ docs/ customer/ eped-form.shtml.
14. web page of Italia Oggi journal. www.italiaoggi.it/giornali/giornali.asp?codici Testate=45&argomento=Circuits.
15. web page of the Sea Smoke Cellars. www.packagingdigest.com/articles/200509/64.php.
16. web page of the TagStream Company. www.tagstreaminc.com.
17. web page on EPCglobal organization. www.epcglobalinc.org/home.
18. Jakobsson M and Wetzel S (2001). Security weakness in Bluetooth. volume 2020 of LNCS. Springer Verlang.

Content Trust Model for Detecting Web Spam

Wei Wang, Guosun Zeng

Department of Computer Science and Technology, Tongji University,
Shanghai 201804, China
Tongji Branch, National Engineering & Technology Center of High
Performance Computer, Shanghai 201804, China

willtongji@gmail.com

Abstract. As it gets easier to add information to the web via html pages, wikis, blogs, and other documents, it gets tougher to distinguish accurate or trustworthy information from inaccurate or untrustworthy information. Moreover, apart from inaccurate or untrustworthy information, we also need to anticipate web spam – where spammers publish false facts and scams to deliberately mislead users. Creating an effective spam detection method is a challenge. In this paper, we use the notion of content trust for spam detection, and regard it as a ranking problem. Evidence is utilized to define the feature of spam web pages, and machine learning techniques are employed to combine the evidence to create a highly efficient and reasonably-accurate spam detection algorithm. Experiments on real web data are carried out, which show the proposed method performs very well in practice.

Key words: web spam; content trust; ranking; SVM; machine learning

1 Introduction

Information retrieval (IR) is the study of helping users to find information that matches their information needs. Technically, information retrieval studies the acquisition, organization, storage, retrieval, and distribution of information [1]. However, as it gets easier to add information to the web via html pages, wikis, blogs, and other documents, it gets tougher to distinguish accurate or trustworthy information from inaccurate or untrustworthy information. A search engine query usually results in several hits that are outdated and/or from unreliable sources and the user is forced to go through the results and pick what he/she trust requirements.

Please use the following format when citing this chapter:

Wang, W. and Zeng, G., 2007, in IFIP International Federation for Information Processing, Volume 238, Trust Management, eds. Etalle, S., Marsh, S., (Boston: Springer), pp. 139–152.

Moreover, apart from inaccurate or untrustworthy information, we also need to anticipate web spam – where spammers publish false facts and scams to deliberately mislead users. Creating an effective spam detection method is a challenge.

In the context of search engines, a spam web page is a page that is used for spamming or receives a substantial amount of its score from other spam pages. Spam can be great harmful for several reasons. First, spamming is annoying for users because it makes it harder to find truly and trustworthy information and leads to frustrating search experiences. Second, if a user searches for information that is relevant to your pages but your pages are ranked low by search engines, then the user may not see the pages because one seldom clicks a large number of returned pages. Finally, a search engine may waste significant resources on spam pages because spam pages consume crawling bandwidth, pollute the web, and distort search ranking [2].

In this paper, we explore a novel content trust model based on evidence for detecting spam. The notion of content trust was first introduced by Gil et al. to solve the problem of reliability of the web resource [3]. But they only proposed the preliminary notion of content trust, and did not take the information content into account actually. In our opinion, spam web pages are a salient kind of distrusted web resource which can utilize content trust to model it. So, we developed a content trust model with ranking algorithms to detect web spam. Experiments show that our method performs very well in finding spam web pages.

The main contributions of this paper are follows:

- A novel content trust model is proposed for web spam detection
- A ranking algorithm is adapted to the model for spam detection
- Experiments of real web data are carried out to evaluate the proposed method

The rest of this paper is organized as follows. We introduce some background and review some related work in Section 2. Section 3 introduces the proposed content trust model for detecting web spam. We first describe the key evidence for the model, and then a rank learning algorithm is proposed to detect web spam. We evaluate our approach and analyze the experiments results in Section 4. Section 5 concludes the paper.

2   Background and Related Work

2.1   Web Spam and Ranking Problem

Web search has become very important in the information age. Increased exposure of pages on the Web can result in significant financial gains and/or fames for organizations and individuals. Unfortunately, this also results in spamming, which refers to human activities that deliberately mislead search engines to rank some pages higher than they deserve. The following description of web spam taxonomy is based on [1], [2], [5] and [12].

Content-based spamming methods basically tailor the contents of the text fields in HTML pages to make spam pages more relevant to some queries. This kind of spamming can also be called *term spamming*, and there are two main term spam techniques: repeating some important terms and dumping of many unrelated terms [1].

Link spam is the practice of adding extraneous and misleading links to web pages, or adding extraneous pages just to contain links. An early paper investigating link spam is Davison [6], which considered nepotistic links. Baeza-Yates et al. [7] present a study of collusion topologies designed tot boost PageRank [8] while Adali et al. [9] show that generating pages with links targeting a single page is the most effective means of link spam. Gyongyi et al. [10] introduce TrustRank which finds non-spam pages by following links from an initial seed set of trusted pages. In [4] Fetterly et al. showed ways of identifying link spam based on divergence of sites from power laws. Finally, Mishne et al. [11] present a probabilistic method operating on word frequencies, which identifies the special case of link spam within blog comments.

Hiding techniques is also used by spammers who want to conceal or to hide the spamming sentences, terms and links so that Web users do not see them [1]. *Content hiding* is used to make spam items invisible. One simple method is to make the spam terms the same color as the background color. In *cloaking*, Spam Web servers return a HTML document to the user and a different document to a Web crawler. In this way, the spammer can present the Web user with the intended content and send a spam pages to the search engine for indexing.

There are pages on the Web that do not try to deceive search engines at all and provide useful and reliably contents to Web users; there are pages on the Web that include many artificial aspects that can only be interpreted as attempts to deceive search engines, while not providing useful information at all and of course can be regarded as distrusted information; finally, there are pages that do not clearly belong to any of these two categories [12]. So, in our opinion, web spam detection can not be simply considered as a problem of classification which most of the traditional work do [2, 4]. In fact, it can be regarded as a ranking problem which arises recently in the social science and in information retrieval where human preferences play a major role [13, 14]. The detail of ranking problem will be introduced in section 3.2.

2.2   Trust, Content Trust and Spam Detection

On the other hand, trust is an integral component in many kinds of human interaction, allowing people to act under uncertainty and with the risk of negative consequences. Human users, software agents, and increasingly, the machines that provide services all need to be trusted in various applications or situations. Trust can be used to protect data, to find accurate information, to get the best quality service, and even to bootstrap other trust evaluations [3]. In order to evaluate the reliability of the web resource, content trust was proposed as a promising way to solve the problem. So, it is promising to use content trust to model the reliability of the information, and solve the problem of web spam detection. Content trust was first introduced by Gil et al. on the International World Wide Web Conference in 2006. They discussed content trust as an aggregate of other trust measure, such as reputation, in the context of Semantic Web, and introduced several factors that users consider in detecting whether to trust the content provided by a web resource. The authors also described a simulation environment to study the models of content trust. In fact, the real value of their work is to provide a starting point for further exploration of how to acquire and use content trust on the web.

Trust has been utilized as a promising mechanism to solve the problem of spam detection, and this kind of work including [10], [15], [16], [17] and [18]. TrustRank [10] proposed by Gyongyi et al. maybe the first mechanisms to calculate a measure of trust for Web pages. It is based on the idea that good sites seldom point to spam sites and people trust these good sites, and in their more recent paper [16], the concept of "spam mass" is introduced to estimate a page's likehood to be spam. B. Wu et al. [15] expand on this approach to form a better performing Topic TrustRank. It combines topical information with the notion of trust on the Web based on link analysis techniques. Metaxas et al. [17] also describe an effective method to detect link spam using trust, which propagate from a seed set of spam pages along incoming links. Further more, L. Nie et al. [18] describe and compare various trust propagation methods to estimate the trustworthiness of each Web pages. They propose how to incorporate a given trust estimate into the process of calculating authority for a cautious surfer.

In fact, before trust was introduced into the effort of fighting web spam, it has been used in other system, such as reputation systems and peer-to-peer systems. Kamvar et al. [19] proposed a trust-based method to determine reputation in peer-to-peer systems. Guha et al. [20] study how to propagate trust scores among a connected network of people. Moreover, varieties of trust metrics have been studied, as well as algorithms for transmission of trust across individual webs of trust, including ours previous research [21, 22].

Compared to the research summarized above, we utilize trust mechanism based on actual content of the web pages, and explore a set of evidence to denote the content trust of the web pages, and propose a novel content trust model with ranking algorithm for detecting spam.

3   Content Trust Model for Spam Detection

In human society, evidence for trust plays a critical role in people's everyday life, and historians, juries and others rely on evidence to make judgments about the past and trust what will happen in the future. In a legal setting, evidence is defined as follows:

(Oxford English Dictionary) *"Evidence is information, whether in the form of personal testimony, the language of documents, or the production of material objects that is given in a legal investigation, to establish the fact or point in question"*

In light of this, based on previous research, we explore a set of salient evidences which can help to tell a web page is a spam or not, and most of them based on the content of web pages. Moreover, some of these evidences are independent of the language a page is written in, others use language-dependent statistical properties.

The overview of the proposed content trust model can be descried in Figure 1.

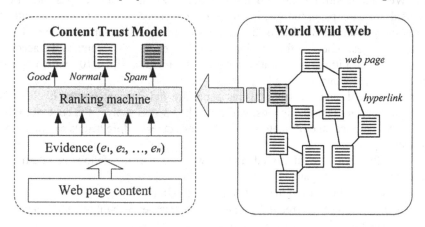

Figure 1 Overview of the content trust model

We first analysis the content of the web page, and extract some salient evidence which can be used to evaluate the reliability of the content. Then, we train a ranking machine using the evidence as the feature to predict the trustworthy of the future web pages. It is obvious that the evidence extraction and the rank machine training is the key. We descript them in more detail in the following section.

3.1   Evidence for detecting web spam

There are many salient factors that affect how users determine trust in content provided by Web pages. So we extract the following evidence for detecting web spam based on previous research [2, 4, 5].

One popular practice when creating spam pages is "keyword stuffing". During keyword stuffing, the content of a web page is stuffed with a number of popular words. So, the first evidence can be number of words in the page. Evidence of an excessive number of words in the title of a page is a better indicator of spam than the number of words in the full page, which can be defined as the second evidence. The third evidence takes keyword stuffing one step further, concatenating a small number (2 to 4) of words to form longer composite words.

Another common practice among search engines is to consider the anchor text of a link in a page as annotation describing the content of the target page of that link. Evidence of higher fractions of anchor text may imply higher prevalence of spam, which can be defined as the fourth evidence. Some search engines use information from certain HTML elements in the pages that are not rendered by browsers. We define the fifth evidence of fraction of visible content. Some spam pages replicate their content several times in an attempt to rank higher. To locating redundant content within a page, we measure the redundancy of web pages by the compression ratio, which defined as the sixth evidence.

The seventh evidence is to examine where the keywords in spam pages come from. We first identified the 100 most frequent words in our corpus, and then computed, for each page, the fraction of words contained in that page found among the 100 most common words. For the eighth evidence, we examined the prevalence of spam in pages, based on the fraction of stop-words that they contain. To account for this potential pitfall, and we also measure the fraction of the 100 most popular words contained within a particular page.

The ninth and tenth evidence in this paper are Independent n-gram likelihoods and Conditional n-gram likelihoods, which can be used to analyze the content of the page for grammatical and ultimately semantic correctness. More details can be found in reference [2].

Except the evidence discussed above, we also use the following additional evidence to detect web spam.

-     Various features of the host component of a URL
-     IP addresses referred to by an excessive number of symbolic host names
-     The rate of evolution of web pages on a given site
-     Excessive replication of content

Table 1 describes the major evidence used in this paper.

Table 1 Evidence for spam detection

	Name	How to calculate
1	Number of words in the page	the number of words in the page
2	Number of words in the page title	the number of words in title
3	Average length of words	$\dfrac{\sum \text{the length (in characters) of each non-markup words}}{\text{the number of the words}}$
4	Amount of anchor text	$\dfrac{\text{all words (excluding markup) contained in anchor text}}{\text{all words (excluding markup) contained in the page}}$
5	Fraction of visible content	$\dfrac{\text{the aggregate length of all non-markup words on a page}}{\text{the total size of the page}}$
6	Compressibility	$\dfrac{\text{the size of the compressed page}}{\text{the size of the uncompressed page}}$
7	Fraction of page drawn from globally popular words	$\dfrac{\sum \text{the number of each words among the N most common words}}{\text{the number of all the words}}$

8	Fraction of globally popular words	$\dfrac{\text{the number of the words among the N most common words}}{N}$
11	Various features of the host component of a URL	
12	IP addresses referred to by an excessive number of symbolic host names	
13	Outliers in the distribution of in-degrees and out-degrees of the graph induced by web pages and the hyperlinks between them	
14	The rate of evolution of web pages on a given site	
15	Excessive replication of content	
...	...	

3.2   Ranking machine for spam detection

As we have discussed above. One way of combining our evidence methods is to view the spam detection as a ranking problem. In this case, we want to create a ranking model which, given a web page, will use the page's features jointly in order to correctly rank it in one of several ordered classes, such as good, normal and spam. We follow a standard machine learning process to build out ranking model. In general, constructing a ranking machine involves a training phase during which the parameters of the classifier are determined, and a testing phase during which the performance of the ranking machine is evaluated. The whole process can be described in Figure 2.

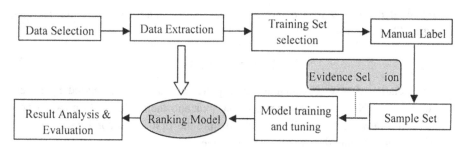

Figure 2 Process of factoid/definition mining from content

The most important process in Figure 2 is evidence selection which forms the features of the proposed ranking model. Besides evidence described above, we also use some normal text features. The total number of the feature is 24 in our implementation of the model. For every web page in the data set, we calculated the value for each of the features, and we subsequently used these values along with the class label for the training of our ranking machine.

In ranking problem, a number of candidates are given and a total order is assumed to exist over the categories. Labeled instances are provided. Each instance is represented by a feature vector, and each label denotes a rank. Ranking SVM [14] is a method which formalizes learning to rank as learning for classification on pairs of instances and tackles the classification issue by using SVM. The reason why we use ranking SVM is because it performs best compare to the other method, such as Naïve Bayesian [24] and decision tree [23] for ranking problem. The experiments result is described in section 4 lately. Here, we only introduce our method of adapting ranking SVM to the problem of spam detection.

In formally, assume that there exists an input space $X \in R^n$, where n denotes number of features. There exists an output space of ranks (categories) represented by labels $Y = \{r_1, r_2, \cdots, r_q\}$ where q denotes number of ranks. Further assume that there exists a total order between the ranks $r_q \succ r_{q-1} \succ \cdots \succ r_1$, where $\succ$ denotes a preference relationship. A set of ranking functions $f \Box F$ exists and each of them can determine the preference relations between instances:

$$\bar{x}_i \succ \bar{x}_j \Leftrightarrow f(\bar{x}_i) \succ f(\bar{x}_j) \tag{1}$$

Suppose that we are given a set of ranked instances $S = \{(\bar{x}_i, y_i)\}_{i=1}^{t}$ from the space $X \times Y$. The task here is to select the best function f' from F that minimizes a given loss function with respect to the given ranked instances.

Herbrich et al. [14] propose formalizing the rank learning problem as that of learning for classification on pairs of instances in the field of information retrieval. We can adapt this method to the spam detection problem in a similar way. First, we assume that f is a linear function.

$$f_{\bar{w}}(\bar{w}, \bar{x}) \tag{2}$$

where $\bar{w}$ denotes a vector of weights and $<\cdot, \cdot>$ stands for an inner product. Plugging (2) into (1) we obtain

$$\bar{x}_i \succ \bar{x}_j \Leftrightarrow \langle \bar{w}, \bar{x}_i - \bar{x}_j \rangle > 0 \tag{3}$$

The relation $\bar{x}_i \succ \bar{x}_j$ between instance pairs $\bar{x}_i$ and $\bar{x}_j$ is expressed by a new vector $\bar{x}_i - \bar{x}_j$. Next, we take any instance pair and their relation to create a new vector and a new label. Let $\bar{x}^{(1)}$ and $\bar{x}^{(2)}$ denote the first and second instances, and let $y^{(1)}$ and $y^{(2)}$ denote their ranks, then we have

$$\left(\bar{x}^{(1)} - \bar{x}^{(2)}, z \right), z = \begin{cases} +1, y^{(1)} \succ y^{(2)} \\ -1, y^{(1)} \prec y^{(2)} \end{cases} \tag{4}$$

From the given training data set S, we create a new training data set S' containing m labeled vectors.

$$S' = \{\bar{x}_i^{(1)} - \bar{x}_i^{(2)}, z_i\}_{i=1}^{m} \tag{5}$$

Next, we take S' as classification data and construct a SVM model that can assign either positive label $z = +1$ or negative label $z = -1$ to any vector $\bar{x}^{(1)} - \bar{x}^{(2)}$.

Constructing the SVM model is equivalent to solving the following Quadratic Optimization problem [14]:

$$\min_{\vec{w}} \sum_{i-1}^{m} \left[1 - z_i \left\langle \vec{w}, \vec{x}_i^{(1)} - \vec{x}_i^{(2)} \right\rangle \right] + \lambda \|\vec{w}\|^2 \qquad (6)$$

The first term is the so-called empirical Hinge Loss and the second term is regularizer.

Suppose that $\vec{w}^*$ is the weights in the SVM solution. Geometrically $\vec{w}^*$ forms a vector orthogonal to the hyperplane of Ranking SVM. We utilize $\vec{w}^*$ to form a ranking function $f_{\vec{w}^*}$ for ranking instances.

$$f_{\vec{w}^*}(\vec{x}) = \left\langle \vec{w}^*, \vec{x} \right\rangle \qquad (7)$$

When Ranking SVM is applied to spam detection, an instance is created from the evidence we proposed in Section 3.1. Each feature is defined as a function of the document content.

4   Simulation Results and Performance Evaluation

4.1   Data configuration

The data set in the following experiments is collected through Google search engine follow the whole process showed in Figure 3. The process of assembling this collection consists of the following two phases: web crawling and then labeling, which are described in the rest of this section.

Figure 3 Process of web spam data collection

We follow the whole spam data collection process proposed in [12]. The crawl was done using the *TrustCrawler* which developed for this research. The crawler was limited to the .cn and .com domain and to 8 levels of depth, with no more than 5,000 pages per host. The obtained collection includes 500,000 million pages, and includes pages from 1000 hosts. The collection was stored in the WARC/0.9 format which is a data format in which each page occupies a record, which includes a plain text header with the page URL, length and other meta-information, and a body with the verbatim response from the Web servers, including the HTTP header. A total of ten volunteer students were involved in the task of spam labeling. The volunteers were provided with the rules of spam web pages described in reference [12], and they were asked to rank a minimum of 200 hosts. Further, we divide out data set in two groups according to the language used in the page. The first data set is composed with English web pages (DS1), and the other is Chinese web pages (DS2).

In order to train our rank machine, we used the pages in the manually ranked data set to serve as our training data set. For our feature set, we used all the metrics described in Section 3. But for Chinese data set, some of the evidence is not suitable, such as "average length of words", and we ignore such features. Here, without loss of generality, every page labeled with three kind of rank: good, normal, and spam. For every web page in the data set, we calculated the value for each of the features, and we subsequently used these values along with the class label for the training of our ranking model.

4.2   Ranking techniques comparison

We experimented with a variety of ranking techniques, and here we only present the following algorithms: decision-tree based ranking techniques (R-DT) [23], Naïve Bayesian based ranker (R-NB) [24] and ranking support vector machine (R-SVM), which modified by us in section 3.2 to suit the problem of spam detection. All algorithms are implemented within the Weka framework [25].

The metric we used to compare the different algorithm here is the ROC (Receiver Operating Characteristics) curve [26], and AUC. An ROC curve is useful for comparing the relative performance among different classifiers, and the area under the ROC (AUC) provides a approach for evaluation which model is better on average. If a ranking is desired and only a dataset with class labels is given, the area under AUC can be used to evaluate the quality of rankings generated by an algorithm. AUC is a good "summary" for comparing two classifiers across the entire range of class distributions and error costs. AUC is actually a measure of the quality of ranking. The AUC of a ranking is 1 (the maximum AUC value) if no positive example precedes any negative example.

Using the metric of AUC, we found that R-SVM based techniques performed best both on DS1 and DS2, but that the other techniques were not far behind. The result is showed in Figure 4. The experiments in the rest of the paper are all carried out with R-SVM.

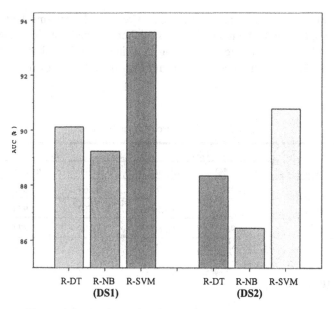

Figure 4 Comparison of varies ranking algorithms on AUC

4.3   Performance of ranking SVM for spam detection

Using all of the aforementioned features, the ranking accuracy after the ten-fold cross validation process is encouraging: 90.13% of our judged pages were ranked correctly, while 9.87% were ranked incorrectly. We can summarize the performance of our ranking machine using a precision- recall matrix (Table 2). More detail about how to calculate recall and precision can be found in reference [1].

The precision-recall matrix shows the recall (the true-positive and true-negative rates), as well as the precision:

Table 2 Recall and precision of our ranking machine

	DS1		DS2	
Rank	Recall (%)	Precision (%)	Recall (%)	Precision (%)
Good	81.34	83.77	83.36	85.95
Normal	95.15	93.84	96.89	91.40
Spam	87.79	88.12	86.04	86.82

Here, the evaluation measure is based on rankings of each web page, which is different from recall and precision measures in traditional classification.

We have also experimented with various techniques for improving the accuracy of our ranking method. Here, we will report on the most popular ones: boosting [13]. This technique essentially creates a set of models, which are then combined to form a composite model. In most cases, the composite model performs better than any individual one (Table 3). More detail of this method can be found in reference [13]

After applying boosting to the ranking machine described above we obtain the following precision/recall values, which improve the accuracy of the method on all the terms.

Table 3 Recall and precision after boosting

	DS1		DS2	
Rank	Recall (%)	Precision (%)	Recall (%)	Precision (%)
Good	84.78	85.95	84.65	86.07
Normal	96.37	95.67	97.67	92.83
Spam	89.96	90.60	86.98	87.05

5 Conclusions

In this paper, we explore a novel content trust model for spam detection algorithm based on evidence of the pages. This method takes the web spam detection task as a ranking problem. And we present how to employ machine learning techniques that combine our evidence to create a highly efficient and reasonably-accurate spam detection algorithm. Experiments show that our method performs very well on the crawled data set. Some of the evidence for spam in this paper may be easily fooled by spammers, so we plan to use more natural language techniques to recognize artificially generated text in our future work, and more accurate machine learning method is also promising to be carried out on real world large-scale datasets.

Acknowledgements

This research was partially supported by the National Natural Science Foundation of China under grant of 60673157, the Ministry of Education key project under grant of 105071 and SEC E-Institute: Shanghai High Institutions Grid under grant of 200301.

References

1. B. Liu, Web Data Mining: Exploring Hyperlinks, Contents, and Usage Data, Springer-Verlag Berlin Heidelberg, (2007)
2. A. Ntoulas, M. Najork, M. Manasse, et al., Detecting Spam Web Pages through Content Analysis. In Proceedings of the 15th International World Wide Web Conference (WWW'06), May 23–26, Edinburgh, Scotland, (2006)

3. Y. Gil, D. Artz, Towards Content Trust of Web Resources. In Proceedings of the 15th International World Wide Web Conference (WWW'06), May 23–26, Edinburgh, Scotland, (2006)

4. D. Fetterly, M. Manasse, M. Najork, Spam, Damn Spam, and Statistics: Using Statistical Analysis to Locate Spam Web Pages. In 7th International Workshop on the Web and Databases, (2004)

5. Z. Gyongyi, H. Garcia-Molina, Web Spam Taxonomy. In 1st International Workshop on Adversarial Information Retrieval on the Web, May (2005)

6. B. Davison, Recognizing Nepotistic Links on the Web. In AAAI-2000 Workshop on Artificial Intelligence for Web Search, July (2000)

7. R. Baeza-Yates, C. Castillo, V. Liopez, PageRank Increase under Different Collusion Topologies. In 1st International Workshop on Adversarial Information Retrieval on the Web, May (2005)

8. L. Page, S. Brin, et al., The PageRank Citation Ranking: Bringing Order to the Web. Stanford Digital Library Technologies Project, (1998)

9. S. Adali, T. Liu, M. Magdon-Ismail, Optimal Link Bombs are Uncoordinated. In 1st International Workshop on Adversarial Information Retrieval on the Web (AIRWeb'05), May (2005)

10. Z. Gyongyi, H. Garcia-Molina, J. Pedersen, Combating Web Spam with TrustRank. In 30th International Conference on Very Large Data Bases, Aug. (2004)

11. G. Mishne, D. Carmel, R. Lempel, Blocking Blog Spam with Language Model Disagreement. In 1st International Workshop on Adversarial Information Retrieval on the Web, May (2005)

12. C. Castillo, D. Donato, L. Becchett, et al., A Reference Collection for Web Spam. SIGIR Forum, 40(2), 11-24 (2006)

13. Y. B Cao, J. Xu, T. Y .Liu et al., Adapting Ranking SVM to Document Retrieval, In Proceedings of the 29th Annual International ACM SIGIR Conference On Research and Development in Information Retrieval, 186-193 (2006)

14. R. Herbrich, T. Graepel, K. Obermayer, Large Margin Rank Boundaries for Ordinal Regression. Advances in Large Margin Classifiers, 115-132 (2000)

15. B. Wu, V. Goel, B. D. Davison, Topical TrustRank: Using Topicality to Combat Web Apam. In Proceedings of the 15th International World Wide Web Conference (WWW'06), May 23–26, Edinburgh, Scotland, (2006)

16. Z. Gyiongyi, P. Berkhin, H. Garcia-Molina, et al, Link Spam Detection Based on Mass Estimation, In Proceedings of the 32nd International Conference on Very Large Databases (VLDB'06), (2006)

17. P. T. Metaxas, J. DeStefano, Web Spam, Propaganda and Trust, In 1st International Workshop on Adversarial Information Retrieval on the Web (AIRWeb'05), May (2005)

18. L. Nie, B. Wu and B. D. Davison. Incorporating Trust into Web Search. Technical Report LU-CSE-07-002, Dept. of Computer Science and Engineering, Lehigh University, (2007)

19. S. D. Kamvar, M. T. Schlosser, H. Garcia-Molina, The Eigentrust Algorithm for Reputation Management in P2P Networks. In Proceedings of the 12th International World Wide Web Conference (WWW'03), Budapest, Hungary,May (2003)

20. R. Guha, R. Kumar, P. Raghavan, and A. Tomkins. Propagation of Trust and Distrust. In Proceedings of the 13th International World Wide Web Conference (WWW'04), New York City, May (2004)

21. W. Wang, G. S. Zeng, L. L. Yuan, A Semantic Reputation Mechanism in P2P Semantic Web, In Proceedings of the 1st Asian Semantic Web Conference (ASWC), LNCS 4185, 682-688 (2006)

22. W. Wang, G. S. Zeng, Trusted Dynamic Level Scheduling Based on Bayes Trust Model. Science in China: Series F Information Sciences, 37(2), 285-296 (2007)

23. F. J. Provost, P. Domingos, Tree Induction for Probability-Based Ranking. Machine Learning, 52(3), 199-215 (2003)

24. H. Zhang, J. Su, Naive Bayesian Classifiers for Ranking, Proceedings of the 15th European Conference on Machine Learning (ECML'04), Springer (2004)

25. I. H. Witten, E. Frank, Data Mining – Practical Machine Learning Tools and Techniques with Java Implementation. Morgan Kaufmann, (2000)

26. F. Provost, T. Fawcett, Analysis and Visualization of Classifier Performance: Comparison under Imprecise Class and Cost Distribution. In Proceedings of the Third International Conference on Knowledge Discovery and Data Mining, AAAI Press, 43-48 (1997)

27. Y. Freund, R. E. Schapire, A Decision-theoretic Generalization of On-line Learning and an Application to Boosting. In European Conference on Computational Learning Theory, (1995)

Applied Computational Trust in Utilities Management: a Case Study on The Town Council of Cava de' Tirreni.

Pierpaolo Dondio[1], Edmondo Manzo[2] and Stephen Barrett[1]
1 Trinity College Dublin, School of Computer Science and Statistics,
Westland Row 2.1 Dublin, Ireland {dondiop,stephen.barrett}@cs.tcd.ie,
WWW home page: http://www.cs.tcd.ie/~dondiop
2 Consultant (until 31.12.2006), City Council of Cava de' Tirreni (SA),
Italy
emanzo@inwind.it
WWW home page: http://www.comune.cava-de-tirreni.sa.it

Abstract. This paper describes an application of computational trust techniques to enhance the water-supply service information system of the Town of Cava de' Tirreni, Italy. The study case covers a population of almost 52 000 people and about 23 000 consumption contracts. The Town Council is responsible for the water supply service and its billing process. A correct billing process requires gathering water consumption data of each citizen, task that is partially not controllable by Town Council personnel and therefore cannot be accomplished properly without the citizen's cooperation. Bad or malicious data are potentially harmful for both parties. The aim of this experimentation is to exploit computational trust techniques to better manage the process of validation of the received data. Computational Trust added value is represented by its autonomic implementation and by its in-depth consideration of social and environmental variables that go beyond simple data validation. The evaluation section, covering 6 years of data, will present the encouraging results obtained.

1 Introduction

This paper proposes an application of computational trust techniques for better managing specific tasks in a large public-sector information system. The study case described here refers to the water supply service in the Town of Cava de' Tirreni, in southern Italy. The Town Council is the only responsible for the water supply service and the billing process. The billing process is computed on the basis of the actual amount of water used by a single user, traced by a counter installed in the user's property. In order to accomplish its tasks, the Town Council needs the collaboration of the citizen.

Please use the following format when citing this chapter:

Dondio, P., Manzo, E. and Barrett S., 2007, in IFIP International Federation for Information Processing, Volume 238, Trust Management, eds. Etalle, S., Marsh, S., (Boston: Springer), pp. 153–168.

The aim of this experimentation is to exploit computational trust techniques to better manage the process of analysing the validity and trustworthiness of the data that the Town Council received from its personnel or from citizens, that can be both affected by human mistaken, maliciousness, lack of experience, failures. An error in the data implies an error on the billing process, damaging the Town Council or the citizen, increasing the claims, delaying the payment process, delaying the Town Council procedures. The water service legislation has recently been changed and the modifications introduced make the present case study more meaningful. Under the new legislation, described in section 2, the right computation of each citizen consumption data became the critical process of the water service management.

Town Council workers are used to gathering consumption data over council territory. However, workers are actually limited in number and not exclusively assigned to this specific task; usually a massive reading of data over the territory requires the employment of fixed term workers and can be accomplished about once a year. External causes (like the lack of accessibility to the property, or the absence of the citizen) can limit the number of data gathered using this channel. Thus, the collaboration of the citizen in such a process is critical.

The analysis of the interactions involved in the service suggested to the authors an enhancement of the process using computational trust. The data transmitted by consumers are partially out of control of the Town Council and malicious values can damage the environment. This satisfies the main requirement for trust to be meaningful: there is a lack of monitoring of an action that may potentially hurt the parties involved or facilitate one party to the detriment of the other.

The authors of this paper chose to use computational trust to enhance the data validation process. Moreover, the automatic way in which computational trust techniques can be embedded in our information system is seen as a helpful added value.

We also expect what S. Marsh called the reduction of complexity [1], obtained by considering only trustworthy possibilities among a set of possible actions.

Finally, the accomplishment of this work is also motivated by the lack of applications of computational trust in information system management and, according to many authors [2], a gap between recommendation/reputation systems and other applications..

The aim of such an experimentation is now described. We seek to investigate the use of computational trust techniques in a new application field, where the same task is accomplished by simple data validation procedures, expecting an improvement. The data available in our study case cover 6 years of service, three of which managed with traditional data validation and three with trust-enhanced techniques. This will allow us to compare the two approaches. Computational trust techniques are expected to obtain more accurate predictions and, as a long-term effect, an increasing trustworthiness of the service perceived by the citizens.

Our application of computational trust techniques to information system management is a first effort to go beyond the data validation one. Many public bodies that manage a scenario similar to ours adopt data validation techniques to test the validity of data. These techniques in general do not go beyond a comparison among data values, possibly using statistical analysis.

On the contrary, we assume that our situation is not a mere problem of data validation (*are these data valid?*), but it should also be treated as a problem of trust (*can I trust these data?*). Stating this means a deeper and broader understanding of the situation. Trust is not only concerned with the validity of the data, its meaning referring to the entity that issued those data and the context in which they were issued, considering past history as well as social interactions, domain-specific expertise, present evidences and other soft factors. In our scenario this means considering if the citizen is a regular payer or if the worker is competent. Thus, the techniques applied in this work range from simple data validation to more trust-specific techniques.

A trust analysis contains more information than simple data validation. For example, data that clearly result out of standard are for data validation techniques simply an error. From a trust perspective, if the data were issued by trustworthy entities, the error could be a mechanical failure or a mistake rather than a malicious attempt, situation more likely when the entity is not trustworthy. This extra information could possibly turn into different actions to correct the anomaly: simply contact the trustworthy citizen for another data reading or warn him of a possible failure; send a Council worker or a legal notice to the untrustworthy user.

By using trust-based techniques we seek to go beyond data validation for two reasons: a better accuracy on the predictions and more motivated and comprehensible reasons to justify the decision-making process. Data validation cannot grant trust, it only detects data anomalies based exclusively on the data value. Trust-added value begins exactly when data validation ends: given that certain data have some anomalies, can I trust them or not? If I grant trust I accept the suspected data anomalies. If the decision was correct – the ultimate goal of trust-based technique - I would avoid additional checking workload without harmful consequences.

Moreover, trust techniques are proactive while data validation is concerned with data only once they have arrived. For example, the generic trust mechanism *pluralism* states that data confirmed by multiple sources, better if independent, are more trustworthy. Thus, this implies to re-organize the process of data collection standing by this principle, in our case the rotation of the personnel over different areas of the Town Council during the data gathering process.

The paper is organized as follows: section 2 describes our scenario and the processes involved in the water supply service, section 3 describes related works that encompass similar approaches in the area of utilities management and computational trust references, section 4 describes the trust techniques that can suit our problem domain, section 5 describes the mechanisms that have been put in place to enhance the data validation procedure, section 6 describes our evaluation and finally we describes our conclusions and possible future extension of the project.

2. Water Supply Management System in Cava de' Tirreni

This section describes the experimentation scenario, explaining the water-supply service processes, actors involved and the dimensions of our study case. The Italian water supply service is generally managed by each Town Council on the territory. In this work we performed our evaluation in collaboration with the Town Council of Cava de' Tirreni, that entirely manages the water-supply service on its territory.

Cava de' Tirreni is a town of about 52 000 people, situated in southern Italy, 50 km south of Naples and 9 km north of Salerno, as shown in fig. 1. Some characteristics of the process are relevant for our experimentation.

The Town has a territory of 36,46 km^2, its population distributed in 19 different districts and a main centre. Water supply service operations are carried on dividing the territory in 30 main areas. The number of contracts up to 31/12/2006 is 24 357: 20658 private and 3699 business. All the customer service operations are carried out by a dedicate office in the Town Council with a personnel of 4 people. The Town Council has also 5 permanent workers, dedicated to counters installation, maintenance and collecting consumption data. In peak periods it also hires 3 or 4 temporary workers for a period of 6 months.

Fig. 1. Campania Region and Cava de' Tirreni.

The water supply service is regulated by a national legislation that changed in 2002. The change, concerning the billing procedure, is very relevant for our scenario. Until 2002, the citizen had to pay his consumption of water according to a fixed minimum per annum, established on the contract. This minimum consumption was paid in any case, regardless of its actual utilization, and only the exceeding part of water was paid according to its actual amount. The minimum consumption was a quite accurate estimation of the expected consumption, and thus the exceeding part had usually a minor impact on the total income.

Between 01/01/2002 and 31/12/2004 the minimum consumption for domestic use was progressively reduced and, since 1st January 2005, this quota has been removed as the new legislation prescribes. The invoice sent to users since 2005 is entirely dependent on the actual quantity of water used. The process of collecting water consumption data becomes essential and, if not properly carried out, much more harmful for the parties involved than before.

The aim of the Town Council Office is to send invoices as accurate as possible, i.e. to collect the exact amount of water consumption for the highest number of users. A lesser amount in the invoice results in damages the Council, generally not because this income goes wasted (it is almost always gathered when the data are collected properly), but because this mistake affects the correctness of the Town Council balance. A higher amount damages the consumer and at the same time the Town Council itself, because the invoice is usually not paid for and claimed. The user will refer to the Council Customer Care, delaying the payment process, triggering extra control procedures done mainly by a Town Council worker and forcing the office to re-calculate some invoices.

The amount of each invoice is established by the data received by the Council or, if not available, on a statistically computed value. The data collection process is now analysed in detail. The water consumption data are traced by counters installed in every user's property. By law, once a year all the citizens' counters must be read by personnel of the Council. This procedure is called the *"massive reading of counter"*, and it is carried out by dividing the Council territory in 30 areas and assigning different areas to permanent or temporary workers. Note that this procedure does not guarantee the complete collection of the data required, since some users may be temporarily absent or the property inaccessible. For each user there are usually multiple data collected in different periods over the years.

During the year data are collected by relying on the collaboration of the users and, in special case (verifications, suspected failures), by resorting to Town Council workers. In order to compute the amount of an invoice, all the consumption data received by the various channel are considered. In 2006 the total number of readings used to compute invoices was 26 192, 57% of which collected during the period of "massive reading" by permanent and temporary workers, 19% by the permanent term workers outside that period and 24% by the citizens. It is clear that users play an important role in the process: they send their consumption data - and that is when malicious users can transmit erroneous data or data in contrast with the reading done by operators.

3. Related Works

This section covers three aspects: computational trust techniques definition, current related applications of computational trust, how other public authorities or utilities manage a process analogous to ours.

3.1 Computational Trust techniques

Computational trust seeks to exploit the human notion of Trust into the digital world. A largely accepted definition of Trust in mathematical terms is the classical definition of Gambetta [3], where Trust is a particular level of the subjective probability with which an agent assesses that another agent will perform a particular action, both before he can monitor such action and in a context in which it affects his own action. Gambetta's definition influences the quantitative representation of trust as a probability, but, as noticed by Castelfranchi and Falcone in [4], it doesn't take into consideration mental processes and mechanisms involved in the quantification of such a probability that represents the ingredients of a trust-based decision. In our paper we underline the need to give clear justifications for a trust-based decision by making explicit motivations and listing the evidence behind a decision.

Fig. 2 represents the elements of a computational trust solution. A trust-based decision in a specific domain is a multi-stage process: the selection of the required input data (trust evidences) by mean of a notion of trust (trust model); the processing of the inputs producing a trust value, and the actual decision considering computed outputs and exogenous factors, like disposition or risk assessments. As a dedicated trust infrastructure (PKI, Recommendations) is not part of the system considered in this paper (and its utility should be investigated), evidences must be directly collected and exploited selecting appropriate domain elements and dynamics. We apply evidence-based trust where the trust computation is supported entirely by elements of the application. One of the authors of this work performed previous application-contained trust computation in the Wikipedia project [5].

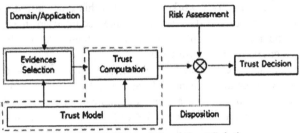

Fig. 2 A Computational Trust Solution

Computational trust identifies trust-based techniques that humans adopt in the decisions whenever trust or distrust is involved. These techniques are taken from interdisciplinary study of Trust, encompassing social science, psychology, cognitive approaches. In section 4 we will describe how we fit some of this mechanisms to our specific domain; here we briefly review the general patterns of these mechanisms referring to some researches in the area that used such mechanisms. The aim of this section is to give a reference to the mechanisms we implemented in our work.

The importance of memory and past history has been largely recognized in many trust models. For instance, the *trustcomp* community defined trust as "a non enforceable prediction of the future behaviour of an entity based on past evidence" [6]. In the *past-evidence paradigm*, implemented for example in the Secure trust engine [7], the trustor collects outcomes of past interactions to compute a trust value for the trustee. Past evidences should be collected in significant numbers, the external conditions should remain stable for the evidences to have sense. The entity with which we are interacting must be recognized in order to bind entity and outcomes. Outcomes (or trust values) can be received and shared with other entities in order to exploit third party experience to assess trust. The sharing of information is related to the Recommendation system, largely studied in centralized and decentralized environment. Related problems studied encompass privacy protection and the identification of malicious users. By exploiting the transitivity of trust values, a Social Network [8] can be constructed and trust values propagated through the links of the network.

A significant approach to trust is represented by the *probability-based* approach. Probability-based trust performs trust calculation by applying the theory of probability over relevant sets of data. In general, the underlying idea is that trust is the probability that the trustee will fulfil the expectation of the trustor. The method required that a sufficient set of triples (trustee, action, outcome) are collected in order to estimate the probability associated with a specific couple entity-action. Examples include Despotovic [9], who used the maximum likelihood theorem to predict good outcomes in a p2p recommendation system for ebusiness, and Wuang [10], who applied the bayesian probability in eBay.

Similarity between entities is another mechanism to propagate trust values. Similarity as a source of trust was studied by Ziegler and Golbeck in [11]. In [12], Castelfranchi and Falcone proposed a computational model of their cognitive approach to trust, encompassing similarity in the sources of the mental believes composing trust. *Categorization* was indicated as another mechanism, where trust values are propagated among categories of entities. Their work consider also the concept of the *pluralism* and *multiplicity of sources* to enforce the trustworthiness, especially when many independent sources confirm the same data in different situations. Finally, risk management and assessment is often coupled with trust analysis (see Secure [7]), since the action of trust towards an entity could be not convenient from a risk point of view.

3.2 Computational Trust and Security application and Consumption Data collection in Utilities management.

Many formal trust models have been defined since 1996, when Stephen Marsh proposed the first model of computational trust. Despite these well-established researches, according to Seigneur [2], a "big effort has been put in defining a formal model of trust, but there are still many applications that needs to be considered and many evidences that need to be identified and processed".

Computational trust methods have gained successful applications in e-commerce scenarios like amazon.com, online auctions systems like ebay, spam email filtering, recommendations and rating systems like epinions.com, movietrust.com (in the social network variant), online forums.

In business, computational trust has a lesser range of application as compared to parallel researches of risk management, security and privacy. The authors find it difficult to identify applications similar to the one presented in this paper, especially due to the peculiar field of application. While reputation-based and recommendation techniques seem to have several applications, the application of trust in business is mainly security-oriented: digital signature protection, privacy management, clustering of customers and sellers [13]. The latter approach, involving collaborative filtering, fuzzy logic-based classification is relevant to some classification models used in this paper. In general, computational trust techniques are not still exploited in the management of information systems specifically for an administrative task like ours. In this system, information is inserted relying on users' cooperation, and lack of control and malicious actions are possible. Data have often been kept safe using key infrastructures, but they do not guarantee their trustworthiness.

Many public Utilities manage a scenario similar to ours adopting only data validation. In the Province of Salerno many public companies are managing water supply services for cities up to 20.000 users [14]. Our survey of the used methods (limited to the Italian territory) showed how techniques beyond data validation are not implemented. The techniques adopted by the institution we analysed can be summarized in a common scheme. The consumption data received, collected by a wide type of channel, are rejected by the system if :

a) in the consumptions database there are previous data greater than the last data consumption (situation technically impossible)

b) the consumption database contains data equal to the previous one

c) the reading data are lower than those already involved in an invoice process.

If the data do not belong to any of the above situations they will be saved in the database, otherwise they will be rejected. The procedure guarantees data consistency and prevents only a mismatching event during the invoice calculation process, since the data rejected will not be involved in any invoice calculation. No other information except the data value is considered.

The same system is applied to other utilities management. Enel [15], the national Italian supplier of energy, based its billing on the same process.

In 1998 the Italian Ministry of Treasure established the *redditometro* ("income evaluation meter"), [16] a mechanism to identify tax returns with anomalous values. On a larger scale, this example is conceptually similar to ours: tax return is done by citizens and it is partially out of control by the state, since controls are obviously not possible on every single citizen. The mechanism works using the presumptive value that every citizen should pay their taxes according to their category. Each category of workers, assets or properties has an estimated expected revenue attached to it, computed performing average among categories of workers, the so called *ministerial study of professional categories*. The value of a tax return should not exceed a certain threshold for the expected values. If it does, more controls should be done. The system reflects the idea of having a predetermined amount, similar to the water supply system preceding 2002. Anyway, clear differences make our scenario more complex: the need for accurate values (expected values are not enough), the possibility of claims by the citizen in the short time, yearly balance requirements.

4. Fitting Computational Trust Techniques

In this paragraph we underline the elements of the process that we found useful for the application of the trust mechanism.

Categorization of users. The Town Council contracts are divided into two general categories: private and business. For each category there are some sub-categories that better specify the water utilization. Private sub-categories are defined as follows: residential home, secondary home, private garage, loft etc. If a house is not the users' habitual residence (it is the case of a holiday house, for instance), then it is classified as a secondary residence; commercial or business sub-categories differ according to water utilization: restaurants, hotels, hospitals, hospices, laundries, industries, agriculture, cinemas, shops, etc. The categorization of the users will sustain the application of *categorization* and *similarity* trust mechanisms. The category specified by the contract is not merely a classification of the users but it implies the utilization of the water for the correct and declared scope.

Sources of consumption data. We can identify three channels of consumption data acquisition. The first channel ("O") is represented by the data collected by permanent Council workers while carrying out their normal tasks. The second channel ("L") is represented by the data acquired by the temporary (L1) and permanent (L2) workers during the "massive reading" period. The third channel ("A") is data collected by the users. Data are collected dividing the council territory in 30 areas. The division is made to better manage the workers over the Council territory and to enhance the prediction of the reading, if necessary. In fact, in this last case, the workers collect the reading data at least once a year in a default period in the same area. The classification of data sources allows binding past data analysis to its relative source of acquisition (past evidence mechanism), while the possibility of having different types of sources over the different areas sustains the use of *multiple sources* mechanisms.

Past history (consumption data). Each user's past data are recorded. Past invoices are recorded, along with all the data consumption readings used to compute each invoice. These historical data are the input required by statistical trust mechanism. We shall consider the number of data acquired, but also the number of data accepted and rejected by the system for each customer, from which we can deduct the quality of the users' data. The minimum consumption quota, that in the year before 2002 was the key datum used for computing the invoice, is also taken into account as a statistical reference.

Family Composition. Trust mechanisms based on past data or past interactions rely on the stability of the entity under analysis: a change in entity's properties can invalidate past data and trust computation. The number of people in a family is an essential information to estimate the consumption data. Components' number may vary during the year and the contract may not have been updated (or there is no possibility to change it). This is why we linked our information system with the council registry database, to avoid that a change in the family composition could invalidate past data and erroneously alter the reputation of a user.

Payments Status and Invoices Status. Past payment dates and status are an important piece of information. We can understand if the user usually pays regularly, with delays or if he was forced to pay. There are five levels of notice that the Town Council can issues, from the simple warning to various legal notices and contract suspension. We considered also if the citizen received some reimbursement due to an erroneously overcharged invoice. These data represent the past interaction between the citizen and the Town Council and an important source of mutual trust evaluation.

Failures: The Town Council is responsible for the maintenance of the public pipeline network; each possible failure in the public network is monitored and controlled by the Town Council, while the end-users' pipes, from the counter to the domestic network, are the users' responsibility. Only a Town Council operator can change a counter; thus it is possible to trace the counter installation and reparation done by a specific operator. Using this information, if a counter has just been replaced, it is unlikely that the transmitted data are erroneous because multiple failures are unlikely. In this case trust is coupled with event probability.

5. A trust-based enhanced system

In order to provide a computational trust solution, we had to identify which elements of the domain are trust evidence, as we did in section 4, define one or more trust metrics, i.e. how to evaluate the trust evidence gathered to produce a trust value TV and decide to trust or not according to the trust value and the set of evidence.

Table 1 shows the elements used in our trust metric. The relative importance of each element in the final aggregated trust value is specified. Our trust metric is case-sensitive, and it computes trust values usually in two stages. Stage 2 is considered only if the resulting trust value after stage 1 is not enough to accept data.

Table 1. Trust factors table. The impact of each factor is shown in the 3 general cases, with the stage of computation (in brackets).

Trust Factor	Case a	Case b		Case C	
		Stage 1	Stage 2	Stage 1	Stage 2
Sub-category		High		Medium	
Past Consumption Data		Medium		High	
Past Payments	Low		Medium		Medium
Number of Readings		Low		Medium	
Channel of acquisition	Low	Medium			High
Source Rotation		Low		Low	
Minimum Quota				Medium	
User's past data rejection rate					Medium
Counter Maintenance	Low		Low		Medium
Family Status				High	

Besides the trust value for a specific data, our system keeps track also of a global trust value, not referring to specific consumption data but to the users, i.e. a value that summarizes all users' previous data validation sessions.

The trust-based system can be used in many ways. A trust value can be produced in an autonomic way, represented by a numeric value in [0..1]. However, this is a limited representation that may hide (or lose) details. That is why the system can list all the reasons behind a computation, showing all the trust evidences used and their individual value for the user under analysis.

All the information is also available to the help-desk operator trough a new user-end interface, in order to facilitate a human-based analysis. The operator can query the system and handle special and fuzzy cases, usually in front of the user in the Help-Desk office, using soft skills and direct knowledge of the user.

The consumption data for each contract are saved in a *consumption database* that we enhanced to support our trust information. The database shows, for each consumption datum, the date of acquisition, the counter's value, if the data are involved in any invoice, the acquisition's channel, the worker who collected them and their state (active/not active). Active data are valid and they contribute to invoice calculation while non active data are data rejected by the invoice calculation process.

For the Town Council operator, two data panels (reading data panel and user panel) have been added to facilitate the analysis of data and support the decision making process. The panels contains information on the family composition as well, taken from the civil registry database that we linked. The examination is helped by the use of the *consumption data panel* application: it allows the operator to divide the cases of evaluation and it gives each contract a complete overview of water consumption. The panel presents three different filter: a) invalid consumption; b) zero consumption: c) greater or lower than expected. These are the three general cases, that are treated differently: case a is a clear situation that can be faced with simple data validation, while case b and c are complex cases requiring a trust-based analysis. The aim is to validate consumption data, that should be the exact amount, or to predict the water consumption. The evaluation system of the reading data is shown in figure 4 .

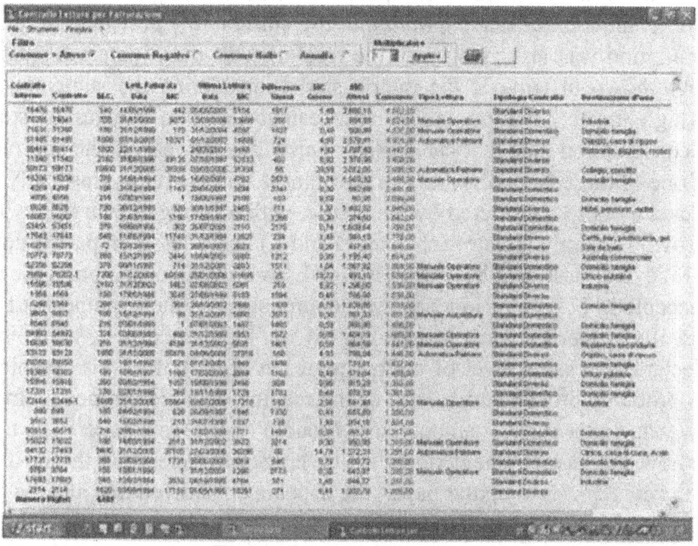

Fig. 3. Consumption data panel

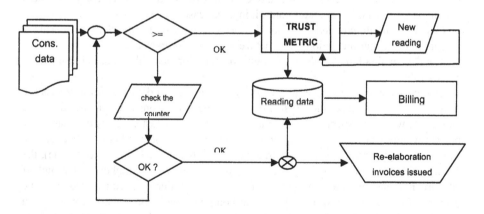

Fig. 4. Evaluation system

Case a: last consumption data are lower than the previous. In this case data are invalid and rejected (total consumption cannot obviously decrease). Trust is not applied to this situation, but only mere data comparison. Invalid data may be a consequence of the citizen makes confusion with other counters like gas. New reading data are collected by a permanent worker (only permanent workers can check and, if needed, replace the counter). These new data are compared by the rejected one and, if the situation is confirmed and the counter is working properly, this means that past data and correspondent invoices were overestimated. The operator re-calculates the last one and, if necessary, also the previous water consumption invoices, issuing a reimbursement note in favour of the citizen.

The consumption data accepted by the process (case b and c) are subject to the "data evaluation system" based on computational trust techniques.

Case b: evaluation of reading data that are equal to the previous. In this case, the data consumption was less than 1 m^3, the resolution of the counter. A trust metric is applied. As shown in table 1, the metric starts considering the sub-category of the contract (high impact): only some specific categories, like garages or stores, have expected consumption data that can be less than 1 m^3 per year. If the contract doesn't belong to one of these categories its trustworthiness will decrease drastically. Anyway, past user data are also considered by the metric, with a strong impact if they have been done by Town Council Operator (channel O and L) and a lesser impact if collected by the user. If several past data by channel O or L confirm a consumption close to zero, data are accepted. In case of low trust value after stage 1, the hypothesis of malicious data is usually discarded since, according to our domain expert, a malicious user usually declares the same level of consumption, in order not to raise suspicions. The counter is probably broken and halted, or the reading data are erroneous. In this case, with a low value after stage 1, an operator is sent to check the counter. The trust metric considers now the past payment status of the citizen to determine the next user trust value. If the citizen was a regular payer, the data are considered true and the possibility of a mistake or failure higher. The user trust value is not lessened. If the citizen had a bad payment history or a recently replaced counter, user's trust value is lessened and, if the user's trust value reaches a lower threshold, the Town council may decide to send a legal notice instead of an operator control, in many case useless.

Case c: evaluation of reading data that are greater than the previous ones. This is the core of our experimentation, the most frequent and complex case.

The data evaluation module verifies the consumption data, like in case b. Sub-cases are possible:

1) Data are as expected (i.e. trustworthy), so the reading data successfully pass the evaluation. In this case the trust metric computation considers if the data are compatible with the expected data, computed on statistical past consumption data used in past invoices (thus accepted). The trust metric considers the number of data available (more data, higher trust value), the period covered (short period, lower trust value), the channel of acquisition (more acquisitions by permanent worker, higher trust value). If data are not enough, the old minimum consumption quota is considered, but the resulting trust value is lower than the one computed with user-related consumption data. The sub-category is considered as well, enforcing or decreasing the trust value with a medium impact. According to this consideration, data may have enough trust value to be accepted, increasing the user's trust value.

2) greater/lower than expected. The data consumption is not applicable from a data validation point of view. We need a more sophisticated trust-based analysis to understand its meaning.

Data are greater than expected. Trust metric starts evaluating how much the data are above the old minimum consumption quota. If the data are compatible, the metric considers the sub-category. Even if the data are correct, the consumption may not be compatible for the category. For example, this is the case of a contract declared for a specific use (such as a shop) and actually applied to a factory. This affects the general user trust value, since the user is not using the water as his contract allows. This reason, when the user's trust values are decreased several times for this reason, can lead to an inspection by the Town Council operator and the user can be forced to change contract and pay a penalty fee.

After stage 1, the trust metric considers now the payment status of the user and the channel of acquisition. If the data were taken by a the citizen and the citizen is a regular payer, the user's trust value is not changed and usually the system suggests to contact the user for another data transmission, to double check it. The user is trustworthy; there is no need to send an operator. If everything is confirmed, the data are accepted and user's trust value is unchanged, since the situation is considered anomalous. In fact, only case a) can increase the user's trust value. The trustworthy user may have a leakage in his pipe network he did not realize and by contacting him the Council increases its Service Quality in the respect of its citizens. If the user is not a good payer - for example the user doesn't pay the invoices because he thinks the consumption invoiced is not right -, a Town Council Operator is sent to check the reading.

Data are lower than expected. If the data are lower than expected, the subcategory and the channel of acquisition play an important role in the trust metric. The other trust factors (table 1) are similar to the previous case and the procedure followed is the same. The difference is that this case has a worse impact on the user trust value than in previous cases. In case the counter is checked by a Town Council operator and the low consumption is not confirmed, the user's trust value decreases. Note that, from the Council point of view, the previous case is more critical, since the Council is a public body and thus considers better to underestimate an invoice than to make the user pay more than the right amount.

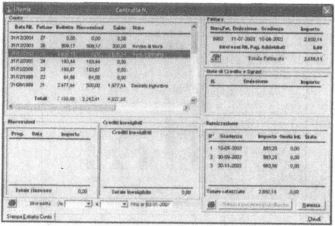

Fig. 5. Consumer overview panel

Finally, for the cases in which a trust metric is used (b,c), the trust value decreases gradually in time until there is a Town Council Operator intervention. For instance, even if the data successfully passed the validation, if the last reading by an operator was two years ago, all the trust values are reduced. When the trust value decreases under a certain threshold, a reading by a Town Council operator is needed to boost the trust value again. When this analysis is done interactively by a help desk operator, the consumer overview panel permits to see the majority of the requested information. This panel (fig. 5) allows the operator to know the total invoice issued, the payment status, the credit notes issued, the irrevocable credits, the collected credits for each contract.

6. Evaluation

Our evaluation covers six years of data, from 2000 to 2005. Our enhanced mechanism became fully operative in 2003. Before applying computational trust techniques the Town Council Customer Care experienced (i) long queues at the help desk, (ii) frequent claims by consumers, that implied extra workload for Council desk operators, (iii) the claims were usually accepted by the Customer Care, meaning the issue of loads of reimbursement notes and deteriorating the level of trust of the citizen towards the Town Council. The introduction of computational trust techniques should give a more accurate estimation and thus reduce the claims. Our evaluation is based on the percentage of income estimated over the actual total income received by the Town Council. The difference between these two values is the total amount of invoices claimed by the citizen and reimbursed. If this percentage is low, this means that predictions were accurate and few invoices were claimed. The total amount of income is not a valid metric, since it could vary, and it is not a Town Council goal to increase the total income (a public bodies is non-profit) but to predict the right income. Our system, started in the year 2002, in few years provided the following advantages:

1. reduction of claims at the customer care desk;
2. reduction of the total amount of credit notes issued;
3. reduction of the difference between estimated and actual incoming

Graph 1. Actual and Estimated Incoming.

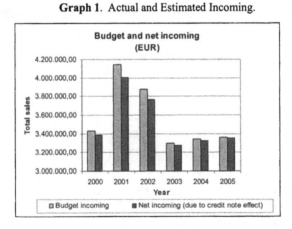

Graphs 1 and 2 display the result of our experimentation. Before proceeding to discuss the graphs it is advisable to underline that in the fiscal year 2000 most of the invoices were calculated according to the minimum quota consumption. In the year 2001 the Council introduced the *"massive reading of counters"* that become fully operative in the year 2002. With this new process a greater number of reading data was acquired than in the past. Consequently, the invoices issued for the fiscal year 2001 and 2002 contained also the extra consumption of the previous years (max 5 years before)

if the user exceeded the minimum quota. In fact, only when consumption data are available is it possible to calculate the exceeding part of the water. This explains the high income of the fiscal years 2001 and 2002. Since 2003 the income has been almost constant (some increments on the charges and a growth of total users explain the small increase), which by itself represents a good result: big variance in the amount means bad previous estimations, as is the case of the remarkable gap in year 2000, 2001 and 2002.

Graph 2 summarizes the reduction of the total amount of reimbursements. This is directly linked to the claims done by the citizens, and their number (since the amount of reimbursement has a low variance). Graph 2 shows the percentage of reimbursement over the total yearly amount. We can notice that in the fiscal year 2000 most invoices were based on fixed - minimum consumption and that year credit notes were issued for 1.27% of the total budget income. For the years 2001 and 2002 this percentage strongly increased while it began to decrease after the introduction of our enhanced system. In the year 2005 the total amount of credit notes issued is 0.17%, a clearly encouraging low value. We believe these results are not only due to a more precise system, but also to a better cooperation on the side of the users, even if quantitative metric for evaluating this cooperation is not yet implemented.

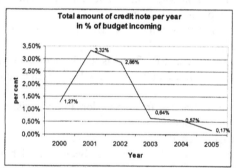

Graph 2. Percentage of income reimbursed over the actual total income.

7. Conclusions and Future Works

In this paper we described an application of computational trust techniques to enhance the water supply information system of Cava de' Tirreni, a middle size Town Council in Italy. We described the water consumption invoice system in detail, a process where citizens' collaboration plays a critical role. We showed how the process of water consumption validation, necessary for a correct invoice system, can be enhanced by introducing, along with usual data validation techniques, computational trust techniques. Using the latter approach data are accepted or rejected not only on the basis of their numerical values, but also considering the quality of the source by which the data have been collected, the reliability of the identity issuing the data and some statistical and environmental variables that may affect the data.

The experimentation has covered a period of observation of 6 years. Our results showed how the trust-enhanced predictions have achieved better results: the difference between the estimated income, based on predictions, and the real income – after the necessary checks – has continuously decreased. This is reflected on the number of invoices claimed by the citizens and cancelled by the system. These results have brought many benefits for the Town Council, such as lesser delays in payments and a reduced workload for Council customer care operators. In our future developments, we will focus on a more detailed tracking of the process and we will seek to make the process more autonomic. We will also seek to apply the system on a larger scale, involving water supply companies that are managing several Town Councils services. In a larger scale experiment, several processes that in our experiment are still carried out manually because of the limited number of variables –such as the management of Town Council operators - will be regulated by autonomic trust procedures based on past history and recommendations.

8. References

[1] Marsh, S. Formalizing Trust as a Computational Concept. PhD thesis, University of Stirling, D. of Mathematics 1994

[2] Seigneur J.M. Ambitrust? Immutable and Context Aware Trust Fusion. Technical Report, Univ. of Geneva, 2006

[3] D. Gambetta, Trust: Making and Breaking Co-operative Relations Basil Blackwell, Oxford 1988.

[4] Castelfranchi, C., Falcone, R.. Trust is much more than subjective probability: Mental components and sources of trust. 32nd Hawaii International Conference on System Sciences, 2000.

[5] P. Dondio et al. Extracting trust from domain analysis: a study on Wikipedia, IEEE ATC, Wuhan, China, 2006

[6] Trustcomp group. Website www.trustcomp.org

[7] V. Cahill et al., Using Trust for Secure Collaboration in Uncertain Environments. IEEE Pervasive Computing, Vol. 2, N. 3, July-September 2003

[8] Golbeck, J., Hendler, J., and Parsia, B., Trust Networks on the Semantic Web. University of Maryland, College Park, USA, 2002

[9] Z. Despotovic, Maximum Likelihood Estimation of Peers performance in a P2P network. CIA, Erfurt, Germany, 2006

[10] Wuang Y. et al. Bayesian Network Based Trust Management, IEEE ATC, Wuhan, China, 2006

[11] Castelfranchi, C., Falcone, R., Peluzzo, G. Trust in information sources as a source for trust: a fuzzy approach. AAMAS, Melbourne, Australia, 2003

[12] C. Ziegler, Golbeck J. Investigating correlation between Trust and Similarity. Decision support system 2005.

[13] Meier A., Werro N. Extending a WebShop with fuzzy classification model for online customer. IADIS eSociety Conference, Dublin, Ireland, 2006.

[14] www.atosele.it Water Supply Service Consortium (ATO4) of the Province of Salerno, Italy

[15] Enel, Ente Nazionale Energia Elettrica, www.enel.it

[16] www.agenziaentrate.it, website of the Italian Ministry of Tresaure

A trust protocol for community collaboration

Samuel Galice[1], Marine Minier[1], and Stéphane Ubéda[1]

CITI INSA-Lyon - ARES INRIA Project
CITI, INSA de Lyon, Bâtiment Léonard de Vinci
21 Avenue Jean Capelle, 69621 Villeurbanne Cedex
FirstName.Name@insa-lyon.fr

Abstract. In ambient environments, new security challenges that are not adequately addressed by existing security models appear. In such context, intelligent communication devices participate to spontaneous and self-organized networks where unexpected interactions with unknown devices take place. Without centralized organization, security turns in a risk management problem.

In this paper we propose and analyze a computational model of trust that captures trust dynamics of the human society. In our model, past experiences and recommendations are aggregated in the notion of *history of past interactions* which are protected by cryptographic material. To avoid the trust dissemination, each entity is viewed as an autonomous device and a trust level is computed based only upon selfish evaluation of common trustworthy nodes. Our proposal reduces the complexity of the decision-making process by providing *proved data* that can be the foundation of the final decision. The proposed trust model is described together with an overview of the cryptographic protocol and its security analysis. The trust function is analyzed through intensive simulations depending on the impact of the chosen parameters of the trust evaluation and on the dynamics of the studied groups.

Keywords: trust management framework, cryptographic protocol, Identity-based cryptosystems.

1 Introduction

Nowadays, smart devices such as mobile phones, personal digital assistants and the like, act in a more and more ubiquitous environment. Their wireless communications capabilities grow up very quickly like their computing capacities. New types of services come out from dynamic groups of objects which can act together cooperatively facing various interaction contexts.

Smart communications objects belong to group with long term relations of size scaling from very few (objects belonging to unique person), to hundred of devices. Those objects hosted by people are organized in a social group with common rules. Those communication devices participate to spontaneous and self-organized networks with encountered other mobiles devices and with an always more and more intelligent environment. Contexts of interaction range

Please use the following format when citing this chapter:

Galice, S., Minier, M. and Ubéda, S., 2007, in IFIP International Federation for Information Processing, Volume 238, Trust Management, eds. Etalle, S., Marsh, S., (Boston: Springer), pp. 169–184.

from access to authenticated servers to unexpected interactions with unknown devices.

Such an environment introduces new security challenges that are not adequately addressed by existing security models. Without centralized organization, security turns in a risk management problem where specific trust model and associated cryptographic techniques are required. Each device needs to carry self-contained information and methods to be able to make fully autonomous trust decisions.

In human interaction, trust is a *continuous variable* that is compared to the aim of the interaction to evaluate the risk of the operation. Our computational model of trust captures trust dynamics of the human society. As mentioned in [6], trust is subjective and individual as suggested according to Gambetta's definition [9]: "Trust is the subjective probability by which an individual, Alice, expects that another individual, Bob, performs a given action on which its welfare depends". Trust also depends on stable groups such as family, friends or colleagues at work defining subjective trusted communities.

The aim of this paper is to describe and analyze a complete trust model dedicated to smart mobile communicating devices. Our proposal holds all the desired properties for a distributed trust framework. First of all, the proposed framework *derives from human social system* in order to be socially accepted. Human evaluation of trust is a complex system and is difficult to mimic in a computational model. Therefore, we know that this evaluation is a combination of past experiences and external information that can be simplified as recommendation information. Human evaluation of trust is also depending on the *context of interaction.*

In our trust model, past experiences and recommendations are aggregated in the notion of *history of past interactions* (as proposed in [6]) which are protected by cryptographic material. Context may be derived by collecting past history of objects in the environment. In our model, the acting peer tries to forge a direct experience with the target party using the content of their own histories. We avoid the trust dissemination, each entity is viewed as an autonomous device and the trust evaluation is based only upon selfish evaluation of common trustworthy nodes. The trust level is then computed only after successful transactions corresponding with a positive reputation mechanism as described in [18]. Our proposal reduces the complexity of the decision-making process by providing *proved data* that can be the foundation of the final decision.

Besides already presented properties, our trust model is highly adaptable and parameters can be set to correspond to various model of communities, each with its own trust policy. Our model is also *robust to classical security attacks* like Sybil and man in the middle attacks. And last, our proposal can be fitted in a *light weight* decision module, both in term of required computing capability and bandwidth requirement.

This paper is organized as follows: section 2 presents relevant approaches concerning trust and trust management framework. Section 3 specifies the proposed history based trust approach and provides an overview of our protocol (already described in [8]) with a dedicated security analysis. Section 4 gives the trust metric and explains the impact of the parameters associated with the metric. Section 5 shows using intensive simulations the effect of the parameters on the dynamics of groups using our model.

2 Related Work

According to [18], trust management systems are classified into three categories: credential and policy-based trust management, reputation-based trust management, and social network-based trust management. This approach depends on the way trust relationships between nodes are established and evaluated. In credential and policy-based trust management system [2–4], a node uses credential verification to establish a trust relationship with other nodes. The concept of trust management is limited to verifying credentials and restricting access to resources according to application-defined policies: they aim to enable access control [10]. A resource-owner provides a requesting node access to a restricted resource only if it can verify the credentials of the requesting node either directly or through a web of trust [11]. This is useful by itself only for those applications that assume implicit trust in the resource owner. Since these policy-based access control trust mechanisms do not incorporate the need of the requesting peer to establish trust in the resource-owner, they by themselves do not provide a complete generic trust management solution for all decentralized applications. Reputation-based trust management systems on the other hand provide a mechanism by which a node requesting a resource may evaluate its trust in the reliability of the resource and the node providing the resource. Trust value assigned to a trust relationship is a function of the combination of the nodes global reputation and the evaluating nodes perception of that node. The third kind of trust management systems, in addition, utilize social relationships between nodes when computing trust and reputation values. In particular, they analyze the social network which represents the relationships existing within a community and they form conclusions about nodes reputations based on different aspects of the social network. Examples of such trust management systems include Regret [16,17] that identifies groups using the social network, and NodeRanking [14] that identifies experts using the social network.

Ambient networks are environments where only a distributed reputation system is allowed [13]: there is neither centralized functions nor central location for submitting the ratings or for obtaining the reputation scores of nodes. Each participant simply records his opinion deduced from his own experience about another party. A node, in order to protect itself from potential malicious nodes, trusts only information which is obtained locally: a communication protocol allows all participants to obtain ratings from each other. The reputation of a target party is computed by a specific agent with the help of requested ratings and possibly from other sources of information. Of course, proper experiences with a target party carry a weight higher than the received ratings. But it is not always the case and the main difficulty is thus to find the distributed stores which deliver these specific ratings considering that the trust data is disseminated in numerous stores. Nevertheless, this information is easily provided on request for a relying party.

3 Our trust management framework

3.1 Our model

General Overview Current trust management systems suppose that most of the encountered terminals are honest so that the number of malicious information is not enough important to mislead the trust decision process. If this assumption is true in some general context, it does no longer hold for personal communicating devices in ambient and intelligent environment. Except in the case of direct interactions between each mobile device such as in personal experiences, all knowledge comes from uncertified devices. Moreover, the availability of this information is limited because of the restricted size of storage of these mobiles.

Our trust management framework is thus designed for decentralized environment where only partial information is available. Trust is evaluated and derived from the following types of information: past personal experiences, encountered device recommendations, and contextual information such as the moment and the place where the interaction takes place. A history based approach (as in [6,12]) is used in combination with some cryptographic materials: in case of a successful interaction, each involved node stores a *history element* signed by both parties. The number of interactions with a node called *intensity* of interaction, is also stored. The semantics of a history element is important but this is out of the scope of this paper (see [8]). Each node also carries a *blacklist* which takes into account the untrustworthy nodes. This situation may occur because these nodes were dishonest during several interactions or the service did not repeatedly proceed properly. The full management policy of this blacklist is also out of the scope of this paper.

Thus, a history implies that trust decision process is based on the validity of exchanged information since it not only relies on the honesty of the transmitted information, but also it depends on fully *certified* data: the mobiles are thus incited to be honest regarding transmitted information. In the case of multiple interactions with the same node, the device has to keep only the last proof of interaction to lower the volume of recorded data and the computing overhead.

To sum up our proposition, a node A evaluates the trustworthiness in a node B using only local information: its history H_A, the intensity $I_A(B)$ of the relation with B, its own blacklist BL_A, and the history H_B transmitted by B. With the help of cryptographic algorithms (see section 3.2), node A can check the validity of any history element in H_B as soon as it has the knowledge of the public identity of the involved nodes. As explained later, the verification is restricted to $H_A \cap H_B$ which corresponds to the known common devices between A and B. Conserve a history element relating A and B means *node A recommends node B* but unlike classical recommendation framework, this assumption can be verified.

The lifetime approach In an environment where exists neither a central regulating entity nor authorizing accreditations or the revocation of objects, a possibility is to let make time: the data elements are automatically revoked after their lifespans expire [15]. A temporal semantics can easily be added to a history element if both nodes agree on a creation and an expiration date. This information is simply concatenated with existent data before the signature. Nevertheless, nothing guarantees that the both entities will choose correct values for this information: the reality may be different (dishonest nodes or malfunction). But there is no real benefit to cheat on these values. Indeed, each entity may filter a received history element according to its local trust policy: an element can be rejected if its creation date is too old, its validity period is considered to be abnormally long although being still valid or if its lifespan is of course expired. No information having an infinite lifespan in the system is guaranteed by this timestamp.

Identity and impregnation It is of course impossible in absolute to avoid the compromise of a node either by a technical action (hacking) or by a social engineering attack (stealing of password, ...). Consequently, an attacker who compromises a mobile has a direct access on the history elements present on this device. This problem is addressed in our model through the impregnation of a device with an identity.

Identity is set at the birth of the mobile device and is the result of a collaboration between the node (or the owner) and a special device called *imprinting station*. Although this imprinting station implements the trust model but it is not certified by any authority. Each imprinting station defines a domain of security which corresponds to a dedicated social group. A domain may contain a large group of mobile devices or just a single smart mobile device embedding its own imprinting station.

At the end, a node A can easily check that an encounter B either belong to the same community or not by verifying their respective imprinted signatures. Then, we could define the $C(A, B)$ parameter which is a Boolean value assigned to true if and only if A and B belong to the same community. We call this value the *community parameter*. Depending of the social model underlying a community, this parameters can be included or not in the trust function.

To mitigate the impact of compromised nodes, the identity has also a lifespan. Before its expiration time, a node needs to be re-initiated by its imprinting station in order to update its new identity lifespan. A cryptographic link is created between two consecutive identities ID_1 and ID_2 (as explained in the section 3.2). While there exists some elements that are non expired or signed with the older identity, this identity is yet presented to check previous history elements. The new identity is used to sign new history elements.

3.2 A detailed approach of our protocol

An entity of our model is equipped at least with a *cryptographic package* what will make it compatible de facto with any other entity of our model, i.e. other objects which implicitly accept the model. When an object received this package and the initial parameters, it can then initiate sessions of communication by the means of the CHE protocol (detailed in [8]). If a session is accepted, the two involved nodes estimate, considering their security policies, that they can trust each other during this interaction.

Starting from an empty history, a node records all the successful interactions made with other nodes in order to support the future spontaneous interactions. To prove the past interactions, it creates with each met node an element of history related to their respective identities and signed by the two parts. Before any interactions, nodes must build a *trust germ*, by counting the number of common nodes they have in their history, or by manually forcing the relation: this is the *bootstrap* phase of our model. If the number of common interactions is sufficient (greater than a threshold p which is a function of the size n of the community and the maximum size H_{max} of the history), they can then interact.

The initial seed of trust Each device receives an initial *trust germ* from its *imprinting station*. It is composed by the following information: an identifier ID_u chosen by the device owner (eMail address or IP address or just a simple name or pseudonym) supposed to be unique within the security domain built by this imprinting station, an identity which is obtained from this identifier by concatenating it with a date d and a lifespan T ($ID = ID_u||d||T$), a first pair of private/public key (S_{ID}, Q_{ID}) for cipher operations, a second pair of keys (S_{ID}^S, Q_{ID}^S) for the signature and a set representing all the public parameters of the elliptic curves required along computations:

$$\text{Params: } \Omega := \langle \mathbb{F}_p, a, b, P, h, G_1, G_2, e, H_1, H_2, H_1', H_2'; P_{pub}, \Omega \rangle$$

where: a and b are the parameters of a particular elliptic curve $y^2 = x^3 + ax + b$ on $\mathbb{F}_p$; P, a particular point of this curve of prime order q; h, the cofactor defined as $h = \#E(\mathbb{F}_p)/q$; G_1, is a first additive cyclic group of prime order q built using the P point; G_2, a multiplicative cyclic group of the same order; e, a bi-linear pairing from $G_1 \times G_1$ to G_2; $H_1 : \{0,1\}^* \to G_1^*$ and $H_2 : G_2 \to \{0,1\}^n$, two map-to-point hash functions required for the Boneh-Franklin's Identity Based Encryption (BF-IBE) (see [5] for more details); and $H_1' : \{0,1\}^* \times G_1 \to G_1$ and $H_2' : \{0,1\}^* \times G_1 \to \mathbb{Z}_q$, two hash functions required for the Chen-Zhang-Kim IBS signature scheme (CZK-IBS) (see [7] for more details). Notice that the node public keys are directly derived from their identities due to the use of Identity-Based cryptosystems.

Another important point is that each smart device shares the same following cryptographic algorithms and protocols downloaded from the imprinting station: a fingerprint algorithm, a signature algorithm, a zero-knowledge protocol, a protocol to construct secure channel and the public parameters.

Ω-values are the domain identifier values provided to each node imprinted by the same imprinting station. Every imprinting station possesses the same Ω-values except $P_{pub,\Omega} = sP$ varying along the parameter s, the master key of a station. This value depends on each station and must be absolutely kept secret by it. None of these imprinting stations is supposed to be certified by any authority. Moreover, an independent mobile imprinting itself may be its own standalone security domain. The only values that each smart device has to keep secret is S_{ID} and S_{ID}^S as usually in cryptosystems.

Notice that if a first identity is $\text{ID}_1 = (\text{ID}_u||d_1||T_1)$ where ID_u represents the name or a pseudonym, d_1 a date and T_1 a lifespan, this identity allows to generate the first corresponding key pairs. Then, the updated identity ID_2 is equal to $\text{ID}_2 = ((\text{ID}_u||d_2||T_2)||MAC((\text{ID}_1||\text{ID}_u||d_2||T_2), P_{pub,\Omega}))$ where d_2 represents a second date, T_2 another lifespan and MAC is a MAC algorithm. And so on, the next identities are created using the same operations, generating a MAC chain.

The reciprocal trust Once the initialization phase is done, a node may interact with other nodes without any contacts with its imprinting station. This forms a second phase in the protocol.

The first step of our protocol supposes that both entities Alice and Bob have already interacted at least once and have built a trust bond: this is a message m signed by Bob that Alice publishes in the public part of her history $(m, sign_B(m))$ while Bob publishes $(m, sign_A(m))$ in its own history. This bond could be created by forcing by the hand the beginning interaction as in a Bluetooth like system if the number of common elements of their history were insufficient. Let us note that if Alice and Bob have already met and if this new interaction is successful, they just have to modify the respective values of the intensity and to rebuild a new history element to replace the old one because it contains a timestamp. Suppose now that in the same way Bob and Charlie have built a secure channel to exchange a common message of mutual trust m'.

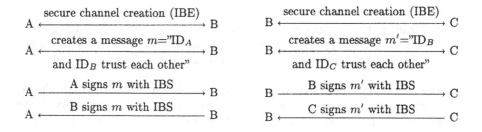

The second step of our protocol describes a trust bond establishment using history contents between two entities (here Alice and Charlie) that have never met. Thus, when Alice meets Charlie for the first time, they exchange the concatenation of all the public keys Q_{ID} contained in their history. Once this first exchange carried out, Alice and Charlie realize that they have both met before Bob and want to mutually prove this common meeting. Charlie, first, proves to Alice that Bob trusts him using the message m'. Alice could verify the contents of m' because she knows Bob's public keys from her own previous meeting.

$$A \xrightarrow{\quad\text{did you meet Bob before ?}\quad} C$$

$$A \xleftarrow{\quad (m', sign_{S_B^S}(m')) \quad} C$$

verifies m'

The reciprocal process will be then repeated by Alice.

3.3 Security analysis

Security requirements The following traditional cryptographic properties are guaranteed by our protocol: an offline authentication (users performs each other a weak authentication using the IBE scheme and as Charlie knows the Bob's public keys, he could authenticate his signature), integrity is guaranteed by the hash function used in the IBS scheme as in the classical case of a certificate, confidentiality is guaranteed by the use of the cryptographic IDs. Those IDs also permit to guarantee that the first phase of our protocol was correctly done. The secure channel built at the beginning of the exchange in the first phase also prevents a man-in-the-middle attack.

The user could preserve its anonymity because he is free to choose his own pseudonyms according the context and could have several pseudonyms distributed by different imprinting stations. Those pseudonyms are certified through the used identity-based schemes and they preserve the real identity of their owner, even if his meetings when he acts in the network are known with other peers with pseudonyms. Moreover, each identity defines its own history and all the pseudonyms are certified, thus tackling "Sybil attacks". Our model also guarantees the non-repudiation: each user is preventing from denying previous meetings or actions. Revocation is also possible using the timestamp linked with an ID and included in the key pairs (as previously described in 3.2).

Classical attacks As mentioned in [8] and due to the use of the IBE-scheme, the well known key escrow drawback is inherently present in our protocol. We then suppose that all the imprinting stations must be trusted entities. Otherwise, they can read and send messages instead of nodes. However, the signature scheme used here prevents such an attack from happening because the signature key pair generated is unknown from the imprinting station.

Our trust management framework is a cross-domain protocol: two nodes, not belonging to the same domain (or to the same imprinting station) could nevertheless interact by comparing the contents of their respective histories once they exchange the public key of their security domains (we suppose here that all the other parameters are the same).

Our protocol also guarantees the non-transferability of the history because only the knowledge of the secret keys allows to use the content of the history (the secure channel initially built prevents the use of the history elements). Then, stolen identities or pseudonyms or histories could not be useful.

Sybil-like attacks A node or a user could using our protocol forges several identities or pseudonyms from the same or different imprinting stations and then uses them in Sybil-like attacks. However, in our model, one identity or pseudonym could only be linked with a particular history.

For example, suppose that an attacker (Eve) wants to attack a single entity Alice, then she creates first several pseudonyms $S_1, \cdots, S_n$. Alice asks her a particular service, they realize that they have enough common history elements to interact. Suppose now that Eve does not provide the corresponding service to Alice with her S_1 pseudonym, Alice then decides to blacklist the S_1 Eve's pseudonym. So, Eve must use an other pseudonym, S_2 for example, if she wants to interact and attack Alice again. To manage this operation, she must build an other time a sufficient number of history elements common with Alice. Even if, she knows the pseudonyms of nodes to meet again with her second pseudonym, she must play an active and positive role inside the "Alice's friends". The attack using several pseudonyms is then very expensive in our case and requires lots of social engineering.

Clone attacks As mentioned in [8], a major attack against our model is the clone one where Alice clones herself with some other terminals. Those clones with exactly the same keys could build a very strong history and have lots of recorded elements and could interact more easily than the others. Therefore, Alice cloned devices could be carried by different persons visiting different places in order to have different histories. This is not considered by us as a major risk since it is a social engineering attack which is difficult to conduct as well as difficult to surround by cryptographic methods.

4 General Context of our analysis

Having presented the basic block of our trust management framework and having discussed its security requirements, we then describe the general context of our framework main processes: how a node A really computes the trust value concerning the node B, supposing that the node A is the service provider - the trusty - whereas the node B is the trustor.

First, we give a general overview of our notations and then we introduce a function which rates the trustfulness between each node.

4.1 General context

For sake of simplicity, we consider a unique community which is characterized by its *size* n. The community dynamics depends of the *interaction rate* of each individual node, i.e. the average number of interactions by unit of time. The other parameters are H_{max} the maximal size of a history which is the same for all nodes and BL_{max} the maximal size of the blacklist which is also the same for all nodes. The node A stores its trusted nodes in its history H_A and reciprocally, it stores untrustworthy nodes in its blacklist BL_A. Hence, to a trusted node B corresponds an element $h_A(B)$ in the history H_A. In addition, each element is tagged with two fields: the first one, denoted by $I_A(B)$, represents the intensity of the relation with B, the second, denoted by $U_A(B)$, represents the *utility* of B, i.e. the usefulness of the node B with respect to the node A. This last notion is related to the number of times this element contributes in the computation of common elements.

In a more general framework, with different communities, trust policy could be different according to either an interaction takes place with a member of its community or not, taking into account the $C(A, B)$ *community parameter*. More deeply, the internal structure of a community could also modify the trust policy: for instance, through the social degree of the community, initial trust may be total: each node is valid and active in the community (for example for objects belonging to a same family). On the contrary, the initial trust may be partial or even non-existent if the social degree of these communities is loose (for example for objects belonging to members of a national sporting federation with several thousand of members). In this case, the weight given to the *community parameter* could no more be the same and the behavior of a mobile in such a community depends essentially of its own experiences through its history.

4.2 Trust function

Direct trust value We first introduce the main element of our trust function. Suppose now that A and B are two nodes belonging or not to the same community. The main element of trust in our model is the threshold of common history elements. To compute this value, we need to introduce the direct trust value:

$$d(A, B) = \alpha|H_A \cap H_B| + (\alpha - 1)|BL_A \cap H_B|$$

where α varies in the interval $[0, 1]$.

This coefficient indicates the weight of the number of common elements $|H_A \cap H_B|$ versus the number of untrustworthy nodes of A that B considers trustfulness. This value obviously admits negative value for some values of $|BL_A \cap H_B|$, but we consider that if its value exceeds a positive threshold p, then the associated value $T(A, B)$, representing the direct trust level, is equal to one, otherwise it is equal to 0. The parameter p defines thus the threshold for a direct trust.

General trust function A trust value is also context-dependent, so we need to combine the direct trust value with other values given by the context of the interaction, limited here to the *intensity* of the relation between the two involved nodes and to the *community parameter*. We then compute the general trust function about the node B viewed by the node A using the following formula:

$$TF_A(B) = \frac{\beta_A T(A, B) + \gamma_A \frac{I_A(B)}{I_{max}(A)} + \delta_A C(A, B)}{\beta_A + \gamma_A + \delta_A}$$

with $T(A, B) = 1$ if $d(A, B) \geq p$, 0 otherwise and with $C(A, B) = 1$ if $\Omega_A = \Omega_B$, 0 otherwise; where β_A, γ_A and δ_A are three parameters that belong to $[0, 1]$; and where $I_{max}(A)$ represents the maximal intensity admitted by A. Then, The general trust function gives a trust notation that belongs to $[0, 1]$. According this value and the trust threshold t_{ID} defined by each node, the involved nodes could decide to interact or not.

The β, γ and δ values represent the weights of each parameter we want to take into account. They depend on the local trust policy of the node. For example, a node will prefer, if it has never met a node C (then, the corresponding $I_A(C)$ value is equal to 0), to take into account the number of encountered nodes represented by the β parameter than the community one (they belong to the same tennis club). More precisely, the δ parameter represents the degree of structure of a community and will depend on the type of the community.

5 Experiments and Simulation results

We aim here to propose a set of rules for the management of a group by evaluating the various parameters in order to make the mobiles as autonomous as possible: we seek for instance to lower the duration from which the dynamic process takes the top compared to the bootstrap phase (Fig. 1) by adjusting the different parameters (the maximum history size H_{max}, the metric threshold p,...).

In this section, the presented simulations only compute the $d(A, B)$ parameter, the most important one, considering the other ones as some bonus of interactions. An evaluation including the blacklist process efect is also presented. Let us recall also that two nodes having interacted jointly several times keep only one element of history: this element is updated each time as necessary. For needs of the performed simulations, two types of network were considered: the first type was built upon a uniform random distribution which selects the pairs of interacting nodes, while for the second type, the pairs of nodes are picked with respect to a power law distribution.

The bootstrap phase The bootstrap phase of a node is very important in our proposition and requires the intervention of its owner. At initial step, the history of the node A is empty of trusted elements. And thus, the metric above is useless since no terms can be evaluate. Hence, each trusted element $h_A(B)$

(resp. each blacklisted element B) which is added by the user in the history
(resp. in the blacklist) of A has a great impact in the dynamics of this node.

It is also important to notice that this phase implicitly has an impact on the
defense mechanism of a group: a group may protect itself by imposing a strong
social activity to users belonging to another groups. A malevolent user which
has compromised an object, must act inside the group in order to avoid losing
the benefit of his situation. The situation is quite the same for a benevolent
user who leaves for a long time his group: if he does not anymore maintain
his relations and wants to be reintegrated, he must undertake one more time
the *bootstrap* phase. This fact can be seen as a disadvantage of our protocol,
nevertheless, initiate a *bootstrap* phase is easier for an authorized user than for
an attacker.

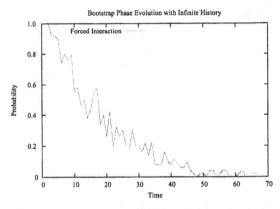

Fig. 1. Evolution of forced interactions by section of 50 steps of time for a community
of size $n = 100$ nodes considering a history with an infinite size.

Eviction policy of the history A major element of the policy management of
a community is the rule to apply for incorporating a new element in a saturated
history. Indeed, the size of the history is necessarily limited for a mobile with
small resources. We plan here to set up two modes of replacement. The first
mode, which is denoted by FIFO (*First In, First Out*), removes the *oldest*
element out of a considered node history: the first withdrawn element has the
oldest date. Such a policy allows thus to make disappear the mobiles which
are no longer active in the community. The second mode, which is denoted
by LFU (*Least Frequently Used*), withdraws the useless elements which appear
in the computation of common elements. To measure the importance of each
history element, we take into account the number of times this element is used
to compute the number of common elements: each common element between
the two parts i and j is credited with one point, this corresponds to the value
$U_i(j)$ that represents the *utility* of an element. A history element having the

lowest points account is purged and replaced by the partner of the interaction if the current interaction succeeds. We focus on the study of the probability that two distinct nodes have a sufficient number of common elements in their respective histories at time t. This probability is: $P(t) = \frac{2}{n(n-1)} \sum_{i \neq j} T(i,j)$ with $n(n-1)/2$ corresponding to the total number of distinct nodes pairs and $T(i,j)$ is the Boolean value previously defined without taking into account the blacklist process.

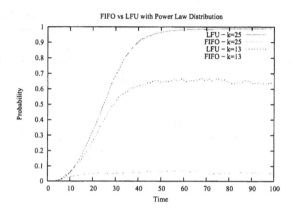

Fig. 2. Evolution of the P probability during time t for several k values (history size) according the eviction mode used (LFU or FIFO). Threshold: $p = 3$ for $n = 100$ nodes).

We have also computed such a probability by using the birthday paradox for several values of H_{max} ranging from $0,5 \times n/\ln(n)$ to $1,2 \times n/\ln(n)$, whereas the threshold p ranging from $0,5 \times \sqrt{n/\ln(n)}$ to $1,5 \times \sqrt{n/\ln(n)}$. On the one hand, a quick analysis shows that the obtained computation results are not really different as well as the case of a random distribution as the case of a power law distribution (however, with a light profit for this last). On the other hand, there is a great difference in behavior of the model according to the mode of replacement used (LFU or FIFO) as shown in Figure 2.

In conclusion, this analysis shows as results that the LFU mode is more efficient to keep the cohesion of a regular interacting nodes group than the FIFO mode. Indeed, the FIFO policy does not take into account the importance of the history elements. On the contrary, if we only keep the most active and useful elements, the chances to find them in other histories are increased. Their number is thus often greater than the threshold p. In consequence, the choice of an eviction policy is very clear: the LFU mode using the $U_i(j)$ value is opted. In addition, fixing a threshold at 3 or 4 is reasonable for communities of 100 or 200 nodes. Beyond, the protocol would require too many user interventions to be viable. Another information from this analysis is the choice of a power law distribution versus a uniform random distribution to describe the behavior of the nodes activities in the community is negligible.

Impact of blacklist As we announced in the description of the model, the use of a blacklist is highly desirable. In a fully distributed environment, adding a node in a blacklist is the only possible sanction if its behavior is considered to be incorrect. It corresponds to a perfectly identified social behavior. In a risk evaluation approach, it can appear logical to penalize the nodes which present recommendation coming from nodes which are blacklisted.

The disadvantage of the blacklist policy is to prohibit some interaction with honest nodes only because some element of their history have been locally blacklisted. There is thus a balance to find between a very strict policy which will have a very negative impact on the whole of the community and permissive policy which will imply a too important taking risk.

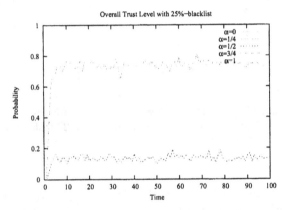

Fig. 3. This figure describes overall trust level of a 25-nodes community according to whether the blacklist elements are considered or not. Each node has a fixed history size $BL_{max} + H_{max} = 10$.

The figure 3 shows evolution of the overall trust along the time for a 25-nodes community. We observe that as the coefficient α decreases as does overall trust. Such a behavior is what expected. This observation could be extended for all values of α: for its small values, the dynamics of the system is stopped due to the higher importance of blacklisted elements than common elements in the history of each node. In contrast, for values around one, the dynamics of the system is not impacted by the presence of these blacklisted elements.

context awareness As we announced at the beginning of this paper, our model allows the introduction of context awareness evaluation. A node A can carry out easily a passive listening of the elements of the histories H_B and H_C exchanged by two nodes which apply our protocol in its radio range. The node can compute the cardinality of both $H_A \cap H_B$ and $H_A \cap H_C$. By carrying out regular listening, the node can evaluate the social situation in which it is embedded. If the cardinality of intersected histories is always high the node could consider that it acts in a well known environment and may adapt its security policy to this context. The use of our protocol confers on the model two major advantages. First of all, context awareness evaluation is made of data that can by checked cryptographically. Secondly, with only some listening nodes obtain a large list of history elements what enables us to acquire this information very quickly. This second point is important to reduce the cost of such a listing and of the evaluation process.

Let us consider a node A belonging to a community C and 3 contexts where the proportion of C nodes surrounding A are respectively 80%, 50% and 10%. The objective of a context awareness evaluation for the node A is to detect as quick as possible in which A is really embedded. As we explained at the beginning of this section, with a bounded history, even while being in its own community, the intersection of history is not always sufficient for spontaneous interaction. This detection can be established by the gap in the ratio of known nodes over unknown nodes. Known nodes mean here those stored in its history. This ratio may be accurate with few samples. This could be proved analytically using again the birthday paradox.

6 Conclusion

We have proposed a distributed framework that produces trust assessments based on proved direct experience. Our cross-domain scheme supports a weak authentication process, user anonymity and resists to lots of attacks, especially the Sybil-like one. From this basis, we have designed a trust notation that takes into account a local blacklist process and that is context awareness. Finally, we have conducted experiments which show that this framework is suitable for large communities, the bootstrap phase being not an obstacle and that the blacklist process well prevents trusted nodes from the malicious behavior of some peers. As part of future work, we will investigate the dynamics of our model behavior for some special social cases.

References

1. *The First International Joint Conference on Autonomous Agents & Multiagent Systems, AAMAS 2002, July 15-19, 2002, Bologna, Italy, Proceedings*. ACM, 2002.
2. Matt Blaze, Joan Feigenbaum, John Ioannidis, and Angelos D. Keromytis. The KeyNote Trust-Management System Version 2 - RFC 2704. RFC 2704, Available from http://www.faqs.org/rfcs/rfc2704.html, September 1999.
3. Matt Blaze, Joan Feigenbaum, and Angelos D. Keromytis. The role of trust management in distributed systems security. In Jan Vitek and Christian Damsgaard

Jensen, editors, *Secure Internet Programming*, volume 1603 of *Lecture Notes in Computer Science*, pages 185–210. Springer, 1999.

4. Matt Blaze, Joan Feigenbaum, and Jack Lacy. Decentralized trust management. In *IEEE Symposium on Security and Privacy*, pages 164–173. IEEE Computer Society, 1996.

5. Dan Boneh and Matthew K. Franklin. Identity-based encryption from the weil pairing. In *Advances in Cryptology - Crypto'2001*, volume 2139 of *Lecture Notes in Computer Science*, pages 213–229. Springer, 2001.

6. Licia Capra. Engineering human trust in mobile system collaborations. In Richard N. Taylor and Matthew B. Dwyer, editors, *SIGSOFT FSE*, pages 107–116. ACM, 2004.

7. Xiofeng Chen, Fangguo Zhang, and Kwandjo Kim. A new ID-based group signature scheme from bilinear pairings. In *Information Security Applications, 4th International Workshop - WISA'03*, volume 2908 of *Lecture Notes in Computer Science*, pages 585–592. Springer-Verlag, 2003.

8. Samuel Galice, Marine Minier, John Mullins, and Stéphane Ubéda. Cryptographic protocol to establish trusted history of interactions. In *Third European Workshop on Security and Privacy in Ad hoc and Sensor Networks*, page LNCS 4357, september 2006.

9. Diego Gambetta. Can we trust trust? In Diego Gambetta, editor, *Trust: Making and Breaking Cooperative Relatioins*, chapter 13, pages 213–237. Published Online, 2000.

10. Tyrone Grandison and Morris Sloman. A survey of trust in internet applications. *IEEE Communications Surveys and Tutorials*, 3(4), 2000.

11. Rohit Khare and Adam Rifkin. Weaving a Web of trust. issue of the World Wide Web Journal (Volume 2, Number 3, Pages 77-112), Summer 1997.

12. Véronique Legrand, Dana Hooshmand, and Stéphane Ubéda. Trusted ambient community for self-securing hybrid networks. Research Report 5027, INRIA, 2003.

13. Filip Perich, Jeffrey Undercoffer, Lalana Kagal, Anupam Joshi, Timothy Finin, and Yelena Yesha. In reputation we believe: Query processing in mobile ad-hoc networks. *mobiquitous*, 00:326–334, 2004.

14. Josep M. Pujol, Ramon Sangüesa, and Jordi Delgado. Extracting reputation in multi agent systems by means of social network topology. In *AAMAS* [1], pages 467–474.

15. Daniele Quercia, Stephen Hailes, and Licia Capra. Tata: Towards anonymous trusted authentication. In Ketil Stølen, William H. Winsborough, Fabio Martinelli, and Fabio Massacci, editors, *iTrust*, volume 3986 of *Lecture Notes in Computer Science*, pages 313–323. Springer, 2006.

16. Jordi Sabater and Carles Sierra. Regret: reputation in gregarious societies. In *Agents*, pages 194–195, 2001.

17. Jordi Sabater and Carles Sierra. Reputation and social network analysis in multi-agent systems. In *AAMAS* [1], pages 475–482.

18. Girish Suryanarayana and Richard N. Taylor. A survey of trust management and resource discovery technologies in peer-to-peer applications.

Towards an Understanding of Security, Privacy and Safety in Maritime Self-Reporting Systems

Mark McIntyre, Lynne Genik, Peter Mason, and Tim Hammond
Defence R&D Canada
http://www.drdc-rddc.gc.ca/

Abstract. Global satellite navigation systems such as GPS enable precise tracking of vessels worldwide and pervasive global networks such as the Internet allow sharing of this information almost instantaneously between locations anywhere on Earth. This ability to monitor vessels globally is a topic of current debate among those concerned with national security, those who are mainly interested in safety at sea and those who advocate for privacy rights at the personal, commercial and national level. In this paper we discuss two maritime self-reporting systems, namely the Automatic Identification System and Long Range Identification and Tracking, which have given rise to this debate. The benefits and drawbacks of each are discussed with safety, security and privacy in mind. Also, some connections are drawn between these systems and Mobile Ad Hoc Networks and Radio Frequency Identification where security and privacy are also of current interest.

1 Introduction

Global satellite navigation systems such as the Global Positioning System (GPS) have revolutionized our ability to precisely locate entities in both time and space in a common global reference system. Modern communication and networking systems, such as cell-phone networks, the INMARSAT satellite system and the Internet, provide the capability to access this precise track information, together with other ancillary information about the entity, virtually anywhere on

Please use the following format when citing this chapter:

McIntyre, M., Genik, L., Mason, P. and Hammond, T., 2007, in IFIP International Federation for Information Processing, Volume 238, Trust Management, eds. Etalle, S., Marsh, S., (Boston: Springer), pp. 185–206.

earth. Taken together, these systems offer tremendous potential for improving the efficiency and safety of any enterprise that relies on movement of goods and/or people. This is especially true for sea and air transportation – those transportation modes for which navigation systems like GPS were originally designed. But, the benefits of geospatial reporting systems are being realized much more broadly to include many land applications and there are examples proposed where these technologies can be used to continuously monitor individuals thorough the course of their daily lives [1]. Such examples suggest the impact that geospatial reporting systems could have in national security applications but equally they raise concerns about the potentially invasive nature of such systems on personal privacy.

Because terrorists have exploited commercial transportation systems in the past, there is concern that they will do it again. Since September 11, 2001 significant advances have been made towards securing the air transportation system and land border security issues have been a high priority. However, particular attention is now being paid to the maritime environment since the seas have been relatively unregulated in the past and a tremendous amount of trade flows into, and out of, North America in a globalized economy. Unregulated flow of goods and people in the maritime domain raises fears of terrorist threats but it also provides a vector for illegal smuggling of goods and people, for proliferation of traditional weapons and weapons of mass destruction and for environmental exploitation and crime. Because of these worries, measures are being taken both nationally and internationally to improve general awareness of activity on the world's oceans and waterways.

There are three objectives of this paper. The first is to provide a general discussion of two self-reporting systems (SRS) that have been recently introduced in the maritime domain - namely the Automatic Identification System (AIS) and Long Range Identification and Tracking (LRIT). Through a discussion of self-reporting systems in general and the safety, security and privacy issues that are currently under debate regarding AIS and LRIT we hope to stimulate interest in the academic community to address some of these concerns. Secondly, we attempt to draw parallels between these maritime self-reporting systems and two fields of current interest in information and network security – namely Mobile Ad Hoc Networks (MANETs) and Radio Frequency Identification (RFID) systems. Security and privacy investigations for MANETs and RFID systems may be directly applicable to AIS and LRIT. Finally, we try to identify some key questions that need to be addressed in order to understand the tradeoffs between privacy, security and safety properties in self-reporting systems such as AIS and LRIT.

In Section 2 the general concept of a geospatial self-reporting system is introduced and several properties that characterize them are discussed. In Section 3, AIS and LRIT are presented in sufficient detail to allow a discussion of the drawbacks and benefits of each with respect to security, privacy and safety in Section 4. Next we discuss MANETs and RFID systems in Section 5 and discuss some parallels between these classes of systems and both AIS and LRIT.

2   Self-Reporting Systems

Self-reporting systems enable sharing of position, velocity, time and identity information among parties that either need or want such information. Specifically, we define self-reports as messages, in some pre-defined format, that include at least position, velocity and identity information about some entity. Other ancillary information, such as status or intention information may be included in self-reports. A self-reporting system is characterized by the form of its self-reports in conjunction with a well-defined communication system used for passing these messages between participating parties. Typically, defining a communication system involves defining a communication path together with a protocol for passing the self-report messages. A simple example is one where operators on a ship at sea are expected to fill out a paper form with self-report information and fax the information to some central site that requires the information at regular intervals. This is current practice for all ships that wish to visit ports in North America – a notification report must be filed with national authorities at least 96 hours before arrival in a port. We will use this highly-manual example to motivate the following section where we discuss the characteristics of more automated SRSs. Another example of a self-reporting system is one in use by the crab fishing industry as illustrated in Figure 1. The figure shows the history of self-reports from fishing boats that are collected by the crab fishing authority.

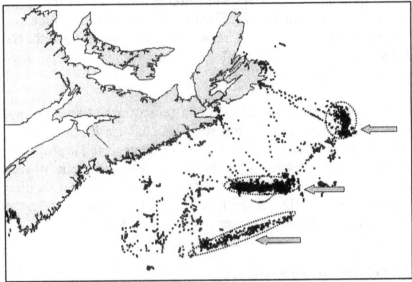

Figure 1. Vessel Monitoring System (VMS) data from 35 vessels of the snow crab fishery off the coast of Nova Scotia [2]. The black dots indicate position reports and the arrows show concentrated areas.

2.1 Characteristics of Self-Reporting Systems

There are a number of properties that characterize automated or semi-automated self-reporting systems and here we attempt to characterize them from the point of view of the entity providing the self-reports. The goal in this section is to provide a general characterization that will be made more concrete in the following section where two specific maritime SRSs are discussed.

The first characteristic of an SRS is the information *content* provided in the self-reports. As mentioned earlier, the key information considered here is position, velocity and time information, together with identity information, related to each of the participating entities. Furthermore, there may be some form of intention information contained in a self-report such as the intended track for that entity. This information is distinguished by the fact that it is information about the future. Ancillary static information about each entity will also be considered but only as amplifying information.

A second important characteristic of an SRS is the class of entities that provide self-reports. In practical terms this determines which entities must participate in an SRS. For example, certain classes of maritime vessels are required by international marine law to carry certain self-reporting systems while others may participate by choice alone. We will refer to this as *carriage* requirements. Note that entities that are not required to carry an SRS system may still benefit from the information available from the system if they have access to it

Two other characteristics of a SRS are *coverage* and *resolution* and these can be broken down into spatial and temporal components. The *spatial coverage* is roughly the geographic area over which a SRS is expected to operate. From the reporting entities viewpoint, this is the geographic region over which self-reports are required to be available. *Spatial resolution* is the accuracy with which entities are expected to report their geospatial information while *temporal resolution* is the accuracy of the temporal component of the self-reports. Finally, *temporal coverage* is the period of time over which an SRS is meant to operate.

Finally, we characterize an SRS by its *enrolment policies and protocols* and the *information sharing policies and protocols* used to exchange information between two entities within the SRS. The joining policy determines what new entities are permitted to join an SRS and the enrolment protocol specifies the procedure that new entities must follow to join an SRS. Information sharing policies determine what information can be shared among entities within an SRS and the information sharing protocols determine how this sharing takes place. These in turn help to determine the information sharing architecture that is needed to support an SRS.

3. Examples of Maritime Geospatial Self-Reporting Systems

Two self-reporting systems that are of topical interest to the maritime community are discussed in this section and described using the characteristics discussed in the previous section. The Long Range Identification and Tracking system is planned for initial operation in January 2008 while the Automatic Identification System has been in limited operation since 2004 with full scale operation due in 2007.

3.1 Long Range Identification and Tracking (LRIT)

Long Range Identification and Tracking (LRIT) is a self-reporting system mandated for worldwide adoption that is designed to allow maritime nations to achieve three objectives. The first is to allow a maritime nation (referred to as flag states) to maintain global, continuous awareness of the location and movements of ships that are flagged under that country. Secondly, it will allow countries (port states) to maintain a detailed awareness of the ships that are destined for their national ports. And lastly, it will allow maritime nations (coastal states) to achieve much better awareness than they currently have of vessels that transit past their coastlines, largely for reasons of national security [3]. The main technology enabler for this system is the growing availability of global communication networks, particularly satellite systems, that allow a flag state to communicate with vessels worldwide. It is noteworthy that the adoption of technologies to improve awareness of vessels at sea has been slow compared to that of airspace awareness for the aerospace community.

The content of LRIT messages is specified by the International Maritime Organization (IMO) which requires vessels to provide time-stamped position and identity reports when requested by an authorized agency. Passenger ships and cargo ships larger than 300 gross tonnes on international voyages as well as mobile off-shore drilling units will be required to carry LRIT information systems [4]. These carriage requirements are also decided by the IMO. The spatial coverage is meant to be global to insure that flag states and vessel owners can access LRIT reports from wherever a vessel may be. As well the system is meant to operate continuously to provide full temporal coverage. However, there are provisions to allow delays of up to four hours for LRIT message reporting, depending on the distance a vessel is from a state requiring the reports [3].

The LRIT information collection policies, together with the policies for sharing LRIT reports nationally and internationally, have been quite contentious issues over the past few years. The main contention has been the coastal state requirements. The desire by some coastal states to access LRIT reports for ships transiting up to 2000 nautical miles off their coasts [3] appears to contravene a long-standing "right of innocent passage" for marine vessels. This boundary is well outside the traditional 12 nautical mile national maritime boundaries and is also well beyond the 200 nm exclusive economic zone of maritime nations, suggested by the Russian Federation [5]. The range of 1000 nm was finally adopted in 2006 [4].

The LRIT system architecture is shown in Figure 2. LRIT information is transferred from the ship to the Application Service Provider (ASP) by a Communication Service Provider (CSP). The ASP adds additional information and sends the data to the LRIT Data Centre (DC), where it is stored. The International LRIT Data Exchange is effectively a router that routes messages between DCs without processing or storing the position data within the messages. The LRIT Data Distribution Plan defines how LRIT information will be distributed to other governments.

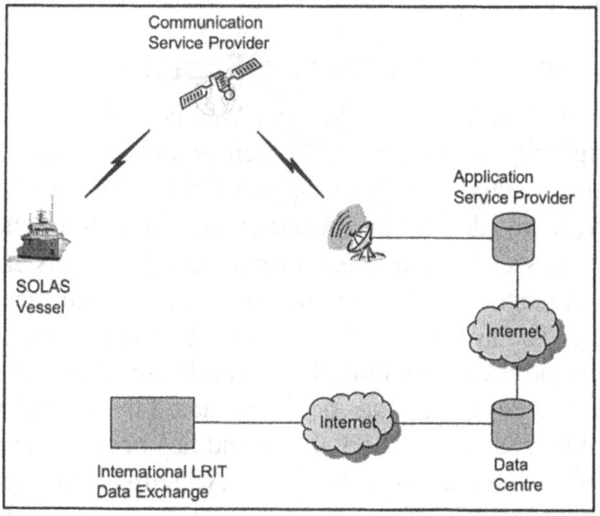

Figure 2. Typical LRIT System Architecture

The LRIT Coordinator helps to establish the international components of the system and performs administrative functions, reviews and audits. In late 2006 the Maritime Safety Committee (MSC) appointed the International Mobile Satellite Organization (IMSO) as the LRIT Coordinator, who had offered to take on the role "at no cost" to the participants although the details of the cost structure remain to be confirmed [6]. The overwhelming majority of nations supported this.

It should be noted that LRIT is an example of general vessel tracking / vessel management systems that have been in use for many years for various reasons. Companies that own fleets of vessels have been employing modern vessel tracking technologies based on self reporting for fleet awareness and efficiency reasons for some time. They have tended to keep this information to themselves as commercially sensitive information although they are often willing to share the information for safety at sea reasons as is the case in the Automated Mutual-Assistance Vessel Rescue (AMVER) system. In ecologically and environmentally sensitive marine regions governments or other responsible agencies may require self-reporting while within a protected area. These areas will generally be quite small in size to protect, for example, breeding grounds of marine mammals, but they could be much larger as is the case of a self-reporting system known as Reef Rep put in place to insure awareness of vessel activity on the Great Barrier Reef [7].

3.2 Automatic Identification System

The Automatic Identification System (AIS) is a self-reporting system that was originally developed in Sweden as an inter-vessel maritime information exchange system to support safety of navigation. Specifically, it was designed as a self-reporting system where participating vessels continuously broadcast self-reports and exchange collision avoidance information once they are in radio reception range of each other. The system has been in development since 1992 and has been strongly promoted by both the US and Canadian Coast Guards. Carriage of AIS equipment has been mandated by the IMO for all vessels of 300 gross tonnes and above and has been in the process of being phased in since 2004 with all SOLAS ships expected to carry AIS equipment by 2007. Smaller vessels are not required to carry the system although a significant number choose to. There is also growing interest in so-called Class-B AIS for use on small boats. Interestingly, fishing vessels of all kinds are not required to employ AIS.

There are in fact many types of AIS reports [8], depending on the reporting scenario and the type of transmitter, but we will focus on basic AIS vessel position reports which are most directly comparable to LRIT position reports. The content of an AIS self-report is similar to that of an LRIT self-report but has additional information. It contains static information such as vessel identification in the form of its Maritime Mobile Service Identity (MMSI) number, which is meant to be a unique identification number assigned to a vessel and encoded in the AIS transceiver. These numbers are controlled by the telecommunications regulations agency in the various countries and are overseen by the International Telecommunications Union. The static information also includes the size and type of ship as well as the positioning information for the AIS antenna on the ship. This information is required for high-accuracy collision avoidance calculations. Vessel self-reports contain dynamic data such as GPS position and velocity information as well as rate of turn. They also include rough time information although it is not meant to be an accurate time stamp on the information. Finally, AIS reports may also include voyage-related data such as next port and information regarding hazardous goods onboard.

With respect to spatial coverage of the AIS system, it is mandated as a global system and two frequencies in the VHF band have been reserved. Although there were some difficulties with reserving this spectrum worldwide, the importance of the system for both safety at sea and awareness of maritime activity facilitated international agreement and the system has been operating since 2004. The spatial resolution of the system is that of the underlying GPS position data. Without spatial information of this quality, the system could not be relied on as a collision avoidance system.

The temporal coverage of the AIS system has to be continuous while a vessel is at sea in order to insure that it provides the safety benefits (although one could argue that the safety mandate could be met by a system that could be turned on in designated areas that are deemed to be high-traffic). Furthermore the temporal resolution has to be high in order to guarantee collision avoidance when vessels are in close proximity. Typically the frequency of vessel reports vary between once every 2 seconds to once every 10 seconds and the information is transmitted immediately without any delay.

As discussed earlier, carriage of AIS is mandated for most large vessels that travel internationally but other vessels can install the equipment on a voluntary basis. The equipment is relatively inexpensive and the enrolment procedure simply involves applying for an MMSI number from the national authorities. Sharing of AIS vessel reports once the system is operating on a ship is completely open as it needs to be for safety purposes. The broadcast nature of the AIS system insures that any vessel in RF reception range of the transmitter will be able to make use of the AIS information. There are AIS messages that can be directed to specific vessels via MMSI addressing.

4. Benefits and Drawbacks of AIS and LRIT

Major distinctions between AIS and LRIT are the short range of AIS versus the long range of LRIT, the peer-to-peer nature of AIS as opposed to the centralized architecture of LRIT, and the end-to-end security features of LRIT for point-to-point communications versus the unsecured broadcasts of AIS. As outlined in the previous section, AIS was intended to support safety at sea and is now being considered for maritime domain awareness (MDA), while LRIT is being developed to provide MDA for national security and can provide location information for search and rescue missions. These different purposes and capabilities lead to a series of benefits and drawbacks for each.

4. 1 AIS

A primary benefit of AIS is safety, providing ships with a means for exchanging identity, location and other important information to prevent at-sea collisions and facilitate traffic management in ports, and aiding in search and rescue missions [9]. The system offers a substantial improvement over radar tracks in providing situational awareness and institutes automatic reporting between devices without human intervention/operation, which reduces the need for radio voice communications, especially in high traffic areas. It should be noted, however, that there is still a fair bit of manual input required on set-up, which is a potential cause of errors.

The wealth of information provided in AIS transmissions significantly enhances maritime domain awareness. The Maritime Domain Awareness Data Sharing Community of Interest (COI) was formed in February 2006 with members from the US Department of Defense and Department of Homeland Security (including the US Coast Guard) [10]. Under this COI, a pilot working group was formed to share AIS data between members. The goal is to evolve the pilot into an operational capability, leading to a national coastal AIS capability. Canada also has an AIS pilot project that, similarly to the US, is based primarily on AIS collection networks that have been set up for research and evaluation purposes. Discussions are underway to share local and regional AIS information to provide more complete coastal AIS coverage across North America.

AIS devices range from US $1500 to $5000 [11], with installation costs ranging from CA $5000 to $10000. The cost is considered to be relatively inexpensive. Governments can also benefit economically since traffic monitoring helps in enforcing pollution regulations and managing fisheries [9].

Safety-related text messages and short binary text messages can be sent via AIS, and can either be broadcast or sent to a specific station[1]. Through the binary text messages there is potential to carry other, non-AIS data, which means that information could be piggy-backed on the AIS system and may reduce other communications costs. AIS can also play a role in assisting search and rescue missions.

At present there appear to be no nationally and internationally accepted guidelines with respect to the collection and handling of AIS data. This has privacy implications associated with it. AIS information is broadcast in the clear and is accessible by any receiver within range. This means that anyone with the proper equipment can collect information on an individual ship and its history. For example, the UK

---

[1] http://emmel.alfahosting.org/english/message_en.htm

company AIS Live Ltd.[2] collects AIS information worldwide and sells access to it online. This information could be used in clandestine activities such as developing a competitive advantage between shipping companies, determining prime fishing areas, pirate attacks, etc. Given that vessels broadcast AIS information in the clear, should they have an expectation of privacy? On the other hand, given that the intent of the information is for safety purposes, one could expect that it only be used as intended, and not for MDA. These issues have yet to be resolved.

From a technical standpoint, AIS is vulnerable to both unintentional and intentional misreporting. Devices are not required to authenticate to each other and there is nothing to ensure the integrity of a ship's data. This allows for malicious activity, such as false identity and/or location information reporting. Steps taken to make the system more robust against accidental misreporting can often make intentional misreporting more difficult; however, devices can be powered off at any time, resulting in no reports.

AIS is dependent on GPS for time-slot governance and position fixing[3] [12] and GPS is susceptible to interference. Therefore, adequate backup systems (for example, Loran, a network of coastal transmitters put in place for marine navigation) and procedures must be in place. The AIS frequencies are also susceptible to intentional and unintentional interference. If there is significant interference on the AIS frequencies the system becomes virtually useless.

AIS is considered to be a short-range system (typically on the order of 20-30 nm) [2]. Methods of significantly extending its range, such as by using satellite and high altitude balloons, are currently being investigated, but this is usually for passive reception of the signals only. At this point it is not clear who would be responsible for supporting any infrastructure costs for receptions past the close coastal areas.

---

[2] http://www.aislive.com/AISLivePortal/DesktopDefault.aspx
[3] If GPS, as opposed to Differential GPS, is being used a ship's position may be off by up to 100 m, http://www.esri.com/news/arcuser/0103/differential1of2.html

Fishing boats are not obligated to use AIS. This is a case where vessel owners may trade safety for privacy. Typically fishermen are not concerned with national security but are very concerned with preserving privacy (for example, of their fishing areas). They may opt to forego the safety features of AIS rather than make their location and other details known.

4.2 LRIT

LRIT was designed to enhance national security and is being spearheaded by the US with support from other coast guards. As previously noted, LRIT will provide awareness of the location and movements of ships intending to enter a nation's ports, ships traversing a nation's coastal waters within 1000 nm, and global awareness of ships flying a country's flag (hence the "long" range). Data will be stored for up to two years for auditing purposes. By providing maritime domain awareness, LRIT can aid in thwarting potential maritime attacks. Although the full economic impact of a successful attack would be difficult to project, Cairns states that an attack on US west coast ports is estimated to be $140 million to $2 billion over eleven days [3].

The IMO claims that only recipients who are entitled to receive LRIT information will have access and that safeguards regarding confidentiality have been built into the regulatory provisions[4]. The MSC's performance standards for LRIT address the security of LRIT data in transit and in storage [13]. ASPs must ensure the reliable and secure collection, storage and routing of LRIT information, CSPs are responsible for the secure point-to-point transfer of LRIT information, and DCs need a secure transmission method with the International LRIT Data Exchange and a secure authentication method with data users. The International LRIT Data Exchange is required to use a secure access method with the DCs and cannot archive LRIT information. Landline communications must provide security using methods such as authorization, authentication, confidentiality and integrity [13].

---

[4] http://www.imo.org/Safety/mainframe.asp?topic_id=905

The technical specifications for LRIT contained in [14] are more precise when it comes to system security. LRIT components must authenticate each other using digital certificates and information can only be shared with authorized components. Digital cryptography with a minimum 128 bit key length must be employed during data transit. However, no anti-spoofing mechanisms have been designed into the system.

Governments are expected to protect the LRIT information they receive from unauthorized access or disclosure [4]. Nations are able to prevent governments from receiving LRIT information when traversing their coastal waters for security or other reasons [4]. This is specified in their Data Distribution Plan, which is shared with the IMO and subsequently all contracting governments. This caveat only holds for coastal water traversal. For safety purposes, LRIT DCs must provide LRIT information for all transmitting ships in any geographic region specified by a search and rescue (SAR) service [13]. The LRIT information is to be used only for SAR and not for any other reason, which may require special handling.

Unlike AIS, data storage policy for LRIT is fairly well defined. LRIT information can only be stored by the data centre receiving the ship's information, which for many countries will be the national data centre. There has been mention of the establishment of a European (that is, regional) Data Centre [6], which could store LRIT information for small European countries, such as Cyprus. Brazil may also be utilized as a regional data centre. In the event that a country cannot afford to establish and maintain a national data centre and is not supported by a regional data centre, the data would go to the International Data Centre (IDC).

The US has offered to build and operate an IDC and International LRIT Data Exchange. This has met with opposition, likely due in part to the US Patriot Act[5] but also for political and other reasons. Several countries expressed the view that the IDC and exchange should be neutral and truly international. A Request for Proposal has gone out for

---

[5] In particular, Section 215: Access to Records and Other Items Under the Foreign Intelligence Surveillance Act

the International LRIT Data Exchange and IDC and it is expected that the IMSO, as LRIT Coordinator, will make a decision on the location in the fall of this year.

Cost and billing issues are complicated and have not yet been resolved. The LRIT Ad Hoc Engineering Group identified billing as a major policy issue needing to be addressed by the MSC [15], and the absence of billing discussions was raised as a concern by International Radio-Maritime Committee (CIRM) members working on LRIT. In their view communications costs and billing need to be studied in order for LRIT to be implemented [6]. It was suggested that the issue of communications billing be added to the Ad Hoc Engineering Group's Terms of Reference. One of the biggest issues is the cost and support of the International Data Centre.

5. Mapping to Other Wireless Broadcast Systems

As discussed previously, both LRIT and AIS are self-reporting systems that enable the sharing of information with specific purposes in mind. The security and privacy issues of these systems should be addressed while keeping in mind some lessons learned in other wireless broadcast systems. AIS was designed with safety as the primary benefit while LRIT is intended for enhancing the coastal security of nation states. This difference in purpose naturally leads to the divergences in the structure/protocol of each system as described above. It can be argued that through aggregation and persistence of data, leakage of information and subsequent analysis that the lines between the two systems blur to the point that either could, potentially, be used to accomplish many of the goals set out for each. The entities enrolled in the self-reporting system must be aware that the information they are providing may be used for purposes other than that stated as the primary goal.

To assist with the understanding of the tradeoffs among security, privacy and safety, we can map these two systems onto more developed areas of wireless research that have grappled with these same issues. LRIT can be seen to be analogous to a Radio Frequency

Identification (RFID) tag system. With RFID systems, an RFID tag is embedded into an object and filled with information tied to that object. The tag can be active, periodically broadcasting its information, or passive, responding only to a poll from an RFID reader. With LRIT, ships report their position periodically and can respond to polls from their flag states or states whose coasts are within the specified range, so they can be seen to be mimicking both passive and active RFID systems. Like RFIDs, which only communicate with a reader (not with other tags), LRIT does not facilitate inter-ship communication. In contrast, AIS is an active, periodic, broadcast system specifically designed to enable ship-to-ship reporting with no mandate to report information back to a centralised data collection centre. AIS message routing also allows for base stations to have a repeat mode that enables a base station to essentially route AIS packets between mobile units (ships) [9]. From this perspective, AIS consists of peer-to-peer connections and can be viewed as a very basic instantiation of a Mobile Ad Hoc Network (MANET). In particular, MANETs with proactive routing protocols send out periodic messages for the purposes of neighbour discovery. The information compiled from, and provided in, these periodic messages is then used for constructing an awareness of the local environment and for building routing tables for the network as a whole. Having access to reports beyond the local range of AIS does not enhance the safety of a vessel, so AIS may not require multihop exchange of information. However, nations can (and do) deploy AIS sensors to collect AIS messages and feed them back to data centres. The result is that the AIS reports are often captured by an external sensor network, a reality that dramatically alters the range of functionality of the system. Subsequent traffic analysis of this report data is one concern – a well-known problem in MANETs [16].

Privacy and confidentiality concerns of RFID systems are also well documented [17, 18, 19 (and references therein)]. The use of RFID tags by the US military to control and maintain their inventory and supply chain provides a prime example of the caveats of such systems. An adversary can themselves scan tagged items or eavesdrop while an item is legitimately scanned. Information illicitly collected at the point of scanning may itself be of local value, for example knowing that a specific container carries munitions while another simply food supplies, but aggregated information on flows of goods may be even more concerning, revealing information about troop movements and mobilisations. To protect against the former, information can be secured through encryption so that it is recognisable only by an authorised reader. The second problem, which is essentially one of traffic analysis, is much more difficult to deal with. Even if the information is encrypted the fact that it is broadcast means that it constitutes an event. These events can be aggregated, correlated and analysed for patterns and meaning. Therefore, a self-reporting system like RFIDs naturally sacrifices privacy for some end goal. Researchers are actively working on solutions (see [17] for a recent example) but they are generally application-dependent.

LRIT is designed with security as the primary goal and the self-reports can have three different destinations – the flag state, the port state, or the coastal nations within range. However, a ship that is dutifully broadcasting reports that go to a coastal nation when within its limits cannot expect that it can no longer be tracked when it moves outside these limits and is reporting back to its flag state only. Even though the flag state information is encrypted, given the information a coastal nation has already received it could continue to monitor the traffic intended for the flag state and, with some effort, tie the information back to the appropriate vessel. This would essentially give a coastal nation the ability to track worldwide every ship that passes through its reporting zone until that ship reaches its port of call. While subscribers and proponents of LRIT may be comfortable with self-reporting for legitimate security purposes, it is unlikely they would agree to having their movements continuously tracked by every coastal nation they pass by.

The primary intent of AIS as a system designed for safety purposes accentuates some of the concerns mentioned above. There are two safety components – avoiding ship-to-ship collisions and tracking of the last known location of a vessel should it become lost or disabled. The first issue is solved by the local peer-to-peer exchange of the shorter-range (compared to LRIT) messages which allow ships to have situational awareness within the range of their messages. The second requires the deployment of the AIS sensor network by a coastal state to collect the (unsolicited) periodic broadcasts. In effect, this system is like a simple single-hop MANET with each node simultaneously reporting back to the AIS sensor network, connected to a central server. If it is accepted that AIS exists solely for safety reasons it could be argued, then, that the only information collected by the sensor network that serves this purposes is the last known location of the vessel. If privacy is truly a concern, the nodes in the sensor network could simply buffer self-reports, storing only a single report per vessel. When a new report is received from an existing contact, the previous report could be overwritten. Only when a new report is not received within a certain timeframe (given by the protocol) should a safety alert be raised and the information transmitted back to the centralised authority. If, instead, all AIS reports are intercepted, stored, and shared among nations, it could be argued that many of the aims of the LRIT system could be achieved by AIS. That is, sacrificing the privacy of a local broadcast system greatly enhances its ability to function as a security system. Using AIS explicitly for such purposes would almost certainly require participant permission. A further complication is that broadcast AIS information can be captured by third parties who can publish it. There are already companies that could facilitate such a scenario (ICAN[6], Shine Micro[7]).

A party interested in preserving its privacy within AIS may purposely alter its reports to provide misinformation. The problem of authentication and establishment of trust in peer-to-peer systems such as MANETs is complex [20]. Without access to a centralised authentication server or the distribution of pre-shared keys or certificates bound to each vessel, the possibility of inaccurate (deliberate or accidental) information compromising the safety of a vessel remains a possibility. If trust can be established between participants, they may choose to share more information in their self-reports if they feel it can enhance the effectiveness to their benefit. Effective ways in which this can be done is an open area for research.

6. Discussion and Conclusions

[6] http://www.icanmarine.com/maritimeadmins.htm
[7] http://www.shinemicro.com/Govt.asp

There remain a number of important questions to be addressed in both LRIT and AIS with respect to the tradeoffs among security, privacy and safety. These questions are more than academic as the functionality of the systems and the user "buy-in" depend strongly on the details of the implementations. It may prove to be a useful exercise to consider the lessons from other self-reporting wireless systems, such as RFIDs and MANETs, when examining the interplay among these three features, as security, privacy and safety concerns have been the objects of investigation by many researchers in these areas. In both of these analogous systems, many problems remain unresolved.

For AIS, of paramount importance is the authenticity of the self-reports. Without assurance of authenticity, neither safety nor security is achievable. Mutual authentication enhances security but does not appear to be well-considered in the current implementation of AIS. A host of other problems such as eavesdropping, message alteration, spoofing, traffic analysis and attacks (such as replays) should also be given consideration. Some of these problems may also apply to LRIT. A great deal of policy work needs to be done regarding the collection, storage and exchange of data in order to address the legitimate privacy concerns of participants. AIS information is being used for maritime domain awareness and takes the system beyond its original intent at the price of privacy. Researchers in other areas, such as radar systems, may find AIS data to be of great benefit to their work, but measures may need to be taken to anonymize (at least partially) historical data in order to obscure information that infringes upon privacy. This is a common practice for network data being analysed by security researchers.

With LRIT, privacy is willingly sacrificed for security purposes but only under certain circumstances (for example, within 1000 nm of a coastal state). This does not mean, however, that privacy is always preserved. The nature of a wireless broadcast system makes it vulnerable to traffic analysis and once LRIT information is divulged, privacy may be compromised indefinitely. The issue of the location of the International Data Centre and International LRIT Data Exchange are still in question, in large part because of concerns of who has access to the information.

One goal of this paper has been to introduce both the AIS and LRIT systems to the information security and privacy community in the hope that some of the security and privacy concerns for these systems can be addressed. A second goal has been to begin to draw links between these two maritime self-reporting systems and both RFID systems and MANETs. This goal has been partially accomplished but further work is needed to better understand the linkages and draw conclusions about the applicability of security and privacy results for RFIDs and MANETs to both AIS and LRIT.

7. References

[1] K.R. Foster and J. Jaeger, RFID Inside: The Murky Ethics of Implanted Chips, *IEEE Spectrum*, March 2007, pp. 41-48

[2] Fisheries and Oceans Canada, Vessel Monitoring System (VMS), (2005), retrieved June 2006 from http://www.glf.dfo-mpo.gc.ca/fm-gp/cp-cp/vms-ssn/vms_presentation-e.pdf

[3] W.R. Cairns, AIS and Long Range Identification and Tracking, *The Journal of Navigation* (2005), 58, pp. 181–189.

[4] Adoption of Amendments to the International Convention for the Safety of Life at Sea, 1974, as Amended, Annex 2 Resolution MSC.202(81), adopted May 19, 2006, retrieved April 2007 from http://www.imo.org/includes/blastDataOnly.asp/data_id%3D15576/20 2%2881%29.pdf

[5] Development of the Draft SOLAS Amendments on Long Range Identification and Tracking, Submitted by the Russian Federation, IMO Intersessional MSC Working Group on Long Range Identification and Tracking, MSC/ISWG/LRIT 1/3/4, September 20, 2005, retrieved April 2007 from http://www.state.gov/documents/organization/58690.pdf

[6] Draft Report of the Maritime Safety Committee on its Eighty-Second Session (continued), IMO MSC 82/Wp.8/Add.1, December 8, 2006

[7] K. Abercrombie, N. Trainor and J. Huggett, Enhancing Navigation Safety and Protection of the Marine Environment of the Great Barrier Reef and Torres Strait Region, Australian Maritime Safety Authority, retrieved April 2007 from
http://www.amsa.gov.au/About_AMSA/Corporate_information/AMSA_speeches/Austmarine_East_conf.pdf

[8] W.R. Cairns, On Watch: Vessel Tracking Technologies for Maritime Security, *US Coast Guard Proceedings*, Spring 2006, pp 32-35.

[9] T. Hammond, R. Kessel, The Implications of the Universal Shipborne Automatic Identification System (AIS) for Maritime Intelligence, Surveillance, and Reconnaissance, Defence R&D Canada – Atlantic Technical Memorandum, DRDC Atlantic TM 2003-143, August 2003.

[10] Macaluso, Capt J.J., "Maritime Domain Awareness Data Sharing Community of Interest: A new partnership explores net-centricity", The Coast Guard Journal of Safety & Security at Sea Proceedings of the Maritime Safety & Security Council, Vol. 63, Number 3, Fall 2006, pp 62-64.

[11] AIS Frequently Asked Questions, US Coast Guard Navigation Center, available April 2007 from
http://www.navcen.uscg.gov/enav/ais/AISFAQ.HTM#0.4_7

[12] Review of AIS, International Sailing Federation, available April 2007 from
http://www.sailing.org/default.asp?ID=j/qFni6v&MenuID=t67mGMn on~824QM6/%60xAM4Y1TU0d6YZUhv~JMBMq/RNTdbdlYpYP3P Wct8Ulz4

[13] Performance Standards and Functional Requirements for the Long Range Identification and Tracking of Ships, Annex 13 Resolution MSC.210(81), adopted May 19, 2006, retrieved April 2007 from http://www.emsa.eu.int/Docs/LRIT/msc210_81_lrit_ps.pdf

[14] Interim LRIT Technical Specifications and Other Matters, IMO Ref. T2-OSS/1.4, MSC.1/Circ.1219, December 15, 2006, retrieved April 2007 from http://www.imo.org/includes/blastDataOnly.asp/data_id%3D16797/12 19.pdf

[15] Informal Record of Discussions, LRIT Ad Hoc Engineering Group, June 2006, available April 2007 from http://www.emsa.eu.int/Docs/LRIT/lrit_ad_hoc_engineer_vancouver.p df

[16] H. Yang, H. Luo, F. Ye, S. Lu, and L. Zhang, Security in mobile ad hoc networks: challenges and solutions, *IEEE Wireless Communications*, Vol 11, Issue 1, Feb 2004, pp 38- 47.

[17] J. Cichon, M. Klonowski, and M. Kutylowski. Privacy Protection in Dynamic Systems Based on RFID Tags, *PerSec 07*, March 2007.

[18] S.A. Weis, S.E, Sarma, R.L. Rivest, D.W. Engels, Security and Privacy Aspects of Low-Cost Radio Frequency Identification Systems, *Security in Pervasive Computing (SPC) 2003*, LNCS 2802, 201-212.

[19] A. Juels, RFID security and privacy: a research survey, *IEEE Journal on Selected Areas in Communications*, Vol. 24, Issue 2, Feb 2006, pp 381-294.

[20] N. Aboudagga, M. T. Refaei, M. Eltoweissy, L. A. DaSilva, J-J. Quisquater, Authentication protocols for ad hoc networks: Taxonomy and research issues, *Proceedings of the 1st ACM international workshop on Quality of service & security in wireless and mobile networks*, October 2005.

Dismantling the Twelve Privacy Purposes

Sabah Al-Fedaghi

Computer Engineering Department , Kuwait University

P.O. Box 5969 Safat 13060 Kuwait

sabah@eng.kuniv.edu.kw

Abstract. *Purpose* appears in all privacy guidelines, codes, policies, and legislations. It plays a central role in many privacy-related systems such as P3P, Hippocratic databases, EPAL, and XACML. We show that the P3P 12 standard purposes mix uses of personal information with acts on personal information and mix uses of personal information privacy with other states of affairs that have several interpretations. Some purposes are not even strongly privacy-related purposes. In this paper, P3P is singled out as the object of study; however, the implication applies similarly to other projects. We propose to use chains of information handling that let the user exercise more control on the use of his/her PI and allow the personal information gatherer to excise more control on the processing and accessing of information in its procession.

1. Introduction

The privacy landscape is rich with privacy-enhancing technology in response to concern about privacy erosion caused by the increased appetite for personal information in all aspects of life. The Platform for Privacy Preferences (P3P) provides means for policy privacy specification and exchange [13]. The Enterprise Privacy Authorization Language (EPAL) concentrates on privacy authorization in enterprise-internal privacy policies [7]. The eXtensible Access Control Markup Language (XACML) supports directly-enforceable policies both for privacy and for access control in general [10]. Hippocratic databases have been introduced as systems that integrate privacy protection within relational database systems [1].

We claim that in spite of these impressive systems, insufficient attention is directed to fundamental terms of informational privacy. In this paper, we single out P3P since it is the oldest of these projects that is supposed to reach a mature foundation of specification. We direct our efforts on the most important notion in P3P and other systems: purpose.

Please use the following format when citing this chapter:

Al-Fedaghi, S., 2007, in IFIP International Federation for Information Processing, Volume 238, Trust Management, eds. Etalle, S., Marsh, S., (Boston: Springer), pp. 207–222.

2. Problem

Purpose commonly is defined in general terms as how the collected data can be used, or the intended use of the data element, or a description of the reason(s) for data collection and data access [8]. According to Thibadeau,

> Because P3P is an outstanding work, it deserves serious critique. It is essential to know what it does, and what it does not do. For a period of time, P3P will be a work in progress. There is opportunity to hone the edge on this knife so beautifully made [15].

One edge to be honed is more specificity in declaring the purpose. Purpose is defined in the 2006 W3C Working P3P Draft as "The reason(s) for data collection and use." Reasons are given in response to why questions. Why do you collect my personal information? Because I want to use it in "telemarketing," "delivery," etc. This is analogous to "Why do you want to take my money?" "Because I want to use it in trading, investing, etc."

(1) I need to know how
However, there remains the equally important how question:
How do you use my money for this purpose?
To answer this question, you don't give me reasons but actions. For example,
- I will use it to buy and sell stocks, or
- I will buy with it old houses to renovate and sell for profit.
I would be foolish if I were satisfied with only the answer to the why question.
- Why do you want my money?
- To invest it for you.
- OK, here it is.

This is approximately the logic of personal information exchange in P3P. We will propose a mechanism to specify the answer to the how and why questions concurrently.

(2) Separating the why from the how
We investigate the semantics of the P3P 12 purposes and show that their specifications sometimes reflect the answer to the why question rather than reasons that answer the why question. Take, for example, the P3P purpose "I collect personal information 'to determine the habits, interests, or other characteristics of individuals and combine it with identified data to make a decision that directly affects that individual'" [15]. The determination of habits, interests, or other characteristics of individuals, and combining them with identified data, is an answer to the how question, while making a decision is subject to the answer to the why question. As we will see later, this separation is important because there are a limited number of ways of how to use personal information; hence, the answer to the why question can be specified in a precise manner.

(3) Several interpretations of the same purpose
The interpretation of the 12 P3P purposes is overly verbose. According to Thibadeau,

We could have hundreds of very specific purposes. For people who know about the science of human intentionality, it makes sense to be able to list many specific purposes...and the writers of the 1.0 working draft specification...understand that a purpose or intent is actually a simple thing to state and evaluate [15].

Answering the *how* question uncovers multiple interpretations of the answer to the question "Why are you collecting and using my personal information?"

(4) Is this a privacy-related purpose?

The 12 P3P purposes sometimes sway away from privacy-related situations. A P3P purpose, "Information may be used to...without tying identified data," doesn't deal with personal information defined as personally-identifying information. If these purposes are necessary, then they should not be mixed in the same basket with personal information use purposes. This point will be discussed in section nine

3. Background

This section summarizes published works that give the definition of personal information (PI) and its flow model [3] [4]. The purpose is to make the paper a self-contained work since these publications are very recent.

3.1 Personal Information

Personal information theory assumes two fundamental types of entities: *Individuals* and *Non-individuals* [6]. *Individuals* represents the set of natural persons and *Non-individuals* represents the set of non-persons. Personal information (PI) is any linguistic expression that has referent(s) in *Individuals*. There are two types of PI:

(1) *Atomic* personal information is an expression that has a single human referent (e.g., *John is 25 years old, Bob is a poor guy*). "Referent," here, implies an identifiable (natural) person.

(2) *Compound* personal information is an expression that has more than one human referent (e.g., *John loves Mary*).

The relationship between individuals and their own atomic personal information is called *proprietorship*. If p is a piece of atomic personal information of v ∈ *Individuals*, then p is proprietary personal information of v, and v is its *proprietor*. An Example of non-personal information is *Spare part 123456 is in store XYZ*. Any compound personal statement is privacy-reducible to a set of atomic personal statements. Personal information privacy involves acts on personal information in the context of creating, collecting, processing, disclosing, and communicating this type of information.

3.2 Personal Information Flow Model (PIFM)

The personal information flow model divides the functionality handling PI into four stages that include informational privacy entities and processes, as shown in Figure 1.

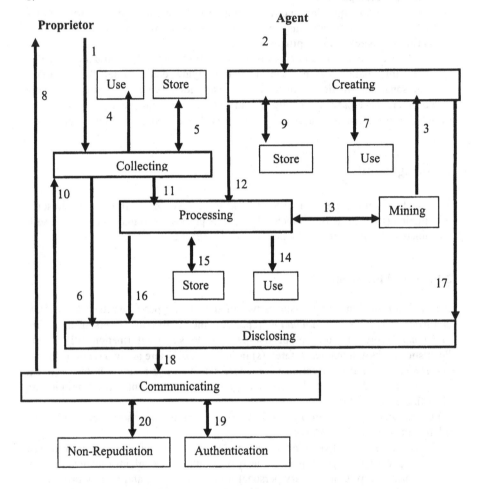

Figure 1. The PI Flow Model (PIFM).

New PI is created at Points 1, 2, and 3 by proprietors or non-proprietors (e.g., medical diagnostics by physicians) or is deduced by someone (e.g., data mining that generates new information from existing information). The created information is utilized either at Point 4 (e.g., use: decision-making), Point 5 (stored), or Point 6, where it is disclosed immediately. Processing the personal information stage involves acting (e.g., anonymization, data mining, summarizing, translating) on PI that includes using and storing processed PI (Points 14 and 15). The disclosure stage involves releasing PI to insiders or outsiders (Points 18, 19, and 20). The "disposal" or disappearance of PI can happen anywhere in the model, such as in the transformation to an anonymous form in the processing stage. "Store" in Figure 1 denotes both storing and retrieving operations.

Using the PI flow model, we can build a system that involves a proprietor on one side and others (other persons, agencies, companies, etc.) who perform different types of activities in the PI transformations among the four stages of PIFM. We will refer to any of these as PI agents. PI agents may include anyone who participates in activities over PI.

How many ways to act on PI? Types are distinguished as acts on PI as follows:
- Gathering personal information from: (1) proprietor him/her, (2) an agent who possesses the personal information.
- Storing/retrieval of personal information: (5) raw (as collected) data, (15) processed data, (9) created data.
- Processing personal information: (11) non-mining processing of collected PI, (12) non-mining processing of created PI, (13) mining that produces implied PI, (3) mining that creates new PI (e.g., *John is risk*).
- Creating personal information: (3) automatically (mining), (1) manually by proprietor, (2) manually by non-proprietor.
- Disclosing personal information: (6) gathered (collected) data, (16) processed data, (17) created data, (8) disclosing to proprietor, (10) disclosing to non-proprietor.
- Use: (4) raw (as collected) data, (14) processed data, (7) created data.
- Communicating personal information: (18) sending through the communication channel, (19) and (20) characteristics of communication channel.

These acts form ordered sequences or *chains*, as will be discussed later.

4. Purposes and P3P

In P3P, we find 12 declared standard purposes: current, admin, develop, tailoring, pseudo-analysis, pseudo-decision, individual-analysis, individual-decision, contact, historical, telemarketing, and other-purpose. The purpose element in P3P contains one or more of these pre-defined values and can be qualified with values such as opt-in, opt-out, and always. These purposes suffer from the following shortcomings:
- Not specific, since it is possible to produce an infinite number of these purposes.
- Mixing uses of personal information with acts on personal information.
- Mixing uses of personal information privacy with other states of affairs that have several interpretations.

In order to dismantle these purposes, we need to construct a framework for the semantics of acts and uses.

5. Framework

Acts perform an action on something, while *Uses* refers to putting something to a particular purpose. Consider the case of acts and uses with respect to grapes:
(1) Acts on grape: Plant it; Eat it; Collect it, Store it, Dry it …

(2) Uses of grape: Medical treatment of a person, Decorating cakes (eyes in a face), Celebrating [I/others], Teaching students addition and subtraction, Fueling cars (bioethanol fuel).

To distinguish between acts and uses, we adopt the structure of agent/action/patient shown in Figure 2. It includes an agent who acts on a patient. "Patient" is a term used in ethics to refer to the object that receives the action. For *acts*, this agent/action/patient becomes actor/acts-on/patient, as shown in 3. For *uses*, the model involves a third entity: the usee, as shown in Figure 4. The usee is the one used by the user to act on a patient. For example, a physician uses information to treat a patient.

Agent —act→ Patient	Actor —act→ Patient
Figure 2. Basic agent/patient.	**Figure 3. Binary relationship in acts.**

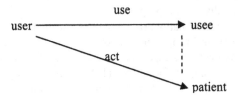

Figure 4. Ternary relationship of uses.

Here, we have a feature that distinguishes acts on personal information from its uses. In acts, the patient is personal information, while in uses, the patient is not personal information.

6. Dismantling "CURRENT"

According to P3P, the purpose "current" refers to:

> Completion and Support of Activity For Which Data Was Provided: Information may be used by the service provider to complete the activity for which it was provided, whether a one-time activity such as returning the results from a Web search, forwarding an email message, or placing an order; or a recurring activity such as providing a subscription service; or allowing access to an online address book or electronic wallet [16].

We show that this purpose:
- Mixes uses and acts
- Displays uses that have several interpretations (several possible chains)
- Displays acts that have several interpretations (several possible chains)

Mixing Uses and Acts

The definition of P3P purposes mixes acts and uses, as shown in Table 1.

Table 1. Acts and uses in purpose: current.

Example given by P3P	Type
Returning the results from a Web search	use
Forwarding an email message	act
Placing an order	use
Providing a subscription service	use
Allowing access to an online address book or electronic wallet	use

Example: Consider the phrase "Completion and Support of Activity For Which Data Was Provided." Analogously, we can introduce the following scenario:

- I am taking your money to complete and support activities for which you give me your money.

- I give you money to buy laptop from you.

- I am taking your money to complete and support delivering the laptop to you (use).

In this case, *acts* on money can include paying money to my employees, paying money for others (DHL, manufacturer), charging money, converting money …

Table 2 shows the five examples given in P3P purpose and the equivalent money-scenario actions. In (2), "Forwarding an email message" and "Transferring money" are *acts* where PI and money are patients, respectively. Forwarding an email message is a communicating act because the message is the patient, i.e., the object of forwarding. In contrast, in (1), "returning the results from a Web search" and "delivering laptop," the PI and money are used to perform non-PI actions.

This discussion shows that P3P purpose "current" mixes uses and acts.

Table 2

	P3P Examples	Money examples
1	Returning the results from a Web search	Delivering laptop
2	Forwarding an email message	Transferring money
3	Placing an order	Placing an order for laptop
4	Providing a subscription service	Providing a maintenance service for laptop
5	Allowing access to an online address book or electronic wallet	Allowing access to workshop

Uses have several interpretations

In P3P's purpose "current": *uses* have several interpretations. Figure 5 shows one possible interpretation. PI is collected and then used without processing it or disclosing it. Yet, another interpretation is possible in another stage.

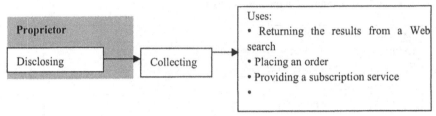

Figure 5. Uses on col

Acts have several interpretations

The P3P's example "Forwarding an email message" ((2) in table 2)) depends on whether the email contains PI or otherwise. "Forwarding a non-PI email message" is a mix of use and a chain of acts, as shown in Figure 6.

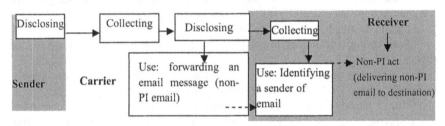

Figure 6. A mix of use and a chain of acts.

If the email contains PI, then the mail itself is part of the PI flow, as shown in Figure 7. P3P "forwarding an email message" hides important differences related to the type of email. When I say *give me your PI in order to forward an email message*, then this may mean:

(1) Forwarding that involves personal information.
(2) Forwarding that involves non-personal information

P3P's purposes mix these two different actions.

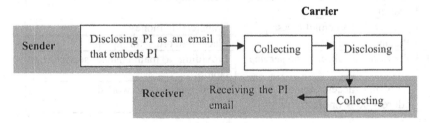

Figure 7. A chain of acts.

7. Dismantling "ADMIN"

P3P "Admin" purpose refers to:

> Web Site and System Administration: Information may be used for the technical support of the Web site and its computer system. This would include processing computer account information, information used in the course of securing and maintaining the site, and verification of Web site activity.

This would include
(1) Processing computer account information,
(2) Information used in the course of securing and maintaining the site,
(3) Verification of Web site activity by the site or its agents.

This method of description juxtaposes acts and uses. It can be written (or graphed) systematically thus: PI is *gathered, processed*, and *used* [acts on PI] for [uses of PI]: (1) The technical support of the Web site and its computer system

(2) Securing and maintaining the site

Notice how such a statement reflects the subgraph in the PIFM: gathering → processing →using →different types of usage. The term "processing" here may be interpreted to involve mining. In this case, the wording will be:

PI is *gathered, processed, mined*, and *used* for…

Item (3) raises doubt about the meaning of "its agents." If these agents are different entities than the collecting entity then the PI in the PIFM crosses borders to another region of PIFM through *disclosing*.

This purpose, in addition to its juxtaposing description, is also vague.

Example: According to P3Pbook.com [9],

> We … collect … the information contained in standard web server logs … The information in these logs will be used only by us and the server administrators for website and system administration and for improving this site. It will not be disclosed unless required by law. We may retain these log files indefinitely.

But "will be used only by us and the server administrators for website and system administration and for improving this site" can mean anything except disclosing the information to others. The chain (1)(4)(5)(11)(13)(3)(9) means that we will collect your information, process it, mine it, and generate new information about you to be stored indefinitely. We can see that the current P3P method of specification of purpose expresses little to the user. In [5], *chains* is used to replace "business purpose."

8. Dismantling "DEVELOP"

P3P "develop" purpose refers to:

> Research and Development: Information may be used to enhance, evaluate, or otherwise review the site, service, product, or market. This does not include personal information used to tailor or modify the content to the specific individual nor information used to evaluate, target, profile, or contact the individual.

Using PI "to enhance, evaluate, or otherwise review the site, service, product, or market" can have two types of interpretation: good and bad. These two interpretations are shown in Figures 8 and 9. The exceptions in the statement of the P3P purpose try to avoid the bad interpretation. However, the exceptions by themselves do not exclude the possibility of disclosure to a third party.

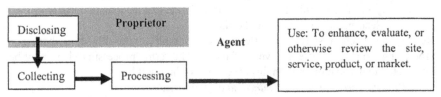

Figure 8. Good interpretation of purpose "develop."

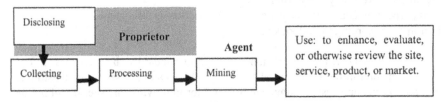

Figure 9. Bad interpretation of purpose "develop."

We can see how the fragmented P3P method of specifying purposes is where exceptions are specified in a non-systematic way. PIFM forces the specification of all of the trail of flow from source of creating PI to the destination where PI is used.

9. Where is the Personal Information?

The P3P purpose "Pseudonymous Analysis" refers to:

> Information may be used to create or build a record of a particular individual or computer that is tied to a pseudonymous identifier without tying identified data (such as name, address, phone number, or email address) to the record...

If the requested personal information will be merely anonymized, then why not asking for de-identified information in the first place. This purpose does not involve personal information. The situation is as collecting information about the shopping of a completely veiled woman. You do not need any personal information to accomplish that. Thus, the collected information is not covered by the PI flow model. This purpose is mixing privacy with ethics and etiquettes.

10. Telemarketing

The P3P purpose "Telemarketing" refers to

> Contacting Visitors for Marketing of Services or Products Via Telephone: Information may be used to contact the individual via a voice telephone call for promotion of a product or service.

But which telemarketing? Telemarketing use of gathered (raw) data, processed data, mined data ...? The P3P purpose "Telemarketing" specifies the end point of several possible chains in the PIFM. An important issue in this context is the completeness of specification of acts and uses. The telemarketing purpose is an example of a chain without acts but with use. The following example gives acts without use.
Example: Consider the following sentence from 2002 Doubleclick's policy: "DoubleClick does use information about your browser and Web surfing to determine which ads to show your browser." According to Hogben,

> P3P would cover the preceding sentence with the Element <customization/> and possibly <individual-decision/> and <tailoring/> however it is not clear from any of these, and it cannot be expressed, that it is for the purposes of advertising third-party products [1?].

In PIFM, "processing" involves many standard processing of information such as tailoring, anonymization, modification, translation, summarization, and generalization. The "patient" in each case is the personal information. The problem in Doubleclick's statement is that the chain of acts on PI is incomplete where the chain does not end in a *use*. The processing of PI "to determine which ads to show your browser" in Doubleclick's policy informs the proprietor of an act (mapping PI to ads) on his/her PI without completing the chain to such use as "advertising third-party products" or without completing the chain through crossing the boundary of disclosure to another advertising agent. We can say that the issue here is a matter of specifying (complete) chains. The specification of chains of acts on PI forces the agent to fully acknowledge all of its acts on and uses of PI.

11. Alternative Approach

The PIFM provides a foundation for developing an alternative approach. Each purpose can be translated to a set of chains of acts/uses. Chains of acts on PI are chains of *information handling* that start with one of the following acts:
- A proprietor discloses his/her PI. This act also can be described as an agent collecting PI from a proprietor.
- An agent collects PI from another agent. This act may be preceded by the act of a disclosing agent to indicate where the PI is coming from.
- A non-proprietor creates PI.
These three acts are the only sources that supply any agent with PI. Suppose that a company has a piece of personal information. This piece of information is collected either from its proprietor, from another agent, or created internally by the agent. Starting with any of these sources, that piece of PI flows into the PI information handling system (manual or automatic) subjected to different acts such as processing, utilization, mining, and so forth. This track of acts can be traced through *chains*.

In our system, we envision a Proprietor Agent (called PRAG) as an agent that examines the policy of those who request collecting or gathering the personal information. PRAG represents the proprietor in order to reach a decision about whether he/she should disclose his/her personal information. We also represent any of the others as a PI agent (called PIAG). PIAG represents anyone who participates in activities over PI except the proprietor. Figure 10 illustrates this mode of operation on PI. Of course, a proprietor can have the role of an agent (his/her own agent) and any of the others also can be its own PI agent.

Figure 10. PRAG and PIAG relation.

Both PRAG and PIAG know the PIFM. Thus, they can communicate with each other according to this knowledge. General Procedure for the dialogue between PRAG and PIAG is as follows:

1. PIAG requests PI from PRAG and sends a subgraph representing the set of acts and uses that would be performed on the requested PI.

2. PRAG examines the subgraph, and a dialogue is initiated with PIAG regarding different acts in the subgraph.

3. The results of such a dialogue may lead to: agreeing to and accepting the transaction, refusing to complete the transaction, or hanging some parts of the subgraph according to the proprietor preferences.

Example: Consider the following dialogue between PIAG and PRAG
   - PIAG requests certain PI from PRAG.
   - PRAG asks for the set of acts/uses on the requested PI.
   - PIAG sends a sub-graph.

We assume here, without loss of generality, that there is one sub-graph associated with the requested PI. Also, we assume that the sub-graph contains the specific acts and uses. For example: Use is "delivery," Processing is "statistical analysis," and Disclosure is "to XYZ crediting company."
- PRAG then asks whether it is possible to have another sub-graph that indicates that there is objection to disclosing the PI to any third party.
- PIAG answers YES if you (PRAG – its user) pay in e-cash "because we disclose your PI to check your credit."
- Etc.

From this dialogue, we see that PRAG knows PIFM. So, in general, PRAG can ask any question about PIFM. Notice that we present here the general methodology of using chains to specify the operations on PI performed on the enterprise side. The issue of user friendliness reflects a different problem that concerns the type of communication between PRAG and the proprietor. Our approach does not only allow the user to excise more control on the use of his/her PI, which he/she may elect not to do, but also allows the PI gatherer to excise more control on the processing and accessing of PI in its procession. The PIFM, for instance, can be used to define access control policy to the PI databases [2].

To compare the chains approach with the proposed W3C Platform for Privacy Preferences [16], we utilize the following scenario used in the W3C Working Draft:

Claudia has decided to check out a store called CatalogExample, located at http://www.catalog.example.com/. Let us assume that CatalogExample has placed P3P policies on all of their pages, and that Claudia is using a Web browser with P3P built in. Claudia types the address for CatalogExample into her Web browser. Her browser is able to automatically fetch the P3P policy for that page.... Then she proceeds to the checkout page. The checkout page of CatalogExample requires some additional information: Claudia's name, address, credit card number, and telephone number. Another P3P policy is available that describes the data that is collected here and states that her data will be used only for completing the current transaction, her order [16].

Assuming that the credit card has been issued by different company, the phrase "her data will be used only for completing the current transaction, her order" means on the face the chain $(1_x)(4_x)(5_x)(6_x)(10)(11)_z(16)_z(6)_z(10)_x$ where the subscript x refers to CatalogExample and z refers to the crediting company (RECIPIENT element). The parenthesis in the chain denotes a don't care sequence. The chain represents a well-understood series of acts. In English, this chain expresses the following: *Your personal information will be stored and used for delivery by us and disclosed to your credit company, which solely will process it to check your credit and return OK/not OK for us. Accordingly, your merchandise will be delivered to you by us and your PI will be kept as a record of the transaction for (say) a year.*

The chain method is an explicit specification of this instance of acting on personal information (supplemented with retention period, etc.), while "her data will be used only for completing the current transaction, her order" is ambiguous specification. "Completing the current transaction" can mean for CatalogExample many things that cover different chains in CatalogExample's region of actions and the credit card company's region of acts and beyond these two companies. According to the W3C, "P3P declarations are positive, meaning that sites state what they do, rather than what they do not do," [16] simply because it is impractical to list "what they do not do." In contrast, the PI flow model represents a "closed system" that excludes what is not specified. Thus, the specified chains are the permitted acts on PI, while the rest of the chains are not permitted.

A policy specification and its "privacy statements" can be made in chain language instead of an imprecise list of items. The PI flow model is simple to understand with a limited number of acts on personal information that can be used in designing a privacy preference language.

According to the W3C Working Draft's scenario,

> Claudia's browser examines this P3P policy. Imagine that Claudia has told her browser that she wants to be warned whenever a site asks for her telephone number. In this case, the browser will pop up a message saying that this Web site is asking for her telephone number and explaining the contents of the P3P statement. Claudia then can decide if this is acceptable to her. If it is acceptable, she can continue with her order; otherwise, she can cancel the transaction.

But how can Claudia decide? The telephone number can be used in many chains that can be interpreted as "the current transaction." The usual behavior is obeying the maximum entropy law (uncertainty means 50% opportunity for misuse; hence, cancel the transaction). However, if she is given explicit information that her phone will be used only in the chain (1)(4)(5) (store: until delivery time and use: guarantee delivery), she probably would be more willing to complete the transaction. The basic thesis here is that the clearer picture people have regarding the fate of their personal information, the more they are willing to expend their privacy. The chain method provides the user with a full general description of what is being performed on his/her PI. According to Hogben, "P3P cannot guarantee that the promise matches the practice and presents a solution that can be compared to the solution adopted by restaurants, who wish to make clients trust their hygiene practices. They put the kitchen in full view of their customers. In the same way, given a sufficiently standardized system, perhaps based on P3P..." [12]. The PIFM certainly improves the transparency of PI handling and puts "the kitchen in full view of their customers"; nevertheless, it is not specific for particular circumstances.

According to the W3C Working Draft's scenario,

> Alternatively, Claudia could have told her browser that she wanted to be warned only if a site is asking for her telephone number and was going to give it to third parties and/or use it for uses other than completing the current transaction. In that case, she would have received no prompts from her browser at all, and she could proceed with completing her order.

Again, "giving it to third parties" and "use it for uses other than completing the current transaction" are descriptive specifications that can mean many things. "Third party" may mean the credit company that already has Claudia's number or a marketing company. The method of specification of a different third party is ambiguous. Even if these third parties are specified, what type of acts will be performed on personal information? The phrase "use it for uses other than completing the current transaction" does not specify whether the uses involved are informational acts or non-informational acts.

12. Privacy and Secrecy

In P3P, you "enumerate the types of data or data elements collected and explain how the data will be used" [16]. According to the W3C Draft,

> Identified data is information in a record or profile that can reasonably be tied to an individual... The P3P specification uses the term "identified" to describe a subset of this data that reasonably can be used by a data collector *without assistance from other parties to identify an individual.*

This means that the equation $a^2=b^2+c^2$ is "personal information" of Pythagoras because it "reasonably can be tied" to him. In another passage, it is stated that:

> IP addresses are not considered identified even though it is possible for someone (e.g., law enforcement agents with proper subpoena powers) to identify the individual based on the stored data... However, if a Web site collects IP addresses but actively deletes all but the last four digits of this information in order to determine short-term use, but insure that a particular individual or computer cannot be identified consistently, then the data collector can and should call this information non-identifiable.

This approach generates confusion between the definition of personal information and subsets of, restrictions on, and exceptional situation of this information. The definition involves, in addition to previous criticisms, ambiguity. What about the case of *John has bought Mary's laptop*? Is it *John's identifiable information* or *Mary's information*? Consider the information *John F. Kennedy is a very busy airport.* Is it identifiable information of John F. Kennedy?

Our definition of personal information provides a better formalism to specify this type of information. With its foundation, it is possible to add certain restrictions to make the information suitable in certain applications. According to the P3P Draft,

> The Working Group decided against an identified or identifiable label for particular types of data. However, user agent implementers have the option of assigning these or other labels themselves and building user interfaces that allow users to make decisions about web sites on the basis of how they collect and use certain types of data.

So, any data that you have can be "personal information" if you choose to call it so. Such an approach mixes personal information with non-personal (but may be personally owned) information. If I have a proof that P=NP, then this is not personal information. Personal information *refers* to its proprietor.

13. Conclusion

The personal information flow model or similar theoretical framework ought to be given more attention in order to build a foundation for personal information handling policies and systems. Many issues remain to be addressed, including concerns related to syntax specification, mapping to a user's purposes, effects on access control privacy negotiation, and privacy policy enforcement.

REFERENCES

[1] Agrawal, R. Kiernan, J. Srikant, R. and Xu, Y. (2002). Hippocratic databases. In The 28th International Conference on Very Large Databases (VLDB), Hong Kong, China, August.

[2] Al-Fedaghi, S. (2007). Beyond Purpose-Based Privacy Access Control. The 18th Australasian Database Conference, Ballarat, Australia, January 29th - 2nd February.

[3] Al-Fedaghi, S. (2006a). Anatomy of Personal Information Processing: Application to the EU Privacy Directive, Inter. Conf. on Business, Law and Technology (IBLT 2006), Copenhagen, December..

[4] Al-Fedaghi, S. (2006b). Aspects of Personal Information Theory, 7th, The Seventh Annual IEEE Information Assurance Workshop (IEEE-IAW), West Point, NY: US Military Academy, June 20-23.

[5] Al-Fedaghi, S. (2006c). Personal Information Model for P3P, W3C Workshop on Languages for Privacy Policy Negotiation and Semantics-Driven Enforcement, 17 and 18 October 2006, Ispra/Italy.

[6] Al-Fedaghi, S. (2005). How to Calculate the Information Privacy, The Third Annual Conference on Privacy, Security and Trust, St. Andrews, New Brunswick, Canada.

[7] Ashley P., Hada S., Karjoth G., Powers C., and Schunter, M. Enterprise Privacy Authorization Language, W3C Submission 10 November 2003. http://www.w3.org/Submission/EPAL/.

[8] Byun, J. Bertino, E. and Li, N. (2005). Purpose Based Access Control of Complex Data for Privacy Protection, SACMAT'05, June 1–3, 2005, Stockholm, Sweden.

[9] Cranor, L.F. Web Privacy with P3P, 2002, O'Reilly & Associateshttp://p3pbook.com/examples.html.

[10] Cover, R. (Editor), Extensible Access Control Markup Language (XACML), October 10, 2006. http://xml.coverpages.org/xacml.html#v20CD.

[11] EU Directive (1995). DIRECTIVE 95/46/EC OF THE EUROPEAN PARLIAMENT AND OF THE COUNCIL, 24 October. http://eur-lex.europa.eu/LexUriServ/LexUriServ.do?uri=CELEX:31995L0046:EN:HTML.

[12] Hogben, G. A technical analysis of problems with P3P v1.0 and possible solutions, "Future of P3P" workshop, Virginia, USA, 12-13 November, 2002. http://www.w3.org/2002/p3p-ws/pp/jrc.html.

[13] OECD (1980). Guidelines on the Protection of Privacy and Transborder Flows of Personal Data, http://www.oecd.org/document/18/0,2340,en_2649_34255_1815186_1_1_1_1,00.html.

[14] P3P (2002). The Platform for Privacy Preferences 1.0 (P3P1.0) Specification, The World Wide Web Consortium, April 16, 2002, http://www.w3.org/p3p/.

[15] Thibadeau, R., A Critique of P3P: Privacy on the Web, Aug 23, 2000 (Postscript, April 20, 2004). http://dollar.ecom.cmu.edu/p3pcritique/#postscript.

[16] W3C Working Draft 10, The Platform for Privacy Preferences 1.1 (P3P1.1) Specification, February 2006. http://www.w3.org/TR/P3P11/.

A Framework for Privacy-Preserving E-learning

Esma AÏMEUR, Hicham HAGE and Flavien Serge MANI ONANA
Département d'informatique et de recherche opérationnelle
Université de Montréal
{aimeur, hagehich, manionaf}@iro.umontreal.ca

Abstract. E-learning systems have made considerable progress within the last few years. Nonetheless, the issue of learner privacy has been practically ignored. The security of E-learning systems offers some privacy protection, but remains unsatisfactory on several levels. In this work, we corroborate the need for privacy in E-learning systems. In particular, we introduce a framework for privacy preserving E-learning to provide the learner with the possibility of combining different levels of Privacy and *Tracking* to satisfy his personal privacy concerns. This allows the learner to perform learning activities and to prove his achievements (such as with anonymous transcripts and anonymous degrees) without exposing various aspects of his private data. In addition, we introduce the *Blind Digital Certificate*, a digital certificate that does not reveal the learner's identity. Finally, we report on the implementation and validation of our approach in the context of an E-testing system.

1   Introduction

E-learning emerged over 20 years ago. At first, it consisted solely of text, like a book on a screen, and was ineffective and unpopular with learners. Today, E-learning has become richer with multimedia content and more interactive. In a typical E-learning system, other than the Tutor and Learner interfaces, there are many components collaborating in order to analyze the learner's skills, develop and deliver proper training material, and evaluate the learning process. Nonetheless, for simplicity, we group these components into four major components: the Tutor Environment, the Learner Environment, Data Storage and the System Manager (Fig. 1). The Tutor Environment is composed of tools and functionalities that can be grouped into three major parts: Content Authoring to create learning objects and assessments or to import/export learning material from other systems. Course

Please use the following format when citing this chapter:

Aïmeur, E., Hage, H. and Mani Onana, F. S., 2007, in IFIP International Federation for Information Processing, Volume 238, Trust Management, eds. Etalle, S., Marsh, S., (Boston: Springer), pp. 223–238.

Management offers class management tools such as electronic grade books, and splitting the class for group work. Finally, Learner Tracking allows the tutor to track learner (or group) activities and performance, and to offer personalized feedback. The Learner Environment on the other hand offers the learner a Learning Environment to perform the learning tasks assigned by the tutor, a set of Productivity Tools such as to track his progress and performance, search tools, and a forum. In addition, Evaluation and Assessment tools allow the learner to take un-graded practice tests and quizzes, and to actually take a graded assessment.

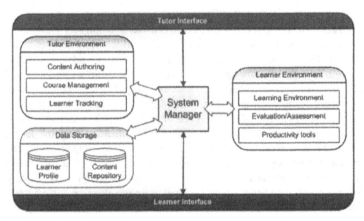

Fig. 1. Generic E-learning architecture

The Data Storage components contain all the necessary data and information. The Learner Profile stores all the relevant information about the learner such as identification data (name, age, gender, etc.), learning style, preferences and the courses the learner has passed/failed. On the other hand, the Content Repository contains the learning objects and assessments. The System Manager is a set of tools and protocols to handle communication and access privileges. For example the System Manager assures that a learner does not have access to the tutor environment and vice versa. Moreover, the System Manager arbitrates the access to the Data Storage so as to verify that each module or component is accessing the proper data.

One of the main advantages of E-learning is its adaptability to the learner's specific needs and preferences. But in order to do so, the E-learning systems must collect large amounts of information about the learner [1], thus violating his *privacy*, which is the claim of individuals to determine what information about themselves is known to others, as well as when and how it is used [2]. The security aspects of E-learning systems do offer some privacy protection; nonetheless it remains unsatisfactory on several levels. Other than the case of Head-in-the-sand privacy (by which the learner wants to keep secret his ignorance even from himself), learners might need to keep private different parts of their profile for different reasons. For example, a learner who is following a professional training course, for competitive reasons, would rather keep his identity hidden; yet, he wouldn't mind leaving a trace of his activities in the E-learning system. On the other hand, a secret agent would rather take the training course for a top-secret mission without revealing his identity and without even leaving a trace that someone took this training. Thus, in order to satisfy various privacy needs, we adapt the levels of Privacy and the levels of Tracking introduced in [3-4] to the context of E-learning. In particular, learners are able to receive anonymous transcripts and anonymous degrees such as to prove their accomplishments and achievements to third entities (employers, other E-learning systems, etc.) without compromising their private data. Moreover, in order for the learner to prove that he is the rightful owner of the anonymous transcript or degree, we introduce the concept of *Blind Digital Certificates*, a digital certificate that does not reveal the learner's identity. Although issuing anonymous credentials and certificates is not a new idea, *Blind Digital Certificates* are designed for the specific structure of the e-learning environment. We are aware that not everybody will embrace our wish for privacy. Nevertheless, as many would agree, we consider privacy to be a fundamental human right: it is not negotiable! This is why we introduce Privacy-Preserving E-learning as an alternative to standard E-learning. Of course, the final choice belongs to each learner. As a proof of concept, we use public-key cryptography as well as digital signatures to implement and validate an E-testing system (the Evaluation/Assessment component in Fig. 1) along with the Privacy-Preserving Processes to satisfy the various privacy and tracking levels. In this E testing setting, depending on the selected privacy level, some of the learner profile's data is encrypted, and the remaining data is stored in the clear. Moreover, based on the learner's learning objectives, the E-testing system signs and authenticates his achievements.

The paper is organized as follows: Section 2 highlights the existing literature on privacy in E-learning and offers some preliminaries on Pseudonymous and Anonymous Credentials. Section 3 raises privacy issues in E-learning and our proposed framework to solve these issues. In Section 4, we introduce Privacy-Preserving E-learning. Section 5 details the implementation and validation of our approach in the context of E-testing. Section 6 offers a discussion of further issues to consider and Section 7 concludes the paper and offers pointers to future works.

2   Related work

2.1   Related work on privacy in E-learning

Although learner privacy is barely addressed within E-learning systems, there were concerns raised with regards to security. There exists literature, such as [5], on how to achieve two key security requirements: *confidentiality* and *integrity*, which provide a certain level of privacy. **Integrity** guarantees that the data is not maliciously or accidentally tampered with or modified: for example, when the learner submits his test, he requires the guarantee that his test answers are not modified after his submission. **Confidentiality** assures that the data and information is kept secret and private and is disclosed only to the authorized person(s): for example, test scores must be accessible only to the appropriate tutor. The confidentiality of the information is considered at two different stages: while it is being transmitted to/from the E-learning system, and when it is stored within the E-learning system. In the first case, the data can be encrypted using Public Key Encryption such that only the appropriate receiver can read the data. In the second case, the use of access control mechanisms [6] can be employed to restrict access to the data. Access control cannot totally guarantee the privacy of the learner: first of all, it does not protect against a *super user* with full access privileges. Second, the learner has no control on which information about him is being gathered by the E-learning system. Although Privacy Policies have been provided for this purpose [7], they cannot restrict unwanted access to the data. One cannot preserve the learner's privacy without first identifying the issues and then defining the proper framework to solve these issues (Section 3.1 and 3.2).

2.2   Pseudonymous and Anonymous Credentials

Certificate Authorities (CA) are trusted entities whose central responsibility is certifying the authenticity of entities (persons or organizations) and their public keys. More precisely, an entity certificate issued and signed by a CA acts as proof that the legitimate public key is associated with the entity. Usually, the CA makes the decision to issue a digital certificate based on evidence or knowledge obtained in verifying the identity of the owner. In the context of privacy-preserving systems, the CA cannot be used to protect user private data and transactions. Therefore, new approaches are considered.

In 1985, Chaum [8] introduced the concept of pseudonymous credentials to protect individual privacy. More precisely, the resulting system enables users to engage in several anonymous and untraceable electronic transactions with organizations. Two years later, the implementation of this concept was proposed by Chaum and Evertse [9]. However, it was not suitable in practice because it relied on the existence of a semi-trusted third party participating in all communications.

In 2000, Brand [10] used several properties of Chaum's original concept to introduce a privacy-enhanced certificate system. Here, the system consists of two entities (Organizations and Users) and two protocols (Issue and Show). Unfortunately, Brand's approach is also limited for practical implementations. For instance, every Brand's credential is unique, thus it can be showed only once; otherwise, transactions by the same user could be linked. To overcome this limitation, the system needs to be extended by introducing recertification or batch issuing mechanisms [10].

Another implementation of Chaum's proposal is the credential system proposed by Camenisch and Lysyanskaya [11], which is based on previous work by Lysyanskaya et al. [12]. Here, users first register with the root pseudonym authority before using the system. Thus, users are unable to build up several parallel identities and they can be traced in case of fraudulent transactions. Users are limited to at most one pseudonym per organization. Each credential is related to a single attribute and an expiry date. Moreover, users are able to choose which statement to prove about an attribute, such as choosing to prove that the value of attribute "age" is greater than 18. While considered an interesting implementation of the concept of pseudonyms and credentials, Brand's solution has the drawback of being based on zero knowledge proofs, thus the system is difficult to implement in environments with limited resources.

Although the previous general solutions for anonymity, pseudonyms and credentials can be used to solve issues related to user privacy in various domains, we aim to use the specific structure of an E-learning setting in order to seek more efficient solutions. Therefore, we introduce the concept of Blind Digital Certificates, to enable privacy-enhanced access to E-learning data.

3   Privacy in E-learning

3.1   Issues to solve

Privacy is nearly absent in current E-learning systems. Only primitive forms of privacy are offered in some platforms, such as not allowing the tutor any access to information about auto-evaluations performed by the learners. Nonetheless, the tutor has access to virtually all the remaining information including who are the students, what parts of the course they referred to, how many times and for how long, all the messages in the forums, and all the information about the quizzes and tests the learner took in his course. There are many reasons why a learner would like to keep his information private. We group these reasons under two main categories: *Competitive* and *Personal*. In the **Competitive** context, the learner requires his privacy due to competitive considerations. Consider, for example, a prominent politician taking a course to increase his knowledge in a certain domain, which will give him an advantage over his opponents. Other than for protecting himself from any prejudice from the part of the tutor, he has the right and interest in keeping this fact hidden, and his performance results private, from public knowledge and scrutiny, especially from his opponents. As another example, consider a company that uses E-learning for employee training purposes. If competitors have knowledge of the training and the performance of the employees, it could seriously affect the competitiveness of the company and its reputation, especially if the employees performed poorly. Finally, in the case of a military training E-learning system, just knowing that secret agents performed a specific training (such as desert or jungle survival techniques) could jeopardize their mission objectives. In the **Personal** context, the learner requires his privacy due to personal considerations. For example, he may wish to protect himself from a biased tutor. The bias of the tutor might stem from prejudice or stereotyping, based on a previous encounter with the learner, or even from personal reasons. Another reason a learner would prefer to keep his privacy is the increased pressure and stress due to performance anxiety; a learner might feel more comfortable and relaxed knowing the tutor will not know how he performed in the test.

In addition, there are issues to consider with regards to the learner's educational goal. An employee must be able to prove to his manager that he completed the training successfully without exposing his privacy. Moreover, a learner must be able to prove that he finished the prerequisites for a certain course, to assert that he has the required degree to obtain a job, and he should be able to pursue higher education while maintaining his privacy.

3.2   Framework for solving the issues

Our task is to provide an architecture for E-learning systems in which privacy issues can be addressed. With this in mind, we consider the following components of the learner's data, which are of interest from a privacy point of view.

- **The identity (id):** refers to information that makes it possible to determine physically who the learner is (or at least to seriously circumscribe the possibilities). This includes data such as his name, address, and student id number.
- **The demographic profile (dp):** refers to demographic characteristics of the learner, such as age, gender, weight, race, ethnic origin, language, etc.
- **The learning profile (lp):** refers to information such as the learner's qualifications, his learning style, interests, goal and aspirations.
- **The course history (ch):** lists the courses the learner has followed in the past, and their respective information such as the learner's activities within the course and his final grade.
- **The current courses (cc):** lists the courses in which the learner is currently registered and those he is attending, as well as the courses' respective information such as the learner's activities within the course.

These elements constitute the Learner Profile, $L = (id, dp, lp, ch, cc)$. Moreover, we define, in this context, a learner's activity within a course as being any act involving one of the course's tools or resources. For example, an activity might involve the posting of a message in the forum, using one of the course's learning objects, or even taking a quiz or a test.

The above elements constitute the personal information on which we base our privacy framework for E-learning systems. Since different learners prefer different degrees of privacy, we adapt the four levels of privacy introduced in [3] to the context of E-learning.

1. **No Privacy:** the learner doesn't wish, or doesn't care to keep private any of his information. He does not mind the compilation of a dossier about him that consists of his identity, demographic information as well as his learning history.
2. **Soft Privacy:** the learner wants to keep his identity and demographic profile private, but he does not mind if the tutor has access to his learning profile, course history and current courses.

3. **Hard Privacy:** the learner wants to keep his identity, demographic profile, course history and learning profile private, but he does not mind if his current courses are known.

4. **Full Privacy:** the learner wants to keep secret every component of his personal data.

Another dimension to consider, which is independent of the personal data listed above, is the tracking of learners within a course. Even under soft, hard or full-privacy constraints, some learners might not want the tutor to know their activities and navigation within the system. Thus, we introduce the following terminology, inspired by [4], to account for the levels of tracking that different learners might accept.

1. **Strong Tracking:** the system can relate the activities performed within all the courses to the specific learner, even though that learner may be anonymous. In this case, the system can track the same learner u and his access to courses c_1, c_2 ... c_n.

2. **Average Tracking:** the system can relate the activities within a course to the same learner u, but cannot relate them to other activities within other courses. In this case, the system can relate the activity of u_1 in c_1, of u_2 in c_2 ... and of u_n in c_n, but cannot link u_1 to u_2 to ... u_n.

3. **Weak Tracking:** in this case, although the system recognizes the learner u as a regular visitor, it cannot link him to a course nor trace his activities.

4. **No Tracking:** in this case, the system cannot even recognize the learner u as a recurring user of the system.

For example, a learner, Alice, is using a privacy-aware E-learning system to take the following courses: CSC101 and CSC102. In the case of **Strong Tracking**, Alice creates a pseudonym, A, and uses it to access and perform the learning activities in CSC101 and CSC102. In the case of **Average Tracking**, Alice creates two pseudonyms, A1 and A2, one for each course, such that the system cannot relate A1 and A2 to Alice, nor to each other. Hence, whenever Alice needs to access and perform the learning activities in CSC101 or CSC102, she uses respectively A1 or A2. In the case of **Weak Tracking**, the system only records that Alice was logged in, but leaves no trace of her activity (nor identity). And, in the case of **No Tracking**, the system cannot even trace that Alice was logged in at all. Selecting No Tracking is similar to using a guest account to access a demo of the E-learning system. If the learner requires a proof of his achievements (Section 4.1), he must select at least Weak Tracking.

4 Privacy-Preserving E-learning

Now that the privacy issues are defined and the framework to solve these issues is set, we present our solution: Privacy-Preserving E-learning. We first introduce the tools we use to protect learner privacy, and then we present our solution, which utilizes Public Key Cryptosystems (PKCs). In the remainder of this work, we use the following notation: E is an Encryption Algorithm which computes the ciphertext $c = E_{pk}(m)$ of a message m, given a public key pk; and D is a Decryption Algorithm which computes the cleartext message $m = D_{sk}(c) = D_{sk}(E_{pk}(m))$, back from the ciphertext c, given the secret key sk.

4.1   Anonymous Transcripts, Anonymous Degree and Blind Digital Certificate

There are many situations in which the learner will require some official document from the E-learning system to prove his achievements (to a third party or the E-learning system itself). Among other such documents are his transcripts as well as his degrees obtained within the E-learning system. For privacy purposes, these documents must remain anonymous, while being able to prove the credentials of the learner:

- **Anonymous transcripts:** the grades attributed for exams and assignments are grouped in the same document to form the learner's transcript, which remains an anonymous transcript since the E-learning system cannot identify the learner.
- **Anonymous degree:** similarly, an anonymous degree is a degree delivered to the learner by the E-learning system, such that the learner can prove that he earned this degree without revealing his identity.

In order to deliver an anonymous transcript or degree, the E-learning system uses the blind digital certificate as the learner's identifier, and uses its own private key to sign the anonymous transcript or anonymous degree. It is important to note that the anonymity of the degree and transcript does not increase the risk of *consensual impersonation* (where the actual learner asks someone else to take the course or perform the learning task in his stead), since it is an existing issue in traditional E-learning.

Moreover, in the context of privacy-preserving E-learning, the learner needs to prove to a third party (an employer, another E-learning system, etc.) that he is the rightful owner of a number of anonymous documents. Recall that a *Digital Certificate* is a certificate that uses a digital signature to bind a public key to an entity's (a person's or an organization's) identification data, which includes information such as name, address, etc. The main objective of the certificate is to prove that a public key belongs to a certain entity. Since the learner wishes to protect his privacy, a conventional digital certificate cannot be used. Therefore, we introduce the concept of *blind digital certificates*. We define a **blind digital certificate** as a certificate that binds together the learner's public key with the *encrypted* components of his profile (depending on the level of privacy). In particular, the learner's identity and demographic data will always be encrypted. For example, if $L = (id, dp, lp, ch, cc)$ is the learner's profile, and (pk, sk) is his public/private key-pair, then the corresponding blind digital certificate in the case of full privacy is the digital signature apposed by the CA on $[pk, E_{pk}(id), E_{pk}(dp), E_{pk}(lp), E_{pk}(ch), E_{pk}(cc)]$, where

$E_{pk}(x)$ is the public key encryption (Section 2.2) of x using the public key pk. Similarly, the corresponding blind digital certificate in the case of soft privacy is the digital signature apposed by the CA on $[pk, E_{pk}(id), E_{pk}(dp), lp, ch, cc]$. Please take note that instead of having only one id, the learner could create several identifiers $id_1,..., id_n$, if he wishes to prove his achievements to n entities, so that each pseudonym or identifier is used for only one entity. This is greatly inspired from Chaum's seminal fight against Big Brother [8], with his proposition of giving different pseudonyms to each organization with which he does business, so that it is impossible for organizations to link records from different sources and then generate dossiers on him.

4.2 Architecture

Fig. 2 illustrates a Privacy-Preserving E-learning architecture. Compared to the architecture in Fig. 1, the difference, although very subtle, is clear: since the System Manager controls data flow between the Tutor/Learner Environments and the Data Storage, it is only logical to include the Privacy-Preserving Processes into the System Manager. Moreover, the Learner Profile was split into two parts: the Basic Learner Profile and the Anonymous Learner Profile. The Basic Learner Profile functions as in any privacy-deprived E-learning environment, storing the data in the clear. On the other hand, the Anonymous Learner Profile stores the Learner's profile and information privately. In this case, a tutor has access only to the data in the Basic Learner Profile. Even if the tutor can access the Anonymous Learner Profile, he cannot decrypt it and view the learner's data. Similarly, the Privacy-Preserving System Manager performs a Privacy-Preserving Process, depending on the learner's privacy preference, before updating the learner's profile. The next section details the Privacy-Preserving Processes in the case of Soft Privacy.

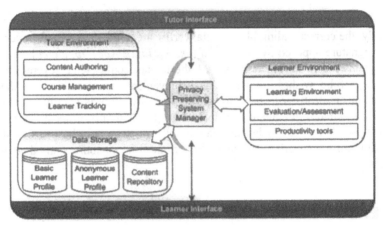

Fig. 2. Privacy-Preserving E-learning architecture

4.3   Soft Privacy learning process

Currently, we only consider the learning process for soft privacy with strong tracking. However, we leave the generalization of this process for the other levels of privacy and tracking for future work. In the context of soft privacy, the blind digital certificate (BDC) consists of the learner's public key and the encrypted form of his identity and demographic data. The learning process is as follows:

SoftPrivacyLearningProcess(Learner U)
1. U obtains a BDC from the CA
2. U registers in the E-learning system:
    a. Presents the BDC.
    b. Provides his learning profile information such as his goals, preferences and qualifications.
3. Repeat until the learner reaches his goals:
    a. U selects the courses he wishes to take.
        i.   His learning profile proves that he has the necessary qualifications and skills.
        ii. His course history proves that he has the necessary prerequisites.
    b. U completes the course's learning activities.
        i.   The E-learning system takes into account U's learning profile during the learning process.
        ii. The E-learning system records the activities, and updates the learning profile accordingly.
4. Upon request
    a. U obtains an anonymous transcript.
    b. U obtains his anonymous degree.
    c. U updates his goals.

4.4   Satisfying the Learning Objectives

The learning process is usually defined by the learning objectives. These objectives are either professional or academic. Suppose, for instance, that the learner must prove to his manager that he completed the training course, without revealing his personal data to the E-learning system. In this case, the learning process is as follows: The learner goes through the *SoftPrivacyLearningProcess*(), and performs the required activities. Thus, at this stage, the E-learning system is in possession of the learner's BDC, and the learner's activities are evaluated by the E-learning system without compromising his privacy since his identity is unknown to the system. In particular, the E-learning system grades the learner's assignments and exams and uses its private key to sign the learner's BDC together with his results. This signed data is sent to the learner, who forwards it to his manager, along with the E-learning system's digital certificate. The manager verifies the authenticity of the E-learning system's digital certificate. He then verifies the validity of the signature on the learner's data. This last verification confirms that learning was achieved by an individual identified by the BDC. If the learner used his real identity, *rid*, when creating the BDC, then the manager can easily verify this identity by computing $E_{pk}(rid)$ and comparing this value with $E_{pk}(id)$ contained in the BDC. During the creation of the BDC, to avoid a guessing attack, the learner chooses *id* such that *id* = (*rid,randVal*), where *randVal* is a random value that the learner reveals only to his manager for the BDC validation. If the learner did not use his real identity, then he provides the manager with the identifier *id*, which is encrypted as $E_{pk}(id)$ in his BDC, and the manager can then verify the authenticity of this identifier.

In addition, if the learner wishes to pursue further training activities within the same E-learning system, then he only needs to select the level of privacy/tracking. For instance, if the learner doesn't want the E-learning system to link his previous activities to new ones, he could ask for an anonymous transcript and use it to create a new account to follow new learning activities. On the other hand, if the learner decides to pursue learning activities in another E-learning system, then the current E-learning system delivers an anonymous transcript, and/or an anonymous degree to the learner. Based on these anonymous documents, the learner can prove to the new E-learning system that he possesses the required credentials and qualifications to continue his learning activities.

5   Implementation and Validation

In order to validate our approach, we implemented an E-testing prototype that supports Soft Privacy and Strong Tracking. Moreover, to keep things simple, our E-testing system only contains an Auto-Evaluation tool. At registration, the new learner is introduced to the concepts of No Privacy and Soft Privacy, and is asked to select one of them. If the new learner selects No Privacy, his Identification and Demographic data is collected and stored in the system. One the other hand, if the learner opts for Soft Privacy, the registration will proceed as highlighted by steps 1 and 2 in the SoftPrivacyLearningProcess (Section 4.3). To implement the BDC we simulate the CA and provide the learner with a Java applet that generates the public/private key pair and encrypts his identification and demographic data at client side. Now that the learner has access to the E-testing system, he must perform at least one Auto-Evaluation test on the Java programming language. When the learner decides that he performed enough tests, he is represented with an account of the activities he performed in the E-testing system along with any information the system has on him. If the learner in question had opted for No Privacy, the system asks if he would like to switch to Soft Privacy. The purpose of this question is to determine the percentage of learners who took the issue of privacy lightly and then changed their minds after realizing the kind of information gathered about them. If the learner decides to protect his personal data, he goes through the process highlighted earlier. At this stage, learners are invited to answer a short questionnaire. First, all four privacy levels (Section 3.2) are presented and explained to the learners who are requested to choose their preferred privacy level (Fig. 3).

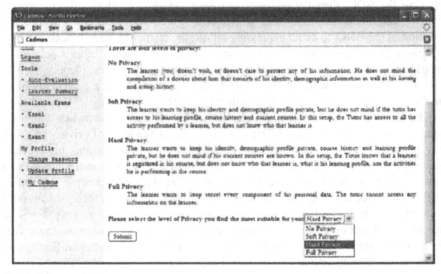

Fig. 3. Privacy selection

This question determined the interest of learners in each privacy level: none of the learners selected No Privacy and most selected Soft Privacy (Fig. 4). Afterwards, learners are introduced to the four tracking levels (Section 3.2) and they are requested to choose their preferred tracking level. Finally, learners are requested to give an overall evaluation of the system with regards to Privacy.

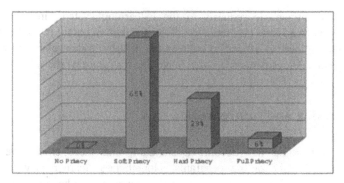

Fig. 4. Privacy Preference distribution

In summary, there were a total of 34 learners who tested the system. Among those, 82% of the learners selected Soft Privacy at registration time; 12% of the learners selected No Privacy at registration but changed their mind after seeing the kind of information the system gathers about them. Moreover, 35% of the learners who originally selected Soft Privacy selected a higher level of privacy when the four levels were introduced. Tracking preferences were almost evenly distributed across the four levels.

6 Discussion

In Section 3.2, we introduced a framework to solve privacy issues in the context of E-learning. However, we only focused on the case of soft privacy and strong tracking for the prototype implementation purpose. The hard and full privacy options are more challenging and require more cryptographic tools. For instance, in the case of full privacy, not only has the E-learning system no information about the courses currently taken by the learner, but the system must also evaluates the learner's activities for these unknown courses! Nonetheless, this can be achieved by performing the computations with encrypted functions (CEF) [13]. However, we leave the adaptation of the CEF technique, as well as a prototype for a more complete privacy-preserving E-learning system for future work.

In addition, in this work we provided tools and methods to protect learner privacy within an E-learning system. Admittedly, there are other aspects to consider: since most E-learning systems are web-based, a learner could be easily tracked through his IP address, thus violating his privacy. However, this issue can be addressed by using well-known anonymous Web surfing systems. Anonymous surfing implies that the learner can send information to and receive from the E-learning system without being traced. If the learner is in an Internet café, the learning activities can be performed somewhat anonymously. If the learner trusts a third party (such as an identity proxy [14-15]), then he can perform the learning activities from his home or office. If no single party can be trusted, Chaum's mix-nets [16] can be used to send untraceable requests to the E-learning system, in which case an untraceable return address can serve to deliver the learning activity contents. In more general context, there is a need to address the privacy issues related to tracking as stated in Section 3.1. However, we also leave this for future work.

7 Conclusion and future work

Today, E-learning has become a standard, and there exist several virtual universities that offer online programs. Nonetheless, learner privacy is barely considered within E-learning systems, at a time when people have growing concerns about their privacy. In this work, we have presented a framework to address various learner privacy concerns in an E-learning environment. Moreover, we have implemented and tested an E-testing system to offer Soft Privacy along with Strong Tracking. Our privacy preservation approach is more robust than approaches in existing E-learning systems since, in our case, the learner alone can unlock his private data. Moreover, preliminary testing results are encouraging where 94% of the learners selected to protect their privacy, and 2 learners out of 3 who first selected No Privacy, changed their mind after seeing a sample of the data collected about them. Nonetheless, there is still work to be done in this field. Hard and Full Privacy still require implementation, while keeping in mind that E-learning systems need to gather information about the learner in order to provide a better learning experience.

Acknowledgements

We are most grateful to the three anonymous referees for suggestions that allowed us to greatly improve this paper. This gratitude covers also Professor Gilles Brassard for his valued guidance and feedback.

References

1. Arroyo, I., and Park Woolf, B.: "Inferring Learning and Attitudes from a Bayesian Network of Log File Data". *International Conference on Artificial Intelligence in Education (AIED 2005)*, pp 33–40, Amsterdam, 2005.

2. Westin, A.: *Privacy and Freedom* (Atheneum, New York, 1967).

3. Aïmeur, E., Brassard, G., Fernandez, J.M., and Mani Onana, F. S.: "Privacy-Preserving demographic filtering". *The 21st Annual ACM Symposium on Applied Computing*, pp 872–878, Dijon, 2006.

4. Mani Onana, F. S.: "Vie privée en commerce électronique". Ph.D. Thesis, Département d'informatique et de recherche opérationnelle, Université de Montréal, Mai 2006.

5. Raitman, R., Ngo, L., Augar, N., and Zhou, W.: "Security in the online e-learning environment". *IEEE International Conference on Advanced Learning Technologies (ICALT 2005)*, 5(8), pp 702–706, 2005.

6. Franz, E., Wahrig, H., Boettcher, A., and Borcea-Pfitzmann, K.: "Access Control in a Privacy-Aware eLearning Environment". *International Conference on Availability, Reliability and Security (ARES 2006)*, pp 879–886, Vienna, 2006.

7. Yee, G., and Korba, L.: "The Negotiation of Privacy Policies in Distance Education". *Information Resources Management Association International Conference (IRMA 2003)*, Philadelphia, 2003.

8. Chaum, D.: "Security without identification: Transaction systems to make Big Brother obsolete". *Communications of the ACM*, 28(10), pp 1030–1044, 1985.

9. Chaum, D., and Evertse, J.: A Secure and Privacy-protecting Protocol for Transmitting Personal Information Between Organizations. In Andrew M. Odlyzko, editor, *Advances in Cryptology – CRYPTO '86*, volume 263 of *Lecture Notes in Computer Science*, pp 118–167 (Springer, Berlin, 1987).

10. Brands, S.: *Rethinking Public Key Infrastructure and Digital Certificates – Building in Privacy*. (MIT Press, Cambridge, 2000).

11 Camenish, J., and Lysyanskaya, A.: An Efficient System for None-transferable Anonymous Credentials with Optional Anonymity Revocation. In Birgit Pfitzmann, editor, *Advances in Cryptology – EUROCRYPT 2001*, volume 2045 of *Lecture Notes in Computer Science*, pp 93–118 (Springer, Berlin, 2001).

12 Lysyanskaya, A., Rivest, R. L., Sahai, A., and Wolf S.: In Howard Heys and Carlisle Adams, editors, *Selected Areas in Cryptography*, volume 1758 of *Lecture Notes in Computer Science*, pp 184–199 (Springer, Berlin, 1999).

13. Sander, T., and Tschudin, C.: "Towards mobile cryptography". *Proceedings of the IEEE Symposium on Security and Privacy*, IEEE Computer Society Press, pp 215–224, Oakland, 1998.

14. Boyan, J.: "The Anonymizer: Protecting user privacy on theWeb". *Computer-Mediated Communication Magazine*, 4(9), 1997.

15. Gabber, E., Gibbons, P.B., Kristol, D.M., Matias Y. and Mayer A.J.: "Consistent, yet anonymous, web access with LPWA". *Communications of the ACM*, 42(2), pp. 42–47, 1999.

16. Chaum, D.: "Untraceable electronic mail, return addresses, and digital pseudonyms". *Communications of the ACM*, 24(2), pp. 84–90, 1981.

Exploiting Trust and Suspicion for Real-time Attack Recognition in Recommender Applications

Ebrahim Bagheri and Ali A. Ghorbani
Faculty of Computer Science,
University of New Brunswick
Fredericton, N.B., Canada
{e.bagheri, ghorbani}@unb.ca

Abstract. As is widely practiced in real world societies, fraud and deception are also ubiquitous in the virtual world. Tracking and detecting such malicious activities in the cyber space is much more challenging due to veiled identities and imperfect knowledge of the environment. Recommender systems are one of the most attractive applications widely used for helping users find their interests from a wide range of interesting choices that makes them highly vulnerable to malicious attacks. In this paper we propose a three dimensional trust based filtering model that detects noise and attacks on recommender systems through calculating three major factors: Importance, Frequency, and Quality. The results obtained from our experiments show that the proposed approach is capable of correctly detecting noise and attack and is hence able to decrease the absolute error of the predicted item rating value.

1 Introduction

The rapid growth of online virtual communities has resulted in new types of collaboration and communication between the members of such societies. The main purpose of these interactions revolves around information sharing and data distribution. Any single person can disseminate his preferred information in the cyber world. The open atmosphere provides suitable grounds for free flow of information and an equal opportunity for every one to express or convey their knowledge, information, beliefs, or ideas. People can even exploit this opportunity as a means for marketing their products as has been practiced in e-commerce. With

Please use the following format when citing this chapter:

Bagheri, E. and Ghorbani, A., 2007, in IFIP International Federation for Information Processing, Volume 238, Trust Management, eds. Etalle, S., Marsh, S., (Boston: Springer), pp. 239–254.

no doubt the Internet, as the major medium resembling the cyber space has been overly populated with tremendous amounts of information from different sources. It would be hence a tiresome or even at times impossible attempt to find the appropriate information in the right time. Recommender systems are one of the most attractive applications widely used for helping users find their interests from a wide range of interesting choices [1].

One of the major worries in uncontrolled information society is the aspects of privacy and security. Security in cyberspace can have two very different aspects. Its first face that seems more obvious is restricting the use of the shared information only to authorized users. In order for users to become authorized, it is most likely that the information source or owner has to explicitly or implicitly grant the access. This type of security is referred to as hard security. Hard security; however, is not the only security requirement in such a setting. Protecting the users from malicious sources of information is also a challenging task. Since information is freely distributed by any person without proving its credibility, shielding users from spiteful information sources is highly desirable [2]. Johnson [3] states that 90% of the children encounter pornography online while doing their homework which elucidates the need for protecting children from deceit in the wild, undiscovered, and unregulated frontier called the Internet.

Fraud and deception are not only related to virtual communities, but also pervasive in real societies and actual life [4]. Different attempts have been made to create a methodology for detecting deceit, fraud, slander, and cheat with respect to different contexts [5, 6]. Zhao et al [7] believe that deception in a multiagent environment can be classified into three major categories. In the first category the agents are not sincere in expressing their abilities. This type of deception is called Agent Ability Declaration Deception. In the second category, Agent Information Deception, the agent spreads false information to mislead others or disguise reality. In an Imposter Deception an agent spawns many fake agents to interact with others to broadcast rumor or a special thought in the agent society.

From a formal logic point of view; Sun et al [4] have stated that an agent is a combination of knowledge and inference. For instance suppose a_i is an agent, therefore it will have a knowledge base K_{ai} and a set of reasoning methods R_{ai}. Exploiting such definition allows us to define three circumstances that deceit would occur. It would either be an expression of knowledge base contradiction (*i*), reasoning opposition (*ii*) or both (*iii*), which have been named Knowledge base Deception, Inference based Deception, and Hybrid Deception, respectively.

- $K_{ai} \neq K_{aj}$ and $R_{ai} = R_{aj}$ (*i*)
- $K_{ai} = K_{aj}$ and $R_{ai} \neq R_{aj}$ (*ii*)
- $K_{ai} \neq K_{aj}$ and $R_{ai} \neq R_{aj}$ (*iii*)

In an e-commerce environment deceit can be employed to defame rivals. False information or partially true facts can be spread out by biased buyers or sellers to defame a specific product or seller. Bitting and Ghorbani [8] propose a defamation protection model based on the concept of reputation. In their model, whenever a transaction takes place between two parties, a buyer and a seller, the buyer can become suspicious of the information provided to him. If the received quotes cause his perception of some other seller (or sellers) to change to a significant enough degree, that quote is deemed suspicious. Similarly, if any of the quoted prices differ significantly from what the buyer believes to be real, the information is taken as an indication for becoming suspicious to that seller. If the buyer is suspicious to the information received from a specific seller, he can call for a consensus. Reaching confidence based on the conclusion of the consensus that defamation has taken place, the buyer can decrease the seller's reputation. Participants with low reputation value are overlooked in this model; therefore different parties try to promote their social face by providing truthful information.

Electronic commerce systems need to suggest the most relevant set of items to the users to increase their sales and customer satisfaction. Recommender systems can serve this purpose by exploiting the opinions of the community to aid individual members effectively identify their appropriate needs from an overwhelming set of choices [9]. Content based and collaborative filtering are the two most widely used methods that are employed in different recommender systems. Each of these methods suffers from different problems. Content based filtering recommends a set of items that are conceptually closest to the items that have been previously selected by the user. One of the deficiencies of this model is that it requires a correct human aided classification and proper ontological categorization of all items. Since this categorization procedure is human centric, it is time consuming and error prune [10]. There are also cases in which items cannot be clearly classified into specific categories. Jokes are a clear example of such instances [11].

It is not only the content based filtering that experiences certain difficulties, but collaborative filtering has also its own deficiencies. Collaborative filtering provides recommendation to the end users through inter-user rating pattern similarities. The cold start problem, recommendation sparseness, and attack vulnerability are the major issues in this class of recommender systems. Cold start refers to the fact that since new comers have not rated sufficiently enough number of items, the recommender algorithm is unable to direct appropriate recommendations at the user. This results in a poor recommendation list for the people with fewer ratings. As is the case for many recommender systems, when there are only a few people with the similar rating patterns to the current user, poor recommendations are given that is a consequence of the sparseness problem. Collaborative filtering algorithms are also vulnerable to malicious attacks. By attacks we mean that malicious users can insert unfaithful ratings to deceive others. This can be a tool for people to advertise their own products while degrading other people's goods.

In collaborative filtering based recommender systems users provide ratings for four specific reasons: improve their profile, express themselves, help others, or influence others [12]. The first group of people believe that their contribution to the system will benefit them through receiving much more accurate recommendations. A user within the second class however, provides rating to express himself in the community; while in the third group, people tend to assist others make the right decisions. On the contrary to these three groups of users, the fourth group tries to influence the recommender system's behavior by providing unfaithful ratings. Their ratings may aim at pushing an item's conceptual coordinates in a well-connected position in the virtual correlation space that the recommender system would recommend the item to many other users. Nuke attacks may also be pursued to devalue products of other competitors. Some of the users in the fourth category only have the intention to harm the recommender system itself. This type of attack will affect the overall behavior of the recommender system and be undertaken for fun or defaming the recommender system amongst many other recommender applications.

An attack can be analyzed from many different points of view [13]. It can be firstly analyzed from the intention aspect to see whether it is aiming to push or nuke a set of items or is it aiming at the recommender system as a whole. The target of the attack should also be considered. An attack may aim specific users or items. Any guided attack requires some level of knowledge and expertise which is very much algorithm dependent and needs information of the rating datasets. Some of this information may be collected from the interfaces of recommender systems that provide the average rating of every specific item. It is also important to increase the cost of attack in a recommender system so that fewer people are willing to launch an attack. Social costs are paid through idea elicitation and reputation endangerment [14]. Monetary costs have also been applied in e-commerce systems such as eBay [15] that giving ratings requires a user to have at least one financial transaction. In such situations, users prefer not to waste their rating chances for defaming others.

O'Mahony et al [16] have proposed a model to detect natural and malicious noise in a dataset of recommender systems. In this approach they exploit the *Mean Absolute Error* (*MAE*) between the actual and the predicted rating as the consistency measure. Any rating that falls below a given threshold (φ) is deemed to be classified as one of the before mentioned noises. Let $r_{u,v}$ be a rating value, $p_{u,v}$ be the predicted rating for the user-item pair, and r_{min}/r_{max} be the minimum and maximum permissible ratings. Consistency c is calculated using Equation 1.

$$c_{u,v} = \frac{\left| r_{u,v-}p_{u,v} \right|}{r_{max} - r_{min}} \qquad (1)$$

$$c_{u,v} > \varphi \qquad (2)$$

In this paper we propose a layered model for detecting noise in a recommender dataset. The most important feature of the algorithm is that it is performed online and during the recommender system execution. As a new rating is provided in the systems a trust value is ascribed to the rating. Trust is formalized in this context through three major constituent elements:

1. Importance (ζ),
2. Frequency (γ),
3. Quality (λ).

Importance (ζ) measures the degree of conformance between the asserted rating value for *item j* in the given rating and the overall trend towards rating the same item in all previous interactions from all other users. This factor focuses on the social aspect of trust and has been incorporated into the model to reflect the real world fact that ratings which fall far from the general trend of rating in the history of a specific item should not heavily affect the rating behavior of the recommender algorithm. Frequency, γ, determines how often a user participates in the activities of the community. This factor implicitly encompasses both the longevity and interaction roles [17] of a user in a recommender system. This constituent element of the formalized trust value targets the behavior of the user that has asserted the rating. Quality (λ) is also the other component of the proposed trust model that addresses the excellence degree of a user's past behavior and interaction with regard to the current recommender system. We formalize the trust value ascribed to every rating asserted by a user through a 3-Tuple $T = (\zeta, \gamma, \lambda)$. In this way, and with the help of signal processing theory each rating in the recommender system can be quantified as a signal. Any of the signals that have an altitude lower than the average trend of the overall signal altitudes that is calculated by the autoregressive moving average (ARMA) model is regarded as *Suspicious*. By suspicious we mean that it is considered as a distrustful rating. Any suspicious rating that descends below the standard deviation of the overall signal altitude will then be regarded as attack or natural noise and will be discarded from the dataset.

The rest of the paper is organized as follows. In the next section we will analyze the structure of the proposed trust model for detecting noise and malicious attacks. In Section 3 the structure of the employed datasets for evaluating the model, different types of attacks and simulation results have been provided. The paper then concludes in Section 4.

2. Trust Formalization for Noise Filtering

Any recommender system can be a target for malicious activity. Although malicious activity causes serious worries for the accuracy and the ability of a recommender system in giving precise and at the same time useful recommendations, but natural noise is also the other factor that may affect the functionality of the recommender system. Hill et al [18] have shown that users may provide inconsistent ratings for the same item at different points of time. For this reason, a specific rating cannot undoubtedly be classified as malicious or attack, and hence punish the corresponding user for unfaithful recommender system manipulation, since it may well be a natural noise that has occurred due to the misalignment of the user with his normal behavior at that certain time.

It would also be unfair to basically cluster the set of ratings related to a specific item and consider the outliers as noise or attack. Although this approach seems to give good insight into how different ratings are spread out for a particular item, but cannot be exploited as a sole factor in the detection procedure. For example other factors such as the asserting user's past behavior, his overall contribution in prior interactions, and longevity may compensate for this poor rating and even make it the decisive rating in certain circumstances. Suppose that an attacker has launched an Imposter Deception attack on the recommender system. In this attack he creates numerous imposters to nuke item χ. All these imposters would hence rate item χ with very low rating. If user υ, that has a high reputation value based on his previous interaction, rates item χ with a high value, the detection mechanism which is based on a simple clustering technique will be easily misleaded to decide that the rating provided by user υ is either noise or malicious attack (Figure 1). This misdetection has two major repercussions which are Incorrect User Devaluation, and False Rating Disposal. In incorrect user devaluation a user with loyal rating will be devaluated because of incorrect attack detection. Disposing the correct rating values under the suppression caused by imposters can further disable the recommender system from giving suitable ratings. The major risk that threatens the recommender system as an effect of these two side effects is that the recommender system itself will assist the imposters by devaluating reliable users and disposing correct ratings.

In our proposed methodology we exploit a three dimensional factor for detecting natural noise or malicious activity in a recommender system dataset. Whenever a new rating is entered into the system by a specific user, the rating is analyzed in a real-time fashion. The rating is then tagged with a trust value showing how much confidence the system has on the new rating. The lower the trust value is, the more the system will be suspicious of the rating as being noise or attack. As it can be seen in Equation 3, suspicion has a inverse relationship with trust.

$$Suspicion = (Trust)^{-1} \qquad (3)$$

We have applied an adaptive threshold for filtering suspicious ratings. This means that not all suspicious ratings are disposed, but only those who fall lower than the threshold would be deleted. The reason for why we have applied a threshold instead of deleting suspicious ratings is the fact that some degree of uncertainty exists in the decision making process. Josang et al [19] state that due to a system's imperfect knowledge, it would be unreasonable to think that every opinion is strictly classified into belief or disbelief (or in our case trust or distrust); hence uncertainty should also be taken into account. Lack of evidence, vague user rating process, external factors affecting the user's behavior and many other factors can contribute in establishing uncertainty and lead us to devising a more conservative filtering approach.

To track each user's behavior in the system, an implicit reputation ascription process has also been devised. Reputation is a distributed, socially ascribed, and collective belief of the society towards the stand point of a single person within the context of that society [20]. For this reason we exploit user reputation values as one of the dimensions of rating trust ascription. The employed reputation management model is centralized and handled by the trust management process. A user with higher reputation would have a privilege over other users and has the chance to affect the overall ratings in the system.

Trust has been formalized as a three dimensional vector in the proposed malicious attack detection strategy. It consists of Importance (ζ), Frequency (γ), and

Quality (λ). Unlike Frequency, and Quality, that address some of the features of the user who has expressed the rating, Importance is directly related to the rating itself. It compares the altitude of the generated signal by the rating with the expected altitude. The weaker the signal is, the less it would have the ability to manipulate the system status. For instance if the recommender system has reached a stable rating for a given item, a very powerful input signal is required to interrupt the equilibrium. Algorithm 1 shows the overall behavior of our proposed filtering module.

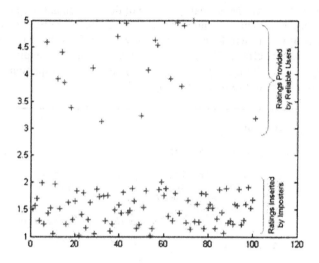

Fig. 1. The colony of ratings inserted by imposters easily deceives a naive attack detection algorithm

2.1. Importance

Importance calculates the potency of the input rating as a normalized signal. To determine the altitude of the input signal every rating is normalized in the first stage. In the normalization phase the input rating $rating_{i,j}$ that has been expressed by user i for rating item j will be compared with the previous rating behavior of user i. It is obvious that the ratings provided by each user for a specific item cannot simply be compared. For example if user υ_1 and υ_2 rate the same item χ with 2, and 5, respectively, in a 10 scale rating scheme, these ratings cannot be simply used to infer that $\upsilon 1$ has a lower belief to χ compared with υ_2. For this reason we normalize the rating value based on the prior rating behavior of the user.

$$NormalizedRate_{i,j} = \frac{rating_{i,j} - \dfrac{\sum_{k=1}^{n} rating_{i,k}}{n}}{\sqrt{\dfrac{1}{n}\sum_{k=1}^{n}(Rating_{i,k} - \overline{Rating_i})^2}} \qquad (4)$$

In Equation 4, n represents the number of items that have been previously rated by user i. Having calculated the normalized value of the input signal, we plot the overall rating trend in rating item j. In this phase the ratings that have been given to item j from the start of its life will be considered. However ratings that have an older age will have a lower effect. Using this trend and with the application of the Autoregressive and Moving Average (ARMA) model (see Equation 5), we will estimate a possible rating value for this stage.

```
While Running(RS)

   If Received (Rating)

      ζ=Importance(Rating->Rate,Rating->Item)
      γ=Frequency(Rating->User,RS->History(User))
      λ=Quality(Rating->User,Rating->Date)

         // The trust value is calculated based on
         // ζ, γ, λ
         Trust = f (ζ, γ, λ)

         // Weaker input signals than what is
         // expected will be filtered
         if (Trust < (ExpectedTrust - Threshold) )
            FilterRating (Rating)
         End

   End //end if
   End  // end while
```

Algorithm 1. Overall Behavior of the Proposed Filtering Module

Given a time series consisting of the ratings for a specific item, the ARMA model will provide the basic tools for understanding and predicting future values in this series. The ARMA model consists of two parts, an autoregressive (AR) part and a moving average or (MA) part. The model is usually referred to as the ARMA (p, q) model where p is the order of the autoregressive part and q is the order of the moving average. We employ ARMA (2, 1) in our experiments. The predicted value through ARMA will show the importance of the input signal that the system expects from a faithful user regardless of his rating behavior (since signals show normalized ratings).

$$X_t = \varepsilon_t + \sum_{i=1}^{p} \phi_i X_{t-i} + \sum_{i=1}^{q} \theta_i \varepsilon_{t-i} \qquad (5)$$

In Equation 5, ε_t is the error term, while the first and second summations calculate the AR and MA parts of the ARMA model, respectively.

The predicted signal altitude will then be used as the center of a Gaussian distribution like function (see Equation 6) to decrease the value of the input signals that are far from the predicted value. The altitude of the input signal calculated by Equation 6 will represent the Importance of the current rating.

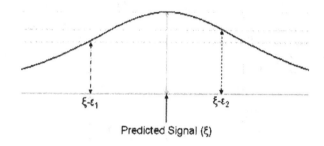

Predicted Signal (ξ)

Fig. 2. ξ Shows the predicted signal value calculated by the ARMA model

$$\zeta = \frac{2}{e^{\Theta(\Delta\xi)} + e^{-\Theta(\Delta\xi)}} \qquad (6)$$

$$\Delta\xi = \xi - \varepsilon \qquad (7)$$

In Equation 6, Θ is a constant regulating factor that controls the gradient of the importance function. ξ and ε represent predicted signal value and the input signal in Equation 7, respectively.

2.2. Frequency

Frequency (γ) determines how often a user participates in the rating process in a recommender system. This factor implicitly encompasses and verifies both the longevity and interaction role fulfillment of the user. The more rates are contributed to the recommender system, the more successful it will be. Therefore the ratings of the users that have provided more ratings in the system should be valued more than other negligent users. Respecting these users will also have another benefit by guarding their ratings from deceitful attacks of imposters. Since imposters start an attack without any prior interaction with the system, the proposed algorithm will not value their ratings as much as it does for more frequent raters. There are cases where the imposters commence their attack by providing fair ratings for a few items so that they gain enough reputation in the system to enable them to attack a specific item later on. In this case other factors of the trust model will contribute to the attack prediction process.

The frequency of a user participating in the activities of a recommender system is calculated through the ratio of signals (ratings) that he has recently emitted into the system with regard to all input signals. An aging factor (β) has been employed to value the users that have a continuous rating behavior. $\Psi_{i,t}$ shows the number of contributions of user i at time t.

$$\lim_{x \to \infty} \int_0^x \left(\frac{1}{1+e^x}\right) = 1 \qquad (8)$$

$$\Phi_i = \sum_{t=1}^{now} \frac{\Psi_{i,t}}{1+e^{(now-t) \times \beta}} \qquad (9)$$

$$\gamma_j = \frac{\Phi_i}{\dfrac{\sum_{j \in |\{users\}|} \Phi_j}{|\{users\}|}} \qquad (10)$$

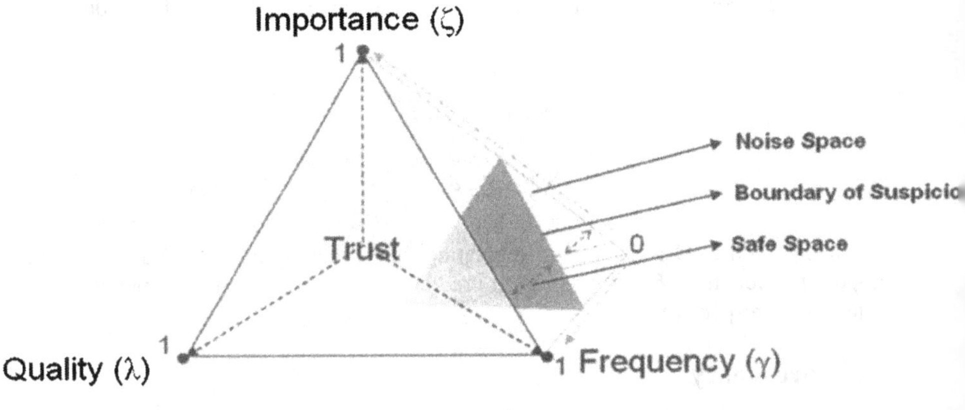

Fig. 3. The proposed model exploits a three dimensional trust value

2.3. Quality

Quality refers to the degree of excellence of a user in his rating history compared with the rest of the users in the recommender system. The calculation of this factor is achieved through counting the number of positive ratings (the ratings that the system has detected as clean) to the total number of his ratings compared with the behavior of others.

$$\alpha_i = \sum_{t=1}^{now} \frac{1}{1 + e^{(now-t) \times \beta}} \times \frac{|\, CleanRatings_i \,|}{|\, Ratings_i \,|} \qquad (11)$$

To find out the general trend between the users as to what percentage of their rating contains noise; we follow a similar approach to Figure 2 and Equation 6. In this way a value is calculated that shows that a specific degree of noise in the rating is legitimate. This value is based on both the current user's past behavior and the other users' previous rating performance. If the current input signal contains more noise than the expected rate, it would be assigned a lower quality value.

The proposed trust model is a three dimensional concept that comprises Importance, Frequency, and Quality as its building blocks. Figure 3 clearly depicts the notion of Trust and Suspicion and their relationship with the three introduced factors. As the value of each factor decreases the trust value also diminishes and reaches towards the *Boundary of Suspicion*. We name the area between complete trust and the boundary of suspicion as *Safe Space*. The ratings that have a trust value in this area will be regarded as clean; however ratings with trust values in the *Noise Space* will be regarded as noise or malicious attack.

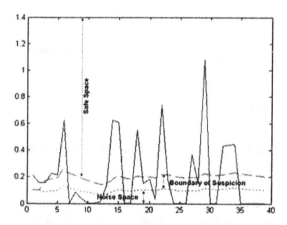

Fig. 4. A sample trust signal for a specific item (The item has 39 ratings in the dataset)

To specify the exact placement of the boundary of suspicion we employ an adaptive approach. In this approach we use the ARMA (2, 1) model again, to predict the next tolerable trust value. We also apply some degree of tolerance which is based on the standard deviation of the overall trust values calculated from the input signals for a specific item. As Figure 4 depicts, stronger signals have higher altitudes that makes them more trustworthy and less suspicious of being noise or attack. Other signals that have a lower altitude are suspicious of being noise or attack; but are tolerated. The last set of signals that fall below the boundary of suspicion are tagged as noise or attack and are hence filtered out.

We currently do not devalue the signals that fall in the boundary of suspicion, but further research can be conducted to see the effect of applying a fading factor to such signals.

3. Experiments and Results

In this section we will initially analyze the dataset that we have employed for our simulations. Different types of attacks that have been launched against the dataset in different periods of time will also be explained. The improvements achieved through the application of the trust model have also been depicted that are based on the Absolute Error (AE) between the predicted and the actual rating.

We have calculated the final trust value by building a vector (Equation 12) from the attributes of the trust model: Importance, Quality, and Frequency. Two sample trust vectors are shown in Figure 5.

$$Trust = vector(\varsigma, \lambda, \gamma) \tag{12}$$

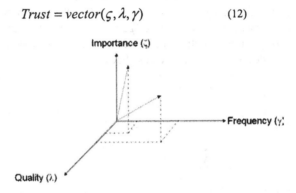

Fig. 5. The trust values as three dimensional vectors

3.1. Dataset

There are several recommender system datasets freely available on the web such as EachMovie and MovieLens. The Eachmovie dataset consists of 72,916 users that have provided 2,811,983 ratings for 1,682 movies. The MovieLens dataset is a smaller dataset that comprises 100,000 ratings from 943 users for 1,682 movies. In our simulations we generated a sample dataset consisting of 12,000 ratings for 300 items by 60 users over 20 days. The ratings were on a scale of {1, 2... 5}. Our initial experimentations were conducted based on this dataset since we were doubtful that the previously introduced datasets may themselves contain noisy data. For this reason and because of their probable internal noise (or even malicious attack data that may be the result of attacks launched against these datasets at the time of their preparation) we decided to generate a new dataset for our simulations. In this way we are able to analyze the behavior of our proposed model under different attack strategies without having to worry about unknown noise that may affect the behavior of the algorithm.

The users in our generated dataset are categorized into 6 main classes. Each user depending on its class and the certain condition that he is in will show a specific behavior. Some users tend to rate the items they encounter with a high rating (class1) while the others prefer to give lower ratings (class 2). The rest of the user classes (classes 3 through to 6) conceptually differentiate between the items and rate each category of items in a different manner (e.g. a class of users may rate philosophical books with a high rating while they rate mathematic books very low.).

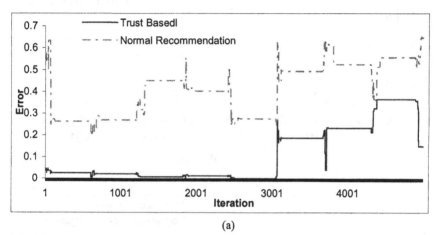

(a)

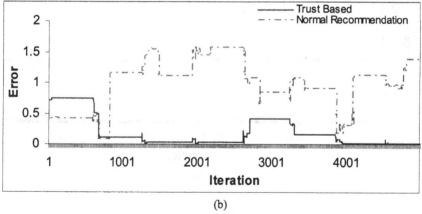

(b)

3.2.   Attack Strategies and Evaluation

O'Mahony et al [16] have introduced various attack strategies on recommender system datasets from which we have adopted four: Natural Noise, Random Attack, Probe Attack, and AverageBot. In the simulations conducted with the natural noise strategy we did not add any extra ratings into the dataset, and the algorithm was applied to the dataset in a temporal manner. Recommendations were made in each iteration for a random item, and the difference between the real rating value assigned by the user and the predicted value by the same recommendation algorithm [21], but with the application of the trust based filtering model were calculated. The recommendation error of each method, with and without noise detection, is shown in Figure 6(a). The proposed filtering method shows a much better performance compared with its counterpart.

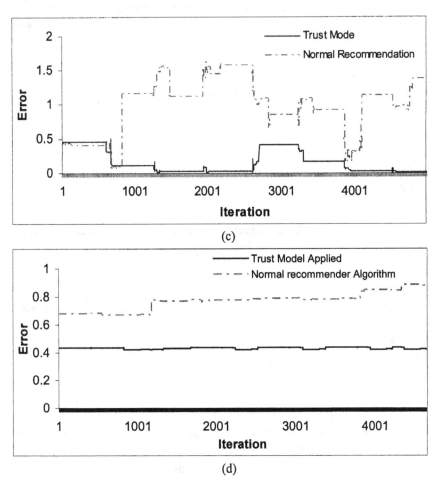

(c)

(d)

Fig. 6. Graphs from (a) to (d) show the Absolute Error of the recommender application

The random attack strategy is the simplest type of attack that we consider. In this strategy $m-1$ items are selected at random from the item set. These items are rated in a normal fashion, while one other item is either rated as r_{max} or r_{min} based on the average rating that the other users have ascribed to the item (Figure 6(b)). The popular attack attempts to ruin the attraction of the most popular items within the recommender dataset. These items are good candidates for attacks since they are likely to be in a neighborhood of many other items and users, in this way damage to such an item can propagate to others that results in decreasing the cost of an attack (Figure 6(c)). The last type of attack that we undertake is the AverageBot attack. In this strategy the attack profile consists of all the items in the systems (or in our case a small portion of it). The attacked item receives r_{min} or r_{max}, while the other items receive a random rate on a normal distribution with the mean equal to the average rating of the item being rated and the standard deviation of all items in the dataset (Figure 6(d)).

4. Conclusions

Recommender systems are very attractive for malicious activity and vulnerable to attack. There are three major sources of threat intimidating recommender systems. The first source of such threats is the inconsistency of user's behavior in providing reliable and steady ratings.   Although this type of risk causes concerns, but malicious activities that aim to nuke or push a certain item or groups of users arouse much more serious worries. In this paper we have proposed a three dimensional trust model comprising Importance, Frequency, and Quality to distinguish between noisy and clean ratings in a dataset of a recommender system. The model has a dynamic nature and analyzes incoming ratings in a real-time fashion. The results show great improvement from the perspective of reducing the absolute error between the real ratings and the predicted ratings. We would like to analyze the behavior of the proposed model on other datasets to understand its behavior under various conditions. It would also be provoking to measure the time complexity of the recommender system with the application of the proposed trust based filtering algorithm.

5. Reference

1. Rashid, A.M., Karypis, G., and Riedl, J., Influence in Ratings-Based Recommender Systems: An Algorithm-Independent Approach. SIAM International Conference on Data Mining, 2005.
2. Golbeck, J., Hendler, J.A., Accuracy of Metrics for Inferring Trust and Reputation in Semantic Web-Based Social Networks. EKAW 2004.
3. Johnson, S., Keep Your Kids Safe on the Internet, McGraw-Hill Osborne Media, 2004.
4. Sun, Z., Finnie, G., "Experience Based Reasoning for Recognising Fraud and Deception," Fourth International Conference on Hybrid Intelligent Systems (HIS'04), 2004.
5. Cristiano Castelfranchi, Yao-Hua Tan, The Role of Trust and Deception in Virtual Societies, International Journal of Electronic Commerce, Volume 6, Number 3 / Spring 2002.

6. Schillo, M., and Funk, P., Who can you trust: Dealing with deception. In Proceedings of the Autonomous Agents Workshop on Deception, Fraud and Trust in Agent Societies, 1999.
7. Zhao, S., Jiang, G., Huang, T., Yang, X., "The Deception Detection and Restraint in Multi-agent System," 17th IEEE International Conference on Tools with Artificial Intelligence (ICTAI'05), 2005.
8. Bitting, E., Ghorbani A., Protecting e-commerce agents from defamation. Electronic Commerce Research and Applications 3(1): 21-38, 2004.
9. Schafer, J. B., Konstan, J., and Riedi, J., Recommender systems in e-commerce. In Proceedings of the 1st ACM Conference on Electronic Commerce, 1999.
10. Massa, P., and Avesani, P., Trust-aware collaborative filtering for recommender systems. To Appear in: Proceedings of International Conference on Cooperative Information Systems, 2004.
11. Goldberg, L., Roeder, T., Gupta, D., Perkins, C., Eigentaste: A Constant Time Collaborative Filtering Algorithm, Information Retrieval, Volume 4, Issue 2, Jul 2001.
12. Herlocker, J. L., Konstan, J. A., Terveen, L. G., and Riedl, J. T., Evaluating collaborative filtering recommender systems. *ACM Trans. Inf. Syst.* 22, 1, 2004.
13. Lam, S. K. and Riedl, J., Shilling recommender systems for fun and profit. In Proceedings of the 13th international Conference on World Wide Web, 2004.
14. Donath, J., and Boyd, D., Public displays of connection, BT Technology Journal 22(4):pp. 71-82, 2004.
15. Resnick, P., and Zeckhauser, R., Trust Among Strangers in Internet Transactions: Empirical Analysis of eBay's Reputation System. The Economics of the Internet and E-Commerce. Michael R. Baye, editor. Volume 11 of Advances in Applied Microeconomics. Amsterdam, pages 127- 157, Elsevier Science, 2002.
16. P.O'Mahony, M., J. Hurley, N., Silvestre, N., Detecting Noise in Recommender System Databases, IUI'06, 2006.
17. Carter, J., Bitting, E., Ghorbani, A., Reputation Formalization for an Information–Sharing Multi–Agent System, Computational Intelligence 18 (4), pages 515-534, 2002.
18. Hill, W., Stead, L., Rosenstein, M., and Furnas, G. 1995. Recommending and evaluating choices in a virtual community of use. In Proceedings of the SIGCHI Conference on Human Factors in Computing System, 1995.
19. Josang, A., Modeling Trust in Information Security. PhD thesis, Norwegian University of Science and Technology, 1997.
20. Jøsang, A., Ismail, R., and Boyd, C., A Survey of Trust and Reputation Systems for Online Service Provision, Decision Support Systems, 2005.
21. Resnick, P., Iacovou, N., Suchak, M., Bergstrom, P., Riedl, J., GroupLens: An Open Architecture for Collaborative Filtering of Netnews, Proceedings of ACM 1994 Conference on Computer Supported Cooperative Work, 1994.

Self-Selection Bias in Reputation Systems

Mark A. Kramer

MITRE Corporation, 202 Burlington Road, Bedford, MA 01730 USA
mkramer@mitre.org

Abstract. Reputation systems appear to be inherently biased towards better-than-average ratings. We explain this as a consequence of self-selection, where reviewers are drawn disproportionately from the subset of potential consumers favorably predisposed toward the resource. Inflated ratings tend to attract consumers with lower expected value, who have a greater chance of disappointment. Paradoxically, the more accurate the ratings, the greater the degree of self-selection, and the faster the ratings become biased. We derive sufficient conditions under which biased ratings occur. Finally, we outline a potential solution to this problem that involves stating expectations before interaction with the resource, and expressing subsequent ratings in terms of delight or disappointment.

1 Introduction

Trust management involves several different functions: helping a system determine whether to grant a consumer access to a resource ("hard" trust), helping to enforce behavioral norms by providing accountability (sanctioning), and helping a consumer decide whether to employ a resource (signaling). Signaling represents conveyance of information to the consumer about a resource, in support of a decision on whether to employ the resource (which can be practically any service, information, or artifact). The signal must contain information that allows future consumers to estimate the value of the resource, for example, by expressing the likelihood of success of the transaction, the quality of the artifact, or the nature of the information.

Typically, reputation scores are based on reviews of consumer-resource interactions. Because reviews are provided only by the subset of consumers who have selected and interacted with the resource, the group of reviewers may not be representative of the larger group of potential consumers.

Self-selection bias is a classic experimental problem, defined as a false result introduced by having the subjects of an experiment decide for themselves whether or not they will participate [1]. The effect is that the test group may not be representative of the ultimate target population, and therefore the experimental

Please use the following format when citing this chapter:

Kramer, M., 2007, in IFIP International Federation for Information Processing, Volume 238, Trust Management, eds. Etalle, S., Marsh, S., (Boston: Springer), pp. 255–268.

results cannot be extrapolated to the target population. This is precisely the case in most reputation systems. Reviewers are disproportionately drawn from the subset of potential consumers who are favorably predisposed toward the resource, making it difficult to extrapolate the result to the general population. The self-selection effect in consumer ratings has been previously noted by Li and Hitt [2], but not thoroughly explored.

It is easy to observe positive bias in reputation and rating systems. For example, the average user rating on NetFlix [3] is 3.6 out of 5.0[1]. On Amazon.com, it is 3.9 out of 5.0 [2]. To put the issue in sharper focus, NetFlix users rate SpongeBob SquarePants videos approximately 4 out of 5 stars (Fig. 1). As popular as this cartoon may be among 6-12 year-olds, it is unlikely that the average user of NetFlix would concur with this rating. If the rating seems out of line with expectations, then what value is this rating, and to whom? What "discount" must be applied, if you suspect you are not demographically matched with the average reviewer? Does this rating indicate you might be pleasantly surprised, or severely disappointed?

There might be a tendency to downplay the problem of biased ratings, on the grounds that (a) you already "know" whether or not you would like the SpongeBob movie, (b) you could look at written reviews, or (c) one could get personalized guidance from a recommendation engine. Clearly, if you adore the denizens of Bikini Bottom, then neither reviews nor recommendations are necessary. However, the ubiquity of reviews is evidence that our prior knowledge has limits, and we do not always "know" what we want without them. Surveys of web consumers conducted by BizRate indicate that 44% consult opinion sites before making an online purchase, and 59% consider consumer reviews more valuable than expert reviews [4]. As far as using written reviews instead of ratings, it is true that better choices may result if one can discern the nature of the resource and the motivations or biases of the writer from the review. However, there is every reason to believe that bias pervades opinions expressed in written reviews as much as numerical ratings, and hence we believe the key arguments of this paper apply equally to qualitative and quantitative ratings. In addition, discarding quantitative ratings would eliminate a convenient shorthand and time saver; it may be impractical to read enough reviews to draw appropriate conclusions. Finally, recommendation engines may guide you (as an adult) to more suitable fare than SpongeBob, but even so, reviews and ratings of the recommended movies still play a role in your decisions. No recommendation engine will ever totally replace browsing as a method of finding resources.

In this paper, we explore the reasons that reputation management systems (RMS) are inherently biased, and introduce the *paradox of subjective reputation*, which can be stated as follows: <u>accurate ratings render ratings inaccurate</u>. The nub of the

---

[1] This number was calculated from over 100 million user ratings collected between October 1998 and December 2005 using the dataset provided for the NetFlix Prize competition. For details, see http://www.netflixprize.com.

paradox is that, while the purpose of a RMS is to support self-selection (allowing consumers to match themselves with resources they value the most); achieving that purpose results in biased reviews, which prevents the RMS from achieving its purpose. The practical effect of this paradox is overly-optimistic ratings driving elevated levels of consumer disappointment.

We begin by creating a model of the self-selection process, and show that under mild assumptions, ratings will be biased. We then explore the dynamics of ratings over time, and present evidence of the effect. Finally, we suggest ways of creating rating systems resistant to self-selection bias.

SpongeBob SquarePants: The Movie
(2004) PG
 SpongeBob SquarePants, star of the popular animated Nickelodeon television series, is an optimistic, free-spirited, rectangular sponge. Living at the bottom of the sea in a pineapple in the ... Read More

SpongeBob SquarePants: Halloween
(2002) NR
 Nickelodeon's hit animated series is ready for a spirited Halloween filled with costumes and fun and adventure for kids! SpongeBob and his pals Squidward, Patrick, Mr. Krabs and others become ... Read More

SpongeBob SquarePants: Season 1 (3-Disc Series)
(1999) NR
Deep down in the Pacific Ocean, in the subterranean city of Bikini Bottom, lives a square yellow sea sponge named SpongeBob SquarePants. SpongeBob lives in a pineapple with his pet snail, Gary, ... Read More

SpongeBob SquarePants: Lost in Time
(2005) NR
"Who lives in a pineapple under the sea?" It's none other than SpongeBob SquarePants. Residing in beautiful Bikini Bottom, the immensely likable aquatic star of the hit Nickelodeon series continues ... Read More

Fig. 1. SpongeBob boasts four-star ratings, but does he deserve it?

2   Expectation and Self-Selection

2.1   Model of Self-Selection

Self-selection happens at a number of different stages in the resource selection process. It occurs when a consumer decides to seek a certain type of resource, when the consumer selects one or more resources for further investigation, when the consumer selects a specific resource to employ, and finally when the consumer decides to review or provide feedback about the resource. For the purposes of analyzing the phenomenon of self-selection, we are concerned with two populations: the population evaluating a resource (evaluation group $\mathcal{E}$), and the population providing ratings and reviews of the resource (feedback group $\mathcal{F}$). The feedback group might not be a representative sample of those employing the resource; for example, those who are particularly pleased or disappointed might be more likely to provide reviews. However, for simplicity, we will consider population $\mathcal{F}$ to be statistically identical to the population employing the resource.

A typical RMS captures the reviews from the feedback group and provides this data to the evaluation group. As indicated above, $\mathcal{F}$ is not a random sample of $\mathcal{E}$; rather it is a self-selected group containing individuals who, on average, value the resource more highly on average than members of group $\mathcal{E}$. Therefore the ratings awarded by group $\mathcal{F}$ do not represent the latent distribution of opinions in $\mathcal{E}$.

To model this situation, define:

R = resource selected
E = expected satisfaction with the resource
S = actual satisfaction with the resource
P(S) = probability of satisfaction in the evaluation group
$P(S_F) = P(S|R)$ = probability of satisfaction in the feedback group

R, E, and S are propositional variables, either true or false. P(S) represents a hypothetical probability that would result if every member of the evaluation group would employ and rate the resource. P(S) represents the "right" answer for someone in the evaluation mode, in the sense that it represents the likelihood that a consumer will get a satisfactory outcome, independent of the decision whether to employ the resource. Since P(S) is not observable, the question is whether $P(S_F)$ is a reasonable proxy for P(S).

In real life, consumers base their decisions on whether or not to employ a resource on indicators such as price, reputation, and apparent quality, transmitted via advertisement, word-of-mouth, and reviews. This information helps the consumer form a preliminary opinion of the resource, which we represent as the expected satisfaction, E. Because of differences in values, tastes, and priorities, there will be a distribution of expectations within the evaluation group.

If there is a strong expectation of satisfaction, a consumer will be more likely to select the resource. In our binary satisfaction model, we describe self-selection in term of the inequality:

$$P(R|E) > P(R|\sim E) \qquad \text{(Self-selection)}$$

This simply says, in a group of consumers, those that expect to be satisfied with a resource are more likely to select the resource than those who do not expect to be satisfied with the resource. If these expectations turn out to be more right than wrong, consumer expectations will correlate with the achieved satisfaction, S, after employing the resource:

P(S|E) > P(S|~E)   (Realization of expectations)

As shown in the Appendix, *these two simple conditions are sufficient to prove the resulting feedback will be biased, overestimating the satisfaction in the resource.* Bias is defined as the probability of satisfaction in the feedback group being greater than the satisfaction in the evaluation group:

$$P(S_F) = P(S|R) > P(S)   \text{(Biased Rating)}$$

While the proof given in the Appendix shows that bias is a mathematical consequence of the two prior inequalities, the effect can be readily understood without formulae. Consider choosing a movie. The consumers are exposed to some prior information, e.g. a movie review, which appeals to some consumers more than to others. The consumers who expect to like the movie are the ones most likely to see it, and when they see it, they are more likely to enjoy it than those who chose not to see it. In the end, the opinions of the viewers are fed back to the pool of available information. This is illustrated in Fig. 2.

In the following, we quantify the cost of bias in terms of *dissatisfaction* and *lost opportunity*. Dissatisfaction is defined as the probability of not being satisfied after selecting the resource, $P(\sim S|R)$. Lost opportunity is defined as not employing the resource when the consumer would have been satisfied with the resource, $P(S|\sim R)$.

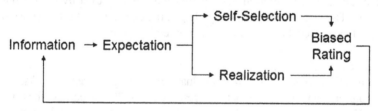

Fig. 2. Causal model of self-selection bias with feedback of ratings

2.2   Effect of Self-Selection on Ratings

If there were no information to form expectations, then consumers could do no better than random selection of resources. If such were the case, the feedback group would be a random sample of the overall population; the reviews would reflect the opinions of the overall population. In this case, reviews would be fair, but disappointment would be maximized, since there would be no opportunity for self-selection. In the other extreme, if there were perfect information, consumers would always know in advance if they would be satisfied with the resource, and self-selection would be perfect, reviews would be uniformly glowing, and there would be no dissatisfaction whatever.

Anchored by these two extremes, it can be seen that increasing (accurate) information increases self-selection, increases ratings bias, and decreases dissatisfaction. Conversely, reduced, biased, or inaccurate information decreases self-selection, decreases ratings bias leading to fairer ratings, and increases dissatisfaction.

To put this in perspective, imagine what could happen when 10 people land on the NetFlix page shown in Fig. 1:

- Three consumers are SpongeBob fans who see the movie, and rate it five stars.
- Six consumers don't like SpongeBob, ignore the high ratings, and do not go see the movie.
- One consumer who has no prior opinion about porous invertebrates inhabiting undersea pineapples, is impressed by the high ratings, and sees the movie. He rates the movie one star.

The average new rating is $(5+5+5+1)/4 = 4$ stars, so the rating remains unchanged; the "trap" remains baited for subsequent consumers. Seven of the ten consumers have reason to be skeptical of the rating system and are less likely to believe it in the future. Nine of ten consumers with strong prior beliefs and depended very little on the ratings system. Only one consumer depended on the ratings system, and to him it was the cause of disappointment, wasted time and money.

If the ratings were unbiased, they would indicate approval by only 3 out of 10 consumers. This data could potentially change the decision of the 10th consumer - or at least, reduce his level of surprise if the movie disappoints.

Example:
A population consists of 100 individuals evaluating a resource. Assume they have enough information to evaluate the resource with 80% accuracy, for both type I and type II errors ($P(S|E) = P(\sim S|\sim E) = 0.8$). Suppose that when these individuals are provided with *unbiased* information about the resource, 50 expect to be satisfied with the resource. For simplicity, assume the same individuals go on to employ the resource. Of the 50 employing the resource, 40 of these individuals will be satisfied. Of the 50 who are not expecting to be satisfied, 10 would have been satisfied if they had elected to employ the resource. With biased information, assume an additional 10 individuals are persuaded to employ the resource. In the feedback group of 60 individuals, 40 of the first 50 are satisfied (as before), but only 2 of the additional 10 are satisfied. Therefore, the probability of satisfaction falls to 42/60, or 70%. Among the remaining 40 consumers not selecting the resource, the lost opportunity is 8/40, or 20%. This is summarized in Table 1.

We see from this Example that biased feedback increases the rate and quantity of disappointed individuals. This is not surprising since biased information decreases the efficiency of self-selection. What is surprising is that the group provided with unbiased information actually produces ratings that are *more* biased than the group presented with biased information (80% positive versus 70% positive). This is because unbiased (accurate) rating information creates efficient self-selection, which enhances the ratings bias.

Table 1. Data for Example

	Unbiased Information	Biased Information
Evaluating Population	100	100
# Expecting satisfaction (E)	50	60
# Selecting resource (R)	50	60
Feedback group satisfaction	40/50 = 80%	42/60 = 70%
Disappointment	10/50 = 20%	18/60 = 30%
Lost opportunity	10/50 = 20%	8/40 = 20%

2.3   Effect of Bias on Self-Selection

In the preceding section, we examined how self-selection affects ratings.   In this section, we examine how ratings affect self-selection.   Our assumption is that the primary action of biased feedback is to increase the number of consumers employing the resource.   Chevalier and Mayzlin [5] have shown that online book ratings do affect book sales.   The consumers most likely to be influenced by biased feedback are those without strong preexisting opinions.   As a group, these "swing" consumers have lower expectations than the group who would select the resource based on unbiased feedback.   If expectations are well-calibrated, the likelihood of dissatisfaction in the "swing" group will be higher than in the first feedback group. By delving deeper into the group of consumers, bias tends to decrease the selectivity of the feedback group.   This is consistent with the previous observation that less (or inaccurate) information decreases self-selection, and results in less biased ratings.

As shown in Fig. 2, ratings systems involve a feedback loop.   It is a negative feedback loop because increasing information tends to increase self-selection, which tends to increase ratings bias, which tends to decrease information.   Systems with negative feedback can show a variety of interesting dynamics, including overdamped (asymptotic approach to steady state) and underdamped responses (overshoot followed by asymptotic approach to steady state).

To demonstrate the effect of feeding back biased ratings, we have to use a more complex model than the binary satisfaction model used above.   Assume the following simple deterministic situation:

- A resource whose latent satisfaction (S) is uniformly distributed between 0 and 100
- Perfectly-calibrated consumer expectations (E=S)
- Average rating equal to average satisfaction
- Sequential subgroups of 100 consumers
- Number selecting the resource in each subgroup proportional to the average rating thus far received, i.e. if the resource has earned a perfect rating of 100, then all consumers in the subgroup will select the resource
- Initial group of 10 random "pioneers" rating the resource

In this situation, we might expect an average rating of 50, since this corresponds to the average latent satisfaction of all consumers. Furthermore, the initial rating of the resource is fair (50), because the pioneers are randomly selected. In the round immediately following the pioneers, 50 consumers whose expectation exceeds 50 employ the resource. Among this group, the average rating is 75. Thus, the cumulative average rating rises to (50*10 + 75*50)/60 = 70.8. This demonstrates the paradox: *accurate ratings render ratings inaccurate.* Table 2 shows the evolution of the average rating through five rounds of consumers, and shows that the steady state is reached at cumulative average rating of 67.

A variation on this scenario is when the initial group consists of a group of enthusiasts, fans, or shills who award maximum ratings, either as a sincere endorsement or calculated attempt to expand the audience for a resource. In this case, the initial ratings are maximal, which draws large group of consumers in round 2. However, the average rating plummets when many in the group are disappointed (Table 3).

Table 2. Dynamic evolution of ratings seeded by random pioneer group

Round	Total Subgroup Size	# Selecting Resource	Average Rating	Cumulative Average Rating
1 (Pioneer Group)	10	10	50	50
2	100	50	75	70.8
3	100	70	65	67.7
4	100	67	66.5	67.3
5	100	67	66.5	67.1
6	100	67	66.5	67.0
Steady state	100	66	67.0	67.0

Table 3. Dynamic evolution of ratings seeded by shill (or enthusiast) group

Round	Total Subgroup Size	# Selecting Resource	Average Rating	Cumulative Average Rating
1 (Shill Group)	10	10	100	100
2	100	100	50	54.5
3	100	54	73	60.6
4	100	60	70	63.1
5	100	63	68.5	65.0
6	100	64	68.0	65.4
Steady state	100	66	67.0	67.0

Figure 3 shows this data in graphical form, for two initial conditions (pioneer and shill), and different subgroup sizes. The larger the subgroup, the larger the overshoot effect in the opposite direction from the initial rating. In both cases, the final steady state is approximately 67/100 (slight differences are due to round-off effects). We can see this analytically, because given a fraction f of the subgroup, the average rating is given by r = 1 - f/2.   If the rating draws an equivalent fraction of the subgroup, then f = r, so r = 1 - r/2, or r = 0.67.   Also notes that small subgroups lead to overdamped behavior, while larger subgroups lead to underdamped (overshoot) behavior.

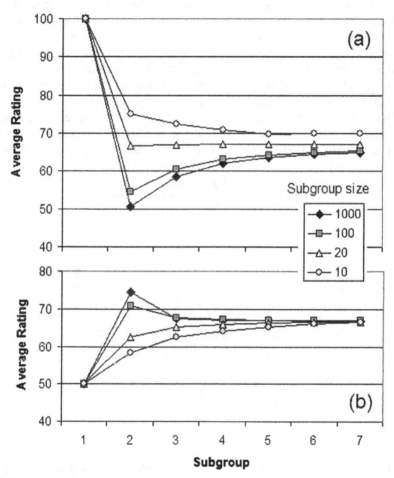

Fig. 3. Dynamic evolution of ratings as a function of subgroup size for (a) initial shill (or enthusiast) group and (b) initial pioneer (fair rating) group

2.4   Steady-State Bias

Steady state is achieved at the point where the available information, including ratings, recruits a new group of consumers whose composition is such that the average rating from the new group matches the existing rating. The steady state is the fixed point of the function r = R(G(r)), where g = G(r) is a function that generates a group of consumers employing the resource given an average rating r, and r = R(g) is a function that generates ratings for a group, g. As we have already shown, under a few easily-satisfied assumptions, this fixed point is biased in favor of the resource. How large is the steady-state bias?

Suppose the distribution of user expectations is given by a standard normal distribution, and the final ratings are correlated to the expectations via a correlation coefficient between 0 and 1. Assume a fraction f of the overall population, drawn from the top of the expectation distribution, become the reviewers. In this case, we can determine the bias between the unbiased rating and the observed rating through simulation, where we generate a Gaussian distribution of expectations, select the reviewers from the top of the distribution, and simulate their final ratings according to the given correlation between expected and actual ratings.

Figure 4 shows the results of this simulation. Bias is higher when a smaller fraction of the population selects the resource, and higher with stronger correlation between expected and actual ratings. Without realization of expectations, there is no bias.

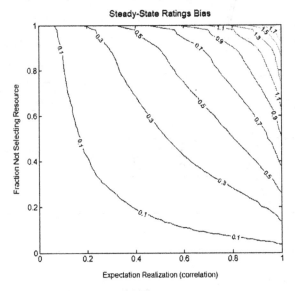

Fig. 4. Extent of steady-state ratings bias for normal distribution of expectations, as a function of correlation between expected and actual ratings (x-axis), and the fraction of population not selecting the resource (y-axis).

3. Evidence from Ratings Systems

At this time, the existence of bias due to self-selection can be considered a hypothesis. However, the predictions are easily testable, by comparing the ratings from a group of randomly-selected consumers against ratings from a group of self-selected consumers. It is possible that effects ignored here might cancel out the expected bias; for example, fans of SpongeBob might be hypercritical and give lower ratings if the SpongeBob movie is not up to snuff, resulting in ratings equal to or lower than randomly-selected people.

However, if self-selection bias did not exist, one would expect the average rating in rating systems to be close to the median value (2.5/5.0 stars). As mentioned in the introduction, in NetFlix, the average rating is 3.6/5.0. At Amazon, the average book rating is even higher, 3.9/5.0 [2]. People are evidently very satisfied with the books and movies they choose; self-selection is indeed working to some extent.

One can also look at the dynamic evolution of ratings in these systems. Li and Hitt [3] gathered data from 2651 hardback books published from 2000-2004 reviewed on Amazon.com in a 5-month period in 2004. They correlated average rating against the time the since the book was published, correcting for the average rating of a book, and discovered a clear declining trend. The average rating conformed to a negative exponential:

$$\text{Rating for book } i = 3.90 + 0.45*\exp(-0.746\ t) + \alpha_i$$

where t is the amount of time (in months) after publication, and α_i is the steady-state rating of book i above or below the overall average of 3.9 (out of 5.0). The average rating drop is approximately half a point on this scale. Li and Hitt also conclude that the time-variant component of the rating has a "significant impact on book sales, which leads to the conclusion that consumers did not fully account for the positive bias of early reviewers". If our analysis is correct, the positive bias is not just an early effect, but a steady-state effect as well.

We analyzed data from the NetFlix challenge problem in a similar manner. This data shows an average increase of about 0.2 points (out of 5.0) during the lifetime of a typical movie. A large majority, 765 of 1000 randomly-selected movies, showed an increase in ratings over time. In terms of our model, this suggests that the initial audience is more random than the audience that develops over time -- i.e., it takes time for a movie to "find its audience". It is possible that shill reviews are more common and influential in the book domain than the movie domain.

4. Avoiding Bias in Reputation Management Systems

Since ratings systems have a built-in bias in favor of the resource, alternative designs that are more resistant to self-selection bias are of interest. Personalization is well-known approach improving ratings. The most obvious way to achieve personalization is using demographics, for example, correlating SpongeBob preference to viewer age. However, dividing consumers into demographic subgroups does not eliminate self-selection bias, because within each demographic, self-selection is still the prime determiner of who selects the resource and becomes a reviewer. Furthermore, available demographics might not create useful subsets of consumers with different preferences for a resource (for example, determining who is interested in a particular technical topic). The other common approach to personalization is collaborative filtering. However, as we argued in the introduction, while consumers may appreciate personalized recommendations, they also expect to be able to discover resources by browsing, consulting both aggregate ratings and individual reviews. The problem of consumers failing to discount biased aggregate ratings (as well as biased written review), does not go away.

In closing, we mention a novel approach for eliminating bias. It involves dividing the reviewers into subgroups according to their prior expectations. Instead of rating the resource in absolute terms, the rating is collected in two parts: the prior expectation E and the posterior satisfaction S. The latter can be collected in terms of surprise (whether the encounter was worse, better, or the same as expected). Collecting these two pieces of data allows the reputation system to build up approximations to the conditional probability $P(S|E,R)$. We have already argued that S is conditionally independent of resource selection (R) given E, and therefore $P(S|E,R) \approx P(S|E)$. Conditioning on E takes the resource selection decision literally and figuratively out of the equation. Making the expectation explicit bridges the gap between the satisfaction of the evaluation group $\mathcal{E}$ and the feedback group $\mathcal{F}$.

Here is one way this approach might work in the context of a movie recommendation system. Consumers browse or use recommendation engines to find and select resources in the typical manner. However, instead of the aggregate rating, data is presented in conditional form:

Among people who thought they would love this movie:
- *40% loved it*
- *30% liked it*
- *20% neither liked nor disliked it*
- *10% disliked it*

Among people who thought they would like this movie:
- *5% loved it...*

When a resource is selected (for example, when a user adds a movie onto his or her queue in NetFlix), he or she is solicited for an expectation. The expectation scale could be the similar to the five-star rating scheme, or a verbal scale ("I think I'll love this movie", "I think I'll like this movie", "I somewhat doubt I'll like this movie", etc.). The elicitation of expectation information can take other forms, for example, asking the viewer if he or she is an "avid SpongeBob fan", "neutral to SpongeBob", etc. or even "dying to see this movie", "looking forward to seeing this movie", or "not looking forward to seeing this movie".

After viewing the movie, feedback can be collected in conventional form, or in terms of delight or disappointment, for example:

I liked this movie:
- *Much more than expected*
- *A little more than expected*
- *About the same as expected*
- *A little less than expected*
- *Much less than expected*

This approach reduces or eliminates self-selection bias because, although the majority of responses are collected from those who expect to like or love the movie, these responses are never pooled with the smaller number of respondents who have lower prior expectations. Therefore, the information represented by these viewpoints is not overwhelmed by sheer numbers.

5. Conclusions

The problem of ratings bias and the market inefficiency (consumer disappointment) that results has not been widely recognized or analyzed. We have shown that if prior expectations exist and are used to select resources, and these expectations positively correlate with results obtained, then biased ratings will result.   We have also explored the dynamics of ratings under the assumption that higher ratings attract more consumers. The analysis reveals a paradoxical situation, where biased ratings tend to attract a broader cross-section of consumers and drive the ratings to become less biased, and unbiased ratings tend to attract a focused set of consumers who value the resource highly, which drives towards more biased ratings. These countervailing forces explain the time trends in ratings.

Creating a fair and unbiased rating system remains an open problem.   The framework presented here suggests an approach centered on collecting prior expectations, as well as after-the-fact ratings.   There is also scope for further investigation into data collected by existing systems to try and determine the extent of actual bias, and to what extent consumers are recruited by biased ratings.

Acknowledgement
The author gratefully acknowledges the sponsorship of MITRE Corporation, thoughtful input from the SezHoo research group (Roger Costello, Andrew Gregorowicz, Dino Konstantopoulos, and Marcia Lazo), and the support of Harry Sleeper, Tom Gannon and Ed Palo.

References

1. J.J. Heckerman, Sample Selection Bias as a Specification Error, *Econometrica*, **47**(1), 153-162 (1997).

2. Xinxin Li and L.M. Hitt, Self Selection and Information Role of Online Product Reviews, Working Paper, Wharton School of Management, University of Pennsylvania (2004); http://opim-sun.wharton.upenn.edu/wise2004/sat321.pdf.

3. Netflix, Inc. (January 17, 2007); http://www.netflix.com.

4. C. Piller, Everyone Is A Critic in Cyberspace, Los Angeles Times (December 3, 1999).

5. J. Chevalier and D. Mayzlin, The Effect of Word of Mouth on Sales: Online Book Reviews, Working Paper, Yale School of Management (2003).

Appendix

As described in the text, we assume consumer expectation predicts selection of the resource, and likewise, expectation predicts satisfaction with the resource:

1) $P(R|E) > P(R|{\sim}E)$ (self-selection)
2) $P(S|E) > P(S|{\sim}E)$ (fulfillment of expectations)

From (1), noting that $P(R) = P(R|E)P(E)+P(R|{\sim}E)P({\sim}E) < P(R|E)P(E)+ P(R|E)P({\sim}E)$, it follows that $P(R|E) > P(R)$. By Bayes theorem, $P(E|R)P(R)/P(E) > P(R)$, and therefore:

3) $P(E|R) > P(E)$.   Combining (2) and (3),
4) $(P(E|R) - P(E))(P(S|E) - P(S|{\sim}E)) > 0$

Expanding algebraically, and simplifying:

5) $(P(S|E)P(E|R)+P(S|{\sim}E)-P(S|{\sim}E)P(E|R)) - (P(S|E)P(E)+P(S|{\sim}E)-P(S|{\sim}E)P(E)) > 0$

Noting that $1-P(E|R) = P({\sim}E|R)$ and $1-P(E)=P({\sim}E)$, then:

6) $(P(S|E)P(E|R)+P(S|{\sim}E)P({\sim}E|R)) - (P(S|E)P(E)+P(S|{\sim}E)P({\sim}E)) > 0$

We can identify the second term as $P(S)$. If we assume that S is conditionally independent of R given E, i.e. $P(S|E,R) = P(S|E)$, the first term is recognized as $P(S|R)$. Conditional independence is a good assumption since once the consumer decides whether he is likely to be satisfied by the resource, the selection decision does not influence the likelihood of being actually satisfied with the resource. Therefore:

7) $P(S|R) - P(S) > 0$, and finally
8) $P(S_F) > P(S)$

This shows that biased feedback (8) will result whenever there is self-selection based on expectations (1) and greater-than-random fulfillment of expectations (2).

Resisting Sybils in Peer-to-peer Markets

Jonathan Traupman

Computer Science Division
University of California, Berkeley
jont@cs.berkeley.edu

Summary. We describe two techniques for reducing the effectiveness of sybil attacks, in which an attacker uses a large number of fake user accounts to increase his reputation. The first technique uses a novel transformation of the ranks returned by the PageRank system. This transformation not only reduces susceptibility to sybil attacks but also provides an intuitive and easily interpreted reputation score. The second technique, called RAW, eliminates remaining vulnerabilities and allows full personalization of reputations, a necessary condition for a sybilproof reputation system.

1 Introduction

Reputation systems are a key component of many large peer-to-peer and distributed applications, such as online markets, file sharing systems, and ad hoc networks. As these networks grow in size and importance, the value of a high reputation will also increase. While most users build their reputation through consistent, honest behavior, there will always be some who will attempt to manipulate the system to extract maximum benefit with minimum effort and expense. One common technique for gaming reputation systems is the sybil attack, which exploits the fact that most online applications allow the inexpensive creation of new identities. A nefarious user can easily manufacture an army of fake user accounts, the sybils, and exploit them to increase his reputation by engaging in bogus transactions and leaving undeserved positive feedback.

One proposed solution is to enforce a one-to-one correspondence between online pseudonyms and real people using a third party service created to guarantee the authenticity of pseudonyms. [8] To date, no such services have been created, and few sites implement any sort of rigorous identity screening when creating an account.

An alternative solution is to use economic effects to control the creation of sybils. If we attach a cost to creating user accounts and conducting transactions, it may be possible to render both sybil attacks and fake transactions between real users uneconomical. Bhattacharjee and Goel [2] derive the conditions necessary for a transaction fee to prevent fake feedbacks. It remains unclear, though, whether the fees needed to

---

Please use the following format when citing this chapter:

Traupman, J., 2007, in IFIP International Federation for Information Processing, Volume 238, Trust Management, eds. Etalle, S., Marsh, S., (Boston: Springer), pp. 269–284.

prevent bad behavior will be low enough so as not to discourage legitimate participation in the system. A related approach [14] makes users pay a computational cost or pass a CAPTCHA when creating an account in order to foil automated attempts to register hundreds of accounts.

If we cannot stop people from creating sybil users, then the best defense is to detect them, so that we can discount reputation information coming from sybil sources. A recent result [4] proved that any system where reputation is symmetric (i.e. where reputations are invariant under relabeling of nodes) is theoretically vulnerable to sybil attacks. Feldman et al. [6] demonstrate a scheme that uses maximum flow to form reputations in a simulated file sharing network, which is non-symmetric and effectively resists sybil attacks. Unfortunately, computing maximum flow is expensive: the fastest general algorithm requires $O(nm \log(n^2/m))$ time for a n-vertex, m-edge graph. [10] The amortized constant time approximate algorithm of [6] limits the total number of iterations of the $O(n^3)$ preflow-push algorithm [9], but they present no evidence that this approach will scale effectively to web scale networks.

The EigenTrust system [11] applies the well-known PageRank [12] algorithm to the problem of trust and reputation in peer-to-peer systems. EigenTrust's authors claim it to be resistant to not just sybils but also to collusion by otherwise legitimate users. We show in Section 2 that these claims are false and show several mechanisms for using sybils to attack EigenTrust.

We then describe a novel transformation of EigenTrust, Relative Rank, that realizes two important goals. First, it returns reputation metrics suitable for peer-to-peer markets, where both parties need to simultaneously make a decision to interact or not based on the other's reputation. Second, the reputations returned by Relative Rank resist sybil attacks.

Finally, we propose a new algorithm, RAW, that replaces PageRank within the Relative Rank framework. We prove that RAW combined with Relative Rank is secure against one main class of sybil attack and also provide a strong bound the effectiveness of the other type. Furthermore, RAW is fully personalizable: it can easily return reputations that are specific to the querying user. RAW is thus able to meet the conditions set forward by [4] as a necessary condition for a sybilproof reputation algorithm.

2 PageRank as a Reputation System

In order to understand the extensions to PageRank that confer sybil resistance, we must first look at the PageRank algorithm itself. This section serves as a brief summary of PageRank and of EigenTrust, an application of PageRank as a reputation system. For more details on these algorithms, we refer the interested reader to the original PageRank [12] and EigenTrust [11] papers.

2.1 The PageRank Algorithm

Let $G = (E, V)$ be a directed graph where every vertex has at least one out-going edge[1]. Let S, the *start set*, be a vector of length $|V|$ with $||S||_1 = 1$, which defines a distribution across V. Let A be a $|V| \times |V|$ matrix with each element $a_{ij} = 1/|\text{succ}(j)|$ if there is a link from j to i and 0 otherwise, where $\text{succ}(i) = \{j|(i, j) \in E\}$. The matrix A is thus a stochastic matrix that represents the link structure of G.

Define the random walk process $\{X_t\}_{t=1...\infty}$ on G with constant *damping factor* $c \in (0, 1)$:

1. $\Pr\{X_0 = i\} = S_i$
2. With probability c, take a step such that $\Pr\{X_{t+1} = i|X_t = j\} = a_{ij}$.
3. Otherwise, restart at a random node: $\Pr\{X_{t+1} = i\} = S_i$.

The process $\{X_t\}_{t=1...\infty}$ is an irreducible, aperiodic, persistent Markov process with a finite state. By the Perron-Frobenius theorem, the process's stationary distribution, R, is the first eigenvector of the matrix $(1 - c)S \times 1 + cA$, and can be computed with a simple iterative algorithm.

Definition 1. R_i *is the* rank *or* PageRank score *of node* i.

Details of the PageRank algorithm and its applications to web search can be found in [12].

EigenTrust [11] uses PageRank as a reputation system for peer-to-peer file sharing networks. While web links are binary (either a link is present or it is not), trust relationships are described using a range of values, both positive and negative. When constructing the A matrix, EigenTrust therefore uses a more complex normalization procedure. A user i defines his satisfaction with user j, s_{ij} as:

$$s_{ij} = \text{sat}(i, j) - \text{unsat}(i, j)$$

where $\text{sat}(i, j)$ and $\text{unsat}(i, j)$ represent respectively the number of satisfactory and unsatisfactory interactions that user i has had with user j. The elements of the A matrix are defined by:

$$a_{ij} = \frac{\max(s_{ij}, 0)}{\sum_k \max(s_{ik}, 0)}$$

Two important consequences of this normalization process are (1) that the random walk now chooses an outgoing link with probability proportional to the user's satisfaction instead of uniformly and (2) that negative satisfaction ratings are essentially discarded: negative trust is treated the same as no trust.

The creators of EigenTrust propose two decision procedures to use when applying this reputation information. In the first procedure, the user always picks the partner who has the highest EigenTrust score. In the second, the user chooses randomly with probability proportional to the potential partners' scores.

---

[1] In real networks, some nodes may not have outgoing links. There are several possible solutions to this problem: we could trim out nodes that link to no one, or we could add a link from a node to all the start set nodes. In our implementation, we do the latter.

2.2 Problems with EigenTrust

Despite the optimistic claims in [11], EigenTrust has a number of problems as a reputation algorithm for peer-to-peer markets:

EigenTrust is vulnerable to collusion and sybils. While [11] claim to demonstrate that EigenTrust is robust to collusion, their evaluation is flawed. Consider the simple collusion scenario where a set of users all agree to form a "feedback clique:" they each leave a maximally positive rating for all other members of the clique. Under such an attack, our tests have shown that each member's rank increases. Furthermore, even a single user can construct a network of sybils that will increase his rank as shown in the next section.

EigenTrust does not have a clear decision procedure. In peer-to-peer markets, users need to be able to look at a potential partner's reputation and decide whether to interact or not. EigenTrust scores are more or less a measure of the degree to which a node is "linked in" to the rest of the graph, and this score grows roughly linearly with the number of transactions. Consequently, the decision procedures proposed by [11] are flawed: they tend to select more experienced, but not necessary more trustworthy, partners.

EigenTrust does not use negative feedback. Most online markets allow both positive and negative feedback. EigenTrust's strategy of discarding this negative information is sub-optimal. Because EigenTrust scores grow linearly with the number of positive links and ignore the negative ones, a user with a fairly high rate of negative feedback can still see unbounded grown in his EigenTrust score.

EigenTrust is vulnerable to attacks by users in the start set. The vertices with positive probability in the start set distribution fill a special role in PageRank-like algorithms. As the starting point for the random walk, these nodes are the source of all authority in the graph. In classical implementations of PageRank, this start set contains all top level domains, weighted uniformly. In EigenTrust, the start set is a set of "trustworthy" nodes established by the management of the reputation system. In both cases, this start set remains the same for all queries, resulting in a symmetric reputation function, which is provably not sybilproof [4]. While the cost of top-level domains [5] and careful selection of trustworthy nodes in EigenTrust can raise the cost and reduce the effectiveness of sybil attacks, they cannot be eliminated. Furthermore, the power wielded by start set members is an invitation for corruption.

Fortunately, none of these pitfalls is insurmountable. We spend the remainder of this report examining these weaknesses and their solutions in detail.

3 Sybil Attacks

Broadly speaking, there are two ways in which sybils can be helpful: the attacker can use use them to increase his own reputation or he can use a sybil, rather than his main identity, to conduct transactions with other users. We concentrate first on attacks designed to increase the attacker's reputation. With PageRank or EigenTrust, if an attacker can alter the random walk process to increase the amount of time it spends at his node, then he can increase his rank. We assume that the only way an attacker can affect the random walk is by engaging in fake transactions with sybils, thus adding links among his main node and the sybils. It is also possible to use the sybils to engage in transactions with other users, but this tactic is counter-productive if the attacker's goal is to increase his main node's reputation:

Proposition 1. *Let $G = (E, V)$ be the trust graph excluding the attacker node and all its sybils. Let $G_a = (E_a, V_a)$ be the graph of the attacker node $v_a \in V_a$ and its sybils $\{s_0, \ldots, s_n\} \subset V_a$. Let $G_C = (E_C, V_C)$ be the complete graph with $V_C = V \cup V_a$ and $E_C = E \cup E_a \cup \{(i, j) : i \in V, j \in V_a\}$.*

The rank of the attacker v_a is maximized when all edges (i, j) between nodes in G and nodes in G_a are connected to v_a.

Proof (informal). Consider incoming edges (i, j) where $i \in V$ and $j \in V_a$. If $j = v_a$, then on each transit of (i, j), the random walk will visit v_a, increasing its rank. However, if $j \neq v_a$, then the probability that the random walk visits v_a after transiting (i, j) is strictly less than one. So, to maximize its rank, an attacker would want to have edges incoming from G to G_a to go to his main node, not one of the sybils.

Outgoing edges (i, j), where $i \in V_a$ and $j \in V$, fall under a similar argument. If $i = v_a$, then all random walks exiting G_a must first visit v_a increasing its rank. If $i \neq v_a$, then it is possible for a random walk to exit G_a without visiting v_a. So to maximize its rank, the attacker should have all outgoing edges connected to v_a.

A more formal proof of this result can be found in [3].

3.1 Attack Types

While Proposition 1 shows that an attacker cannot increase his reputation through cleverly choosing sybils to engage in transactions, it is nevertheless possible to engineer a network of sybils that increases the attacker's score. Informally, a node's EigenTrust score is the ratio of visits to the node to the total number of steps in the process, so there are two strategies for increasing it: increase the number of visits to the node or make fewer visits to other nodes.

A *Type I* attack uses sybils to redirect the random walk back at the attacker's node, increasing the number of visits to it. A simple configuration that implements this attack creates N sybils and adds both in- and outgoing links between each sybil and the attacker. Provided the attacker has no other outgoing links (or N is much larger than the number of outgoing links), once the process enters the sybil network, it will spend approximately half its time visiting the attacker until it resets to a new start set node.

In the *Type II* attack, the attacker links to each sybil but does not link back to his main node: each sybil is a dead end. This attack forces the process to restart at a start set node more frequently, preventing visits to nodes outside the sybil network. Sybils are not strictly necessary in this attack: an attacker with no outgoing links at all also achieves the same end. However, if the attacker has outlinks to non-sybil nodes, he

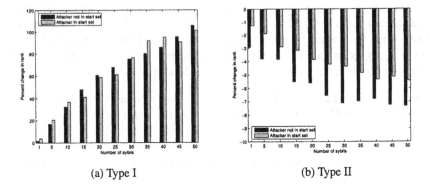

(a) Type I   (b) Type II

Fig. 1: Effectiveness sybil attacks against the EigenTrust reputation system.

will need a significantly larger number of links to dead-end sybils to cause a high restart probability. While forcing a reset of the process does prevent visits to other nodes after it sees the attacker, the low probability of returning to the attacker render it unclear whether this attack is of much use. In practice, we have seen little benefit to using this attack, but we include it for completeness.

The *Type III* attack, which uses the same network topology as the Type II attack, has a different goal. Instead of increasing the attacker's reputation, the purpose of this attack is to create sybils with high reputations that can then be spent engaging in uncooperative behavior without affecting the attacker's primary reputation. Once a negative feedback diminishes a sybil's reputation, the attacker simply discards it.

3.2 EigenTrust is not Sybilproof

To investigate the effect of these three sybil attacks on the EigenTrust algorithm, we implemented them in our marketplace simulator (described in detail in [13]). We measure the effectiveness of the first two attack types by looking at the percentage change in reputation. For the Type III attack, we simply look at the mean reputation of the created sybils. For each test, we ran 10 independent simulations, each with 10 attackers with the final results obtained by taking the mean of all 100 attackers.

Figure 1 shows the results of this test. The Type I attack is clearly effective: even a single sybil causes a measurable increase in reputation and 50 sybils allows the attacker to more than double his reputation. The effectiveness of this attack strictly increases with the number of sybils, although the incremental benefit is less with more sybils. The attack is roughly equally effective whether the attacker belongs to the start set or not; however, the members of the start set begin with much higher reputations, so the absolute increase is greater.

The Type II attack (Figure 1b) is not effective at all, with sybils causing a decrease in reputation at all levels. It is slightly less ineffective if the attacker is a member of the start set, since the chances of returning to the attacker after restarting a random walk is much higher. While of some theoretical interest, this attack does not appear to be of much concern for practical systems.

It is difficult to evaluate the effectiveness of the third attack (see Figure 6 below) because, as we discussed in Section 2.2, it is unclear exactly what constitutes a *good* or *bad* reputation under EigenTrust. However, sybils do receive a positive reputation, though more sybils means each sybil's reputation is slightly lower. More troubling is that the reputations of sybils created by a start set member are, on average, nine times higher than those created by a non-member. Since the configuration of sybils in the Type III attack is identical to that of the Type II attack, we note that a start set member can trade off a small (roughly 5%) decrease in his main identity's reputation in order to create an army of relatively high reputation sybils.

4 Relative Rank: PageRank for Markets

We now introduce our technique of *Relative Rank*, a transformation of EigenTrust scores with several desirable properties:

- Relative Rank has a clear decision procedure. Honest users, regardless of their experience, receive high Relative Rank scores, while dishonest ones receive low scores, permitting users to use a simple constant threshold.
- Relative Rank uses negative feedback. A user with a steady rate of bad behavior will have a lower Relative Rank than one whose behavior is consistently honest.
- Relative Rank resists sybil attacks. For users that are not members of the start set, Relative Rank does not increase with either Type I or Type II sybil attacks. Furthermore, the sybils created in a Type III attack have reputation too low to reliably engage in transactions on the attacker's behalf.

4.1 Relative Rank Defined

The original motivation for Relative Rank was to transform PageRank into a reputation system suitable for use in peer-to-peer markets. In typical markets, potential buyers and sellers examine each others' reputations and try to decide whether or not it is safe to interact. In systems like Percent Positive Feedback, used by eBay, a high reputation corresponds to a high estimated success rate, allowing users to apply a simple threshold when deciding whether or not to interact.

Under EigenTrust, a user's score increases with the number of positive feedbacks received, not with the success rate of the user. Additionally, users in the start set begin with much higher rank than non-members. However, enlarging the start set to include all users allows a new, trivial sybil attack. [5]

Figure 2 plots EigenTrust score against the number of transactions for all users in two simulated markets. In the first market, we use a bimodal distribution of agent honesty:[2] 95% of users are honest and behave honestly an average of 98% of the

---

[2] We use the term "honesty" as a shorthand for "probability of acceptable performance." As suggested by [1], we do not try to assess user motivation or make a distinction between incompetence and malice.

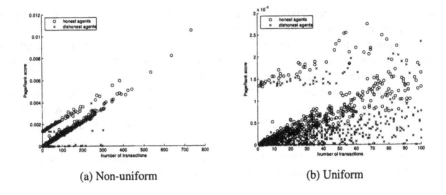

(a) Non-uniform   (b) Uniform

Fig. 2: EigenTrust score vs. number of transactions for all users in two simulated markets.

time. The remainder average honest behavior only 2% of the time. We believe that this distribution captures the essence of real networks where users tend to either play by rules or cheat all the time, and not use some mixed strategy. The overall mean honesty in this market is 93.2%. In the second market, user honesties are distributed uniformly. Honest users are those that behave honestly at least as often as the mean.

Examining Figure 2a, we see four major regimes:

1. Honest agents whose rank follow a line with positive slope and intercept 0.0015
2. Honest agents whose rank follow a line with positive slope and intercept 0
3. Dishonest agents whose rank lies around 0.0015, regardless of experience
4. Dishonest agents whose rank lies around 0, regardless of experience

Similar patterns exist in the uniformly honest market (Figure 2b) as well.

Encouragingly, the rank of dishonest agents behaves differently than that of honest ones. However, it is clear that a simple threshold won't work very well: a threshold less than 0.0015 will miss many dishonest users, while one much greater than 0 will classify a large number of honest agents incorrectly. Groups 1 and 3 represent users that belong to the start set and the other groups consist of non-members. However, even if we divide the users based on start set membership, any threshold we set will likely exclude a large portion of users with low experience.

If we plot only users of a fixed level of honesty, we observe that the plotted points roughly follow a ray beginning at the origin (or at $(0, 0.0015)$ for start set members) and extending into the first quadrant. The angle this ray forms with the x axis is proportional the user's honesty. This observation forms intuition behind the Relative Rank algorithm:

1. Run EigenTrust.
2. Separate start set members from other users.
3. For each feedback count k, including *both* positive and negative feedback, find the non-start-set user i_k that has the highest observed rank, r_{i_k} among users who have received k feedbacks.

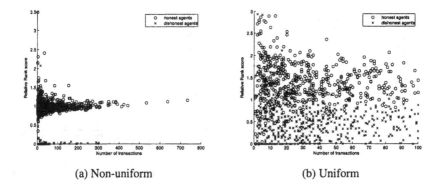

(a) Non-uniform   (b) Uniform

Fig. 3: Relative Rank versus number of transactions in the two example markets.

4. Fit a line to the pairs (k, r_{i_k}) and obtain a slope, $\beta_{\bar{S}}$, and intercept, $\alpha_{\bar{S}}$.
5. Repeat steps 3 and 4 for start set members to obtain a separate intercept and slope, α_S and β_S.

For a non-start-set user i with k feedbacks, define the *Relative Rank score* as:

$$s_i = \frac{r_i - \alpha_{\bar{S}}}{\beta_{\bar{S}} k}$$

The same definition holds for start set members, except that α_S and β_S are used.

Similar plots of Relative Rank versus number of transactions for the two example markets can be found in Figure 3. Clearly, a simple linear separation between honest and dishonest users appears to be a good approach in both of these markets.

4.2 Reputation System Performance

Before we look at its performance with sybils, we examine how well Relative Rank serves as a reputation metric. Certainly, the ability to resist sybils is moot if the system cannot sort out good users from bad.

Figure 4a presents a ROC curve that illustrates the trade-off between detecting dishonest users and incorrectly labeling honest users as dishonest when using Relative Rank with a simple fixed threshold in our two example markets. The area under this curve is considered a good non-parametric estimation of a classification algorithm's performance, with an ideal system having area 1. For Relative Rank, the area under the curve is .9306 for the market with uniform honesty and .9212 for the market with a bimodal honesty distribution. In both cases, we define an honest user as one whose rate of successful transactions is equal or greater to the mean. If we relax this definition somewhat so that an honest user is one that behaves correctly 90% of the time, the area under the curve for the bimodal market increases to 0.996.

In Figure 4b, we measure the transaction success rate (the percentage of transactions where both parties behave honestly) in the example markets. We compared

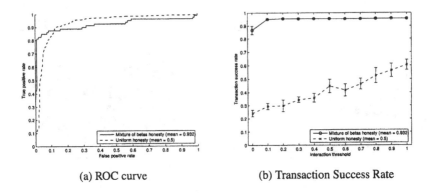

(a) ROC curve   (b) Transaction Success Rate

Fig. 4: Performance of the Relative Rank algorithm in our example markets. Error bars in (b) indicate standard deviation across ten trials.

the market's performance with several different interaction thresholds (the minimum reputation an agent must have before being allowed to interact). Even with a relatively low interaction threshold, Relative Rank was able to roughly halve the number of failed transactions in both markets.

Relative Rank nearly perfectly separates the two modes in the bimodal market: with a threshold of 0 (all users always interact) the observed transaction success rate was .866, very close to the expected rate of .869. However, with Relative Rank and a moderate positive threshold (0.4–0.6), the success rate increased to .956, just slightly less than the .960 rate expected if only the honest users were permitted to operate. However, Relative Rank seems less capable of making fine discrimination between agent honesties: increasing the threshold further does not provide a significant benefit. This is not unexpected: with roughly equal honesty and experience, there will be some variation in users' Relative Rank scores depending on the local topology of the graph in which they operate. We do not view this as a problem — there is ample evidence that suggests that a bimodal distribution of users with a mostly honest majority and a dishonest minority is a reasonable model of real user behavior. Furthermore, it is exactly this sensitivity to graph structure that gives Relative Rank its resistance to sybil attacks.

4.3 Relative Rank and Sybils

Now that we have established that Relative Rank is a useful reputation algorithm for peer-to-peer markets, we examine its behavior under the three sybil attack scenarios described in Section 3.1. The results of this experiment are shown in Figure 5. Comparing these graphs with the results for EigenTrust (Figure 1), we see that Relative Rank is significantly more resistant to sybil attacks.

The Type I attack (Figure 5a) is completely ineffective for users that do not belong to that start set but remains a viable means for start set members to increase their reputations. The Type II attack (Figure 5b) is, once again, more or less useless:

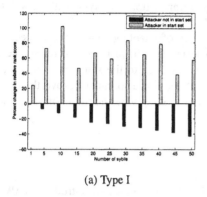

(a) Type I

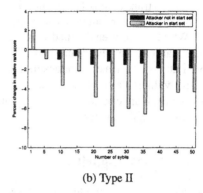

(b) Type II

Fig. 5: Performance of Relative Rank under the sybil attack scenarios described in Section 3.1 in the bimodal example market.

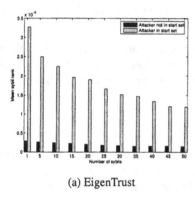

(a) EigenTrust

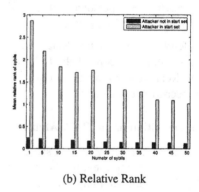

(b) Relative Rank

Fig. 6: Performance of (a) EigenTrust and (b) Relative Rank under the Type III attack.

nearly all attackers see their Relative Rank fall with sybils. One exception is for start set nodes with only one sybil, which gives a very small reputation increase, but this small increase is of little practical benefit to the attacker.

Since, unlike EigenTrust, we have an interaction decision procedure for Relative Rank, we can analyze the impact of the Type III attack (Figure 6b) more thoroughly. The results of the previous section suggest that a good interaction threshold for this example market is around 0.5. All of the sybils created by non-start set users are thus useless: their reputation is below the interaction threshold, so it is unlikely that the attacker can use them to engage in any transactions.

However, sybils created by start set members have very high reputations. If used to commit fraudulent transactions, f negative feedbacks will reduce a sybil's Relative Rank by a factor of $1/f$. An attacker can thus create a large number of sybils with only minimal effect on his main identity's reputation and conduct a large number of fraudulent transactions (e.g. approximately 3 transactions per sybil with 25 sybils) before the sybils' reputations are expended.

While initially envisioned as merely a way of adapting EigenTrust to peer-to-peer markets, Relative Rank had the unexpected benefit of increased resistance to sybil attacks, at least by attackers that do not belong to the start set. However, it is still vulnerable to abuse by start set members. We also cannot prove this sybil resistance: it appears to be generally true, but may simply be an artifact of our choice of simulation parameters.

5 The RAW Algorithm

To address the few remaining concerns with Relative Rank, we introduce RAW, a PageRank-like algorithm with two important properties:

1. Provable immunity to Type I attacks and a provable bound on the effectiveness of Type II sybil attacks.
2. Asymmetric, personalized reputations, which render attacks that rely on start set membership ineffective.

RAW does not replace Relative Rank; rather, it replaces the PageRank implementation within the core of the Relative Rank framework. The combination of RAW with Relative Rank achieves our goal of a highly sybil resistant reputation system for peer-to-peer markets.

5.1 Definition of the RAW Algorithm

The setup for RAW is the same as for PageRank: we have a directed graph, $G = (E, V)$, representing the users and their trust relations as well as a start set, S and constant damping factor, $c \in (0, 1)$. The RAW process, $\{(X_t, H_t)\}_{t=1\ldots\infty}$ is a random walk on the graph that proceeds according to the following rules:

1. $H_0 = \emptyset$, $\Pr\{X_0 = i\} = S_i$.
2. With probability c, set $H_{t+1} = H_t \cup \{X_t\}$ and take a step such that $\Pr\{X_{t+1} = i | i \in H_t\} = 0$ and $\Pr\{X_{t+1} = i | X_t = j, i \notin H_t\} = a_{ij} / \sum_{k \in \text{succ}(j) \setminus H_{t+1}} a_{kj}$.
3. Otherwise, $H_{t+1} = \emptyset$ and $\Pr\{X_{t+1} = i\} = S_i$.

Definition 2. *If R is the length $|V|$ vector describing the stationary distribution of X_t in the process $\{(X_t, H_t)\}_{t=1\ldots\infty}$ defined above, then R_i is the RAW score of node i.*

This process is very similar to the one used to define PageRank with one important difference: the process cannot visit the same node more than once between resets to a random start set node. This property is the key to RAW's sybil resistance. No configuration of edges can cause the process to revisit a node, so the Type I attack is impossible by definition.

RAW behaves very similarly to PageRank in the absence of Sybils and can be used as a "drop-in" replacement in EigenTrust, Relative Rank, or any other system that uses PageRank.

5.2 Implementation and Personalization

The addition of history obviously renders the RAW process non-Markov, so simple close-form or iterative formulations of its stationary distribution are not readily apparent. For the experiments in this paper, we use a Monte Carlo implementation that directly simulates the random walk process.

For deployment in a web-scale marketplace, it will be necessary to efficiently scale up this implementation from thousands to millions of nodes. Similar techniques have been proposed for Personalized PageRank web search systems [7], and these systems can be readily adapted to computing RAW scores instead.

A key benefit of this implementation of RAW is that it can be fully personalized. To accomplish this, we create a collection of start sets, each with only a single member. We then run the Monte Carlo simulation of the RAW random walk to build a "fingerprint" of ranks for that user — in essence the RAW scores using just that single node as the start set. These fingerprints are stored in a database for easy access.

At query time, the user chooses which nodes to include in the start set and looks up the RAW scores of the target in the fingerprint database. The user then constructs a personalized RAW score by taking the (optionally weighted) average of the queried fingerprint values. In this way, the user creates the start set dynamically for each query. A proposition in [7] proves that a start set built up in this fashion is equivalent to a start set chosen in the standard way.

In a practical system, the market administration will want to build a fingerprint database large enough to offer a user a wide choice of start set nodes, yet small enough to make the Monte Carlo RAW calculation tractable. Users then choose unique subsets of this "meta-start set" for individual queries. Provided the meta-start set is large enough, a user will be able to find a sufficiently large start set that does not include either the node whose reputation is being queried or any of its immediate neighbors, drastically reducing the effectiveness of sybil attacks that rely on start set membership or proximity.

5.3 RAW and Sybils

The proof of RAW's immunity to Type I attacks is by definition: RAW prohibits multiple visits to the same vertex between resets to a start set node, so any configuration of sybils that attempts such a redirection will fail. Obviously, this immunity to Type I attacks also carries over to RAW Relative Rank: feedback from sybils cannot increase the RAW score, but it does increase the feedback count, thus decreasing Relative Rank score.

Type II attacks are theoretically possible against RAW; however, we can prove a tight bound on their effectiveness.

Proposition 2. *Let r_i be the RAW rank of a user, i, without any sybils and let r_i' be the RAW rank of the same user after creating sybils in a Type II configuration. If c is the chosen damping factor, then the effectiveness of the attack is bounded by $\mathbb{E}[r'/r] < (1 - c^3)^{-1}$.*

Proof. We consider the worst case: there is a single start set node, s, that is the source of all random walks. It is connected directly to i and to no other nodes. This configuration maximizes the number of visits to i, because i lies along the path of all walks of length 2 or more. The attacker has connections to n non-sybil nodes.

The expected number of visits to i on each walk is simply the damping factor c. The expected walk length given a visit to i is $1 + c + c^2(1 + l)$, where l is the expected length of a random walk in the non-sybil portion of the graph. So, the expected rank of i without sybils is:

$$\mathbb{E}[r] = \frac{c}{1 + c + c^2(1 + l)}$$

When i creates m sybils in a type II configuration, the walk transitions from i to a sybil with probability $m/(m + n)$, so the expected rank with sybils is:

$$\mathbb{E}[r'] = \frac{c}{1 + c + c^2(1 + \frac{m}{m+n}l)}$$

If we take the limit as $m \to \infty$, we get that:

$$\mathbb{E}[\frac{r'}{r}] = \frac{1 + c + c^2(1 + l)}{1 + c + c^2}$$

If the random walk never hits a dead end, then $\mathbb{E}[l] = c/(1 - c)$. Because dead ends are possible, $\mathbb{E}[l]$ is strictly less than this value. Making this substitution for l gives us our bound.

For the choice of $c = 0.85$ used in our experiments, the maximum increase in reputation with an attack of this type is approximately 2.6. We can also solve the above equation for c given a desired bound on r'/r.

In practice, attacks of this form are even less effective because there are many start set nodes, making the probability of returning to the attacker extremely low. Furthermore, with personalization, the membership of the start set can change arbitrarily often, making it essentially impossible to consistently gain a practical increase in reputation.

5.4 Results

Figure 7a plots the transaction success rate against the interaction threshold for RAW Relative Rank in our simulated market. Compared to standard Relative Rank (Figure 1), there are few differences. Both systems are about equally effective at preventing failing transactions. However, the RAW version experiences a slight reduction in transaction success with high (> 0.8) interaction thresholds, due to higher score variances introduced by the Monte Carlo implementation. Once again, a moderate interaction threshold of around 0.5–0.7 makes the best trade-off between preventing failed transactions and not deactivating too many honest agents.

Performance with sybils (Figure 7b) is as predicted by theory. Neither Type I nor Type II sybil attacks achieve any practical measure of success in increasing the

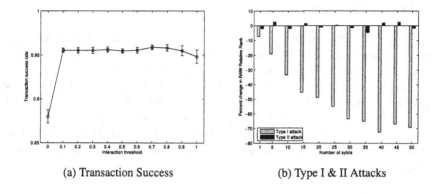

(a) Transaction Success   (b) Type I & II Attacks

Fig. 7: Evaluation of RAW Relative Ranks used as a reputation system.

attacker's RAW Relative Rank. Sybils created in a Type III attack have RAW relative ranks in the 0.25–0.35 range, similar to what we saw with standard Relative Rank for non-start set members. However, with RAW Relative Rank, the "start set" disappears as a concept, so it is not possible for an attacker to exploit his start set membership to launch a successful Type III attack.

6 Conclusion

In this report, we presented two techniques that make considerable progress towards the goal of a fully robust reputation system for peer-to-peer markets. The Relative Rank algorithm takes the widely studied PageRank algorithm and adapts it for use as a marketplace reputation system. It transforms users' EigenTrust scores, which are dependent on their experience level, into a reputation metric that can be easily thresholded against for making trust decisions. Furthermore, it incorporates negative feedback so that users must maintain a high degree of honesty in order to be judged worthy of interacting. Finally, Relative Rank is more resistant to sybil attacks than PageRank: for non-start set users, all three of the sybil attacks we identified fail.

The RAW algorithm replaces PageRank within the Relative Rank framework resulting in several key benefits. Unlike PageRank, RAW is, by definition, invulnerable to Type I sybil attacks. Type II attack success can be bounded, and in practice is far lower than even the bound suggests. Finally, RAW is completely personalized: the querier can choose the start set, so reputations are asymmetric. Combined with Relative Rank, RAW becomes a reputation algorithm with a simple decision procedure for peer-to-peer markets, resistance to all three classes of sybil attacks, and no opportunity for corruption by start set members.

Acknowledgments

The research contained in this report was performed in collaboration with Prof. Robert Wilensky of U.C. Berkeley. While he was unable to participate in writing this report, we would like to acknowledge his many contributions to it.

This work was supported in part by TRUST (The Team for Research in Ubiquitous Secure Technology), which receives support from the National Science Foundation (NSF award number CCF-0424422) and the following organizations: AFOSR (#FA9550-06-1-0244) Cisco, British Telecom, ESCHER, HP, IBM, iCAST, Intel, Microsoft, ORNL, Pirelli, Qualcomm, Sun, Symantec, Telecom Italia and United Technologies.

References

1. K. S. Barber, K. Fullam, and J. Kim. Challenges for trust, fraud and deception research in multi-agent systems. *Trust, Reputation, and Security: Theories and Practice*, pages 8–14, 2003.
2. R. Bhattacharjee and A. Goel. Avoiding ballot stuffing in ebay-like reputation systems. In *Proc. SIGCOMM '05 P2P-ECON Workshop*, 2005.
3. M. Bianchini, M. Gori, and F. Scarselli. Inside pagerank. *ACM Transactions on Internet Technology*, 5(1), February 2005.
4. A. Cheng and E. Friedman. Sybilproof reputation mechanisms. In *Proc. SIGCOMM '05 P2P-ECON Workshop*, August 2005.
5. A. Clausen. The cost of attack of pagerank. In *Proc. International Conference on Agents, Web Technologies and Internet Commerce (IAWTIC)*, 2004.
6. M. Feldman, K. Lai, I. Stoica, and J. Chuang. Robust incentives for peer-to-peer networks. In *Proc. ACM E-Commerce Conference (EC'04)*, May 2004.
7. D. Fogaras, B. Rácz, K. Csalogány, and T. Sarlós. Toward scaling fully personalized pagerank: Algorithms, lower bounds, and experiments. *Internet Mathematics*, 2(3):333–358, 2005.
8. E. Friedman and P. Resnick. The social cost of cheap pseudonyms. *Journal of Economics and Management Strategy*, 10:173–199, 2001.
9. A. V. Goldberg. *Efficient Graph Algorithms for Sequential and Parallel Computers*. PhD thesis, MIT, 1987.
10. A. V. Goldberg and R. E. Tarjan. A new approach to the maximum-flow problem. *J. ACM*, 35(4):921–940, 1988.
11. S. D. Kamvar, M. T. Scholosser, and H. Garcia-Molina. The eigentrust algorithm for reputation management in p2p networks. In *Proc. WWW 2003*, May 2003.
12. L. Page, S. Brin, R. Motwani, and T. Winograd. The pagerank citation ranking: bringing order to the web. Technical Report 1999-66, Stanford University, 1999.
13. J. Traupman and R. Wilensky. Robust reputations for peer-to-peer marketplaces. In *Proc. 4th International Conference on Trust Management (iTrust)*, 2006.
14. L. von Ahn, M. Blum, and J. Langford. Telling humans and computers apart (automatically). Technical Report CMU-CS-02-117, Carnegie Mellon University, School or Computer Science, 2002.

A Trust Model for an Open, Decentralized Reputation System

Andreas Gutscher

Universität Stuttgart,
Institute of Communication Networks and Computer Engineering,
D-70569 Stuttgart, Germany
gutscher@ikr.uni-stuttgart.de

Summary. The use of reputation systems has been proposed for various applications, e. g., to estimate the trustworthiness of sellers and buyers in electronic transactions. Reputation systems collect opinions of users about properties of certain services, subjects and other users and evaluate these opinions. It is important that the results of reputation systems are consistent with intuitive expectations of its users, which highly depends on the properties of the underlying trust model. The trust model defines the representation of the trust values as well as the computation of trust values for derived trust relations.

We propose a new sophisticated computational model of trust which seamlessly integrates authentication verification into the trust evaluation process and which is suitable especially for open, decentralized reputation systems. It consists of definitions of trust and authentication relations, inference rules and three downward compatible trust calculi. It is therefore possible to represent and evaluate trust values with different levels of detail. The model reflects all relevant aspects and properties of trust and authentication relations and therefore avoids any counterintuitive effects.[1]

1 Introduction

1.1 Reputation Systems

A reputation system is an approach to systematically evaluate opinions of online community members on various issues (e. g., products, services, events, etc.) and their opinions on the trustworthiness of other community members.

Reputation systems first collect and combine all relevant opinions, draw conclusions about the trustworthiness of all opinions from the subjective perspective of a given user and calculate the trustworthiness of all opinions referring to certain issues. Then, all opinions referring to a particular issue are combined according to their trustworthiness, and the result is returned to the

---

[1] This work was funded by the German Research Foundation (DFG) through the Center of Excellence (SFB) 627.

Please use the following format when citing this chapter:

Gutscher, A., 2007, in IFIP International Federation for Information Processing, Volume 238, Trust Management, eds. Etalle, S., Marsh, S., (Boston: Springer), pp. 285–300.

requesting user or application, where it can be used to make a decision, e. g., to recommend the highest ranked restaurant.

The use of reputation systems has been proposed for various applications, for example to validate the trustworthiness of sellers and buyers in online auctions, to detect free-riders in peer-to-peer networks and to ensure the authenticity of signature keys in a *web of trust* (e. g., PGP [1]).

Evaluating large sets of different and possibly contradictory opinions is a non-trivial yet crucial process. The *trust model* of a reputation system represents the core concepts of the system. It defines all assumptions on the properties of trust relations and describes how to calculate the resulting trust values.

1.2 Related Work

There exists a large number of propositions for computational models and systems which intend to support humans, agents and applications in deciding whether or not to interact with other parties based on the accumulated opinions of others. However, the field of proposed solutions is quite diversified, so that even surveys [2, 3] have difficulties to cover the whole range from collaborative filtering systems [4], recommender and reputation systems, risk and trust management system [5], deterministic and probabilistic trust models, formal and logic frameworks [6] for trust, distrust [7], uncertainty and forgiveness [8] to experimental sociological studies [9]. Therefore, only selected propositions can be covered here.

Stephen Paul Marsh [10, 7] was one of the first researchers to formalize the concept and various aspects of trust and to represent them by a mathematical model which can be evaluated and used for the implementation of artificial trusting agents.

A trust model that emerged from probability theory is the Dempster-Shafer model [11]. It assigns probabilities to sets and subsets of events. Two values, *belief* and *plausibility*, define the upper and the lower bound of the probability corresponding to a given set of interest. With them, it is possible to express a degree of uncertainty. The *Dempster's rule of combination* defines how to combine the opinions of two independent observers. This rule has been criticized by many researchers for its property to create counterintuitive results, and several alternative combination rules have been proposed [12].

Thomas Beth et al. [13] proposed a model for estimating the trustworthiness of entities in open networks on the basis of recommendations of mediators. An initial trust value is calculated from the number of positive and negative past experiences and direct trust is distinguished from recommendation trust.

Audan Jøsang [14, 15] has developed a mathematical model called "subjective logic." The opinion space corresponds to the area of an *opinion triangle*, the angles represent full *belief, disbelief* and *ignorance* (which is equivalent to the representation of trust values in the Dempster-Shafer model). Jøsang defines a set of operators to calculate with opinions, e. g., operators for the conjunction and disjunction of two opinions as well as consensus and recommendation operators. However, this model and all other trust models with non-distributive operators are not applicable to arbitrary trust structures but only to *directed series-parallel graphs* [16].

One of the currently most widely deployed trust models for public key validation is the model used in the PGP *Web of Trust* [1]. Trust and authenticity statements can be expressed and distributed via digitally signed certificates. The strength of trust and key authenticity can be expressed by discrete trust levels. A set of rules defines how to derive new trust and authenticity relations starting from an initial set of trusted relations specified by the user. A limit for the length of the trust chains can only be specified globally by the validator, but not by the issuer of the trust certificates. It has been shown in [17] that this model can produce counterintuitive results.

Ueli Maurer [18] has proposed a model for trust and authenticity relations for public key authentication in PKIs and introduces recommendation levels for trust relations. Unlike the models using operators to combine two opinions, Maurer proposes to calculate the resulting trust value on the basis of probability calculus instead and avoids thus the above-mentioned trust graph evaluation problem. However, the trust model is limited to public key authentication, and it has been criticised to make the restricting implicit assumption, that each principal holds exactly one key pair [19].

An important yet difficult task is the evaluation and validation of trust models. Several design principles and validation criteria for trust models have been proposed in [20, 19] and [17], but there is no consensus on whether all trust models should follow these principles or whether trust models for different applications may have different requirements [21].

1.3 Contributions

Due to the above mentioned problems and limitations of existing trust models we propose a new trust model (basing on Maurer's trust model [18]), which tries to overcome these issues and which is better suited especially for open decentralized reputation systems. The model integrates public key authenticity verification into the trust model, it avoids any counterintuitive effects, it may be used to evaluate arbitrary trust structures, it supports multiple keys (and identity descriptions) per user, it enables the signer of a trust certificate to limit the length trust chains, it does not force users to stick to a limited number of discrete trust values and clearly defines the semantic of the trust values. Moreover, it offers three different trust calculi basing on the same relations and inference rules but offering different levels of detail. The trust model can therefore serve as a sophisticated replacement for currently used trust models in various open decentralized reputation and public key validation systems (e. g., the PGP trust model).

The remainder of this paper is organized as follows. Section 2 describes the scenario and attacker model, in section 3 we discuss properties of trust relations. An overview on the trust model is given in section 4. In section 5 the trust and authenticity relations and in section 6 the inference rules of the model are described. In section 7 three trust calculi are proposed. We discuss our approach in section 8 and conclude in section 9.

2 Problem Description

We consider an open system without a central authority. *Entities* (the users of the reputation system, e. g., humans, agents, etc.) can join and leave the system at any time and may use different identities (or pseudonyms). Entities can generate multiple asymmetric *key pairs*, sign statements and verify signatures. We assume, that entities have some kind of distinct names, addresses, attributes, etc. so that it is possible to compose *descriptions* which refer unambiguously to the current identity of an entity. Several different descriptions may refer to the same identity.

Entities can formulate *ratings*. A rating is a statement describing the subjective opinion of an entity on some *issues* (e. g., "I believe that pizzas from X are very tasty"). Each issue corresponds to one or more *capabilities* which are considered necessary to formulate a useful rating. An entity cannot definitely determine whether or to which extend an other entity possess a particular capability, but it can determine the initial *trustworthiness* of the entity with respect to this capability. The trustworthiness is a measure for the *subjective estimation* of whether the other entity has this capability (competence and goodwill), based on own experience and knowledge. Similarly, an entity can make subjective estimations about the authenticity of public keys. Entities may use different, application-dependent strategies to determine these estimations (e. g., [13]), however, a discussion is out of scope. Entities can sign ratings as well as trust and authenticity statements and publish those certificates. All entities can retrieve and analyze all published certificates.

Each entity (or a trusted reputation service) can *evaluate* own trust and authenticity statements together with all public trust and authenticity certificates from other entities in order to determine the trustworthiness of all entities for all capabilities and the authenticity of all public keys. Then, the trustworthiness of all ratings can be determined, and finally all ratings for the same issue can be merged according to their respective trustworthiness. This merged rating can then serve as basis for decision-making.

Note that we consider the uncertainty which originates from the subjective estimations as predominant factor for the reliability and usefulness of the result. Therefore, the trust model is designed to capture and trace the impact of uncertainty which originates from the subjective estimations and to determine the most likely conclusion. We do *not* try to measure, whether the system is resistant to attacks against the dissemination of trust or authentication information (e. g., by forcing entities to revoke already issued certificates) [2].

Attackers may try to influence the result of the evaluations by publishing arbitrary rating, trust and authenticity certificates as regular entities, but we assume that attackers cannot prevent other entities from publishing their certificates. Cryptographic mechanisms are assumed to be secure, and private keys are never disclosed.

3 Trust

In general, trust is often described as *the subjective belief of someone in the character, ability, strength, reliability, honesty or truth of someone or something* [3]. In this paper, however, we adopt the following, more technical working definitions (based on [22]):

Trust (or a trust relation) *is a unidirectional relation between a truster and a trustee expressing the strong belief of the truster that the trustee will behave as expected with respect to a particular capability within a particular context.*

Trustworthiness (or a trust value) *is a quantitative measure of the strength of a trust relation representing the subjective estimation of the likelihood that the trustee will behave as expected with respect to a particular capability within a particular context.*

We do not discuss finer grained classifications for trust (e. g., distinguish *competence* and *goodwill*) as they do not have direct implications on our model.

Trust relations have a number of properties, which must be properly reflected by trust models in order to avoid counterintuitive results.

Specificity Trust is specific for a particular *capability* c within a particular context[3]. Trust for a particular capability does in general not imply trust for other capabilities. This can be illustrated by the following example: The fact, that Alice trusts Bobs for giving useful recommendations on recent movies does *not* imply that she trusts him for giving medical advice. In our model, the capability c may either be

- the pre-defined capability c_{PKI} representing the capability, that the trustee will honestly and carefully verify that a given description of an entity refers to the holder of a particular public key, or
- an arbitrary application specific capability, e. g., c_1, c_2, etc.

---

[2] In the latter case you might wish to have a look at the trust model proposed in [19]

[3] in the following, we simplifyingly use the term "capability" only

Direct and Indirect Trust Trust relations can be divided into *direct* and *indirect trust* relations. *Direct trust* (or *functional trust*) represents the opinion of the truster, that the trustee *has* the specified capability, e. g., "Bob trusts Carol to be a good dentist." *Indirect trust* (or *recommender trust*) represents the opinion of the truster, that the trustee will give useful *recommendations* for this capability, e. g., "Alice trusts Bob to recommend good dentists." Note that Alice does not express her opinion on Bobs qualities as dentist, Bob does not even have to be a dentist at all in order to give useful recommendations. For indirect trust relations, we can further distinguish recommendations with different numbers of *recommendation hops* (or *levels*) $h > 0$:

- An indirect trust relation with $h = 1$ expresses, that the truster trusts the trustee for recommending a third entity which has the specified capability.
- An indirect trust relation with $h = 2$ expresses, that the truster trusts the trustee for recommending a third entity which is trustworthy for recommending a forth entity which has the specified capability.
- etc.

A value of $h = 0$ denotes a direct trust relation. Note that values for h are normally very small (typically $h \leq 2$).

Symmetry Trust relations are in general *not symmetric*. The fact, that Alice trusts Bob does not imply that Bob trusts Alice. Trust relations must thus be modeled as *unidirectional* relations.

Reflexivity Trust relations are in general *not reflexive*, i. e., an entity does not always trust itself. This apparently implausible property can be illustrated by the following example: Alice might consider herself to be not trustworthy with respect to the capability of doing surgery (because she knows that she has no medical skills).

Transitivity Many trustmodels are based on the assumption that trust relations are transitive. Although it seems to be intuitive and correct to rely on recommendations of trustworthy entities in some cases, we emphasize that trust relations are *not necessarily always transitive*. This can be illustrated by the following example: Alice beliefs that Bob is gullible but honest, and she trusts Bob for lending money. Bob considers Carol to be trustworthy for lending money and recommends Carol to Alice. However, Alice beliefs, that Bob is not able to judge whether Carol is honest or not. Thus, in this case it is reasonable for Alice not to trust Carol for lending money. This apparent contradiction disappears if we distinguish more clearly between direct and indirect trust [23]. Trust shows transitive properties *only for specific combinations of direct and indirect trust relations*. These conditions and the parameters of the resulting trust relations are definded by the transitive trust inference rule in section 6.1.

Time Variability Trust may change over time, either due to new experiences or due to inactivity of the trustee. Therefore, the usual certificate update and recovery mechanisms (time-stamps, validity periods, certificate revocation lists, etc.) should be deployed. These mechanisms (as well as their problems) have been well-investigated and will be omitted in the following for simplicity.

4 Trust Model Overview

Our trust model is composed of four building blocks and it allows to choose between three calculi (see Figure 1). The basic two blocks are independent of the chosen calculus. They define all existing *trust and authentication relations* (section 5) and describe *inference rules* to combine the relations (section 6).

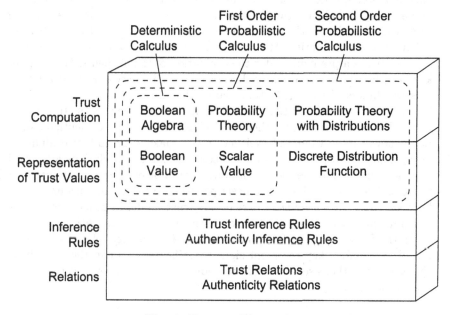

Fig. 1. Trust model overview

The other two blocks are calculus-specific. They describe how to *represent trust values* and how to *compute the trust values* of derived trust relations (section 7). For simple applications, which do not need to distinguish multiple trust levels, the simple *deterministic calculus* will be sufficient. The *first-order probabilistic trust calculus* operates on trust values which correspond to probabilities. The most flexible calculus is the *second-order probabilistic trust calculus* Here, trust values can be expressed by discrete probability distribution functions. Note that the format of *ratings* is not defined within the trust model because it may be application specific.

5 Trust and Authenticity Relations

Users decide whether they trust other entities, e. g., a human being, an organization, a server etc. However, in order to share these trust opinions with other users they typically have to be exchanged via digitally signed trust certificates. In these certificates, users have to reference the entities by unique identifiers or descriptions. In open systems either the public keys of the entities may serve as unique identifiers or some kind of description may be used, e. g., first and last names or host names, postal or network addresses, profession and affiliation or even photos. Humans often prefer to use descriptions because they consider it much easier to associate an entity with a description than with it's public key.

Thus, the authenticity of a public key or a description of an entity can constitute a prerequisite for the evaluation of trust certificates, because it may be necessary to validate that the key used to sign a trust certificate belongs to a trusted entity or that public keys and descriptions in these certificates belong to the same entity. At the same time, the trustworthiness of an entity can constitute a prerequisite for the evaluation of the authenticity of a public key or a description of an entity because it may be necessary to validate the trustworthiness of the entity that claims that a public key or a description belongs to a particular entity. Therefore, it does not make sense to first evaluate all trust relations and then to decide whether the authenticity of the public keys can be validated. Neither does it make sense to first evaluate the authenticity of all public keys and to consider the trust relations afterwards. Instead, trust and authenticity relations have to be evaluated in an integrated process. Therefore, public keys, descriptions of entities and various relations between them are an integral part of our trust model in order to seamlessly integrate the authenticity verification with the trust computation.

In the following, we define nine trust and authenticity relations. Relations issued by a public key represent signed certificates and can therefore be exchanged with other users, whereas relations issued by an entity serve for local evaluation only.

5.1 Trust Relations

Trust Relation Between Two Entities An entity E_A can express trust in another entity E_B for the capability c for h recommendation hops with the trust relation:

$$E_A : Trust(E_B, c, h) \qquad (h \geq 0) \qquad (1)$$

Trust Referring to a Public Key An entity E_A can express trust in the *entity possessing the private key* corresponding to the public key K_B for the capability c and h recommendation hops with the trust relation:

$$E_A : Trust(K_B, c, h) \qquad (h \geq 0) \qquad (2)$$

Trust Certificate Referring to a Public Key A *trust certificate referring to a public key* expresses (similarly to equation 2) that the owner of the private key corresponding to the public key K_A trusts the entity possessing the private key corresponding to the public key K_B for the capability c and h recommendation hops:

$$K_A : Trust(K_B, c, h) \qquad (h \geq 0) \qquad (3)$$

Trust Referring to a Description An entity E_A can express trust in the entity matching the description D_B for the capability c and h recommendation hops with the trust relation:

$$E_A : Trust(D_B, c, h) \qquad (h \geq 0) \qquad (4)$$

Trust Certificate Referring to a Description A *trust certificate referring to an entity description* expresses (similarly to equation 4) that the owner of the private key corresponding to the public key K_A trusts the entity matching the description D_B for the capability c and h recommendation hops.

$$K_A : Trust(D_B, c, h) \qquad (h \geq 0) \qquad (5)$$

5.2 Authenticity Relations

Authenticity of Public Keys An entity E_A can express its belief that the entity E_B is the owner of the private key corresponding to the public key K_B with the authenticity relation:

$$E_A : Auth(K_B, E_B) \qquad (6)$$

Authenticity of Entity Descriptions An entity E_A can express its belief that the description D_B refers non-ambiguously to the entity E_B with the authenticity relation:

$$E_A : Auth(D_B, E_B) \qquad (7)$$

Relationship between Public Keys and Descriptions An entity E_A can express its belief that the description D_B refers non-ambiguously to the entity which is the owner of the private key corresponding to the public key K_B with the authenticity relation:

$$E_A : Auth(K_B, D_B) \qquad (8)$$

Identity Certificates An *identity certificate* expresses (similarly to equation 8) that the owner of the private key corresponding to the public key K_A beliefs that the description D_B refers non-ambiguously to the entity which is the owner of the private key corresponding to the public key K_B:

$$K_A : Auth(K_B, D_B) \qquad (9)$$

6 Trust and Authenticity Inference Rules

The following set of rules describes the logic of the trust model. These rules define whether and which relations one can derive from a set of given relations, i. e., which conclusions result from a set of given relations.

It is important to distinguish clearly between relations from different origins: *First-hand relations* are relations which have been issued by users based only on own experience and knowledge and which are independent from other issued relations. *Second-hand relations* are relations which have been derived from other relations using inference rules. Note that only first-hand relations may be published in certificates. Second-hand relations must not be disseminated to other users.

The evaluation process starts with an *initial set* V of first-hand relations, which consists of all first-hand relations expressed by the user himself and all available published certificates[4]. The inference rules can then be applied repeatedly to the initial set expanded by all previously derived second-hand relations. This procedure is repeated until no more new relations can be derived. The set of relations consisting of the initial set V and all relations which can be derived from V is denoted by $\bar{V}$.

6.1 Trust Inference

Trust Inference for Lower Hops Indirect trust for more than one hop implies indirect trust for fewer hops:

$$A : Trust(B, c, h) \quad \wedge \quad h > 1 \quad \Rightarrow \quad A : Trust(B, c, h - 1)$$

The truster A can be an entity (E_A) or a public key (K_A). The trustee B can be an entity (E_B), a public key (K_B) or a description (D_B).

Transitive Trust Inference The following rule describes the *transitivity* property of trust relations. It defines in which cases two trust relations can be combined in order to derive a new trust relation from the truster of the first relation to the trustee of the second relation. This rule summarizes two cases. It describes how direct trust can be derived from an indirect and a direct trust relation ($h_2 = 0$), and how indirect trust can be derived from two indirect trust relations ($h_2 > 0$):

$$A : Trust(B, c, h_1) \quad \wedge \quad B : Trust(C, c, h_2)$$
$$\wedge \quad ((h_2 = 0 \quad \wedge \quad h_1 > 0) \quad \vee \quad (h_2 > 0 \quad \wedge \quad h_1 > 1))$$
$$\Rightarrow \quad A : Trust(C, c, min(h_1 - 1, h_2))$$

The truster A can be an entity (E_A) or a public key (K_A). The second relation can be a trust relation or a trust certificate, i. e., B can be an entity (E_B) or a public key (K_B). The final trustee C can be an entity (E_C), a public key (K_C) or a description (D_C).

---

[4] relations with trust value *no trust* can be removed from V immediately

Trust in Entities, Keys and Descriptions If an entity is trusted then an authentic key of the entity can be trusted, too (and vice versa):

$$E_A : Trust(E_C, c, h) \quad \wedge \quad E_A : Auth(K_C, E_C) \quad \Rightarrow \quad E_A : Trust(K_C, c, h)$$
$$E_A : Trust(K_C, c, h) \quad \wedge \quad E_A : Auth(K_C, E_C) \quad \Rightarrow \quad E_A : Trust(E_C, c, h)$$

If an entity is trusted then an authentic description of the entity can be trusted, too (and vice versa):

$$E_A : Trust(E_C, c, h) \quad \wedge \quad E_A : Auth(D_C, E_C) \quad \Rightarrow \quad E_A : Trust(D_C, c, h)$$
$$E_A : Trust(D_C, c, h) \quad \wedge \quad E_A : Auth(D_C, E_C) \quad \Rightarrow \quad E_A : Trust(E_C, c, h)$$

If a key of an entity is trusted then an authentic description of the entity can be trusted, too (and vice versa):

$$E_A : Trust(K_C, c, h) \quad \wedge \quad E_A : Auth(K_C, D_C) \quad \Rightarrow \quad E_A : Trust(D_C, c, h)$$
$$E_A : Trust(D_C, c, h) \quad \wedge \quad E_A : Auth(K_C, D_C) \quad \Rightarrow \quad E_A : Trust(K_C, c, h)$$

6.2 Authenticity Inference

Local Authenticity Inference If two corresponding authenticity relations are known, a third authenticity relation can be derived:

$$E_A : Auth(K_C, D_C) \quad \wedge \quad E_A : Auth(K_C, E_C) \quad \Rightarrow \quad E_A : Auth(D_C, E_C)$$
$$E_A : Auth(K_C, D_C) \quad \wedge \quad E_A : Auth(D_C, E_C) \quad \Rightarrow \quad E_A : Auth(K_C, E_C)$$
$$E_A : Auth(K_C, E_C) \quad \wedge \quad E_A : Auth(D_C, E_C) \quad \Rightarrow \quad E_A : Auth(K_C, D_C)$$

Authenticity Inference with Identity Certificates If an entity directly trusts a certification authority for issuing identity certificates (c_{PKI}), then the entity can consider the authenticity statements published in identity certificates signed by this certification authority to be valid:

$$E_A : Trust(K_B, c_{PKI}, 0) \quad \wedge \quad K_B : Auth(K_C, D_C) \quad \Rightarrow \quad E_A : Auth(K_C, D_C)$$

7 Trust Calculi

Users associate each trust relation r with a trust value $t = \text{conf}(r)$. Propositions for valid trust values reach from *positive trust* ("I trust X") via *no trust* ("I have no indication that X is trustworthy", also called *ignorance* or *uncertainty*) to *negative trust* ("I distrust X"). We started from the assumption of an open system, i. e., users may discard their current identity whenever they earn bad reputation and rejoin later with a new, clean identity. Therefore, we propose to refrain from using *negative trust* and to use instead *no trust* as the lowest trust value, which will be used as default value for strangers.

7.1 Deterministic Calculus

This calculi is based on boolean algebra. It is very simple to implement and intended for applications which do not need to distinguish multiple trust levels. Trust values are represented by boolean values: $t = 0$ represents *no trust* and $t = 1$ represents *full trust*.

The trust values of derived trust relations can be determined as follows: A derived relation r is *fully trusted* $(t = 1)$ if and only if it can be derived from an initial set V of *fully trusted* trust relations (i. e., if $r \in \bar{V}$), else r is *not trusted* $(t = 0)$. Note that it is sufficient to find a single trust path (i. e., a minimal set of trusted relations and a sequence of inference steps to derive r) in order to decide that r is *fully trusted*. Other (even trusted) opinions suggesting *no trust* do not reduce the trust value of r.

7.2 First-Order Probabilistic Trust Calculus

The *first-order probabilistic trust calculus* is based on probability theory and has similarities to the probabilistic model in [18]. The deterministic calculus is a special case of the first-order probabilistic trust calculus.

Trust values of relations are represented by real numbers within the interval $[0, 1]$. The lowest possible value $t = 0$ represents *no trust* and the highest possible value $t = 1$ represents *full trust*. Trust values are interpreted as probabilities, which represent the subjective estimation of the probability that the concerning relation is valid.

As we interpret trust values as probabilities, the computation of trust values of derived relations is performed according to probability theory. We consider the following random experiment: Each relation r_i $(i = 1, 2, \ldots, n)$ of the initial set V is considered valid with a probability equal to its trust value $t_i = \mathrm{conf}(r_i)$. The resulting trust value t of a derived relation r is then equal to the probability that r can be derived from the set of valid relations

$$t = P\{r \in \bar{V}\}$$

An algorithm for the calculation of $P\{r \in \bar{V}\}$ can be constructed on the basis of the following consideration: Each relation r_i can either be valid (with probability $\mathrm{conf}(r_i)$) or invalid (with probability $1 - \mathrm{conf}(r_i)$). Therefore, we can construct 2^n different subsets of valid relations of V (*"possible worlds"*), which we denote by S_j $(j = 1, 2, \ldots, 2^n)$. The probability, that the world S_j is the existing world, is

$$w_j = \prod_{r_i \in S_j} \mathrm{conf}(r_i) \cdot \prod_{r_i \notin S_j} 1 - \mathrm{conf}(r_i)$$

The trust value of r is the sum of the probabilities w_j of all worlds S_j, in which r can be derived from S_j:

$$t = \sum_{r \in \bar{S}_j} w_j$$

An algorithm for an efficient implementation of this computation has been proposed by Ueli Maurer [18].

7.3 Second-Order Probabilistic Trust Calculus

The *second-order probabilistic trust calculus* makes use of discrete probability distributions to represent trust values. The first-order probabilistic trust calculus is a special case of the second-order probabilistic trust calculus.

A trust value can be represented by a discrete probability distribution function, which allows to express uncertainty. The discrete probability distribution can be represented by a finite list of trust values t^i with an associated probability value p^i.

$$t = \{(t^1, p^1), (t^2, p^2), \ldots, (t^k, p^k)\} \qquad t^i, \, p^i \in [0, 1], \qquad \sum_{i=1}^{k} p^i = 1$$

The lowest possible value $t = \{(0, 1)\}$ represents *no trust* and the highest possible value $t = \{(1, 1)\}$ represents *full trust*.

The trust value of a derived relation can be calculated as follows: We consider all possible combinations of all trust values of the first relation r_1 $t_1^1, t_1^2, \ldots t_1^{k_1}$ with all trust values of the second relation r_2 $t_2^1, t_2^2, \ldots t_2^{k_2}$ etc. with all trust values of the last relation r_n $t_n^1, t_n^2, \ldots t_n^{k_n}$ ($\prod_{i=1}^{n} k_i$ combinations). For each combination $(t_1^1, t_2^1, \ldots t_n^1), (t_1^2, t_2^1, \ldots, t_n^1), \ldots, (t_1^{k_1}, t_2^{k_2}, \ldots, t_n^{k_n})$ we perform the same computation as in the case of the first-order probabilistic trust calculus. Finally, we construct the discrete probability distribution function: For each of the previous combination we get a resulting trust value from the computation. The associated probability value is computed as product of the probability values associated with the involved trust values of the relations from the initial set. If the trust value computation for two or more combinations return the same trust value, then the trust-probability-pairs can be merged by adding the associated probabilities.

The expectation $E[t] = \sum_i t^i p^i$ of a distribution function can be used if a scalar trust value is required, e. g., to compare two distribution functions or to merge ratings.

8 Discussion

Trust models for reputation systems should not be designed to *emulate* the sometimes irrational behaviour of humans. Instead, they should *improve* the ability of users to evaluate opinions and to come to the most beneficial decision. Therefore, it is not useful to check, whether agents using a particular trust model show the same behaviour as humans (i. e., whether they would pass a "trust touring test" [21]). Instead, we believe that it is important to validate, that the models fulfill functional requirements, that they comply with rational principles and that the results do not show counterintuitive effects.

Therefore, we validate our model on the basis of some relevant principles (e. g., proposed in [20, 19] and [17]) and on aspects, which have been criticized in other trust models.

8.1 Features

The model is able to *evaluate arbitrary trust structures*. It supports *multiple key pairs* and *multiple descriptions* per entity, and is able to express *uncertainty* in trust opinions (with the second-order probabilistic trust calculus). It is based on a *sound mathematical basis* (probability theory), and the *meaning* of trust values is well-defined (trust value corresponds to a probability) and can directly be used in risk analysis. The model allows to specify the number of *recommendation hops* for each indirect trust relation. It *integrates authentication* of public keys and it supports *three downward compatible calculi* with different representations of trust.

8.2 Intuitive Behaviour

The model does not violate any of the following *rational intuitive principles*: *Adding* arbitrary trust or authentication relations does not decrease trust. *Concatenation* of trust relations does not increase trust. Trust relations, which are *not part of any valid trust path* have no influence on the resulting trust value. Trust based on *multiple recommendations* from a single source is not higher than that from independent sources.

8.3 Complexity and Implementation Aspects

The complexity of evaluation algorithms and other implementation aspects are of course important factors. However, we believe that the first (and apparently not yet satisfactorily completed) step is to find trust models which offer the required functionality and which show no counterintuitive behaviour. The question, whether computation complexity is a prior issue or not, may depend on the application. Even if a trust model turns out to be unsuitable for efficient implementation, there can be room for optimizations and simplifications and it may be as well a valuable reference to validate simpler estimation algorithms.

The deterministic calculus shows low complexity. The first-order probabilistic trust calculus can lead to a high complexity if the number of relations in the valid trust paths is high. The complexity can be reduced significantly by summarizing parallel relations and concatenations before the final trust value computation. The second-order probabilistic trust calculus will have a high complexity if the number of trust values per distribution function is high. However, we believe that users will seldom require more than two trust values per distribution function to represent their opinions.

Incremental evaluation (i. e., reusing parts of the previous evaluations when new trust or authentication relations become available) is possible and efficient for the search of valid trust paths, but not for the computation of the resulting trust value.

First *prototypical implementations* in Java and in stored procedures of a relational database have shown, that the performance highly depends on the chosen data structures and that optimizations (e. g., as proposed in [18]) have the potential to speed up the computation by orders of magnitude.

9 Conclusion and Outlook

We have presented a new sophisticated computational model of trust for the evaluation of trust and authentication relations from the view of a user. Due to the integrated authenticity verification of public keys used to sign trust certificates, it is especially suitable for open, decentralized reputation systems and other applications, in which the authenticity of public keys is not verified otherwise. We discussed properties of trust relations and proposed a new trust model. It defines all possible trust and authenticity relations and their parameters, inference rules to draw conclusions and three downward compatible trust calculi which allow for representations of trust values with a different level of detail and complexity. Finally, we have shown that it provides a multitude of important functional aspects, that it complies with requirements for intuitive trust evaluation results and discussed complexity and implementation issues.

Some remaining challenges are algorithms and optimizations for the efficient computation of trust values as well as the discussion and evaluation of further principles of trust models.

References

1. Ashley, J.M., Copeland, M., Grahn, J., Wheeler, D.A.: The GNU Privacy Handbook. The Free Software Foundation. (1999)
2. Jøsang, A., Ismail, R., Boyd, C.: A survey of trust and reputation systems for online service provision. In: Decision Support Systems. (2007)
3. Grandison, T., Sloman, M.: A survey of trust in internet application. IEEE Communications Surveys & Tutorials 3(4) (2000)
4. Good, N., Schafer, J.B., Konstan, J.A., Borchers, A., Sarwar, B., Herlocker, J., Riedl, J.: Combining collaborative filtering with personal agents for better recommendations. In: Proceedings of the Sixteenth National Conference on Artificial Intelligence. (1999) 439–446
5. Suryanarayana, G., Taylor, R.N.: A survey of trust management and resource discovery technologies in peer-to-peer applications. Technical Report UCI-ISR-04-6, Institute for Software Research, University of California (2004)

6. Demolombe, R.: Reasoning about trust: A formal logical framework. In: Proceedings of the Second International Conference of Trust Management (iTrust 2004). (2004) 291–303

7. Marsh, S., Dibben, M.R.: Trust, Untrust, Distrust and Mistrust – An Exploration of the Dark(er) Side. In Herrmann, P., Issarny, V., Shiu, S., eds.: Proceedings of Third iTrust International Conference (iTrust 2005), Paris, France, May 23-26, 2005. Volume 3477., Springer (May 2005) 17–33

8. Vasalou, A., Pitt, J.: Reinventing forgiveness: A formal investigation of moral facilitation. In: Proceedings of the Third International Conference of Trust Management (iTrust 2005). (2005) 146–160

9. Jonker, C.M., Schalken, J.J.P., Theeuwes, J., Treur, J.: Human experiments in trust dynamics. In: Proceedings of the Second International Conference of Trust Management (iTrust 2004). (2004) 206–220

10. Marsh, S.P.: Formalising Trust as a Computational Concept. PhD thesis, Department of Mathematics and Computer Science, University of Stirling (1994)

11. Shafer, G.: A Mathematical Theory of Evidence. Princeton Univ. Press (1976)

12. Sentz, K., Ferson, S.: Combination of Evidence in Dempster-Shafer Theory (2002)

13. Beth, T., Borcherding, M., Klein, B.: Valuation of Trust in Open Networks. In: Proceedings 3rd European Symposium on Research in Computer Security (ESORICS) 1994, Springer-Verlag (1994) 3–18

14. Jøsang, A.: Artificial Reasoning with Subjective Logic (1997)

15. Jøsang, A., Knapskog, S.: A Metric for Trusted Systems. In: Proceedings 21st National Security Conference 1998. (1998)

16. Jøsang, A., Gray, E., Kinateder, M.: Simplification and analysis of transitive trust networks. In: Web Intelligence and Agent Systems Journal. (2006) 139–161

17. Kohlas, R., Maurer, U.: Confidence Valuation in a Public-key Infrastructure Based on Uncertain Evidence. In: In the proceedings of Public Key Cryptography 2000. Volume 1751 of Lecture Notes in Computer Science. (January 2000) 93–112

18. Maurer, U.: Modelling a Public-Key Infrastructure. In Bertino, E., ed.: Proc. 1996 European Symposium on Research in Computer Security (ESORICS' 96). Volume 1146 of Lecture Notes in Computer Science., Springer-Verlag (1996) 325–350

19. Reiter, M.K., Stubblebine, S.: Toward acceptable metrics of authentication. In: Proceedings of IEEE Symposium on Security and Privacy. (1997) 10–20

20. Sun, Y.L., Yu, W., Han, Z., Liu, K.J.R.: Information Theoretic Framework of Trust Modeling and Evaluation for Ad Hoc Networks. In: IEEE Journal on Selected Areas in Communications, Volume 24, Issue 2. (Feb 2006) 305–317

21. Langheinrich, M.: When Trust Does Not Compute The Role of Trust in Ubiquitous Computing. Workshop on Privacy at Ubicomp 2003 (October 2003)

22. Gambetta, D. In: Can We Trust Trust? Basil Blackwell (1988) 213–237 Reprinted in electronic edition from Department of Sociology, University of Oxford, chapter 13, pp. 213-237.

23. Jøsang, A., Gray, E., Kinateder, M.: Analysing Topologies of Transitive Trust. In Dimitrakos, T., Martinelli, F., eds.: Proceedings of the First International Workshop on Formal Aspects in Security & Trust (FAST2003), Pisa, Italy (September 2003) 9–22

Control Flow Based Pointcuts for Security Hardening Concerns

Marc-André Laverdière, Azzam Mourad, Andrei Soeanu, and Mourad
Debbabi *

Computer Security Laboratory,
Concordia Institute for Information Systems Engineering,
Concordia University, Montreal (QC), Canada
{ma_laver,mourad,a_soeanu,debbabi}@ciise.concordia.ca

Abstract. In this paper, we present two new control flow based pointcuts to Aspect-Oriented Programming (AOP) languages that are needed
for systematic hardening of security concerns. They allow to identify
particular join points in a program's control flow graph (CFG). The
first proposed primitive is the *GAFlow*, the closest guaranteed ancestor, which returns the closest ancestor join point to the pointcuts of
interest that is on all their runtime paths. The second proposed primitive is the *GDFlow*, the closest guaranteed descendant, which returns
the closest child join point that can be reached by all paths starting
from the pointcuts of interest. We find these pointcuts to be necessary
because they are needed to perform many security hardening practices
and, to the best of our knowledge, none of the existing pointcuts can
provide their functionalities. Moreover, we show the viability and correctness of our proposed pointcuts by elaborating and implementing
their algorithms and presenting the results of a testing case study.

1 Motivations & Background

In today's computing world, security takes an increasingly predominant role.
The industry is facing challenges in public confidence at the discovery of vulnerabilities, and customers are expecting security to be delivered out of the
box, even on programs that were not designed with security in mind. The challenge is even greater when legacy systems must be adapted to networked/web
environments, while they are not originally designed to fit into such high-risk
environments. Tools and guidelines have been available for developers for a few
years already, but their practical adoption is limited so far. Software maintain-
ers must face the challenge to improve program security and are often under-
equipped to do so. In some cases, little can be done to improve the situation,

---

* This research is the result of a fruitful collaboration between CSL (Computer Security Laboratory) of Concordia University, DRDC (Defence Research and Development Canada) Valcartier and Bell Canada under the NSERC DND Research
Partnership Program.

Please use the following format when citing this chapter:

Laverdière, M.-A., Mourad, A., Soeanu, A. and Debbabi, M., 2007, in IFIP International Federation for Information
Processing, Volume 238, Trust Management, eds. Etalle, S., Marsh, S., (Boston: Springer), pp. 301–316.

especially for Commercial-Off-The-Shelf (COTS) software products that are no longer supported, or for in-house programs for which their source code is lost. However, whenever the source code is available, as it is the case for Free and Open-Source Software (FOSS), a wide range of security improvements could be applied once a focus on security is decided.

Very few concepts and approaches emerged in the literature to help and guide developers to harden security into software. In this context, AOP appears to be a promising paradigm for software security hardening, which is an issue that has not been adequately addressed by previous programming models such as object-oriented programming (OOP). It is based on the idea that computer systems are better programmed by separately specifying the various concerns, and then relying on underlying infrastructure to compose them together. The techniques in this paradigm were precisely introduced to address the development problems that are inherent to crosscutting concerns. Aspects allow us to precisely and selectively define and integrate security objects, methods and events within application, which make them interesting solutions for many security issues [3, 5, 9, 16, 17].

However, AOP was not initially designed to address security issues, which resulted in many shortcomings in the current technologies [11, 7]. We were not able to apply some security hardening activities due to missing features. Such limitations forced us, when applying security hardening practices, to perform programming gymnastics, resulting in additional modules that must be integrated within the application, at a definitive runtime, memory and development cost. Moreover, the resulting code after applying this strategy of coding is of higher level of complexity as regards to auditing and evaluation.

The specification of new security-related pointcuts is becoming a very challenging and interesting domain of research [14, 4, 10]. Pointcuts are used in order to specify where code should be injected, and can informally be defined as a subset of the points in a programs' execution flow. In this context, we propose in this paper AOP pointcuts that are needed for security hardening concerns and allow one to identify join points in a program's control flow graph (CFG). The proposed primitives are *GAFlow*, and *GDFlow*. *GAFlow* returns the closest ancestor join point to the pointcuts of interest that is on all their runtime paths. *GDFlow* returns the closest child join point that can be reached by all paths starting from the pointcuts of interest. These poincuts are needed to develop many security hardening solutions. Moreover, we combined all the deployed and proposed pointcuts in the literature, and, as far as we know, were not able to find a method that would isolate a single node in our CFG that satisfies the criteria we define for *GAFlow* and *GDFlow*.

This paper is organized as follows: we first cast a quick glance at security hardening and the problem that we address in Section 2. In Sections 3 and 4 we show the usefulness of our proposal and its advantages. Afterwards, in Section 5, we describe and specify the *GAFlow* and *GDFlow* pointcuts. In Section 6, we present the algorithms necessary for implementing the proposed pointcuts, together with the required hierarchical graph labeling method. This section also shows the results of our implementation in a case study. We move on to the related work in Section 7, and then conclude in Section 8.

2 Security Hardening

In our prior work [12], we proposed that software security hardening be defined as *any process, methodology, product or combination thereof that is used to add security functionalities and/or remove vulnerabilities or prevent their exploitation in existing software.* This definition focuses on the solving of vulnerabilities, not on their detection. In this context, the following constitutes the classification of security hardening methods:

Code-Level Hardening Changes in the source code in a way that prevents vulnerabilities without altering the design. For example, we can add bound-checking on array operations, and use bounded string operations.

Software Process Hardening Addition of security features in the software build process without changes in the original source code. For instance, the use of compiler-generated canary words and compiler options against double-freeing of memory would be considered as Software Process Hardening.

Design-Level Hardening Re-engineering of the application in order to integrate security features that were absent or insufficient. Design-level changes would be, for example, adding an access control feature, changing communication protocol, or replacing temporary files with interprocess communication mechanisms.

Operating Environment Hardening Improvements to the security of the execution context (network, operating systems, libraries, utilities, etc.) that is relied upon by the software. Examples would be deploying `libsafe`, using hardened memory managers and enabling security features of middleware.

Security hardening practices are usually applied manually by injecting security code into the software [2, 8, 15, 18]. This task requires from the security architects to have a deep knowledge of the code inner working of the software, which is not available all the time. In this context, we elaborated in [13] an approach based on aspect orientation to perform security hardening in a systematic and automatic way. The primary objective of this approach is to allow the security architects to perform security hardening of software by applying proven solutions so far and without the need to have expertise in the low-level security solution domain. At the same time, the security hardening is applied in an organized and systematic way in order not to alter the original functionalities of the software. This is done by providing an abstraction over the actions required to improve the security of the program and adopting AOP to build our solutions. The result of our experimental results explored the usefulness of AOP to reach the objective of having systematic security hardening. During our work, we have developed security hardening solutions to secure connections in a client-server application, added access control features to a program, encrypted memory contents for protection and corrected some low-level security issues in C programs. On the other hand, we have also concluded the shortcomings of the available AOP technologies in security and the need to elaborate new pointcuts for security hardening concerns.

3 Usefulness of *GAFlow* and *GDFlow* for Security Hardening

Many security hardening practices require the injection of code around a set of join points or possible execution paths [2, 8, 15, 18]. Examples of such cases would be the injection of security library initialization/deinitialization, privilege level changes, atomicity guarantee, logging, etc. The current AOP models only allow us to identify a set join points in the program, and therefore inject code before, after and/or around each one of them. However, to the best of our knowledge, none of the current pointcuts enable the identification a join point common to a set of other join points where we can inject the code once for all of them. In the sequel, we present briefly the necessity and usefulness of our proposed pointcuts for some security hardening activities.

3.1 Security Library Initialization/Deinitialization

In the case of security library initialization (e.g. access control, authorization, cryptography, etc.), our primitives allow us to initialize the needed library only for the branches of code where they are needed by identifying their *GAFlow* and/or *GDFlow*. Having both primitives would also avoid the need to keep global state variables about the current state of library initialization. We use as example part of an aspect that we elaborated for securing the connections of a client application. With the current AOP pointcuts, the aspect targets the main as the location for the TLS library initialization and deinitialization as depicted in Listing 1. Another possible solution could be the loading and unloading of the library before and after its use, which may cause runtime problems since api-specific data structures could be needed for other functions. However, in the case of large applications, especially for embedded ones, the two solutions create an accumulation of code injection statements that would create a significant, and possibly useless, waste of system resources. In listing 2, we see an improved aspect that would yield to more efficient and wider applicable result using the proposed pointcuts.

Listing 1. Excerpt of Hardening Aspect for Securing Connections Using GnuTLS

```
advice execution ("%␣␣main␣(...)␣") : around () {
    hardening_socketInfoStorageInit ();hardening_initGnuTLSSubsystem(NONE);
    tjp -> proceed ();
    hardening_deinitGnuTLSSubsystem ();hardening_socketInfoStorageDeinit();
    *tjp -> result () = 0;
}
```

Listing 2. Excerpt of Improved Hardening Aspect for Securing Connections Using GnuTLS

```
advice gaflow(call("%␣connect(...)") || call("%␣send(...)") || call("%␣
    recv(...)")): before(){
  hardening_socketInfoStorageInit();  hardening_initGnuTLSSubsystem(NONE);
  }

advice gdflow(call("%␣connect(...)") || call("%␣send(...)") || call("%␣
    recv(...)") || call("%␣close(...)")): after(){
  hardening_deinitGnuTLSSubsystem();  hardening_socketInfoStorageDeinit();
  }
```

3.2 Principle of Least Privilege

For processes implementing the principle of least privilege, it is necessary to increase the active rights before the execution of a sensitive operation, and to relinquish such rights directly after it was accomplished. Our primitives can be used to deal with a group of operations requiring the same privilege by injecting the privilege adjustment code at the *GAFlow* and *GDFlow* join points. This is applicable only in the case where no unprivileged operations are in the execution path between the initialization and the deinitialization points. The example in Listing 3 (made using combined code examples from [8]) shows an aspect implementing a lowering of privilege around certain operations. It uses restrict tokens and the SAFER API available in Windows XP. This solution injects code before and after each of the corresponding operations, incurring overhead, particularly in the case where the operations a, b and c would be executed consecutively. This could be avoided by using *GAFlow* and *GDFlow*, as we show in Listing 4.

Listing 3. Hypothetical Aspect Implementing Least Privilege

```
pointcut abc: call("%␣a(...)") || call("%␣b(...)") || call("%␣c(...)");

advice abc: around(){
  SAFER_LEVEL_HANDLE hAuthzLevel;
  // Create a normal user level.
  if (SaferCreateLevel(SAFER_SCOPEID_USER, SAFER_LEVELID_CONSTRAINED,
                       0, &hAuthzLevel, NULL)){
    // Generate the restricted token that we will use.
    HANDLE hToken = NULL;
    if (SaferComputeTokenFromLevel(hAuthzLevel, NULL, &hToken,0,NULL)){
      //sets the restrict token for the current thread
      HANDLE hThread = GetCurrentThread();
      if (SetThreadToken(&hThread,hToken)){
        tjp->proceed();
        SetThreadToken(&hThread,NULL); //removes restrict token
      }
      else{//error handling}
    }
    SaferCloseLevel(hAuthzLevel);
  }
}
```

Listing 4. Improved Aspect Implementing Least Privilege

```
pointcut abc: call("%ua(...)") || call("%ub(...)") || call("%uc(...)");

advice gaflow(abc): before(){
  SAFER_LEVEL_HANDLE hAuthzLevel;
  // Create a normal user level.
  if (SaferCreateLevel(SAFER_SCOPEID_USER, SAFER_LEVELID_CONSTRAINED,
                       0, &hAuthzLevel, NULL)){
    // Generate the restricted token that we will use.
    HANDLE hToken = NULL;
    if (SaferComputeTokenFromLevel(hAuthzLevel, NULL, &hToken,0,NULL)){
      //sets the restrict token for the current thread
      HANDLE hThread = GetCurrentThread();
      SetThreadToken(&hThread,NULL);
    }
    SaferCloseLevel(hAuthzLevel);
  }
}
advice gdflow(abc): after(){
  HANDLE hThread = GetCurrentThread();
  SetThreadToken(&hThread,NULL); //removes restrict token
}
```

3.3 Atomicity

In the case where a critical section may span across multiple program elements
(such as function calls), there is a need to enforce mutual exclusion using tools
such as semaphores around the critical section. The beginning and end of the
critical section can be targeted using the *GAFlow* and *GDFlow* join points.

Listing 5. Aspect Adding Atomicity

```
static Semaphore sem = new Semaphore(1);

pointcut abc: call("%ua(...)") || call("%ub(...)") || call("%uc(...)");

advice abc: before(){
  try{
    sem.acquire();
  } catch(InterruptedException e) {//...}
}

advice abc: after(){
  sem.release();
}
```

Listing 5, although correct-looking, can create unwanted side effects if two
calls (say, a and b) were intended to be part of the same critical section (i.e.
in the same execution path), as the lock would be released after a, and acquired again before b, allowing for the execution of another unwanted critical
section, possibly damaging b's internal state. Improving this aspect to deal with
this case requires knowledge of the program's flow of event, contradicting the
core principle of separation of concerns, and thus complicating maintenance
and preventing aspect reuse. Using our proposal, however, the lock is acquired
and released independently of the individual join points, but guarantees that

they will be, altogether, considered as one critical section. Listing 6 shows this improvement.

Listing 6. Improved Aspect Adding Atomicity

```
pointcut abc: call("%_a(...)") && call("%_b(...)") && call("%_c(...)");

advice gaflow(abc): before(){
  static Semaphore sem = new Semaphore(1);
  try{
  sem.acquire();
  } catch(InterruptedException e) {//...}
}

advice gaflow(abc): after(){
  sem.release();
}
```

3.4 Logging

It is possible that a set of operation are of interest for logging purposes, but that their individual log entry would be redundant or of little use. This is why it is desirable to use *GAFlow* and/or *GDFlow* in order to insert log statements before or after a set of interesting transactions.

4 General Advantages of *GAFlow* and *GDFlow*

It is clear that our proposed primitives support the principle of separation of concerns by allowing to implement program modification on sets of join points based on a specific concern (as previously exemplified). We now present some general advantages of our proposed pointcuts:

– *Ease of use*: Programmers can target places in the application's control flow graph where to inject code before or after a set of join points without needing to manually determine the precise point where to do so.
– *Ease of Maintenance*: Programmers can change the program structure without needing to rewrite the associated aspects that were relying on explicit knowledge of the structure in order to pinpoint where the advice code would be injected. For example, if we need to change the execution path to a particular function (e.g. when performing refactoring), we also need to find manually the new common ancestor and/or descendant, whereas this would be done automatically using our proposed pointcuts.
– *Optimization*: Programmers can inject certain pre-operations and post-operations only where needed in the program, without having to resort to injection in the catch-all main. This can improve the apparent responsiveness of the application. Certain lengthy operations (such as library initialization) can be avoided if the branches of code requiring them are not executed, thus saving CPU cycles and memory usage. Also, this avoids the execution of the

pre-operations and post-operations needed around each targeted join point, which is the default solution using actual AOP techniques. This is replaced by executing them only once around the *GAFlow* and *GDFlow.*

- **Raising the Abstraction Level**: Programmers can develop more abstract and reusable aspect libraries.

5 Pointcut Definitions

We provide here the syntax that defines a pointcut *p* after adding our proposed pointcuts:

$$p ::= \texttt{call}(s) \mid \texttt{execution}(s) \mid \texttt{gaflow}(p) \mid \texttt{gdflow}(p) \mid p \mid\mid p \mid p \texttt{\&\&} p$$

where *s* is a function signature. The *GAFlow* and the *GDFlow* are the new control flow based pointcut primitives. Their parameter is also a pointcut *p*.

The *GAFlow* primitive operates on the CFG of a program. Its input is a set of join points defined as a pointcut and its output is a single join point. In other words, if we are considering the CFG notations, the input is a set of nodes and the output is one node. This output is the closest common ancestor that constitutes (1) the closest common parent node of all the nodes specified in the input set (2) and through which passes all the possible paths that reach them. In the worst case, the closest common ancestor will be the starting point in the program.

The *GDFlow* primitive operates on the CFG of a program. Its input is a set of join points defined as a pointcut and its output is a join point. In other words, if we are considering the CFG notations, the input is a set of nodes and the output is one node. This output (1) is a common descendant of the selected nodes and (2) constitutes the first common node reached by all the possible paths emanating from the selected nodes. In the worst case, the first common descendant will be the end point in the program.

6 Algorithms and Implementation

In this section, we present the elaborated algorithms for graph labeling, *GAFlow* and *GDFlow*. We assume that our CFG is shaped in the traditional form, with a single start node and a single end node. In the case of program with multiple starting points, we consider each starting point as a different program in our analysis. In the case of multiple ending points, we also consider them as one end point. Most of these assumptions have been used so far [6]. With these assumptions in place, we ensure that our algorithms will return a result (in the worst case, the start node or the end node) and that this result will be a single and unique node for all inputs.

6.1 Graph Labeling

Algorithms that operate on graphs have been developed for decades now, and many graph operations (such as finding ancestors, finding descendants, finding paths and so on) are considered to be common knowledge in computer science. Despite this theoretical richness, we are not aware of existing methods allowing to efficiently determine the *GAFlow* and *GDFlow* for a particular set of join points in a CFG by considering all the possible paths. Some approaches use lattice theory to efficiently compute a Least Upper Bound (LUB) and Greatest Lower Bound (GLB) over lattices [1]. However, their results do not guarantee that all paths will be traversed by the results of LUB and GLB, which is a central requirement for *GAFlow* and *GDFlow*. Moreover, the lattices do not support the full range of expression provided by the CFG, as the latter can be a directed cyclic graph. In order to determine the *GAFlow* and *GDFlow*, we chose to use a graph labeling algorithm developed by our colleagues that we slightly modified in order to meet our requirements. Algorithm 1 describes our graph labeling method.

Each node down the hierarchy is labeled in the same manner as the table of contents of a book (e.g. 1., 1.1., 1.2., 1.2.1., ...), as depicted by Algorithm 1, where the operator $+_c$ denotes string concatenation (with implicit operand type conversion). To that effect, the labeling is done by executing algorithm 1 on *start* node with label "0.", thus recursively labeling all nodes.

We implemented Algorithm 1 and tested it on a sample hypothetical CFG. The result is displayed in Figure 1. This example will be used throughout the rest of this paper.

6.2 *GAFlow*

In order to compute the *GAFlow*, we developed a mechanism that operates on the labeled graph. We compare all the hierarchical labels of the selected nodes in the input set and find the largest common prefix they share. The node labeled with this largest common prefix is the closest guaranteed ancestor. We insured that the *GAFlow* result is a node through which all the paths that reach the selected nodes pass by considering all the labels of each node. This is elaborated in Algorithm 2. Please note that the FindCommonPrefix function was specified recursively for the sake of simplicity

Moreover, we implemented Algorithm 2 and we applied it on the labeled graph in Figure 1. We selected, as case study, some nodes in the graph for various combinations. Our results, are summarized in Table 1 and Figure 2.

6.3 *GDFlow*

The closest guaranteed descendant is determined by elaborating a mechanism that operates on a labeled CFG of a program. By using Algorithm 3, we obtain the sorted list of all the common descendants of the selected nodes in the input

---

Algorithm 1 Hierarchical Graph Labeling Algorithm

1: labelNode(Node s, Label l):
2:   $s.labels \leftarrow s.labels \cup \{l\}$
3:   $childrenSequence = s.children()$
4:   **for** $k = 0$ to $|childrenSequence| - 1$ **do**
5:     $child \leftarrow childrenSequence_k$
6:     **if** $\neg hasProperPrefix(child, s.labels)$ **then**
7:       $labelNode(child, l +_c k +_c ".")$;
8:     **end if**
9: **end for**
10:
11: hasProperPrefix(Node s, LabelSet $parentLabels$):
12: **if** $s.label = \epsilon$ **then**
13:     **return false**
14: **end if**
15: **if** $\exists s \in Prefixes(s.label) : s \in parentLabels$ **then**
16:     **return true**
17: **else**
18:     **return false**
19: **end if**
20:
21: Prefixes(Label l):
22: $StringSetlabels \leftarrow \emptyset$
23: $Stringcurrent \leftarrow "$"
24: **for** $i \leftarrow 0$ to $l.length()$ **do**
25:     $current.append(l.charAt(i)$
26:     **if** $Label1.charAt(i) = '.'$ **then**
27:       $labels.add(current.clone())$
28:     **end if**
29: **end for**

Selected Nodes	GAFlow
N2, N8, N13	N1
N6, N11	N2
N14, N13	N1
N14, N15	N14

Table 1. Results of the Execution of Algorithm 2 on Figure 1

list of the pointcut. The principle of this algorithm is to calculate the set of descendants of each of the input nodes and then perform the intersection operation on them. The resulting set contains the common descendants of all the input nodes. Then, we sorted them based on their path lengths.

Algorithm 4 determines the closest guaranteed descendant. It takes first the result of Algorithm 3, which its considers as its list of possible solutions. Then, it iterates on the list until it reaches the node for which all paths coming from the selected nodes pass through it. During the verification, we operates on

---

Algorithm 2 Algorithm to determine *GAFlow*

Require: *SelectedNodes* is initialized with the contents of the pointcut match
Require: *Graph* has all its nodes labeled
 1: **gaflow**(NodeSet SelectedNodes):
 2: *Labels* ← ∅
 3: **for all** *node* ∈ *SelectedNodes* **do**
 4:   *Labels* ← *Labels* ∪ *node.labels*()
 5: **end for**
 6: **return** *GetNodeByLabel*(*FindCommonPrefix*(*Labels*))
 7:
 8: **FindCommonPrefix** (LabelVector Labels):
 9: **if** *Labels.size*() = 0 **then**
10:   **return** error
11: **else if** *Labels.size*() = 1 **then**
12:   **return** *Labels.removeHead*()
13: **else**
14:   *Label1* ← *Labels.removeHead*()
15:   *Label2* ← *Labels.removeHead*()
16:   **if** *Labels.size*() = 2 **then**
17:     **for** i ← 0 to *min*(*Label.length*(), *Label2.length*()) **do**
18:       **if** *Label1.charAt*(i) ≠ *Label2.charAt*(i) **then**
19:         **return** *Label1.substring*(0, $i - 1$)
20:       **end if**
21:     **end for**
22:     **return** *Label1.substring*(0, *min*(*Label.length*(), *Label2.length*()))
23:   **else**
24:     *PartialSolution* ← *FindCommonPrefix*(*Label1*, *Label2*)
25:     *Labels.Append*(*PartialSolution*)
26:     **return** *FindCommonPrefix*(*Labels*)
27:   **end if**
28: **end if**

Algorithm 3 Algorithm to Determine the Common Descendants

Require: *SelectedNodes* is initialized with the contents of the pointcut match
Require: *Graph* has all its nodes labeled
 1: **findCommonDescendants**(NodeSet SelectedNodes):
 2: *PossibleSolutions* ← *Graph.allNodes*()
 3: **for all** *node* ∈ *SelectedNodes* **do**
 4:   *PossibleSolutions* ← *PossibleSolutions* ∩ *node.AllDescendants*()
 5: **end for**
 6: Create *OrderedSolutions* by sorting *PossibleSolutions* by increasing path length
    between the solution and the nodes in *SelectedNodes*
 7: **return** *OrderedSolutions*

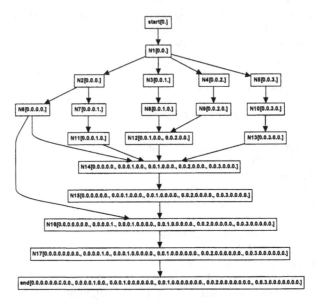

Fig. 1. Labeled Graph

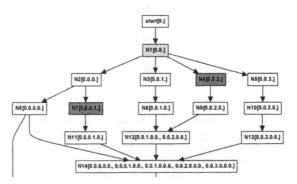

Fig. 2. Excerpt of Graph Illustrating the *GAFlow* of N4 and N7

the labels of each node in the list, which we call candidate. For each selected node, we count the number of labels of the candidate that have proper prefixes identical to the labels of the considered selected node. The resulting candidate of the first iteration is the first encountered node with the largest label count. This candidate is the starting one of the next iteration and so on until all the selected nodes are examined. The final candidate of the last iteration is returned by the algorithm as the closest guaranteed descendant.

Algorithm 4 Algorithm to Determine the *GDFlow*

Require: *SelectedNodes* is initialized with the contents of the pointcut match
Require: *Graph* has all its nodes labeled
1: gdflow(NodeSet SelectedNodes):
2:   *PossibleSolutions* ← *findCommonDescendants(SelectedNodes)*
3:   *Candidate* ← 0
4: **for all** *node* ∈ *SelectedNodes* **do**
5:     *Candidate* ← *findBestCandidate(PossibleSolutions, Candidate, node)*
6: **end for**
7: **return** *PossibleSolutions$_{Candidate}$*
8:
9: findBestCandidate(NodeQueue   *possibleSolutions*,   int   *Candidate*,   Node   *selectedNode*)
10: *PreviousFoundPrefixes* ← 0
11: **for** *i* ← *Candidate* to *possibleSolutions.size()* − 1 **do**
12:   *sol* ← *possibleSolutions$_i$*
13:   *foundPrefixes* ← *countProperPrefixes(sol, node)*
14:   **if** (*PreviousFoundPrefixes* < *foundPrefixes*) ∨ ∃*child* ∈ *sol.children()* : *hasProperPrefix(sol, child.labels())* **then**
15:     *Candidate* ← *i*
16:   **end if**
17: **end for**
18: **return** *Candidate*
19:
20: countProperPrefixes(Node *candidate*, Node *selectedNode*):
21: *count* ← 0
22: **for all** *candidateLabel* ∈ *candidate.labels()* **do**
23:   **for all** *selectedNodeLabel* ∈ *selectedNode.labels()* **do**
24:     **if** ∃*p* ∈ *prefixes(candidateLabel)* : *p* = *selectedNodeLabel* **then**
25:       *count* + +
26:     **end if**
27:   **end for**
28: **end for**
29: **return** *count*

We used the same implementation of Algorithm 1 and case study illustrated in Figure 1. With this, we first implemented Algorithm 3 to determine the list of common descendants for different selected nodes, as summarized in Table 2. Then, we implemented Algorithm 4 to calculate the *GDFlow* for the list of common descendants previously computed by applying the aforementioned conditions. Table 2 contains the results for this algorithm. Figures 3 and 4 illustrate these as well.

Selected Nodes	Common Descendants	*GDFlow*
N2, N8, N13	N14, N15, N16, N17, end	N16
N6, N11	N14, N15, N16, N17, end	N16
N14, N13	N15, N16, N17, end	N15
N14, N15	N16, N17, end	N16

Table 2. Results of the Execution of Algorithm 3 and 4 on Figure 1

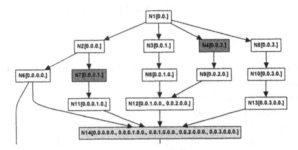

Fig. 3. Illustration of the *GDFlow* of N4 and N7 as N14

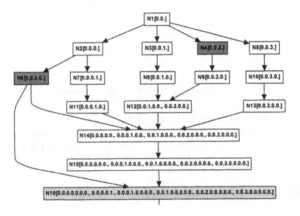

Fig. 4. Illustration of the *GDFlow* of N4 and N6 as N16

7 Related Work

Many shortcomings of AOP for security concerns have been documented and some improvements have been suggested so far. In the sequel, we present the most noteworthy.

A dataflow pointcut that is used to identify join points based on the origin of values is defined and formulated in [11] for security purposes. This poincut is not fully implemented yet. For instance, such pointcut detects if the data sent over the network depends on information read from a confidential file.

In [7], Harbulot and Gurd proposed a model of a loop pointcut that explores the need for a loop join point that predicts infinite loops, which are used by attackers to perform denial of service of attacks.

Another approach, that discusses local variables set and get poincut, has been proposed in [14]. He claims that this pointcut is necessary to increase the efficiency of AOP in security since it allows to track the values of local variables inside a method. It seems that this poincut can be used to protect the confidentiality of local variables.

In [4], Bonér discussed a poincut that is needed to detect the beginning of a synchronized block and add some security code that limits the CPU usage or the number of instructions executed. He also explored in his paper the usefulness of capturing synchronized block in calculating the time acquired by a lock and thread management. This usefulness applies also in the security context and can help in preventing many denial of service attacks.

A predicted control flow (pcflow) pointcut was introduced by Kiczales in a keynote address [10] without a precise definition. Such pointcut may allow to select points within the control flow of a join point starting from the root of the execution to the parameter join point. In the same presentation, he introduced an operator allowing to obtain the minimum of two pcflow pointcuts, but never clearly defined what this min can be or how it can be obtained. These proposals could be used for software security, in the enforcement of policies that prohibit the execution of a given function in the context of the execution of another one.

8 Conclusion

AOP appears to be a very promising paradigm for software security hardening. However, this technology was not initially designed to address security issues and many research work showed its limitations in such domain. Similarly, we explored in this paper the shortcomings of the AOP in applying many security hardening practices and the need to extend this technology with new pointcuts. In this context, we proposed two new pointcuts to AOP for security hardening concerns: The *GAFlow* and *GDFlow*. The *GAFlow* returns the closest ancestor join point to the pointcuts of interest that is on all their runtime paths. The *GDFlow* returns the closest child join point that can be reached by all paths starting from the pointcuts of interest. We first showed the limitations of the current AOP languages for many security issues. Then, we illustrated the usefulness of our proposed pointcuts for performing security hardening activities. Afterwards, we defined the new pointcuts and we presented their elaborated algorithms. Finally, we presented our implementation of pointcuts and a case study that explore their correctness.

References

1. Hassan Ait-Kaci, Robert S. Boyer, Patrick Lincoln, and Roger Nasr. Efficient implementation of lattice operations. *Programming Languages and Systems*, 11(1):115–146, 1989.

2. Matt Bishop. How Attackers Break Programs, and How to Write More Secure Programs. http://nob.cs.ucdavis.edu/~bishop/secprog/sans2002/index.html (accessed 2007/04/19).

3. Ron Bodkin. Enterprise security aspects, 2004. http://citeseer.ist.psu.edu/702193.html (accessed 2007/04/19).

4. J. Bonér. Semantics for a synchronized block join point, 2005. http://jonasboner.com/2005/07/18/semantics-for-a-synchronized-block-joint-point/ (accessed 2007/04/19).

5. B. DeWin. *Engineering Application Level Security through Aspect Oriented Software Development.* PhD thesis, Katholieke Universiteit Leuven, 2004.

6. Ernesto Gomez. Cs624- notes on control flow graph. http://www.csci.csusb.edu/egomez/cs624/cfg.pdf.

7. B. harbulot and J.R. Gurd. A join point for loops in AspectJ. In *Proceedings of the 4th workshop on Foundations of Aspect-Oriented Languages (FOAL 2005), March,* 2005.

8. Michael Howard and David E. Leblanc. *Writing Secure Code.* Microsoft Press, Redmond, WA, USA, 2002.

9. M. Huang, C. Wang, and L. Zhang. Toward a reusable and generic security aspect library. In *AOSD:AOSDSEC 04: AOSD Technology for Application level Security, March,* 2004.

10. G. Kiczales. The fun has just begun, keynote talk at AOSD 2003, 2003. http://www.cs.ubc.ca/~gregor/papers/kiczales-aosd-2003.ppt (accessed 2007/04/19).

11. H. Masuhara and K. Kawauchi. Dataflow pointcut in aspect-oriented programming. In *Proceedings of The First Asian Symposium on Programming Languages and Systems (APLAS'03),* pages 105–121, 2003.

12. A. Mourad, M-A. Laverdière, and M. Debbabi. Security hardening of open source software. In *Proceedings of the 2006 International Conference on Privacy, Security and Trust (PST 2006).* ACM, 2006.

13. A. Mourad, M-A. Laverdière, and M. Debbabi. Towards an aspect oriented approach for the security hardening of code. In *To appear in the Proceedings of the 3rd IEEE International Symposium on Security in Networks and Distributed Systems.* IEEE Press, 2007.

14. Andrew C. Myers. JFlow: Practical mostly-static information flow control. In *Symposium on Principles of Programming Languages,* pages 228–241, 1999.

15. R. Seacord. *Secure Coding in C and C++.* SEI Series. Addison-Wesley, 2005.

16. Viren Shah. An aspect-oriented security assurance solution. Technical Report AFRL-IF-RS-TR-2003-254, Cigital Labs, 2003.

17. Pawel Slowikowski and Krzysztof Zielinski. Comparison study of aspect-oriented and container managed security. In *Proceedings of the ECCOP workshop on Analysis of Aspect-Oriented Software,* 2003.

18. D. Wheeler. *Secure Programming for Linux and Unix HOWTO – Creating Secure Software v3.010.* 2003. http://www.dwheeler.com/secure-programs/ (accessed 2007/04/19).

Design of Trusted Systems
with Reusable Collaboration Models

Peter Herrmann and Frank Alexander Kræmer

Norwegian University of Science and Technology (NTNU)
Telematics Department, 7491 Trondheim, Norway
herrmann@item.ntnu.no, kraemer@item.ntnu.no

Abstract. We describe the application of our collaboration-oriented
software engineering approach to the design of trust-aware systems. In
this model-based technique, a specification does not describe a physical
system component but the collaboration between various components
which achieve system functions by cooperation. A system model is composed from these collaboration specifications. By a set of transformations, executable code can be automatically generated. As a modeling
language, we use UML 2.0 collaborations and activities, for which we
defined a semantics based on temporal logic. Thus, formal refinement
and property proofs can be provided by applying model checkers as
well. We consider our approach to be well-suited for the development of
trust-based systems since the trust relations between different parties
can be nicely modeled by the collaborations. This ability facilitates also
a tight cooperation between trust management and software engineering
experts which are both needed to create scalable trust-aware applications. The engineering approach is introduced by means of an electronic
auction system executing different policies which are guided by the mutual trust of its principals. While the approach can be used for various
trust models, we apply Jøsang's Subjective Logic in the example.

1 Introduction

Since the turn of the millenium, the management of trust has gained more
and more momentum. While this field is inherently multi-disciplinary and researchers from psychology, sociology, philosophy, law and economics work on
trust issues for many years, computer science seems to be the driving force behind the current advances. An important reason for that is the maturing of the
internet-based consumer commerce [1]. The acceptance of e-commerce services
depends directly on the trust the different parties involved in it can build up in
each other. In the internet, however, commerce partners are often unknown, live
in another country with a different legal system, and are selected on an ad hoc
basis guided by the best offer. Therefore, traditional trust building mechanisms
like personal experience, recommendations by friends, or the general reputation "in town" cannot be used in the same way as in traditional commerce.
The trust management community started to overcome this deficiency by de-

Please use the following format when citing this chapter:

Herrmann, P. and Kraemer, F. A., 2007, in IFIP International Federation for Information Processing, Volume 238, Trust
Management, eds. Etalle, S., Marsh, S., (Boston: Springer), pp. 317–332.

veloping trust models consisting of both representations for trust in computers and related mechanisms specifying the building of trust. Some of these models describe trust in a more general way from either a mathematical-philosophical perspective (e.g., [2, 3]) or from a sociological-cognitive view (e.g., [4, 5]). Other approaches are devoted to realize trust building mechanisms which take the practical limits of computer systems and networks into account [6, 7, 8, 9, 10].

The invention of computer-readable trust mechanisms facilitates the design of applications incorporating trust. Most approaches enhance or replace traditional security mechanisms at points where they are not suitable for modern ad hoc-networks. In particular, a number of solutions were developed for access control of both peer-to-peer networks [11, 12, 13] and business processes for web services [14, 15, 16] while other tools approach authorization [17], authentication and identity management [18] as well as privacy [19]. A second field of application design is devoted to federate systems combined of separate partners and, in particular, to determine the kind of mutual protection of the partners. Here, a wide field starting at security-protecting routing algorithms [20] via the formation of virtual organizations [21] to the trust-based protection of component-structured software [22, 23] and the protection of collaborations of pervasive devices [24] is covered. It does not require prophetic skills to expect that there will be a lot more trust-encompassing systems to come in various application domains.

As the design of trust-based systems can be quite complex, it has to incorporate typical software engineering techniques. The application of these techniques is usually so difficult that experienced software engineers are required. Thus, to develop a trust-aware system, we need experts both for the trust management and for software engineering who have to cooperate very closely since the trust management functions of a system are tightly interwoven with the rest of the system logic. Ideally, the trust management developer should be able to integrate trust models into a system design process without necessarily understanding the full application logic, while the software designer should be capable to make the general software engineering decisions without comprehending the complete functionality of the underlying trust management model.

We consider our software engineering approach based on collaboration-oriented formal system models [25] as a solution to this problem. Most modeling techniques combine system specifications from models specifying a separate physical software component each. In contrast, in our technique a specification building block describes a partial system functionality which is provided by the joint effort of several components cooperating with each other. Every component taking part in a collaboration is represented in the form of a so-called collaboration role. The behavior models of collaborations specify both the interactions between the collaboration roles as well as local behavior of collaboration roles needed to provide the modeled functionality. Collaborations may be composed with each other to more comprehensive collaborations by means of collaboration uses. Thus, hierarchical system models are possible.

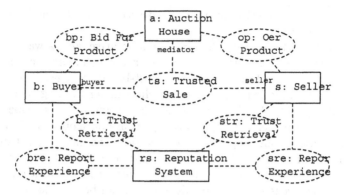

Fig. 1. Collaboration of the *Trusted Auction System*

As an example, we depict in Fig. 1 the collaboration uses of the highest hierarchical level to model a trusted electronic auction system which will be introduced in detail in sections 3 and 4. The system specifies an automatic internet-based auction system which could, for instance, be built upon the web services offered by eBay. From a trust management perspective, the major problem of such a system is the sale between the winning buyer and the seller after the auction since the reluctance of one party to pay resp. to deliver the product may cause damage to the other side. As a solution, we provide a trust-encompassing application based on a reputation system (e.g., the eBay feedback forum). According to their mutual trust, both parties can decide how to carry out the sale. As a consequence, the example system incorporates four major components: the winning buyer, the seller, the reputation system and the auction house. Its functionality is expressed by means of seven collaboration uses depicted in Fig. 1. The collaboration use *btr* models the access to the reputation system by the buyer in order to retrieve the current trust of the community in the seller. We will see in Sect. 4 that this retrieval is done before bidding for the product. Likewise, the collaboration use *str* describes the retrieval of the buyer's trust value by the seller which takes place after the auction. According to the mutual trust, the buyer and seller perform the sale which is modeled by *ts*. Indeed, this collaboration is a composition from more basic collaborations specifying four different modes which depend on the trust of the participants in each other. After finishing the sale, both parties report their mutual experiences to the reputation system which is expressed by the collaboration uses *bre* and *sre*. The remaining collaboration uses *op* and *bp* describe the offering of goods by the seller and the bidding of the buyer. As these collaboration uses are not relevant from a trust management perspective, they are not discussed further.

Fig. 1 is a collaboration in the popular graphical modeling language UML 2.0 (Unified Modeling Language [26, 27]). These diagrams are used to describe the basic structure of a collaboration (i.e., the collaboration uses forming it and the relation between the roles of the collaboration uses and those of the comprehensive collaboration). To specify the behavior of the collaborations and the logic combining collaboration uses is described by UML activities which are introduced in Sect. 3.

As trust relations are inherently collaborative and always comprise at least a trustor and a trustee, we consider the collaboration-oriented specification style very helpful to develop trust-based systems. The reduction of systems to sub-functionalities supports their understanding to a high degree (cf. [25, 28, 29, 30]). As discussed in Sect. 2, we consider this property useful to provide trust management experts and software developers with a fundament for tightly interwoven cooperation. In addition, the model structure enables a higher reuse of collaborations. In many distributed application domains, the system components cooperate with each other by means of a relatively small number of recurrent sub-functionalities which can be specified once and thereafter stored in a library. System developers can create their specifications in a relatively simple way by selecting collaborations from the library, instantiating them, and composing them to a system description. In our example, *btr*, *str*, *bre*, and *sre* are instantiations of the collaborations *Trust Retrieval* resp. *Report Experience* which are suitable building blocks to create applications using reputation systems.

By means of an algorithm [31], we can automatically transform the collaboration-oriented models into executable state machines from which in a second step executable code can be generated [32]. Moreover, we currently develop a transformation to TLA$^+$ [33], the input syntax of the model checker TLC [34] which facilitates formal proofs of system properties. This will be further discussed in Sect. 5. Before that, we discuss in Sect. 2 the benefit of our approach for the generation of trust management-based systems. Thereafter, the specification of collaborations by UML collaboration diagrams and activities is introduced by means of the trusted auction example in Sect. 3. The coupling of collaboration uses to more comprehensive collaborations is outlined in Sect. 4.

2 Trust Management Aspects

In recent years, numerous definitions for trust have been published. A significant one was introduced by Jøsang [35] who distinguishes between trust in humans and trust in computers. He calls humans as well as organizations formed by humans with a free will *passionate entities*. In contrast, computers and other entities without a free will are named *rational entities*. Trust in a passionate entity is defined as *"the belief that it will behave without malicious intent"* while trust in a rational entity is *"the belief that it will resist attacks from malicious agents"* [35]. Both definitions have in common that a trustor can only be a passionate entity since trust needs a free will. Nevertheless, in specific application domains both the building of trust and its deployment selecting different policies to deal with the trustee is so rational that it can be handed over to a computer. A good example is the decision making process of banks whether to provide loans or not. A bank's behavior is basically guided by its trust in a debtor that he will be able to pay back a loan. To build this trust, typical mechanisms as the debtor's behavior in previous cases (i.e., the debtor's reputation) are taken into account and the decision is made according to fixed policies. These policies can be implemented on a computer as already applied in some banks.

For the representation of trust one can apply trust values. For instance, Jøsang introduces so-called opinion triangles [2, 36]. These are effectively triples of probability values, the sum of which is always 1. Two of these values describe the belief resp. disbelief in the trustee while the third one states the uncertainty based on missing knowledge on the trustee. The building of trust is, in consequence, described by traces of changing trust values. In between, a lot of trust models were developed which are suited for computers (cf. [2, 5, 6, 7, 8, 9, 10]). The utilization of trust in dealing with a trustee can also be realized on a computer by defining trust-related policies. The actual policy can then be selected based on the current trust value.

Our collaboration-oriented software development approach is well-suited to model the mechanisms used to describe the building of trust. A collaboration is appropriate to describe the various functions of a trust model since every function affects more than one partner. Moreover, the collaborations can be used as building blocks for trust-encompassing applications. For instance, the collaborations *Trust Retrieval* and *Report Experience* used in the trusted auction model (see Fig. 1) describe the two aspects typically used in dealing with a reputation system, i.e., the decision about how to deal with the trustee depending on its current trust value as well as improving the trustee's assessment by sending the reputation system a positive or negative experience report. Similar collaborations can be defined to model other trust gaining mechanisms such as considering one's own experience or the recommendation by third parties. In addition, to support the design of more complex trust building mechanisms, one can add building blocks enabling the combination of different trust values.

The method is also useful to simplify the cooperation between the trust management experts and the software engineers. A trust expert can specify the trust building functions of the system on its own by utilizing collaborations from a library. The outcome will be a set of collaboration uses that the software engineers can integrate into the overall system model without fully understanding their internal behavior. The engineers only need to recognize that different trust-based policies are possible but not the steps to decide which actual policy should be used.

Somehow more difficult is the support of the cooperation between the two expert groups in modeling the enforcement of the different trust policies. Here, aspects of the general application functionality and special trust-related properties have to be combined. This can be achieved by a twofold proceeding. First, characteristic trust-based functions may be used to enforce policies. These functions can also be modeled by collaborations and used in several system models. For instance, a sale between two parties with a low degree of trust in each other can be performed by including a trusted third party which mediates the sale by guaranteeing that a buyer cannot receive the product before sending the money, while the seller must send the product before receiving the payment. It is easy to model this as a collaboration which can be used by the software engineer without understanding the exact functionality (see also Sect. 4).

Second, the trust expert can inform the software engineer about trust-related functionalities the application has to follow. For instance, a requirement of the trusted sale should be that the buyer only issues the money transfer to the seller without having evidence of receiving the product in time if her trust in the seller is high. The software engineer considers these properties in the system development. Afterwards, the trust expert can check that the system complies with the properties by, for instance, proving them with the model checker TLC [34]. In the following, we will clarify how trust-based systems like the trusted auction example can be developed using the collaboration-oriented specification style.

3 Activity-Based Collaboration Models

As depicted in Fig. 1, we use UML collaborations to specify the overall structure of system models composed from collaboration uses. In particular, a collaboration describes the different components forming a system and the assignment of the roles of the collaboration uses to the components. To model the behavior of a collaboration, UML offers various diagram types like state machines, sequence diagrams, and activities [27]. We decided to use activities mainly for two reasons: First, activities are based on Petri Nets and specify behavior as flows of tokens passing nodes and edges of a graph. This proved to represent flows of behavior quite naturally and is therefore easy to understand (cf. [25]). Second, activities are self-contained. Sequence diagrams, for instance, typically describe in one diagram only a set of system scenarios rather than the complete behavior. In contrast, activities facilitate the specification of the full behavior of a collaboration within one diagram.

A typical example for an activity is *Trust Retrieval* which models the behavior of the collaborations *btr* and *str* in the trusted auction example[1] (see Fig. 1). It is listed on the left side of Fig. 2 and describes the access of a caller to a reputation system in order to retrieve a trustee's reputation. Moreover, it models the decision about a certain level of trust which may lead to different trust policies. Since the collaboration comprises two different roles, the client of the reputation system and the reputation system itself, we use two activity partitions in the diagram which are named by the role identifiers. The interface of the collaboration to its environment is located at the activity partition of the client and consists of three output pins each describing a certain level of trust[2].

---

[1] We use Jøsang's approach [2, 37] to specify trust and trust building in the example but could adopt the specifications easily to other trust models.

[2] As these output pins are mutual exclusive, they belong to different parameter sets shown by the additional box around them.

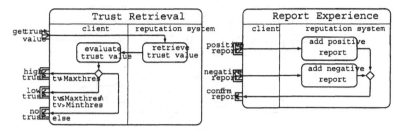

Fig. 2. Activities *Trust Retrieval* and *Report Experience*

The behavior of the activity is described by a token flow which is started at the input node in the partition of the client. It passes a token from the client via the partition border to the reputation system. The token contains an identifier of the trustee which is computed in the call operation action *retrieve trust value*. This call operation action contains the logic to access the number of good and bad experiences with the trustee and to generate the current trust value. The trust value is thereafter forwarded back to the caller and evaluated in the call operation action *evaluate trust value* (i.e., the trust value is copied to the auxiliary collaboration variable *tv*). Thereafter, the token proceeds to a decision node (◇) from which it branches to one of three edges. The branching is guided by the conditions of the decision node, which depend on two thresholds. Finally, the token is forwarded to the activity environment via one of the output pins *high trust*, *low trust*, or *no trust*. By passing one of the output pins, the overall activity is terminated. A trust management expert can instantiate *Trust Retrieval* simply by defining suitable thresholds.

Activity *Report Experience* (on the right side of Fig. 2) models the report of positive or negative experiences with a trustee to the reputation system adjusting the trustee's reputation. It is started with a token passing one of the input pins *positive report* or *negative report*. The tokens are forwarded to the reputation system which adapts the trustee's data base entry in the call operation actions. The edges leaving the two call operation actions lead to a merge node (◇) that merges its incoming flows by forwarding all incoming tokens to the only outgoing edge. In this way, after registering either a positive or negative report, the token is passed back to the client's output pin *confirm report* describing the confirmation of the experience report.

The activity *Mediated Sale* introduced in Fig. 3 expresses a functionality with several parallel flows. As discussed before, a mediator acts here as a trusted third party which assures a fair sale by collecting the payment and the product which are delivered to their recipients not before both are received by the mediator. The activity consists of three partitions for the buyer, the seller and the mediator. It is started by two separate tokens arriving from the buyer through the input pin *send payment* and from the seller via *send product*. The token from the buyer heads to the fork node f_1. In a fork node every incoming token is reproduced and one copy is sent via every outgoing edge. One of the tokens

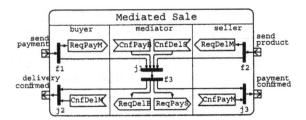

Fig. 3. Activity *Mediated Sale*

leaving f_1 reaches the send action *ReqPayM*. We use send actions to model the transfer of signals to external applications which are not an inherent part of the modeled application. For instance, the accounting unit of the buyer is an example of an external system which is notified by *ReqPayM* to issue the payment to the mediator. The other token leaving f_1 is forwarded to the mediator which is notified thereby about the start of the payment. Likewise, the seller calls its delivery unit to send the product to the mediator which is expressed by the send action *RegDelM* and notifies the mediator as well. When the payment arrives at the mediator, it is notified by its accounting unit using the receive action *CnfPayM* while *CnfDelS* reports the reception of the product. Similar to send actions, we use receive actions to model incoming signals from the environment. All tokens coming from the two receive actions and from the buyer resp. seller lead to the join node[3] j_1. A flow may only leave a join if tokens have arrived on all of its incoming edges. During the execution of the join, all but one token are removed and the remaining token leaves it via its outgoing edge. The token leaving j_1 continues to the fork f_3 from which both deliveries to the final recipients and the notifications are issued. Thus, by the combination of j_1 and f_3 we guarantee that deliveries are only carried out if both the payment and the product have arrived at the mediator.

The notification for the buyer heads to the join node j_2 and can only be forwarded if the buyer's delivery unit reports the product's reception which is specified by the receive action *CnfDelM*. The token passing j_2 leaves the activity via the output pin *delivery confirmed*. Likewise, the seller sends a confirmation of the payment via *payment confirmed* after receiving the money. As the two activities introduced above, *Mediated Sale* can be provided by the trust management expert. The only necessary cooperation with the software engineer is to agree about the formats of the transmissions with the various accounting and delivery units.

---

[3] UML uses identical symbols for join and fork nodes. They can be distinguished by the number of incoming and outgoing edges. Fork nodes have exactly one incoming edge while join nodes have exactly one outgoing edge.

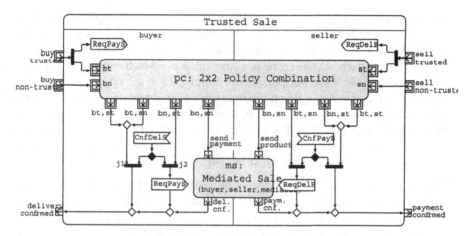

Fig. 4. Activity *Trusted Sale*

4 Coupling Activities

Activities are especially powerful for the composition of behaviors from existing ones. This is done by means of call behavior actions that refer to other activities. The events of the activities may be coupled using all kinds of control nodes and edges, so that arbitrary dependencies between the sub-activities may be described. As activities are used in our approach to describe the behavior of collaborations, this technique is applied to compose the collaborations behaviorally (while the UML collaboration in Fig. 1 shows the structural aspect of this composition.) An example of a composed activity is *Trusted Sale* in Fig. 4 which is composed from the call behavior actions *ms* and *pc* referring to the behavior of subordinate activities (resp. collaborations).

Trusted Sale describes the functionality of selling a product between a buyer and a seller after finishing an auction. The two parties in the sale may either have a high or a low degree of trust in the other one, which is modeled by the two input pins in both the buyer and the seller partition. If the buyer has a high degree of trust in the seller, she is willing to send the payment immediately without waiting for the partner. That is described by the send action *ReqPayS* to which a token is forwarded directly after entering the activity via *buy trusted*. By this send action, the accounting unit of the buyer is notified to start the payment to the seller. Likewise, the seller is ready to send the product to the buyer immediately if he has a high level of trust which is expressed by the flow to the send action *ReqDelB*.

Since both parties may either have high or low trust in each other, four different trust relations between the two parties are possible and for each one a separate sale policy is defined. Nevertheless, to decide about a sale policy, both parties have to know the partner's trust in themselves. As a mutual distributed combination of policies is a quite common function in many networked systems, we have a collaboration and a corresponding activity *2×2 Policy Combination* available from our general pattern library which can be applied here in the form of the call behavior action pc. This activity has two input pins and four output pins on each side. The two parties define the selected input policy by transferring a token via the corresponding input pin which causes the delivery of tokens through those output pins describing the combination of the two policies (e.g., if the buyer sends a token via input pin bt (for *buy trusted*) and the seller via sn (for *sell non-trusted*), the tokens will eventually arrive at the output pins bt,sn). The input nodes of *Trusted Sale* are connected with the corresponding ones of pc and its output pins can be used as the starting points to model the four sale policies (bt,st; bt,sn; bn,st; bn,sn):

- If both partners have a high degree of mutual trust (bt,st), they simply send the payment resp. the product without waiting for the other. Each partner completes the sale after the delivery has arrived. As the payment has already been started, the buyer has to wait for a token arriving via output pin bt,st in join j_1 for the delivery of the product. The reception of the product is described by the accept signal action *ConfDelS* forwarding a token to j_1 as well[4]. Thus, j_1 can be triggered and a token leaves the activity *Trusted Sale* via the output pin *delivery confirmed* which specifies the completion of the sale on the buyer's side. The behavior in the partition of the seller is similar.
- If the buyer has only a low trust in the seller but the seller a high one in the buyer (bn,st), we use a policy in which the seller transfers the product first and the buyer initiates the payment not before receiving the product. Thus, the buyer does not send the payment initially, but waits for the delivery of the product which is expressed by the token in join j_2. After the delivery is notified as modeled by a token heading from *ConfDelS* to j_2, the buyer initiates the payment, which is described by the send action *ReqPayS*, and finishes the sale. The handling of this policy on the seller's side is identical to the first one since it behaves similarly in both policies.
- If the buyer has a high degree of trust in the seller which, however, trusts the buyer only lowly (bt,sn), we use the reciprocal policy to that listed above. Here, the seller does not send the product before receiving the payment. As the effective behavior for the buyer is the same as for the policy (bt,st), the flow from bt,sn is simply merged into the behavior for bt,st.
- If both partners have a low degree of trust in each other (bn,sn), they decide to rely on a mediator. This can be modeled by applying the activity *Mediated Sale* introduced in Sect. 3. The pins bn,sn are simply connected with the input pins of *Mediated Sale* and its output pins with the output pins of *Trusted Sale*.

When one of the partners cheats by not sending anything, the activity is not finished correctly but stops somewhere. We will see below that this case leads to a negative rating of the partner.

The activity *Trusted Sale* exemplifies the interplay between both expert groups. The trust management expert provides the software engineer with the

---

[4] The token leaving *ConfDelS* is stored in a so-called waiting node (♦, cf. [31]) which forwards it to join j_1 or j_2 depending on which join can be executed first.

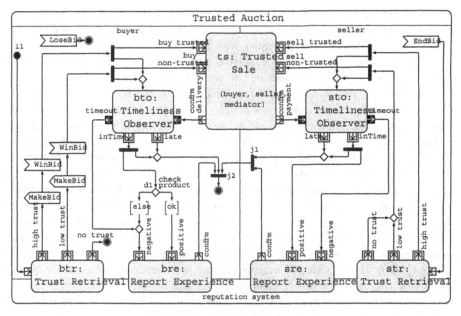

Fig. 5. Activity *Trusted Auction*

activity *Mediated Sale* and describes the four sale policies. Based on this information, the software engineer accomplishes the overall model of the trusted sale which can be added to the library of building blocks for trusted systems facilitating a later usage in other applications.

The last activity introduced here is *Trusted Auction* depicted in Fig. 5 which describes the behavior of the overall system. The collaboration uses it is composed of (see Fig. 1) are represented by the call behavior actions *btr*, *str*, *bre*, *sre*, and *ts*. While an electronic auction encompasses an arbitrary number of buyers and sellers, we laid out the activity in a way that only the relation between exactly one buyer and one seller is modeled by the activity. In consequence, the whole application is described by multiple instances of *Trusted Auction*. For the sake of brevity, we omitted the part in which the seller registers the product since that is not relevant for trust management. Thus, the activity is started by the buyer, who becomes active if she finds an interesting product. This is expressed by the initial node i_1 from which, at first, the trust level of the seller is retrieved by accessing *btr*. If the reputation of the seller is so bad that there is almost no trust, the buyer decides not to bid and the activity is terminated by a final node (●). If the buyer trusts the seller to at least some degree, she makes a bid[5] which is modeled by the send action *MakeBid* and waits in the receive node *WinBid* for the end of the bidding. If the bid is not sufficient, a token is received via the accept signal action *LoseBid* and the activity is terminated since no further action is necessary. If the bid won, a token leaves *WinBid* and

---

[5] For brevity, we assume that a buyer makes only one bid in an auction.

the trusted sale is started by forwarding a token to *ts*. Moreover, the instance *bto* of activity *Timeliness Observer* is started. It specifies a timeout process to detect late deliveries of the product which will be discussed below.

On the seller's side, a flow is started after the auction is finished which is expressed by *EndBid*. Thereafter, the reputation of the buyer is retrieved in *str* and the trusted sale is started as well. Due to the nature of an electronic auction system, the seller has to start the sale process even if he does not trust the buyer at all. Furthermore, *sto* is initiated starting a timer as well. In the case of a timeout, a token leaves the output pin *timeout* immediately, meaning that the payment did not arrive in due time, and via *sre* a negative report on the buyer is sent to the reputation system. The confirmation is forwarded to the join node j_1 used to synchronize the activity termination in the seller partition. If the payment is confirmed, a token proceeds from *ts* to *sto*. If this confirmation arrives at *sto* after the timeout, a token is issued at the output pin *late* which is forwarded to j_1. If the negative report was already confirmed, j_1 can fire which notifies the buyer's side that the seller can accept to terminate the activity. If the payment confirmation arrives in time, a token leaves the output pin *in-Time* of *sto*, issuing a positive report about the buyer. In addition, a token is forwarded to j_1 such that the buyer can be notified about the readiness for termination after the experience report was confirmed.

The behavior after finishing the sale on the buyer's side is similar except for the decision d_1. We assume that the delivery unit of the buyer attaches information to the token sent to the activity *Trusted Sale* describing if the quality of the product is sufficient. In that case, a positive report is triggered while a bad condition of the product leads to a negative report. The join j_2 can only be executed if the delivery of the product was confirmed, the report about the seller was attested and the seller reported that it is ready to terminate. The execution of j_2 causes the termination of the activity.

As in the activity *Trusted Sale*, this activity can be developed combining the competence of the two expert groups. The trust management expert delivers the activities describing the access to the reputation system as well as some policies defining, for instance, which reports have to be issued to the reputation system under which circumstances. This provides the software engineer with the sufficient knowledge to develop the behavioral model specified by the activity.

5 Implementation and Verification

The fact that activities render a complete system behavior facilitates automatic generation of code from the collaboration-oriented model which is performed in a series of steps: At first, we apply the algorithm introduced in [31] which transforms the activities into a set of UML state machines each describing a system component. As we defined both the semantics of the activities and the state machines based on the compositional Temporal Logic of Actions (cTLA) [38], the correctness of the transformation could be verified by a cTLA refinement proof sketch (cf. [31]). For our example, the algorithm in its current version creates separate state machines modeling the behavior of the buyer, the seller, the reputation system and the auction house acting as mediator. Due to the varying complexity of the four components, the state machines have a quite different size. Since the behavior of the reputation system is stateless, its state machine consists only of one control state and three transitions modeling the retrieval of trust values as well as the addition of positive and negative experience report. In contrast, the state machine of the mediator consists of 15 control states, while that of the buyer models the most complex functionality using 64 control states.

The state machines have a special "executable" form in which, except for the initialization, all transitions are triggered by incoming signals from the environment or from local timers. Since, in addition, the enabling condition of a transition depends only on the control state of the state machine but not on its auxiliary variables, very efficient executable code can be generated. This kind of code generator has been built for nearly 30 years now (see, for instance, [39, 40]). To implement our example, we used a generator creating Java code which is executed on the middleware platform JavaFrame [41]. During testing the application, we could not detect any significant overhead. The application of the code generators, the related middleware platforms, and a cTLA-based correctness proof are described in [32].

The trust expert can check if the produced collaboration-oriented model fulfills the trust-related properties passed to the software engineer by applying an animation tool. Moreover, due to defining the semantics of the activities by cTLA, formal refinement and invariant proofs are also facilitated. For instance, the property that the buyer may only start a payment to the seller immediately if she has high trust in him can be expressed by an invariant. This excludes a state in which (1) the trust level is low, (2) the payment was already sent to the seller and (3) the product is not yet delivered. By a cTLA proof, one can verify that the cTLA formula specifying the activity *Trusted Sale* always fulfills the invariant. In the context of trusted systems, this kind of proof was introduced in [42]. We currently develop a tool transforming activities directly into the input syntax TLA$^+$ [33] of the model checker TLC [34] carrying out the proofs automatically. Of course, model checkers are subject to the state space explosion problem. Thus, the number of states to be inspected in a scalable system can be too large to be handled by the checker. cTLA, however, supports a coupling style reflecting the activity combinations in a quite natural way. For each activity, a separate cTLA model is created and, in a proof, only those models realizing the verified property need to be considered. For instance, to prove the invariant listed above, only the states of the cTLA model representing the activity *Trusted Sale* must be checked. This quality of cTLA makes our approach not only well-suited for the design and implementation of realistic trust-based systems but also enables formal property proofs in a relatively user-friendly way.

6 Concluding Remarks

In this paper we introduced our collaboration-oriented software development approach which facilitates system modeling by specifying the various cooperations between the system components separately. We consider the approach well-suited for the design of trust-aware systems since trust relations between principals can be directly modeled as collaborations. This property enables the tight cooperation of trust management experts and software engineers without affording a too close insight in the competence of the other expert group. The collaboration-oriented development approach is supported by the Research Council of Norway (RCN) that approved the research and development project ISIS (Infrastructure for Integrated Services). ISIS is mainly devoted to the creation of a tool set supporting the suitable design of collaboration-oriented systems. Moreover, we want to combine the methodologies of collaboration-oriented software design and security protocol composition. As a result of this project, we expect methods facilitating the engineering and deployment of secure and trust-aware distributed systems. The work presented above is considered as a major cornerstone for these research goals.

References

1. Cheskin Research and Studio Archetype/Sapient, eCommerce Trust Study (1999).
2. A. Jøsang, A Logic for Uncertain Probabilities, *International Journal of Uncertainty, Fuzziness and Knowledge-Based Systems* **9**, 279-311 (2001).
3. A.J.I. Jones and B.S. Firozabadi, On the Characterisation of a Trusting Agent — Aspects of a Formal Approach, in: Trust and Deception in Virtual Societies, edited by C. Castelfranchi and Y.H. Tan (Kluwer Academic Publishers, 2001), pp. 157-168.
4. R. Falcone and C. Castelfranchi, Social Trust: A Cognitive Approach, in: Trust and Deception in Virtual Societies, edited by C. Castelfranchi and Y.H. Tan (Kluwer Academic Publishers, 2001), pp. 55-90.
5. N. Mezzetti, A Socially Inspired Reputation Model, in: 1st European Workshop on Public Key Infrastructure (EuroPKI 2004), Samos, edited by S.K. Katsikas, S. Gritzalis and J. Lopez, LNCS 3093 (Springer-Verlag, 2004), pp. 191-204.
6. M. Blaze, J. Feigenbaum, and J. Lacy, Decentralized Trust Management, in: Proc. 17th Symposium on Security and Privacy, Oakland (IEEE Computer, 1996), pp. 164-173.
7. T. Grandison and M. Sloman, Specifying and Analysing Trust for Internet Applications, in: Proc. 2nd IFIP Conference on E-Commerce, E-Business & E-Government (I3E), Lisbon (Kluwer Academic, 2002), pp. 145-157.
8. A. Abdul-Rahman and S. Hailes, Supporting Trust in Virtual Communities, in: Proc. 33rd Hawaii International Conference, Volume 6., Maui, Hawaii (IEEE Computer, 2000).
9. K. Aberer and Z. Despotovic, Managing Trust in a Peer-2-Peer Information System. in: Proc. 10th International Conference on Information and Knowledge Management (CIKM'01), New York, edited by H. Paques et al. (ACM Press, 2001), pp. 310-317.

10. F. Azzedin and M. Maheswaran, A TrustBrokering System and Its Application to Resource Management in Public-Resource Grids, in: Proc. 18th International Parallel and Distributed Processing Symposium (IPDPS'04), Santa Fe (IEEE Computer, 2004).

11. L. Xiong and L. Liu, Building Trust in Decentralized Peer-to-Peer Electronic Communities, in: Proc. 5th International Conference on Electronic Commerce Research (ICECR-5), Dallas (ATSMA, 2002).

12. S.D. Kamvar, M.T., Schlosser, and H. Garcia-Molina, The EigenTrust Algorithm for Reputation Management in P2P Networks, in: Proc. 12th International World Wide Web Conference, Budapest (ACM Press, 2003).

13. D. Ingram, An Evidence Based Architecture for Efficient, Attack-Resistant Computational Trust Dissemination in Peer-to-Peer Networks, in: Proc. 3rd International Conference on Trust Management, Paris, edited by P. Herrmann et al., LNCS 3477 (Springer-Verlag, 2005), pp. 273-288.

14. P. Bonatti and P. Samarati, A Unified Framework for Regulating Access and Information Release on the Web, *Journal of Computer Security* **10** 241-272 (2002).

15. T. Yu, M. Winslett, and K.E. Seamons, Supporting Structured Credentials and Sensitive Policies through Interoperable Strategies for Automated Trust Negotiation, *ACM Transactions on Information and System Security* **6** 1-42 (2003).

16. H. Koshutanski and F. Massacci, Interactive Access Control for Web Services, in: Proc. 19th IFIP Information Security Conference (SEC 2004), Toulouse (Kluwer Academic, 2004), pp. 151-166.

17. A.J. Lee, M. Winslett, J. Basney, and V. Welch, Traust: A Trust Negotiation Based Authorization Service, in: Proc. 4th International Conference on Trust Management, Pisa, edited by K. Stølen et al., LNCS 3986 (Springer-Verlag, 2006), pp. 458-462.

18. S. Pearson and M.C. Mont, Provision of Trusted Identity Management Using Trust Credentials, in: Proc. 4th International Conference on Trust Management, Pisa, edited by K. Stølen et al., LNCS 3986 (Springer-Verlag, 2006), pp. 267-282.

19. S. Pearson, Trusted Computing: Strengths, Weaknesses and Further Opportunities for Enhancing Privacy, in: Proc. 3rd International Conference on Trust Management, Paris, edited by P. Herrmann et al., LNCS 3477 (Springer-Verlag, 2005), pp. 305-320.

20. C.D. Jensen and P. O Connell, Trust-Based Route Selection in Dynamic Source Routing, in: Proc. 4th International Conference on Trust Management, Pisa, edited by K. Stølen et al., LNCS 3986 (Springer-Verlag, 2006), pp. 150-163.

21. F. Kerschbaum, J. Haller, Y. Karabulut, and P. Robinson, PathTrust: A Trust-Based Reputation Service for Virtual Organization Formation, in: Proc. 4th International Conference on Trust Management, Pisa, edited by K. Stølen et al., LNCS 3986 (Springer-Verlag, 2006), pp. 193-205.

22. P. Herrmann, Trust-Based Protection of Software Component Users and Designers, in: Proc. 1st International Conference on Trust Management, Heraklion, edited by P. Nixon and S. Terzis, S., LNCS 2692 (Springer-Verlag, 2003), pp. 75-90.

23. G. Lenzini, A. Tokmakoff, and J. Muskens, Managing Trustworthiness in Component-Based Embedded Systems, in: Proc. 2nd International Workshop on Security and Trust Management, Hamburg (2006).

24. D. Quercia, S. Hailes, and L. Capra, B- Trust: Bayesian Trust Framework for Pervasive Computing, in: Proc. 4th International Conference on Trust Manage-

ment, Pisa, edited by K. Stølen et al., LNCS 3986 (Springer-Verlag, 2006), pp. 298-312.

25. F.A. Kraemer and P. Herrmann, Service Specification by Composition of Collaborations — An Example, in: 2nd International Workshop on Service Composition (Sercomp), Hong Kong (IEEE Computer, 2006).

26. G. Booch, J. Rumbaugh, and I. Jacobson, *The Unified Modeling Language User Guide* (Addison-Wesley, 1999).

27. Object Management Group, Unified Modeling Language: Superstructure (2006).

28. R.T. Sanders, H.N. Castejón, F.A. Kraemer, and R. Bræk, Using UML 2.0 Collaborations for Compositional Service Specification, in: ACM / IEEE 8th International Conference on Model Driven Engineering Languages and Systems (2005).

29. J.E.Y. Rossebø and R. Bræk, Towards a Framework of Authentication and Authorization Patterns for Ensuring Availability in Service Composition, in: Proc. 1st International Conference on Availability, Reliability and Security (ARES'06) (IEEE Computer, 2006), pp. 206-215.

30. H.N. Castejón and R. Bræk, A Collaboration-based Approach to Service Specification and Detection of Implied Scenarios, in: ICSE's 5th Workshop on Scenarios and State Machines: Models, Algorithms and Tools (SCESM'06) (2006).

31. F.A. Kraemer and P. Herrmann, Transforming Collaborative Service Specifications into Efficiently Executable State Machines, to appear in: *Electronic Communications of the EASST* (2007).

32. F.A. Kraemer, P. Herrmann, and R. Bræk, Aligning UML 2.0 State Machines and Temporal Logic for the Efficient Execution of Services, in: Proc. 8th International Symposium on Distributed Objects and Applications (DOA), Montpellier, edited by R. Meersmann and Z. Tari, LNCS 4276 (Springer-Verlag, 2006), pp. 1613-1632.

33. L. Lamport, *Specifying Systems* (Addison-Wesley, 2002).

34. Y. Yu, P. Manolios, and L. Lamport, Model Checking TLA$^+$ Specifications, in: Correct Hardware Design and Verification Methods (CHARME '99), edited by L. Pierre and T. Kropf, LNCS 1703, (Springer-Verlag, 1999), pp. 54-66.

35. A. Jøsang, The right type of trust for distributed systems, in: Proc. UCLA conference on New security paradigms workshops, Lake Arrowhead (ACM Press, 1996), pp. 119-131.

36. A. Jøsang, An Algebra for Assessing Trust in Certification Chains, in: Proc. Network and Distributed Systems Security Symposium (NDSS'99), edited by J. Kochmar (The Internet Society, 1999).

37. A. Jøsang and S.J. Knapskog, A Metric for Trusted Systems, in: Proc. 21st National Security Conference (NSA, 1998).

38. P. Herrmann and H. Krumm, A Framework for Modeling Transfer Protocols, *Computer Networks* **34**, 317-337 (2000).

39. R. Bræk, Unified System Modelling and Implementation, in: International Switching Symposium, Paris (1979), pp. 1180-1187.

40. R. Bræk, J. Gorman, Ø. Haugen, G. Melby, B. Møller-Pedersen, and R.T. Sanders, Quality by Construction Exemplified by TIMe — The Integrated Methodology, *Telektronikk* **95**, 73-82 (1997).

41. Ø. Haugen and B. Møller-Pedersen, JavaFrame — Framework for Java Enabled Modelling, in: Proc. Ericsson Conference on Software Engineering, Stockholm, (Ericsson, 2000).

42. P. Herrmann, Temporal Logic-Based Specification and Verification of Trust Models, in: Proc. 4th International Conference on Trust Management, Pisa, edited by K. Stølen et al., LNCS 3986 (Springer-Verlag, 2006), pp. 105-119.

MUQAMI: A Locally Distributed Key Management Scheme for Clustered Sensor Networks

[1]Syed Muhammad Khaliq-ur-Rahman Raazi, [1]Adil Mehmood Khan, [2]Faraz Idris Khan, [1]Sung Young Lee,[3]Young Jae Song, [1]Young Koo Lee[†]
[1]Ubiquitous Computing Lab, Department of Computer Engineering, Kyung Hee University, 449-701 Suwon, South Korea {raazi, adil, sylee, yklee}@oslab.khu.ac.kr
[2]Internet Computing and Security Lab, Department of Computer Engineering, Kyung Hee University, 449-701 Suwon, South Korea {faraz}@khu.ac.kr
[3]Software Engineering Lab, Department of Computer Engineering, Kyung Hee University, 449-701 Suwon, South Korea, {yjsong}@khu.ac.kr

Abstract. In many of the sensor network applications like natural habitat monitoring and international border monitoring, sensor networks are deployed in areas, where there is a high possibility of node capture and network level attacks. Specifically in such applications, the sensor nodes are severely limited in resources. We propose MUQAMI, a locally distributed key management scheme for resilience against the node capture in wireless sensor networks. Our scheme is efficient both in case of keying, re-keying and node compromise. Beauty of our scheme is that it requires minimal message transmission outside the cluster. We base our Scheme on Exclusion Basis System (EBS).

1 Introduction

Wireless Sensor Networks (WSN) differs from other distributed systems in a way that they have to work in real-time with an added constraint of energy. They are mostly data centric and are used to monitors their surroundings, gather information and filter it [1]. A sensor network will typically consist of a large number of sensor nodes

---

[†] Corresponding author.

Please use the following format when citing this chapter:

Raazi, S. M. K., Khan, A. M., Khan, F. I., Lee, S. Y., Song, Y. J. and Lee, Y. K., 2007, in IFIP International Federation for Information Processing, Volume 238, Trust Management, eds. Etalle, S., Marsh, S., (Boston: Springer), pp. 333–348.

working together for collection of data in a central node, using wireless communications [2].

WSN should also be cost effective, as their energy may not be replenished. This limits their memory and computational power also. In effect, resource conscious techniques should be employed in the WSNs. Sensor networks can be deployed in different areas for surveillance activities. WSNs are required to work unattended. Adversary may attack externally i.e. capture the node or jam the traffic signals. Internal attacks such as collusion can be made through loopholes in protocols. In addition to the energy constraint, WSNs have dynamic topologies. Due to these constraints, traditional security techniques can not be applied to WSNs.

Sensor nodes work collectively to perform a common task. Group communications are performed for efficient operations. In this case, groups of nodes share common keys. If a node is compromised and acts abnormally, it should be evicted from the group. In case of node compromise, re-keying must be done. During the re-keying process all the communication and administrative keys, known to the compromised node, should be revoked. After re-keying, the group should be in such a state that the compromised node is not part of the group i.e. it can't infer anything from the communication going on within the group.

In this paper we present MUQAMI, a lightweight and locally distributed key management scheme for clustered sensor networks. MUQAMI is based on Exclusion Basis System (EBS) matrix [3] and key-chains [4], which is an authentication mechanism based on Lamport's one-time passwords [5]. Our scheme is an improvement on SHELL [6], which is a hierarchical, distributed and collusion resistant key management scheme for WSN. In addition to the advantages offered by SHELL, our scheme offers lesser communication and computation overhead. Also, it is more resilient and scalable as compared to SHELL.

This paper is organized as follows. Section 2 describes models and assumptions of our system. Section 3 outlines related work and relevant schemes, which will help in understanding our solution. In section 4, we will present our scheme. In section 5, we will analyze our scheme and compare it with SHELL. We'll conclude our discussion in Section 6.

2   Models and Assumptions

2.1   System Model

WSN consist of a command node connected to a number of sensor nodes, which can be grouped into clusters. In case of clusters, there is a cluster head, which aggregates information from other sensor nodes and sends it back to the command node. Cluster head is also called a gateway. We will use both the terms interchangeably. Clustering of nodes can be based upon their location and other criteria [7] [8]. We are assuming clustered sensor networks in our scheme. Sensor nodes sense their environment and relay information to their cluster heads. Sensor nodes relay their messages directly or indirectly, depending upon their reach [9] [10].

We are assuming that all nodes, including the cluster heads, are stationary. Communication range and physical locations of all nodes are known to the nodes at the higher layer. We assume that sensors can only communicate within their clusters. Their processing and memory capabilities are also very limited. The cluster heads are designed with more energy capabilities as compared to lowest level sensor nodes. Cluster heads have to communicate with the command node, which can be situated at a larger distance.

Data aggregation is carried out at the clustered heads and not low level sensor nodes, due to their limited processing capabilities. Data aggregation at cluster heads considerably reduces size of messages, which need to be transmitted to the command node. This hierarchy can be extended to any number of levels depending upon the requirements. Command node is even more resource rich as compared to the cluster heads.

Higher we go in a hierarchy, higher is the energy consumed in transmitting a message. Due to this reason, we were motivated to delegate the message exchange for security as low as possible in the hierarchy of sensor nodes. Delegating message to lower levels is not as trivial. Special care should be taken not to overload sensor nodes in this process.

2.2 Adversity Assumptions

We assume that an adversary can capture a node and use its memory in any way possible. The sensor nodes are not assumed to be tamper resistant. We also assume that initially, the adversary does not have any knowledge about the contents of nodes' memory or messages, being exchanged between nodes. Another assumption is that higher we go in hierarchy, difficult it gets for an adversary to capture a node. Moreover, command node can not be compromised and every node has a unique identifier.

Moreover, we assume that a compromised node does not have any information about any other compromised nodes except its neighbours. Our last assumption is that compromised nodes can not communicate through any external communication channel. No assumptions are made on trust and collusion. According to our model, the adversary will try to get hold of keys so that it can attack actively or passively. In order to get hold of the keys, adversary can even capture a node and read or edit its memory.

3 Relevant schemes

In this section, we will briefly describe Exclusion Basis System (EBS) and Key-chains, which are the basic building blocks of MUQAMI. We will also briefly explain SHELL as our scheme is an improvement over SHELL.

3.1 Exclusion Basis System (EBS)

EBS was developed by Eltoweissy et. al[3], in which they used combinatorial optimization for key management. EBS is found to be very scalable for large networks. Basically, EBS plays between two variables 'k' and 'm'. To support a set of 'N' nodes, a set of "k+m" keys are required in EBS. Out of the total of "k+m" keys, each node knows 'k' keys. No two nodes should know the same set of 'k' keys. Any new node can be added if a distinct set of 'k' keys is still available. Values of 'k' and 'm' can be adjusted according to the network requirements. In order to evict a compromised node, new keys are distributed using 'm' keys that the node does not know. Clearly, communication overhead increases with the value of 'm'.

EBS scheme is very susceptible to collusion attacks. Younis et. al[6] has devised a scheme, which tends to mollify collusion attacks on EBS-based key management schemes. Details of EBS scheme can be found in [3].

Table 1: Example of an EBS Matrix

	N_0	N_1	N_2	N_3	N_4	N_5	N_6	N_7	N_8	N_9
K_1	1	1	1	1	1	1	0	0	0	0
K_2	1	1	1	0	0	0	1	1	1	0
K_3	1	0	0	1	1	0	1	1	0	1
K_4	0	1	0	1	0	1	1	0	1	1
K_5	0	0	1	0	1	1	0	1	1	1

3.2 Key-chains

G. Dini et al [4] uses key-chains, whose authentication mechanisms are based on one-way hash functions. These one-way hash functions are light weight and several orders of magnitude more efficient than RSA [11], an example of Public Key Cryptography.

One-way hash function [12] uses a key to compute its previous one. We can't use the current key to compute the next one. If we give the end key and the start key, sensor node can iteratively apply the one-way hash function to find the intermediate keys starting from the end key. We can adjust the number of keys that the sensor node produces before it needs to be given the new set of start and end keys. The number of keys produced by a sensor node in one such episode can be optimized. Optimum value will depend upon the node's power and memory capabilities.

3.3 SHELL

In SHELL, each sensor node has a discovery key K_{sg} and two preloaded keys KS_{CH} and KS_{Key} initially. K_{sg} is recomputed with one-way hashing function, such as SHA1 [13] or MD5 [14], stored in the node. The one-way hashing function is only known to the sensor node and the command node. K_{sg} helps later on, when the network needs to be recovered after gateway compromise. KS_{CH} and KS_{Key} are used for initial key distribution.

Apart from K_{sg} of every node in its cluster, the gateway also has a preloaded key K_{gc}. K_{gc} is used for communication between the gateway and the command node. Gateways can also communicate between themselves. In SHELL, gateway is responsible for the following: -

- Formation of EBS matrix and generation of communication keys of its own cluster. Also, it is responsible for refreshment of its cluster's data keys.
- On request generation of administrative keys of other clusters.
- It is also responsible for detection and eviction of compromised nodes within its cluster.

Whenever a node is deployed initially or afterwards, it is authenticated by the command node. Inter-gateway communication keys are also generated and renewed by the command node.

Key Distribution: In the key distribution phase, gateways form their EBS matrices first. Each EBS matrix, along with the list of sensors in that cluster, is shared between the gateways and the command node. Command node designates more than one cluster for each cluster to generate administrative keys. The gateway or the cluster head shares its EBS matrix with the gateways designated by the command node.

Command node shares the key KS_{CH} of each sensor node with its cluster head. It also shares their keys KS_{Key} with the neighbouring cluster heads i.e. the one's who are supposed to generate their administrative keys. For key distribution, each neighbouring gateway generates one message per individual administrative key in its cluster for each sensor node. The message is first encrypted with the KS_{Key} of the node and then the administrative key of the sensor node's gateway. Gateway decrypts the message, encrypts it with KS_{CH} of the node and sends it to the sensor node.

Cluster heads/gateways share their communication keys in a similar fashion. They generate communication keys and send them to their neighbouring cluster heads. Neighbouring clusters then send them to sensor nodes in the way described above.

For addition of new sensor nodes, command node informs the relevant gateways about their IDs and keys K_{sg}. Gateways register the new nodes and authenticate them from the command node. Command nodes then provide the gateways with keys KS_{CH} and KS_{Key} of the new nodes. Rest of the procedure is same as in the initial key distribution phase.

Failure Recovery: If a gateway is compromised, it is either replaced or its sensors are redistributed. If replaced, the command node establishes new keys for communication between existing gateways and the newly deployed one. Then the new gateway makes a new EBS matrix, repeats initialization process and generates administrative keys for other clusters. The other option is that sensor nodes join other clusters with the help of new K_{sg} that they generated after initial deployment.

If a sensor node is compromised, keys known to the compromised node must be changed so that the compromised node doesn't get to know the new key. For this purpose, we encrypt new keys with their older versions and then again encrypt them in a key that is not known to the compromised node. This way, the compromised node can not decrypt the message. Assumptions of SHELL scheme and its complete details can be found in [6].

4   MUQAMI

In our scheme also, the command node stores the database of all node IDs as in SHELL. All sensor nodes have a basic key K_{bsc} along with a one-way hashing function. The one-way hashing function is used to compute new values of K_{bsc}. We assume that the nodes have enough memory to store the keys required for their normal operation. K_{bsc} is used for communication between the sensor and the command node in case the gateway or a key-generating node is compromised.

Apart from K_{bsc}, each sensor also has another set of keys $K_{kgs}[n]$ for administrative purposes. $K_{kgs}[n]$ are used by key-generating nodes to communicate with the sensor nodes. Some of the sensor nodes are given an additional responsibility of generating a key. We refer to such nodes as key-generating nodes. Key-generating nodes use lightweight one-way hashing functions to generate keys. One-way hashing functions are as described in [4]. As required by the one-way hashing function, the key-generating nodes also need to store the hashing function and the keys it generate in a chain. Key-generating nodes store one other key for administrative purposes K_{chs}, which is used by the cluster head to communicate with the key-generating node.

The same scheme is not employed in the upper hierarchy i.e. at the level of gateways. Analogy of a gateway and a sensor can not be applied to the command node and a gateway. The reason is that we assume the command node to have unlimited energy unlike gateways. In effect we think that we should move as much responsibility to the command node as possible. If we have more than three-level hierarchy, we can use the same scheme at every level, except the top most.

Initially, the gateway has its K_{bsc} stored in it. For key management, communication between gateways is not necessary in our scheme. Command node authenticates all the nodes, which are initially deployed or added to the network later on.

4.1   Network Initialization

Gateways are deployed in the beginning. They communicate with the command node with the help of their basic keys K_{bsc}. The command node then sends the gateway a list of sensor IDs along with their basic keys K_{bsc}. These are the sensors that are to be deployed within the cluster of this gateway. We assume that the sensors are deployed carefully under their desired cluster heads.

In the second phase, sensors are deployed in the desired regions. Sensor nodes try to communicate with their cluster heads with the help of their basic Keys K_{bsc}. On getting the initial messages from sensor nodes, cluster heads authenticate them from the command node. Command node authenticates valid sensors to their cluster heads and also informs which one will also generate keys in their cluster. In addition to that, the command node communicates the K_{chs} of nodes to their cluster head. In case of simple sensors i.e. those that are not key-generating nodes, command node sends list of IDs of key-generators that are responsible for generating its keys. After authentication, the cluster heads form EBS matrices for key management. EBS matrices are shared between the cluster heads and the command node.

4.2 Initial Key Distribution

In the first phase, EBS matrices are formed in gateways and the command node. We know that in EBS matrix, values of 'k' and 'm' are to be decided, which depends upon factors like storage requirements, number of re-keying messages, size of the cluster and frequency with which the sensor nodes are to be evicted. It is evident that in our case, command node predominantly decides the whole EBS matrix and communicates with the gateways during the authentication phase.

We propose a little change in the representation of EBS matrix. Usually, we use '0' if a node does not know a key and '1' if a node knows a key. In this case, we make an addition. We use a '2' if a node generates a key. For our case, example shown in table 1 can be modified as shown in table 2.

Table 2: Updated EBS matirx example for MUQAMI scheme

	N_0	N_1	N_2	N_3	N_4	N_5	N_6	N_7	N_8	N_9
K_1	2	1	1	1	1	1	0	0	0	0
K_2	1	2	1	0	0	0	1	1	1	0
K_3	1	0	0	2	1	0	1	1	0	1
K_4	0	1	0	1	0	2	1	0	1	1
K_5	0	0	1	0	2	1	0	1	1	1

Note that after the formation of EBS matrix in the gateway and the command node, initial keys of the EBS matrix are already distributed among the sensor nodes. Moreover, also the gateway does not have any idea about the administrative keys being used in the sensor nodes just as in SHELL. In order to send its communication key to the cluster, the cluster head encrypts it with keys K_{chs} of all key-generating nodes and send it to all of them. In turn, the key-generating nodes decrypt, then encrypt with their generated keys and broadcast the encrypted communication key in their cluster.

4.3 Node addition and Re-keying

Re-keying is not very complicated in our scheme. If the cluster head wants to refresh its communication key, it encrypts in keys K_{chs} and sends the new communication key to the key-generating nodes. The key-generating nodes then broadcast the new communication key in the cluster using their generated keys. In order to refresh the administrative keys, the cluster head just needs to send a very short message to the key-generator, whose key needs to be refreshed. In turn, the key-generator sends new key encrypted in the old one. The short message need not be encrypted as it does not contain any key. Even if an adversary comes to know that a key is being refreshed, it will not be able to do anything as it wouldn't know any of the new and old keys. We know that the key-generator uses one-way hashing function. If the key-generating node is running out of keys it has generated and stored, it communicates with the command through cluster head using its K_{bsc}. Command node sends it a new seed for calculating the key.

Sometimes, it may be necessary to add new nodes into the cluster. For this purpose, we should have an EBS matrix such that there is a key combination available for the new node. The command node possesses a copy of EBS matrix. The new node can be a simple node or it can be a node with key-generating capability. A group of new nodes including both can also be added.

First of all, adjustments in the EBS matrices are made in the command node. Then relevant gateways are sent IDs and K_{bsc} of the nodes, which it should expect in its cluster. The gateway halts re-keying and for every key, tells the command node how many times it has been changed. Command node calculates the current keys relevant to the new sensors and encrypts them with the second key in their respective key rings. Then the new keys are sent to the cluster head, which stores until the new node is authenticated and registered completely.

In case of simple sensor nodes i.e. without key-generating capability, the sensor node communicates with its cluster head. Cluster head authenticates the new node from the command node. Command node authenticates and specifies which nodes should generate key for it, so that the gateway can also update its EBS matrix. Then the cluster head forwards current administrative keys to the new sensor node. In the end, the network returns to its normal state. The command node also sends its key K_{chs} to the cluster head. As already stated, cluster head uses K_{chs} keys to spread its communication key in the cluster.

4.4 Node compromise

We assume that the system has enough capability to find out the compromised node. In this subsection, we describe how to evict compromised node from the network. We need to keep all further communications secret from the compromised nodes such that they can only act as an outsider when trying to interfere in the network's normal operation. There are three types of nodes, so we will discuss each of them one by one.

Cluster head compromise: Command node is responsible for detecting the compromise of gateways. There are three methods to cater for the compromise of gateways. First option is that we deploy a replacement. Second one is that we redistribute nodes among neighbouring clusters. These two methods are discussed in detail in [6].

If our scheme is applied in the network, command node can designate another nearby gateway as a caretaker in case of gateway compromise. We assume that this is possible because we have taken off the burden of administrative key generation from cluster heads. In this case, command node evicts the compromised gateway and communicates ID of the caretaker to the nodes in the compromised gateway's cluster. Then the command node assigns a new K_{chs} to the key-generating nodes in the cluster of compromised gateway. This is done with the help of K_{bsc} of the nodes. Then the command node provides the cluster's EBS matrix and all K_{chs} keys, to the caretaker node. Network continues its normal operation until new gateways are deployed. In case there is no nearby cluster head, or it does not have enough resources to manage two clusters, we can use other methods.

Sensor Compromise: In case of sensor node compromise, all the keys that are known to the compromised sensor node must be changed. Cluster head informs all the key-generators, whose keys need to be changed, to change their keys, encrypt them using previous ones and then further encrypt in their respective K_{chs} and send them back to the cluster head. Cluster head is not able to find out the new keys as it does not know the old ones. Also the compromised node is not able to find out the new key as it does not know the K_{chs} keys of the key-generating gateways. All this is possible because in our scheme, the same key is used both for encryption and decryption.

After receiving all the keys, which were demanded from key-generating nodes, the gateway aggregates them into one message. From the EBS matrix, it finds out the key-generating nodes, whose keys are required for spreading the new keys. It then sends this aggregated message to each of those key-generating nodes using their respective K_{chs}. Upon receiving the aggregated message, the key-generator node decrypts the message and then encrypts it again with the key it generates. Eventually, the message is forwarded to all the cluster in such a way that only the relevant node knows about the new key.

As an example, consider the scenario in table 2. Suppose the node N_2 is compromised. Cluster head will ask the nodes N_0, N_1 and N_4 to send the new keys encrypted in the old ones. Cluster head will then aggregate all three messages into one and send to nodes N_3 and N_5. N_3 and N_5 use their keys to spread the new keys to whole cluster. Cluster head does not come to know the new keys as it does not know the old keys. All the nodes, which know the old keys, can use them to find out the new ones except N_2. As N_2 does not know keys K_3 and K_4, it does not come to know the new values of keys K_1, K_2 and K_5 and thus it is effectively evicted from the network.

Key-generator Compromise: In case a key-generating node is compromised, it can either be replaced by a new key-generating node, or some other node can take over the responsibility of key-generation. Cluster head can also hold this responsibility temporarily but cluster heads can only take this responsibility up to a certain number of keys. After that, they might become a single point of failure. We assume that the cluster head and nodes, for which it generates key, immediately come to know that the node has been compromised. In effect, they cease any re-keying and wait for corrective actions. If a key-generator is compromised, the cluster head tells the command node how many times the key has been changed. Command node then calculates the current value of the key.

In case the compromised node is to be replaced, a new key-generator node is added to the network. Method for addition of a new node is described in section 4.3. After addition of the new node, command node sends the current value of key to the newly deployed key-generator node. The newly deployed key-generator node changes the key, encrypts in the old one and send it to the cluster head using its K_{chs} key.

In case some other node is to be given the responsibility of generating the key, then the command node informs the cluster head and provides it with the current value of key encrypted in its current K_{bsc}. Cluster head forwards it to the responsible node. The responsible node then calculates the new value of key, encrypt it in the old one and send it to the cluster head using its K_{chs} key.

In case the cluster head is given the responsibility of this key, the command node simply provides the current value of key to the cluster head. Cluster head then calculates new value and encrypts it in the old one. It is recommended to use this method temporarily and that too when above two methods can't be applied. As soon as a capable node is deployed, responsibility should be shifted on it and administrative keys should be deleted from the cluster head. This is because in our scheme, the management of administrative keys is not the responsibility of gateways.

The compromised node also knows some other keys, which it does not generate. Cluster head asks generators of those keys to change them encrypt in the previous ones and send using their K_{chs} to the cluster head. After getting all the keys, the gateway aggregates them into one message. From the EBS matrix, it finds out the key-generating nodes, whose keys are required for spreading the new keys. It then sends this aggregated message to each of those key-generating nodes using their respective K_{chs}. Upon receiving the aggregated message, the key-generator node decrypts the message and then encrypts it again with the key it generates. Eventually, the message is forwarded to all the cluster in such a way that only the relevant node knows about the new key.

5   Comparison

As compared to shell, we have moved the generation of administrative keys to key-generating nodes within our cluster. We have been able to take this responsibility down to sensor nodes due to the use of key-chains [4]. Also, we have maintained the condition that there is no single point of failure in our scheme. In this section, we will compare the number and length of messages exchanged in each stage in both SHELL and MUQAMI.

5.1   Storage Requirements

Sensor Nodes: Equal numbers of EBS keys are stored in each node in both schemes. However, if we compare storage requirement of the two schemes on lowest level sensor nodes, we see that we have to store three administrative keys (K_{sg}, KS_{CH} and KS_{Key}) in case of SHELL and only two (K_{bsc} and K_{chs}) in case of our scheme

MUQAMI. On the contrary, storage requirements of the key-generating nodes are more in case of MUQAMI. In addition to the keys that are stored in the simple sensor nodes, key-generating nodes also have to store K_{chs} along with the series of key values that it uses for managing the key it generates.

In key-generating nodes, we use one-way hashing function to generate and store 'n' key values at a time. When all 'n' values are exhausted, command node provides the key-generator with another seed value to generate 'n' keys. Value of 'n' depends upon storage capabilities of the key-generating node. We have to store only K_{chs} and K_{bsc} in MUQAMI as compared to SHELL, in which we had to store Ksg, KSCH and KS_{Key}. This provides us with one more slot for storing a key. We assume that in the key-generating node, each key uses 'm' bits of memory.

$$SR_{kg} = m \times (n - 1) \; bits \qquad (1)$$

where SR_{kg} is the additional storage requirement for the key-generating node in MUQAMI as compared to SHELL. If we assume that every key takes 128 bits (16 bytes) and re-keying is done after every 500 seconds as in SHELL, then a key-generating node requires mere 512 bytes for managing its generated keys for more than four and a half hours before contacting the command node for a new seed. We should also keep in mind that the number of such key-generating nodes wouldn't be too high as we show in the storage requirements analysis of the cluster heads.

Cluster Heads: As opposed to SHELL, cluster heads in our scheme need not store any key to communicate with other cluster heads. Moreover, gateways in our scheme also do not need to generate and store EBS keys for other clusters. If we assume that the key management capability was equally distributed among all gateways in SHELL and size of clusters both in our scheme and SHELL are same then

$$SR_{ch}^{SHELL} - SR_{ch}^{MUQAMI} = (\sum_{i}^{k+m+r} n[i]) keys \qquad (2)$$

where SR_{ch}^{SHELL} and SR_{ch}^{MUQAMI} are the storage requirements of cluster head nodes in SHELL and MUQAMI schemes respectively, 'k' and 'm' are the EBS parameters, 'r' is the number of gateways, with which a gateway communicates in SHELL, and 'n[i]' is the number of key values that SHELL stores for key. We assume that SHELL also uses one-way hashing function for key management. In SHELL, cluster size is assumed to be between 500 and 900. Assuming the value of 'k' and 'm' to be 7 each we get more than 3000 key combinations, which looks to be quite safe if we need to deploy more sensor nodes afterwards. This also shows that we do not require a large ratio of key-generating nodes either. If we assume value of 'r' to be 2 and each n[i] to be 32 on average (as assumed above),

$$SR_{ch}^{SHELL} - SR_{ch}^{MUQAMI} = 16 \times 32 = 512 \; keys \qquad (3)$$

Further, if we assume each key to be 128 bits (16 bytes) as in SHELL, storage difference becomes

$$SR_{ch}^{SHELL} - SR_{ch}^{MUQAMI} = 8KB \qquad (4)$$

Storage cost at cluster head is increased a little bit in our scheme. In addition to '0' or '1', now we also have to incorporate '2' to indicate the key-generating nodes. Storage cost also depends upon the storage scheme applied for storing the EBS matrix.

If we apply SHELL, then our cluster heads need to have double the size of memory that we have in typical MICA mote just for key management purposes. On the contrary, if we apply MUQAMI, we do not require very high memory both in cluster head and the sensor nodes.

5.2 Computation Requirements

Sensor Nodes: In SHELL, sensor nodes used to do two decryptions per administrative message received, while in our scheme, only key-generating nodes are required to do one encryption and one decryption. Other nodes only need to do one decryption. However, key-generating nodes would have to bear some additional computation cost due to the calculation of keys through one-way hashing function.

Cluster Heads: Computation requirements are also higher in case of SHELL. Computation cost of calculating the EBS matrix is lower in MUQAMI than SHELL. This is because in our scheme, the command node explicitly informs the cluster head about the keys stored and generated by every node. For the distribution of keys in SHELL, it requires four encryptions and four decryptions. Two of the decryptions are done at sensor level and rest is done at gateway level. On the contrary, our scheme requires only two encryptions and two decryptions for the distribution of keys. Out of these four computations, only one is done at the gateway level.

In SHELL, all sensor nodes required two decryptions, while in our scheme only key-generating gateways require one decryption and one encryption. Other sensor nodes only require one decryption. So, if we have to distribute 'k+m' administrative keys inside a cluster,

$$COMP_{ch}^{SHELL} = ((r \times 2) + ((k + m) \times 4)) computations \qquad (5)$$

where $COMP_{ch}^{SHELL}$ denotes the number of computations required by cluster head in SHELL for computing all the administrative keys once. Rest of the variables is the same as above. By computation, we mean one encryption or decryption. In MUQAMI, the number of computations comes out to be

$$COMP_{ch}^{MUQAMI} = (k + m) computations \qquad (6)$$

as the cluster head just needs to encrypt and send one message for key distribution. In effect, we see the following difference in the number of computations for each cluster head on average

$$COMP_{ch}^{SHELL} - COMP_{ch}^{MUQAMI} = ((r \times 2) + ((k + m) \times 3)) computations \qquad (7)$$

Considering similar values of 'r', 'k' and 'm' as above the average computation difference at the cluster head, for computing all administrative key once, becomes 46. We need 60 computations in case of SHELL and just 14 in case of MUQAMI.

In case of node compromise also, MUQAMI overshadows SHELL. For redistributing the keys in SHELL, we need to initiate the jilting process that requires $r \times 2$ computations. Then for every key in 'k', neighbouring cluster head encrypts twice and sends to the cluster head. Then the cluster head decrypts and aggregates. This requires $k \times 3$ computations. Then for every 'm', cluster head encrypts and sends to neighbouring cluster head. Neighbouring cluster head decrypts, encrypts in another key and then further encrypts in the cluster head's key. Cluster head decrypts and then broadcasts the message. This requires $m \times 5$ computations. Sensor nodes only need to decrypt twice for finding out a new key. $COMP_c^{SHELL}$ denotes the computations in case of node compromise. $COMP_c^{SHELL}$ can be calculated as

$$COMP_c^{SHELL} = ((r \times 2) + (k \times 3) + (m \times 5)) computations \qquad (8)$$

For sensor node compromise in MUQAMI, only 'k' key generating nodes are required to do one decryption and two encryptions (one extra computation). No extra computation is required in case of key-generating node compromise. Cluster head is required to do at maximum 'k' encryptions for asking key-generating nodes for new keys. This is followed by 'k' decryptions of reply messages and then further m encryptions after aggregation. So $COMP_c^{MUQAMI}$ comes out to be

$$COMP_c^{MUQAMI} = (2k + m) computations \qquad (9)$$

we see that the difference in the computations at each node comes out to be

$$COMP_c^{SHELL} - COMP_c^{MUQAMI} = ((r \times 2) + k + (m \times 4)) computations \qquad (10)$$

Considering similar values of 'r', 'k' and 'm' as above, the difference comes out to be 39. In case of SHELL, we need 60 computations while in case of MUQAMI, we just need 21. The difference in the cost of encryption and decryption is evident from these figures. Despite the fact that cluster heads have more power, we think it is a good idea to take off a large burden from cluster heads and put a small burden on a few key-generating nodes inside the cluster.

5.3 Communication Requirements

In this section, we will compare the number of communication messages that the sensor nodes have to transmit in each phase of our scheme. We assume that most of the energy is consumed in transmitting a message and thus it should be minimized.

Sensor Nodes: Network initialization phase for the sensor nodes is similar in both schemes, so there is not much to compare. As evident from the scheme, administrative keys are already stored on each node. Each key-generating node is required to broadcast one message encrypted in its generated key for re-keying of administrative keys, initial distribution of communication keys and re-keying of communication keys. Note that the transmission of one such message from each key-generating node causes significant decrease in the communication overhead of the cluster heads. Similar analysis is applicable to the re-keying methodology in both schemes. For node addition, similar analysis is required as in network initialization and initial key distribution. In case of the compromise of sensor nodes, no transmission is required by sensor nodes in SHELL scheme. In our scheme, all key-generating nodes are required to broadcast one message each.

Cluster Heads: In the network initialization phase of MUQAMI, command node computes most of the EBS matrix itself and communicates it to the cluster heads. In case of SHELL, command node sends inter-gateway keys to the cluster heads. Cluster heads also use these keys to find out the working and broken links. In the initialization phase, at least 'r' communication messages are transmitted from each node in SHELL where 'r' is the number of neighbouring cluster heads, with which each cluster head communicates. On the other hand, MUQAMI requires no communication messages to be transmitted from cluster heads. MUQAMI requires the cluster heads to receive significant EBS related information from the command node. On the other hand, before the initial key distribution phase in SHELL, cluster head transmits the complete EBS matrix to the command node. This requires almost the exact opposite of what happens in MUQAMI. MUQAMI is better because it requires command node to transmit and cluster head to only receive.

Apart from communicating the EBS matrix to the command node, SHELL requires each cluster head to share its EBS matrix with 'r' other cluster heads. On average, each cluster head transmits and also receives one complete EBS matrix just before the initial key distribution phase. In SHELL, each cluster head has to receive one additional key per sensor node in some other cluster. Since we are not considering the reception of messages, we establish that one extra inter-cluster transmission of whole EBS matrix by each cluster head is required in SHELL just before initial key distribution phase. Analysis of the overhead due to EBS matrix exchange depends upon the storage scheme used. Storage scheme are out of the scope of this paper.

Initial administrative keys are already stored in MUQAMI. Analyzing the administrative key distribution of SHELL, we see that neighbouring cluster heads generate one message per individual administrative key. This message is transmitted to the cluster head. Keeping in mind that the number of administrative keys is 'k+m', we observe

$$TRANSMISSIONS_{CH,CH}^{ADMIN,INI} = (k+m) transmissions \qquad (11)$$

where $TRANSMISSIONS_{CH,CH}^{ADMIN,INI}$ is the number of inter-gateway transmissions required from each cluster head in the initial distribution of administrative keys. Each neighbouring cluster can aggregate all such messages into one large message. After the cluster head receives one such message, it sends one message to each of the sensor nodes in its cluster head. So,

$$TRANSMISSIONS_{CH,S}^{ADMIN,INI} = ((k+m) \times S_n) transmissions \qquad (12)$$

where $TRANSMISSION_{CH,S}^{ADMIN,INI}$ is the number of transmissions required by cluster head to communicate with the sensor nodes in initial distribution of administrative keys and Sn is the average number of sensor nodes inside a cluster. For each communication key, cluster head first transmits it to 'r' neighbouring cluster heads. Each neighbouring cluster head encrypts each communications key in the administrative keys that it has, and sends it back to the cluster head. If we assume that there are 'l' communication keys,

$$TRANSMISSIONS_{CH,CH}^{COMM,INI} = (l \times (r + k + m)) transmissions \qquad (13)$$

where TRNASMISSIONS$_{CH,CH}^{COMM,INI}$ is the number of transmissions required by cluster head to communicate with other cluster heads in initial distribution of communication keys. Value of TRANSMISSIONS$_{CH,S}^{COMM,INI}$ is also same as TRNASMISSIONS$_{CH,CH}^{COMM,INI}$ because every message in broadcasted inside the cluster.

In case of MUQAMI, there is no inter-cluster communication required. For each communication key, cluster head is required to send just one transmission to each key-generating node. So,

$$TRANSMISSION_{CH,S}^{COMM,INI} = (l \times (k + m)) transmissions \qquad (14)$$

In case of communication between cluster head and sensor nodes, difference between the two schemes for initial distribution of communication keys become

$$DIFF\_TRANS_{CH,S}^{COMM,INI} = (l \times r) transmissions \qquad (15)$$

In both schemes, node addition phase is the same as network initialization phase. So, the same analysis is applicable in both phases.

When a sensor node is compromised, SHELL sends one message per neighbouring cluster head, informing them about the keys to be changed. Neighbouring cluster heads send new keys encrypted in old ones to the cluster heads. Cluster head aggregates them and sends back to the neighbouring cluster heads, so that the aggregated message can be encrypted in keys that are not known to the compromised node. Neighbouring nodes encrypt the aggregated message and send back to the original cluster head. This shows that we require four inter-cluster transmissions in case of SHELL. Eventually, the cluster head broadcasts the aggregated message one by one in every key that is not known to the compromised node. One broadcast communication in every key is required in MUQAMI also. Effectively, in case of node compromise the inter-cluster communications are avoided in our scheme.

6 Conclusion and Future work

From our discussion in section 5, we see that if we give a little responsibility to a small ratio of nodes in a cluster, we can take off a lot of burden from cluster heads. We have freed the cluster heads of inter-cluster communication and key management. In addition to that, we also take away from the cluster heads, the burden of communicating EBS matrix to the command node and neighbouring cluster heads. We achieve two goals by doing this. Firstly, our cluster heads will have a longer life as their power will mainly be used for long-range communications with the command node. Secondly, we have reduced the vulnerability of cluster heads as it is more costly to deploy cluster heads rather than simple sensor nodes.

Acknowledgement

This research was supported by the MIC (Ministry of Information and Communication), Korea, Under the ITFSIP (IT Foreign Specialist Inviting Program) supervised by the IITA(Institute of Information Technology Advancement).

7 References

1. I.F. Akyildiz, W. Su, Y. Sankarasubramaniam, and E. Cayirci, Wireless Sensor Networks: A Survey, Computer Networks 38(4), 393-422 (2002).
2. S. Tilak, N.B. Abu-Ghazaleh, and W. Heinzelman, A Taxonomy of Wireless Microsensor Network Models, ACM Mobile Computing and Comm. Rev. 6(2), 1-8 (2002).
3. M. Eltoweissy, H. Heydari, L. Morales, and H. Sadborough, Combinatorial Optimization of Group Key Management, J. Network and Systems Management 12(1), 33-50 (2004).
4. G. Dini and I.M. Savino, An Efficient Key Revocation Protocol for Wireless Sensor Networks, International Workshop on Wireless Mobile Multimedia, Proceedings of the 2006 International Symposium on World of Wireless, Mobile and Multimedia Networks, 450-452 (2006).
5. L. Lamport, Password authentication with insecure communication, Communications of the ACM 24(11), 770–772 (1981).
6. M. Younis, K. Ghumman, and M. Eltoweissy, Location aware Combinatorial Key Management Scheme for Clustered Sensor Networks, IEEE Trans. Parallel and Distrib. Sys. 17(8), 865-882 (2006).
7. G. Gupta and M. Younis, Load-Balanced Clustering of Wireless Sensor Networks, Proc. Int'l Conf. Comm. (ICC '03), 1848-1852 (2003).
8. O. Younis and S. Fahmy, HEED: A Hybrid, Energy-Efficient, Distributed lustering Approach for Ad Hoc Sensor Networks, IEEE Trans. Mobile Computing 3(4), 366-379 (2004).
9. K. Langendoen and N. Reijers, Distributed Localization in Wireless Sensor Networks: A Quantitative Comparison, Computer Networks 43(4), 499-518 (2003).
10. A. Youssef, A. Agrawala, and M. Younis, Accurate Anchor-Free Localization in Wireless Sensor Networks, Proc. First IEEE Workshop Information Assurance in Wireless Sensor Networks (WSNIA '05), (2005).
11. R.L. Rivest, A. Shamir, and L. Adleman, A method for obtaining digital signatures and public-key cryptosystems, Comm. of the ACM 21(2), 120-126 (1978).
12. A.J. Menezes, P.C.V. Oorschot, and S.A. Vanstone, Handbook of Applied Cryptography, CRC Press, (1996).
13. D. Eastlake and P. Jones, US Secure Hash Algorithm 1 (SHA-1), RFC 3174, IETF, (2001).
14. R. Rivest, The MD5 Message-Digest Algorithm, RFC 1320, MIT and RSA Data Security Inc., (1992).

Trust based Approach for Improving Data Reliability in Industrial Sensor Networks

Tatyana Ryutov and Clifford Neuman
Information Sciences Institute
University of Southern California
4676 Admiralty Way, Suite 1001, Marina del Rey, CA 90292

Abstract. The resource constraints and unattended operation of wireless sensor networks make it difficult to protect nodes against capture and compromise. While cryptographic techniques provide some protection, they do not address the complementary problem of resilience to corrupted sensor data generated by failed or compromised sensors. Trusting data from unattended sensor nodes in critical applications can have disastrous consequences. We propose a behavior-based trust mechanism to address this problem in static sensor networks, in which the location of nodes is known. We take advantage of domain knowledge which includes: (i) physical constraints imposed by the local environment where sensors are located, (ii) expectations of the monitored physical phenomena; and (iii) sensor design and deployment characteristics. The system diagnoses and isolates faulty/malicious nodes even when readings of neighboring nodes are faulty. The goal of this system is to increase work effort and capabilities required by an attacker. The framework and related techniques of behavior-based trust are discussed in this paper.

1 Introduction

Sensor network technology has great value for many industrial applications, including oil and gas production, industrial plant monitoring and maintenance [1]. Use of permanent sensors mounted on industrial equipment enables facilities to gather operational data and to send it to analytical tools that examine critical operating parameters (e.g., casing gas pressure, temperature, pump torque, etc). This enables proactive management of operations by adjusting settings to maintain steady state conditions.

While remote asset monitoring and control dramatically enhance operating efficiencies, use of untrusted data from unattended sensor nodes in critical

Please use the following format when citing this chapter:

Ryutov, T. and Neuman, C., 2007, in IFIP International Federation for Information Processing, Volume 238, Trust Management, eds. Etalle, S., Marsh, S., (Boston: Springer), pp. 349–365.

applications can have disastrous consequences. An inherent assumption that all nodes are trusted leaves the nodes at the mercy of an adversary who can insert faulty data by exploiting access in the physical environment (e.g., placing a source of heat close to a sensor) or by compromising the sensor. In the absence of adequate physical and cyber security, an adversary can mislead a process control system responsible for procedures that are critical to productivity and safety of the plant facilities.

While cryptographic techniques [3], [4], [7], [13] and [20] make sensor networks more secure, they do not address the complementary problem of resilience to corrupted sensor data generated by failed or compromised sensors. The difficult issue that needs to be addressed is falsification of sensor data due to node capture, compromise or abuse of the physical environment.

Because sensed events are ambiguous with respect to causes, diagnosing normal and malicious/faulty sensor behavior in a distributed industrial environment is a difficult technical problem. Consider, for example, a Weatherford's optical flow meter system that provides real-time measurements of oil flow rate in a section of a production pipe. The meter employs an array of sensors mounted on the outside of the flow pipe to measure the velocity and speed of sound of the flowing stream. The differences in the incoming and outgoing flows may suggest that (i) some of the sensed data is corrupted or (ii) there is an oil leak. Since the pipeline might be situated in a physically unprotected area, an attacker can easily compromise the external sensors in order to report a false oil leak event or, even worse, hide a real one.

Current approaches [5], [6], [8], [9], [10], [11], [14] and [21] for detecting and correcting malicious/faulty sensor readings suffer from reliance on the node neighbors. A common underlying assumption about sensor faults being uncorrelated is not practical. An attacker could compromise a number of sensors located in a physically insecure place, or some natural event could impact a group of sensors in close proximity to the event. Accurate real time detection of malicious/faulty sensors requires contextual information, such as deployment parameters, baseline system and sensor behavior, and underlying process models.

This paper targets the identification of malicious/faulty sensors and detecting abnormal events in static, context aware sensor networks deployed in industrial facilities. In such environments, the location of a single node is known and the spatial temporal correlations in the underlying physical process are known as well. We propose a behavior-based trust solution that ensures that only trusted sensor readings are accepted even when a group of neighboring sensors misbehaves. The goal of this system is to increase the work effort and capabilities required by an attacker. With this system in place, an attacker must simultaneously compromise a number of sensors of different types deployed at various locations. Some of the locations can be physically protected, be difficult to reach or unknown to the attacker. The effects of the compromise are contained to be those that effectively duplicate the expected relationships between the readings of different sensor groups. However, the behavior of maliciously cooperating nodes will be different from the arbitrary nature of failure of faulty but non-malicious nodes. With this knowledge, we can find correlations between compromised sensors belonging to different groups and detect malicious node collaborations.

The main contributions of this paper can be summarized as follows: (1) a scheme for representing and evaluating trust (suspicion levels) based on conformance of empirical observations to a set of expectations; (2) an approach for defining and representing contextual information (expectations); (3) a methodology for determining data trustworthiness and updating suspicion levels even when the readings of neighboring nodes are faulty.

2   The Trust Model

In this section, we describe our approach to representing and computing trust given a set of pre-defined expectations and direct observations of sensor performance.

2.1   User Expectations and Trust

In static industrial environments, sensor nodes are deployed to monitor a particular facility. We can build a set of accurate expectations using extensive domain knowledge: deployment parameters, baseline facility and sensor behavior, and underlying process models. This is different from more dynamic applications of sensor networks that observe unknown environments (e.g., habitat monitoring). In such cases we may not have exact knowledge of the phenomenon behavior or pre-collected sensor readings.

We need mathematical tools to represent expectations, continuously confirm system performance to the expectations based on direct observations and finally, make a transition from confirmation level to trust metric of a node. Trust is an overloaded term used with a variety of meanings in different contexts. In our approach, we are concerned with a particular type of trust - **trust in behavior** that reflects strict conformance to a set of pre-defined **expectations**:

- Sensor nodes report correct real world readings that reflect the behavior of the observed facility;
- Sensor nodes confirm appropriate behavior consistent with the sensor design characteristics (e.g., expected sending rate, sensing radius, natural error rate);
- Readings of sensors monitoring different aspects of physical phenomena (e.g., pressure/temperature, torque/flux) must conform to temporal and spatial dependencies according to the expectations that we have developed based on past experiences and laws of physics.

2.2   Suspicion Level as a Metric of Distrust

We associate a Suspicion Level (SL) with each sensor. SL represents the belief that the sensor is not acting reliably according to the expectations of sensor behavior formed before the actual interactions with the sensor. During the interaction, the system assesses perceived sensor performance against the original expectations and determines the extent to which the expectations are confirmed. When results are not as expected, the system increases the SL for the sensor of concern.

SL for a node is a variable taking values on the interval (0, 1], that represents the accumulative performance of the node in past interactions. To calculate a SL for a node S_i during the evaluation phase N, we adopt the approach described in [8]. Assume that the natural error rate for the node S_i is $0<NER<<1$. The system maintains a nonnegative variable α for each node that is used to update the SL during each evaluation phase N. Each time a node does not act according to the expectations, its α is incremented by $1-NER^{S_i}$. Each time a node behavior is assumed correct, its α is decreased by NER^{S_i}. Thus correctly functioning nodes will have a SL approaching 0 while faulty and malicious nodes will have a higher SL. The SL is calculated as:

$$SL_N^{S_i} = 1 - e^{-\omega_{S_i}\alpha_N}, \alpha_N = \alpha_{N-1} + (1 - NER^{S_i}) \ or \ \alpha_N = \max(0, \alpha_{N-1} - NER^{S_i}) \ (1)$$

Here ω^{S_i} is a proportionality constant that depends on the sensor S_i design and deployment parameters. Sensor data may have different "value" to an end user depending on the sensor design and deployment characteristics, such as reliability and the data paths used to obtain data from the sensor. These characteristics are represented by ω^{S_i} for each sensor and are used to bootstrap initial SL values for each sensor. At system initialization time $N=0$, the SL assigned to each node S_i is given by an initialization function f: $SL_0^{S_i} = f(\omega^{S_i})$.

Note that ω^{S_i} influences the convergence of SL to distrust: the higher the value ω^{S_i}, the more suspicious we are when we detect that node S_i misbehaves. Figure 1 shows the effects of different values taken by ω^{S_i} on the shape of the function $SL_N^{S_i} = 1 - e^{-\omega_{S_i}\alpha_N}$. Krasniewski et al [8] show that SL for an uncompromised node is expected to remain at the same value.

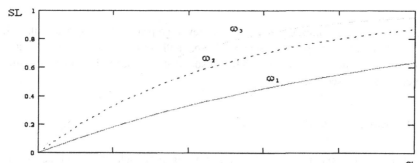

Fig. 1. The effects of ω ($\omega_1<\omega_2<\omega_3$) on the shape of the function $SL_N^{S_i} = 1 - e^{-\omega_{s_i} \alpha_N}$

In this paper, we consider the following types of malicious sensor behavior that causes the system to increase the SL of a sensor:

- False event reports (e.g., false fire alarm);
- Not reported events (e.g., an oil leak);
- Excessive reports;
- Incorrect reports: incorrect data (e.g., temperature, pressure) or event.

Note that if a node faults once, it does not mean that the node is considered faulty/malicious for the rest of the time. If the subsequent readings of the node are assumed valid by the system, the suspicion level will decrease according to the formula (1).

SL is the core of our behavior-based trust framework. Process control and security policies that govern operation of a monitored facility are conditioned on suspicion levels in order to deemphasize results from malicious or faulty sensors. The readings of a sensor with a high value of SL are treated with suspicion. If node's SL exceeds a certain threshold (specified in the policies), the node is deemed untrustworthy and is blacklisted.

3   Basic System Design

We consider a sensor network that consists of individual sensors permanently mounted on industrial equipment. The nodes of different types sense real world phenomena (e.g., temperature, pressure, flux) and forward observed measurements to a base station. We place trust with the base station, which has sufficient resources to resist attacks and is located in a physically secure place. The individual sensors are not trusted. The underlying network assumptions include the following:

- sensors are stationary (immobile);
- the location of each node is known;
- sensors can be securely and uniquely identified;
- each message is integrity protected and authenticated.

To make these assumptions practical, we leverage prior efforts. In particular, SPINS [13] protocols can provide secure sensor authentication and message integrity protection. The location of each sensor can be securely verified using the mechanisms described in [12].

3.1   Categories of Expectations

We use deployment knowledge, baseline facility behavior, and sensor design parameters to construct internal representations of the three categories of expectations:

1. **Expected Individual Sensor Behavior** is represented as follows according to sensor design characteristics and deployment parameters:

$$E^{S_i} = \{NER, RR, DR, L, r\},$$

where NER - natural error rate that nodes are allowed to make due to natural causes, $0 < NER << 1$;
RR - reporting rate, i.e. expected number of reports per specified time interval;
DR - data range of values that the reported data can take;
L - position of the sensor;
r - sensing radius within which a node can detect the occurrence of an event or take measure. We refer to the sensing area of a node S as a sphere with a sensing radius r centered at the location of the node.

2. **Expected Sensor Group Behavior** describes dependencies between data reported by different groups of sensors.

Sensor data redundancy
We assume that a phenomenon of a particular type can be correctly sensed by n sensors of the same type which form a group of neighbors G_i due to redundant node placement. The system maintains information about all groups and the membership in the groups. This is possible due to the static nature of the nodes.

Consider a simple example of a sensor network deployed in a pipeline system used to transport crude oil to a refinery (Figure 2). The network is tasked with pipeline monitoring and oil leak detection. The pump pushes the crude oil into the pipeline. The pipeline monitoring system ensures leak detection by either observing presence of oil in the surrounding area or by measuring pressure and flux simultaneously. When oil is transmitted in an encapsulated pipe, the flux at both ends of the oil-transporting pipes should remain steady [19].

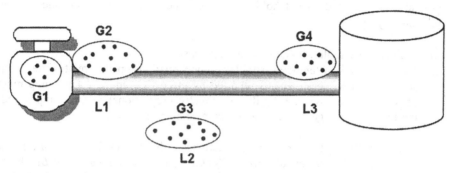

Fig. 2. The Pipeline Example

In our example, there are four sensor groups installed in the field equipment:
1) G_1 measures speed of the pump's impeller, it reports data D^{G1};
2) G_2 measures oil flux in the pipe at the location L_1, it reports data D^{G2};
3) G_3 detects the presence of oil in the soil at the location L_2, it reports data D^{G3};
4) G_4 measures oil flux in the pipe at the location L_3, it reports data D^{G4}.

Reading of sensors comprising group G_3 are binary: $D^{G3} = 1$ if G_3 detects oil in the soil at the location L_2, otherwise $D^{G3} = 0$. The readings of all other sensor groups are continuous. We expect that all sensors within a group must report the same data, but are allowed to make errors only within a specified bound defined by *NER*.

Complimentary Analysis
We consider temporal and spatial dependencies between different groups of sensors in order to detect anomalies due to faulty or malicious nodes. In our example, measurements reported by groups G_1 and G_2 provide complementary analyses and verifications of the pipeline operation. If the pump speed sensor indicates an unusually high speed, the flux sensors at the location L_1 must display a corresponding anomaly. Alternatively, if the torque sensor indicates a "normal" level of torque, the flux must be within a normal range. Deviations of data reported by one of the groups indicate a potential problem with the sensors.

The expectations about temporal and spatial correlations are encoded as a set of relationships. A relationship $R(e_1, e_2) \rightarrow T$ or F is a Boolean function that indicates dependency between two entities e_1 and e_2. An entity can represent readings of a group or another relationship. A *simple relationship* links readings of two groups of sensors. A *compound relationship* either links readings of a group of sensors with another relationship, or relates two other relationships. A relationship R holds if it evaluates to T (a Boolean true), R does not hold if it evaluates to F (a Boolean false).

Some relationships must always hold due to, for example, laws of physics or empirical knowledge. We call such relations - *ground relationships*. The fact that a ground relationship does not hold means that one of the groups included in the relation is lying.

In our pipeline example, we define three relationships:
1) $R_1(D^{G1}, D^{G2})$ is a temporal, simple, ground relationship that relates the pump speed and flux measurements reported by groups G_1 and G_2. The pump must obey the pump law: the oil flux is directly proportional to the pump speed, therefore the changes in speed and flux must be proportional [19].

2) $R_2(D^{G2}, D^{G4})$ is a temporal, simple relationship that relates the levels of oil flux measured by the groups of sensors G_2 and G_4 at the locations L_1 and L_3. Under normal pipeline operation, the flux at both locations must be equal.

3) $R_3(D^{G3}, R_2)$ is a temporal, ground, compound relationship that describes the dependencies between the results of soil tests for oil contamination at the location L_2 and the differences in flux at the locations L_1 and L_3. R_3 holds if the levels of flux at L_1 and L_2 are equal within an acceptable error range.
   $R_3 \rightarrow T$ if:
     1) $D^{G3} = 0$ and $R_2 \rightarrow T$, **OR**
     2) $D^{G3} = 1$ and $R_2 \rightarrow F$.
   Otherwise, $R_3 \rightarrow F$.

3   Expected Facility Behavior describes the expected system behavior based on prior experience and desired facility state (e.g., baseline flux/pressure/torque range). For each group of sensors, the expected facility behavior describes a range of expected values:
   D^{G1}should be within normal pump speed range $[S_1, S_n]$;
   $D^{G2}$and D^{G4} should be within normal flux range $[F_1, F_n]$;
   $D^{G3} = 0$ (no oil contamination should be reported).

The system detects abnormal state of the monitored facility by comparing the observed readings (perceived trustworthy) against the Expected Facility Behavior. If any anomalies are detected, the system reacts according to policies that govern the operation of the monitored facility (e.g., adjust pump speed).

3.2   Determining Data Trustworthiness and Updating SLs

The system evaluates sensor data and updates SLs for all sensors periodically. Each evaluation phase consists of two steps. First, the system considers each individual sensor and updates corresponding SL if the sensor behavior does not comply with the expectations. Next, the system averages the data reported by each group and calculates SL for each group. The system employs the averaged data to determine which ground relationships do not hold and which groups report wrong data. For the groups deemed to be wrong, the SLs of each sensor in the group are further increased. During the third step the system acts according to trust-based policies. We next describe each step in detail.

Step 1

During each evaluation phase N, the system waits for a predefined interval of time Δ to receive reports from deployed nodes. After Δ has elapsed, the system assesses the conformance of each sensor to the Expected Individual Sensor Behavior E^{S_i}. Some types of malicious/faulty behavior can be detected at this step. For example, if the report sending rate RR considerably exceeds the expected rate, the system may suspect a Denial of Service Attack (DoS) on behalf of the sensor and take an appropriate action. On the other hand, if perceived RR is lower than expected, the system may suspect an aging node due to battery energy depletion. If the sensor readings are out of the expected data range DR, the data is assumed invalid and is not used for evaluation. In all these cases, the SL for the node is updated according to the formula (1). Note that a node may continue to report correct data even if we suspect a DoS or a dying battery. If we know that the node might have been compromised or is aging, we will treat the data from that node with suspicion, until it can be manually verified that the node is benign.

However, not all types of abnormal behavior (discussed in Section 2.2) can be detected at this point. For example, detecting false alarms or incorrect reports (e.g., false temperature reading) requires additional knowledge. So, the next step is to employ the Expected Sensor Group Behavior in order to determine the quality of the data reported by each node.

Step 2

Binary Data
For each group G_i which reports binary events, the system decides whether an event actually occurred by partitioning the sensors into two sets based on whether the sensor reported the occurrence of the event or not. The SLs of sensors in each set are summed and the set with the lower cumulative SL wins [8]. If the group G_i reading is decided to be correct during this step, the suspicion levels of the sensors comprising the faulty set is increased according to formula (1).

Continuous data
For each group G_i consisting of n sensors, during each evaluation stage N the system calculates the weighted mean of the data $D_N^{G_i}$ reported by $m \leq n$ sensors. m is less or equal to n because (i) some sensors might have missed their reports; (ii) data reported by certain sensors fell out of the expected data range DR and was discarded, as described above.

$$D_N^{G_i} = \frac{\sum\limits_{j=1}^{m} SL_N^{S_j} D_N^{S_j}}{\sum\limits_{j=1}^{m} SL_N^{S_j}} \quad (2)$$

For each node S_j in the group G_i the system uses a threshold δ to determine whether the node reading is correct. If the absolute difference between the sensor reading and weighted mean exceeds the threshold $|D_N^{G_i} - D_N^{S_j}| > \delta$, the data is assumed incorrect. If the system decides that the group G_i reading is accurate during this step, SLs for the incorrect nodes are updated according to the formula (1).

Next, the system employs a decision tree approach to determine whether the expectations about group and facility behavior hold. The system assumes that during each data evaluation phase N, only one sensor group can lie. Under this assumption, the decision tree either detects the lying group (if any) or provides us with a list of candidates. The decision tree is constructed a priori (e.g., using automatic decision tree construction tools such as ID3 which employs greedy top-down algorithm [15]). An internal node denotes a test on a relationship. A branch represents an outcome of the test: binary True or False. Leaf nodes represent outcome class labels, such as facility is in normal state, oil leak is detected, particular sensor group is lying.

The expectations about group and facility behavior are used to construct a decision tree. The most common method for learning decision trees is top-down induction: start from the entire set of training examples (relationships and corresponding outcome classes), partition it into subsets by testing whether a relationship holds, and then recursively call the induction algorithm for each subset [15]. The constructed tree is stored along with a set of functions that implement methods for determining whether relationships hold.

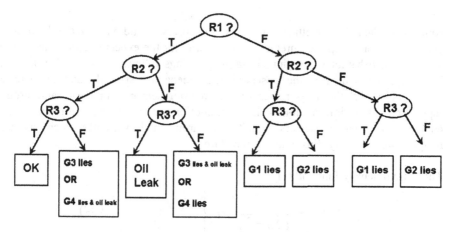

Fig. 3. The Decision Tree for the Pipeline Example

Figure 3 shows a decision tree constructed for our pipeline example. Note that R_1 and R_3 are ground relationships and must always hold; R_2 may or may not hold. If R_2 does not hold and neither group G_2, nor group G_4 is lying, then there is an oil leak. There are two situations when we can not tell whether group G_3 or G_4 is lying. Consider two cases:

1) $R_1 \rightarrow T$, $R_2 \rightarrow T$ and $R_3 \rightarrow F$
2) $R_1 \rightarrow T$, $R_2 \rightarrow F$ and $R_3 \rightarrow F$

<u>Case 1:</u> if G_3 lies (it reports 1 while R_2 holds), it means that the facility is in the normal state and G_3 reported a false oil leak. If we assume that G_4 lies, then R_2 does not hold and there is an oil leak.

<u>Case 2:</u> if G_3 lies (it reports 0 while R_2 does not hold), it means that the there is an oil leak (G_3 must have had reported 1). If we assume that G_4 lies, then R_2 and R_3 hold and the facility is in the normal state.

To decide which group from the candidate set is faulty the system calculates a SL for each group by taking a mean of the SLs of all nodes in the group calculated during the step 1.

$$SL_N^{G_i} = \frac{1}{n} \sum_{i=1}^{n} SL_N^{S_i} \quad (3)$$

Next the system compares the SL for each candidate group and decides that the one with the highest SL is lying.

Breaking the ties

If SLs differ insignificantly, we utilize a simple sequential parameter estimation method as a tie breaker. Note that this method works only for groups who report continuous data. The method compares the observed and predicted relationship between sensor group measurements and determines the expected group value. We assume that behavior of continuous sensor readings follows a normal distribution. This approach works if the observed phenomena are spatially and temporally consistent, so that the measurements at neighboring sensors within the same group report common information. This assumption is reasonable for industrial environments where sensors monitor environmental variables such as air temperature, humidity, flux, and soil moisture.

The normal density function [2] is:

$$p(D_N^{G_k}) = \frac{1}{(2\pi\sigma^2)} \exp\left\{-\frac{(D_N^{G_k} - \mu)^2}{2\sigma^2}\right\} \quad (4)$$

From the maximum likelihood estimate we can find the mean and variance of a normal distribution in one dimension:

$$\hat{\mu} = \frac{1}{N}\sum_{n=1}^{N} D_N^{G_k\,n}, \hat{\sigma}^2 = \frac{1}{N}\sum_{n=1}^{N}(D_N^{G_k\,n} - \hat{\mu}) \quad \text{[2], or alternatively:}$$

$$\hat{\mu}_{N+1} = \hat{\mu}_N + \frac{1}{N+1}(D_N^{G_k\,N+1} - \hat{\mu}_N)$$

$$\hat{\sigma}^2_{N+1} = \hat{\sigma}^2_N + \frac{1}{N+1}(D_N^{G_k\,N+1} - \hat{\mu}_{N+1})^2$$

For each group G_k from the candidate set, we calculate the probability $p(D_N^{G_k})$ of observing data $D_N^{G_k}$ according to formula (4). The group with the lowest probability is decided to be faulty. Note that we do not have to store the complete set of sensor data since each data point can be discarded once it has been used and only $\hat{\mu}$ and $\hat{\sigma}^2$ are saved. In our pipeline example, G_3 reports binary data and G_4 reports continuous data. If the values of the suspicion levels SL_N^{G3} and SL_N^{G4} are very close, we calculate $p(D_N^{G_4})$. If the probability p is lower than a threshold γ, we decide that G_4 is faulty.

Note that this method of breaking the ties must be used with caution. To confuse the system, an adversary needs to compromise most of the sensors in one of the groups (which is a valid assumption in our paper) and make the suspicion levels of the two groups equal. In our example, if an adversary compromises the majority of the sensors in the group G_3, the system cannot tell G_3 or G_4 is lying, as analyzed in Figure 3. Second, when resorting to maximum likelihood estimate, the probability of data reported by G_3 in (4) can still be high. Therefore, if the suspicion levels of the groups are low, the system should report this case to an operator. Ideally, sensor group types, placements, and the corresponding set of relationships should be defined to eliminate (or at least reduce) the number of inconclusive cases.

Next, the system updates SLs according to formula (1). For all groups deemed to be faulty, the system increases SL for each sensor in the group. For all groups who reported correct data, the SL of each sensor from the correct set is decreased.

Step 3

The system employs trust-based security policies [15], [16] to activate fine-grained real time responses (conditioned on SLs). For example, the system may blacklist sensors that are believed to send corrupted data or report incorrect/false events. However, if the system suspects a Denial of Service attack on behalf of a sensor, just blacklisting the sensor does not solve the problem because the links will still be saturated with malicious traffic. To address this issue, the reaction should isolate the misbehaving node and drop messages originated by this node.

Mistrusted nodes can regain trust dynamically over the time by reporting data that the system assumes valid. As the result, the SL will gradually decrease. However, the treatment of blacklisted nodes must be carefully regulated by domain and organization specific policies. The system should report blacklisted nodes to an operator for analysis. Most of the problems that cause node banishment require a manual resolution. For example, a non-malicious node was blacklisted because its battery was dying and needed replacement, or a tilted light sensor needed correct orientation. The blacklisted compromised sensors require physical adjustment or replacement. For some blacklisted nodes policies can specify a predetermined time period after which the nodes are unlocked with a high SL value assigned. Another issue that policies should consider is the number of blacklisted nodes in a particular group. If the number is large the policy can require a manual action. If just a few nodes were isolated, the policy can employ the time out mechanism discussed above.

4   Related Work

Considerable attention has been given to developing localized, distributed methods for fault recognition is sensor networks. The majority of these approaches rely on the neighboring nodes to calculate reputation, trustworthiness, opinion and other classes of trust-related metrics.

Krasniewski et al [8] designed a TibFit protocol to diagnose and mask arbitrary node failures in event-driven wireless sensor networks. The protocol determines whether a binary event has occurred and the location of the event by analyzing reports from the event neighbors. TibFit maintains a Trust Index for each node that represents the reliability of previous event reports of that node. Our notion of suspicion level extends the concept of the trust index. We maintain a SL for sensors which report binary and continuous data. Furthermore, the SL is updated based on the conformance of node behavior to individual- and group-level expectations.

Elnahraway et al [5] present an approach to handling outliers and missing information in sensor networks based on exploiting contextual information of the networks. This information includes spatial dependencies between spatially adjacent nodes as well as the temporal dependencies between history readings of the same sensor node. The context is used by each sensor to locally predict its current readings given its own past readings and current readings of the neighbors. This work is the closest to our approach because it relies on contextual information to detect fault readings. However, in our approach the context includes relationships among different groups of sensors (not just two neighboring sensors). We also maintain a distrust metric that allows us to deemphasize data reported by untrusted nodes.

Ganeriwal et al [6] developed a reputation system for sensor networks that uses a Bayesian formulation for reputation representation, updates, integration and trust evolution. Each node monitors behavior of other nodes and builds their reputation over time in order to characterize them as cooperative or non-cooperative. The problem of what constitutes co-operative or non-cooperative behavior has not been sufficiently explored. In our paper we explicitly specify non-compliant node behavior as non-conformance to the set of expectations.

Krishnamachari and Iyengar [9] proposed a solution to the recognition of faulty sensor readings based on a combination of shortest-path routing, and the construction of a spanning tree as a clustering mechanism. This work assumes that a node can rely on its neighbors to accept its own reading as correct if at least half of its neighbors have the same reading. Larkey et al [11] present a distributed algorithm for detecting measurement errors and inferring missing readings in sensor networks based on statistical distributions of differences between sensor readings and the readings of its neighbors.

Distributed fault-tolerance for event detection using the assumption of spatial correlation is considered in [10]. The sensor measurements are assumed to be spatially correlated. Using this principle, faulty readings are eliminated. For fault recognition, the assumption is made that sensor faults are uncorrelated. This assumption is unrealistic. It is possible that all the sensors in a particular area fail due to some external event, and generate faulty readings.

Trappe et al [18] present a high-level framework for assessing the trustworthiness of the data reported by sensors. A monitor applies consistency checks to sensed data to determine the reliability of the data. The processed data is tagged with a class (suspicious or reliable) and confidence (how sure the monitor is) values. The consistency checks may examine relationships between several physical properties. The framework is discussed at a very high level, lacking a language for expressing consistency rules and rules for updating the confidence level. In our work, we explicitly define the relationship between different sensor readings. Furthermore, we assess the reliability of the data based on the trustworthiness of the sensor. Dynamic assessment and update of a SL for each sensor allows us to detect and rule out misbehaving sensors. Such stateful SL calculation increases system resilience to compromised/faulty nodes.

Pirzada and McDonald [14] introduce a trust model that evaluates the reliability of routes in ad-hoc networks, using only direct node observations. Trust is calculated by analyzing different categories of the events, such as received, forwarded and overheard packets. The categories signify the specific aspect of trust that is relevant to a particular relationship.

Zourdaki et al [21] propose a conceptual framework for trust establishment with respect to reliable packet delivery in the presence of potentially malicious nodes. They introduce a concept of trustworthiness which combines the computed trust metric and statistical confidence associated with a trust value. Trustworthiness is computed using a Bayesian method based on observations of packet forwarding behavior by neighbor nodes.

5   Conclusions and Future Work

We presented a system that diagnoses and isolates faulty/malicious nodes even when the readings of neighboring nodes are faulty. We map the problem of identifying and isolating faulty/compromised sensors to the problem of comparing observed behavior to a set of expectations, making inferences, and updating the suspicion level associated with each sensor. The suspicion level is used to deemphasize results collected from untrusted sensors. Observed deviations from expected behavior help us to detect sensor errors or system malfunctions.

Our future work includes experiments with the system in a simulated environment and extending the framework. In our current approach, we do not take into account differences in the reporting rates of different sensors. In wireless sensor networks, it is critical to conserve energy by minimizing the idle listening time with asymmetric sleep or activity duty cycles. This approach may lead to variations of active/sleep duty cycles of different types of sensors: some sensors report almost constantly, others only according to a schedule or after an explicit query. These incompatible time scales will be taken into account when assigning a static SL and weighting the adjustment of dynamic SL to reduce the bias.

Failures due to compromised nodes can be correlated. This is different from the arbitrary nature of failure of faulty nodes. We plan to develop an approach that will look for correlations between mistrusted sensors to detect malicious node collaboration. Currently, we assume that only one group could be faulty if a ground relationship does not hold. We will consider a more complex situation where more than one group could be wrong and will develop a set of rules and constraints to determine the faulty groups.

6 Acknowledgements

This research was supported by funding the National Science Foundation under grants no. CCR-0325951 and ACI-0325409. The views and conclusions contained herein are those of the authors and should not be interpreted as representing the official policies or endorsement of the funding agencies.

7 References

1. R. Adler, P. Buonadonna, J. Chhabra, M. Flanigan, L. Krishnamurthy, N. Kushalnagar, L. Nachman, M. Yarvis. Design and Deployment of Industrial Sensor Networks: Experiences from the North Sea and a Semiconductor Plant, Sensys 2005.

2. C. M. Bishop, Neural Networks for Pattern Recognition, Oxford University Press, ISBN: 0198538642, 1995.

3. M. Bohge and W. Trappe. An Authentication Framework for Hierarchical Ad Hoc Sensor Networks. In Proc. of ACM workshop on Wireless Security, 2003.

4. W. Du, J. Deng, Y. S. Han, P. Varshney, J. Katz, A. Khalili, A Pairwise Key Pre-distribution Scheme for Wireless Sensor Networks. The ACM Transactions on Information and System Security, 2005.

5. E. Elnahrawy, and B. Nath. Context-aware sensors. In Lecture Notes in Computer Science, H. Karl, A. Willig, and A. Wolisz, Eds. Vol. 2920. Springer-Verlag, 77–93, 2004.

6. S. Ganeriwal and M. B. Srivastava, Reputation-based framework for high integrity sensor networks. In Proceedings of the 2nd ACM workshop on Security of ad hoc and sensor networks, 66-77, 2004.

7. G. Gaubatz, J.-P. Kaps, and B. Sunar. Public key cryptography in sensor networks revisited, 1st European Workshop on Security in Ad-Hoc and Sensor Networks, LNCS 3313, 2004.

8. M. Krasniewski, P. Varadharajan, B. Rabeler, S. Bagchi, Y. C. Hu. TibFit: Trust Index Based Fault Tolerance for Arbitrary Data Faults in Sensor Networks. In Proceedings of the International Conference on Dependable Systems and Networks, 2005.

9. B. Krishnamachari and S. Iyengar, Distributed Bayesian algorithms for fault-tolerant event region detection in wireless sensor networks. IEEE Transactions on Computers, Vol.53, No.3, 2004.

10. B. Krishnamachari, S. Iyengar. Efficient and Fault-Tolerant Feature Extraction in Wireless Sensor Networks, Proceedings of Information Processing in Sensor Networks, 2003.

11. L. B. Larkey and A. A. Hagberg and L. M. A. Bettencourt. In-Situ Data Quality Assurance for Environmental Applications of Wireless Sensor Networks, Report LA-UR-06-1117, 2006.

12. D. Liu, Peng Ning and W. Du. Attack-Resistant Location Estimation in Sensor Networks. In Proceedings of The Fourth International Conference on Information Processing in Sensor Networks, 2005.

13. A. Perrig, R. Szewczyk, V. Wen, D. Culler, and J. D. Tygar. SPINS: Security protocols for sensor networks, Wireless Networks Journal , 8(5):521–534, 2002.

14. Pirzada and C. McDonald. Establishing trust in pure ad-hoc networks, In Proceedings of the 27th Australasian Computer Science Conference, 47-54, 2004.

15. J. R. Quinlan. Induction of decision trees. Machine Learning 1:81–106, 1986.

16. T. Ryutov, L. Zhou, N. Foukia, C. Neuman, T. Leithead, K. E. Seamons. Adaptive Trust Negotiation and Access Control for Grids. In proceedings of the Grid 6th IEEE/ACM International Workshop on Grid Computing, 2005.

17. T. Ryutov, L. Zhou, C. Neuman, T. Leithead, and K. Seamons. Adaptive Trust Negotiation and Access Control. In Proceedings of SACMAT, 2005.

18. W. Trappe, Y Zhang, and B. Nath. MIAMI: Methods and Infrastructure for the Assurance of Measurement Information, In DMSN, 2005.

19. S. Q. Zhang, S J Jin, F. L Yang, X Q Wang and Q. Y. Bai. Crucial Technologies of Oil Transporting Pipe Leak Detection and Location Based on Wavelet and Chaos, 7th ISMTII2005(UK), 2005.

20. S. Zhu, S. Setia, S. Jajodia, and P. Ning. An Interleaved Hop-by-Hop Authentication Scheme for Filtering of Injected False Data in Sensor Networks, Proceedings of IEEE Symposium on Security and Privacy, 2004.

21. C. Zouridaki, B. L. Mark, M. Hejmo, R. K. Thomas. A quantitative trust establishment framework for reliable data packet delivery in MANETs, SASN 2005.

The AI Hardness of CAPTCHAs does not imply Robust Network Security

Allan Caine and Urs Hengartner

University of Waterloo, Canada
{adcaine, uhengart}@cs.uwaterloo.ca

Abstract. A CAPTCHA is a special kind of AI hard test to prevent bots from logging into computer systems. We define an AI hard test to be a problem which is intractable for a computer to solve as a matter of general consensus of the AI community. On the Internet, CAPTCHAs are typically used to prevent bots from signing up for illegitimate e-mail accounts or to prevent ticket scalping on e-commerce web sites. We have found that a popular and distributed architecture for implementing CAPTCHAs used on the Internet has a flawed protocol. Consequently, the security that the CAPTCHA ought to provide does not work and is ineffective at keeping bots out. This paper discusses the flaw in the distributed architecture's protocol. We propose an improved protocol while keeping the current architecture intact. We implemented a bot, which is 100% effective at breaking CAPTCHAs that use this flawed protocol. Furthermore, our implementation of the improved protocol proves that it is not vulnerable to attack. We use two popular web sites, tickets.com and youtube.com, to demonstrate our point.

1 Introduction

A CAPTCHA is a special kind of AI hard test used to prohibit bots from gaining unauthorized access to web sites and computer systems. Using a definition similar to von Ahn *et al.* [1], we say that an AI problem is *hard* if it is the general consensus of the AI community that the problem is intractable when using a computer to solve it. CAPTCHAs are used by Yahoo! [2] to prevent bots from signing up for illegitimate e-mail accounts. Similarly, e-commerce web sites like the Minnesota Twins Major League Baseball Club [3] use CAPTCHAs to prevent ticket scalping by bots.

The word CAPTCHA stands for Completely Automated Public Turing test to tell Computers and Humans Apart. Its basic operation is illustrated in Fig. 1. The central idea is simple: it is assumed that only humans can solve CAPTCHAs; bots cannot. There are two principals involved: the prover and the verifier. The verifier is an automated system. It generates a CAPTCHA image and evaluates the prover's response. If the prover's response is correct, the prover is admitted to the next step of the authentication process. If the prover's response is incorrect, the verifier bars the prover from proceeding any

Please use the following format when citing this chapter:

Caine, A. and Hengartner, U., 2007, in IFIP International Federation for Information Processing, Volume 238, Trust Management, eds. Etalle, S., Marsh, S., (Boston: Springer), pp. 367–382.

368   Allan Caine and Urs Hengartner

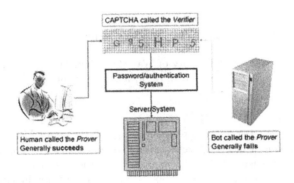

Fig. 1. The verifier issues a visual test to the prover. In general, only human provers can solve CAPTCHAs.

further. If the prover is a human, the prover will generally succeed in solving the CAPTCHA; if the prover is a bot, the bot will generally fail.

There exists a popular architecture used by web sites that use CAPTCHAs for security. In this architecture, the security task is distributed amongst two servers: the Sales Server and the CAPTCHA Server. The Sales Server is responsible for the conduct of the e-commerce sales transaction; the CAPTCHA Server for generating the CAPTCHA image. This distributed approach is used so that many Sales Servers can utilize a single CAPTCHA Server.

In this paper,

- we show that the current protocol used in this architecture is insecure;
- we propose an improved and secure protocol while preserving the current distributed architecture;
- using a bot that we implemented, we prove that the current protocol is indeed insecure and subject to attack; and
- we prove that our implementation of our proposed protocol is indeed effective against the same attack.

The authors von Ahn *et al.* [1] suggest that a good CAPTCHA must be AI hard. Our research shows that their suggestion must be qualified. True, an AI hard CAPTCHA is a necessary condition but it is not a sufficient condition for robust network security. If the protocol is set up improperly, the CAPTCHA can be broken by an attacker with greater ease all things being equal. The problem rests with what we call a repeating CAPTCHA. Repeating CAPTCHAs are discussed in Sect. 2.

Our paper is organized as follows: Sect. 2 discusses the popular architecture and its insecure protocol. We show that the insecurity is the result of a repeating CAPTCHA. Section 3 discusses the attack, which exploits the insecurity identified in Sect. 2.

In Sect. 4 we propose a new and secure protocol. Our proposed protocol eliminates the repeating CAPTCHA. However, the current architecture is preserved.

Our experimental results are given in Sect. 5. It consists of three major subsections: the experimental results from our bot's attack on e-commerce web sites using a major U.S. ticket selling agent as our example; a demonstration of our implementation of our proposed protocol; and a discussion of youtube.com's insecure protocol.

Section 6 discusses related work, and Sect. 7 sets out our conclusions.

2 Current Protocol

The current protocol is given in Fig. 2. It is used by web sites that employ CAPTCHAs for security and it involves three entities: the Sales Server, the CAPTCHA Server, and the Client. We learned of this protocol by examining HTML source code using tickets.com and youtube.com as our primary examples.

$$\text{Sales Server : Chooses random solution } s \tag{2.1}$$
$$\text{Sales Server} \to \text{Client} : E_c\big(s||\text{ID}||\,\text{MAC}_h(s||\text{ID})\big) \tag{2.2}$$
$$\text{Client} \to \text{CAPTCHA Server} : E_c\big(s||\text{ID}||\,\text{MAC}_h(s||\text{ID})\big) \tag{2.3}$$
$$\text{CAPTCHA Server : Generates CAPTCHA image with solution } s \tag{2.4}$$
$$\text{CAPTCHA Server} \to \text{Client} : \text{CAPTCHA image} \tag{2.5}$$
$$\text{Client} \to \text{Sales Server} : s',\,E_c\big(s||\text{ID}||\,\text{MAC}_h(s||\text{ID})\big) \tag{2.6}$$
$$\text{Sales Server : Proceed if } s = s' \wedge \exists\,\text{ID} \tag{2.7}$$

Fig. 2. The current and popular protocol

The Sales Server is responsible for processing the sale, selecting a solution for the CAPTCHA image, and evaluating the Client's response. The CAPTCHA Server is responsible for generating the CAPTCHA image. The Client is the purchaser. The servers share a secret called c, which is used in a symmetric encryption function $E_c(\cdot)$ such as AES in CBC mode with a random initialization vector; and a shared secret h, which is used in a message authentication code $\text{MAC}_h(\cdot)$ such as HMAC [4]. There is a pre-existing session identifier ID. The servers trust each other, because the introduction of any distrust between the servers would undermine their effectiveness in providing the intended security. Finally, we note that the session ID is encrypted; otherwise, an attacker could build a database that would map IDs to CAPTCHAs and their solutions with the view to an on-line attack on the Sales Server.

If $s = s'$, the Sales Server allows the sale to proceed; otherwise, the sale is prohibited. The sale is also prohibited if the message from the Client to the Sales Server has expired. The message expires when the session ID expires. Fig. 3 shows the protocol graphically. The numbers correspond to the transaction numbers in Fig. 2.

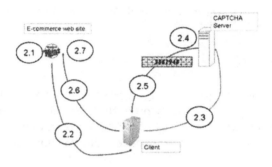

Fig. 3. Diagram of the current protocol

There is a flaw in message (2.3). An attacker can repeatedly send the message to the CAPTCHA Server, because the CAPTCHA Server does not keep state. The CAPTCHA Server is unaware that it has previously seen message (2.3). Each time the CAPTCHA Server receives message (2.3) from the Client, the CAPTCHA Server responds with a new CAPTCHA image.

Repeatedly sending message (2.3) generates a set of similar CAPTCHAs. We say that two CAPTCHAs are similar if they have the same solution, but they differ in terms of the transformation used. Fig. 4 illustrates two similar CAPTCHAs. The CAPTCHAs in Figs. 4(a) and 4(b) both have the solution 8370193, but each is rendered in a different font and a different background. We define a CAPTCHA Server which can be made to produce a set of similar CAPTCHAs a repeating CAPTCHA. We show in Sect. 3 that a repeating CAPTCHA places the attacker in a very advantageous position.

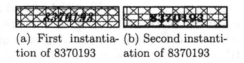

(a) First instantia-   (b) Second instanti-
tion of 8370193   ation of 8370193

Fig. 4. Two similar CAPTCHAs.

3 Attack

There are two steps in the attack: 1) collecting a representative sample of the characters used in the CAPTCHA and; 2) downloading a set of similar CAPT-CHAs by repeatedly sending message (2.3) to the CAPTCHA Server and looking for patterns across that set of images.

We take `tickets.com`, a major U.S. ticket agent, as our example. They use CAPTCHAs to prevent ticket scalping by bots. The characters that are used in their CAPTCHAs are the digits zero to nine. Before we start running our attack, we download a number of CAPTCHAs and cut out the digits until a representative for each digit is found. Such a set is depicted in Fig. 5. These representative digits are called templates. Fig. 5 shows the templates after the noise has been removed by visual inspection on a commercially available photo editor. The templates are said to be clean. The templates are stored for re-use.

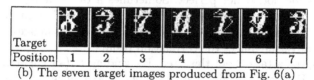

Fig. 5. Clean Templates

Once clean templates have been generated, the attack itself can begin. The bot downloads from the CAPTCHA Server a CAPTCHA image such as the one depicted in Fig. 4(a). Using a heuristic, the bot crops back the image as shown in Fig. 6(a). Next, the digits need to be segmented from each other.

(a) The cropped image.
It reads 8370193.

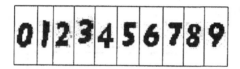

Target							
Position	1	2	3	4	5	6	7

(b) The seven target images produced from Fig. 6(a)

Fig. 6. The character segmentation process.

Since the digits are proportionally spaced, it is not possible to segment the digits by simply dividing up the image shown in Fig. 6(a) into equal segments along its width. Rather, the segmentation is done using k-means clustering [5] with the centroids equally spaced across the width of the image in Fig. 6(a). This segmentation produces seven target images as shown in Fig. 6(b).

The last step is to use the normalized cross correlation [5] to recognize the digit itself. We apply the normalized cross correlation, which gives us a score, S, each time we compare a template to a target image. The score is computed as

$$S = \max_{(u,v)} \left\{ \frac{\sum_{x,y} \left(I(u-x, v-y) - \bar{I}_{u,v} \right) \hat{T}(x,y)}{\sum_{x,y} \left(I(u-x, v-y) - \bar{I}_{u,v} \right)^2 \sum_{x,y} \hat{T}(x,y)^2} \right\} \tag{3.1}$$

where $\hat{T}$ is the template, I is the target, and $\bar{I}_{(u,v)}$ is the local average. The local average means the average of all of the pixels of I falling under $\hat{T}$ taking (u,v) as the upper left-hand corner of the template.

For example, if we compare the ten templates against a target image that actually contains a six, we get the scores shown in the bar chart of Fig. 7. As can be seen, template six obtains the best score. So, the target image would be judged to be a six.

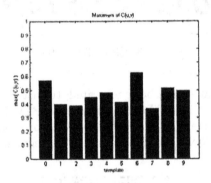

Fig. 7. The correlation scores for matching each of the templates 0 to 9 against a target known to contain a 6.

Yet, this method is not perfect. Sometimes a target image may be misinterpreted. For example, 3's are similar to 8's; 1's are similar to 7's; and 5's are similar to 6's. Also as can be seen in Fig. 6(b), the target images contain noise, which may adversely affect the correlation results.

Even so, the attack is not thwarted. By sending $E_c(s||\text{ID}|| \text{MAC}_h(s||\text{ID}))$ to the CAPTCHA Server again, a similar CAPTCHA image can be downloaded as illustrated in Fig. 4(b). Through every iteration, tallies are kept of the best interpretations. A sample final result is given in Fig. 8. Voting for more than one possibility in any given character position is evidence of occasional misinterpretation. For example, in the Position 1 histogram given in Fig. 8, we can see voting for the 6 and the 7, although most of the votes were given to the 6 — the correct interpretation. Since there is a clear favorite interpretation in each of the seven positions, an attacker can determine the correct solution to the CAPTCHA. In Fig. 8, the correct solution is 6674846.

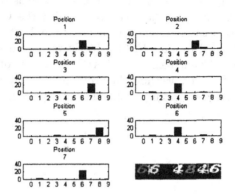

Fig. 8. The voting results on CAPTCHA "6674846"

4 Proposed Protocol

Essentially, the current protocol has one major downfall: the CAPTCHA Server depends upon the Sales Server to determine the solution to the CAPTCHA image. The attacker exploits this by sending message (2.3) repeatedly to the CAPTCHA Server. The attacker collects a set of similar CAPTCHA images, which she uses to break the CAPTCHA. The problem is cured by reassigning responsibilities. The CAPTCHA Server determines the solution instead of the Sales Server. Our proposed protocol is given in Fig. 9.

$$\text{Sales Server} \rightarrow \text{Client} : E_c\big(\text{ID}||\,\text{MAC}_h(\text{ID})\big) \tag{4.1}$$

$$\text{Client} \rightarrow \text{CAPTCHA Server} : E_c\big(\text{ID}||\,\text{MAC}_h(\text{ID})\big) \tag{4.2}$$

$$\text{CAPTCHA Server} : \text{Chooses solution } s, \text{ and generates a CAPTCHA}$$
$$\text{image with that solution} \tag{4.3}$$

$$\text{CAPTCHA Server} \rightarrow \text{Client} : \text{CAPTCHA image}, E_c\big(s||\text{ID}||\,\text{MAC}_h(s||\text{ID})\big) \tag{4.4}$$

$$\text{Client} \rightarrow \text{Sales Server} : s', E_c\big(s||\text{ID}||\,\text{MAC}_h(s||\text{ID})\big) \tag{4.5}$$

$$\text{Sales Server} : \text{Proceed if } s = s' \wedge \exists\,\text{ID} \tag{4.6}$$

Fig. 9. Our Proposed Protocol.

We make largely the same assumptions as we do in Sect. 2: there is a symmetric encryption function $E_c(\cdot)$ using a shared secret c; a message authentication code $\text{MAC}_h(\cdot)$ using a shared secret h. The variable s is the chosen solution; s' is the Client's attempt at the solution. There is a pre-existing session identifier.

To determine if the client has passed or failed the CAPTCHA test, the Sales Server confirms the message's authenticity and integrity. If $s = s'$ and the Session ID returned by the CAPTCHA Server is the same as the current Session ID, then the Client passes the CAPTCHA test; otherwise, the Client fails. For the sake of clarity, we show the protocol in diagrammed form with the numbers in Fig. 10 corresponding to the message numbers in Fig. 9.

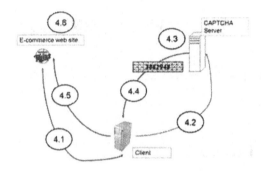

Fig. 10. Diagram of the proposed protocol

As pointed out earlier in Sect. 2, it is imperative that the ID be encrypted. Otherwise, the attacker can off-line query the CAPTCHA server for CAPTCHAs, solve them, build a database that maps IDs to CAPTCHAs and their solutions, and use this database in an on-line attack on the Sales Server

5 Experimental Results

This section consists of three major subsections. The first subsection discusses our attack. We prove that the security vulnerability in Sect. 2 truly exists. The second subsection demonstrates our implementation of our proposed protocol mentioned in Sect. 4 to show that the attack can be defeated. The third subsection discusses youtube.com's repeating CAPTCHA and the security vulnerability it implies.

5.1 Attacking tickets.com

In our experiments designed to attack tickets.com, we wanted to find the answers to the following questions:

1. Is the attack as mentioned in Sect. 3 a realistic way of attacking CAPT-CHAs?
2. Can the attack be conducted with a high probability of success?
3. If the attack is largely successful, does it place all of the clients of tickets.com in jeopardy or just some of them?

We built a bot to test our ability to break tickets.com's CAPTCHA. We found that

1. It took on average 9.89 seconds and 7.2 queries to the CAPTCHA Server to break the CAPTCHA.
2. The attack was 100% successful.
3. All of the clients of tickets.com are at risk.

Setup of the Experiment For ethical reasons, we did not actually attack tickets.com's clients directly over the Internet. Rather, we downloaded 20 different CAPTCHAs with identical solutions for each of the 40 experiments we conducted. As it turned out, downloading 20 images for each experiment was generally more than necessary. On average, only the first 7.2 images were needed by the bot to break the CAPTCHA.

The images were stored on our computer. Each image was given an index number reflecting the image's download order. Our bot strictly obeyed this ordering when fetching the images for processing.

Our bot ran on a Pentium 4 running at 3.2 GHz. The bot was written in the Matlab programming language. We used MATLAB Version 7.0.4.365 (R14) Service Pack 2 together with the statistics and image processing toolboxes. We used the statistics toolbox to have access to the k-means function, and the image processing toolbox for access to the image read function. The data we used can be found on our web page [6]. This web page periodically refreshes to reveal a new set of similar CAPTCHAs.

Our Bot's Success Rate and Running Time We ran 40 simulated attacks. They were all successful taking an average of 7.2 queries to the CAPTCHA Server. The minimum number of queries was 4; the maximum 20. Our results are summarized in Fig 11(a). It shows the average number of correct characters in all 40 attacks versus the number of queries made to the CAPTCHA Server. After one query, the bot knows 5.4 characters on average. After ten queries, the bot knows 6.925 characters on average with 38 out of the 40 experiments solved correctly. After examining 15 CAPTCHAs, our bot has determined the solution in all cases but the 11th. In retrospect, our bot had actually determined the correct answer in experiment 11 after examining 15 CAPTCHA images but it decided to increase its confidence in its answer by examining the remaining five CAPTCHAs.

While we were impressed with the bot's 100% success rate, we wanted to ensure that the bot was breaking the CAPTCHA in a reasonable period of time. It is the case that tickets.com allows the client only 60 seconds to solve the CAPTCHA. Our bot must break the CAPTCHA within that time limit.

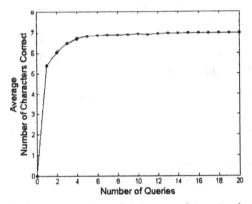

(a) Average number of characters determined versus number of CAPTCHAs examined.

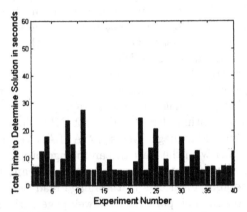

(b) Time to download and process images

Fig. 11. Experimental Results $N = 40$

The bot's average processing time is 7.85 seconds implying that 52.2 seconds are left to download on average 7.2 images. Each image is about 2.3 kB. Based on downloading 800 images, our experimental results show that it takes on average 0.2836 seconds to download one image. So, it would take 2.0419 seconds on average to download 7.2 images, which is far less time than the 52.2 seconds available.

Finally, we took the actual time reported by the bot to process the images and added 0.2836 seconds for each image that the bot reported having had processed. Our results are illustrated in Fig. 11(b). The average time to both download and process the images is 9.89 seconds, well within the 60-second time limit. Even in the worst case, the total time taken in experiment 11, including an estimate of network time, is 27.51 seconds. We claim that if the average download time of 0.2836 seconds per image prevails in an actual direct attack, our bot would succeed in breaking every CAPTCHA.

Risk to ticket.com's Clients Our experiments show that when a Client is making a purchase through tickets.com, the Client always calls a script located at http://pvoimages.tickets.com/buy/NVImageGen to fetch the CAPTCHA image. Our data set [6] is quite broad. It covers Major League baseball games, rock concerts, circuses, and children's entertainment to name a few. While it is true that the name of the e-commerce web site is passed to the CAPTCHA Server through the URL, this information is not used in determining the CAPTCHA image. As illustrated in Fig. 4(a), tickets.com's CAPTCHAs are always characterized by a seven-digit number written in some font with a mesh of lines behind it. It is our view that our attack would succeed against any e-commerce web site supported by tickets.com.

5.2 Implementation of our Proposed Protocol

To demonstrate that our proposed protocol works, we implemented it as if it were being used on an e-commerce web site with anti-scalping security. We assumed that the Client had already selected her purchases and was ready to place her order.

We wrote two scripts in php: SalesServer.php and CAPTCHAserver.php. Each script emulates the roles of the Sales Server and CAPTCHA Server respectively. To avoid confusing the client as she moves from server to server, we used an embedded frame (iframe). In HTML, an iframe is essentially a browser within the Client's main browser window. The servers' output is directed to the iframe — not to the main browser window itself. Consequently, as the servers take turns responding to the Client's input, the change in servers is not reflected in the Client's address bar. From the Client's perspective, she would see herself as always being on the Sales Server's web page albeit with dynamic content. On the other hand, we admit that if the Client's browser does not support iframes, then the Client would be able to see the change in her browser's address bar.

Fig. 12(a) shows the opening page on wrapper.html [7]. At this point, message (4.1) of Fig. 9 is sent. The text inside the beveled border is actually code produced by SalesServer.php within the iframe. In practice, the beveled border would not normally be visible to the Client. The beveled border is being shown for the sake of clarity.

When the Client clicks on the BUY!!! button shown in Fig. 12(a), messages (4.2), (4.3), and (4.4) of Fig. 9 are sent. In Fig. 12(b), the HTML form shown within the beveled border is produced by the CAPTCHAserver.php script. Yet, the Client's address bar indicates that she is still on wrapper.html. So, while we have preserved the distributed architecture, we made it invisible to the Client.

The client enters her response to the CAPTCHA image and clicks on the SEND SOLUTION button shown in Fig. 12(b). With this mouse click, message (4.5) of Fig. 9 is sent. As illustrated in Fig. 12(c), if the Client enters the

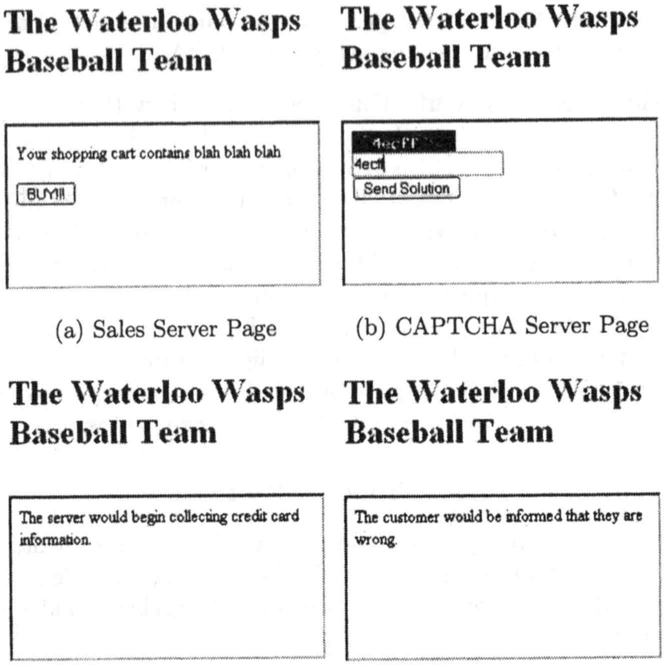

The Waterloo Wasps Baseball Team

The Waterloo Wasps Baseball Team

Your shopping cart contains blah blah blah

[BUY!!!]

4ecff

4ecff

[Send Solution]

(a) Sales Server Page   (b) CAPTCHA Server Page

The Waterloo Wasps Baseball Team

The Waterloo Wasps Baseball Team

The server would begin collecting credit card information.

The customer would be informed that they are wrong.

(c) Success   (d) Failure

Fig. 12. The HTML Pages from our implementation of our proposed protocol

correct solution, she receives an affirmative message and credit card information would now be taken from the Client. If the Client enters the wrong solution, the Client receives a negative indication from the Sales Server as in Fig. 12(d). Of course, in an actual implementation, the Sales Server would do more than simply post pass or fail messages in the window of the Client's browser.

If the Client should attempt to run the CAPTCHA Server script directly, the CAPTCHAserver.php script will detect that either message (4.2) is phony or non-existent. In either case, the script redirects the Client's browser to wrapper.html. Since the default of wrapper.html's iframe is the Sales Server, the redirect is tantamount to compelling the Client to always go to the Sales Server first before going the CAPTCHA Server. The Client must follow the protocol. Unlike the current protocol, steps in our protocol cannot be circumvented or skipped to the attacker's advantage. They must be done in order from first to last.

Alternatively, even if an attacker should succeed in circumventing the message authentication, the script unconditionally chooses a new and random solution. The algorithm is given in the right-hand column of Fig. 13. The CAPTCHA will never repeat.

As earlier indicated in Sect. 5.1, at least four similar CAPTCHAs are needed by our bot to defeat `tickets.com`'s CAPTCHA. Our attack would not succeed against a non-repeating CAPTCHA. So, our attack has been defeated and `tickets.com`'s security vulnerability fixed using our proposed protocol. Yet, it remains to be seen if their CAPTCHA could be defeated without depending upon a repeating CAPTCHA; `tickets.com`'s CAPTCHA may still be vulnerable to other kinds of attacks.

Figure 13 gives the two php scripts as pseudo code. In the interests of clarity, we have left out the message authentication steps. We use c for the shared secret, and ID for the session identifier. The `SalesServer.php` script keeps state. Keeping state can be justified because the Sales Server needs keep track of the merchandise in the Client's electronic shopping basket anyway. On the other hand, `CAPTCHAserver.php` is stateless.

`SalesServer.php`

- Open the session
- if $\not\exists$ ID
  - Generate session identifier ID
  - Echo out an HTML form with
  - $E_c(\text{ID})$ in a hidden field
  - a BUY!!! button
  - action attribute `CAPTCHAserver.php`.
- if $\exists$ ID
  - Compute $D_c\big(E_c(s)\big)$
  - If $s = s'$ then admit the client; otherwise reject.
  - The script stops

`CAPTCHAserver.php`

- Choose a random s
- Compute $E_c(s)$
- Generate CAPTCHA image
- Echo out an HTML form with
  - $E_c(s)$ in a hidden field,
  - a text field for the client's solution (s'),
  - the CAPTCHA image,
  - a SUBMIT SOLUTION button
  - action attribute of `SalesServer.php`

Fig. 13. Algorithms for `SalesServer.php` and `CAPTCHAserver.php`. The HMAC steps have been omitted.

Hidden fields in the HTML forms are used for aesthetic reasons so that the form does not show the cypher text in the Client's browser window and possibly confuse the Client. It is not a security threat that the Client has a copy of the cypher text. If the Client attempts to alter the cypher text, the HMAC test of the server receiving the message will detect the alteration.

The advantage of our solution is that it maintains the existing architecture as closely as possible. As well, the distributed nature of the architecture is normally not apparent to the Client. On the other hand, we do admit that our proposed protocol requires two trips to the CAPTCHA Server: one trip to fetch the iframe and a second trip to fetch the CAPTCHA image. In the current protocol, only one trip is necessary. In addition, the CAPTCHA image must be of the form *uniqueName*.jpeg; some background process must generate those unique file names. Also, a background process must periodically clear away any old image files.

5.3 youtube.com

A new and popular web site for personal video sharing is called youtube.com. Our research shows that they too have a repeating CAPTCHA. They leave themselves vulnerable to attack. Their vulnerability seems to stem from a bug in their CAPTCHA server. To get their CAPTCHA to repeat, it is a simple matter of clicking on the "Can't read?" link soon after the sign up page loads [8]. Clicking the "Can't read?" link is analogous to sending message (2.3). Consequently, youtube.com has a repeating CAPTCHA.

Curiously, the window of opportunity eventually closes after a few minutes. Their CAPTCHA reverts from a repeating CAPTCHA to a non-repeating CAPTCHA. We suggest that youtube.com needs to examine their CAPTCHA server with a view to correcting this bug and resolving this security vulnerability.

6 Related Work

This paper focuses strictly upon text-based types of CAPTCHAs. However, there are other types of CAPTCHAs in existence. Examples of these other types can be found at The CAPTCHA Project [9].

We do not claim to be the first to have ever broken a CAPTCHA. It is unlikely that we will be the last. An extensive list of broken CAPTCHAs can be found at PWNtcha [10].

A major criticism of visual CAPTCHAs is that they are difficult if not impossible for the visually impaired to use. This point is brought up by Fukuda et al. [11]. From the authors' report, it does not appear that there currently exists any adequate solution to this problem without compromising security.

Mori and Malik [12] provide a detailed discussion regarding how they broke two other CAPTCHAs: GIMPY and EZ-GIMPY. [9] Our approach differs from theirs in that while they are looking at shape cues, we looking at correlation-based matching. They used tests to hypothesize the locations of characters while we used k-means clustering. Since GIMPY and EZ-GIMPY use English words, Mori and Malik could use that fact essentially as a conditional probability to determine the likelihood of the existence of a particular letter given the neighboring letters. On the other hand, we had no such similar advantage. The appearance of a digit in one location did not suggest the likelihood of a particular digit appearing in another location.

We also found it interesting that Mori and Malik [12] had a copy of the EZ-GIMPY and GIMPY software. Consequently, they could generate an unlimited number of CAPTCHA images. It is our contention that this kind of unlimited access can be a CAPTCHA's undoing. Indeed, our attack succeeded in part because we had virtually unlimited access to the CAPTCHA server at `tickets.com`. Yet, for us, we broke `tickets.com`'s CAPTCHA in spite of not being able to see their code.

Another ingenious way to solve CAPTCHAs is through free porn [13]. The user is enticed into the site, but the user's progress is occasionally blocked. The site presents the user with a CAPTCHA to be solved. However, the user is actually solving a CAPTCHA on an unrelated site. The attacker can then break the CAPTCHA on the other unrelated site.

There is quite a range of opinion on what constitutes success in breaking a CAPTCHA. The authors von Ahn *et al.* [14] suggest a success rate nearly as good as a human, while the W3C suggest a success rate as little as 10% [11]. Mori and Malik [12] declared success over GIMPY, the more difficult version of EZ-GIMPY, with a success rate of only 33%. We suggest that these differences in opinion stem from each author's implied threat model. For example, in our particular case, we suggest that a scalper needs a success rate near 100%, because the scalper must be able to buy up tickets quickly as soon as they go on sale. Otherwise, the scalper may be stuck with a small handful to tickets, which have not affected the market price and which are worth little more than their face value.

Finally, we agree fully with von Ahn *et al.* [14] that researching and breaking CAPTCHAs is a win-win scenario for both the AI community and for practitioners in network security. For the AI community, this research is profitable in the study of computer vision and object recognition. For the network security community, this research is beneficial in terms of designing better access control measures, which use AI as a means of telling humans and computers apart.

7 Conclusions

In this paper, we have shown that it is a security flaw to make the CAPTCHA Server dependent upon an outside entity to determine the solution for a CAPTCHA. This kind of protocol may lead to a repeating CAPTCHA. A repeating CAPTCHA may place the attacker in an advantageous position. We have also shown that it is important that web sites which employ CAPTCHAs ensure that no bugs exist in their scripts, which might cause the CAPTCHA to repeat even for a period of time.

We both proposed and implemented a protocol which can resist the outlined attack. We discovered that the attack is one which can succeed against any customer of `tickets.com`. This happens because all of `tickets.com`'s customers use the same CAPTCHA server.

We argue that our results are important in terms of the issues of trust and assurance. For example, in the context of ticket selling, a seller will not use a web site if the seller believes that she will expose herself to ticket scalping. Buyers, on the other hand, will become disillusioned with a web site if all of the best tickets are generally unavailable for sale. Companies like `tickets.com` must protect its principals from ticket scalping through the use of authentication protocols like CAPTCHAs.

Yet, for a CAPTCHA to be useful, it must be AI hard. In this paper, we have shown that while AI hardness is a necessary condition, it is not a sufficient condition for having a good CAPTCHA. A poorly implemented CAPTCHA can be AI softened; it becomes relatively easy to break. We have shown that a CAPTCHA that can be made to repeat itself is insecure. The attacker can use the numerous examples as a kind of sanity check before offering a response.

Acknowledgements

The authors wish to thank the reviewers for their helpful comments and feedback. We extend our thanks to Ian Goldberg for his suggestion to use embedded frames in our implementation, and to Richard Mann for his comments and suggestions regarding the computer vision portion of our paper.

References

1. von Ahn, L., Blum, M., Langford, J.: Telling humans and computers apart automatically. Commnications of the ACM **47**(2) (2004) 57 – 60
2. Yahoo! Inc.: Yahoo e-mail sign up. http://www.yahoo.com (2007)
3. Minnesota Twins Major League Baseball: Minnesota twins electronic ticketing. http://minnesota.twins.mlb.com/ (2007)
4. Krawczyk, H., Bellare, M., Canetti, R.: HMAC: Keyed-hashing for message authentication. Internet RFC 2104 (1997)
5. Lewis, J.P.: Fast template matching. Vision Interface (1995) 120 – 123
6. Caine, A., Hengartner, U.: Data set. http://www.cs.uwaterloo.ca/~adcaine/php/demo.htm (2007)
7. Caine, A., Hengartner, U.: Implementation of proposed protocol. http://www.cs.uwaterloo.ca/~adcaine/php/wrapper.html (2007)
8. Youtube: Sign up page for youtube.com. http://www.youtube.com/signup (2007)
9. The CAPTCHA Project at Carnegie Mellon University. http://www.captcha.net/ (2006)
10. PWNtcha captcha decoder. http://sam.zoy.org/pwntcha/ (2006)
11. Fukuda, K., Garrigue, M.A., Gilman, A.: Inaccessibility of CAPTCHA. W3C (2005)
12. Mori, G., Malik, J.: Recognizing objects in adversarial clutter: Breaking a visual CAPTCHA. In: CVPR. Volume 1. (2003) 134–141
13. Doctorow, C.: Solving and creating captchas with free porn. http://boingboing.net/2004/01/27/solving_and_creating.html (2004)
14. von Ahn, L., Blum, M., Hopper, N., Langford, J.: CAPTCHA: Using hard AI problems for security. Eurocrypt (2003)

Resilia: a Safe and Secure Distributed Backup System for Small and Medium Enterprises

Christian Damsgaard Jensen, Fernando Meira, and Jacob Nittegaard-Nielsen

Informatics and Mathematical Modeling
Technical University of Denmark
Christian.Jensen@imm.dtu.dk

Abstract. Most small and medium-sized enterprises (SME) operate from a single address, which means that backups are normally kept at the same physical location as the company's computers. This means that fire, flooding or other disasters are likely to destroy both computers and the backups that were meant to ensure the continued operation of the company.
The price per Giga-byte of hard disk storage is falling and at the same time the bandwidth of the connection from small companies to the Internet is increasing, so it appears logical for small companies to achieve improved availability of their backups by storing backups on the hard disk of one or more remote computers. However, storing business-critical information or customer data on a foreign computer requires a mechanism that preserves the secrecy and ensures the integrity of the stored data.
This paper presents Resilia, which is a safe and secure backup system that allows a company to distribute its backup among a number of remote servers, thereby ensuring availability, without compromising the confidentiality and the integrity of the backup. The confidentiality of data in Resilia is ensured with an encryption technique known as threshold cryptography, which means that a backup can be restored even if all cryptographic keys are lost in a disaster. We describe a working prototype of Resilia and report initial performance numbers for the developed prototype.

1 Introduction

The main goals of computer security are normally defined as ensuring the *confidentiality*, *integrity* and *availability* of resources managed by the computer system (these are commonly known as the *CIA properties*). Much of the existing research into computer security has focused on the first two goals, because they are easier to ensure from within the system, but loss of availability, in particular the loss of data stored in business information systems, may have devastating consequences for a company. It is widely reported that companies that experience major data loss face serious problems and may even be forced to close. Examples of such statistics found on the Internet [1] are: "30% of all businesses that have a major fire go out of business within a year.

---

[1] Many of these quotes are found on the websites of companies that offer backup software or services, but they are normally attributed to an independent source.

Please use the following format when citing this chapter:

Jensen, C. D., Meira, F. and Nittegaard-Neilsen, J., 2007, in IFIP International Federation for Information Processing, Volume 238, Trust Management, eds. Etalle, S., Marsh, S., (Boston: Springer), pp. 383–398.

70% fail within five years"[2], "50% of companies that lose their data in a disaster never open their doors again"[3], "93% of companies that lost their data center for 10 days or more due to a disaster filed for bankruptcy within one year of the disaster. 50% of businesses that found themselves without data management for this same time period filed for bankruptcy immediately"[4] and similar statistics can be found in the press: "Data loss costs U.S. businesses more than $18 billion a year, according to the Pepperdine study. That 2003 study is the most recent estimate available, but Smith says the number is probably much higher today."[1] It is therefore obvious that protecting a company against major data loss is of vital importance to the continued operation of that company.

Frequent and reliable backups have proven to be an important element in the protection against major data loss. By replicating data, it is possible to restore an operational system from the latest backup if the original system is destroyed. Keeping all the replicas in the same location, however, means that whatever happens to one may also happen to the other. Many small and medium enterprises operate from a single address which means that backups are normally kept at the same physical location as the company's computers. This means that fire, flooding or other disasters are likely to destroy both computers and the backups that were meant to ensure the continued operation of the company. Moreover, taking regular backups and managing the (off site) location and rotation of backup media is a cumbersome and repetitive job. While larger companies generally have the resources to accomplish this task, smaller companies generally struggle just to take backups, e.g., "40% of Small and Medium Sized Businesses don't back up their data at all"[5]. Furthermore, the dramatic increase in secondary storage (hard disk space) on most computers, mean that the volume of backups has exploded during the past decade, so backup to magnetic media is not always feasible. The growth in hard disk capacity is matched by a similar growth in bandwidth on the networks that connect small companies to the Internet, so service companies that offer remote storage for network backups have emerged. These service companies solve the problem of ensuring availability of the primary backup data, but they introduce a new problem of protecting the cryptographic keys used to protect the confidentiality and integrity of the backup data. Moreover, these services are charged at a price that exceeds the cost of the hardware needed to host the service within a few months. Developing a relatively simple and cheap networked backup service that ensures the availability of a company's backups without compromising the confidentiality and integrity of its data would therefore benefit many small and medium enterprises.

It is generally agreed that confidentiality is best ensured by keeping a single well guarded copy of the data, while availability is best ensured by keeping many replicas in different physical locations, so there appears to be an inherent conflict between confidentiality and availability. However, there exist cryptographic techniques known as *threshold cryptography schemes*, where the secret information is split into several sets of data known as *shares*, where each share in itself conveys no information about

---

[2] Attributed to the journal "Home Office Computing Magazine".

[3] Attributed to "University of Texas for research into Info systems".

[4] Attributed to the "National Archives & Records Administration in Washington".

[5] Found on the web site of the Data Deposit Box [2], attributed to the journal "Realty Times".

the secret, but a previously defined fraction of the shares are enough to reconstruct the original data. The application of such schemes to a distributed backup system means that individual share can be distributed to different backup nodes, which will learn nothing about the secret. If the backup needs to be restored, shares from the predefined fraction of backup nodes have to be retrieved in order to reconstruct the original backup. This addresses the inherent conflict between confidentiality and availability in distributed backup systems. It is easy to imagine that every member of the local commerce council makes backup space available on their servers to the other members of the commerce council. This backup space can then be used in a peer-to-peer (P2P) backup system in the same way that other digital content is shared across the Internet. Other members of the local commerce council can be assumed to be honest about storing and returning data (i.e., integrity and availability), but competitors are likely to try learning the trade secrets of each other. The encryption performed though threshold cryptography, however, means that backups may even be stored on competitors' computers, because each share conveys no information about the overall content.

Different threshold cryptography schemes have been proposed in the literature. We have developed a prototype backup system for small and medium enterprises, called Resilia, which implements two different types of schemes: *secret sharing* and Rabin's *information dispersal algorithm*. These schemes have different properties and allow us to experiment with different trade-offs between computational power and network/storage requirements. Resilia is implemented in Java [3], using the JXTA [4] platform for P2P applications, which ensures platform independency.

The rest of this paper is organized in the following way. Section 2 examines the requirements for network based backup systems. Section 3 provides an overview of threshold cryptography and the Resilia prototype is described in Section 4. The prototype is evaluated in Section 5, related work is surveyed in Section 6 and our conclusions are presented in Section 7.

2 Secure Distributed Backup Systems

Backing up data and information is probably one of the most important aspects of security on a personal computer and for any computer belonging to a distributed system. Every user wants to assure that his work does not evaporate into thin air if some unexpected event happens.

2.1 Network Storage for Backup

Any distributed backup system consists of a local agent on the machine where the backup is made, a number of remote agents on the machines where the backup is stored and a network infrastructure needed to transport the backup from the node where the backup is made to the nodes where the backup is stored.

The backup agent on the client machine is responsible for creating the backup, locating one or more remote nodes that will store the backup, transfer the backup to those nodes in a reliable way and possibly receiving a receipt from the remote backup node indicating that the backup was received. If the backup needs to be restored, the client requests the remote backup node to return the backup data to the client, which is then able to restore the data.

The backup agent on the remote backup node is responsible for receiving the backup from the client, committing the backup to persistent storage and possibly issuing a receipt to the client. If the client requests the backup, the remote backup node must retrieve the data from persistent storage and return it to the client. This architecture is illustrated in Figure 1.

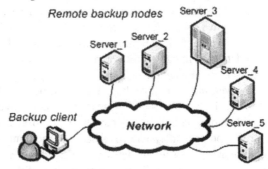

Fig. 1. Backup Network

In order to ensure the availability of the backup, data may be replicated on multiple remote backup nodes. This may either be the task of the backup agent on the client machine or the backup agent on the first remote node that receives a replica of the backup. In the first case, the client negotiates, possibly independent, service level agreements with each remote backup node, while in the second case the remote backup nodes have some predefined agreement between them to store replicas for each other. This agreement is implicit in most cases where the remote backup nodes belong to the same organisation.

2.2 Security Goals

Backups are primarily about ensuring availability and integrity. Having the ability to replace a file by a previous version limits the damage that can be done to the information stored in the file, so the security of the backup system is vital to a company's security strategy. Thus, a *secure backup* can be defined as a backup that has the following proprieties:

Confidentiality: Backups that contain sensitive data should be stored in a way that prevents unauthorised access to the stored data. In particular, backups stored on an insecure site should be protected from unauthorised access. This is normally achieved by encrypting the backup before it is stored on the insecure site, which means that the data received from the insecure site must be decrypted before the backup can be restored.

Integrity: The original data should be returned when a backup is restored. There are several ways that a backup can be modified in a distributed backup system: it may be affected by transmission errors when it is sent over the network, it may be affected by disk errors on the remote backup node or it may be modified by a malicious node that handles the backup data. Integrity is normally achieved by cryptographic means, such as message integrity codes and digital signatures.

Availability: It must always be possible to restore the backup, so the backup system must be able to function despite a fraction of the backup nodes becomes unavailable. The fraction of backup nodes that must be available determines the robustness of the backup system; if this fraction is close to one most nodes must be available and the system is considered *brittle*, but if it is close to zero most nodes may fail and the system is considered *robust*.

Survivability: It must be possible to restore the backup from any machine without special information, such as passwords or cryptographic keys. This ensures that the backup can be restored on a new computer even if all the computers and media belonging to the client's organisation are stolen or destroyed. Survivability is an essential requirement if the backup strategy forms part of a company's business continuity plan.

As mentioned above, confidentiality and integrity are normally achieved by means of cryptography. This introduces the problem of managing the keys needed to encrypt, decrypt or sign data, because these keys cannot be stored locally on the computer. Otherwise, the keys will be lost along with the system in the disaster that caused the need to restore the backup.[6] It is therefore important to develop a secure backup system that does not store cryptographic keys locally on the computer, in order to ensure the survivability of the system.

Although not considered in the definition of a secure backup, *efficiency* is a very important property of any backup-system. Backups are often made when the system is otherwise idle, i.e., during the night. This means that there is a limited time to create the backup and transfer it to the remote backup nodes. Moreover, the system may still be accessed by employees from home or by visitors to the organization's web site, so the backup system cannot utilize the full bandwidth of the organization's Internet connection. The size of the backup should therefore be as small as possible in order to conserve both disk space on the backup nodes and network bandwidth.

2.3 Threat Model

We assume that the client machine has not been compromised; otherwise an attacker would already have access to all the original data in unencrypted form. This means that there are two possible targets for an attacker: the network and the remote backup nodes.

We assume that an attacker may obtain complete control over the network, but that he cannot break strong cryptographic algorithms with brute force (this is commonly known as the Dolev-Yao threat model [5]).

---

[6] We do not here consider accidental deletion of individual files, which may cause problems, but rarely forces a company into closure.

With respect to the remote backup nodes, we assume that an attacker may have complete control over a limited number of these nodes, e.g., she may have hacked into the node or she may be the legitimate, but untrustworthy, operator of some of the nodes. Hacking systems belonging to different organisations, i.e., where systems configurations and passwords are different, is considerably more difficult than breaking into a set of homogeneous systems belonging to the same organization.

An effective countermeasure against both types of threats to remote backup nodes is therefore to ensure that the remote backup nodes belong to as many different organisations as possible. This also means that backups are likely to disperse over a larger physical area, which improves availability in the case of area specific disasters, such as earthquakes, fires and floods

2.4 Trust Model

We defined four security goals above, where the first three (CIA) concerns the security of the backup while the survivability goal concerns the design and implementation of the backup system itself. If the backup is physically stored by colleagues or competitors, we must assume that they will try to learn any sensitive information stored in the backup, they may also attempt to modify the backup in any way that cannot be detected, but we expect them to return the backup if the client attempts a restore operation. This means that we should not trust the remote backup nodes to maintain confidentiality and integrity, but we do trust that they will actually return backup data when requested, i.e., we trust that help maintain availability.

Consider a small and medium enterprise called ACME, a realistic scenario would be to form a backup network with other companies within the local council of commerce, trade association or professional organisation. Potential competitors are likely to try and obtain trade secrets or customer information from the backup data that they store, so the distributed backup system must protect against this threat. Furthermore, business partners may want to reduce the debt that they owe to ACME or either introduce or increase any debts owed by ACME to the company that stores the backup. The backup system should therefore also have effective integrity protection mechanisms. Finally, the fear of social and commercial ostracism is likely to ensure that they will actually return backup data at ACME's request. In order to sanction backup nodes that do not return backup data when requested and, at the same time, eliminate the risk of framing, the system must the protocol that transfers backup data ensures the non-repudiation of both parties.

3 Threshold Cryptography

A *threshold cryptosystem* requires a number of parties collaborate in the decryption of encrypted data. In the following, we describe two types of threshold cryptosystems, which have the desired property that decryption is possible by combining the encrypted data from the right number of participants, i.e., without requiring a cryptographic key. These types of threshold cryptosystems are a class of algorithms known as *secret sharing* schemes and a single *information dispersal algorithm*.

3.1 Secret Sharing

A *secret sharing scheme* is a model for distributing a *secret* among a group of participants. The secret information is divided into n shares, where n is the number of participants, in such a way that with any m valid shares, where $m \leq n$, it is possible to reconstruct the secret. Any attempt to reconstruct the secret using up to $m - 1$ shares is unfeasible and discloses no information about the secret. This is known as a (m, n)-*threshold scheme*.

A secret sharing scheme is limited in two ways: the size of the shares and random bits. Each share needs to be of at least the same size as the secret itself. If this is not the case, an attacker holding $m - 1$ shares will be able to learn some information about the secret. Assuming that the final share is secret, all $m - 1$ shares still reveal some information. This information cannot be secret, therefore must be random.

Secret sharing was first introduced by Shamir [6] and Blakley [7] independently in 1979. Shamir's secret sharing scheme (SSS) is based on polynomial interpolation, where $n + 1$ points uniquely determine an n-degree polynomial. Knowledge of m shares should suffice to restore the data, so a $(m - 1)$-degree polynomial is generated, which is defined by

$$f(x) = a_0 + a_1 x + a_2 x^2 + a_3 x^3 + \ldots a_{m-1} x^{m-1}$$

over a finite field. The coefficient $a0$ represents the secret, which is the polynomial intersection with the y-axis. Any other point of the polynomial may be distributed to the n participants. Figure 2 illustrates two examples of polynomials that may be used to implement schemes for $m = 2$ and $m = 3$. The figure shows the secret, point $(0, s)$, and other points that would be distributed to participants of the sharing.

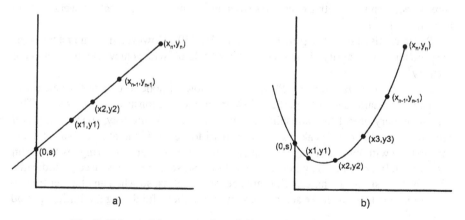

Fig. 2. Polynomials representing: a) $(2, n)$-scheme b) $(3, n)$-scheme

This scheme has two interesting proprieties. It allows different levels of control over the secret, by giving more than one share to selected participants. The more shares a single participant holds, the more control he has over the shared secret, since fewer participants are needed to reconstruct the secret. The second propriety is that the scheme allows new participants to be added to the sharing after the initial distribution has been made, without affecting the existing shares. Finally, SSS is relatively space efficient; each share only needs to be the same size as the original secret because the x-coordinates of each share can be known to everyone.

Blakley's secret sharing scheme (BSS) is based on the fact that n n-dimensional hyperplanes intersect in a single point. The secret is encoded as a single coordinate of that point, to prevent anyone who knows one or more of the hyperplanes from learning something about the secret. Each participant is given enough information to construct a hyperplane and the secret is recovered by finding the intersection of the planes and selecting the right coordinate.

Both secret sharing schemes have information theoretical security, but BSS requires m times as much storage as SSS and since we have to distribute the shares across the network as part of our backup, we have decided to focus on Shamir's scheme.

Although the secret sharing scheme presented above protects data against passive attacks, like missing shares, there are times when it is necessary to protect against active attacks, such as someone sending incorrect or corrupt shares when distributing shares or even receiving incorrect shares when restoring. This may be accomplished with *verifiable secret sharing* (VSS) schemes. Feldman's VSS scheme [8] is a well-known example that works in the following way: the distribution operation is performed the same way as Shamir's scheme, with the backup client sending each share to each remote backup node in private and also broadcasting a set of values that allows each recipient to verify that their share has not been corrupted in transit. If a user receives a corrupt share a complaint should go back to the backup client. If the backup client receives m or more complaints, then the process fails, otherwise the sender is required to broadcast correct shares to complaining users. Therefore, this scheme ensures a secure system with a cheating sender and at most $m - 1$ cheating users, as long as $2(m - 1) < n$.

Pedersen also presents a scheme to handle VSS [9]. However, his scheme weakens the protection of integrity of the secret (x) in a trade-off with achieving a true semantic security[7].

A *proactive secret sharing* (PSS) scheme allows a node to generate a new set of shares for the same secret from the old shares without reconstructing the secret. This scheme is very useful for refreshing secret shares in a secure way, such as in server recovery cases. Server break-ins are very hard to detect if the attacker steals some information without modifying anything on the victim host and covering his tracks on his way out. In order to strengthen the security, a PSS scheme may be used periodically. Thus, by refreshing all shares, old shares become useless, so when an attacker tries to steal m shares to recover the secret, these will only be valid during the limited period

---

[7] A scheme is *semantically secure* if for any function k computable on the secret, the difference $(p_1^{(k)} - p_0^{(k)})$ between the amount of knowledge learned by the adversary by watching the execution of the protocol is negligible, where $p_0^{(k)}$ and $p_1^{(k)}$ are the probabilities that an adversary correctly computes the value $k(x)$ when fed with public information and with additional information gathered during the run of the protocol, respectively.

of time between the start of two PSS operations, i.e., an attacker has to recover all m shares belonging to the same period. With an (m, n) secret sharing scheme, each server holds a share for the entire lifetime of the service, which means that the share is more exposed to threats than a system using PSS.

A safe and secure proactive secret sharing scheme is achieve by combining VSS and PSS schemes, offering a way to protect the secrecy and integrity of sensitive information. One such scheme (the one used in Resilia) was proposed by Herzberg, Jarecki, Krawczyk and Yung [10].

3.2 Information Dispersal Algorithm

The information dispersal algorithm (IDA) was proposed by Rabin [11] in 1987. It is a similar technique to SSS, but it allows a reduction of the communications overhead and the amount of information kept at each site, by sending only partial information to sites. The IDA makes use of a secret key vector, which can be seen as an $n \times m$ matrix, to process the input data. As in the SSS scheme, n stands for the number of participants of the sharing and m the number of required participants to recover the secret. For the main operation in the algorithm, the key matrix is repeatedly multiplied by fix-sized blocks of input data, which can be seen as an $m \times 1$ matrix, until all the data is processed.

We define the key vector as a set of n vectors, $V_1, V_2, \ldots, V_n$, each of length m, $(V_i = (a_{i_1}, \ldots, a_{i_m}))$, with the condition that any subset of m vectors are linearly independent, and the input data as $b_1, b_2, \ldots, b_N$, then the IDA result, c, is achieved by combining values in the following way, for $i = 1, \ldots, n$ and $k = 1, \ldots, N/m$:

$$c_{i_k} = a_{i_1} \cdot b_{(k-1)_{m+1}} + \ldots + a_{i_m} \cdot b_{k_m}$$

The IDA process adds some bits of redundancy that allows some communication errors to be corrected at the reconstruction stage. From each block of a complete key vector computation, that is $c_1, \ldots, c_n$, a value c_i is sent to each participant. It is important to note that there is a link between all n key vectors, all n participants and all n values of each resulting block. Participant number two must always receive value number two of each resulting block, which is represented by vector key number two. This relationship is important at the reconstruction stage.

Thus, each site will store a share of the size $|F|/m$, where $|F|$ is the size of the original data. This represents a total overhead of $((n/m) - 1) \cdot 100$ percent of the size of the original data.

To reconstruct the original data m valid shares are required. With less than m shares, it is infeasible to restore the data. The reconstruction of the data is done by:

$$b_j = a_{i_1} \cdot c_{(1)_k} + \ldots + a_{i_m} \cdot c_{m_k}$$

where $1 \le j \le N$. The key vector used for the reconstruction is composed by only the vectors that correspond to the participants' shares used. This results in an $m \times m$ matrix, which is inverted before of the reconstruction of the data.

The advantage of IDA over SSS is that IDA can tolerate the failure of k remote backup nodes by adding $k \cdot |F|/m$ bits to the backup, where SSS requires $k \cdot |F|$ bits to be added.

4 Resilia

The existing prototype of Resilia implements a safe and secure distributed peer-to-peer backup system for small and medium enterprises. Resilia has been designed to satisfy the four security requirements for distributed backup systems (cf. Section 2.2), where traditional cryptography may be used to ensure confidentiality and integrity while threshold cryptography is used to ensure the availability and survivability requirements. The current version of Resilia supports both a combination of a verifiable secret sharing (VSS)[8] scheme and a proactive secret sharing (PSS) scheme [10] and Rabin's information dispersal algorithm (IDA)[9]. The following description of Resilia is very short and we refer to the reports [12, 13] for further details.

Resilia allows any group of users to set up a P2P network, to establish peer groups and to distribute, restore, delete and update their backup files in a secure way. The physical dispersion of the nodes in these peer groups determines the extent of the disaster that the system can tolerate.

A file backup can be performed in two different ways, either using the SSS or the IDA. An overview of the backup agent architecture (both client and remote node) is shown in Figure 3.

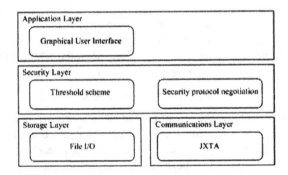

Fig. 3. Resilia Agent Architecture

The Resilia agent architecture is divided into three layers, the *Application Layer*, which manages interaction with the users, the *Security Layer*, which performs the threshold cryptography, authenticates the other nodes in the backup system and establishes secure communication channels with the remote backup nodes.

4.1 Backup and Restore Operations

When a user wishes to backup (part of) her system, she selects the files to be backed up and the threshold scheme to be used in the graphical user interface. The Secu-

---

[8] The implementation of VSS was developed as part of Jacob Nittegaard-Nielsen's Master Thesis project [12].

[9] The implementation of Rabin's IDA was introduced by Fernando Meira as part of his Final Year project [13].

rity Layer then instantiates the right threshold cryptosystem and starts locating remote backup nodes. The Storage Layer then reads the selected files and creates a backup file, which is handed to the threshold cryptosystem, which performs the necessary threshold cryptography operations [10] and send the shares to the remote backup nodes through the Communication Layer.

If a backup needs to be restored after a disaster, the user selects the restore option from the graphical user interface. The system will then use the lookup service in the Communication Layer to find remote backup nodes that store backups from this node. This requires that the remote backup nodes are able to identify user and authenticate the backup client (cf. Section 4.2). The backup agent will determine which backups can be restored, i.e., where m of n remote backup nodes have responded, and presents them in a list to the user. The user decides which backups to restore (there may be old backups in the list) and starts the restore operation, which performs the necessary threshold cryptography operations to retrieve the backup file. The backup file is then handed to the Storage Layer, which restores the backup on disk.

4.2 Resilia Node Authentication

In order to prevent a malicious backup client from broadcasting a request to restore the backup of another machine, the nodes in the backup system needs an authentication mechanism. Resilia implements an authentication mechanism based on certificates, which contain the identity of the backup agent and the public-key needed in the authentication protocol. It is important to note that we do not require a full public key infrastructure, because certificates may be distributed by other means, e.g., through a mechanism similar to PGP [14] or at certificate exchange sessions at the local council of commerce.

The client certificate prevents malicious backup agents from restoring the backup from another machine, but it also helps ensure availability because, if a client machine is stolen or destroyed, the user may revoke the existing certificate and request a new certificate from the same source where she got the original certificate. This new certificate contains the same ID as the original certificate, which is all that is needed to allow the client to restore the backup.

Servers also have certificates, which prevent a malicious user from flooding the backup network with (virtual) backup servers, in order to receive enough shares to restore the backup of client machines.

5 Evaluation

In the following we present a short analysis of some security properties of the developed prototype, but the main focus will be on a performance evaluation of the two

---

[10] The operations required to perform threshold cryptography are computation-intensive, but in the case of SSS, we simply encrypt the file using a block cipher (in our case AES) and a randomly generated session-key. This means that we only perform threshold cryptography on a small data structure containing the session-key and some other meta-data describing the backup, so our implementation of SSS is significantly less computation-intensive than IDA.

threshold cryptography schemes, which allows us to compare their relative merit for a backup system designed for small and medium enterprises.

5.1 Security Analysis

Different attacks can be performed to breach the security of both backup clients and servers. An attacker may also attempt to compromise packets send across the network in different ways. Some of these attacks and the countermeasures implemented in Resilia are analysed in the following.

A network packet holds important information, but an attacker has to gather m correct packets in order to compromise a backup file. By "correct" we mean any m of the n packets corresponding to the same backup file. This corresponds to an attacker controlling the right m remote backup nodes for a particular backup. As there are several potential backup nodes for every backup file, the odds that an attacker guesses where to find all shares and breaking in to all those hosts are minimal. If the attacker is able to intercept all packets originating from a backup client, she will know all the shares and will be able to reconstruct the backup, this is why communication between backup agents has to be authenticated and encrypted.

As mentioned before, we expect a fraction of the remote backup nodes to be under the control of one or more attackers. Keeping the number of shares needed to restore the backup relatively high, means that many nodes have to be compromised by the same attacker or different attackers have to collude in order to restore the backup. This does not provide strong security in itself, but it increases the risk of discovery and therefore acts as an effective deterrent against collusion between malicious backup servers.

5.2 Performance Evaluation

The two threshold cryptosystems implemented in Resilia have different requirements with respect to computational power, network bandwidth and storage capacity. We examine these differences in the following.

We have conducted a series of experiments with backup on a local area network, but we have chosen to present the results of a single experiment, where a 5 Kilobyte backup was distributed to 6 nodes where 4 were needed to restore the backup, i.e., we perform threshold cryptography with $n = 6$ and $m = 4$.

The amount of data transmitted over the network and stored on the remote backup nodes is shown in Figure 4. The IDA is expected to distribute $6/4 \cdot 5$ KB, which is effectively what can be seen in Figure 4. The SSS distributes the full encrypted backup and a share of the meta-data to all nodes which means that the total amount of data transmitted is a little more than $6 \cdot 5$ KB, which is also seen in Figure 4. Figure 5 shows the same results, but focus on a different aspect: the data overhead achieved by each scheme. Using the IDA, the defined parameters generate a 50% of added redundancy to the file, which means that total data dispersed over the 6 nodes is equal to the size of the file plus an overhead of 33%. The resulting overhead using the SSS scheme is $|F| \cdot (n - 1)$, which represents more than 80% of the total transmitted data.

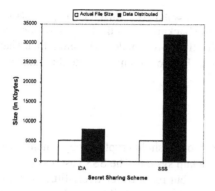

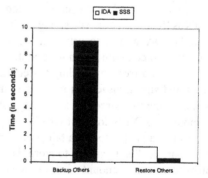

Fig. 4. Volume of backup data distributed to remote nodes.

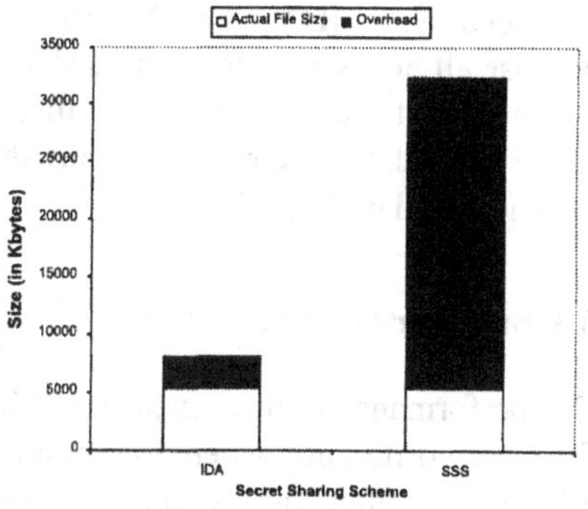

Fig. 5. Communications and storage overhead.

The SSS runs over a small amount of data, the session-key and the meta-data, so the computational power required to construct a share is relatively small. The IDA, on the other hand, runs over the whole file which requires significantly more processing power. We have measured the time needed to perform the necessary threshold cryptography operations on both clients and servers. Figure 6 and 7 show the results of these measurements for backing up and restoring a file. The measured times include all operations on the client that performs the backup and the backup nodes that receive the backup shares and reply with a confirmation message.

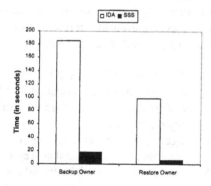

Fig. 6. Computation required on backup client.

Fig. 7. Computation required on remote backup node

The results, shown in Figure 6, illustrates that if the IDA is used, the backup client has to perform an expensive IDA operation on the entire backup-file for both backup and restore operations, while the SSS only needs to operate on the meta-data which is significantly faster (about 10% of the time required for the IDA). However, the use of a verifiable secret sharing scheme means that some computation is required by the remote backup node when it receives a backup using the SSS, while little processing is needed by the IDA. The IDA is slightly more expensive when a backup is restored because all nodes have to return a share of the backup file. In the SSS, only one node has to return the encrypted backup file, while all the other nodes only return their share of the meta-data. The measurements shown in Figure 7 do not include the transfer of the encrypted backup file.

5.3 Summary of Evaluation

Our performance evaluation shows that the two threshold cryptography schemes perform very differently when used in a P2P backup system. The SSS based system has a large communications and storage overhead, but requires relatively little computational power. The IDA provides similar availability with significantly less communication and storage overhead, but the IDA has to be applied to the entire backup file, which is a computationally expensive operation.

If the client has limited processing power but a high bandwidth network connection, the SSS should probably be used. On the other hand, plenty of processing power but a network connection with limited bandwidth, then the IDA is probably the best solution.

6 Related Work

A number of secure P2P backup systems have been proposed in the research literature.

pStore combines peer-to-peer systems with techniques for incremental backup systems, which include file encryption and versioning [15]. It shares many of the same goals as Resilia, but off-site storage is fully replicated, requiring higher resource-usage than the IDA, and its security relies on ownership tags. Furthermore, pStore is a pure research project, with no implementation.

DIBS is a freeware backup system that uses Gnu Privacy Control (GPG)[11] to encrypt and sign transactions in order to achieve confidentiality and authenticity [16]. Restore operations require knowledge of the cryptographic keys stored on the local computer, so DIBS does not satisfy the survivability requirement.

Samsara [17] enforces a fair peer-to-peer storage system without requiring trusted third-parties. Peers willing to store data in Samsara have to guarantee that they can provide the same amount of disk space to other peers. It ensures availability and durability through replication, and is used as punishment mechanism for cheating nodes, that have eventually lost data. Samsara was designed as an extension of Pastiche [18].

The CleverSafe Dispersed Storage [19] is an open-source application that is able to disperse a document to 11 storage locations throughout the world. It is implemented in C++ programming language and uses a version of Rabin's IDA to disperse the information. The storage locations are part of a grid, which keeps data private and safe from natural disasters.

---

[11] GPG is an open source implementation of the well known PGP system.

CleverSafe IDA, also named CleverSafe Turbo IDA, disperses the data into 11 slices, each slice is stored in a different node of the grid. To retrieve the information, at least 6 nodes need to be available. This setup is fixed and cannot be modified. A default grid is already set up and available to users, but users are free to set up their own grid. The advantage of restricting the IDA setup to a 6-out-of-11 scheme for all users is mainly in the ability to optimize the algorithm for this specific case. The optimized algorithm performs significantly better than the general implementation of Rabin's IDA. Although a 6-out-of-11 scheme represents a good balance between availability and storage overhead, it is not possible to shift this balance to suit a particular application. In other words, it is not possible to increase the availability of an important backup, nor reducing the amount of space used to store less important but large backups. Moreover, CleverSafe only supports IDA which we have shown requires significant computational power compared to an implementation of the SSS which only performs threshold cryptography operations on the meta-data.

Another P2P backups system based on IDA is presented by Bella at al. [20]. This work is based on the Chord [21] P2P protocol, which is a proven protocol that supports a dynamic configuration of peers, i.e., new peers may join the network and existing peers may leave the network. The system uses a "meta data file" stored by the backup client, which ensures that only the owner may initiate a restore operation. However, this also means that the backup cannot be restored if the client is stolen or completely destroyed, so their system does not meet the survivability requirement that we defined for Resilia. Finally, no evaluation of the implementation has been reported, so it is unclear to what degree the system actually works.

7 Conclusions

In this paper we addressed the problem of maintaining safe and secure off-site backups in small and medium enterprises. We proposed to build a safe and secure backup service based on threshold cryptography, and presented Resilia which is our prototype implementation of this proposal.

Resilia implements two types of threshold cryptography, secret sharing and Rabin's information dispersal algorithm. We showed that combining efficient block ciphers with secret sharing of keys and meta-data produces a system with low computational overhead, but full copies of all backup data have to be distributed to and stored on all the remote backup nodes. The implementation of Rabin's IDA requires significantly less communication and remote storage, but requires significantly more computational power. The best choice of threshold cryptography therefore depends on the backup client's environment.

Although Resilia was developed for small and medium enterprises, we believe that the techniques presented in this paper may also benefit large providers of backup services, who would only need to operate a single facility and rely on mutual arrangements with competitors to ensure replication of their clients' data.

References

1. S. Armour (2006) Lost digital data cost businesses billions. In USA TODAY 12 June 2006.
2. Data Deposit Box (2007) Data Loss Quotes and Statistics. Available at URL: http://www.datadepositbox.com/media/data-loss-statistics.asp, visited 21 February 2007.
3. Sun Developer Network (2007) Java Tecchnology: Reference. Available at URL: http://java.sun.com/reference/index.html, visited 21 February 2007
4. J. D. Gradecki (2002) Mastering JXTA: building Java peer-to-peer applications. Wiley Publishing
5. D. Dolev, A. C. Yao (1981) On the security of public key protocols. In Proceedings of the IEEE 22nd Annual Symposium on Foundations of Computer Science, pp. 350–357
6. A. Shamir (1979) How to share a secret. In Communications of the ACM, vol. 22, no. 11, pp. 612–613
7. G. R. Blakley (1979) Safeguarding cryptographic keys. In AFIPS 1979 NCC, Vol. 48, pp. 313–317.
8. P. Feldman (1987) A practical scheme for non-interactive verifiable secret sharing. In Proceedings of the 28th IEEE Symposium on Foundations of Computer Science (FOCS '87)
9. T. P. Pedersen (1991) Non-interactive and information-theoretic secure verifiable secret sharing. In Proceedings of Crypto'91 (LNCS 576), pp. 129–140
10. A. Herzberg, S. Jarecki, H. Krawczyk, and M. Yung (1995) Proactive secret sharing or: How to cope with perpetual leakage. In Proceedings of Crypto'95 (LNCS 963)
11. M. O. Rabin (1989) Efficient dispersal of information for security, load balancing, and fault tolerance. In Journal of the ACM, Vol. 36, No. 2, pp. 335–348
12. J. Nittegaard-Nielsen (2004) Sikkert og plideligt peer-to-peer filsystem. Master's thesis, Technical University of Denmark (in Danish)
13. F. Meira (2005) Resilia: A safe & secure backup-system. Final year project, Engineerng Faculty of the University of Porto
14. S. Garfinkel (1994) PGP: Pretty Good Privacy. O'Reilly
15. C. Batten, K. Barr, A. Saraf, and S. Trepetin (2002) pStore: A secure peer-to-peer backup system. Technical Memo MIT-LCS-TM-632, Massachusetts Institute of Technology Laboratory for Computer Science
16. E. Martinian (2007) Distributed internet backup system (dibs). Available at URL http://www.csua.berkeley.edu/~emin/source_code/dibs
17. L. P. Cox and B. D. Noble (2003) Samsara: honor among thieves in peer-to-peer storage. In Proceedings of the nineteenth ACM symposium on Operating systems principles
18. L. P. Cox, C. D. Murray, and B. D. Noble (2002) Pastiche: making backup cheap and easy. SIGOPS Opererating Systems Review, 36(SI):285–298
19. CleverSafe Project (2007) Cleversafe dispersed storage project. Available at URL http://www.cleversafe.org/wiki/Cleversafe_Dispersed_Storage
20. G. Bella, C. Pistagna, S. Riccobene (2006) Distributed Backup through Information Dispersal. In Electronic Notes in Theoretical Computer Science, Vol 142:63–77
21. I. Stoica, R. Morris, D. Karger, M. F. Kaashoek, H. Balakrishnan (2001) Chord: A Scalable Peer-to-peer Lookup Service for Internet Applications. In Proceedings of the 2001 ACM SIGCOMM Conference

All websites were last visited in February 2007.

Integrity in Open Collaborative Authoring Systems

Christian Damsgaard Jensen

Informatics and Mathematical Modelling
Technical University of Denmark
Christian.Jensen@imm.dtu.dk

Abstract. Open collaborative authoring systems have become increasingly popular within the past decade. The benefits of such systems is best demonstrated by the Wiki and some of the tremendously popular applications build on Wiki technology, in particular the Wikipedia, which is a free encyclopaedia collaboratively edited by Internet users with a minimum of administration.

One of the most serious problems that have emerged in open collaborative authoring systems relates to the quality, especially completeness and correctness of information. Inaccuracies in the Wikipedia have been rumoured to cause students to fail courses, innocent people have been associated with the killing of John F. Kennedy, etc. Improving the correctness, completeness and integrity of information in collaboratively authored documents is therefore of vital importance to the continued success of such systems. In this paper we propose an integrity mechanism for open collaborative authoring systems based on a combination of classic integrity mechanisms from computer security and reputation systems. While the mechanism provides a reputation based assessment of the trustworthiness of the information in a document, the primary purpose is to prevent untrustworthy authors from compromising the integrity of the document.

1 Collaborative Authoring Systems

Collaborative authoring systems which support an open and dynamic population of authors, such as the Wiki [1], have become increasingly popular over the past couple of years. Large pieces of documentation, such as the Wikipedia [2], have been compiled using this type of technology and the Wiki technology has become an indispensable part of many computer supported collaborative work (CSCW) tools that support a distributed user base. The Wikipedia project has demonstrated the benefits of this approach by compiling a comprehensive and largely accurate encyclopaedia from the contributions of individual people located around the world. However, the Wikipedia has also exposed one of the weaknesses of collaborative authoring, which is that malicious or incompetent users may compromise the integrity of the document by introducing erroneous entries or corrupting existing entries, e.g., a public figure has found that the entry describing them in the Wikipedia had been modified to defame him [3].

The quality of a collaboratively authored document is determined by a few simple properties, such as whether the document is complete, correct and unbiased. Some of these properties correspond to the properties ensured by existing integrity mechanisms

Please use the following format when citing this chapter:

Jensen, C. D., 2007, in IFIP International Federation for Information Processing, Volume 238, Trust Management, eds. Etalle, S., Marsh, S., (Boston: Springer), pp. 399–402.

in computer security, so we intend to leverage this work when designing an integrity mechanism for open collaborative authoring systems. Classic integrity mechanisms [4, 5] associate an integrity level with every author (subject) and document (object), so that authors are assigned the integrity level of the documents that they work on and authors with low integrity are prevented from updating documents with higher integrity levels. Data protected by an integrity mechanism, however, normally have well defined syntax and semantics, whereas the syntax and semantics of collaboratively authored documents are difficult to define. This means that existing integrity mechanisms cannot be used directly. The obvious answer to this problem is to rely on feedback from the users, i.e., some reputation system similar to the ones used by Amazon [6], which corresponds to the approach that is already used in a Wiki. Reputation systems have previously been proposed as an effective means to assess the quality of information from uncertain sources [7, 8], but they only help automate detection of undesirable content and are generally unable to prevent undesirable content from being introduced into the document.

2 A Reputation-based Integrity Mechanism

We propose a combination of reputation systems to assess the quality of collaboratively authored documents and traditional integrity mechanisms to prevent unknown or untrusted users from modifying the documents in the collaborative authoring system. The mechanism automatically assigns a "quality rating" to every document in the system, based on the reputation of the last user who updated the document. In order to enforce integrity, we want that only users with a similar or higher reputation than the past user will be able to modify the entry. This means that users with a poor reputation will be unable to update most of the documents in the systems, but more importantly that documents that have a high quality rating may only be modified by the few users who have an equally high reputation. The integrity mechanism is based on two fundamental integrity models: the static integrity model and the dynamic integrity model, which capture respectively the static and dynamic properties of integrity control.

2.1 Static Integrity Model

All authors must have an identifier (possibly a pseudonym) which will allow the system to recognise authors and associate them with a quality confidence value (QCV), which indicates the normal level of correctness, completeness and lack of bias in documents by that author, i.e., it encodes the reputation of that author.

Each section of the document has an integrity level (IL) associated with it, which corresponds to the QCV of the latest author. This means that it is the integrity level (QCV) of the author that determines the current integrity level (IL) of the document, the integrity label of a document is modified to reflect the integrity label of the author, which is the opposite of the low watermark policy [5]. Moreover, authors are only allowed to modify a document if their QCV is higher than the IL of the document, so authors with a poor reputation cannot modify high integrity documents. We believe that it is reasonable to assume that authors who have a history of writing complete, correct and unbiased documents are likely to continue in that style, so new documents edited by such authors will benefit from their involvement, i.e., the document will be raised to the higher level of the author.

2.2 Dynamic Integrity Model

New accounts are created with a QCV which is lower than any other integrity label in the system. This means that newly created accounts are only able to modify documents by other new authors and create new documents at the lowest integrity level. Authors who create enough quality documents will eventually be promoted, so they will be allowed to contribute to documents with higher integrity levels.

Authors are promoted as a consequence of the promotion of documents that they have authored. This requires a mechanism to assess the quality of their work, which can be done automatically, e.g., at regular intervals using some of the existing information rating techniques [7, 8], or manually using feedback from the users (readers and/or other authors). While the automatic techniques look promising, we believe that they are not yet sufficiently mature for general use, so we propose a simpler and more transparent manual approach, which is initiated by the author who wishes to promote one of his documents.[1] The documents are forwarded to a number of higher integrity authors who use a voting mechanism to decide on the promotion. The group of higher integrity authors who are asked to vote on the promotion, should include a decreasing number of members with an increasing QCV in order to prevent a hoard of vandals from promoting each other. If one of the documents are promoted, then the QCV of the author is updated to the new IL of the document.

Finally, we need a mechanism to deal with any documents that are mistakenly promoted. Any author whose QCV dominates the IL of the document may request that the document is demoted, using essentially the same mechanism as promotion. If a document is demoted, so are the integrity labels of the latest author to modify the document and the author who initiated the promotion.

3 Discussion

In this paper, we proposed a mechanism which combines existing assessment techniques with integrity control mechanisms from computer security, in order to provide quality information to the reader and prevent untrustworthy users from corrupting high quality documents.

Documents are internally labelled with an integrity label, which provides the reader with an idea about the provenance of the document and whether the content should be trusted. The system also associates integrity labels with authors, which allows the system to prevent authors who have primarily authored low quality documents from

---

[1] The complete details of the protocols and mechanisms needed to promote and demote authors and documents are too lengthy to be included here.

modifying documents with a high integrity (quality) label. The integrity mechanism is designed to ensure that the editing process does not lower the integrity of documents.

The proposed integrity mechanism for open collaborative authoring systems has the following integrity properties:

1. Unknown authors can only modify the documents of other unknown authors
2. Normal authoring procedures will never decrease the integrity label of documents
3. Collaborative filtering techniques are used to promote documents that are complete, correct and unbiased to a higher integrity level

We believe that these properties will help raise the quality of documents produced and stored in open collaborative authoring systems. The system is currently being developed at the Technical University of Denmark and we expect that the implementation of the mechanism in an existing Wiki system will allow us to experiment more with such policies in a real world environment.

References

1. What is Wiki. http://www.wiki.org/wiki.cgi?WhatIsWiki, visited 28 December 2006
2. Wikipedia, the free encyclopedia. http://en.wikipedia.org/wiki/Wiki, visited 28 December 2006
3. John Seigenthaler (2005) A false Wikipedia 'biography'. Editorial in USA TODAY, 29 November 2005
4. K. J. Biba (1977) Integrity Considerations for Secure Computer Systems. Technical Report MTR-3153, The MITRE Corporation, Bedford, Massachusetts, U.S.A.
5. Timothy Fraser (2000) LOMAC: LowWater-Mark Integrity Protection for COTS Environments. In Proceedings of the IEEE Symposium on Security and Privacy, Oakland, California, U.S.A.
6. Amazon website. http://www.amazon.com, visited 28 December 2006
7. Pierpaolo Dondio, Stephen Barrett, Stefan Weber and Jean-Marc Seigneur (2006) Extracting Trust from Domain Analysis: a Case Study on Wikipedia Project. In Proceedings of the 3rd International Conference on Autonomic and Trusted Computing, IEEE, 2006
8. Ilya Zaihrayeu, Paulo Pinheiro da Silva and Deborah L. McGuinness (2005) IWTrust: Improving User Trust in Answers from the Web. In Proceedings of 3rd International Conference on Trust Management, Rocquencourt, France, 2005

Service-Oriented Approach to Visualize IT Security Performance Metrics

Clemens Martin, Mustapha Refai

1 University of Ontario Institute of Technology, Canada
clemens.martin@uoit.ca

2 University of Ontario Institute of Technology, Canada
mustapha.refai@mycampus.uoit.ca

Abstract. In this paper we propose a metrics visualization system design. Visualization is a key component in our Policy-Based Metrics Framework for Information Security Performance Measurement. To achieve openness and interoperability we have based our approach on a Service Oriented Architecture. The tight integration of a visualization component into our framework allows improved control of the metrics collection process, gives continuous access to security performance information, shows deviations between current data and set targets and displays developing trends. Thus management is enabled to more thoroughly understand their business' security posture and is supported in their IT security related decision making processes.

1 Introduction

Measuring security performance is slowly becoming a more and more accepted tool to management, because "if you cannot measure performance, you cannot control it and if you cannot control it, you cannot improve it" as [1] expresses it.

We observe that businesses deploy more and more security measures throughout their organization by installing security products, establishing security teams and following security programs; however, little work has been done with regard to measure the effectiveness of these measures. Moreover, the automation of the performance measurement processes resulting in solid metrics becomes a necessary tool that management will depend on to understand their business' security posture at any given time. Although metrics programs have been accepted as a valid approach to measure overall IT security performance, the lack of a comprehensive approach supporting the development and automating the collection of security metrics and providing a clear view of the overall IT security posture is indisputable [2].

We present a visualization approach as a key component in our Policy-Based Metrics Framework for Information Security Performance Measurement. To achieve openness and interoperability we have based our approach on a Service Oriented

Please use the following format when citing this chapter:

Martin, C. and Refai, M., 2007, in IFIP International Federation for Information Processing, Volume 238, Trust Management, eds. Etalle, S., Marsh, S., (Boston: Springer), pp. 403–406.

Architecture. Our approach is embedded in our framework that is based on the seventeen security control areas as proposed by the U.S. National Institute of Standards and Technology (NIST) in [3, 4] to measure security performance because these controls are widely accepted as the minimum requirements for metrics programs.

This paper is organized as follows: Section 2 contains a brief discussion of our approach for a Policy Based Security Metrics Framework. We detail the Service Oriented Architecture Approach to Metrics Visualization in Section 3. We discuss the results of our work and present our conclusions in the final section.

2 Framework for a Policy-Based Metrics Approach

We base our approach on the seventeen security controls areas as proposed by NIST in [3, 4] to measure security performance because these controls are widely accepted as the minimum requirements for metrics programs. We propose to expand these controls by one additional control a Policy Performance Control. This control is intended to monitor and measure organization security policies vis-à-vis their completeness and effectiveness to the business' IT security goals. The framework is a starting point for our policy-based metrics approach. Establishing an organization's security policy entails capturing mission and objectives of the organization. We introduce a set of modules and components that interact in providing a comprehensive overview of an organization's security posture.

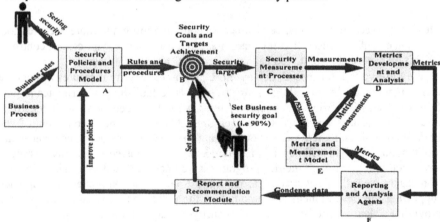

Fig. 1. Security performance framework

Improving the security performance of an organization has to be based on a good understanding of the current security situation with respect to all of the security controls. This level of security can be considered as the baseline toward achieving the next desired security goal set by the organization (Fig. 1).

The framework is composed of the following components: Security Policies and Procedures Model, Security Goals and Targets Achievement, Security Measurement Processes, Metrics Development and Analysis, Metrics and Measurement Model, Reporting and Analysis Agents, and Report and Recommendation Module.

3   Metrics Visualization

The power of visualization is the ability to combine and condense complex information for the stakeholder in an easily understandable way. The visual components we are proposing attempt to simplify the complexity of the results of IT security measurement processes, and provide snapshots of the organization's security posture at any given point in time. We present the underlying data in a set of situation-adjusted graphical representations alongside recommendations to address identified security problems. Reports and recommendations are derived from the NIST guides and recommendations [3-6].

We have designed our metrics framework to work on a distributed system that includes all running systems within the organization's network that need to be monitored and analyzed for security performance measurement purposes.

The overall system is composed of three major components: Control Manager, Agents, and the Reporting and User Interface. The Control Manager is the central component within the metrics framework. Its role is to manage and control communication with different services, such as communicating with agents on different systems, or with another instance of the Control Manager on a different server. It is responsible for the persistence of the relevant metrics data, the question and role-based survey pools, the infrastructure and organizational models, as well as configuration settings for distributed Agents and roles. The Control Manager interacts with the Agents to distribute measurement, data collection, and condensation tasks and retrieve results from them.

The Control Manager consists of the Access Control Manager, Central Processing Services, Reporting, and User Interface Support Services. It plays an important role in providing an interface between the services, Agents, and systems. The design of all system components has been chosen to be service-oriented to achieve interoperability and scalability. Thus, we can separate the services that produce and expose functionality from the consumers that use the services, enabling the extensibility and adaptability of the framework.

Agents on the other hand are services that perform data analysis on logs, reports, or events generated by the system in the network. Once Agents are satisfied with analysis and metrics extraction, they communicate their findings back to the central services. The design has the form of pyramid view where the base represents the system that holds the data to be analyzed and extract metrics from. The middle layer represents information that is extracted from the data layer. The top layer represents the information that can be presented through the user interface components as reports, recommendations, and security posture diagrams.

Agents can be deployed on organization machines/devices to monitor the security performance of the security application running on those devices - Intrusion Detection/Prevention, vulnerability scanner, firewall, etc. They can be configured and instructed by the Control Manager, and then report their findings back to it. A flexible Agent system can accommodate a wide variety of devices and their performance capabilities. One of the main advantages of this design is the ability and flexibility of Agents' deployment across the network. Furthermore, it offers an excellent way of automating the data collection from the systems in question without the need for human interference. In a similar fashion, the Reporting and User Interface subsystem is constructed in an Agent-based approach. Thus, it can easily be deployed on display devices on the network and communicate with the Control Manager for its visualization tasks. The diagram represents the level of achievement with respect to the 17 NIST controls, as well as our newly introduced policy performance control. We also present an overall security posture of the organization as a weighted mean of the individual control achievement levels.

4   Conclusion and Future Work

We attempt to provide an answer to the question about the current state of organizational security – its security posture – by collecting and condensing data to visual representations of past and current situations and bring them in context with future goals. Our design approach is a step toward achieving this goal. Its advantage is the automation of data collection whenever possible to avoid human error and improve the trustworthiness of the end result. It is based on a service-oriented architecture approach that provides flexibility and scalability. Furthermore, it is designed with security in mind and we have implemented and tested the services that support the notion of XML digital signature and encryption, as well as XACML access control process service. We are currently implementing the remaining modules of the framework in order to demonstrate an integrated IT security performance measurement methodology across a complete organization.

Acknowledgment

This work is currently being funded by the Bell University Labs and the Faculty of Business & Information Technology at the University of Ontario Institute of Technology.

References

1. T. Bahil and D. Frank. (2006, May 19, 2006). What is systems engineering? A consensus of senior systems engineers. [Online]. 2006(June 2), pp. 13. Available: http://www.sie.arizona.edu/sysengr/whatis/whatis.html

2. F. Robrt. (2004, April 09, 2004). Collecting effective security metrics. [Online]. 2006(May 20), pp. 5. Available: http://www.csoonline.com/analyst/report2412.html

3. NIST 800-53. (2006, July 2006). Security metrics guide for information technology system. [Online]. 2006(May 15), pp. 159. Available: http://csrc.nist.gov/publications/drafts/800-53-rev1-clean-sz.pdf

4. NIST SP 800-80. (2006, May 2006). Guide for developing performance metrics for information security. [Online]. 2006(June 1), Available: http://csrc.nist.gov/publications/drafts/draft-sp800-80-ipd.pdf

5. NIST 800-26. (2005, August 2005). Security metrics guide for information technology system. [Online]. 2006(May 15), pp. 106. Available: http://csrc.nist.gov/publications/drafts/Draft-sp800-26Rev1.pdf

6. NIST 800-55. (2003, July 2003). Security metrics guide for information technology system. [Online]. 2006(May 15), pp. 99. Available: http://csrc.nist.gov/publications/nistpubs/800-55/sp800-55.pdf

From Early Requirements Analysis towards Secure Workflows [*]

Ganna Frankova[1], Fabio Massacci[1], and Magali Seguran[2]

[1] DIT - University of Trento
email: {ganna.frankova,fabio.massacci}@unitn.it
[2] SAP Labs France, SAP Research - Security and Trust
email: magali.seguran@sap.com

Abstract. Requirements engineering is a key step in the software development process that has little counterpart in the design of secure business processes and secure workflows for web services. This paper presents a methodology that allows a business process designer to derive the skeleton of the concrete coarse grained secure business process, that can be further refined into workflows, from the early requirements analysis.

1 Introduction

There are many requirements engineering frameworks for modeling and analysing security requirements, such as *SI**/Secure Tropos, UMLsec, MisuseCase, and AntiGoals. There are several methodologies aim to web services and business processes design [8, 4, 9]. We noticed that there is a gap among the requirements engineering methodologies and the actual production of software and business processes based on a Service-Oriented Architecture (SOA). Business processes and security issues are developed separately and often do not follow the same strategy [6]. The existing design methodologies for web services do not address the issue of developing secure business processes and secure workflows. An overview of approaches aimed to use requirements engineering methodologies in the context of web services can be found in [1]. There are a number of security standards in the area of SOA. For instance, WS-Federation defines the mechanisms for federating trust, WS-Trust enables security token interoperability, WS-Security covers the low level details such as message content integrity and confidentiality. The question we address in this paper is "How to obtain a secure workflow from the early requirements analysis?".

We address the issue of secure workflows design based on early requirements analysis by presenting a methodology that bridges the gap between early requirements analysis and secure workflows for web services development. We introduce a language for secure business processes description, which is a dialect of WS-BPEL for the functional parts and abstracts away low level implementation details from WS-Trust, WS-Security and WS-Federation specifications.

---

[*] This work has been partly supported by the IST-FP6-IP-SERENITY project

---

Please use the following format when citing this chapter:

Frankova, G., Massacci, F. and Seguran, M., 2007, in IFIP International Federation for Information Processing, Volume 238, Trust Management, eds. Etalle, S., Marsh, S., (Boston: Springer), pp. 407–410.

2 The *SI**/Secure Tropos framework

SI*/Secure Tropos is a formal framework and a methodology for modelling and analysing security requirements [2, 5]. In this work we employ the early security requirements analysis to design secure business process and secure workflow. *SI**/Secure Tropos uses the concepts of actor and goal. Actors can be *agents* or *roles*. *SI**/Secure Tropos also supports the notion of *delegation of permission* and *delegation of execution* to model the transfer of entitlements and responsibilities from an actor to another. *Trust of permission* and *trust of execution* are used to model the expectation of one actor about the behavior and capabilities of another actor. The meaning of trust of permission is that a trustor trusts that trustee will at least fulfill a service while trust of execution means that trustor trusts that trustee will at most fulfill a service, but will not overstep it.

From a methodological perspective, *SI**/Secure Tropos is based on the idea of building a model of the system that is incrementally refined and extended. Specifically, goal analysis consists of refining goals and eliciting new social relationships among actors. They are conducted from the perspective of single actors using AND/OR decomposition. In case an actor does not have the capabilities to achieve his own objectives or assigned responsibilities by himself, he has to delegate them to other actors making their achievement outside his direct control.

3 Secure workflows design based on early requirements

A secure business process is originated by the early requirements analysis and then is used to the development of an appropriate workflow.

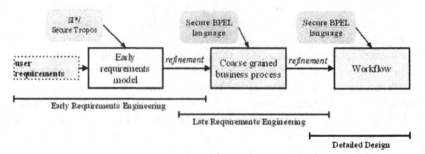

Fig. 1. Relations among early requirements, business process and workflow levels.

The process of deriving a secure workflow from early requirements is presented in Figure 1. The process includes three phases, namely, (1) early requirements engineering, (2) late requirements engineering and (3) detailed design.

Early requirements engineering. During early requirements analysis the domain actors and their dependencies on other actors for goals to be fulfilled are identified. For early requirements elicitation, one need to reason about trust relationships and delegation of authority. We employ *SI**/Secure Tropos modelling framework to derive and analyse both functional dependencies and security and trust requirements. Various activities contribute to the acquisition of the early requirements model, namely:

Actor modelling aims at identifying actors and analysing their goals.

Functional dependency modelling aims at identifying actors depending on other actors for obtaining services, and actors which are able to provide services.

Permission delegation modelling aims at identifying actors delegating to other actors the permission on services.

Trust modelling aims at identifying actors trusting other actors for services, and actors which own services.

A graphical representation of the model obtained in these modelling activities is given through the actor, functional dependency, authorization, and trust diagrams [2], respectively.

Late requirements engineering. Late requirements engineering is concerned with a definition of the functional and non-functional requirements of the system-to-be. In this work the proposed refinement methodology aims to obtain an appropriate coarse grained business process and workflow based on early requirements. The refinement is processed by diagrams created in the early requirements engineering phase. The methodology takes the components of the diagrams and derives a secure business process constructs from them that is described by the proposed Secure BPEL language.

Considering actor diagram, the notion of actor is refined into partner in Secure BPEL, a root goal is refined into business process while AND/OR goal decomposition with delegation are refined into orchestration. We assume that each actor has a single root goal that can be decomposed by AND/OR goal decomposition. The notions of delegation of execution and delegation of permission presented in dependency and authorization diagrams are refined into choreography of services and authorization respectively. As for trust diagram, trust on execution and permission are refined into choreography of attestation that is further refined into attestation of integrity for the notion of trust on execution and attestation of reporting for trust on permission. The concept of attestation characterizes the process of vouching for the accuracy of information [3]. Attestation of integrity provides proof that an actor can be trusted to report integrity and performed using the set or subset of the credentials associated with the actor. Attestation of reporting is the process of attesting to the contents of integrity reporting.

Secure BPEL Language. Secure BPEL is a language for secure business processes and workflows description. Secure BPEL is a dialect of Web Services Business Process Execution Language (WS-BPEL) [7] for the functional parts and abstracts away low level implementation details from WS-Security and WS-Federation specifications.

For the lack of space we do not present the details of Secure BPEL in this paper, refer to [1] for the language description and illustration with a typical loan origination process scenario. Here we do not have space to present the whole scenario. We focus on the concept of delegation of execution that is relevant to the security requirement such as separation of duties and introduce the refinement of the dependency diagram in order to give an example. The loan origination process describes a customer applying for a loan to the BBB bank. Several external ratings conducted by the Credit Bureau need to be obtained by the processing clerk in order to check the credit worthiness of the customer. Delegation of execution appears when the processing clerk delegates the external rating analysing to the Credit Bureau. The concept of delegation of execution is refined as follows. At the delegater side, the partner processing clerk invokes the service creditWorthinessCheck (by the <invoke> construct) from the partner Credit Bureau. While at the delegatee side, the partner Credit Bureau, the delegatee responds to a service invocation (the <pick> construct) accepting the message of service invocation and execute the creditWorthinessCheck service.

4 Concluding remarks

The main contribution of the paper is to bridge the gap between early requirements analysis and the design of secure workflows based on SOA. In particular, we have proposed a methodology that allows to derive the concrete secure business processes from the early requirements analysis. Furthermore, the secure business processes are refined in order to obtain the appropriate secure workflows that can be described by the proposed language for secure business processes description called Secure BPEL. The proposal is illustrated with an e-business banking case study, a working scenario of the SERENITY project.

The research presented in this work is still in progress. Currently we are diving into the details of the low level secure requirements of messages integrity and confidentiality that will be included in the next release of the language.

References

1. G. Frankova, F. Massacci, and M. Seguran. From Early Requirements Analysis towards Secure Workflows. Technical report, University of Trento, 2007.
2. P. Giorgini, F. Massacci, J. Mylopoulos, and N. Zannone. Requirements Engineering for Trust Management: Model, Methodology, and Reasoning. *International Journal of Information Security*, 5(4):257–274, October 2006.
3. Trusted Computing Group. TCG Specification Architecture Overview Revision 1.2, April 2003.
4. D. Lau and J. Mylopoulos. Designing Web Services with Tropos. In *Proceedings of IEEE International Conference on Web Services*, San Diego, USA, July 6-9 2004.
5. F. Massacci, J. Mylopoulos, and N. Zannone. An Ontology for Secure Socio-Technical Systems. *Handbook of Ontologies for Business Interaction*, 2007.
6. T. Neubauer, M. Klemen, and S. Biffl. Secure Business Process Management: A Roadmap. In *Proceedings of International Conference on Availability, Reliability and Security*, Vienna, Austria, April 2006.
7. OASIS. Web Services Business Process Execution Language Version 2.0, August 2006. Public Review Draft, http://docs.oasis-open.org/wsbpel/2.0/.
8. M.P. Papazoglou and J. Yang. Design Methodology for Web Services and Business Processes. In *Proceedings of the International Workshop on Technologies for E-Services*, Hong Kong, China, August 2002.
9. L. Penserini, A. Perini, A. Susi, and J. Mylopoulos. From Stakeholder Needs to Service Requirements. In *Proceeding of International Workshop on Service-Oriented Computing: Consequences for Engineering Requirements*, Minneapolis, Minnesota, USA, September 2006.

Monitors for Usage Control

M. Hilty[1], A. Pretschner[1], D. Basin[1], C. Schaefer[2], and T. Walter[2]

[1] Dept. of Computer Science, ETH Zürich, Switzerland
{hiltym,pretscha,basin}@inf.ethz.ch
[2] DoCoMo Euro-Labs, Munich, Germany
{schaefer,walter}@docomolab-euro.com

Abstract. Distributed usage control is concerned with controlling how data may or may not be used after it has been given away. One strategy for enforcing usage control requirements is based on monitoring data usage and reacting to policy violations by imposing penalties. We show how to implement monitors for usage control requirements using run-time verification technology.

1 Introduction

The vast amount of data collected in digital form necessitates controlling the usage of sensitive data. The use of *personal data* is governed by data protection regulations. Likewise, the protection of *intellectual property* such as copyrighted artworks or trade secrets is in the financial interest of the data owners. Usage control [8, 9] is an extension of access control that not only addresses who may access which data, but also what may or may not happen with the data afterwards. We study usage control in the context of distributed systems where the participating subjects can take the roles of data providers (who give data away) and data consumers (who request and receive data). When a data provider gives data to a data consumer, the latter must adhere to obligations, which are conditions on the future usage of data. Examples include "do not distribute document D," "play movie M at most 5 times," "delete document D after 30 days," and "notify the author whenever document D is modified."

There are two basic strategies that data providers can employ for enforcing obligations. With *control mechanisms*, they can restrict the usage of objects or ensure that certain actions are executed at a certain point in time, thus preventing obligation violations. The second strategy is based on *monitoring* whether an obligation is violated and penalizing the data consumer when this happens. This is similar to law enforcement where the police cannot always prevent people from breaking the law but fine or sentence delinquents when catching them. This strategy is implemented by *observation mechanisms*, which consist of two parts. Provider-side *obligation monitors* are used to decide whether an obligation is adhered to, and consumer-side *signaling mechanisms* notify the data provider about events that happen at the data consumer's side.

In this paper, we present the implementation of an obligation monitor that adapts run-time verification techniques. The obligation monitor has been de-

Please use the following format when citing this chapter:

Hilty, M., Pretschner, A., Basin, D., Schaefer, C., and Walter, T., 2007, in IFIP International Federation for Information Processing, Volume 238, Trust Management, eds. Etalle, S., Marsh, S., (Boston: Springer), pp. 411–414.

signed to monitor a wide range of usage control requirements that were identified in earlier studies. This is the first application of run-time monitoring to usage control to the best of our knowledge.

2 Background

Obligations The Obligation Specification Language (OSL) [6] is a language for expressing obligations in usage control. OSL is a temporal logic similar to LTL and includes constructs for expressions that frequently occur in usage control requirements and that are difficult to express with standard LTL operators. In particular, OSL is able to express cardinality conditions, conditions on the accumulated usage time, and both permissions and prohibitions. An obligation expressed in OSL formulates a property that every execution trace of a data consumer must satisfy.

We call an obligation *o* *fulfilled* in a trace *t* at time *n* if *t* with every possible extension after *n* satisfies *o*. In contrast, *o* is *violated* in *t* at time *n* if *t* with every possible extension after *n* does not satisfy *o* [5]. Violation and fulfillment correspond to the notions of bad and good prefixes introduced by Kupferman and Vardi [7]. We use them to decide the points in time when penalties should be triggered (i.e., when an obligation is violated) or when the monitoring of an obligation can be stopped (when it is either violated or fulfilled).

Related Work Monitoring as an enforcement strategy for obligations has been proposed by Bettini et al. [1]. There are many different approaches to the monitoring of temporal formulae. These approaches differ depending on the expressiveness of the input language and the techniques used for monitoring. General overviews of such systems are given in [2, 3]. In terms of the implemented techniques, we can differentiate between rewriting-based and automata-based approaches. Automata-based algorithms have an initialization overhead that results from building the automata, and this overhead is usually exponential in the length of the monitored formula. However, they are only linear in the size of the formula at run-time, whereas the rewriting-based algorithms do not have any initialization overhead but are less efficient at runtime [10].

3 Observation Mechanisms

An observation mechanism consists of a provider-side *obligation monitor* and a consumer-side *signaling mechanism*. The signaling mechanism observes the actions of a data consumer and informs the monitor about these observations by sending dedicated *signals*. If the monitor detects the violation of an obligation, the corresponding penalty is triggered. If an obligation is fulfilled or violated, its monitoring is stopped. The signaling mechanism may send signals corresponding to single actions or sequences of actions. In the latter case, obligation monitors can also be deployed at the consumer side. In the extreme case, the whole monitoring functionality may be included in the signaling mechanism, which then informs the data provider in case an obligation is violated.

The signals received by the data provider must be trustworthy in the following sense: (1) the observations of the signaling mechanism must correspond to what really happens at the data consumer (correctness and completeness); (2) the signaling mechanism itself must not be tampered with; and (3) the signals must not be altered or blocked during transmission. How these guarantees can be provided is outside the scope of this paper. However, monitoring also makes sense even when only some of them hold. If signals cannot always be transmitted, for example, then the monitoring functionality can be integrated into the signaling mechanism. This way, the signaling mechanism can go online periodically and tell the data provider whether violations have occurred.

4 Obligation Monitors

Monitoring Algorithm The process of finding good and bad prefixes for temporal formulae has been studied in the discipline of run-time verification [2, 3]. An important criterion for selecting an algorithm was efficient support for all operators of OSL. While all OSL formulae can be translated into LTL formulae, direct translation results in poor performance. For instance, OSL can express exclusive permissions such as the obligation that a given data item may only be sent to two subjects. Enumerating all subjects that are not allowed, which is necessary when translating permission expressions to LTL, not only makes the resulting monitors potentially very large, but also poses problems when new subjects are dynamically added to the system. Thus, such exclusive permissions should be directly supported by the monitoring algorithm as well.

The algorithm we have chosen is based on the work of Geilen and Dams [4]. It is a tableau construction that constructs a timed automaton for every obligation. When a transition is not defined, this indicates the violation of the obligation, and when a special state is reached, then the obligation is fulfilled. We have extended the algorithm to efficiently support cardinality conditions by introducing dedicated counters, which are similar to timers. Further, we have introduced special support for the permission operators of OSL.

Implementation We have prototypically implemented the obligation monitor in Java. Tests have shown that the following factors impact the monitoring performance: the number of simultaneously monitored obligations, the size of the obligations, the frequency at which signals are received, and the duration of the clock cycle. The number of actions that are prohibited by an exclusive permission does not have an effect on the performance of the monitor, and neither does the size of the number in a cardinality condition. Determining the exact performance of the monitor is outside the scope of this paper, especially as the implementation itself is not yet optimized towards heavy workloads.

414   M. Hilty, A. Pretschner, D. Basin, C. Schaefer, and T. Walter

However, tests on a Pentium M with 1.6GHZ and 1GB of RAM where 1000 obligations were monitored simultaneously and signals were sent every 150ms on average showed that the monitor was able to process all signals within less than 100ms. The fact that we have achieved this performance on a low-end system, without dedicated performance optimizations of the code and the platform, suggests that creating industrial-strength obligation monitors is not an illusion.

5 Conclusion

Observation mechanisms are an important means for usage control enforcement. A widespread adoption of observation mechanisms will lead to a wider applicability of usage control enforcement. We have characterized those mechanisms and have shown how to adapt existing run-time verification techniques for obligation monitoring in usage control. We have also built a prototype of an obligation monitor based on these ideas. Future work includes creating a performance-optimized implementation of the monitor, determining how trustworthy signaling mechanisms can be built, and integrating observation mechanisms into business information systems.

References

1. C. Bettini, S. Jajodia, X. S. Wang, and D. Wijesekera. Provisions and obligations in policy rule management. *Journal of Network and System Management*, 11(3):351–372, 2003.
2. S. Colin and L. Mariani. *Model-Based Testing of Reactive Systems*, chapter 18: Run-Time Verification, pages 525–555. LNCS 3472. 2005.
3. N. Delgado, A. Q. Gates, and S. Roach. A taxonomy and catalog of runtime software-fault monitoring tools. *IEEE Transactions on Software Engineering*, 30(12):859–872, 2004.
4. M. Geilen and D. Dams. An on-the-fly tableau construction for a real-time temporal logic. In *Proc. 6th International Symposium on Formal Techniques in Real-Time and Fault-Tolerant Systems*, LNCS 1926, pages 276–290, 2000.
5. M. Hilty, D. Basin, and A. Pretschner. On obligations. In *10th European Symposium on Research in Computer Security*, LNCS 3679, pages 98–117, 2005.
6. M. Hilty, A. Pretschner, C. Schaefer, and T. Walter. A system model and an obligation lanugage for distributed usage control. Technical Report I-ST-20, DoCoMo Euro-Labs, 2006.
7. O. Kupferman and M. Y. Vardi. Model checking of safety properties. *Formal Methods in System Design*, 19:291–314, 2001.
8. J. Park and R. Sandhu. The UCON ABC Usage Control Model. *ACM Transactions on Information and Systems Security*, 7:128–174, 2004.
9. A. Pretschner, M. Hilty, and D. Basin. Distributed Usage Control. *Communications of the ACM*, September 2006.
10. G. Roşu and K. Havelund. Rewriting-based techniques for runtime verification. *Automated Software Engineering*, 12:151–197, 2005.

Author Index

Adams, William 91
Adnane, Asmaa 75
Aïmeur, Esma 223
Al-Fedaghi, Sabah 207
Almulhem, Ahmad 47

Bagheri, Ebrahim 239
Barrett, Stephen 153
Basin, David 411
Bidan, Christophe 75

Caine, Allan 367
Cardoso, Roberto Speicys 59
Costantini, Stefania 123

Davis, Nathaniel 91
De Sousa Jr., Rafael Timóteo 75
Debbabi, Mourad 301
Deriaz, Michel 31
Dondio, Pierpaolo 153
Dong, Changyu 17
Dulay, Naranker 17

Frankova, Ganna 407

Galice, Samuel 169
Genik, Lynne 185
Ghorbani, Ali 239
Guosun, Zeng 139
Gutscher, Andreas 285

Hage, Hicham 223
Hammond, Tim 185
Hengartner, Urs 367
Herrmann, Peter 317
Hilty, Manuel 411

Inverardi, Paola 123
Issarny, Valérie 59

Jensen, Christian Damsgaard 383, 399

Khan, Faraz Idris 333
Khan, Adil Mehmood 333
Kraemer, Frank Alexander 317
Kramer, Mark 255

Laverdière, Marc-André 301
Lee, Sungyoung 333
Lee, Young Koo 333

Mani Onana, Flavien Serge 223
Manzo, Edmondo 153
Martin, Clemens 403
Mason, Peter 185
Massacci, Fabio 407
McIntyre, Mark 185
Mé, Ludovic 75
Meira, Fernando 383
Minier, Marine 169
Mostarda, Leonardo 123
Mourad, Azzam 301

Neuman, Clifford 349
Nittegaard-Nielsen, Jacob 383

Paurobally, Shamimabi 107
Pretschner, Alexander 411
Proctor, Seth 1

Raazi, S. M. Khaliq-ur-Rahman 333
Raverdy, Pierre-Guillaume 59
Refai, Mustapha 403
Russello, Giovanni 17
Ryutov, Tatyana 349

Schaefer, Christian 411
Seguran, Magali 407
Soeanu, Andrei 301
Song, Young-Jae 333

Tamassia, Roberto 1
Tocchio, Arianna 123
Traore, Issa 47
Traupman, Jonathan 269

Ubéda, Stéphane 169

Walter, Thomas 411
Wei, Wang 139

Yao, Danfeng 1